My Life

Autobiography of

HAVELOCK ELLIS

BOOKS BY HAVELOCK ELLIS

Paul Bisho

Havelock Ellis

My Life

Autobiography of

HAVELOCK ELLIS

With Illustrations

HOUGHTON MIFFLIN COMPANY . BOSTON
The Riverside Press Cambridge

English

𝕿𝖍𝖊 𝕽𝖎𝖛𝖊𝖗𝖘𝖎𝖉𝖊 𝕻𝖗𝖊𝖘𝖘
CAMBRIDGE · MASSACHUSETTS
PRINTED IN THE U.S.A.

Preface

I⠀T WAS soon after the age of thirty that I privately conceived the idea of writing an intimate account of my own life. At the same time I felt (like Cellini) that such a narrative could not wisely be begun earlier than the age of forty when the greater part of life was already past and it became possible to see the whole in one perspective. As it turned out, I could scarcely have begun it earlier, for I wished to give due weight to the influences of heredity, and it was not until I was forty that my father put into my hands a few old family papers which furnished clues to an investigation of my more remote ancestry, and helped me to understand the sources of my own tendencies. A little later, in that same year (1899), as I had planned, I duly began the narrative.

I wrote it in a leisurely fashion. It seemed to me that in transcribing, with the most delicate precision I was capable of, the process of my growth and progress through life, I was occupied in a task to which only my finest moments should be given. The record was thus slowly set down during a few days of the best summer weeks every year at Carbis Bay, as I reclined on the moor, reserving, without premeditation, one choice and special spot on Sunday mornings for this occupation. There seemed no need for haste; life was still spread spaciously ahead. With this careful choice of time and place the narrative moved so slowly that at the end of some fifteen years I had not advanced beyond the period of adolescence. Then my wife died and the space of life before me seemed suddenly to contract. It became clear that I must speed up my task. I made a fresh start from the time of my marriage, and I wrote at the two sections of the narrative concurrently. Moreover, I wrote at much more frequent intervals, though I still chose my finest moments to write, for if I had from the first taken this record seriously as the most perdurable piece of work I was likely to leave behind, a new sacredness was now infused into it.

With the course of years, however, my conception of the method of my task, though not of its aim, had become modified. I had started with the idea, which I still retain, that of all forms of prose, outside the limits of imaginative art, there is no form so precious in its nature and so permanent in its value as autobiography. But in this form, as I understood it, there were few productions that deserved to rank high. Adequately rendered, the Pilgrim's Progress of the soul through life should be as fascinating, even as noble a record, as Bunyan's, and still more instructive. Yet of how few can this be said! It cannot even be said of Bunyan's own autobiography, while nearly all the lives written in my time, by their subjects or about them, were loathsome in their falsity or unprofitable in their emptiness. Even when I viewed the whole range of such works, the *Confessions* of Saint Augustine, the *Confessions* of Rousseau, the *Memoirs* of Casanova could alone be placed at the summit, though I recognised that each of these is open to criticism, while there are some half-dozen other autobiographical documents of high value, often, indeed, little if at all inferior in quality to these first three. Of all these documents Rousseau's *Confessions* had always come before me — in spite of all the objection brought by the great army of little scribblers — as a model in their kind.

Yet slowly, very slowly, even before I had made much progress in my task, I realised that I could not take Rousseau, or indeed anyone else, as my model. Rousseau, Augustine, Casanova had each in his own special way attained the perfection of more or less sincere intimacy in the record of his individual life and produced a narrative of immortal value and interest. But Rousseau had

been stimulated by the exquisite torture of his need for self-justi-
fication, and Augustine had been carried away by the self-aban-
donment of religious emotion, and Casanova by a certain audacious moral obtrusity. I was conscious of no such grounds for
self-revelation. The very qualities, indeed, of sanity and reasonableness, of critical impartiality, of just analytic precision, which
made the task fascinating and possible for me were incompatible
with those qualities which had assured the success of Rousseau
and Augustine and Casanova, not one of whom had so much as
conceived the scientific spirit applied to life.

Moreover, even if I were to set down the exact facts of my life
in the scientific impersonal spirit not impossible for me, I should
still have to encounter the insuperable prejudices of my con-
temporaries. All literature is a perpetual struggle. Every morning the writer who is truly alive must conquer afresh the liberty
of expression. At his heels is the compact army organised by convention and prudery, ready at any moment to thrust aside or
trample down every straggler. It so happens, also, that for a long
time past, some two centuries or more, my own country and some
others have been passing through a phase of timidity in self-
expression, the outward sign of an increased literary emasculation.
It has been impossible to set down clearly the most vital facts of
life, or always even the most trivial, because they seemed not to
accord with that drawing-room standard of good taste which generally ruled. Under such conditions no immortal book can ever
be written, and I suppose that our prose literature of this period —
for the criteria of poetry may be different — will be as tedious and
unprofitable to posterity as it is already becoming to ourselves. I
cannot accept this standard of taste. Yet I must necessarily write
as a child of my own time.

It has thus come about that I have had to find my own personal
way of telling my own life, a way that is sincere without being
crude, a way that tells all that is essential to tell and yet leaves
many things to be read, clearly enough by intelligent readers,

between the lines. It is not the way I had proposed, it is not an easy way, yet it seems, on the whole, to be my way, and I think that, if need were, I could justify it.

There has been selection in my narrative. In every such narrative there is inevitably selection, and often it is far from being stringent enough. But too often it is a selection by which the insignificant things are recorded and the significant things suppressed. I am indeed concerned mainly with my inner life; I have no wish to write anything but a spiritual biography, and outer events only interest me here in so far as they affected my inner life. I have sought to select the significant things. That requires a certain daring and a certain fortitude, just as much if one happens to be a saint as if one happens to be a sinner, though that is rather a conventional distinction, since most people are, at the same time or at different times, saints when seen from one angle and sinners from another. No doubt it requires also a certain skill if one is to tell the essential truth, at every point, to discerning readers and yet avoid the various risks of truth-telling. I have at least sought to be fair and never to suppress anything — however shameful it might seem to some — which signifies. I have not left it possible for any persons, however miraculously informed, to come forward to discredit my narrative by the revelation of significant facts I had suppressed. Except for the beautiful and prolonged episode of my closing years, which is too near to me to write about, I have left nothing significant of my life untold. No doubt, some shocked old-fashioned prude will comment: 'I should hope not!'

Those who in writing of their own lives concern themselves mainly with outer events are, it would seem, largely moved by vanity, and the outcome is often harmless and agreeable. The motive that seems to have been influential with me — apart from the fundamental impulse of self-expression which may well be deeper — is the desire that my experience of life may help those who come after me to live their own lives. From the age of sixteen at least that motive has been strong, almost instinctive, within me. Certainly and consciously, the leading motive which induced me to take up the chief work of my life was the wish that others might be spared some of the difficulties I had to contend with. That, it may be said, hardly justifies me in extending the same unsparing frankness to the record of my wife's life. I believe, nevertheless, that — sensitively independent as she was — I may now venture to speak for her as well as for myself. Her wisdom of life, as she remarked to an acquaintance during her last week in the world, had been the outcome especially of her experience with me. She desired to help others, she often succeeded in helping others, and she never spared herself, although during the best part of her life she was not without a certain shrewdness and caution, as well as personal reserve. But I knew what her unfulfilled plans and aims were, and I knew that, even as regards the deep-lying anomaly of temperament which meant so much in her character and work, it was one of her dearest wishes to bring light and consolation to others. Now there is nothing left to do but what I have done, in the belief that she would understand and approve, or, at the least, forgive.

I know there are some who exclaim on the indecency of publishing intimate letters which were never written to be published. The love-letters of the Brownings have been used to exploit the indignation of the superior people who make this protest. I have looked into those letters; they were all written before marriage by two people who had never had any opportunity of being intimate; they might all, as my wife once exclaimed in a different connection of a letter she had herself written, have been stuck up on the stable door. But if one publishes letters that once really were intimate, what can it matter when we are both dead? Who can be hurt, if she and I, who might once have been hurt, are now only a few handfuls of ashes flung over the grass and the flowers? To do what I have done here has been an act of prolonged precision in cold blood, beyond anything else that I have ever written. For I know that, to a large extent, the world is inhabited by people to whom one does too much honour by calling them fools. The cost has been great, but I have counted the cost. All mankind may now, if they will, conspire together to hurt us. We shall not feel it. We shall still be in the soft air that bathes them and in the blossoms that burst into beauty beneath their feet. Nothing matters to us who are dead. But we may perhaps have brought a little help and consolation to those who are still alive, and sensitive and suffering.

I have no more to say by way of prelude except to make clear that the period of life I have sought to record is that which covers what I have always regarded as my life-work, the period of struggle and of perpetual advance towards a desired goal. With the completion of that task and, a little later, the loss of that comrade who had been throughout so loyally at my side, the narrative ends. All that matters has been told.

But I do not by any means imply that therewith my life was ended. Far, far from it! Life has never been so beautiful to me as it has become since I could peacefully lay the burden of my accomplished life-work down. With the tension of an unachieved task no longer felt, with a widespread recognition of the significance of that achievement such as I had never even hoped for, with a comparative freedom from anxieties, with loving and lovely friends among, as it has seemed to me, the best people in the world; above all, with the constant companionship of one who has been a perpetual source of comfort and joy, I can say with truth that the last phase of my life has been the happiest.

To say this is also to say that this book is not a mere personal revelation. If it were, I should never have written it. I do not come forward to say: 'This was the real Me — that was the real She.' So to do would merely be to display an indiscretion of intimacy from which the modest reader might desire to turn aside as not concerning him. I say what cannot fail to concern him: 'This is life.' It is an impersonal revelation which I uncover, and had it been possible I would use symbols for all proper names, including my own. The narrative that holds a true picture of life should be helpful to many, and it has seemed to me that, when it represents what may on nearer view seem failure and yet on far view supreme success, it is helpful to all. For novels do not bring to us real life. They inevitably seek to transform life into art, to beautify it or perhaps to uglify it. When one is not concerned with artistic representation, there is no need to do either. For life itself holds all the beauty we can conceive, with all the ugliness, and weaves them together into a final harmony. It is in the desire by self-expression to help others that I find the chief reason for this record; and even though, deeper than that, the heart, as Pascal says, has its reasons, that reason may suffice.

The stuff of our lives is, indeed, a tangled web, yet in the end there is order. It may be long before order becomes clear, for life, when we reach below the surface, is full of complexity and full of contradictions. Thus it has taken me long to find out whether I am of weak or of strong character; I have seemed to those who knew me both the one and the other, and could myself find reasons on either side. But one might ask the same unprofitable question of the water or the wind. I see now that weakness and strength are only names for two necessary aspects of any possible approach, however humble, toward perfection. The man who seems, and he merely seems, all strength is as far from success as the man who seems all weakness may be from failure. Indeed, the whole question of success and failure is of the same blended kind. What from one point of view is tragic failure may from another angle be magnificent success, of which the story of Jesus is the immortal symbol. In the sphere of the practical and in that of the spiritual, the Napoleons of the world and the Beethovens of the world tell the same story of success that was failure, of failure that was success. I know too well my own inefficiency; it has weighed on me from youth, and the disasters I have met have proved greater than even the melancholy of youth could forebode. My life has sometimes seemed a path to Calvary trodden with bleeding feet. Yet the roses of immortal beauty have blossomed wherever I trod. I have tasted the joys of Heaven on every side. The peace that passes all understanding has dwelt at my heart. The life-work I planned in youth I have achieved through half a century — together with the power it has brought to help and to console — in a measure that surpasses my dreams. And now at the threshold of old age the precious unsought balms of love and devotion, almost of worship, that are poured on my head are a perpetual miracle I can only receive with humility, if not with awe. On the foundation of much failure is built success, and there is no defeat left for him who is no longer conscious of defeat. With simplicity and love in one's heart, with truth to one's own deepest natural instincts, we may touch the world where we will and it bursts into radiant beauty. That surely is enough for anyone.

It is certainly enough for me. I have never had ambition as that word is usually understood, and I have never desired praise, nor received more than a moderate satisfaction when it came to me, just as, on the other hand, I have been indifferent to, if not indeed contemptuous of, blame. The attentions of the world, I have found, embarrass more than they flatter. I have been a dreamer and an artist, a great dreamer, for that is easy, not a great artist, for that is hard; but still always an artist, whether in the minor art of writing, or the greater art of comprehending, or the supreme art of living, wherein it is something to have tried even if one fails. So that if I am often sad — for the art of living is finally the art of loving, in which one becomes a master too late — I am always content.

For I have always been instinctively attracted to what is difficult, even in my relations with those I have loved.

HAVELOCK ELLIS

List of Illustrations

Part I

I

Ever since I was a small child, the sea, and a ship sailing on the sea, and nearly all the things that belong to the sea, have had for me a poignant emotional fascination. The sights and sounds and odours of sailing ships, with the memories of harbours and wharves, seem woven into my mental texture. Whenever I come back to them, it is with something of the same emotion that everything still gives me that was once my mother's. I know that as long as I live there will be no more beautiful thing in the world for me than a finely cut ship, sailing with full-bellied sails, bound for mysterious shores. It is perhaps fitting that such a sight should be so moving to one who has been a pioneer on unknown seas of the spirit, haunted by the longing for remote lands that no keel has yet touched.

But to explain the fascination that ships and the sea hold for me, I need not fall back on their symbolism. The real associations have themselves been early enough to explain it all. I was only seven when my father first took me with him to sail round the world, and some ten years later he took me again. I can, moreover, trace the sea far back in the traditions of my family on both sides. My father was a sea-captain who lived for fifty years on the sea. His father and all his brothers spent their lives as officials in the warehouses of the London Docks, in constant contact with ships, and all the rich and wonderful products of the East that are there piled up in legendary profusion. My mother was the daughter of a sea-captain; her only brother was lost on his first voyage at sea, in a ship that was never heard of again; her grandfather was both sailor and shipbuilder, and most of his family were sailors. Thus all my near male relations in the generations immediately preceding me — all whom I ever heard of in youth — have lived on or by the sea.

Behind my sailor ancestors — again along both sides, for my father's father and my mother's mother were first cousins — there are, for the most part, long rows of often scholarly divines and parish priests, away from the sea, and springing mostly from old families seated on the land, and all in Suffolk. It is strange that I knew nothing whatever of this ancestry until, after I had reached the age of forty, my father put some old family papers into my hands. Until then my knowledge of these ancestors had been confined to the bare facts that the names Peppen and Powle, borne by my father and one of his brothers, were surnames which entered into the family history at some unknown period. The few papers my father gave me served as a clue to various lines of ancestry which I am still slowly unravelling.

It has long been my belief that a man's aptitudes and temperament are rooted in fundamental characteristics of even remote ancestors. I know that theoretically nearly the whole of a man's heredity must be supplied by his immediate ascendants: his parents and grandparents, and so, in most cases, I doubt not it practically happens. But the germinal possibilities of heredity from more remote ancestors, it seems to me, though in most people latent throughout life, may here and there in a sensitive perhaps slightly abnormal individual spring into life, rise to the level of consciousness, and enter into new emotional and intellectual combinations. Recent theories of heredity seem to make this more rather than less intelligible. Thus it is, perhaps, that in the sphere of genius, for instance, to which I have given some attention, a man totally unlike his parents may yet appear to us, and truly appear, as a marvellous incarnation of the typical characteristics of his race. For these and the like reasons I have always sought out carefully the ancestry of the men whom I have desired to study. It has been a novel and fascinating task to work out the same problem in myself. I even propose to devote a book to it, and that design, even if never carried out, may dispense me from entering into any tedious details here. It will be enough to set forth briefly what appear to be the main characteristics of the half-dozen families which I regard as the streams which have fed my own fundamental inborn personality. As I knew nothing whatever of them, or their histories before the nineteenth century, until my own life was definitely moulded, and perhaps its chief episodes already lived, there can be no question of the consciously plastic force of tradition; if these people have influenced me at all, as many curious points of contact seem to show, this influence cannot have been that of example, but altogether unconscious and organic.

The document, handed down in my father's family, which awakened in me the desire, never felt in my life before, to make a voyage of exploration among my ancestors, was the parchment will, proved in 1736, of Susannah Peppen, wife of the Reverend Richard Peppen, rector of Great Waldingfield, and daughter of the Reverend William Powle, formerly rector of the same Suffolk village and also of Little Waldingfield near-by. I soon set out for Great Waldingfield, which I had never before heard of, accompanied by my old friend Doctor Barker Smith, and found a pleasant village, a few miles out of Sudbury, once a little centre of

Puritanism and the home of the New England Appletons. No one there had ever heard of Peppens or of Powles, but as we wandered over the churchyard, Barker Smith speedily detected, in perfect preservation, the altar-tomb in slate of William Powle with a long and interesting Latin inscription. That was the starting-point of an investigation which in leisure moments I have pursued with considerable ardour and success, aided by various fortunate and fortuitous circumstances, as well as by a certain sense for re-search, assiduously developed in quite other fields. In a few years I had constructed on a solid foundation the history in its main lines of several families, and elucidated the lives of two or three remarkable men.

A figure I look back at with pleasure is that of Richard Pep-pen's grandfather, the Reverend William Keble, B.D., rector of Ringshall in Suffolk and at one time fellow of Benet (now Corpus Christi), Cambridge, a victim of Puritanism who has his niche in Walker's *Sufferings of the Clergy*. The Kebles were a vigorous and independent stock, a manorial family settled at Old Newton near Stowmarket, perhaps from before the Norman Conquest. The head of the family was always called 'the Heir.' At the end of the sixteenth century the 'Heir' was Giles Keble. William, whose outspoken allegiance to King and Church brought him suffering and temporary deprivation of his living, was a younger son of Giles. A still younger son was Richard, who has his part in the history of England. On leaving the University, Richard entered at Gray's Inn, became in course of time a distinguished judge, and, unlike his brother, took the Parliamentary side; he presided at Lilburne's trial with admirable impartiality, and when the Privy Seal was put into commission he was appointed one of the three commissioners. But he was unable to accept the despotism of Cromwell and retired to his Suffolk estate at Tuddenham near Ipswich a few years later, and long before the Restoration. That doubtless was why he escaped prosecution for treason, though I have not found the slightest reason to suspect that he was (as

some have supposed) one of the Regicides. Some said he fled to
Switzerland, like one of his fellow commissioners who was mur-
dered at Vevey by Royalists; but the men of this stock were not
accustomed to fly from possible dangers; there are various indications that he remained in the absolute seclusion of his Suffolk
home, far from the changes and turmoils of the world, though
there is what seems a deliberate vagueness in the inscription on
the tablet set up to him by his daughter in the chancel of Tuddenham Church.[1]

Naturally the rector of Ringshall's uncompromising attitude
provoked unpleasant attentions from the Puritans. Again and
again they plundered him or at least stole his horses; once they
pounced down on the rectory and on searching it found it full of
pamphlets on the King's side with not one on the other side; and
it was set down that he had said of the Puritans that they 'railed
at the Pope, yet are Popes themselves, doing what they list'; and
again that 'if a cobbler or a tinker get into the pulpit and preach
four or five hours for the Parliament, these are the men nowadays.'[2] Finally, in 1644, he was turned out of his cure, but, as
Walker carefully neglects to say, he was reinstated the next year,
apparently through the intervention of Mr. Keble's brother, the
Judge, who was influential on the Parliamentary side. Possibly he
reconciled himself to the new order. He died at an advanced age,
and in the parish register there is an unusual entry concerning
this 'ancient and revered Divine,' who, we are told, was rector
'by the space of fifty years and upwards' (in reality not more than

---

[1] The biographers of John Keble, author of the *Christian Year*, state that he was
descended from the Right Honorable Richard Keble, but the assertion is baseless.
John Keble belonged to the Gloucestershire family of that name, and, though it is
not unlikely that the Gloucestershire Kebles came from the Suffolk stock, since both
districts were engaged in the same cloth industries (and I find a man of the name of
the rare Peppen family also in Gloucestershire), the separation must have taken
place before the seventeenth century.

[2] John Walker, *An attempt towards recovering an account of the Number and the
Sufferings of the Clergy in the later times of the Great Rebellion* (1914), Part II, p. 289.
There are numerous documents dealing with Keble's affair in the Bodleian Library,
which the Reverend F. Compston has kindly examined and summarised for me.

forty-eight years), and he is described as 'a pastor most faithful in the service of his Master Jesus Christ, most loyal to his prince, very peaceable and exemplary among his parishioners, very pittiful and charitable towards the poore, very charitable to strangers, and most courteous to all honest-minded men.' It is interesting to see the tribute to his loyalty combined with a subsequent statement that his funeral sermon was preached by Fairfax, who was a leading Puritan divine in the eastern counties. Evidently the bitter antagonism of earlier years had been mellowed. This was in 1659. Had old Keble lived a year longer, his ears would have been gladdened by the sound of the bells that announced the return of the King and the Bishops. His will is a concise and businesslike document; there is not a word of complaint, and only one personal note can be traced: the old man — evidently remembering how Gresham had devastated the neighbouring country to get timber for his Royal Exchange — directs that on his estate the trees are not to be felled; the landmarks of the old order had been swept away, but, he seems to say, the trees at least shall remain. He bequeathed the advowson of the living to his daughter Susannah. She speedily presented it and herself to the Reverend George Peppen.

I do not know precisely who was the father of George Peppen, but I can trace him to Wenhaston — a village with an interesting old church some five miles from the Suffolk coast — which was then the home of the Peppen or Pepyn family. They were a small family which never branched out far, though in earlier ages it seems to have been somewhat more numerous, for Pembury in Kent is a corruption of 'Peppenbury.' In the seventeenth century, and after, so far as I can find, there was no other recognisable family of Peppens in England, and now, it is probable, there are no Peppens at all. I imagine that they were Walloons, who, like so many others, came to England at some period earlier than the sixteenth century. Ever since the time of the famous father of Charlemagne, Pepin has been, as it still is, a common name round

Liége. The curious point about these English Peppens is their constant devotion to the Church; we scarcely hear of them in any other connection; at Wenhaston their names are found only as those of church-wardens; just before the Reformation Dom Robertus Pepyn was rector of Knoddeshall, not far away from his native Wenhaston, where he expressed a wish to be buried, a piety towards the past also characteristic of these Peppens. And now George Peppen was the founder of an almost exclusively clerical family, his three sons were all rectors of Suffolk parishes; at Ringshall four generations of Peppens peacefully ruled in succession. The last, who died in 1789, married the daughter of a knight, Sir William Barker, acquired a coat of arms with a Pegasus as crest and now reposes beneath a large gravestone with a long inscription at the west end of Ringshall Church. A son of George Peppen's was that Richard who, like his father, married a wife with a living in her gift and became, as his father had once been, rector of Great Waldingfield. With his arrival, however, the presentation to the living passed into the hands of a Cambridge College so that his son, Powle Peppen, was not brought up to succeed his father. He settled in Edwardstone, the beautiful village in which once John Winthrop, the founder of Massachusetts, was born. There he became a farmer, maltster, and farrier. His two children were both daughters, one noted for her prettiness, the other for her cleverness. They each became my great-grandmother, for the clever one married an Ellis of Sudbury and the pretty one an Oliver of Bury. In abandoning the Church, the Peppens in the male line became extinct.

The Peppens, as I view them, take on a definite family character. Their devotion to the Church seems to have been, on the one hand, without any ecclesiastical ambition and, on the other, it may be, without any extreme religious devotion. They sought and found — on at least two occasions by the road of marriage — Church livings of more than average value which were quiet and comfortable country estates, and they felt no disdain for the worldly advantages of good county alliances and a coat of arms. I take it that they were men of good ability, yet nowise standing conspicuously beyond their fellows. They were all Cambridge men, all content with their M.A. degree. They seem to have been faithful and grateful friends; the Ringshall registers contain a pleasant and, I doubt not, reliable account of the virtues of William Keble, such as one seldom finds in such registers, and there can be little doubt that George Peppen wrote it; while his son, Richard, surely wrote the eloquent Latin epitaph which records the many fine qualities of William Powle. The Peppens had a certain pertinacity of character, even obstinacy, as shown by their attachment to the Church and well illustrated by Richard Peppen, who, before becoming rector of Great Walding-field, was head master of the grammar school at Needham Market. Here he would insist on preaching in neighbouring churches, although the managers of the grammar school maintained that he should devote his whole time and attention to the school. It was a dispute which, I understand, has continued to appear even in modern schools with clerical heads. In this case the head master was repeatedly called to order and severely admonished, but he continued imperturbably on his own way. The history of the conflict was contained in the minute-books of the school which, unfortunately, have disappeared in recent years.

Of all these families it is the Powles I know most about. They belonged to Bury Saint Edmunds and in the fifteenth century they called themselves Bocher, indicating that they had once been butchers (which then meant primarily graziers). They are described as yeomen, but at the beginning of the sixteenth century one of them was a plumber, and that was an important occupation at a time and in a region where church-building was active and churches must be roofed with lead. These sixteenth-century Bochers, men and women, wrote long and detailed wills, all extant in the Bury probate registry, which show that, though they were not more than comfortably well off, they were estimable people, thoughtful and kindly for all whom they came into relation with. One charming old lady of this family, Margaret Powle *alias* Bocher — the women were nearly all Margaries or Margarets in this family — made an unusually long and detailed will which gives the pleasantest picture of her character and surroundings. Every article she possessed, it would seem, every pot and pan, every garment, is separately bequeathed as an affectionate remembrance, often with a befitting word of gratitude or regard, among a large circle of relations, friends, acquaintances, her manservant and her maidservant. To her grandson, Paul Powle, she leaves, not a brass dish or a pair of shirts, but, perhaps with insight into the boy's character, 'ten shillings of good and lawful money,' though I may note that his father, John Powle, left him, in addition to a fair share of his estate in money, 'my other clarichord and my lute and some of my singing-books'; but this Bury yeoman was evidently a most musical man, for besides this clarichord (supposed to be identical with the clavichord which preceded the spinet) he had another as well as two virginals, and singing-books enough to be divided among all his sons. He was a true Elizabethan, this accomplished musical yeoman, nor was he neglectful of his bow and arrows, though he bequeathed them outside the family, realising, no doubt, that they were growing out of date, and that Paul Powle would prefer a gun. Paul Powle, born in 1564, raised the family to a higher social position and acquired a considerable estate. But I regret to say that, though extremely restless and energetic, he was scarcely an amiable or even estimable man. My knowledge of him is extensive and the evidence convincing. He was apparently a lawyer, 'clerk in the King's Bench' (and we hear of him being commissioned to make out a deed of conveyance), with chambers in Fleet Street, himself most litigious, and not always strictly scrupulous. For many years he was the neighbour and friend of Adam Winthrop (father of the great New-Englander), a lawyer also, lord of the manor of Groton and the auditor of two Cambridge colleges, an excellent and pious man. In Adam Winthrop's interesting but still unpublished Diary (deposited in the British Museum since this was first written and now printed), as well as in his Almanachs, there are curious and vivid glimpses of Powle's private life. Moreover, since Powle was constantly figuring as plaintiff or defendant in chancery cases, various aspects of his domestic affairs are thus brought before us. Adam Winthrop never says a word which records his opinion of Powle, but he shows that though they were often in association and on friendly terms, and the affairs of his family and Powle's were intimately connected, there were constant disputes between them over leases and bonds and so forth. Sometimes 'I was arrested at Mr. Powle's suit,' sometimes 'Mr. Powle was arrested at my suit,' but these disputes seem to have been satisfactorily settled. Powle's first wife belonged to the Vintner family, rich Suffolk clothiers, and hereby also he was in hot water. In 1603, Winthrop mentions that at Bury Sessions Powle bailed his brother-in-law, Zachary Vintner — who was a youth of twenty — charged with burglary, and that Ada Winthrop testified against Zachary; we know from other sources that Zachary was hanged for that misdeed. A few months later we hear that Powle, after sitting in a commission at Colchester, 'was in danger to have been killed by Gilbert Vintner, his wife's brother' — it is not clear why — who two days before had been staying at his brother-in-law's house at Groton. Again, much later, Winthrop mentions that Powle 'charged a chimney sweeper with stealing of a silver cup.' It is not certain that Powle was a bad man. I do not think that he was. But he seems to have been a highly energetic and probably neurotic person, devoted to the furtherance of himself and his family, irritable, suspicious, and aggressive, yet constantly regarding himself as the victim of other people's malevolence, a troublesome man for all who had any dealings with him. He is described by his father-in-law after a second marriage as 'always quarrelsome,' and he certainly was so. It must at the same time be said that the wrongs were not all on one side, and it would seem that at that period a considerable proportion of respectable well-to-do people must have been engaged in endeavouring to cheat each other in ways that were often barefaced and sometimes violent. Powle's young brother-in-law of the first marriage, as I have noted, though of a good family, was hanged for burglary. Three years after the death, within a few days of each other, of his first wife and of his only son by her, he married Sarah Corder, a wealthy yeoman's daughter, who, her father admits, was 'much in love.' Her dower was to be four hundred pounds. But twelve years later Corder had not paid his daughter's marriage portion and Powle brought an action in the King's Bench and was awarded only one hundred and fifty pounds by the jury with costs. Then Powle came forward to complain that on that occasion Corder had appeared before the court in such shabby attire that the jury concluded he was poor. A few years later, Powle, having apparently received no satisfaction, brings an action in chancery against Corder, who pleads in his answer that he had always been hoping for 'a better and more friendly disposition' in Powle, but that this hope was not realised, and one Sunday, while Corder and his aged wife (they were both near eighty) were at church, Powle entered their house, debarred their entrance, and thus forced them to seek their lodging in woods and barns. Corder further pleads that Powle had brought an action against him in the Star Chamber which led to his imprisonment in White-chapel Gaol, and while Corder was still there Powle, he alleges, instigated the gaoler's wife with two ruffians to attack him and take his money away. These quarrels are difficult to disentangle. Later in life Powle fell into more serious troubles which are easier to follow.

Powle had purchased the living of Great Waldingfield for the future benefit of his young son, John, whom he was sending to Cambridge, and in the meanwhile he rented the rectory on lease at forty pounds a year, undertaking the repair of the parsonage, boarding and lodging the rector, Clemson, with fire, washing, and attendance to the value of twenty pounds a year, also paying him to instruct two of his children something over two pounds. Almost from the first Powle felt that he was being victimised by Clemson. Always mixed up in so many people's affairs, Powle had been executor to the previous rector, Hindes, whose books to the value of fifty pounds had come into the hands of Powle, and he now found them in possession of Clemson, as Clemson admitted, but said they had been left in the rectory and he knew nothing of Powle's rights to them. Then, in 1624, Clemson absented himself, Powle alleged, from his cure for the space of more than fourscore days, whereupon the lease, according to the law of the realm, becoming void, Powle prepared a new lease, but this disappeared from Powle's desk in the rectory, and since no one in the house was able to read or write except Clemson, Powle opined that he must have taken it. Clemson on his side denied the allegations and pleaded 'that the bill was drawn up in mere malice to vex a poor minister, denies he carried away the lease, and before he carried away his books he allowed Powle to examine them himself to manifest his honesty; he wishes the lease to be void and to pay his own duties, and so forth; says that Powle, when he came to his parsonage house, shut him in unarmed, and Powle's wife [that was the second wife], set upon him with her fists most outrageously and Powle struck him a deadly blow with a gun over the forehead, which swelled immediately to the bigness almost of a hen's egg and the length of a man's finger and bled some few drops of blood, and afterwards the complainant threw a chamber-pot at his head which, had he not fenced off with his arm, it came with such a force, he believeth it would have brained him; then Powle cried "Kill him!" and his wife cried "Shoot him!" and Clemson flew out of the house without his hat or cloak.' It is satisfactory to find that Powle was able to secure such wholehearted allegiance from his wife, but we see, as indeed we know from many other sources, that in the reign of James I the conduct of ladies and gentlemen was not marked by the same prim propriety as in the reign of the highly respectable Victoria, nor was there any undue excess of reverence for the 'sacred cloth.' Clemson held the living, however, for five years longer, and then, over his successor, Nicholas Bloxam, Powle fell into the most lamentable troubles of all, for, as is so often the case with people of his temperament, he was quite incapable of learning by experience. His son, John, was still too young for the living, so Powle endeavoured meanwhile to extract the utmost profit from it and in this effort he committed the grievous ecclesiastical sin of simony, aggravated by breach of promise. (A reliable version of the matter is printed, among other cases in the High Court of Commission, by the historian Gardiner in a Camden Society volume.) The parties injured in the matter reported it to the High Court of Commission. Powle, together with Bloxam, was tried, before Archbishop Abbot, Laud, and many other bishops. He was found guilty, excommunicated, heavily fined, deprived of his lands, and imprisoned. The deprivation and imprisonment were not part of the original sentence, but Powle was not the man to yield weakly, and I expect that he aggravated the original offence by resistance to the court. In his defence he admitted the facts, but sought to justify them. These admitted facts, however, cover the whole case against him, and the sentence of the High Court was not unjust, though it might have been excessive. It is astonishing that a lawyer should have been ignorant of, or indifferent to, so elementary a principle of ecclesiastical law, but in part this may be accounted for by the evil odour which everything ecclesiastical was now acquiring for Puritans, and the Powles, though always Anglican, leaned strongly to the Puritan side which was generally prevalent in Suffolk. The influence of Puritanism in this matter is shown by the fact that eventually the sentence of the Court of Commission in Powle's case was quashed by the House of Lords — surely a much transformed House of Lords — and the case was sent for retrial to the Suffolk Assizes, I believe at his native Bury, and here a jury, evidently composed of Puritans, brought in a verdict against the bishops and in favour of Powle. It was not a sound verdict, but it was, in a sense, a justification of Powle, and it indicates, moreover, that, turbulent and unscrupulous as his methods appear to our more refined age, he had not lost popular esteem among his own fellow citizens; they probably regarded him, indeed, as something of a martyr at the hands of a tyrannical Church. In 1636, evidently no longer a prisoner, I find him petitioning Laud, now become Archbishop of Canterbury for release from the sentence of excommunication. The petition is in the Record Office, and I see Laud has written on it an instruction to the Dean of Arches to report to him before anything is done in the matter, for 'he hath been a very troublesome man.' Therein, I suspect, the Archbishop wrote Paul Powle's epitaph. I can hear little more of him. In 1638 he was living in his house at Felsham, in the full enjoyment of his old litigiousness and persistency; for we find that — recurring to that old grievance of seventeen years back — he brought an action for the return of some of the books left by Hindes in the rectory of Great Waldingfield and since purchased for twenty-four pounds by a clergyman named Bird who knew nothing of Powle's claim. What happened in the matter I do not know, probably nothing. Then in 1642 we hear of him as lending money, but as being at the same time, or a little later when repayment was due, in prison at Bury — it is not stated on what ground — and, again characteristically, because repayment was made a few days late, he insisted that the amount repaid should be considerably increased. Then in a subsequent chancery deposition, in 1652, it is stated that Powle was dead, though the date of his death is not given, and in other chancery pleadings, I am told, it is mentioned that he died in the Fleet Prison in London. Whether, however, these imprisonments arose out of the old trouble with the Court of High Commission seems doubtful, for that court had been abolished in

1641. Thus was his turbulent life gradually extinguished in obscurity and disgrace. He seems already to have lost his devoted wife, and his daughter Sarah, named after her mother, occupied her father's house at Felsham and held the presentation to the living of Great Waldingfield. The Felsham parish registers for that period no longer exist, there is no monument to Powle or his family in the church, and I cannot anywhere find his will. That will was doubtless a document on which Powle spent some trouble, as he had a larger estate to devise than any of his family before or after, but their wills are mostly extant and his has disappeared. He probably died about the beginning of the Civil War troubles and in the general dislocation of those times his will and the memory of his end were both alike lost.

There is one fact which may indicate that Paul Powle was perhaps a more estimable person than the records present to us. He not only came of an estimable stock, but his descendants also were sturdy and admirable men. His son, John Powle, for whom he had purchased the Great Waldingfield living, was of Puritan leanings, a great admirer of Owen, but though, as he said, he would rather have any order in the Church than none, he was for episcopal rule; consequently, after having been parson of Great Waldingfield for a time (though there is no mention of him as rector in the Waldingfield registers or any other official document), he states in his will that he refused to sign the Covenant and fled, never to return, as he honourably refused to turn out the incumbent he had placed there. He became vicar of Dartford — at a time when many travellers, Pepys frequently among them, stopped at this village to change horses and dine at the Bull, as in later years for the old vicar's sake I have done — and here spent a long life, for he was over eighty when he died in 1692, leaving little record of himself in the registers, but making a digressive and amusing will, which exhibits him as a staunch Protestant, and perhaps a rather eccentric personality. His hatred of Popery is pronounced; he lays many evils to its charge,

including the Great Fire of London, and shows a knowledge of the
history of various European countries, partly derived, no doubt,
from his folio copy of Monro's *History of the Wars of the King of
Sweden* which he specially bequeathes to a nephew, and he desires
that no Arminian be presented to the living of Great Waldingfield lest the souls of the people be infected with Pelagian principles which prepare for Popery. He would have no sermon
preached at his funeral; [1] he will have no coffin because of the
risk of being buried alive; and he directs that no stone or railing
shall be placed to mark his grave. He married twice, having a
family by each wife, and he divided among them a considerable
property evidently derived from his father. One of his daughters
married his successor at Dartford. In his son, William, this
circle of clerical ancestors is completed.

William Powle left his fellowship at Pembroke College to
accompany as curate the master of the college, Doctor Coga, who
had chosen to retire from Cambridge to the rich living of Framlingham. Here for many years Powle lived and laboured, the
burden of the cure doubtless sliding more and more from the
shoulders of the aged rector onto his; the entries in the register
are largely in his hand. He married, acquired property in Framlingham, and here nearly all his children were born. In due
course, when his father's incumbent — 'a very careless incumbent,' it is recorded — at length died in 1694, William Powle
migrated to Great Waldingfield. The rectory, today entirely
transformed, stands in spacious and pleasant grounds, approached
through a winding avenue of trees from the church. Here Powle
lived, and in old age died, the finest flower of his race, and the

---

[1] He evidently felt strongly on this point, for he dwells on it at length. 'I will that
there be no sermon at my burial, funeral sermons in the general having done more
harm than good as they have been commonly used, the original of the custom not
commendable, the abuse of it very great, the consequences prejudicial and destructive, being eulogiums unto, and in the hearing of those who were not strangers to,
the deceased, and who finding those placed in Heaven by the Preacher whose conversation was so well known to them to be but civil at best, they hence take liberty
to cast away care of any strict search into their spiritual estate. . . . For these reasons
let me be buried in silence without word spoken except the Office appointed.'

model of an eighteenth-century parish priest, scholar and squire and pastor of souls, simple, just, modest, and practical, loved and esteemed by all. His eldest son, who bore his father's name and was certainly intended to succeed to his father's living, had died immediately after taking his degree. This was evidently a severe blow to the old man, and in his will — an unaffected and straightforward document with none of the quaintly aggressive personal touches we find in his father's will — he directs that he is to be buried near to this son. He had other sons and was married to a third wife (widow of Mark Anthony, a rector of Framlingham), also affectionately mentioned in the will; but it is his daughter Susannah whom he makes his sole executrix with considerable powers and to whom he leaves the presentation to the living which is afterwards to be sold, and become, as it still remains, the property of Clare College. In the male line, after some four centuries of vigorous life, the Powles were now a declining stock; William Powle was the final efflorescence of the family and in his sons it died out. Alike in Kebles and Peppens and Powles the line of hereditary succession has finally been through the women.

Towards the end of the eighteenth century the history of these families became rather featureless, on the whole, indeed, more humble. Powle Peppen, the only child of Richard Peppen and Susannah Powle, spent his whole life quietly at Edwardstone. He had not inherited the Powle property which went to his uncle John, nor, probably, had he inherited any aptitude for business, for the Peppens, as we know, were apt only for the Church, but he seems to have maintained his place in life. I know that he had to borrow money, but I know also that he duly repaid it in instalments, for I hold the receipts. He had married Mary Dodd, of Cockfield in Suffolk, whose father, Merry Dodd, seems to have been in business there. He was somehow related, according to a tradition on both sides of my family, to that brilliant, extravagant, careless Reverend Doctor Dodd who acquired some fame and much notoriety as an eloquent preacher, the skilful editor of the *Beauties of Shakespeare* which served to popularise Shakespeare, and a forger who — so great was the public outcry against the infliction of the penalty on such a person — proved to be the last in England to expiate the offence of forgery by hanging.[1]

I have inherited a miniature said to represent Doctor Dodd, but what his relationship was to Mrs. Powle Peppen neither the genealogy of the Cockfield Dodds, so far as I possess it, nor the biography of the unfortunate divine, suffices to make clear, and it could not have been closer, at nearest, than cousinship. A descendant of the Dodd family with whom I have been in touch had not heard of Merry Dodd.

Mary Peppen died in 1767 — two years before Doctor Dodd's execution at Tyburn — at the early age of twenty-seven, and left two little girls who, though I suppose that they spent their motherless youth with their widowed father (he never seems to have married again) in a small village without social position save a tradition of gentility, possessed fine personal qualities and may be said to have married well, one to my great-grandfather, John Ellis, a burgess, like his father before him, of Sudbury, the other to my great-grandfather, Laver Oliver, burgess of Bury Saint Edmunds, a most energetic and prosperous citizen of the town, where he was an upholsterer besides establishing an extensive carrier system, greatly furthering the fortunes of a now mainly commercial family which still flourishes honourably in Bury and Sudbury.[2]

Ellis is an old Suffolk name, and, though I have not traced the Ellises (I am descended from farther back than William Ellis who was a burgess of Sudbury in the first half of the eighteenth cen-

---

[1] The main facts about Dodd were brought together in a book by Percy Fitzgerald, *A Famous Forgery* (1865). The author remarks that 'no English social event of that character, before or since, ever excited so much absorbing interest.'

[2] In its ramifications the family has been active in many professional and other fields. One of its members, a retired Anglo-Indian, had an extensive genealogical tree prepared. This was once lent me by the head of the Bury family.

tury), I am content to believe that they were the same family who were burgesses of Sudbury in the previous century (when they owned the Swan Inn, later described by Dickens as the Peacock, and demolished in my time) and, indeed, appear prominently in the corporation's records centuries earlier. A family tradition, it is true, reports that the Ellises were descended from an eighteenth-century Mayor of Wrexham in North Wales, but as there were then no mayors of Wrexham, and the tradition in other respects seems inexact, I am inclined to doubt it.[1] I only know certainly that towards the middle of the eighteenth century the family was respectably settled in Sudbury where, from 1731 on, the name duly appears in the registers of baptisms of the ancient Independent chapel, with which at the same time the family of the painter Gainsborough, who was born at Sudbury in 1727, was also connected. In 1764 we hear that William Ellis, my great-great-grandfather, had his 'dwelling house with appurtenances,' situated in the parish of All Saints', Sudbury, 'set apart for the religious worship of Protestant Dissenters by certificate under the Archdeacon.' (The house of John Gainsborough, clothier, in the parish of Saint Peter's, had been similarly set apart in 1756.) At that time William Ellis was described as a staymaker, which was also the occupation of Thomas Paine's father at Thetford almost at the same time; in 1792 he is described in the Universal British Directory, amongst

---

[1] It must be admitted there are points that make the Wrexham tradition plausible. It is derived from my oldest uncle who in youth was much with his grandfather, and it harmonises with some ascertainable facts. The Wrexham Ellises used the same Christian names; they were Congregationalists like those of Sudbury and helped to found a church of which in 1783 a Mr. Jenkin Lewis was minister, and it so happens that my father has informed me he had heard of a family connection with the Lewises, a name not belonging to Suffolk. But the original Sudbury Ellis, if he came from Wrexham, must have left long before this period. Palmer's *History of Wrexham* makes no mention of any Ellis who fulfils the necessary conditions. The settlement of the matter may doubtless be found in the registers of All Saints', Sudbury. Another tradition, also coming through the same uncle, is more intangible. According to this, the Ellises are really Wyatts, a Wyatt at some unstated period having been adopted by an Ellis. In 1743 there was at Sudbury a John Wyatt, apparently like the Ellises a dissenter in religion, but he was not early enough.

the principal inhabitants of Sudbury, as a wool factor. His son, John, my great-grandfather, who married Elizabeth Peppen, became a linen draper in the city of London in 1790 and is so termed on the certificate admitting him to the freedom of the borough of Sudbury and to all the liberties and privileges appertaining. His private address was then in Astley Row, Islington.[1] My grandfather Edward was the second child and the young wife took him as a baby on a visit to her husband's family at Sudbury. I have the fresh and charming letter she wrote to her husband on the occasion; full of delight at the admiration her child has aroused in the stagecoach, and with a trace of gay persiflage of all the old people at Sudbury and their meeting-house. John Ellis established a linen draper's business in Tavistock Street, Covent Garden; his shop seems to have acquired a reputation in the theatrical region in which it was situated; Mrs. Siddons, the great actress, used to come to him for her stockings; an engraving of her — presented, I understand, by herself — has been handed down in the family. It would appear, however, that the business was not successful — only the Olivers among my forebears seem to have had any genuine relish for trade — and at a late date John Ellis became a corn factor. As regards his personal tastes, I only know that he was fond of music and played the organ. My father could just recall him as a tall, dignified, and handsome old gentleman in knee-breeches who called him 'Ned.' One day in chapel, a little later, after joining heartily in the singing, he sat down, stooped to pick up his gloves, and was shortly after found to be dead.

His son Edward, born in 1794, who spent his life as a warehouseman in the London Docks, occupied the spacious, well-built, and pleasant corner house which still stands on the pier head at Wapping; it was later occupied by his eldest son and successor as an official in the Docks, my uncle John, and in child-

---

[1] In 1929 I went to look at this house, once of highly respectable character, now falling to decay, but still facing a pleasant open space.

hood I was often taken there. My father's father — as I gather from what I have heard of him and from his daguerreotype portrait — was thought French in appearance and, unlike his father, was of small size. (His mother referred to his 'dark eyes' even as an infant, and I may perhaps conclude that he took after her and that the Peppens were a small dark race.) He was a gentle and sensitive man of rather nervous and anxious temperament, refined artistic tastes, and versatile intellectual aptitudes. His relations considered him rather indifferent to religion, but, judging from a letter he wrote to my father when a boy, chatty and familiar but with a simply genuine reference to religious matters, I suspect that he was religious at heart. He was fond of flowers and of music, himself playing the flute. He dabbled in mechanical problems, and invented a new kind of buoy which was found by the authorities to be excellent in idea but impracticable, though afterwards it was modified by others and generally adopted. He liked to draw and desired his sons to have a sound education in drawing, for which, however, they had little taste. He amused himself, too, by tinting prints of the old masters with delicate water-colour washes. He was also a good amateur carpenter and made an excellent bookcase which is still in use. He had little affinity with his commonplace wife, the daughter of a yeoman-farmer named Gray in the Isle of Wight, and he was rather worried by her ceaseless household activities on behalf of the family of seven children which filled the fine solid old house on the pier head.

On the whole, the Ellis family seems to me chiefly remarkable for its mediocrity, a golden mediocrity it may possibly be, the mediocrity of people who have no vices and no temptations, who never absolutely fail in life, but have no great ambitions and no great ideals. Their energy is always fairly adequate to carry them along the path of life in which they find themselves, but they are never troubled by any surplus of unused energy. '*In medio tutissimus ibis*,' that is a truth they know by instinct. My own

temperament has in it elements of an extremely other sort —
my tendency is to unite extremes rather than to go between them
— and I owe much to the Ellises for a good dose of this beautiful
mediocrity, to me a harmonising influence of the most precious
character.

Very different were the characteristics of my mother's family,
I mean especially the Olivers, to whom my mother's mother
belonged. Here there was an exuberant energy which displayed
itself in various fields. They wandered over the world as soldiers,
they achieved success in commerce and trade; they were, indeed,
the only family from which I spring which showed any aptitude
for making money. In recent times an Oliver, a cousin of my
mother's, was regarded as the foremost citizen of Bury Saint
Edmunds, the town of the Olivers, though they had originally
come from Sudbury, with which they retained a connection, so
having moved in a reverse direction from the Powles who originated in Bury, to settle later around Sudbury, where Olivers and
Powles both came in contact with Ellises, who seem always to
have belonged to Sudbury or the neighbourhood. That is how it
came to pass that I am doubly descended from the Powles and
the Peppens and the Kebles through the marriages of my two
great-grandmothers, Elizabeth Peppen to John Ellis and Susannah Peppen to Laver Oliver. Thus, so far as I can trace, I am
purely English in the narrowest sense, and on both sides I am
half of Suffolk descent. Of recent years — since I have become
acquainted with these facts and since also I have learnt to know
the characteristics of Suffolk — I have been amused to trace in
myself some of the fundamental traits of the Suffolk character.[1]
East Anglia, as I have found, has some claim to be a focus of
English genius. Much that is most typical in English politics

---

[1] That I am justified in regarding myself as mainly an East Anglian of Suffolk is
indicated by at least one little organic trait. As a child I was worried by finding in
myself a difficulty in pronouncing the sound 'th,' notably in such a combination as
the biblical 'it sufficeth us,' and the difficulty still remains. It is only of recent years
that I have learnt that this difficulty is a recognised East Anglian shibboleth.

and adventure, thought and science and art practice, has come out of East Anglia. The people of Suffolk, sometimes apparently slow, are yet ever exuberant in energy, often bright of eye and quick of action. Cautious, patient, pliant, conciliatory, they can yet be forceful, independent, obstinate. Not superficially brilliant like the people of the southwest, they are not so impenetrably reserved beneath a hard rind like the people of the north; there is a strong emotional undercurrent which makes itself felt, even though it may not be visible, so that they are a friendly people whom it is not difficult to get on with. Women play a large part among them. The solidity these people of Suffolk owed to their Dutch and Flemish affinities has been modified by French Huguenot and other foreign elements. They are practical and materialistic people who delight to make their surroundings spacious and beautiful, a religious and benevolent people, indeed, yet by no means ascetic, scarcely even, in the narrow sense, a severely moral people; their instincts, in life as in science and art, tend to direct them towards Nature.

At many of these points I feel myself to be a true child of Suffolk. I have sometimes been puzzled at my instinctive and seemingly opposed attraction towards science and towards art. But they are both in the Suffolk character and both alike are forms of the love of Nature. The fact, however, that I am a true child of Suffolk is brought home to me by the instinctive attraction which I have often felt towards people who came from the same district as I come from, even before I knew what that district was. As a student, the two fellow students for whom I felt a touch of real personal affection — though from lack of common intellectual interests no permanent friendship was formed — both came, as I afterwards discovered, from the same parts of Suffolk as my own family, while the only fellow student with whom I have formed a lifelong friendship, Doctor Barker Smith, belonged on both sides to the neighbourhood of Castle Hedingham, within a walk of Sudbury where my own ancestral roots are most deeply planted.

Almost the most intimate of my women friends during many years belonged to the same region, and even a girl patient in the hospital, who was once under my care as a student, and seemed so charming to me that I wrote a sonnet about her ('Arabella'), possibly belonged, as I now judge by her type and her name, to Suffolk.

When I consider the character and ability of these various Suffolk forefathers so far as known to me, I seem to trace elements of my own character — of individuality, of persistence, of obstinate fidelity to one's own ideas — in several of the remote country parsons from whom I am doubly descended. William Powle may be said to be the most distinguished figure of my family of whose character very definite record is left. The filial piety of his daughter and the generous and grateful appreciation of his son-in-law, Richard Peppen, perpetuated his memory. They also showed their affectionate piety towards the old man's memory by naming their only child Powle. The Latin epitaph on William Powle's altar-tomb is a precise characterisation which can scarcely be classed with the vague and flowery eulogies so common in such places. I translate as follows: 'Here by his own desire are laid the mortal remains of William Powle, A.M., for thirty-three years the most vigilant rector of this church, a man wise, modest, and learned, simple and without guile, pious without pretence, a theologian to be numbered among the first both for skill in judgment and for power of discourse. He died on the 14th of September in the year of human salvation 1727, aged seventy-two.' I cannot pretend to myself that I am in any field all that is here attributed to this accomplished ancestor who died exactly a century before my father was born. But that impulse which led me as a child to play at being a preacher in church, later to propose, as the only vocation that had any attraction at all for me, to enter the Church, and has ever since made me a preacher in other fields, may well be rooted, since it displayed itself so spontaneously, in an inherited aptitude already displayed in a large number of ancestors from whom I am doubly descended and, it would seem, with especial completeness in William Powle, who seems to have possessed also the reasonableness of character, the judicial temperament, which some have noted as traits of mine. The Peppens were distinguished by their piety towards the past and their obstinacy in going their own way in the present. Both these characteristics are certainly pronounced in me, and I have sometimes wondered whether that un-English (once, at least, Flemish) air, which both English and foreign acquaintances have noted in me, may not be the atavistic reminiscence of Walloon Pepins from whom the Peppens of Wenhaston must assuredly have descended. The Peppens combined their independent character and their ecclesiasticism with a certain eye to the main chance, not only in the branch I belong to, but in the related and also clerical branches; thus, one of these clergymen married a baronet's daughter and assumed a crest, a Pegasus, and what connection he found between Peppens and Pegasus I have sometimes wondered. William Keble combined the Peppens' obstinacy and devotion to principle with an indifference to consequences which arouses my admiration, although I scarcely share his spirit of exclusive partisanship; I specially admire the spirit in which the old man, once driven forth from his living for his staunch opposition to Puritanism, left a will so free from bitterness, and was chiefly concerned that his trees should not be cut down.

Herewith I have presented the salient features of my remote Suffolk ancestry: for the most part a distant crowd of scholars and parsons, in recent times almost hidden from sight by men of the sea.

The Olivers stand apart among these Suffolk families, the most recent and the most apt for worldly success. If, however, they knew how to make money, some of them knew how to waste it. They were often, it seems, self-willed, reckless people, intolerant of restraint. They sometimes met tragic ends; I vaguely recall hearing of one, an officer in the army, who narrowly escaped being buried alive on the West Coast of Africa by the happy thought of someone who before the burial rubbed him with cayenne pepper, but who was shortly after blown up in an explosion at a fort in Jamaica. They were highspirited, perhaps a little insolent as well as reckless. An Oliver, a young officer, once waited on Lord Cornwallis, himself a Suffolk man and then commander-in-chief, to beg his favour in obtaining a commission. 'You look as if you had come to confer a favour rather than ask for it,' Cornwallis observed. Physically they tended to be large, imposing, portly people, not handsome — with a mouth too long in upper lip — but with deliberate vigour, with the air of grave responsibility which sometimes marks the man of large and imperious physical organism. It is a variety of the John Bull type. In their portraits they stand with figures well drawn up and seeming to demand a certain amount of space around them, by no means inviting approach. There is a certain anxiety in their countenances, a certain physiological discomfort, the expression of a massive restless organism, too conscious of itself, which cannot but assert: I am I, in the spirit of Marcus Aurelius's words, 'As though the emerald should say, Whatever happens I must be emerald,' words I have so often found myself murmuring through life, by no means necessarily in the spirit of one who would preserve some immaculate purity, but in the conviction that one's own peculiar instincts, good or bad, cannot be violated. I recall my mother's only surviving uncle who was completely of this type. He lived in Chelsea, having occupied an official position at the Chelsea Hospital. He had formed a relationship with his housekeeper whom he never married, but openly had two sons by her. My mother, inflexible as were her own moral standards, seems to have accepted this situation and I never heard her criticise it. I remember her taking me to Chelsea, and I remember Uncle Oliver visiting us with his older son.

My grandmother, Susannah Oliver (afterwards Wheatley), was born in 1788, the eldest child and only girl in a large family of

brothers who idolised her. In a miniature and two pencil portraits she appears a woman of energy and intelligence and vivacity, with a touch of melancholy in the eyes, but a witty and sensitive curve of the lips, not formally beautiful, but with the attraction that comes of vitality and spirit. Her chief beauty was
considered to be her long and abundant hair, worn in clustered
curls at the front and a large mass on the top of the head, of auburn colour in the miniature, but a soft mousy brown in the brace-
let made of it which I now possess. The women of the Oliver family today, I am told, are still noted in Bury for their beautiful hair.
She was a capable woman and had a high-class school for girls she
had set up in a large old house at Leyton, then a rural suburb
of London. I cannot easily imagine her at the head of the prim
academy for young ladies we hear of as typical of these days, but
I am not surprised at her success. I recall the great gateway and
the avenue of trees leading to Suffolk House, as it was called,
where my mother once took me as a child to see her birthplace;
it was pulled down a few years ago to give place to rows of workmen's houses, but it still figures with other large old vanished
houses in the local histories. Susannah Oliver was a woman of
culture and accomplishments. She painted flowers in the delicate
and commonplace Dutch manner of her day; she played the harp,
on which occasions her beautiful arms aroused much admiration.
Her tastes in literature were fine and wide, ranging over many
fields, scientific and artistic; she seems to have bought the best
literature of her day, and many of the books that fed or aroused
my own early thirst for knowledge had her bookplate in them.
Of these I note especially Rowlandson's *Doctor Syntax* on which
I pored with concentrated interest; Rousseau's *Rêveries*, the
first French book I ever read out of school for my own pleasure;
Maria Edgeworth's *Harry and Lucy*, a cleverly written popular-
isation of science in story-form which I still vividly recall; and
Nature Displayed, a more technical, well-illustrated, but too
concise, summary of scientific knowledge in numerous volumes,

not excluding human anatomy. I know it was too concise, for
there, at the age of twelve, I sought to satisfy my nascent curiosity concerning the sexual organs of woman, but intently as I
studied the brief account given I was baffled, for I could not
understand how a region which, so far as I knew anything of it,
was so bare could yet harbour so many different objects with
definite Latin names. My grandmother was a friend of Miss
Sarah Stickney, afterwards the wife of William Ellis, the missionary whose books on Polynesia are still an ethnological treasure-house, and herself one of the most influential writers of the
time. I doubt, however, if she could have influenced my grandmother, for she was eleven years her junior and had scarcely
begun to publish when my grandmother died. The Stickneys
were a Yorkshire Quaker family, but had relatives in Suffolk,
which doubtless accounts for my grandmother's association with
Sarah. Her mother, Esther Stickney, described in her daughter's
biography as 'a refined and intellectual woman,' died when
Susannah Wheatley was a girl of thirteen, but a miniature, said
to be of Mrs. Stickney, has descended to me, an attractive, good-
looking, mature woman, with calm, observant, self-possessed
eyes, and softly rounded full chin. The Stickneys were Quakers
of the best type. My grandmother was anything but a Quaker;
she was something of a woman of fashion; she wore coal-scuttle
bonnets of the largest size, whence once an embarrassing difficulty in entering a carriage; and on the eve of her wedding-day,
being obliged to have her hair dressed by the hairdresser the day
before, she sat up all night; she impressed her neighbours by
appearing at church every Sunday with a new pair of gloves, and
it was known that she tight-laced by fastening the laces to the
bedpost; this, indeed, it was said, conduced to her death in child-
bed on the birth of her third child at the age of a little over forty.
This child, a girl, died young, and another, a boy, went to sea in
a ship that was never again heard of, so that my mother was the
only surviving child.

Susannah Oliver had married her sailor husband, **John Wheat-** ley, late in life; it is perhaps characteristic of her impulsive and dominating Oliver temperament that when, after the marriage, the moment came for Captain Wheatley to go back to his ship, she found it impossible to let him go; he abandoned the voyage, and indeed gave up the sea altogether for a life of dignified in-dolence; henceforth, instead of his ship's poop, he paced up and down the garden-walks at Leyton — as my father's brother, who sometimes went to see him there when a boy, has described to me — in the leisurely and stately manner natural to the fair, handsome, imposing man whom I only know by his miniature, a very large man, my uncle said, who spoke but little, but, when he spoke, spoke well. He was overwhelmed by grief at his wife's death, which caused indeed an attack of brain fever; he could not bear to look at anything that had belonged to her and rapidly disposed of jewels and much else that should have come later to my mother. But he lived on for more than twenty years, marry-ing again a lively little widow with a large family, named Parr, whom he had engaged to keep on the school.

I know little else of my maternal grandfather, who was born in 1783 and died in 1853, six years before I was born. He had traded chiefly in the Mediterranean, especially to Smyrna, whence he had brought the stuff for his wife's wedding-gown. Early in life he had been taken prisoner during the French wars, and when I was a child my mother would tell me how as a prisoner in France he was given black bread which when thrown against the wall would stick to it, and how he had at last escaped through the good offices of a French girl, a certain Annette, possibly — though of that my mother never hinted and perhaps never knew — the sweetheart of the fair and handsome Englishman. I would gladly have known the story of that episode. (For his grandson also owes much to a French girl.) Doubtless it was due to his imprisonment in France, and in part perhaps to Annette, that my grandfather wrote an easy and fluent though incorrect

French; he would write letters in French to my mother as a schoolgirl — I possess some of them — and playfully sign himself 'Jean Houtclet.'

The Wheatleys generally, as I know them, were a race of large and placid people, imposing to look at in their natural and unostentatious dignity, but, unlike the Olivers, of no great energy intellectual or practical. They had long been settled in Durham and Sunderland. A John de Wheatley figures in the roll of the famous Richard de Bury, Bishop of Durham, in 1337, and John was the favourite Christian name of the family whose surname appears from time to time until a John Wheatley from whom I can definitely trace descent came to light in the seventeenth century and was succeeded by another of the same name who married a Haswell, a prominent landed family of those parts. Their son was my great-grandfather, Ralph Wheatley, who about 1776 married Mary Havelock at Sunderland parish church; the marriage, tradition says, was that of the handsomest couple of their time in the town.

Sunderland was a great shipping centre, during the French wars the chief shipbuilding place in the kingdom, so that many fortunes were made there. The Wheatleys were, above all, sailors (at least two were drowned), merchants, sea-captains or naval officers, shipbuilders, sailmakers. Ralph Wheatley became prosperous and rich, leaving considerable property and a large family, of which my grandfather was the youngest, and owing to that fact, and his absence at sea, he seems to have received but a small share of the paternal fortune. The only story that has come down to me of that prosperous household (unless, indeed, it refers to an earlier generation) has its point in the dignity especially associated with the Wheatley family. It concerns a daughter of the house who, suffering from flatulence, prepared herself a glass of hot spirits-and-water, and laying strict injunctions on the housemaid to admit no one into the drawing-room, there proceeded to pin up her skirts round her waist (no drawers were worn in these days) and leisurely drink her spirits, standing with her back to the fire; while thus engaged a carriage drove up and the negligent housemaid or some other servant showed in one of the most eminently conventional and respectable families in the neighbourhood. This story, however, seems to illustrate the customs of the time rather than the traits of an individual young lady, for there is a charming picture extant by Isaac Cruikshank, presenting a young lady in this attitude. I may remark that in some later collateral branches of the Wheatley family slight eccentricity was manifested. Ralph Wheatley's eldest son, another Ralph, who became a sailmaker at, I think, Greenwich, was said to be a man of unusual character, and of his daughter, who was nicknamed 'Sally Brass,' many pranks were narrated. Another cousin of my mother's may possibly have been subject to those *fugues* which have of recent years been studied as epileptic manifestations, for from time to time he would mysteriously leave his wife and family and disappear. But though there were many Wheatleys, for they tended to have large families, there was no definite insanity! Except, indeed, that an Oliver once became insane in old age, I cannot find traces of insanity, scarcely of any gross nervous disease or pronounced mental abnormality, in any of the families from which I spring and am thus suspicious of the statement, so often made, that there is insanity in every family. It seems to me by no means so evenly distributed, and that while there is a great deal of insanity in some families, there is very little in others.

Ralph Wheatley, my great-grandfather, as I have mentioned, married Mary Havelock. She was the aunt of the famous General Havelock, who was then my grandfather's first cousin. At this time the Havelocks were also gaining prosperity as shipbuilders at Sunderland, where the future general was born nineteen years later. The Havelocks had long been scattered about this region, but the chief centre of the family seems to have been Grimsby, and on the seal of the Grimsby Corporation, beside Grime, the supposed founder of the town, is seen the figure of a crowned youth, Havelock, said in the legendary *Lay of Havelok the Dane* to have been the lost child of a great sea-king who, having been saved by fishermen, became a cook boy at Lincoln, but, being recognised as the stoutest man in England, married the young English princess, Goldeburgh, reigned for sixty years and left fifteen sons and daughters who all became kings and queens. It appears that the boundary stone outside Grimsby is still called the Havelock Stone. According to later tradition the Havelock family descended from Guthrum, the really historical Danish King of East Anglia in the days of Alfred the Great, who converted him to Christianity. It is likely that this tradition was in the mind of my mother's favourite cousin, Nancy Wheatley, who told me in childhood that the Wheatleys were descended from the Danish Kings of England. My mother gave me at birth the name of General Havelock, not because of the relationship, but because of her admiration for him as a hero who, above all soldiers of the time, had the reputation of being a devout Christian. I am not sure that I have a concrete mental representation of Sir Henry Havelock, who was not only a devout Christian, but a stern and capable general of the type of Cromwell's Ironsides, with no objection to blow men from guns, nor am I prepared to say that I have the slightest resemblance to him. The only link I can find is that he was nicknamed by his schoolfellows the Philosopher, which happens to be the name which my wife has often playfully applied to me, and possibly a certain firm moral tenacity which I certainly inherit from my mother. (And I have been amused to note in Havelock's portraits a very pronounced chin-dimple equally marked in me.) Havelock is the chief representative in my family of the fighting element which played a considerable part on my mother's side of the house, both the Wheatleys and the Olivers, several of her uncles having been colonels and naval officers, one of them with Nelson at Copenhagen. But none seem to have been in the direct line of my descent.

One of my four grand-parental families I have still left undescribed. It stands rather apart. I have found difficulties in defining its characteristics and in formulating my own spiritual relation to it, so that I was unable to feel much interest in this family, with which, indeed, I have never come in contact and never heard much about. I refer to the family of my father's mother, the Grays of the Isle of Wight. My grandmother, whom I can barely remember, was an excellent woman of colourless character whose life was completely absorbed by domestic routine, and whose energies, I imagine, would in no case have been conspicuous in any other sphere. But she was the daughter — the sixteenth and youngest child — of a really notable and superior woman, Sarah Gray, the only person among my direct ancestors, so far as I know, of whom anyone has ever thought it worth while to write and publish a biography.[1]

The Grays were farmers long established, I believe, at Vittle Fields Farm near Carisbrook, where in the third quarter of the eighteenth century they were represented by Richard Gray, my great-grandfather. In a neighbouring parish, his future wife, Sarah, the daughter of another farmer (the biographer strangely neglects to mention either her maiden name or the name of the parish), was born in 1759 at Quarry Farm. It is on the religious character of this lady that her biographer chiefly insists, and too much else is omitted, so that I can but echo the remark which Eliza Morris herself puts into the reader's mouth: 'The one half was not told me.'

Sarah was brought up as a member of the Church of England and duly confirmed at the age of fifteen. But religion in these days was a disturbing and even exciting element of life. The clergyman, we are told, was 'a man of very immoral habits,' and so quite incapable of preaching the way of salvation, but he had evidently attracted the enthusiastic devotion of his flock to the

---

[1] *Memoirs of Mrs. Sarah Gray, late of the Isle of Wight.* Written by her granddaughter Eliza Morris Hammersmith, 1831, pp. 62. Price one shilling.

church, for when a preacher — no doubt, though we are not told
so, one of the new sect of Methodists — arrived in 'the now
highly favoured but then destitute Island,' and endeavoured to
preach in her parish, Sarah was desirous to hear him, but was
'prevented by the noise and tumult of the people, who evinced
the malice and enmity of their hearts against everything that was
spiritual by pelting the minister with stones and rotten eggs, and
drowning the sound of his voice by beating drums and kettles,
so that he could not proceed in his discourse, but turning himself
to the scoffing crowd, said with a firm voice, "I shake off the dust
from my feet as a testimony against you, and verily it shall be
more tolerable for Sodom and Gomorrah in the days of Judgment
than for you, but I am absolved from the guilt of your destruction."' The young girl wept much at the awful sentence thus
pronounced by one who evidently possessed the keys of hell, and
not long after her marriage in 1775 she 'cast in her lot with the
people of God,' being therein followed by her husband. 'Being
greatly blessed in their temporal circumstances,' in course of
time, with the aid of a few friends, they built a chapel at Node
Hill, which seems, however, to have been some miles away from
their house. Mrs. Gray brought up sixteen children, not all of
whom, we are told, showed her religious faith, but they were a
family of fine and robust farmers, and my grandmother, who was
the youngest, was also the smallest. Mrs. Gray was something
of a saint, but in the practical English way. Her minister was the
Reverend D. Tyerman, a remarkable man whose name and work
survive; he was sent out on a prolonged tour of missionary inspection in the South Seas and died in Madagascar. Sarah Gray
seems to have accepted the doctrine of her Bible and the Calvin-
istic principles of her sect, but she understood them in her own
personal way, and by the instincts of her own beautiful nature she
developed into a kind of mystic.

'In secret silence of the mind
My Heaven and there my God I find,'

were lines she loved to repeat, and they are of the essence of mysticism. 'She was arrived at the highest state of Christian perfection,' we are told, but she necessarily lived a busy practical life in which every moment was occupied, an industrious, economical, and prudent housewife. 'Her maxim was always to be doing something for this world or the next,' and 'never to her recollection did she lie in bed after the sun had risen.' But while thus labouring indefatigably in the details of domestic life on a farm, her outlook was large. She was not one of the trivially fussy domesticated women. She possessed the gift of love. She never sought to find fault with others and she practised religion rather than talked about it; she was very liberal to the poor, though generally in secret, and 'never did she oppress the hireling in his wages,' but was always the friend of her servants. It was the love of God that made the core of her religion. Upon that she would dwell with ever new delight, and often repeat, 'God is love, and he that dwelleth in love dwelleth in God, and God in him.' She also loved Nature and all the more during the last twelve years of her life when, confined to her bed but unable to lie down — no doubt affected by cardiac disease — she loved to have her curtains open during her restless nights so that she might gaze on the sky. She died in 1830 at the age of seventy. Her husband, who died many years earlier, was the meet companion of this woman with a genius for religion, so full of sweetness and loving-kindness. 'The pilgrims of olden time used to give Mr. Gray the honourable appellation of the hospitable Gaius,' and he always read, we are told, a fragment of the *Pilgrim's Progress* and the Bible every evening after the day's business was over! He was a well-to-do man and left one thousand pounds apiece to his very large family. Several of his children emigrated to America, others were scattered about England (though I have never been in touch with any of their families), and I suppose it was in this way that Sophia met Edward Ellis. They were married at Hackney, the then quiet and dignified London suburb where old John Ellis retired and died (as also later, it so chanced, my mother's father) about the year 1821, and became the parents of six children, four boys and two girls, of whom my father, the fourth, was, I believe, born at Bramley.

Of late I have meditated on the significance that the Grays may have in my own ancestral inheritance. An intuitive woman, by no means a mystic herself, remarked to me the other day that she thought that if I had been less scientific I should have been a mystic. It is not a fact that I have ever wished to obtrude, yet it is a fact that there is no need for me to wait to be less 'scientific,' for I am a natural mystic already by inborn constitution as well as by actual experience. The religion of my numerous clerical ancestors, however admirable and genuine, approved indeed by persecution, was not, so far as can now be discerned, mystical; it was in the best sense ecclesiastical. My mother again, whose evangelical piety was so genuine and so practical, so completely the ruling power of her life, was not a mystic. In this matter I see in myself a faint reflection of that inner light, so spontaneously kindled in the beautiful soul of my great-grandmother, Sarah Gray.

The general distinctive fact about the Grays, however, was that they were farmers or yeomen; Sarah Gray was herself a farmer's daughter. In that respect the Grays were unlike the other families from which I am descended. The Ellises, the Olivers, the Wheatleys had not cultivated the soil for some two centuries, perhaps longer. Putting aside trade and other miscellaneous occupations, the prevailing vocation of my forefathers on both sides was the sea and behind that the Church. The sea has not played a large part in the ancestry of the people who represent England to the world, large as has been the part it has played in the life of England and the English people. In the whole of British genius, in my study of that subject, I have estimated the maritime ancestry as 1.9, less than any other class, and few representative English people proceeded from this ancestry, unless it

may be Byron, William Penn, Bishop Andrewes, and Stamford
Raffles. In recent days I think of Edward Carpenter as belonging
to a naval family, but of no others. My own complicated and
far-spread maritime ancestry thus seems to me rare indeed in
the English spiritual field. To it I am inclined to attribute a
large part of what is in me characteristic. I seem to myself
peculiarly English, yet I have to acknowledge that I am singularly
unlike many other peculiarly English persons. That seems to me
due to the fact that I am English of the sea and they are English
of the land. That fluid, libertarian, adventurous, versatile spirit
I find in myself, the far sight, the wide outlook, is English of the
sea, the characteristic outcome of the sailor's life. I miss the
note of earthiness, so common in the English mind and in the
English style. It is not present in me even when I am sensuous,
even in the touch of the satyr or the faun my friends are sometimes pleased, quite rightly no doubt, to find in me, for it is not
possible to one whose spirit is washed by the salt sea. I am born
of the water and the wind, precisely the elements that raged
furiously on the night I entered the world. The more typical
kind of Englishman is born of the earth; his eyes have been fixed
on its furrows, and not on the horizon; he deals with a hard and
rebellious element not to be conquered mainly by skill, by adjustment, by reliance on Nature, but mainly by force, by muscular toughness, by pertinacity, by stubbornness. There is all
that energy and tenacity in the typical Englishman, derived from
his struggle with the earth, and something of the mud of the
earth usually remains bespattering his spirit. No doubt these
qualities have come to me, too, especially much obstinate tenacity, for men far back in my ancestry tilled the soil; but they
have had time to be transformed and sublimated. The Grays
alone represent — and even then at a distance of three generations — a more recent infusion of the farmer's temperament, an
infusion doubtless useful to qualify the rest.

Of even many details in my disposition it seems to me that

the sea is the ultimate basis. Mountains, which are most remote
from the sea, are antipathetic to me; the sea-like plains of Holland
(made by the sea if one thinks of it) satisfy me more than the
Andes and the Alps. I enjoy heights, but it is because of their
outlook and space and atmosphere;

> 'all waste
> And solitary places; where we taste
> The pleasure of believing what we see
> Is boundless, as we wish our souls to be,'

are words I have always loved of Shelley who was in youth my
poet of predilection, and Shelley — I know not why — is not
the poet of earth so much as of sea and air. My love of purity —
to be sure in no prim and prudish sense — is an attraction to a
quality which is of the sea rather than of the gross and muddy
earth, and the quality of clinging tenacity towards all that I have
ever loved is only a form of that fidelity which Conrad declared
to be the chief virtue of the sailor.

On the whole, it may be seen, I represent, on both sides, the
outcome, in the main, of families of sailors and people connected
with the sea, while farther back, through both sides, is a long line
of parish priests, solid, scholarly, admirable men, tenacious of
their convictions, ready to suffer cheerfully for their devotion to
those convictions. In my blood the two latent streams of tendency have entered into active combination and grown conscious
at last in my brain. So I have become an adventurer in morals
and a pioneer over spiritual seas.

In past years I have often puzzled over my own temperament
and wondered whether I am of weaker or stronger character than
average people. Today I am no longer puzzled by the contra-
dictory elements in myself. I see that they are simply the sum
of the tendencies I have inherited from various families. At the
core, doubtless, is the rather dominating, emotional, and instinctive energy of the Olivers — for I have always felt that I
derive the active side mainly from my mother — but that has

been tempered by the indolent placidity, not without its underlying obstinacy, no doubt, of the Wheatleys and considerably
modified by the easy-going nonchalance of the Ellises with the
latent mysticism beneath it of the Grays. I detect in myself a
tenacious and unyielding fidelity to the end or object or person
that has once touched me deeply enough to affect my emotions
and instincts, but on the surface I yield at a touch, and while I
am prepared to suffer anything for the personal and impersonal
ends that have really fascinated me, I am yet too lazy to move an
inch out of my way for other ends that yet seem to me wholly
worthy. I am not incapable, even, of a considerable dash of
scepticism concerning the ends for which I can never cease to
labour. But any question of weakness or strength becomes meaningless to me when I realise that these various tendencies are
simply the balanced play within me of the Oliver strain, Wheatley
strain, Ellis strain, Gray strain. I can understand what Renan
says of the places occupied in his own temperament by unlike
strains of Gascon and Breton.

I have said that, so far as mental aptitudes and tastes are concerned, I trace my inheritance especially to my father's father and
my mother's mother, more remotely to the Suffolk rectors who
were my ancestors along both lines. The creative and productive
impulse was only latent in both of those grandparents, but they
had the intellectual and artistic temperament, a temperament
which my father and my mother transmitted to me, but themselves showed no trace of. My father, Edward Peppen Ellis, possessed all the mediocrity of his family, though in him it was revealed in an almost golden form. As a child he was described, in
the terms of an old-fashioned mixed metaphor, as 'the flower of
the flock' in the large family, and going to sea early, passing half a
century in a sailor's life, he developed a more open-air and genial
personality than his brothers who all spent their lives in the Docks
like their father before them, and became the typical English sea-
captain of whom Sir William Butler remarks in his *Autobiography*

that he is the very best man that England produces. He never knew what a headache was like; his teeth were perfect until old age; he was never troubled by his digestion; no serious illness or physical disability ever befell him. Neither tobacco nor alcohol had any attraction for him, though on occasion he would accept a cigar or a cigarette and appreciated an occasional sherry and bitter, until old age when he regularly took a little whisky. He was equally cheerful and sociable — always a great favourite with girls; content with what the days brought forth, never seeking to go beyond the surface of the things presented to him, though much contact with many kinds of people had imparted to him a touch of good-humoured scepticism. I doubt if he had ever read any poet but Pope, and, while not uninterested in the natural things which fell directly beneath his notice, the manifold spectacle of life which he had seen under many aspects in many parts of the world had left him almost untouched. He was not shrewd or worldly or businesslike, outside his profession; he had availed himself little of his opportunities to make money and his investments were mostly unfortunate. After he retired from the sea, with a small pension from Trinity House, losing at almost the same time his two chief solaces, his ship and his wife, his life was for some years rather unsettled and troubled, but the Ellis spirit and his own temperament were finally reasserted. He went to live in a boarding-house by the sea belonging to a niece, leading an innocently gay and frivolous life, surrounded by young girls, an Epicurean whose philosophy was unconscious. When well past seventy he became attached to a lady, some thirty years his junior, and their marriage was only prevented at the last moment by the objection of the lady's relatives. But the couple remained affectionate friends; he went to live in her house at Folkestone as a lodger, and here he spent the remaining years of his life peacefully and happy, surrounded by her devoted care, and seeing his children from time to time. Once he went with her to Paris, for he had never been there and he felt it was an experience not to be missed. Frequently they would go up for a few days to London, where he was indefatigable in sight-seeing, an eager visitor to theatres and music-halls. His health remained unimpaired until the age of eighty-seven. Then shortly after the Great War broke out, he passed through a phase of unwonted irritability of mood, and when that disappeared it was found that he was suffering from cancer of the liver. The final illness lasted only a few weeks and his mind remained clear, fully conscious that the end was approaching, but cheerful and even humorous. He never complained, and before the last restless stages of discomfort he would say that he felt ashamed of lying so comfortably in bed when there was so much suffering in the trenches. He would speak to me of all the little arrangements to be made after his death, and was content and willing to go, having, as he put it, 'had a good innings.' Of religion or faith or hope of a future life there was never a word. He had never been either religious or irreligious, having never felt any inner need to be either, for he had never had any violent passions to restrain or any exalted aspirations to pacify. He had simply accepted, quietly and humbly, the religious conventions around him, joining without question in all the devotions of my mother for whom he had the highest reverence. At sea he had conducted religious services whenever he felt it his duty so to do, just as under the like circumstances he had once or twice conducted a midwifery case, for on board his ship, in the absence of the accredited representatives of those professions, the captain is both priest and doctor. In his last years, as I learnt from what he once told me, he had quietly and spontaneously become definitely sceptical in matters of religion, but he was not sufficiently interested in those matters to obtrude his conclusions on those whom they might hurt, and to please the devoted friend with whom he lived he cheerfully agreed to a visit from the parson. On the last day I saw him he had just received the Sacrament and even in a genuinely devout spirit. He was, however, as he certainly felt, in no personal need of the ministrations of the clergy or the efficacy of the ecclesiastical rites, for throughout life the Peace of God had been his by Nature. More than once during these last days he said that at night, when lying awake in the dark, he seemed to see his ship waiting for him to board her. So, at length, he finally set sail.

The Ellises, it may be seen, have no vices, but they buy that exemption at a price, for one is inclined to ask whether, when the right path is so easy to them, they really have any virtues. Their strength lies in their imperturbable mediocrity. This, it seems to me, at all events as here manifested, is a distinctively urban quality. The Ellises, in their various branches, have lived and survived through four or five generations in the heart of London. To do this successfully needs exactly the temperament of the Ellises, an indifference alike to the destroying ambitions and the destroying excesses which ravage the souls and bodies of these city-dwellers to whom the city is new. The Ellises still retain the same qualities. Among my numerous cousins and their children the girls are pretty and lively, the boys, whatever their occupation, have all the qualities of trustworthy bank clerks. They neither rise nor fall.

I owe much to the mediocrity of the Ellises. It is true that, so far from being cheerfully content with the surface of things, I am a restless researcher below surfaces. I never live in the present — my moments of happiness have all been in the past or the future. But yet there has always been the precious modifying influence of that Ellis temperament. The disposition that finds its expression mainly in literary channels is usually tempted to adopt a view of life that is one-sided, excessive, or eccentric. If I have been able on the whole to maintain a wide and sunny view of life, not merely to escape the greed of wealth or of honour, but to temper the ardour of my faith and enthusiasm by a pervading reasonableness — a scepticism which smiles at all my failures — I think I owe it largely to that temperate and cheerful acceptance of the world which is part of the mediocrity of the Ellises. My life would have been happier had I possessed more of it.

Captain Edward Peppen Ellis

Susannah Wheatley Ellis

On that foundation, however, only rather negative qualities can spring up. I have never doubted that I owe my more positive and fundamental qualities to my mother. Intellectually, indeed, my mother was not more distinguished than my father; but by her character, by her instinctive and emotional qualities, she was of an order much more rare and high.

In her early years my mother was a large, restless, active, high-spirited girl; her aunt called her 'volatile,' and her brother nick-named her 'the fish' because her activities led to her drinking much water. (She was, like me, born early in February under the sign of Aquarius.) So that there was clearly more in her of the energy of the Olivers than of the placidity of the Wheatleys, but a quiet, massive energy with no restlessness in it after she reached adult age. She grew up, however, untamed, at Suffolk House, Leyton, in the large garden and orchard that throughout life remained with her a memory of delight, and is now swept away, covered by the eruption of mean streets from London. But at the age of seventeen an event occurred which affected her whole life, and in a way which I have sometimes thought was disastrous. She was 'converted.' No doubt that process of emotional expansion and sublimation was inevitable for one of her temperament; it was so even for me. But with her, as not with me, the acquirement of emotional serenity and joy was combined with adherence to a nar-row and rigid creed. Henceforward she was a strict follower of Evangelical principles and practices. As current in her time, the Evangelical creed was simple; beyond ordinary religious observ-ance, it meant a firm reliance on the Bible with an avoidance of all 'worldliness.' To my mother it was almost a kind of Quakerism without the Quaker's eccentricities. She was naturally too toler-ant and liberal-minded to cherish fads and extravagancies of thought or action. Thus, it was only in later years that she gave up her glass of sherry or ale from a conviction of the evils of drink, and though she never went to a theatre after the age of seventeen, she used no pressure to prevent her children from following their own inclinations in this and similar matters. But she had inevitably cut herself off from the influences which might have made for a larger development of her rich nature; soon after her conversion she refused the attractive invitation of a rich aunt who wished to take her on a visit to Paris; she would rather not go to so wicked a city; for she always consistently acted by the light of her principles. Essentially a Suffolk or at all events East Anglian woman — a type in which vitality and character and fine emotional impulse are sometimes happily combined — her full development was arrested. The 'volatility' of the young girl never found its natural matured expression in the woman's life. Grave, though with no formal solemnity, reserved if not exactly repressed, shy and nervous beneath the imposing presence she had inherited from both her parents, she was yet a woman of unmistakable force of character. Though she sought few friends, I doubt if she ever lost any, and their devotion to her was deep. Her force was unconscious and instinctive, perhaps all the more effective on that account. This was clearly illustrated by her relations with her husband. The affection on both sides was complete. She sincerely cherished all the conventional views of wifely devotion and marital authority. Yet, when my father returned from his long sea-voyages, she instinctively remained the mistress of the house and he instinctively fell into the position of a guest. However bravely he might whistle and loudly call for his boots, it was not with the easy assurance of mastership he shouted his orders on deck or damned the steward below. He felt, rightly enough — for she was an excellent manager and organiser, equable in temper, always firm but always kind — that at home she was the captain. Possibly that may be why I have always been conscious of an element of weakness in him. I know that he was able to live up to the sailor's fidelity to duty and I never heard that he was guilty of any act of weakness in other relations of life. If, however, he came safely through, I am assured it was by the happily balanced temperament of the Ellises and not by virtue of strong character or high principle. But my mother, I always knew, was a tower of strength. Throughout life I have possessed an instinctive and unreasoned faith in women, a natural and easy acceptance of the belief that they are entitled to play a large part in many fields of activity. The spectacle of my mother's great and unconscious power — resting on the fact that the same emergence of capable womanhood occurred among my ancestors and perhaps indeed characterised the region they belonged to, since Suffolk has produced so notable a proportion of English women of ability — certainly counted for much in that faith and that belief.

Although my mother could never have been beautiful — probably less so when young than in the dignity and repose of mature life — she had numerous suitors, certainly by no means drawn merely because she was a ward in chancery with a small portion of two thousand pounds (coming from the Olivers) settled upon her, but by her really attractive qualities of impulsive energy combined with solidity of character. 'Never marry a sailor,' her father used to say to her. A few years after his death, she followed, nevertheless, her mother's example. A sailor alone of her wooers won her hand and she married my father, who had just become captain of his first ship at the age of twenty-eight, while she was two years younger. It was probably the only serious act of disobedience to her father she ever committed, but she certainly never repented. If in later years, as I am inclined to think, she realised with some sadness that her husband was not altogether the ideal she had once dreamed, that happens to most women who possess an emotional and idealistic temperament. I know, nevertheless, that the three months of the year my father spent at home — the voyage usually lasting about nine months — were always to my mother a long-expected period of happiness, a kind of annual honeymoon. Thus, when together they always remained like young lovers. I count it my good fortune that never once in the home-life of my childhood was I the witness of any conjugal jar. The unimpaired reverence for women and respect for domestic relationships, with which I set out, permanently coloured my whole conception of life.

When I survey my ancestral stocks as a whole from the eugenic standpoint, I can find little that seems in the slightest degree unbalanced or unsound. In no direction is there any obvious special liability to disease, and in all branches there is a fair, though not extreme, degree of longevity. I write this in my forty-third year, in good health and in entire freedom from any organic disease, and I consider that — if I am to die a natural death — I may reasonably expect to live until I am sixty. As regards mental soundness, I see no definitely weak point. It has often been said in my time that an insane heredity is without significance because insanity is found in all families. If one goes far enough it is certainly true that one must needs find insanity at last, but in an unqualified shape the statement is misleading. One of my numerous cousins, whose mother was an Ellis, once fell for a time into a condition that might well be called insane, but this girl's father belonged to an unquestionably morbid family. As far as I know, the Grays were a sound family, while such morbid traits as the Wheatleys presented were slight, and the restless energy of the Olivers never degenerated into insanity in any member at all nearly related to me. In my mother there was a latent nervousness which I have inherited in a heightened degree; it renders me in some ways an abnormal person, though scarcely morbid. This nervousness is the servant of my intellect and disciplined by my will; it is never likely to be degraded into insanity. I dimly feel that, however wide and apparently eccentric the orbit in which it seems to move, my life will in the end be found to have followed a rounded harmonious course, at one with Nature.

Part II

II

I WAS the eldest child and only boy of a
family of five, all still living.[1] My birth took place four years after
the marriage of my parents and was, I believe, preceded by a mis-
carriage. The newly married couple had taken a little semi-detached flint house (1 Saint John's Grove) in a quiet street in Old
Croydon leading up to the venerable parish church which had not
then been burnt out and so much of its ancient beauty lost. This
small old Surrey town was then chiefly known as once an ancient
seat of the Archbishop of Canterbury and later of a military academy at Addiscombe which disappeared shortly before my time.
It has since become the chief suburb of London and the healthiest
town of its size in the kingdom, a position it partly owed to Doctor
Alfred Carpenter, an ardent sanitary reformer, who was our family doctor. Throughout the rest of his life he never forgot the wild
stormy night which preceded the second of February, 1859, when
I was born at a quarter past eight in the morning.

[1] My sister Louie has since died (1928).

The year 1859 was long known as the year of the great comet, but it is now more permanently and famously known as the year of the publication of Darwin's *Origin of Species*, one of the greatest dates in the whole history of science. But that is far from exhausting the memorable events which were crowded into that most fruitful year, not only in various branches of science, but in life and art, in thought and literature, even in religion. In the world of action this was the year of Italian Unity; the Red Cross Society was founded by Dumont and the first Cottage Hospital built; Dr. Elizabeth Blackwell, the first English medical woman (whom later I met) was placed on the English Medical Register; the Suez Canal was commenced. In religion it became known among Evangelical revivalists as 'the Glorious Year,' while by the simultaneous publication of *Essays and Reviews* there began also the spiritual revival of the Anglican Church. In the sphere of thought J. S. Mill published his *Essay on Liberty* which has been well described as 'the most splendid statement of the ideal of Individualism.' In literature George Eliot and George Meredith both published what are in some respects their most characteristic and famous novels, *Adam Bede* and *Richard Feverel*, while yet more significant was the publication by Fitzgerald of the *Rubáiyát of Omar Khayyám*, and this immortal little book appeared in the midst of the fine poetic work of Rossetti, William Morris, and Swinburne which marks the close of that decade. It was in 1859, again, that Mistral's beautiful and ever-memorable *Mirèio* appeared. In art Millet painted 'L'Angelus' and Whistler produced his Thames etchings, both works which profoundly influenced the following half-century whatever may be ultimately thought of them, while the date is also historic, Pennell has remarked, for it is that of the publication of *Once A Week* which began the era of good illustration. It is, however, in pure science, after all, that the year 1859 displayed the most varied and memorable activities. The new spectroscopic astronomy began under Kirchhoff and the sun's chemical composition was discovered; Hofmeister laid the foundations of the morphology of plants; the definite triumph of the belief in the antiquity of man took place by Boucher de Perthes' at first questioned discovery of palaeolithic instruments being finally proved, so that in 1859, as Gaudry says, 'the study of fossil man began'; Broca founded the Société d'Anthropologie de Paris and therewith originated the scientific study of anthropology; the first journal of folklore was established in Germany, and Kuhn, the founder of comparative mythology, published his chief work, *Ueber die Herabkunft des Feuers*; Moreau de Tours initiated the psychological study of genius, and Lombroso conceived that idea of the anthropological method of studying criminals and other abnormal groups which in its transformations has proved so fruitful. Nor are the intellectual energies of this great year herewith exhausted. It would probably be difficult to name any one year in the whole history of mankind in which the human spirit was more profoundly stirred to more manifold original achievement. It seemed worth while to me to enumerate some of these achievements in order to indicate the spiritual atmosphere into which I was born, the atmosphere in which I was bathed, for it was as I grew up that the significance of these achievements began to be perceived.

I entered the world in a raging tempest, but however symbolic that omen may or may not have been for my life, there was nothing obviously tempestuous about the infant. I was a large child with a large head, as it still remains, so that labour proved tedious and the forceps were used. I remained a large fine healthy baby, suckled at the breast, and deserving, my mother was told, a prize at the baby-show then being held. In the earliest portrait, a daguerreotype long since lost (I had lent it to Olive Schreiner and in one of her sudden migrations from lodgings she left it behind), I looked out into the world from my mother's lap in all the robust and fearless self-satisfaction of babyhood. It was, however, the only portrait in which I ever manifested that attitude. In the next, dating a year or so later, one sees a rather sad, puz-

zled, and forlorn little child placed on a large chair and carefully
dressed in a frock and an ornamental hat with rosettes coming
down over the ears. It is clearly the same child that stands before
us in the next picture, though now grown more intelligent and
more self-possessed, a little fellow in knickerbockers, no longer fat,
and with a restless, nervous, anxious look on his face. It is a look
of which I seem to find the incipient trace in the Olivers, and
henceforth, even if not obvious, I think it is still usually latent.
The eyes are those of a sensitive traveller in a strange land, eager
indeed for friendly response, but always apprehensive of hostility.
Of Nature I have never been afraid. But the world has always
seemed to me to be full of strange human beings, so unknown,
mysterious, and awe-inspiring, so apt to give joy or pain, so apt
also to receive either. I have always felt a mixed reverence and
fear of human creatures, so that I have sometimes even been afraid
to look into the eyes of strangers; they seemed to me gates into
chambers where intimate and terrible secrets lie bare.

It is probable that the change I have noted in my expression
and appearance was connected with a change in my health. I was
a very robust baby, but I was a somewhat delicate child. I cannot recall what the symptoms were, I think they were rather
vague. But I know that my mother took me from time to time to
a London physician who, so far as I can recall, spoke reassuringly.

My earliest recollection dates from the age of about two years,
or perhaps earlier. We were moving into a new house — evidently the ugly little semi-detached villa now replaced by shops
at the Addiscombe end of Cherry Orchard Road which is the
earliest house I recall — and the nursemaid who was carrying me
placed her burden for a moment on the kitchen dresser. The novelty of that lofty and unusual position furnished the first stimulus to perception strong enough to last permanently in memory.
(Rather similarly, Ibsen's earliest memory was of being carried
by his nurse to the top of a church tower.) There are other recollections that are faint, often trivial. I recall the little Chinese

figure of a crouching monkey in soapstone which my mother would give me from off the mantelpiece, as later to her other infant children in succession, to play with in bed in the early morning; somehow the feel of it seems as though it had moulded my fingers to sensation. I recall, for some unknown reason, when still a small child in a frock, running round and round the table till I was tired. I recall, too, the eldest of my baby sisters who appeared when I was four. 'Take away that piece of dirt and rubbish,' I am said to have exclaimed with the jealousy of childhood. That feeling seems soon to have passed. I can only remember my baby sister as the object of my care and attention.

These memories are vague. The only definite memory of this time is of once accompanying the nurse who was wheeling the perambulator with the baby along Morland Road. The nurse stood still and I heard a mysterious sound as of a stream of water descending to the earth. I recall no feeling of interest or curiosity on my part, but the fact that I recall the incident at all seems to indicate that at that moment I was for the first time touched by the strange mystery of woman. It was not till years later that I felt any interest or curiosity in women or in any aspect of sex, however childish. For my mother I had always an equable and unquestioning affection, which seems to have been entirely free from any of those complications to which the child's affection for his mother is now supposed to be liable, even though it may be in part true that it is out of such affection and on the model of such affection, that the youth's late sexual love of woman is moulded. There was no physical intimacy, her love for her children was not of the petting kind, and there were never any curiosities on my part; when these later arose they were turned in other directions. Nor was there ever any trace of jealousy on my part with regard to my father. That, indeed, may in any case have been excluded by the fact that he was such a stranger in his own house. We saw but little of him, and we always accepted him, as a matter of course and willingly, though there was little or no opportunity for warm affection to spring up, for even during his stays in London he had to be away all day at the ship or the office, and Sundays were too formal and sacred to be conducive to intimacy.

There was, I believe, nothing remarkable or precocious about my childhood, though I easily learned to read at the age of five. I was a fairly active child, and it was noted as a peculiarity of my gait that in running I would take a little leap every few steps; the latent tendency to this movement seems to remain with me still. Perhaps the most characteristic incident in my early childhood, which impressed my mother, for she would refer to it in after years, occurred when I once stood stock-still in the middle of the road, for no obvious reason, and for some time could not be induced to move. I do not recall this manifestation of instinctive obstinacy, but in it I clearly detect myself. It may well be to this grim silent persistence, deaf to persuasion, that I owe whatever little success I may have achieved in preserving intact my own individuality and carrying out my own projects, with indifference to the shifting attitudes of society or the law.

Yet in these trifling childhood memories — my own and those of others in regard to me — there was nothing uncommon to childhood. I was just a rather shy, sensitive, reserved, well-dispositioned child, not goody-goody, but completely free from any of the mischievous tricks of childhood (though once, for no remembered reason, I threw my boots in the fire) and equally without any impulses of pugnacity, such as are regarded as the proper attribute of immature virility. I was more disposed to be helpful than to fight, and I remember how once in the Morland Road a boy and a girl of the working class, carrying a basket of washing, invited me to help by carrying one end which, without question, I immediately did and was afterwards, when I arrived home late, mildly reproved by my mother. In all this I was far from being a weak, sickly, or psychically morbid child, and in physical development I was always above the average. But in what the doctors called 'stamina' I was below the average; I had no exuberance of physical energy, no strong impulse to muscular exercise or games, though I joined in them when it was not easy to refuse, and this was combined with some degree of muscular awkwardness. I was, I believe, naturally left-handed; I have never been able to throw a ball with my right hand, and though I have never written with my left hand, my right-handed use of the pen was always the despair of my teachers. All my energy seems to have been in my brain and that was rather of the massive and receptive than of the impulsive and active sort. With such a temperament it was natural that reading soon became my preferred pleasure, and I had no brothers or boy friends to incite me to more social amusements.

One other trivial incident of childhood, when I was about six, may be mentioned, because it made a clear and lasting impression on my mind and represented my first introduction to art, which later became so keen an interest in my life. The twin villa to ours in Cherry Orchard Road was occupied by a fair, consumptive, newly married young artist called Robert Barnes. He belonged to the great circle which from the year 1859 so brilliantly revived wood engraving in England. Like many others of the group, he was also a painter; we were sometimes in his house, he introduced my sister, who was a pretty child, into some of his drawings, and it was on his easel that I first saw a freshly painted picture; I remember it still, an old woman outside a cottage door with a bird in a basket-cage by her side. He gave me a volume of Mrs. Barbauld's which he had illustrated, and I still possess it. A little later, Robert Barnes became a highly successful artist in black and white; he was prodigiously active and, though he had no great brilliance or originality, there was a delicate individuality in his gracious and homely pictures; when we were children of a little higher age, and he was illustrating many of the current magazines, we had no difficulty in detecting his hand immediately. His health improved, he became prosperous, and had a large family; it so chanced that when finally we moved to the house at Redhill in which my mother died, a house of much the same character as that in Cherry Orchard Road, Robert Barnes and his family were occupying a large and handsome house in the neighbourhood and the old friendly relationship was resumed after an interval of a quarter of a century. I have sometimes thought that I ought myself to have been an artist, but this early contact incited no artistic ambitions, though as a child, like many other children, I delighted in a paint-box and experienced that peculiar sensitive reaction to the qualities of different pigments which is probably common among children.

My mother never cared to make her home on board ship, but when I was seven years old it was decided, doubtless for the benefit of my health, that I should accompany my father on a voyage round the world in the *Empress*, an American-built wooden sailing ship belonging to Houldor Brothers which he then commanded. On this voyage my father was to take from Queenstown to New South Wales a large number of Roman Catholic passengers, including several bishops, numerous priests, and many nuns. Up to this point the memories of childhood that remain with me are few and for the most part trivial. But from this moment they become extremely numerous, indeed almost continuous, and though surrounded as it were by haze they are much more vivid than before.

When I think of these days, a number of pictures come on my mind: Sister Agnes, the gentle, quiet nun who had charge of my education during the passage, and was later, as a priest has since told me, at the head of a convent; [1] the good-natured old Mother Superior, who was always giving me little presents, some of which I still preserve; Father Doyle, a merry middle-aged ecclesiastic

---

[1] More than sixty years later, and after her death, it was stated in Australian newspapers that she remembered me well to the end and used to tell of my little childish pranks. It is strange to me that she should have been able to identify Harry Ellis, the Captain's young son, with the later author Havelock Ellis, and I have wondered if there was not somewhere here a touch of Irish imagination; but I like to think that I may have been with her a pleasant memory to the end, as she also will be to me.

who was never tired of playing innocently mischievous pranks; it may possibly have been he who incited me to pull the whiskers of a solemn gentleman called Walsh who promptly boxed my ears; these are but a few of the many persons on board who all stand out clearly in memory. Not the least vivid of these is the kindly German steward, simple-minded, well-educated, and capable — a most typical German — who was much concerned for my mental improvement and lent me beautifully illustrated books of natural history because he thought I read too many stories. Nothing stands out more clearly in memory than the ship's library in my father's cabin. This was the finest treasure-house I had yet come on, and I was free to search in it as though my own. Here I found Hans Andersen whom I read with delight, but with still greater delight Marryat's *Masterman Ready*, a story of the *Robinson Crusoe* type and by far the most ravishing book I had yet discovered.

Of Sydney, though there my father had various old friends to whom I was taken, my memories are fainter.[1] But from Sydney we sailed to Callao and the Chincha Islands to load guano for Antwerp, and here my memories are much more numerous and vivid than those of Sydney. Here I first came within reach of the far-off echoes of that Old-World Spain which afterwards became so fascinating to me. I recall the penetrating and pungent odour of the guano which filled the air all day long on board ship, the most massive odour I have ever known. I recall the old coloured woman who sold fruit on the island and always gave me a large bunch of black grapes, until at last I grew tired of grapes and refused any longer to accept her presents; even yet I have not recovered any taste for black grapes. I recall, again, how my father

[1] I may here remark that what is perhaps my earliest extant letter was written home from the *Empress* at Sydney in October, 1866. It is substantially much the same kind of letter I might write now. 'I like travelling,' I wrote, 'though I should not wish to be a sailor,' and after expressing admiration for Sydney, I added: 'I was much amused with the trees in the Government Gardens, reading their names and the countries they came from, some of them with more flowers than leaves, and the others very curious.' I still find amusement in a similar occupation. It is strange to note that below my signature appears a flourish which is the obvious original of that I now use.

took me with him to Lima where the great Spanish gateways leading into the *patios* especially appealed to me, and it seems significant to me now that the first really foreign city I ever saw should
have been one of Spanish tradition. Here, too, I first saw great
mountains; the enormous range of the Andes seemed to rise from
the coast and frown over the ship; I used to watch these mountains intensely and remember how I long vainly sought to make
out through the glass the nature of the moving spots my keen eyes
could just discern on the mountain slopes. There are other memories of Callao and the Chinchas. Here I first had a boy companion of about my own age, son of a captain who was an old friend of
my father's; sometimes we were allowed to take the dinghy and
go round among the rocks on the island coast, gathering great
starfish and all the strange living things we could find. My companion, I remember, once confided to me his scatologic interests
in his own person, but I was but mildly interested — not repelled, merely indifferent; the association of grace and beauty
would have been needed to arouse my interest. This same boy
also confided to me his habit of what I, much later, learned to
know was commonly called masturbation, though as he told me,
it was simply a method of promoting the wholesome development
of the organs, an object which seemed to me entirely praise-
worthy; on his recommendation I attempted, with the best motives, to follow his instructions, but the results were fortunately
in every respect completely negative, so that I soon abandoned
my attempts and thought no more of the matter. In this connection I should also mention — for it is all that there is to mention — that during the voyage I sometimes associated with an
amiable, quiet apprentice about fifteen years of age, and I recall
on one or two occasions when we were alone together that he permitted or possibly encouraged me to insert my hand into his
trousers and gently to touch his sexual organs; my feeling was
simply one of reverent admiration for what seemed to my childish
mind their magnitude. There was another apprentice, a clever

youth rather older, who would tell me long stories as we walked up and down the deck; the only one I recall (probably because he told me not to repeat it) was slightly indecent and dealt with the embarrassment of a young married couple over the problem of undressing together on their wedding-night; the story went no further and seemed to me complete; sexual problems had no interest, or rather no existence, for me at this age, and for years after. It was at Callao, or the Chinchas, that I found my first girl playmate, a captain's daughter whose name I no longer remember. But I well remember the hours I spent with her on the poop, hidden in a great sail, where we played at keeping house, always with natural decorum; she was just a congenial playmate for whom I felt no further emotions of affection or admiration; indeed, it is satisfactory to me to recall that throughout my childhood to the age of twelve, however nervous a child I may have seemed, all my emotions were wholesomely undeveloped and blunt, never at any point exasperated into acute sensibility. But it was on this coast of Peru, it seems to me, at the age of seven, that I first gained full self-consciousness; I was beginning to become a person.

On leaving Callao we had a passenger, a young Englishman called Whelock, whose name remains with me because I associate it with one of those unaccountable impulses of obstinacy which seems to have been in my original nature. I recall him as a kind and gentle and well-bred man; there was apparently something to me antipathetic about him. He gave me a novel by Mrs. Craik, *A Noble Life*, in the Tauchnitz Series. It was an altogether kindly act, yet for some reason, which has always been completely obscure to me, I refused to thank him, and for a long time would not touch the book, though I ultimately read it. Some latent cause there must have been for my ungraciousness — possibly it was shyness taking on the form of rudeness — but I have never known what it was. I recall another obscure impulse of a more definite character manifested at some time during the voyage.

There was a large cat on board, a favourite with the sailors who had fastened various objects round its neck. One day I was watching this cat making his way between the rails at the ship's stern; he was surefooted, but the position was perilous, a touch would send him into the sea. Moved by a sudden impulse, when the cat was passing to the seaward side of the rail, I supplied that touch. I at once went to my father and told him the cat had fallen overboard and a rope was thrown over, but the cat had already disappeared. No one suspected me of any part in the cat's death, and I never revealed to anyone — I believe unto this day — that I was guilty in the matter. I have always, however, regarded it as a criminal act. One other action of my childhood — occurring, I think, a little later, after my return home — I may mention here to complete the criminal record. My mother kept a purse containing pence behind the clock on the sitting-room mantelpiece for convenience in paying small household expenses. One day — calmly, without a struggle, and possibly even without sense of wrongdoing — I helped myself to pence from this purse and bought and ate some pears, a fruit for which I still retain a special liking. I was discovered — I am not even sure whether I maintained concealment — and no doubt duly punished. This remains in my mind as an objective incident, and I have no recollection of its subjective side. It was evidently an unreasoning impulse, aroused by a sudden irresistible desire for the pears seen in the shop. But I have no other memories to indicate that I was ever greedy; in this sphere they are only of antipathies, as with the black grapes, and also a permanent dislike of seed-cake and sago pudding and bread and jam; though I had early acquired an ineradicable tendency, which probably contributed to my liability to indigestion, to eat fast, this was not attributable to greediness.

These two incidents of my childhood have been useful to me in showing how impulses which can only be called criminal are always liable to arise in childhood; they clearly have little significance and should not be treated too seriously. They come to me out of the past, detached from their environment, almost like dreams. This also is true of my memory of the first time I saw a corpse. As the ship sailed swiftly past, I observed the floating body as it seemed to me of a negro in a red shirt, though the negro effect may possibly have been due to discoloration; I alone saw it and with my characteristic reticence said nothing about it.

From Callao the *Empress* conveyed its freight of guano round Cape Horn to Antwerp. I recall nothing of the voyage except that one day near the Horn I nearly cried from the bitter cold. But of Antwerp memories crowd too thickly for record. It was the first foreign city I ever really lived in. The magnificent docks and the great promenoirs were not then built, but otherwise the essential features of the riverside seem to remain the same today as they were then. On arrival my father took me on shore with him to stay for a few days at a little hotel facing the quay, kept by Flemish people. I remember the landlady's two buxom daughters, their busy ways, the perpetual 'Ja! Ja!' shouted amid banging doors. An event which is always important in a child's life happened at Antwerp. My father took me and the two girls of the house to my first circus. I vividly recall the unending stream of whooping horsemen who wildly stamped round the ring, disappearing on one side to re-emerge on the other, and I recall, too, how the involuntary exuberance of my delight was enjoyed by the two girls at my side. Evidently at the time I had not acquired the undemonstrative impassibility, which, however strong my emotion, I was subsequently wont to show, just as, also, I had scarcely acquired my shyness, for on the *Empress* I used to sing in public, with much enjoyment, to the accompaniment of the piano, a social achievement I cannot imagine at any later period. A few days later my father took me home with him by Harwich. He was to bring the family back to Antwerp, but my mother doubtless wished to see me without a day's unnecessary delay. It is perhaps characteristic of the random and inconsequent impressions of a child's mind that while I recall vividly my return to the Addiscombe house — the end house on the Croydon side of Addiscombe Terrace — the appearance of the dining-room grown small and unfamiliar in my eyes, the look of the spread table, even the salt-cellars, I have not the faintest memory of the meeting with my mother after a year-long absence. Affection is undeveloped in early life.

We all went over at once, with the nursegirl, to Antwerp, to spend there many weeks of the summer of 1867 while the ship was unloading, a much slower process than it has since become. We lodged in a little house on the outskirts of the city not far from a large bare tract on which ruined forts were still standing, a district which is now probably that covered by fashionable streets. One morning before breakfast, in the gratification of one of my earliest impulses of scientific curiosity, I resolved to count the number of cannon ports in a large deserted old fort. Placing a good-sized stick on the ground, so that I might know when my task was completed, I carefully proceeded to march round, counting the holes as I went. But after continuing this process for some time I realised that I had missed the stick and looking around in bewilderment I had some difficulty in orienting myself. By the time that was accomplished, I fear scientific curiosity had evaporated and I quickly went back to breakfast.

It was a very hot summer, and I recall the sensation of being kept awake by the heat — though I had never suffered from heat in the tropics — in the close bedroom where we children and the nursemaid slept in separate beds, while the interminably long goods-trains (I had succeeded in counting the number of wagons in these) rattled on the railway line not far off. This weather brought on an attack of diarrhoea, and I recall the deliciously blissful sensations, such as I have never experienced since even after a large dose of the same drug, produced by the chlorodyne my mother administered to me. About the same time I had my first attack of the severe nose-bleeding which reappeared at intervals until my departure from Australia fourteen years later; on this first occasion we were out with Jack, the big sailor boy who

sometimes looked after us, and he lent me his huge pocket hand-
kerchief on this long dreary walk. I experienced more illness and
discomfort on this brief visit to Antwerp than during all the vicis-
situdes of the long voyage round the world, which seemed to have
suited me perfectly.

My mother had not been to Antwerp before. I doubt even if
she had been abroad before, though she several times went to
Antwerp and to Hamburg afterwards, and she desired my father
to show her all the sights. I sometimes accompanied my parents
to the churches and to the Picture Gallery, an old-fashioned and
unpretentious building very unlike the present Royal Museum.
Only one picture remains in my memory, and that doubtless
because my mother, who always had an engraving of it in her
bedroom, must have observed it with special attention, Rubens's
'Descent from the Cross' in the Cathedral. I mention this because
a little point of psychological interest in relation to memory is
connected with it. I never visited Antwerp again till fifteen
years later, but when I once more saw the 'Descent' hanging in
the transept, I was astonished to find it was by no means either
so large or so high up as in the memory I retained of it. To the
small child everything seems larger than to the adult and the
world is a different place. (Probably also it is a different place
to the small as compared to the large adult.) Nearly twenty
years elapsed before I saw the picture a third time, but the second
interval involved no readjustment of my impression.

After we returned home to Addiscombe, I was again sent to
Mrs. Granville's school in Saint James's Road, whither I had gone
for a short time before the voyage. At this period the memories
of my life and my school grow ever more numerous and definite.
The persons and characters of my teachers — a Miss Frowde,
a Miss Cox, a Miss Bell — still stand out vividly in my mind;
I could describe their appearance and their widely varying
characters, and one or two of my schoolfellows are almost as
distinct. But this moment of my life scarcely seems of special

significance for later development and it is unnecessary to dwell on it. I have described even trivial details of the voyage on the *Empress* when memory first began to be stable, because there is always a certain interest in the beginnings of things, but it would be tedious, and quite unnecessary, to record minutely the ever-growing stream of later memories, even if such a detailed record were possible.

One or two memories of the school are perhaps of some significance. I remember that a schoolfellow called Smith — it was my first acquaintance with that large and admirable family — took me off with himself and his brother to play cricket, talking seriously to me of the importance of skill in games; he had evidently observed — what I had myself discovered — that I had no natural expertness in physical exercises. I also remember that Mrs. Granville once asked my mother if I was quite right in my head. The idea seems to have been suggested to her by her misapprehension of one of the games played in the school-ground and no defect in school was alleged. My mother was indignant at the suggestion, quite naturally and reasonably, for it was never made by anyone else at that time, however 'odd,' at a later period, some people may have considered me. Still it is possible that this shrewd and intelligent old lady ought to have the credit of first detecting in me whatever strain of mental anomaly I may possess.

At Addiscombe Terrace there was a long though not large garden, with a door in the wall at the end leading into a road at the back. It was well stocked with apple trees and plum trees, and cherry trees against the wall, and a large guelder rose, at the end of the little lawn, always impressed my youthful mind by the vastness of its white globular blossoms. We children had each our own tiny patch of ground to cultivate and we bought little plants to put into them; the polyanthus is associated in my mind with this epoch, and the escholtzia, which, however, I avoided, for its virulent-orange flowers and its strange glabrous stalks with their thin milky juice inspired me with ineffaceable repulsion. My mother was always fond of flowers and gardens and orchards — though she scarcely seems to have been much influenced by this love in her choice of houses — and often spoke of the great garden and orchard at Leyton in which her childhood had been passed. A cottage in the country with a large garden remained her unfulfilled ideal to the last. It has been left to me to attain.

An incident which occurred in this garden may be recorded because, simple as it was, it is unique in my life. It was probably about a year after my return to England, and my mother had gone to be with my father, I think at Hamburg. I was swinging myself in the swing when I heard, with perfect distinctness, my mother's voice twice calling me by name. I believe I ran to the servant to ask if she had called, but with the usual secretiveness of childhood I kept the experience to myself. I have never had any other hallucination of this sort in the course of my life.

I believe, however, that children are nearer than adults to the threshold of hallucination. In this belief I am confirmed by another experience which belongs to this period of my childhood at Addiscombe. A boy cousin of about the same age was spending a few days with us and slept in my bed. Sometimes in the morning we would lie on our stomachs, burying our faces in the pillows, and see visions. These visions — I do not know which of us originated the experiment — were somewhat of the same kind, though less vivid, as those I have since learnt to see on the curtain of the eyelids under the influence of mescal buttons and resembled still more the hypnagogic visions one is specially liable to see at night after a fatiguing day. The remarkable point was that our visions were to some extent under the influence of suggestion; the same series appeared to both of us and we would note aloud any change, which then became visible to the other observer. These visions caused no surprise or questioning to either of us, but I cannot recall their occurrence at any other time.

When I was about nine years old, we moved from Addiscombe to a smaller house at Wimbledon, or rather the low-lying district between Wimbledon and Merton. They are both interesting places, but the intermediate region, between Wimbledon Station and Merton Station, was of no interest and we occupied a house in an unattractive terrace in an unattractive road, which I now find it difficult to recognise, so changed has all this region become. My mother sent me as a day-scholar during the next three years to a school called the French and German College opposite old Merton Church. The house is now slowly being dissolved, if it has not completely gone, but it was a fine old mansion, partly of the Elizabethan age, which deserved a better fate. One entered the house, though not the school, by the great finely designed iron gates, after clanging a loud bell, and approached a low but very broad house with two wings, and beyond, to the left, the schoolhouse with various farm buildings and outhouses; the whole was surrounded by a high wall which also enclosed a large garden. I have never been able to learn the ancient history of the house; in fairly recent times it was said to have been once the home of Sheridan; I find no support for this story in the biographies of Sheridan, but it is clear at all events that Garrick once stayed at Merton, and there was a little old theatre attached to the house, in my time transformed into a combined swimming bath and gymnasium, though still recognisable as a theatre.

The school was entitled to rank as fairly good. I do not know that any of my schoolfellows attained distinction, but a boy who was there before my time, Robert Buchanan, acquired fame in literature during my youth, and later, it so chanced, was, as he wrote me, an admirer of my own early literary work, though neither of us was aware of this link of connection; another boy, rather before my time, later achieved notoriety by becoming an itinerant organ-grinder and claiming the title of Viscount Hinton. These two careers probably owed as little as mine — although all three were unconventional — to De Chastelain, the principal of the school, a pale, compact little man of French descent, though completely anglicised, who made a competent and energetic head master, maintaining his authority with a touch of sarcasm. It was he who first noted the peculiarities of my handwriting. He would ask me if I wrote with the kitchen poker, and sometimes remark that I seemed to keep a tame spider to race over the page. But I knew little intimately of De Chastelain, for being a day-boy and one of the youngsters, I stood rather outside the inner life of the school, if it had any. I am afraid that De Chastelain made an unfavourable personal impression on me because I had acquired the idea that he ill-treated his wife, a rather pretty American with a low voice and a faded, crushed air.

This was probably the earliest occasion on which I conceived, without realising it, a championship of woman's rights. My schoolfellows, so far as I know, felt not the slightest interest in her. To me it was her seeming pathos that appealed; her age, about thirty, I suppose, was far too advanced for me to feel the smallest romantic attraction, for though up to the age of about twenty-three such attraction, when I felt it, was nearly always towards women four or five years older than myself, no greater interval of years was possible. I scarcely remember that I ever exchanged two words with her. I do remember, however, that she once reported me to her husband as having passed her in the street without lifting my cap; my 'manners' were set down in the next quarterly report home as 'passable.' I mention this little episode as the earliest proof known to me of the existence of a trait which has marked me throughout life. Absorbed in my own dreams, all my life long I have passed by without seeing — and frequently, even when seeing, not recognising — people who are perfectly well known to me. I have even passed my own sweetheart who had come to seek me, and who let me pass, not revealing that incident to me until years afterwards. Yet I have sometimes been considered very observant, for attention and observation are capricious and partial, dependent on the interest of the moment, or on one's instinctive permanent interests, so that there may be things one never fails to see, though nearly all other persons may fail to see them.

I remained at the French and German College until I was twelve. The years I spent there were almost altogether uneventful, and so far as they were eventful the school counted for nothing. I learned a little Latin and more French; I played a little cricket without the slightest zest, and duly took my part in all other games. I was occasionally invited with one or two selected boys to join in a game of croquet with De Chastelain's friends on the lawn. I looked on in the little theatre while the boarders used the trapeze or learnt to swim. I was on entirely good terms with my schoolfellows without making any intimate friends. Some of them were much older than I was, but they were a good-natured set; there were no bullies among them, nor did I ever see or hear the slightest hint of any schoolboy vice. The nearest approach to any impropriety I came across was in one of the masters whose admiration was excited by two pretty young dressmakers, sisters, who went to Merton Church, and he asked me to take a letter to one of them at her home. I refused; it evidently seemed to my youthfully virtuous mind too much like encouraging an intrigue, and probably I should think so still; he bore me no grudge. This same master was the first adult man I had seen naked; it was in the swimming bath, and the vision — I can still recall it — of the sexual organs struck me as ugly, almost repulsive. I expect I appeared a quiet rather shy boy of average ability and rather commonplace character. De Chastelain, acute man of the world, would probably have been surprised to learn that I was ever to be heard of outside my own parish. In after years, I sometimes had the vanity to wish to call upon him, but, when in middle age I at length paid a pious visit to Merton, De Chastelain and his school and his family had all long vanished, I knew not whither. At the age of twelve I had left the college for good, without joy and without regrets.

My real self was already emerging, but it was discovering itself along lines that I never revealed at school and could never even dream of revealing. I have already said that my love of reading, it was almost a passion in those days, had appeared at an early age. During the years I was at Merton College reading was my constant delight during all my spare hours and moments. In the holidays it was only with difficulty that my mother, anxious for my health, drove me out of the house for solitary walks in the dreary suburb that contained nothing that appealed to me — except a little when I wandered as far as Wimbledon Common — and I abridged these walks to the lowest limit. Our house bookcase was not too well supplied with the kind of literature I needed, though it contained all the early volumes of the *Penny Magazine* (inherited from my Grandfather Ellis) rich with varied miscellany, notably the old English ballads, including the Robin Hood cycle, for my instruction and delight, and other good books like Cowper's poems and Scott's *Marmion*. My taste was fairly omnivorous, though I rejected sermons and books of religious edification with which the bookcase swarmed. But I found here, as first published serially in a religious periodical, that gracious and beautiful book, Mrs. Charles's *Chronicles of the Schönberg-Cotta Family*, and derived from it a kind of unconscious artistic pleasure. I discovered another source of literary enjoyment in the drawers of a huge old bureau-sideboard. Here were stowed away and neglected by all save me a number of books that had belonged to my grandmother, and had in them the simple bookplate 'Susannah Oliver.' They dated from before her marriage, half a century earlier, and they bore witness to her fine and varied taste. Here were all the volumes of *Nature Displayed*, a conspectus of the whole realm of Nature, doubtless meant for popular use, yet with no sacrifice of scientific honesty and precision; it was full of beautiful plates, and I spent many hours poring over it with minute attention. There are no such books now, for modern taste supposes that 'popular science' must be made easy and vague and sentimental and prudish, but for my part, when I was ten years old much as now when I am sixty years old, I wanted truth presented to me as it is, arduous and honest and implacable. There was, however, a scientific book of quite another sort which I read with pleasure, the first edition, in many volumes, of Maria Edgeworth's *Harry and Lucy*. It is a forgotten book now, even by those who rightly admire Maria Edgeworth, but, I imagine, it may well have been the first attempt to bring the elements of science attractively to children. It is written with vivacity and, though I only read it once and spent no long time over it, I can clearly recall some of its scenes still. Here also I found Rousseau's *Rêveries d'un promeneur solitaire*. It was the first French book I ever read for my own pleasure, and I felt its haunting romantic music. This was probably my earliest intimation of what style means. Not the least precious of these books was to me Rowlandson's *Doctor Syntax in Search of the Picturesque*. I was never weary of those pictures and it may well have been through the genius of Rowlandson — though I must not forget the carefully studied papers of Mrs. Jameson on Italian art, in the *Penny Magazine* and their illustrations delicately worked over in colours by my grandfather — that I first began to attain an insight into art. That volume is the only one of my grandmother's books that I have succeeded in preserving. All the rest melted away by use or in moving from house to house, especially during my absence in Australia, and the like happened to a large number of the rare — as they would now be — and beautiful curios my father brought from time to time from many lands, enough to make an exquisite little museum had they all been carefully preserved. But I have a few of these also, above all a Buddha, one of two which a soldier at Rangoon brought as loot one day to the ship (in which my father had transported troops for the Burmese War) and wanted to know what my father would give for them. He offered a very worn copy of one of Marryat's novels. The offer was accepted.

Now a Hindu gentleman who lately saw my Buddha tells me it is of thirteenth-century style and that if I ever feel disposed to return it to India he will come over to escort it.

In addition to these books I read with care about this time a great many serious modern books, such as Macaulay's *Essays*, which I had selected as a birthday present, and annotated in a critical spirit since my parents were somewhat Conservative in political tendency, and I had so far developed no political or social ideas of my own. Nowadays it is often a difficult matter for me to read at all, since my mind at once begins to work vigorously on every statement set before it; every touch now puts innumerable circuits of thought and emotion and expression into action. But at that time my mind was an empty treasure-house into which every precious thing I could find was eagerly poured. I bought cheap editions of Milton and Burns and religiously read them through at the age of twelve, though as yet with no great relish. Longfellow, whom I also bought in a corresponding sixpenny edition, was the first poet to make a profound and intimate impression upon me. Here for the first time, especially in the more lyrical poems, I seemed to hear a living voice which spoke to me in the language of my own heart. Longfellow was, as it were, the sweet friend of my early boyhood, the only friend I then possessed with whom I could privately commune. My love for him was later submerged in a mightier love for Shelley — though in the first tempestuous spring of adolescence I revelled in the intoxicating poetry of Alexander Smith's *Life-Dreams* and Mrs. Browning's *Aurora Leigh* — but there always remained with me, long after I outgrew his poems, a tender memory for that first friend of wistful and pensive puberty. No other writer so well expressed in my day the ideas and emotions of that period.

The prose author who in these days held me most absolutely enthralled was Scott. I suppose I was about ten when my mother took us for a summer holiday to Shanklin in the Isle of Wight.

She asked the landlady if she had any books to lend me to read
and the original edition of *Woodstock* was by a happy chance
produced. I cannot say that I fell at once under the magician's
spell — that is not my way and *Woodstock* is not one of the best
of the Waverley novels — but I was certainly eager to read more
books of the same author, and very soon all my small pocket-
money (I am not sure that my regular allowance yet exceeded
a penny or twopence a week) was devoted to the gradual purchase of Scott's novels in the sixpenny edition. Here was a vast
world, indeed a whole succession of worlds in which I lost my
own personality, and lived, with never a critical pang, a life of
absolute and pure enjoyment. I delighted more or less in all of
them, but those that were most remote in time and place fascinated me most, though not really the finest, because they opened
the largest vistas to imagination, and *Ivanhoe* seemed to me the
most perfect, while none of them made so intimate an appeal
to me as *The Abbot*, with its romance of Mary of Scots and the
charming figure of Catherine Seyton with whom I fell hopelessly
in love. My pocket-money could not keep pace with my insatiable
thirst for these wonderful books, and the favourites I would read,
re-read, and read once again, when novelties ran short. This
went on with vigour that but slowly flagged for several years,
until I was sixteen and had just reached Australia to begin life
on my own account. I was passing through religious struggles
which had sharpened the accuracy of my critical faculty, and
my interests were at the same time being diverted into other
altogether different channels. Scott's brilliant stage lost its glam-
our; the machinery seemed to creak. I was behind the scenes
and could see how tawdry the machinery often was.

While my capacious appetite for literature enabled me to
devour from end to end some very serious books, I also read
with pleasure some boys' books of travel and adventure. At
some not very early date also, I came upon an old sea chest of
drawers of my father's which contained, with some less attractive

literature, an illustrated edition of *Robinson Crusoe* and translations of some navigators' narratives, notably those of La Pérouse.
(I already knew a book of missionary experience in the Pacific,
with coloured illustrations, which fixed on my mind a permanent
ideal of those islands, scarcely intended by the author, long before
I knew *Typee*.) These books, I remember, were stained with
age and soaked in the fragrance of the wood of the chest, exhaled
by many voyages across the tropics, and this added to their
exotic charm. I was at Merton College, and probably about
ten or eleven years old, when I passed through a literary experience which may seem surprising in a boy who was reading, or
about to read, Milton and Macaulay. I was introduced by a
schoolfellow to the *Boys of England*, a penny weekly full of extravagantly sensational and romantic adventures in wild and
remote lands. The fascination with which this literature held
me was a kind of fever. It was an excitement which overwhelmed
all ordinary considerations. My mother forbade me to read these
things, but though I usually obeyed her in this matter I was dis-
obedient without compunction. Mr. de Chastelain once detected
me reading *The Boys of England* in school hours; during solitary
rambles I read it as I walked; every spare moment, when alone,
it was in my hands. But the fever subsided as suddenly as it
arose — probably it only lasted a few weeks — and left not a
trace behind. It is an experience which enables me to realise
how helpless we are in this matter. If this is the literature a boy
needs, nothing will keep him away from it; if he needs more than
ever it can give, it will leave no mark on him. So far as I remember, *The Boys of England* was innocent enough, though full
of wild and extravagant action. It is doubtless in its appeal to
the latent motor energies of developing youth that its fascination
lies.

My demand to make literature, as apart from reading it, I can
scarcely trace the beginning of. At an early age I would buy
penny notebooks, some of which I still possess, and in these I

entered, in a large childish hand, the record of the occurrences of my life that chiefly interested me, together with the dates when I read particular books, and extracts from them of passages which struck me. These notebooks slowly became more elaborate. I began to index them and to co-ordinate the quoted passages under a few headings. In fact the literary methods I later followed now were already growing up slowly and spontaneously, without the slightest stimulus or assistance from outside, at the age of ten. By the age of twelve I had prepared a little book for publication. It was called *The Precious Stones of the Bible.* It contained nothing original, but was an orderly compilation of all the facts on the subject I could bring together from the small supply of books at my disposition. By this time, however, I was beginning to acquire a library of my own, aided by rather skilful bargaining — sale, purchase, and exchange — in the advertisement columns of *The Exchange and Mart.* In this way I secured a number of bound volumes of an old miscellany of instructive character called *The Visitor*, which proved a source of useful information. I wished to publish my little book, and my mother who, without encouraging me, took a sympathetic interest in my literary activities, was willing to help. In my innocence I supposed that the most economical plan would be to print as few copies as possible, and decided to have only twelve. On applying to a large City printing firm it appeared that the cost would be twelve pounds and the scheme dropped. When I look back now at that little book, I seem to see in it the germ of my later books, I mean those of more scientific character; then, as now, it was my desire to accumulate with an open mind all the information I could acquire and present it in a fair, orderly, and attractive way, though I could not then, as I have since learnt to do, in that act create afresh a form that my own spirit had moulded. In its elements this method, I can now recognise, is that of the East Anglian mind with which my own must largely be identified, the method of Ray, the method which Bacon illuminated with the flame of genius. It is a natural-history method, a method to which some would deny the name of science, and it has always been my instinct to be a natural historian of the soul. So that it interested me once when Doctor Davenport, the distinguished American biologist, told me that I seemed to him the only Englishman who had applied natural-history methods to psychology.

I planned another book, on flowers, and I accumulated much material on trees. These studies remained literary, not scientific; whether jewels or flowers or trees, I failed at that time, in a way that now seems strange to me, to develop any ardour for studying them in Nature. The impulse to handle and explore the actual thing, whether material or psychic, only developed slowly within me during the following twenty years, until now the thing that I cannot come in close contact with has little interest for me.

I also wrote a number of short miscellaneous essays on various topics. Here I had more scope for the development of a personal style and was already unconsciously feeling after a rhythm of my own, at this time rather redundant and rhetorical, as I remember my mother once pointed out to me. I would like to read these little essays aloud, and the most obvious way of doing so seemed to me to regard them as sermons and to preach them to the congregation of my young sisters, using the head of the sofa as a pulpit. Doubtless this was the first manifestation of my hereditary ecclesiasticism, not, I suppose, the last, for it is but a few years since that I read in a review by a brilliant woman critic that there is the atmosphere of *Cranford* around even my most daring books, and though I have never read *Cranford* I understand that the atmosphere in question is of pious clericalism.

Neither in form nor substance were these childish writings original. Their interest is as a clue to my genuine literary temperament. I proceeded throughout from native instinct and without the slightest stimulus or example to impel me along the path I was taking. I had never met an author; people of that kind were

completely unknown in my family circle and never mentioned.
No one I knew would have dreamt of holding up an author as
worthy of my imitation. It was not, moreover, until long afterwards that I realised that authorship is a possible means of livelihood. Indeed, in a sense, I never have so looked upon it. I am
quite pleased to make my living by what I write, but the attempt
to write for my living would be hopeless, for I can write nothing
that is not in itself a pleasure to me to write.

My early literary adventures revealed a preoccupation with
the Bible. Just as all my germinal artistic and scientific aptitudes
went into writing, so all my early emotional activity went into
religion. From our earliest years my mother brought us up religiously. She was so profoundly and sincerely religious herself,
in the old Evangelical manner, that it was inevitable she should.
Such early and constant familiarity with the Bible and the Prayer
Book, and a regular attendance at church services, whether or not
it inspires religious emotion, certainly promotes religious knowledge, and the imagery of the Bible, the phrases and cadences of
the Prayer Book, which glide so easily into my mind and into
my writings, date back to my childhood. For strong emotion,
however, the shock of sudden external stimulus is necessary.
I cannot definitely recall how this shock came to me, but I am
fairly certain that it was through the remarkable personality of
the Reverend John Erck, the vicar of Merton at that time. Old
Merton Church, though immediately opposite the college, was
not the nearest church to our house. But my mother was always
accustomed to choose the church that suited her and not that
which happened to be nearest. Erck — an Irishman, a man of
good family and some property — was an example of the so-
called Celt, short and erect, with black hair, sallow complexion,
and dark, glowing eyes. He had all the perfervid oratorical and
emotional genius of his race, and a thousand years earlier might
have been among the Irish missionary saints. A shy, silent man
in daily life, who walked straight ahead, with his forearm carried

at his back, looking neither to right nor left, in the pulpit he was transformed. I have heard many famous preachers — Liddon and Stanley and Spurgeon and Parker — but never one who possessed so fine a natural eloquence as this man, an eloquence in which passionate sincerity blended with poetic imagination, wholly guided, it seemed, by the inspiration of the moment and yet always the instinct of the artist. I remember him vividly enough to believe that if I were to hear him now my opinion would still be the same. He had a beautiful voice with a wide range between the high and the low tones, and he would modulate this voice with a skill and effect which in a popular preacher must soon have become a self-conscious affectation, but in this unappreciated country parson of a quiet village seemed altogether natural. There come back to me the summer evenings in the dim church — it was only in the evening that his eloquence was fully revealed and when dusk came on the lights were not lit — and the stream of Irish eloquence that rose and fell over the heads of those prim and stolid Anglo-Saxon villagers. I well remember, on the sudden death by a fall from his horse of Bishop Wilberforce — a diocesan whose exceeding personal charm had won the heart of the Low Church vicar — with what impassioned eloquence Erck preached on the Elijah who had been suddenly swept to the clouds in a chariot of fire; and how again, in a very different mood, having apparently found that the tradesmen of his parish were not above the trick of giving false measure, he preached a fierce sermon on this subject: 'People of Merton, repent!' Perhaps more than by his sermons I was moved by Erck's exquisite way of reading the lessons and especially the prayers. He would sometimes subtly graduate and slowly deepen his voice through the various collects of evensong, and the low and grave tones with which at length he reached 'Lighten our darkness' still linger in memory. These influences enabled me to understand something of the reality of the Bible and the beauty of the English Prayer Book, and so to some extent counteracted the dulling effect of familiarity with these things when imposed as a task in early life.

Erck left Merton, I believe, a few years after we left the neighbourhood, disheartened, I understand, by the lack of sympathy, and became English chaplain at Pisa during long years. He is still alive when I write this, in 1905, living at Brighton, and now, when I rewrite these pages in 1921, I can add that he died at an advanced age and that when I visited Merton Church a few years ago I noted with pleasure a brass tablet set up on the wall to his memory.[1]

A certain part of the religious and semi-religious influence of Merton Church upon my young and sensitive mind emanated from the building itself. I never knew its history — I sometimes sought to imagine it — though I knew that Merton had a part in ancient history. The churches I had been familiar with before were modern and uninteresting; this, though small and of no great architectural worth, possessed the charm and beauty of antiquity. The ancient monuments, the old helmet that hung aloft over the reading-desk, the row of blazoned escutcheons and their mottoes — *In Coelo Quies* and the rest — these things vaguely and often stirred my ignorant imagination. The love of old buildings, especially old churches, which has become so strong with me since, certainly began to make itself felt at Merton.

Underlying my interest in the external aspects of religion there was really a personal and intimate kernel. What, if any, intellectual or dogmatic conceptions I attached to religion I cannot recollect; doubtless they were only those I was taught. But at one time I constantly carried a little Testament in my pocket: I studied it devoutly: I was, moreover, seriously anxious to do right, and firmly resolved to train myself in the paths of righteousness. I recall one incident that seems characteristic. I had found among old neglected books in the house a little manual on self-

[1] Perhaps it was set up by his wife. Still later (I now write in 1930) I note in *The Times* the announcement of her death, also in Brighton, a few miles from where I am now living, at the great age of one hundred.

education by, I think, a Mrs. Hope, and a list of faults was herein presented in a tabular form, the author recommending the use of such a table for entering a mark against each fault every time it was committed. I copied out the table for my own use and began duly to follow the instructions. Before long, however, I found that it was often difficult to be quite sure about the definition of one's faults and also realised that in any case the proceeding was unprofitable. I folded up the table of my faults and slipped it down between the boards of my bedroom floor. Maybe it rests there still.

All these little experiences, it must be noted, I went through strictly with myself. I had then in a high degree, as I have always had more or less since — though as one grows old and detached from the world it is less rather than more — an instinctive secretiveness in intimate emotional matters, an almost unconquerable impulse to keep my own personal life to myself. I never desired to take, and certainly never dreamed of taking, any person into my confidence in these matters of religious edification and moral improvement. It must be said that I was, at this age, in all respects a 'good' boy; whether or not the vices of boyhood are virtues in disguise, I certainly had no trace of them; but I was not a goody-goody boy, for it would have been horror to me for anyone to suspect my inner feelings.

So far I have said nothing of my sexual life. On the physical side there was really nothing to say until I had passed boyhood and reached adolescence. There were no spontaneous sexual manifestations, and no companion, no servant girl, ever sought to arouse such phenomena, or to gratify curiosities that before puberty had not come into being. Indeed, strange as it may appear to some, throughout the whole course of my schooldays, until they ended at the age of sixteen, I cannot recall that I heard or saw anything that would have shocked an ordinarily modest schoolgirl. One incident there is to tell at the Chincha Islands, but even that merely shows my innocence.

In recent years I have sometimes looked back at my childhood to observe how it appears in the light of modern views of the more subtle mechanism of sex and its manifestations and repressions in childhood. That much may thus be revealed I am now well aware by my own investigations on others. One cannot fail to find something significant when one turns to explore, in this new light, the child one has known most intimately. A central fact about myself seems to be demonstrated by the incident to which I have just referred. In childhood I was not sexually excitable. It seems to me that, however numerous the exceptions, this complete sexual latency in the pre-pubertal period is probably the rule. But I am not here concerned to generalise, nor am I prepared to assert that I was myself either as child or adult completely normal; on the contrary, I was from the first — beneath a reserved and impassive surface — a highly nervous and sensitive person. I was in some degrees, perhaps, what may be called an 'introverted' child; my timidity, my self-consciousness and self-criticism, perhaps drove me in on myself, not, however, towards day-dreaming, which only began at puberty, but to books. (My wife, as a child, by a more profound sense of inferiority — for those around her took pleasure in making her aware of her small size, her lack of beauty, and her naughtiness — was driven to the opposite extreme of rebellious and energetic self-assertion, and so became an 'extraverted' child.) There were no sexual emotions and not even any sexual curiosities at this period. I remember that at some time — I cannot remember when — I considered the question of the origin of babies and decided that they emerged from their mothers' navels, but this was to me a purely scientific question which involved no morbid feelings nor any undue attention. I was, again, affectionately devoted to my mother, but quite calmly and undemonstratively, without at any time the slightest touch of excess or any cravings for the manifestation of love in her, or any curiosities, and without, also, the slightest hostile feeling towards my father. Moreover, I shared the curious reserved critical aloofness which most children feel towards their parents. I am at the same time able to believe that my mother exerted some moulding influence on my later sexual life, and that this would have been much greater if, as never happened, she had allowed her love for me to become unduly tender; but as it was, her chief influence lay in unconsciously moulding my ideal of womanhood generally.

The question arises whether this seeming absence of sexual phenomena in childhood may not be due to deliberate repression or automatic suppression of such phenomena into the unconscious. If so, they ought when thus repressed or suppressed to give some sign in disorder of the conscious life; but there seem no such signs. Something more, however, I now see, remains to be said. There was no occasion for such repression or suppression. There was no need for it, not entirely because there was nothing to put away, but because the veil of impassive reserve with which I concealed the whole of my intimate personal life rendered repression or suppression completely superfluous. Beneath the veil I was free to think or to feel what I liked; there was no one to say me nay and I saw no reason for saying nay to myself. This fact now seems to me of immense significance for the whole of my life; it is, from one point of view, the key to all my work and my whole attitude towards the world. I have never repressed anything. What others have driven out of consciousness or pushed into the background, as being improper or obscene, I have maintained and even held in honour. It has become wrought into the texture of my whole work. Cultured and intelligent people have privately said of my work that it is quite right but should not have been written and published. If I had acted according to their ideas I should have remained as dumb and as obscure as they remained. What I have done has been less perhaps the outcome of deliberate resolve than the expression of an instinct, only now becoming clear to me. That same impulse is expressed in my whole attitude towards the world, in what may be called my philosophy, if by that word one may mean no accepted system but the manifestation of one's personal attitude towards the universe. I have from the first, beneath my concealing veil, been natural and so I am naturally one with Nature and intimately and essentially in harmony with the course of the universe. It was not until I was nineteen that I became consciously aware of that harmonious union, but the immense satisfaction that the discovery gave me was a sufficient proof of what my real nature had been from the first.

I have said that probably in childhood I was sexually normal. But I think I can trace a slight fibre of what, if possibly normal in childhood, is commonly held — though this I doubt since I have found it so common — not to be so when it persists or even develops after puberty. I mean a slight strain of what I may call urolagnia, which never developed into a real perversity nor ever became a dominant interest and formed no distinguishable part of the chief love-interests of my life. It was not a recognisable emotional interest in childhood, but the clearness with which several small incidents from that period stand out in memory seems to indicate that it was of some interest to me. To this in later childhood a more scientific interest, possibly my earliest scientific interest, was added when I observed the differences in vesical energy among my schoolfellows, my own being below the average, and began to measure it exactly as private opportunities offered. Many years afterwards I continued these observations and published the results in a paper on 'The Bladder as a Dynamometer' in the *American Journal of Dermatology*, May, 1902. Later my vision of this function became in some degree attached to my feeling of tenderness towards women — I was surprised how often women responded to it sympathetically — and to my conception of beauty, for it was never to me a vulgar interest, but rather an ideal interest, a part of the yet unrecognised loveliness of the world, which we already recognise in fountains, though fountains, it is now asserted, have here had their origin. It would be easy to overrate the importance of this interest. But it is necessary to note it.[1]

In later years, I would now further note, it has seemed to me that I may have inherited this trait from my mother, whose early love of water I have already referred to. Once she took me at the age of twelve to spend the day at the London Zoological Gardens. In the afternoon, as we were walking side by side along a gravelled path, in a solitary part of the Gardens, she stood still, and soon I heard a very audible stream falling to the ground. When she moved on I instinctively glanced behind at the pool on the path, and my mother evidently watching my movements, remarked shyly, 'I did not mean you to see that.' I accepted the incident simply and naturally. Much later in life, recalling the incident — I remembered it clearly so it must have made an impression on my mind — I realised that my mother's remark could not be taken at its face value. Nothing would have been easier than to step on the grass, where detection might possibly have been avoided, or to find a pretext for sending me a few yards off, or to enter a Ladies' Room. Her action said clearly, 'I meant you to see that.' Today I probably understand it better than she herself could. No doubt there was a shy alarm as to what her now tall, serious boy would think of this new experience with his mother, but there was also the impulse to heighten a pleasurable experience by blending it with the excitement of

[1] I may be regarded as a pioneer in the recognition of the beauty of the natural act in women when carried out in the erect attitude, and it is described in a passage of my *Impressions and Comments* which some critics consider my best piece of prose, as well as in an early sonnet entitled 'Madonna,' while for the more scientific side my study 'Undinism' is the first serious discussion of the whole subject. But Rembrandt preceded me. There is a fine and admired picture of his in the National Gallery (No. 54) of a woman standing in a pool and holding up her smock, with parted legs, in an attitude which has always seemed to me undoubtedly to represent the act of urination. In recent years I have learnt on good authority that so it really came from the artist's hands, but that at some later date (whether or not before it reached the National Gallery in 1836) the falling stream was painted out. The picture is dated 1654 and experts now consider that it probably represents Hendrickje Stoffels, the charming and beloved figure whom, about that time, Rembrandt painted in various intimate situations. I should like to think that the indignation I feel at this sacrilegious distortion of a supreme artist's work will some day be generally shared.

sharing with her son. There was evidently a touch of exhibitionism, the added pleasure of mixing a private and slightly improper enjoyment with the presence of a beloved male person, for a woman is always a little in love with her first born and only son. Every woman who has a streak of what I call Undinism will understand the fascination of this emotion on the threshold of intimacy. Her real feeling would have been better stated: 'I loved you to see, but I didn't want you to see if you would have been disgusted.' On the next occasion, some time later, there was no longer any shyness and she confided in me beforehand. We had just had dinner at an exhibition, and, as there were people strolling about, this time she really took some precautions. She stood on the grass, and, before she had finished, walked on a few paces and then copiously recommenced, while I spontaneously played a protective part and watched to see that no one was approaching. When in much later life I mentioned this experience to my sister Louie, she told me that our mother had always been extremely reserved with the girls in regard to this function, and remarked, after consideration, 'She was flirting with you!'

I could add various significant details which confirm the presence in my mother of this trait, such as the habit of urinating on her hand, which, she said, was good for the skin, but really, I doubt not, found pleasurable. I should add that there was never, on my part at any time, the slightest impulse of curiosity such as young boys sometimes manifest with regard to their mothers; there was an awe in my affection for her which would have prevented even the feeling of curiosity; it seems significant, however, that I remember clearly these as well as other incidents, earlier in life, when the same subject was presented to me in connection with women, the earliest being at the age of four when the nurse, wheeling my baby sister, stood still to perform this function, with no word either on her part or mine, though I still remember the spot in the Morland Road. It was not until the age of sixteen that this trait became a conscious and active, though always subordinate, element in my mind. It can hardly, therefore be considered either the persistence of an infantile impulse or a regression. It proved of immense intellectual benefit to me, for it was the germ of a perversion and enabled me to understand the nature of perversions. On the emotional side, also, it has been a more or less latent element in that tender sympathy for women which, as I have come to realise, they so greatly appreciate.

Love comes normally to a child through what we call the soul rather than through the body. In this and indeed throughout — with whatever wide variations from the most common types — I was normal. The young boy's love is a spiritual passion generated within by any stray spark from the real world, and so far as his own consciousness extends, even without any sensory, still less any sensual, elements whatever, easy as it might be to detect such elements. A chance encounter of life sets free within him a vision which has danced within the brains of his ancestors to remote generations and has no relation whatever to the careless girl whose playful hand opens the dark casement that reveals the universe.

I was twelve years old, and the summer holidays, after my last term at Merton College, had just begun. Half a century earlier (as I discovered five years afterwards in Australia when reading his attractive *Autobiography*), at the same age, in this same village of Merton, a man of letters more famous than I am ever likely to be, Leigh Hunt, had met his first love. Here I was now to meet mine.

My mother, though on occasion hospitable, cared little to have strangers staying in the house; a girl or boy cousin would sometimes be invited to spend a week, and left no impress on my imagination. The first stranger not of my kin to stay in the house was a girl of sixteen, the only daughter of my mother's stepbrother, who was in a well-to-do position. Agnes, then, for that was her name, was invited to spend a summer week or two with us at Wimbledon in 1871. She was a dark, pretty, vivacious girl, with long black ringlets, of something the same type, I can now see, as her grandmother, the second Mrs. Wheatley, whom I distinctly remember. Old enough to be a woman in my eyes, and yet young enough to be a comrade and equal, she adapted herself instinctively to the relationship and won my heart immediately. I took not the slightest liberty with her, and never had the slightest impulse to do so, but she, on her part, treated me with an easy familiarity which no woman had ever used with me before, and that fact, certainly, though its significance was then beyond me, undoubtedly had its influence. She would play and romp with me in all innocent unreserve, and when we went out together for long walks, as often happened, she would sometimes make me offer her my arm and treat her as a lady, then again asserting her superiority by treating me to lemonade and at the best places she could find. One day, as we strolled arm in arm through the poppied cornfields which then lay between Merton Station and the college — it was in these fields that I first knew the beauty of poppies — my severe little schoolmaster suddenly came round the corner onto us. Timid though I habitually seemed, I raised my cap without flinching or withdrawing my arm under my master's stern eye, and have ever since prided myself on that early little act of moral courage. He doubtless smiled to himself at thus seeing a handsome girl hanging on his quiet pupil's arm, and he subsequently asked my father who she was, but without, I think, mentioning that detail. Agnes returned home, and, strangely enough, I have never seen her since. I lent her Keats's *Poems* when she left and she lent me *The Wide, Wide World*; we exchanged a few notes, but our correspondence speedily withered, without protest on my part, and probably aided by the fact that, through a trivial circumstance connected with this very visit of Agnes — she had once offered to help in the domestic work and been given some peas to shell which her mother resented as too menial a task for her daughter — a certain permanent coldness developed between her mother and mine, each feeling aggrieved. She is still alive, and though she was even then looking forward to marriage as a near probability (for I heard her talk to our servant to that effect), she still remains single, an only child who has devoted her life to the care of her aged parents.

I never saw Agnes again; I never made any effort to see her; I never mentioned her name; no one knew that I even thought of her. But for four years her image moved and lived within me, revealing myself to myself. I had no physical desires and no voluptuous emotions; I never pictured to myself any joy of bodily contact with her or cherished any sensuous dreams. Yet I was devoured by a boy's pure passion. That she should become my wife — though I never tried to imagine what that meant — was a wild and constant aspiration. I would lie awake in bed with streaming eyes praying to God to grant that this might some day be. I have often felt thankful since that our prayers are not heard.

Under the stress of this passion I became a person, and, moreover, in temper a poet. I discovered the beauty of the world, and I discovered a new vein of emotion within myself. I began to write verse. I began to enjoy art, and, at the same time, Nature. In a still vague and rudimentary way, all my literary activities slowly took on a new character. Hitherto they had been impersonal, displaying indeed a certain research, a certain orderly and systematic spirit, perhaps inborn, yet not definitely personal. Now the personal element took shape. The touch of this careless vivacious girl had placed within me a new ferment which began to work through every fibre of my being. It was an epoch-making event in my life and was soon to be succeeded by another of scarcely less importance.

Part III

III

Now that I was twelve years old, my mother decided that I ought to be sent to a boarding-school. It was to be a small private school, for she had heard too much evil of large public schools to care to send her only son to them. Moreover, our means were not sufficient for an expensive education. We lived, indeed, in ease and comfort, from a lower middle-class point of view, on my father's earnings as sea-captain under more prosperous conditions than have always prevailed in the merchant service since, and on a small income of my mother's. Until I left home I never knew what money worries meant, though I have often had occasion to know in the years that have followed; but as my parents always lived well within their means a lavish expenditure even on so important a matter as education was out of the question. My mother accordingly visited a school at Mitcham which, from what she had heard, seemed likely to furnish a desirable education at a moderate cost. The house was

large and old — one of the numerous houses wherein Queen Elizabeth is said once to have slept — and my mother was of course
shown over it with all due consideration. But the ill-ventilated
schoolroom full of boys smelt so fusty and dirty that she conceived a dislike of the place and came away without making any
arrangements. On her way back to Tooting Station she had to
pass another school, The Poplars — a curious old wooden house,
long since pulled down, though the brick schoolroom yet stands
— facing an open triangular space with a pond which we called
Frogs' Marsh. She entered and was so pleased with everything
here that she arranged at once with the head master to send me to
him, although the terms were higher than she had proposed to pay.
I was to be a weekly boarder, for my mother, though she never
made any similar arrangements for her daughters, wished to preserve a home influence over her son and to direct his religious
education.

My mother was pleased with the ways of The Poplars, but it
is not possible to make any high claims for its educational
methods. My head master, Mr. Albert Grover, was an oddity, a
tall middle-aged man, looking much older than his years, with a
long grey beard, a bald head, and a blind eye. He had some resemblance to Darwin, but he cherished much contempt for that
great man's doctrines and even published a little anti-Darwinian
pamphlet in doggerel verse which so nearly verged on the obscene
that it could not be sold on railway bookstalls. Grover had a
weakness for verse; he liked to teach facts and dates in doggerel,
such as

> 'Preston Pans and Fontenoy
> Were fought in 1745, my boy.'

He even introduced that method into his punishments, and I recall how a little boy had to stand on the form during breakfast-
time in the presence of the master's wife and daughter and the
whole of the school, repeating:

> 'Oh! Oh! Oh!
> I'm the little boy who broke the *pot*.'

But Mrs. Grover, too, was an oddity: a queer small boyish woman, with short curly hair, rarely seen then in women, and also frank of speech. It was told how she had once entered a bedroom, at a moment when a boy chanced to be naked, and how, as he modestly placed his hands before him, she reassuringly remarked, 'It's not the first time I've seen a little cuckoo.'

It would be easy to write amusingly of the life at The Poplars, but beneath its eccentricities it was essentially commonplace and old-fashioned, quite comfortable, certainly, and without hardship. So far as my head master was concerned, the influence of school upon me was neither good nor evil. He was a kindly man who always treated me well. I do not remember that he ever punished me or ever had cause to, but he inspired no love for any kind of learning, and I continued, as I had begun, without aptitude for formal studies. (It has always amused me in later life when I have come across references to my 'learning' or my 'scholarship.') I learnt no Greek at all, though I taught myself a little some years later; I plodded blunderingly through Latin, and cannot read any Latin author easily even now; I was, as I always remained, a blockhead at even the simplest mathematical problem; in Euclid, however, I showed a certain facility and rather enjoyed its logic, for reason and clarity have always appealed to me, and I am not surprised when I am told that my writings translate peculiarly well into the Latin tongues in which those qualities most prevail. In any art I may sometimes be fascinated by the romantically obscure, but it is to the classic (though not the pseudo-classic) that my admiration instinctively goes out: I am repelled by the shapeless and the unintelligible. At Merton, with a head master who was himself of French origin, I was well grounded in that language, and now at Mitcham I had the good fortune to find eventually — for he was preceded by three others, one a typical Pole, whose engagement proved brief — a resident French master who really loved his work and taught with thoroughness and enthusiasm. His name was Joseph Stevens; he came from Douai, and was, as his name might lead one to expect, of distinctly Flemish type, slender and fair, a simple single-minded man with no interests beyond his work. I frequently associated with him outside school hours and my knowledge of French literature now began and rapidly progressed. Stevens had some knowledge of other languages besides French, and with a little help from him I began on my own account and in my own time (in which also I was keeping up my practice on the piano) to master the elements of German and Italian. My interest in French, and in modern languages generally, simply as instruments to bring me nearer to contemporary life and contemporary literature and contemporary peoples, has been of inestimable value to my work, as well as a perpetual source of delight and of refreshment, and I am grateful to Joseph Stevens, I do not say for implanting but for stimulating and fostering it.

The English assistant master, however, Angus Mackay, had a far more vital and profound influence upon me than Stevens. He came to the school soon after I entered, and he remained when, four years afterwards, I left. I still recall him as he paced the garden on the first evening of his arrival, a short sturdy figure with bent head. Though scarcely twenty years of age, he had already struggled against many difficulties and seen much of life. A Highlander on one side (his father had been an accomplished 'Royal Piper,' but died early after, I believe, a rather dissolute life), English on the other, he fortunately reaped all the congenital advantages that may sometimes come of such mixture of blood. A dreamer and a poet, eager in intelligence and strong in enthusiasm, he was at the same time keen-sighted, energetic, practical, robust, a man of wholesome and pure instincts, a sanguine optimist, hearty in his friendships, equally downright in his contempt for all shams and pretences wherever they might be found. Struggling in poverty for high education (as also was his sister at the same time and with eventual success, for she founded a prosperous school), he had supported himself first as an office boy, then as a city clerk; now he felt able to take the post of assistant master in a school while further studying for a degree at London University. After that, he proposed to enter the Church. His religious views were those of the so-called Broad Church; that is to say, he followed Carlyle, Ruskin, Charles Kingsley, F. D. Maurice, and F. W. Robertson; while he was also in personal touch with Baldwin Brown, a distinguished divine of the Congregational Church. In politics he was, of course, Liberal, not to say Radical. It was, however, to literature, and especially to poetry, that he had been devoted. He had himself already published two little volumes of verse, strongly marked by the influence of Wordsworth and Tennyson, and one of these, *An Artist's Idylls*, had even gone into a second edition; he knew thoroughly the English poetic literature of the first half of the nineteenth century, and he had some acquaintance with contemporary poetic movements, while he was also familiar with many of the great English novelists and an ardent admirer of several contemporary novelists, especially Thomas Hardy, whose *Far From the Madding Crowd* was then about to appear in the *Cornhill*, which Mackay placed in my hands.

It is evident that to the shy, sensitive, solitary boy of twelve who had just arrived at Mitcham, however precocious in some mental respects he was, this man, full of the life and energy of the outer world, and inspired by its culture, was as it were a God-given revelation. He led me into that world. I had travelled round the earth, but I had never in my life conversed with a cultured intellectual man. My mother was a liberally minded Evangelical and I knew of no other religious views, except as a vague rumour of objectionable things; she was a Conservative in politics, or, as she later used to say, a Liberal-Conservative, and I had no idea that any reasonable creature held any other views. I had read Milton and Keats, Scott's *Marmion*, some of Shakespeare's plays, and various other standard poets with more or less tepid interest, and Longfellow had spoken to my youthful heart;

in Scott's novels I had revelled. But I had scarcely so much as heard the names of Shelley, of Mrs. Browning, of George Eliot, whose works were now placed before me, and for all of whom I was soon to acquire a love that for a period was almost passion. I still remember the day when, during a school-walk, Mackay first mentioned to me the names of Rossetti, Swinburne, and Morris, none of which I had heard before, but all poets destined to mean much to me and one to be known personally. If, indeed, I were to repeat all the names that Mackay first mentioned to me, I should have to cover the whole nineteenth century in England and more. It was not, however, merely that many great manifestations of the human spirit were now first brought before me. That was bound to happen soon. It lay, even more, in the stimulus of contact with my friend's vigorous mind, for our relationship was soon that of friends rather than of master and pupil. It was scarcely possible for him to speak a sentence that did not strike sharply across the beliefs and conventions that I had grown up in, that I had accepted without ever thinking about them. For the first time I realised that there were great questions and problems in life, great aspirations beyond one's own personal longings, great ideals to be passionately fought for. A touch had awakened my soul and my intellect; they were now to work at no man's bidding, not even Mackay's — who indeed never consciously sought to influence me — but in accordance with the laws of their own inborn nature. For years, however, Mackay was a banner that waved before me on the road to fresh spiritual conquests.[1]

I was fortunate in my French master; I was fortunate indeed in my English master; in more recent years it has been a regret to me that I never had an equally congenial science master, or at

---

[1] I wrote this in the summer of 1905, at Carbis. Shortly afterwards, Mackay, who knew nothing of what I had written, came to spend a few days with me in Brixton. It was the last time I saw him. Six months later he died of a rapidly developed cancerous tumour in the brain. At that time he had an Anglican church (Holy Trinity) in Edinburgh, had published several notable books, especially one on the Brontës, and was beginning to make a name for himself.

all events some friend to whom the scientific spirit and scientific methods were a reality. Mackay had no native scientific tastes. I was myself, I believe, instinctively possessed of the scientific spirit and independently anxious to gain scientific knowledge. I obtained and studied elementary manuals of natural philosophy, chemistry, and geology; botany chiefly interested me (there, as in some other respects, I seem to see the East Anglian temperament emerging). I studied flowers with the aid of books. But I never had a single scientific lesson of the most elementary kind at school, and I never met anyone who had learnt to observe, or really loved, Nature in her processes. I was never even taught drawing, to my lifelong regret, for that at all events is a discipline in exact observation, and as a child I had a certain amount of natural taste for it. My mother preferred instead to teach me music at home at the domestic piano and for that I had no real aptitude, though a considerable amount of love. (I even, though entirely ignorant of the science of music, 'composed' and wrote down a few short pieces.) I had as a child read and enjoyed Maria Edgeworth's *Harry and Lucy*, which was written to guide boys and girls into the paths of elementary science by story and play. But if I had personally known someone (like my later friend Barker Smith) who could have shown me how our daily life is full of chemical problems, someone to whom the names, structures, and uses of plants were familiar, someone who would have made me feel the vital mechanism of animals and men, I should probably have been greatly helped and saved from wasting much time. I had an instinct for exact measurement; at the age of twelve, or earlier, I was measuring the varying lengths of the urinary stream, and at seventeen I discovered for myself the fact that stature varies during the day. But it was not until I became a student at Saint Thomas's Hospital, at the age of twenty-one, that I really began to learn to observe accurately and to comprehend the scientific temper. I discovered then how rare that temper is among professional men of science.

So far as my masters were concerned, my life at Mitcham would have been from first to last a peaceful and happy period of more or less spontaneous mental development. But for a considerable time it was made a hell by the influence of one boy. I shared a large bedroom with two boys, both several years older than I was. One of them was of quiet and inoffensive temperament when left to himself, but he was always willing to become the tool and partner of the third boy. This third boy, Willie Orr, may, for all that I know, have possessed many fine latent qualities. But he was one of those youths whose irresistible impulse it is to bully and dominate those who are too young or too timid to resist them. His father was a colonel in the Indian army; young Orr was probably fond of riding (later he appropriately joined the Indian Frontier Mounted Police, dying young) and in the absence of a horse he conceived the idea of using me in that capacity. In order to carry out the idea in a manner quite satisfactory to himself he made spurs in which pins formed the working portion; every night he mounted my back with his spurs on and rode me round and round the room in my nightshirt, handing me over to the other boy when he was himself tired of the exercise. (I should add that nothing else, nothing of the slightest sexual character, ever took place.) To a shy, sensitive, and reserved boy, one, moreover, who had never been harshly treated, these performances were an acute nervous torture, out of all proportion to any pain actually inflicted. I had no instincts of pugnacity, and the idea of attacking or resisting a robust and brutal boy older and bigger than myself never occurred to me. I performed the required duties much as a real animal would have done, without articulate protest or complaint, until my mother, discovering something amiss with me, made me confess what was going on, and came to interview Mr. Grover. I was then placed in another room, which I shared pleasantly with a boy of character congenial to my own. But I am inclined to think that the suffering I had silently endured was not without evil influence on my nervous system. I was just then at the critical period of puberty. While subjected to this treatment, at about the age of thirteen, copious seminal emissions began to take place during sleep, once or twice a week, always without dreams or any sensations, and continued, whenever I was alone, for some thirty years. Doubtless my temperament predisposed me to such manifestations, though my thoughts and my habits were, at this period, alike free from any physically sensual tincture, but I incline to think that the state of nervous excitement in which every night I fell asleep was a factor in causing this lack of nervous stability in the new function then developing. The emissions were themselves a source of nervous apprehension, for I vaguely felt they were something to be ashamed of; I constantly dreaded their occurrence and feared their detection.

I was now entering on the period of adolescence, and it is time to describe what sort of boy I was in the eyes of those with whom I associated. When a baby, I had been, as the son of well-developed, healthy, and mature parents might be expected to be, a large and robust infant, and I have already said how I appeared, on my mother's lap, in all the happy insolence of vigorous babyhood, in my earliest portrait, which Olive Schreiner borrowed and lost, and how in the next portrait, that happy careless air gone, I appear as a small child, in a frock, gazing out at the world of human beings with a look of nervous anxiety and doubt, a look which, whether or not it has gone out of my face, has scarcely yet altogether gone out of my heart. It was a portrait that much appealed to my wife, but foolishly remembering the fate of the earlier portrait, I went on postponing a promise I had made to give it to her, though she often reminded me of it, until it was too late. At the age of seven, in a photograph taken in Sydney, I appear with a sensitive but composed face (at this time it was said of me that I always looked as if I had just been taken out of a bandbox), and again at the beginning of the Mitcham period I am seen, now tall but still with the same expression, and an added air of self-consciousness. My height, I may say, when full grown was five feet, ten and one-half inches. My weight has never been considerable (usually around one hundred and fifty pounds), for I am not thickly developed and have never been stout, though, on the other hand, I am not excessively slight or at all emaciated. Olive Schreiner said once of my nude form that it was like that of Christ in the carpenter's shop in Holman Hunt's 'Shadow of the Cross.' I am fairly well formed and proportioned, without congenital blemish or defect at any point, and the skin is of fine texture, though not, I think, of feminine quality. The legs are well developed, the arch of the instep unusually high, the great toe the longest. The chest is not narrow, but the arms are relatively less developed than the legs, and the knuckles of the fingers are slightly prominent; in this I am unlike my eldest sister whose hands are of aristocratic and fine shape. My eyes are commonly called grey, occasionally blue; I call them green — that is to say, they are blue with brown circles round the irides — and my hair, which was light brown, became a dark brown, and began to turn grey towards the age of forty; it seems intermediate between that of my mother, which was rather auburn approaching sandy in the eyebrows, and that of my father, which in mature life had been a brown approaching black; his eyes in early life were said to be hazel, but in later life they were certainly more nearly blue. My hair was and remains remarkably thick on the head; the beard, lighter in tone, sparse and rather straggling. I may add here that my mother when she kissed me used often to say that my cheeks were scented, and my wife, who has frequently made the same remark, has also said that my cast-off shirts have a distinct odour of cedar. My face was not remarkable in adolescence, and the occasional presence of acne pimples was a source of distress which increased the humble self-consciousness I felt concerning my personal appearance. It is rather a short face; the chin, with the large dimple in it (seemingly inherited from the Havelocks), is, I have been told, lacking in strength; the nostrils are broad and at the base of the nose is a marked indentation which my mother used to think was caused by the forceps at my birth, but that is unlikely, and a similar indentation may be noted in various men of marked intellectual force and large heads. My mouth is broad and opens widely, showing large white teeth, finely formed and regular, but not of strong texture, for they began to decay early, and with the carelessness of youth I neglected them; dentally I resemble my mother, for my father's teeth were almost perfect at the age of seventy. The facility with which my teeth appear caused my schoolfellows to compare me, quite unjustly, with that Roman Egnatius who smiled much to show his good teeth. Internally my palate has a well-marked antero-posterior central ridge, the *torus palatinus*. My head is large, twenty-three inches at the greatest circumference, and I have sometimes had difficulty in finding a hat to fit. In the absence of exact measurements, I should say it is mesocephalic; it is certainly well removed from dolichocephaly. In later days, on the whole, I hear that my head is called 'noble,' and that my eyes are bright and, when I look anyone in the face, beautiful, but that the lower part of my face is rather 'weak.' There is, I may add, a peculiarity in the profile of the lower jaw which is probably characteristic. I have never been able to analyse it precisely, nor to say definitely that it is due to prognathism, but when the head is raised there is, in some aspects, a slightly apelike suggestion. Boys are quick to catch the faintest abnormalities, and my schoolfellows at Mitcham sometimes, quite good-naturedly, would call me 'Baboon.' I must admit the justice of the epithet, for something analogous, both in my face and in my nature, has been visible to those who have known me most intimately and most sympathetically. When in the National Gallery once with Olive Schreiner before Rubens's 'Silenus,' she laughingly noted my resemblance to the eager bright-eyed satyr to the right in the picture; and I must now add that more than thirty years later a dear friend loves to call me 'Faun.' Edward Carpenter, with the quiet twinkle of his luminous eyes, once said of me: 'He is the god Pan.'[1]

At the same time quite as many who have known me well — even among those who called me a satyr — have half-seriously and half in play remarked a resemblance to Jesus Christ. My wife has often told me that I am a mixture of a satyr and Christ. Both points had before been noted by Olive Schreiner. I first heard of the resemblance to Jesus from a fellow-student at Saint Thomas's who, when I was one day sitting on a bench awaiting a surgical demonstration, leant over to me from another bench at right angles where he was sitting and said with a dry smile: 'You remind me of Jesus Christ.' I frequently heard of similar remarks in the years that followed. The fact that, owing to the thickness of my hair, I had adopted the fashion of parting it in the middle, may have had something to do with this. I do not think it was generally taken to be a resemblance flagrantly in contrast with my satyr air. Nor would I myself see any contrast. Pan and the satyrs were divinities of Nature, as was Jesus on another plane. The wild being of the woods who knelt in adoration before the secret beauty of sleeping nymphs was one at heart with the Prophet who could see no more than a passing stain of sin in the wanton woman kissing his feet.

These similitudes may suggest that there was about me something slightly anomalous. It probably was so. Although my ancestry has been English in the narrowest sense for some centuries at least, and probably much longer, my physiognomy is not English. Foreign physicians curious in such matters (like my friend by correspondence Paul Näcke when he received my photograph) have made this remark, and its truth has often been brought home to me. I have been taken for a Spaniard in England, and in Spain Spaniards have often taken me for a fellow-countryman. 'Monsieur est russe?' asked the new landlord when I alighted at

---

[1] Many years later he brought the same point into a personal description in his autobiography, *My Days and Dreams.*

the Hôtel Corneille in Paris. 'Flamand?' It never occurred to him, until his wife suggested it, that I belonged to the nationality most often found abroad. The Russian character of my physiognomy must be marked; a Russian lady in the British Museum once addressed me as evidently a fellow-countryman, and more than one friend has told me that I resembled the early portraits of Tolstoy. It is perhaps significant that the peoples I was thus thought to resemble are peoples with whom I feel a special degree of affinity or sympathy.

It is evident that from boyhood I possessed a rather strongly marked and peculiar face, however emphasised this may have become with years; for it seems due more to its natural structure than to any acquired impress on the muscles. It is curious to me that as a boy I had a great horror of acquiring an artificially moulded and wrinkled face. I used to observe myself carefully in the glass, so as to be able to nip in the bud any wrinkling of forehead or contraction of lips. This was by no means from fear of impairing good looks, for I never imagined I had any, but solely because my natural and instinctive ideal involved a fluid receptivity of mind, an openness to impressions which was hostile to all rigidity and fossilised restraint, and I felt, doubtless rightly, that the hardening of mind and heart had its outward expression in a tightly contracted face. The idea, which thus seems to have arisen in me naturally, persisted for many years, whether or not it had any influence on the character of my face.

Facial variation from the average of one's race and family, however slight, doubtless indicates some degree of nervous and psychic variation. That also was certainly present, and I believe the germ of it was inherited from my mother. My father, with his cheerful and superficial temperament, has always been wholesomely normal, in nervous function as in all else. He never knew what it meant to have a headache, and he seems to have known equally little of nervousness or of shyness. In contrast to me, he was sociable and always able to meet the demands of social life, not indeed brilliantly but adequately and pleasantly; he has always easily won the liking and regard of men and women of all ages and classes. My mother, with all her fine and deep convictions, and a personality outwardly dignified and impressive, was beneath the surface congenitally emotional, shy, nervous, diffident, anxious, frequently uncomfortable in the presence of strangers, and only able to meet many ordinary eventualities of life with an effort of will and, I believe, secret prayer. This is my temperament also, and in a more marked degree. I am bold and fearless in abstract matters, or when questions of principle are involved, but in small practical matters I usually prefer to follow a leader. When left to myself in the details of life, I am apt to be cautious, nervous, self-suspicious, haunted by doubts when I have to choose between two courses of action, and tortured by the thought that the course I have rejected may have been the better. I cannot quite escape this tendency even when it is only a matter of choosing a dish at a restaurant, and my wife is always amused that I wait till she has chosen and then usually make the same choice. This temperament alone would probably have stood in the way of success as a practitioner of medicine, though in art, as in science, it is helpful, since it aids self-criticism. I have never been the victim of any definite morbid impulse, phobia, or obsession, but the mother liquid out of which such things crystallise is forever flowing in my veins. In early life and later I was shy to an almost painful extent. During the whole of adolescence I suffered from a tendency to blush from slight causes or no cause at all. Until late in life I found it difficult to look people in the eye, not, it seems, because I minded them looking into my eyes, but because there seemed to me something intimate and sacred in looking into the eyes of others; to meet a stranger's eye casually gives me a slight nervous shock and has often caused my lips to twitch involuntarily into a sort of momentary pout. Any kind of position or action which would attract public attention I find highly embarrassing, and for the most part impossible, though as a child I seem to have had nothing of this feeling and on the *Empress*, at the age of seven, I would sing to the piano and enjoy the applause. I have never made even the shortest speech in public. This, with the diffidence it involves, renders me inapt for social intercourse; there is nothing I find so depressing and so oppressive, even so absurd, as ordinary social intercourse in a roomful of strangers, as generally practised by the men and women of the age into which I have been born. Whether the twenty-first century will differ in this respect from the twentieth I cannot guess. I am, moreover, awkward in movement, though not to any notable extent. I always find it difficult, as my wife has frequently told me, to conduct myself skilfully at a dinner-table — though I believe I have improved under her training — or even to eat with becoming propriety, and although as a boy I played cricket and the ordinary school games I never achieved any real skill in them and football suited me best. This awkwardness can scarcely be the result of defective training; it seems rooted in an organic inborn lack of nervous stability. Many of my larger muscles, especially of the leg, are in frequent fibrillar activity. (I have just now, at the age of sixty-eight, found it possible to verify this observation, though the movement has become less frequent.) I first observed this at about the age of twenty-three when I was perhaps working too hard at my medical studies. There is also a slight unsteadiness of the smaller muscles, which is not visible but makes finer movements of any kind difficult. My handwriting has always been lacking in backbone and is frequently illegible, though as a small boy, and even now, I could always write a clear and orderly hand by taking the requisite trouble. My first schoolmaster used to say, aptly enough, that I kept a tame spider to write for me, and Grover would remark with an air of resignation: 'You will have a hand of your own, my boy.' In this matter I inherit to some extent from my father, but his handwriting, though invertebrate, was uniform and legible. Although I am right-handed except in the single action of throwing a stone or ball, I am inclined to think that congenitally I may be left-handed, and that my right-handedness is the artificial result of training, the spontaneous tendency only showing itself in the un-trained act of throwing. So much for the anatomical and phys-iological characters, in such degree as I consider them signifi-cant, on which my psychic characteristics have arisen.

To complete the picture I should add something as regards my health during this early period of life. Though a healthy breast-fed baby, at some period in childhood it seems that I ailed some-what and was taken by my mother from time to time to see Lon-don physicians, occasionally to a noted homoeopathist who had been recommended to her. I cannot recall in the slightest degree what my symptoms were; they were certainly not severe, and I gather that the physician sometimes thought that, as is probable, my mother was unduly nervous about me. It is possible, though this I doubt, that the beginning had taken place of a recurrent malady which tortured me at intervals in later boyhood and dur-ing the whole of adolescence.

I cannot remember when this disorder appeared; it certainly occurred at fairly frequent intervals soon after the age of twelve; it would come on rather suddenly with intense pain and tender-ness in (if I remember rightly) the right side of the abdomen, the region of the caecum, a dull sickening unintermittent pain; at its worst I could only lie on my back with thighs flexed, so as to relieve the pressure of the abdominal walls. Vomiting always oc-curred. Eating and sleeping, any mental or physical activity, were alike impossible. Sometimes the attack lasted for hours, sometimes for days, and recovery was always slow, tenderness remaining for some time. The doctors I was taken to could evi-dently make nothing of the case (Doctor Carpenter, I remember, on a second visit to him, mistakenly recalled the seat of pain as being on the opposite side), and they did nothing to relieve it. Nowadays, I feel certain, it would be regarded as a recurrent form of appendicitis. (Half a century later, and long after this narra-

tive was first written, one day when staying at my third sister's
house at Tunbridge Wells, in robust health, after a rapid two-
mile walk to catch a train I had a sudden attack of duodenal ulcer, the presence of which I had not detected, and a night of ex-
cruciating agony, followed by several weeks in bed, the first severe
illness of my life. Appendicitis is regarded as a frequent preceding condition in duodenal ulcer, and this tends to confirm my diagnosis.) As to the cause, I can only suggest that it was connected
with indigestion. My digestion was never vigorous; in that I resembled my mother; my father's has always been perfect, like all
his functions. The attacks occurred most usually when I was at
home, and our midday dinner was a simple and copious meal, of,
most usually, a solid joint of meat, potatoes and cabbage, suet
pudding or fruit pie, with a little English ale until my mother
became a total abstainer. It was an excellent meal for a plough-
boy, but for me such a combination, as I now recognise, is very
like a poison, especially if eaten without care and deliberation.
And unfortunately I was, if I do not still remain, an incurably
rapid eater.

These attacks gradually died down and had almost or quite
disappeared by the time I was twenty; but they merged into a
chronic tendency to dyspepsia which has more or less seriously
incapacitated me and greatly contributed to render me inapt for
social functions. If I am leading a healthy and leisurely existence,
much out in the open air, free from mental strain, able to control
the conditions of my daily life and my meals — which should
consist, if possible, of several small dainty dishes, served at fairly
long intervals, and with rest after the meal — then I am usually
able to escape my demon of dyspepsia. But any slight aberration
may nullify other favourable conditions and then a feeling of gas-
tric swelling and discomfort slowly increases and tends to become
paroxysmal in character; I grow more and more wretched, stupid,
silent, absorbed in the consciousness of visceral conditions, and
unless I am free by a voluntary effort of pseudo-vomiting to re-

lieve the stomach of gas, pressure on the heart causes faintness, and once or twice, in a theatre and in a restaurant, I have actually fainted for a few moments from this cause, the only occasions in my life that I ever have fainted. When the condition becomes intolerable, I usually invent an excuse to escape, but I expect that my unexplained stupidity has sometimes left an ineffaceably bad impression on kind hosts. I am inclined to suspect that, like Nietzsche, I have some dilatation of stomach, but the suspicion remains unverified. It was this constantly recurring dyspepsia which caused me to overlook the symptoms of duodenal ulcer until actual hemorrhage occurred. (With the approach of old age, after the attack of duodenal ulcer, when dieting became imperative and self-control easier, and especially when I had learnt the benefit of avoiding much fluid at meals, the condition improved and seldom caused more than minor inconvenience.)

On the whole, though not robust, I was a fairly healthy boy. As a child I had none of the usual childish fevers, except a slight attack of chicken-pox. I have never throughout life had any long or dangerous illness. (Needless to say, the duodenal attack occurred many years after this was written.) When I was about thirteen I had a slight feverish illness which the family doctor seems to have thought was possibly a touch of typhoid, and he declared that I had 'no stamina' and that I was 'threatened with consumption.' The threat was never realised, though my eldest sister afterwards developed this disease, but the observation about the absence of stamina probably contained an element of truth. I mean to say that there are some persons whose nervous systems seem to be of such tough fibre that they can stand prolonged strain without apparently feeling it, and can work at high tension during long periods, the resulting collapse, when at last it appears, being, however, serious and leaving often a lifelong nervous weakness. I am not of that type; I am sensitive to the earliest signs of nervous stress; rest or rather change speedily becomes a necessity; I bend and so I never break. This kind of temperament is associated with the fact that, for me, all work must be of the nature of play. If it is work, as work is usually understood, I find it arduous. So that when people tell me they wonder at the amount of work I get through, I honestly, if not truthfully, answer: 'Work? Why, I never work at all! I only play.' If I had not always been sensitive to the signs of nervous strain, and almost instinctively careful to guard against them, I might have become a nervous wreck. When I was about twenty-one, living at home at the beginning of my medical studies, while at the same time my literary activity began to develop, my brain became very active, full of ideas I wanted to work out; I began to suffer from sleeplessness which I treated myself by occasional doses of bromide or chloral. I quickly realised the necessity of good hygiene; I made it a rule not to work late at night, and never to occupy myself with any literary work in the evening or to read any exciting book. This rule I have seldom broken; I like to read before going to sleep, but always an unexciting book; an architectural book or magazine just now I find best, for it is always interesting and yet soothing to me. The result is that I have never again suffered seriously from sleeplessness and never again been tempted to take any soporific drug.

This kind of nervous temperament has been allied, happily no doubt, with that instinctive temperance which, as I have already said, I inherit from my father's family. It is the English form of that quality which the Greeks praised, whether or not they possessed it. Not only is every kind of excess repugnant to me, both mentally and emotionally, but I have not the organisation which would lend itself to excess. This seems to me a fundamental characteristic. I think it has coloured the whole of my moral ideal. I am on the side of freedom and nature. I look for the coming of Thelema and I accept its ethical rule, 'Fays ce que voul-dras.' I know that, so far as I am concerned, while I am living a free and healthy life I am not likely to hurt either myself or others by doing what I like, and it seems to me that this is more or less true of most people. But there are some persons — a minority, I feel sure, and perhaps a congenitally abnormal minority — of whom this is not true. These people have the temperament of excess; they seem to crave for the hard bit and the tight rein; there may well be some doubt as to whether my code of morals would suit them. I can only say that if these people are, as I believe, a minority — though, as I well know, often very fascinating, very lovable — we must make our moral rules to suit our majority. The main point, certainly, is to find the law of one's own nature.

I left school at the age of sixteen, and for a time lived at home (now at Wandsworth Common), making myself useful by acting as tutor to my two elder sisters, both younger than I was. What my occupation was to be, how I was to earn my living, I had not the slightest idea. My formal education was over, and though it had been a little above my parents' means, I had not been educated for any profession or employment. Nor, though full of eager interests, was there any career that I wanted to enter. Like the youthful Diderot, I wanted to be nothing, absolutely nothing, though, as for him, 'nothing' for me meant something not very far removed from 'everything.' By inborn temperament I was, and have remained, an English amateur; I have never been able to pursue any aim that no passionate instinct has drawn me towards. At this period I was at the beginning of adolescence. My thoughts were much occupied with ideal dreams of women and love; my attitude towards life was embodied in an 'Ode to Death' in which I implored Death to bear me away from the world on gentle wings, although at the same time I had no thought of taking any steps to aid Death in this task. Yet the lack of vocation on earth troubled me much, and also caused some mild concern to my parents, though they never put any pressure on me to bring this uncertainty to an end. My father was too easy-natured for that, and my mother had too much faith in

God, and too much faith in her son's abilities. 'Do not worry about Harry,' she said to my father, probably about this time, and with a confidence which impressed him, for he told me of it many years later. She was right in her insight, but I have taken a great many years to realise that she was right. It seems likely that, if literature could have presented itself to me as a possible career, that would have been the career to appeal to me. I loved reading; I had been writing verse and prose, out of the love of doing so, for some years. I had even sent letters to religious and other newspapers and seen my letters printed. But literature never presented itself to me as a means of livelihood, and, if it had, I lacked the ambition and self-confidence to believe that I could succeed in it; when, more than ten years later, I actually turned to literature as a vocation, it was as an editor rather than as a writer that I sought my living; I have never written for a living, only out of inner compulsion. Ambition I have never had — it is not a matter either for pride or for shame, but merely of temperament — and the belief that I could win a position in the world never came until, late in life, the position was won. I have a certain dogged persistence in quietly keeping on my own path and working out my own nature; this obstinacy alone has brought me what success I have achieved, and the success thus gained was preceded by no enjoyment in imagination. The only possible career that wavered before my mind was that of religion. My mother, religious as she was, had never suggested it to me, and I was quite ignorant of the perhaps significant fact that many of my ancestors had been parsons. At least four years earlier I had fallen into the habit of carrying a little Testament in my pocket. Moreover, I had been stirred by the preaching of Mr. Erck, the vicar of the neighbouring parish of Merton, whose church my mother attended. I was at Merton Church every Sunday from about the age of twelve to fifteen when we left Wimbledon. I have already mentioned Erck, who only died last year (1910), as an extraordinarily eloquent and typically 'Celtic' Irishman, shy

and silent in private life, but a lion in the pulpit. I vaguely proposed to myself to become a minister, but was not quite sure what
Church I would enter (my friend Mackay at that time was more
closely associated with the Congregationalists than with the
Anglican Church in which later he became a priest) and I still
have a letter from Erck urging me to choose the Church of England on account of the greater 'liberty of prophesying' that
Church offered. I was destined to need an indeed large liberty
of prophesying! Even when I received that letter (about the age
of fifteen), it is probable that my own faith was already being
subtly undermined, and my vague notion of entering the ministry
was rapidly dissipated.

It was in the course of my reading that I slid almost imperceptibly off the foundation of Christian belief. No personal influence entered. I had never talked with an unbeliever on religious matters, indeed, I scarcely knew one, though I was aware
that my uncle Joe, my father's youngest brother was — although
he had a special regard for my mother and she for him — a 'free-
thinker.' [1] While still at school I had bought a cheap reprint of
the English translation of Renan's *Life of Jesus*. It was probably
the first 'infidel' book I ever read. I read it carefully, with considerable admiration, though still from the Christian point of
view, and the notes that I made on the margins of its pages were
critical. But it served to familiarise me with the non-Christian
standpoint. At the age of sixteen, when I left school and was
about to accompany my father on his ship, I purchased, among
other books for the voyage, a second-hand copy of Swinburne's
Songs Before Sunrise, and at the same time, or soon after reaching
Sydney, the notorious *Elements of Social Science* (by George
Drysdale), which I had somehow heard of. They both had an in-

[1] When this was written, in 1911, he was still alive, the affectionate father of a
large family, brought up away from the churches, to which they returned with
avidity. He died of influenza and bronchitis in 1915, a few months after my father,
whose death was a great shock to him, but he remained sprightly and alert to the
last, a remarkable figure in old age; I sometimes met him at concerts, for he was
musical, playing the 'cello and singing in the chorus at Handel festivals.

fluence in stimulating the course of my thought away from Christianity, though the tone of the *Elements* was thoroughly uncongenial to me. To these I should probably add, as a subtler but deeper influence, the volume of Shelley's poems which at this age, and for two years later, was a greatly loved companion, read and often re-read. I now reach the great formative period of my life, when my destiny was finally sealed.

My father was soon to sail for Sydney, in the ship *Surrey* which he then commanded, with a large batch of Government emigrants. I had just left school, and though in fairly good health and free from definite disease, I was not, as I perhaps never have been, robust. My parents doubtless bore in mind the report of the family doctor, as well as my recurring attacks of disabling abdominal pain. It occurred to them that the vigour of my health would probably be established and the way prepared for my settlement in life by a voyage round the world, before I began to earn my living. It was an idea that does credit to the fundamental wisdom of my parents, though they could not know how my whole life may be said to have hinged on this decision of theirs. I cannot recall that I greeted the plan with enthusiasm, for such a voyage was no novelty to me. But I certainly accepted it without demur, for at least it enabled me to postpone that melancholy problem of a money-earning occupation which lay so heavily on my thoughts. The *Surrey* was carrying emigrants, and no ordinary passengers are allowed on an emigrant ship, but the difficulty was overcome by putting me on the ship's articles as 'Captain's clerk,' with the consent of the emigration officials, though one of them remarked at Plymouth, more or less jokingly, that I was a good size for my age and might cause havoc among the single girls. My father afterwards bantered me on the exemplary way in which I proved the groundlessness of that official's fear. Woman occupied an enormous place in my ideal life, but it never occurred to me to identify her with any one of the crowd of emigrant girls on board the *Surrey*.

My preparation for the voyage consisted mainly in a supply of books chosen by myself and bought with the aid of money supplied by my parents. They were mostly literary works of good quality in English and French, with a few in German. Some of the books I took with me I still possess, notably Spenser, Rabelais, and *Faust*. There were no real scientific books, except a few textbooks procured with the object of working for matriculation at London University.

My father added a harmonium to my equipment, at least as much for his own sake as mine, for he sang and, like all his family, had a simple taste for music. I had been taught the piano some years earlier, chiefly by Miss Johnston, my mother's old friend (once a teacher in my grandmother's school), and I specially delighted in strumming some of Beethoven's sonatas, fragments of Schubert, and Mendelssohn's *Songs Without Words*, though the last I outgrew; I never played well, but it was a useful method of emotional relief until the age of eighteen; since that age (when I left Carcoar in Australia) I believe I never touched the piano again. I said to myself that what I could not do well was not worth doing. Perhaps also I ceased to find emotional relief in the piano, since my emotions were ceasing to be diffuse and taking on more definite forms. The harmonium, however, was not a sympathetic instrument to me, and the career of this particular instrument was brief. When we had been only a few weeks at sea a tremendous and abnormal wave struck the stern cabin, my father's and mine, fortunately when we were at breakfast, burst through the ports, swamped the saloon, injured the chronometers, and with much other destruction ruined the harmonium. I seem to have accepted this catastrophe with characteristic coolness, for years afterwards my father used to tell smilingly that my only remark was, 'Does this often happen?' He himself had been perfectly cool, as indeed sailors have to be, for they live habitually in an atmosphere of impending catastrophe.

The *Surrey* left London on the nineteenth of April, 1875. From this date, and during the four years I spent in Australia, I kept a diary in a solid manuscript book purchased to this end, so that for the approaching formation period, when nearly all the seeds of my life's activities were sown, I could if I please — though I have not done so — check my recollection by the entries in this intimate contemporary record.[1] Except Olive Schreiner, no one has ever read this diary, not even my wife, though it contains nothing I had any wish to hide from her; but to Olive, with her large tolerance and her active intellectual receptivity, it seemed in 1884 easy and natural to me to bare my inner self. I sometimes think that with increasing years and ill health she has become less tolerant, less receptive, but we have long been separated by all the waves of the Atlantic.[2]

We proceeded from London to Plymouth to take on board the emigrants. During the few days here I recall that we stayed at Lucey's Hotel (a house which, many years later, I have looked around for in vain) and that one night my father took me to the theatre. I do not remember what we saw, but it was my first visit to the theatre. My mother possessed the moral objections of her Evangelical training to the theatre (though she had once taken me to a play at the Crystal Palace) and my father, when at home, adapted himself to her scruples, but at other times he shared the love of amusement natural to the sailor on shore. More vividly than the theatre I recall a visit to a lady at Devonport who had a charming daughter and a buxom girl friend, both a little over my own age. On the following day they visited the ship. The mother, who had evidently noticed my shy awkwardness, remarked that I needed 'some jolly girl friends.' That remark stayed in my memory. It was certainly true. I had never

---

[1] But now, many years later (1929), I think I may add it as an appendix for the sake of comparison between present impressions and completely independent subsequent recollections.

[2] A few years later, when she came again to live in England, I clearly realised how changed she had become in this respect. I remember how a young woman friend of hers once came to me and in a first interview told me of herself what, she said, one could not tell to Olive because one knew she would not be sympathetic.

had girl friends of my own age; my sisters were much younger and
still children; girl comrades might have despiritualised my ideas
of women, but would have wholesomely harmonised them.

My definite memories of the voyage are few. For the most
part they are fused with all my memories of voyages on the sea,
with the magic of a sailing ship — so exquisitely responsive to
Nature, sometimes idly calm on a glassy ocean, sometimes
swiftly driven onwards, furling and unfurling her canvas wings
to the breeze; of the vast blue foam-crested rhythmic waves of
the South Atlantic; of the wild free birds of the sea, above all
the albatross and the gull. I most clearly picture myself labor-
iously struggling with the first pages of *Faust*, for it was not until
a year or two later that I really gained some mastery of German
through becoming absorbed in Heine. My chief interest during
the voyage was certainly in the adolescent impulse to write verse.
I had written verses from time to time since I first fell in love at
the age of twelve. But now I vaguely had in mind the scheme of
a whole drama. So far, although I had read much poetry, only
three poets had deeply stirred me, first, of course, Longfellow,
the supreme poetic evangelist to boyhood, at all events for my
time, and, after that, Mrs. Browning's *Aurora Leigh* and Alexander Smith's *Life Drama*, two volumes that Mackay had lent
me a year or so before I left England. Passages in *Aurora Leigh*
had aroused my idealistic emotions to the highest point. But the
Life Drama, with its extravagant almost Elizabethan imagery
and its unrestrained emotionalism, probably made the most
intimate appeal to my adolescent soul. The outline and the tone
of the drama I proposed to write — so far as it had any definite
outline and tone — were due to Alexander Smith's romantic
poems, though I may also have been influenced by Bailey's
Festus, which I had bought a little before and carefully read,
with interest though no excitement. A number of fragments in
blank verse were written during the voyage, and after that —
nothing. I quickly realised that I had no strong native impulse

in this direction. I confined myself henceforth in verse to translation and the sonnet, with an occasional lyric. In prose I wrote almost nothing until my last year in Australia; my early crude efforts had ceased before I left England. I learnt how to write verse before I seriously drew near prose. I think now it is the right course and that my instinct was sound.

When the ship entered Sydney Harbour and the port medical officer came on board, he was informed by our ship's surgeon, Doctor Sheridan Hughes, that there were cases of chicken-pox among the emigrants. Hughes had discreetly kept this to himself, so it was a surprise as much to the captain as to everyone to find the *Surrey* ordered to the quarantine station, at a beautiful and solitary cove, in charge of an Irishman called Carroll. Hughes was Irish, too, a genial man and capable, but one to whom the writing of the simplest letter presented almost insuperable difficulties. So in the official correspondence which quarantine involved the 'Captain's clerk' was at last found useful. We were delayed at Spring Cove three weeks.

I have little recollection of the first weeks in Sydney, scarcely more than of my earlier visit to the same city ten years before. I remember that we continued, as was usual, to live on board while the ship was unloading at the Circular Quay which remains familiar to my memory. I remember that very soon after our arrival my father took me to a concert which was largely a recital by some famous violinist whose name I forget; it was the first time I had heard the solo violin, and what a few years later was to become for me the most exquisite music in the world seemed at this first hearing to be really just the scraping of horsehair against catgut and so ludicrous that I could scarcely refrain from laughing. And I remember a visit to the theatre which produced an altogether different effect; Ristori was in Sydney and my father took me to see her in *Pia de Tolomei* and (in English) the sleep-walking scene in *Macbeth*; more than fifty years later (as I rewrite these lines) I can see her still in both parts; for classic simplicity, for concentrated intensity with extreme economy of movement, I have never seen her acting excelled. I remember, again, that we used to go to dinner on Sundays to the house of the ship's agent, the Honourable G. A. Lloyd, a member of the legislative assembly and formerly treasurer of the Colony; he had a tall and numerous family and after dinner we would all solemnly sing hymns round the piano. Of more significance for my fate was another acquaintance of my father's, Alfred Morris. He had been first mate when my father once took emigrants to Australia many years earlier, had married one of the girls on board, thrown up his post, and settled in Australia, where he had practised a number of employments, being a clever and versatile Welshman, well-spoken and of good presence, but superficial and unstable, never able to persevere in the tasks he was fitted for, and, naturally, always failing in the others. At this moment he had just joined forces with another man also living on his wits, one Frederick Bevill, a baronet's son, born in France and lately from Japan, still youthful but enormously fat and correspondingly good-natured. They had taken a little office between Pitt Street and George Street and under a pompous name set up an educational agency. Now it happened that the *Surrey* was to proceed from Sydney to Calcutta, and Doctor Hughes had told my father that the Indian climate would be unsuitable for me. At this point Morris put in a suggestion and proposed that the General Educational Registration Association (that, I think, is what he called his little agency) should find me a post as assistant master at some Sydney school. This proposal was accepted, on my part, it seems, as easily as on my father's. Morris made no attempt to investigate my aptitude for such a position, but in one of his former functions as head master of a little school in Melbourne he wrote a glowing testimonial to my abilities, and therewith (since his name happened to be also that of a distinguished and better known head master in Melbourne) he was able in his function as agent to secure for me at once the post of assistant master at a good salary to Mr. Hole, who had a private school, Fontlands, at Burwood near Sydney. Here I was settled without delay to the apparent satisfaction of everyone.

Therewith the first stage of my life ends. I now entered the world. I entered it indeed very thoroughly, without a single friend (except in so far as I can so count Morris), without anyone who cared for me in the whole southern hemisphere I had been dropped into. I am sure that I never myself realised how important a moment it was; I could not know how my whole fate in life hung on it. A little sign, indeed, I recall which at the outset indicated a new stage of mental development. For it was then, as I have already told, that I read *The Pirate*, brought with me from England, one of the few of Scott's novels I had never read, and then, for the first time, I found Scott wearisome. The inner world of my boyhood had imperceptibly slipped away. I realised with a pang that I should never open a volume of Scott's again. I never have. But I was about to open a book which held greater revelations than Scott could bring, and in Australia to find my own soul.

Part IV

IV

My career at Fontlands was short and inglorious. Mr. Hole soon discovered that I was unable to carry my pupils far in classics, and that I had no interest in games. He gave me notice to leave and reduced my salary to a figure more suitable to a youth of sixteen who was completely inexperienced, not specially well taught himself, and with no aptitude for any schoolmastering art. But he remained friendly, and still found me useful. When I left he gave me a pleasant testimonial in which he referred to my special success in teaching French. It was perhaps the one subject I had myself been fairly well taught.

The apparent blow to my vanity — if I had any — seems to have made no deep wound, and the memory of the months at Burwood is not unpleasant. I was launched into the world, and that brought the agreeable realisation of freedom and the knowledge that I was for the first time earning my own living. I was, too, drinking in impressions of a new and beautiful land. I recall

the evening walks under the large and clear Australian sky to the
quiet country inn where during the first week I had to sleep; I recall myself wandering in my leisure moments through the spacious
school grounds reading the *Faery Queen*, which I had leisurely
begun on board ship; I shall always remember the magnolia tree
that grew by the schoolroom door, and the masses of heliotrope
in the garden beds, for then I first realised the delicious scents that
a warm southern clime can fill the earth with, and ever since
magnolia and heliotrope have held for me a magically entrancing
fragrance.

The boys were a singularly well-disposed set, and after Mr.
Hole had measured my abilities I found my work fairly easy, notwithstanding my constitutional deficiency in disciplinary control
over boys. Then there was the friendly and hospitable Australian
social environment. An invitation from the clergyman's daughter
to spend the evening at the parsonage (an invitation due in the
first place to the belief that I was one of the older boys) remains
memorable. There was a service that evening and I accompanied
the clergyman's family to church. On the way back, while he was
walking at the head of the party with a lantern, I, following behind beside the daughter, suddenly fell into a deep ditch by the
unfamiliar path; I strained my right leg, and, being unable to
rest it during the following days, I bear about with me the mark
of that visit to church, in the shape of a varicose vein, to this day.
I have a more agreeable and perhaps more memorable social recollection of Burwood. Near-by, a retired sea-captain called Fox
was comfortably settled, and once or twice I was invited to his
house. He had several pretty and charming daughters with whom
I was on terms of superficial acquaintance. No more, but without being in love with any one of them I vaguely desired more, yet
felt myself powerless, in my inexperienced awkwardness, to attain
more. All the obscure mysteries of sex stirred dimly and massively
within me; I felt myself groping helplessly among the difficulties
of life. The first faint germ was formed within me of a wish to

penetrate those mysteries and enlighten these difficulties, so that to those who came after me they might be easier than they had been to me. The personal situation was, I suppose, that of nearly every shy and sensitive youth before my time. But — as I look back half a century later — I see that here had come a youth whose impulse it was to intellectualise and moralise his own personal situation, thereby transferring it into an impersonal form, and universalising it. The first gleam of insight was so slight, however, so far from the shape it was to assume later, that it is now only with an effort that I can associate plainly the first resolve to take up the task that has mainly filled my life with the avenue of trees, as I paced up and down it one day, in the school grounds at Fontlands.[1]

There were many preliminaries to be gone through to prepare me for that great task, and I was yet far from realising their difficulty. When I left England I had the idea of matriculating and graduating at London University, after the example of my friend Mackay, still cheerfully unaware how inapt I am for academic exercises. I had brought textbooks with me on the *Surrey* with that end in view and occasionally worked at them. Now I so far modified my intentions as to resolve in the interim to matriculate and perhaps graduate at Sydney University. I knew no Greek, so at Burwood and later I was frequently and strenuously occupied with uncongenial Greek verbs. I duly matriculated, I think in the following year, but not in Greek, and the reason may now seem curious. There was an accomplished classical scholar, locally famed for his eccentricity and sharp tongue, at the head of the University called Badham (whose name and origin I have since learnt to associate with my own ancestral town of Sudbury) and he had set as the Greek book for this examination an Olynthiac oration of Demosthenes. I could not

---

[1] In 1936 my friend Marjorie Ross, in Sydney, explored Burwood, now a populous suburb, on my behalf. But she found that the avenue had been swept away, and an old inhabitant could not even recall Mr. Hole's school.

find a single copy of it left in the bookshops of Sydney, and I was
on this account, at almost the last moment, exempted from Greek,
but I enjoyed the gracious wisdom of Cicero's *De Senectute* which,
with the *De Amicitia*, was set for Latin. In this way it came about
that the only university with which I have ever had any connection whatever has been the University of Sydney. The connection
was useful to me, for it served later as an arts entrance to the
study of medicine.

Shortly after leaving Fontlands, a little tired of school-teaching,
I took a post as tutor in a private family on a station called
Goongerwarrie, a few miles from Carcoar beyond Bathurst. The
journey was by rail across the Blue Mountains and then from
Bathurst by a Cobb's coach, a vehicle somewhat resembling the
European diligence. There was a new rush at that moment to
some lately discovered gold-diggings in the Carcoar district, and
the coach was overcrowded, one young woman having to effect the
journey on the knees of a man she had never before seen. I remember this journey in the cramped and jolting coach, in the
cold darkness, over the rough, irregular roads, where at spots we
had to descend and walk, as one of the worst of many experiences
of wretchedness in my memories of travel — which yet has been
one of my chief joys in life. In the hurry and novelty of this first
long journey alone I forgot my luggage, a large old chest, at the
Bathurst railway station — a lapse which has often occurred to
me since in dream-life but never in real life — and it was not until
many days later that I saw it again.

My new employer was a Government official in Sydney who
had lately retired at a comparatively early age to settle on the
country estate he had acquired. He was a remarkably quiet man
of kindly and considerate disposition, who appreciated my correspondingly quiet nature, and when I left wrote in the testimonial he furnished me with that I 'gave no trouble in the house.'
We suited each other well and never the slightest difficulty arose
between us. Mrs. Platt was of much the same quiet, good-

humored disposition as her husband, a woman of the intelligent but distinctly feminine type which has no ambition to go outside a strictly domestic sphere, and with her also I had no difficulties, though we had little to say to each other. The children, boys and girls ranging from five to fourteen, took after the parents, were easy to manage, and showed no troublesome stupidity and no excessive cleverness.[1] Only one of them has left a vivid memory, and that is the elder girl, ten years of age, a quiet but arch and intelligent child of her mother's type, who exerted an attraction over me which I was myself still too much of a child to understand or to control.

I spent a year at Goongerwarrie. Mr. Platt had, I understood, given his place this name (now, I believe, spelt Goongawarrie), which is the aboriginal word for race-course, because adjacent to the Carcoar race-course where races were held once a year; on this occasion I wandered onto the course, innocently passing through the rails without paying the entrance money I knew nothing about — the only occasion in my life when I have been on a race-course. This was a year of peace externally and for the most part internally. My tasks involved no strain at all; there were no amusements within reach; I cannot recall that visitors ever came to the house. Occasionally I went out with Mr. Platt in the buggy or on horseback; one little expedition I specially recall — as it brought me in contact for the only time with gold-mining — to a crushing works, many miles away, the sound of which could sometimes be heard with a favourable wind even from the Platts' estate.

For the most part I was well content to spend my spare time alone with books. In the morning I would go out for a walk before breakfast through the grounds, a book in hand. Often this early-morning book was Main's *Anthology of English Sonnets* and I

---

[1] More than fifty years later, one of them arrived at the door of my rooms at Brixton, asking me if I remembered the name of Platt. He told me he was an engineer, then making a European tour, and he seemed surprised that his early tutor remembered Goongerwarrie so well.

made it a rule to commit one to memory each such morning. Some
of the sonnets thus learnt, especially those of Shakespeare, Wordsworth, and Mrs. Browning, cling to memory yet. It was certainly
this exercise which inspired me at the same time to begin writing
sonnets. I had written blank verse on the *Surrey*; the sonnets
which I now began to write were more personal and original.

As soon as teaching hours were over in the afternoon, I would
start out again with some other book, often the poems of Shelley
which I was still always re-reading and with undiminished enthusiasm, though after leaving Carcoar my reading of Shelley
came to an end, for I had absorbed all that I could of his spirit.
Yet I was not blind to the typical scene of Australian bush around
me. It was at Carcoar, while revelling in a new adolescent world
of poetry, that I first realised the beauty of Australia. At Burwood it had been the night sky, the clear moonshine, the far
horizons that had fascinated me. At Carcoar it was especially the
wealth of brilliant bird life, and the forms of the trees, with the
curious variety of manna gum I only knew there; but above all
the typical wattles of Australia which there seemed to me to grow
with peculiar loveliness and luxuriance, so that they still float in
my mental vision.

Yet, although the prevailing memories of that year at Goongerwarrie are of calm routine, of an external atmosphere of peace and
beauty, of an internal atmosphere of poetry, there were yet intervals of unrest, even of misery and despair. There was the
trouble of youthful sex and the trouble of youthful religion. I
was a teacher in a responsible position, yet still half a child so far
as sex was concerned, innocent and virginal. My eldest girl pupil,
six years younger than I, was a fascinating, saucy, alert little
maiden, in her instincts quite as old as I was, and older. I felt
her charm, and even showed that I felt it — when sometimes she
stood close beside me, in presence of the others, with her slate or
exercise books — in ways that now seem to me daring and incomprehensible, for they were completely spontaneous and with-

out reflection, so that as I look back on myself at that time I see the revelation of an innocence I could scarcely have credited in another, and others certainly would not credit in me. Fortunately, they were never asked to. The little coquette fell naturally into the woman's part, accepted my attitude and the furtive caresses of my hand, and playfully exerted the authority she knew she had acquired over me. In later days I have wondered how she looked back on her tutor. Sometimes, after she had snuggled up to my side with her slate of sums, and the hours of school were over and I started off alone with my Shelley into the bush, I would feel, for the first time in my life during waking moments, the physical presence of the impulse of sex, manifested so far only as the slight urethrorrhoea which the casuists described, and not yet as actual seminal emission which never occurred in waking life until two years later, as the spontaneous climax of the pleasurable reading of a book. When I look back I realise that we must not sit in judgment on the young. They cannot understand themselves, and their psychoanalytic elders wildly misunderstand them.

These experiences were superficial. They were only the scarcely conscious by-play of a deep instinct not yet fully awakened. Much more poignant were my religious difficulties. A year earlier I had completely lost the large and simple-hearted religious faith I had learnt from my mother and accepted and made my own without reserve. A great blank had been left.

That early religious faith, genuine as it seemed, had fallen off me without any struggle. It was not my own, and when my real self awoke and gazed at it, I found that it would not bear inspection. At fifteen, when I read Renan's *Life of Jesus*, I had not accepted its thesis; I made critical comments on the margins. But a year later, when I read one or two books of a free-thinking and agnostic sort, I found that I agreed with them: my faith was gone. Although it went so easily, that was by no means because I desired it to go, or because I felt that I gained anything by its going. Nothing whatever had replaced it. By following what seemed to be the call of Truth, I had merely entered a blank and empty desert. At about this time I read Friedrich Strauss's *Old Faith and New*, and it seemed to me to represent the world fairly enough, as the world looks when faith has gone, but Strauss's sunny Philistine satisfaction in the 'New Faith' — which to me was no faith at all, but merely the presentation of a cold and dead mechanical world — altogether repelled me. I brooded over it, over this alien universe of whirling machinery in which I seemed to be enmeshed. Sometimes, too, with all the morbid nervousness of an ignorant youth who had been impressed with what Drysdale in his *Elements of Social Science* wrote of the dangers of seminal emissions during sleep, I also brooded over the unknown problems of my own sexual nature. And I recall how, walking up and down the garden path at Goongerwarrie, I reached the conclusion that there was no outcome except by death or possibly by becoming a monk. That was a mood, and I took no practical steps in either of those directions. But such moods characterised my disposition at that period, and corresponded to a real emotional undertone, which continued manifest at intervals, though less strongly than at Carcoar, until the age of nineteen.

During all these years, however, in the background of mental conflicts and in the intervals of depressed moods, there was a perpetual growth in intelligence, a constant broadening and deepening of culture. The conflicts and the moods were helpful, indeed, by adding intensity to my emotional nature and critical acuteness to my intellect. My one luxury, during all this Australian period, was books. I subscribed to the *Literary World* (a habit acquired from Mackay) which kept me informed as to what was being published, and I ordered books from England through Robertsons, and also once or twice had a case of English and foreign books shipped from London; moreover, at the shops of the second-hand Sydney booksellers — there were only two that then counted, Lindsay's and Skinner's — I had some happy finds, notably a complete set of Heine in fresh condition at Lindsay's from which I selected all the volumes I fancied — about a dozen — and Swinburne's first series of *Poems and Ballads* at Skinner's. They both soon meant much to me, and I possess them both still.

Then there was the Sydney Public Library. From the first, whenever I was in Sydney and with nothing else to do, that library was an unfailing source of inspiration and delight. No library has been so influential in guiding and moulding my mental activities. It furnished the pasture for my fresh and eager intellectual appetites, instinctively choosing the food they needed, and was admirably adapted for that purpose. There were many good books, and few readers, and no formalities. I could wander where I would, and settle in some quiet corner to devour what I chose. Here in beautiful dishes — for there were some fine editions on the shelves — the gods bountifully granted to me the nectar and ambrosia on which my spirit was fed. It was here that I learned to love the prose of Landor which I found in a stately row of volumes. Here I began to become acquainted with Stendhal, by reading the early English Life of him (almost the first Life of him ever written) by Paton. Here I came on the dignified volumes holding the works of Brantome. Here also I discovered a very different work, the *Anthropométrie* of Quételet, which responded to my instincts on another side and was the first spur to my active interest in anthropology. I at once began a careful process of self-measurement and soon made for myself the discovery that the morning height differs considerably from the evening height; it was a discovery which had been made before me, but when, many years later, I received a visit from a well-known American anthropologist who had measured the height of thousands of school-children to the millimetre, he was still quite ignorant of a fact which concerned him so much, and which I had discovered at about the age of seventeen.

In another direction I received illumination in the Sydney Public Library. I one day took out of a drawer a large and finely

illustrated volume about modern artists and came upon a re-
production of Burne-Jones's 'Merlin and Vivien.' It seems to
have been the first typical picture of his I had seen, and it was the
immediate revelation to me of a new perception of the world and
a new attitude of art. I had distantly admired Filippo Lippi and
his fellows in London, but here I saw the union of that ancient
almost supernatural beauty with the naturalistic realism of my
own age. The vision of a requickened antique art which then
flashed upon me remained a lasting inspiration. In the years that
followed it eventually happened that I was awakened to other and
quite different manifestations of art which have enabled me to
reach a deeper insight into its possibilities. But I have never
failed to understand the message of the so-called 'Pre-Raphaelites'
(who really derived from Ghent at least as much as from Florence)
for the young generation of fifty years ago, in its revolt against
the dead academicism of that period. For a later generation that
revolt is meaningless; it has itself become vulgarised into banality.
Every young generation needs a new revolt, a fresh inspiration.

One other incident, characteristic enough to mention, is associated with the Sydney Public Library. When I left England
I had brought with me a complete edition of Rabelais in French,
induced to buy it by a reference in Macaulay's *Essays* (which I
had carefully read) to Rabelais, as to a curious and rather indecorous old author not without interest. I had gone but little
way in penetrating the ancient and fantastic French of which
Rabelais was such a master before I made a great discovery.
I discovered that this old author, whom the Puritanic Macaulay
— though he doubtless knew better — had described as an extravagant, if remarkable, buffoon, was in reality a marvellous
genius, a profound thinker, a daring pioneer. In my youthful
innocence I imagined that this was a new and original discovery,
and resolved to write an essay by which to announce it. To begin,
it was clear to me, I must make a thorough study of the age in
which Rabelais lived. During my first months in Sydney I ran-

sacked the Public Library with this end in view. But I soon
found that with every step my task became wider and deeper.
I realised that to write an adequate essay on Rabelais would be
the work of a lifetime. As it was not a task on which I was disposed to spend a lifetime, I dropped it. A few months later I
discovered that, in any case, the task was unnecessary. I had
procured Coleridge's *Table Talk* from England, and in that book
I found a passage about Rabelais, of but a few lines only, but
embodying an estimate indeed unlike that of the Philistinish
Macaulay, an unqualified and enthusiastic recognition of Rabelais's immense genius. Here was a fellow-adventurer who had
discovered the same spiritual continent that I had discovered!
No critical judgment has ever caused me such a leap of joy. I still
treasure my copy of this precious little book.

Thus my first attempt to contribute to literature failed, though
but narrowly, to be an essay on Rabelais. I am sorry, for I could
not have set out under a more congenial banner, and it seems to
me now that I have always sought — instinctively and involuntarily, it may well be, rather than deliberately — to live in the
habit, and follow the rule, of the Abbey of Thelema.

When I was left alone in Australia I began naturally to experience those versatile interests and activities which filled my
life for many years subsequently, and to a considerable extent fill
it still. I call them 'versatile,' but they were far from being
promiscuous, for each was severely tested and only admitted
when found to be a coherent part of my spiritual organism; the
interests that I have accepted are as nothing to those I have
contemplated and rejected. For the rest, I carried out my duties
as a teacher as faithfully as I could, though with no great success,
because I was temperamentally inapt for the teacher's vocation,
save with pupils who are themselves apt to learn. I resolved to
become an assistant master again, and had no difficulty in obtaining a post at the grammar school as it was called — though
that meant merely an ordinary private school needing only a

single assistant teacher — at Grafton on the Clarence. I remember the final interview with the head master who had called on me at my boarding-house in Castlereagh Street to settle preliminaries. I was suffering from one of those more or less acute attacks of what I now believe to have been a form of appendicitis — the last, as it turned out, I ever had — which had affected me at intervals ever since I was a young boy. I was so ill I was obliged to cut short the interview, and I recall that my new employer looked at me with some misgiving, in evident doubt whether he had perhaps made a mistake by engaging an assistant of such uncertain health. He was himself young; he never suspected that, while I should be alive and well half a century later, he himself would be dead in a fortnight. He was a pale, thin, austere young man, possessing in a marked form what I used to call the *facies Christiana* (his father whom I met later was a Presbyterian minister on the Clarence), the face which tells of natural instinct repressed by a perpetual stern control, imprinting on the mouth the fixed lines of high tension. In his case this tension was more than the organism would bear. I never heard all the details of his brief illness, but it appears that on this visit to Sydney he indulged in an unwonted lavish expenditure on furniture and other luxuries, and that outburst was the precursor of a swiftly fatal 'brain fever' which killed him even before the school-term was due to open. It was proposed that I should succeed him as head master, and not a word was said as to any payment by me for the transfer of the school. This, as I now recognise, was a most generous proposal, and if I had possessed any aptitude, and any desire to adopt the teaching profession, my fortune would thus have been made at the outset of my career. My successor, a year later, a capable Scotchman, had no difficulty in creating a large and prosperous school out of what I transferred to him in a worse state than I had received it. But — as I have experienced on many occasions in quite different fields — it is useless for Opportunity to present even the most attractive forelock to one who was not born to seize it. And I was so clearly not born to be a successful head master that I have never for a moment regretted my failure to grasp firmly that particular forelock.

Grafton, situated well up its fine and broad river, is in the north of New South Wales, towards Queensland, and so lies in sub-tropical latitudes, with sugar-canes cultivated on its banks and delicious melons and pineapples in the gardens, being indeed the hottest region I have ever dwelt in for a prolonged period. It was nominally already a city with a mayor and corporation and the seat of a bishopric; the cathedral, indeed, had not yet been built, though stones had been gathered together on the proposed site. But if nominally a city it was actually no more than a straggling village, very unlike what it was later to become, and when in 1929 I received from an old Australian pupil a series of to me un-recognisable views of Grafton, it was hard to believe that the village had grown into so splendid a town. There was, indeed, a real bishop, whom I remember once seeing, though I never went to church, when I chanced to cross the river in the ferryboat with him. I recall the incident because he was accompanied by a young lady just out from England, and never before had I realised the exquisite delicacy and loveliness of the English complexion, which so soon fades into dull sallowness beneath the hot dry sun of Australia; for there are two lovely and delicate things that flourish in England and perish in Australia, the fresh green of our grass and the fresh pink-and-white of our girls' complexions.

For my own part I had no fault to find with the climate of Grafton at any time of the year. Certainly it was hot, sometimes very hot, and then I would take my walks at night; but I never had reason to complain of the heat; my health was excellent (I have noted that it was on coming to Grafton that I lost forever my attacks of supposed appendicitis) and my spirits, as always with me in the heat, remained good, although I had some just cause for depression. I never once experienced that melancholic dejection which occasionally befell me at Carcoar. But though I could not regard myself as a success at Grafton, I enjoyed a comfortable home in the house of a delightful family, ready to receive me hospitably, not merely as a paying guest but as a friend. The schoolhouse was built near the house and in the grounds of Mr. F. W. Chapman, an auctioneer and prominent citizen of Grafton who was completing his term of office as mayor at the time I arrived, and had, I think, been active in establishing the school. He was not altogether prosperous just then, and, having imprudently backed a bill for a considerable sum, he became bankrupt and a compulsory sale of the household goods was held amid much friendly support while I was there. I was one of some half-dozen boarders — men professionally engaged in the town — who were received in the roomy house. I have the pleasantest recollection of Mr. and Mrs. Chapman and their large family. It was, indeed, the only time in which I have lived habitually and on friendly terms with a large family of strangers and I owe to this experience my best insight into the real spirit of Australia, as Australia then was.

The family consisted mostly of girls, still all unmarried, from the age of about twenty-five down to near infancy. They were of diversified character but lived in complete harmony, and organised themselves to carry on the whole work of the large house, and the half-dozen boarders, without servants. This they achieved most efficiently, taking turns, week by week, with some of the harder housework, and, moreover, with no false shame or any feeling that housework could be 'menial,' although I need scarcely say, it was not usual for the prominent people of Grafton to dispense with servants. They were housemaids and cooks, they cleaned the grates and stood at the washtub in the open air, and had no outside aid, except that we boarders would help to wash up after meals. Yet they took their housework easily and were by no means subjected to it. In the afternoon they would perhaps mount their horses and go for a run with their brother, and in the evenings they played and sang (I can still hear distinctly the chief airs of *Maritana*, the opera at that time they liked singing) with considerable accomplishment, and now and then they cleared out the large dining-room and invited a few friends from outside to join them for a little dance.

It was the second daughter, May, twenty years of age, who disturbed my emotions. She was tall and well-made, dignified and reserved. I had not been in love since my boyish misplaced passion for my cousin, seven years previously, and my adoration — it was not passion this time — went out to the graciously imposing May. I worshipped in silence; I would have denied — indeed, I did deny when chaffed by a discerning fellow-boarder — that I worshipped at all. After I left Grafton I made no attempt to see her or communicate with her, but merely wrote some verses, to which I prefaced the words of Goethe: 'Wenn ich dich liebe, was geht's dich an?' I am fairly certain that if I had desired to make any advances they would have been rejected. She was friendly to me, but scarcely sympathetic, cool, perhaps rather quizzical. She seemed, indeed, to be cool to men generally; in late years I have heard that she became the wife of one of the boarders, certainly, as I remember him, the worthiest of that prize. To me nothing tangible remains of my adoration but a hairpin, once fallen from her hair, which I picked up and devoutly preserved. I got on much better with her sister Berta, who was of my own age. She was shorter, with brown, sympathetic eyes, pretty, but far too kind and gentle to have any of May's dignified aloofness. We had much in common; she was an accomplished musician and would play for me my favourite Beethoven sonatas of that period, especially the *Pathétique*. I hear that she now has three sons, distinguished musicians, who tour the world often accompanied by their mother, Mrs. Kennedy, and would have been in London before now if it had not been for the Great War.[1] Though I made no attempt at intimacy with Berta, I felt that we were friends by natural

---

[1] Later I repeatedly met her, as well as her sons; and we remain in a friendly relationship more than fifty years after we first met.

temperament, and when, on finally leaving Grafton, I held her hand to say good-bye, I saw tears gleaming in her tender eyes.[1] Once, when the family went, as the custom was, to spend a fortnight at the Clarence Heads, I asked Berta to keep a diary of the stay for me. This she neatly and cleverly accomplished. I have that diary still, and if she ever visits England, I hope for an opportunity to place it again in her hands.[2] I count my knowledge of the Chapman family the chief gain that came to me from my years at Grafton.[3]

The mention of Clarence Heads recalls a little incident which had its significance as an index to my inner life. During the holidays I went to Sydney, and on the return journey the ship grounded on the bar at the entrance to the river, so that we were delayed on board for a day or so. One of my fellow-passengers — another teacher, if I remember rightly — improved the occasion by flirting with a girl he had become acquainted with on the boat and sat with his arm round her for several hours; towards night, having evidently thus acquired all the satisfaction he desired, he generously introduced her, unasked, to me, also merely an acquaintance by virtue of our sea-passage together, and left us alone. We walked once or twice up and down the deck, and she remarked to me by way of opening the conversation, 'Ain't the moon lovely?' Such a feeling of loathing rose up within me that, in a few moments, after briefly responding, I said it was time to go below, and wished her good night. That was the nearest approach

---

[1] Whence some verses, addressed to her, which I wrote a few months later, but never sent to her until fifty years afterwards, when they were at last printed.

[2] This was duly effected a few years later.

[3] For some years after leaving Grafton, I corresponded with Mrs. Chapman. Her letters ceased, no doubt about the time of her death, and for thirty years there was silence. Then through a young lady at Sydney who admired my books, I again came into touch with old Mr. Chapman, who wrote me several letters until his death about the time of the death of my father, who was the same age. I have lately heard from Mrs. Kennedy that he was of Suffolk origin, and so this family furnishes another example of that instinctive affinity with people of the same race which I seem to find in my experience. There was intermarriage with a Chapman among my Suffolk ancestors, though not in the direct line.

to intimacy with a strange woman during the whole of my four years of adolescence in Australia, where, however, as I had opportunity to observe, the relations of the sexes were often facile.

The Chapmans initiated me into an entirely normal aspect of Australian life. When the boarders were gathered together with one or two professional young men from outside, I learnt to know from the conversation of some of them that freedom of language which is often regarded as peculiarly Australian, though in my experience it was exceptional. In this little group of young men I had to listen to obscene stories of a monstrously crude and impossible type which merely disgusted me, not because I fail to appreciate the obscene, but because licence or extravagance, to be enjoyable, must at least have in it an element of sense or of wit. No doubt my companions were more chaste in life than in speech. One of them, a little lawyer who arrived from Sydney during my stay, aroused some mild curiosity and joking by his visits to an unknown lady who lived in Grafton, but eventually it came out that she was his wife by a secret marriage. The Chapman family, simple and wholesome, was outside this atmosphere, though aware of its existence, and no attempt was made to draw them within it.

As a head master I was distinctly a failure. It was hardly, indeed, the right place for a boy of eighteen. But my chief defects no years would have supplied. I was without the educational equipment, the love of games, the moral control of boys, needed for success as a teacher. Discipline in my school was deplorable; at least one of my pupils was more clever at study than I was myself and doubtless knew it; pupils began to drop off and parents began to make uncomplimentary remarks about the management of the school. Such a state of things was not favourable to friendly relations. I was received with real friendliness in one house only, outside the Chapmans', though that was the kindly and hospitable home of the one man in Grafton who belonged to the wider world in which my spirit moved. He was an old doctor with a charming

wife much younger than himself — their only son being my pupil [1]
— and he had the air of one who had moved in fine society.
Doctor Purdie had, in fact, a considerable knowledge of the
European world, and in youth had studied in Paris. He told me
how once, on the staircase of a Paris hotel, half a century before,
he had accidentally jostled Meyerbeer, who had graciously interrupted his apologies: 'Cela me fait rien.'

Meyerbeer belonged to Heine's world, and at this time — for
my troubles as a head master in no way weakened the ardour of
my absorption in literature — I was soaking myself in Heine. It
was at Grafton that I translated a number of Heine's *lieder* into
English verse; they are as good as most translations, though not
so good that I would desire to publish them, which I have never
attempted to do. It was then probably, or soon after, that I made
a version of some portion of Goethe's *Dichtung und Wahrheit*.
I also translated Musset's *Rolla* into blank verse about the same
time, and made an English rendering of Renan's dramatic version
of *The Song of Songs*. During my stay at Grafton, perhaps more
than at any time in Australia, I indulged in books. They were
indeed my one luxury. I never smoked; in food and drink my
tastes were at that time of the simplest; occasionally, when in
Sydney, I went to an opera or a concert. But I bought all the
books I much wanted to buy.

As I had few friends in Grafton outside the house, and there
was no attractive scenery in the immediate neighbourhood, it
was easy for me to settle down in my schoolroom every day, when
the attempt to educate my pupils was over, and to renew the
never-ceasing and always delightful task of educating myself.
At that time I had become much interested in the technique of
verse. On board the *Surrey* I had begun and laid aside my frag-
mentary attempt at a blank-verse drama and at Carcoar, where

---

[1] More than half a century later I see the notice in the London *Times* of the death
of a young man named Purdie at a house called 'Grafton,' not so very far from where
I am now living, and imagine it to concern the grandson of my old friend and the
son of my pupil.

Main's *Anthology of English Sonnets* was my constant companion,
I found that that form specially appealed to me, and it became
my first congenial medium of intimately personal expression.
But, sensitive as I was to poetry, I felt that I was still largely
ignorant of the technical methods that lay behind the poetry that
impressed me so deeply. I was reading Tennyson much at that
time, never with the passion that Shelley inspired; but, for that
very reason, I could bring to the study a more searching and
intelligent interest, more than I had ever applied to poetry before,
and it was in Tennyson, whether by chance or by sound instinct,
that I studied the mechanism of poetry. For Tennyson was a
great artist as well as a real if not a great poet, though I was at
one time tempted to share the reaction which those of my generation felt to the extravagant estimates of the previous generation.
One cannot but admire an artist who could so well reproduce, in
what is without doubt poetry, the surface and texture of things.
It was, however, chiefly the emotional effects in his best lyrics
which I was at first interested to investigate; also I studied *In
Memoriam* with much care — again moved by intellectual
curiosity, for I had little sympathy with the argument — making
an analysis of it; F. W. Robertson had made one before, but I
had not seen it, though a little earlier I had acquired and read
with interest his sermons and his *Life and Letters*. Taken altogether, during my stay on the Clarence, I was continually extending and deepening my knowledge of literature and especially of
poetry.

At the end of nine months I was ready to leave Grafton. The
school had become impossible and was rapidly dwindling away.
I had only one pupil at Grafton whom I can look back at with
any satisfaction, and she was not a school pupil. A German
doctor outside Grafton, Schroeder by name, being on a visit to
his homeland, sent his daughter, a girl of sixteen, to board with
the Chapmans. She was large and muscular (I recall the grip of
her hand when I was introduced as the most painful handshake I

had ever experienced), the representative, physically and mentally, of a familiar German type, and the first I had encountered. Quite in the German manner, she was to employ her time to educational advantage, and I was asked to give her French lessons. That was a subject I liked teaching, and she was a good pupil, though her personality was of no interest to me; so I was not Abélard and she was not Héloïse.

I resolved to sell my school. The audacity of this resolve, under all the circumstances, now appals me; but the idea was suggested by my friends, Morris and Bevill, who, as educational agents, saw therein a profit. It so happened, however, that I discovered a buyer for myself, a Mr. Mackintosh in South Australia. Messrs. Morris and Bevill sent in their bill for commission, nevertheless, and I paid it without demur, for that is the penalty for doing business with friends. When, however, Mackintosh arrived in Grafton, he refused to pay me more than a small portion of the sum agreed upon, for, as he truly pointed out, he would have had most of my pupils in any case. I agreed without protest and bore him no ill-will. I even lent him, at his request, a curious book on sex I had found in Sydney and have never seen a copy of since, and he, on his part, failed to return it. He was a capable man in whose hands the school flourished and in a few years' time was finely housed.

My brief career as head master of the Grafton Grammar School thus came to an end. It was not a post to which I had been born, and I should not have succeeded much better even if my years had been many more than seventeen when I took it up. I said good-bye to my good friends in Grafton, and the last definite vision I have is of the tears that stood in Berta's tender brown eyes. I was not to meet her again till more than forty years later when she was a grandmother, though wonderfully little changed. Of the passage in the boat back to Sydney I have no recollection at all.

Soon after my return I resolved to enter the Government

service, and become a qualified teacher under the Council of Education which at that time controlled elementary education in New South Wales. I suppose it was Morris who suggested this career, which was really a good one, and, indeed, it proved for me of incalculable benefit. It meant at the outset a three months' period of training at the Fort Street School in Sydney, and I am not at all sure that this may not have weighed with Morris, for I had little money left after my experiment in head-mastership, I could not afford to stay long at my usual boarding-house, and Morris could take me as a lodger on moderate terms which yet meant a helpful profit in his own state of chronic financial depletion. He had a high opinion of my moral character as well as of my intelligence and general knowledge; I recall how once, in the course of some scientific or philosophic argument in which I had held my own against him, he remarked at the end, in the words of Festus, that much learning had made me mad. In practical matters I expect he regarded me as a fool; once he took me to a bank where I wished to open my first banking account, and when the formalities, in which I was of course a tyro, were over, and we were leaving, Morris looked back, and I glanced round just in time to catch a grin and a wink — which I affected not to notice — addressed to the clerk behind the counter. It was not in my nature to feel resentment, and I recognised that Morris was, after all, a friend and indeed a sort of guardian in my absence from home; so if I was sometimes made a fool of by him it was with open eyes. I could, if I liked, retort on him. For he made a greater muddle of his life all through than I have ever done at any period. From the time (and even I believe earlier) when he threw up his position as mate on my father's ship to marry a penniless and ordinary emigrant girl and settle in Australia, he had been a perpetually rolling stone. Meanwhile children were growing up around his meek and much-fatigued wife, and the house was scarcely a happy one; one day, on returning home late and meeting a mild reproach, he took up his hat again, without a

word, and went to a public house. All this was new to me; I
accepted it without even internal comment and without seeming
to notice.

So these three months of training were not pleasantly spent,
though I cannot say that they were acutely distressing. I wandered all day about the classrooms at Fort Street, following the
prescribed routine with my fellow-students (one depressed,
ambiguous man confided to me, I remember, that he had previously been a private detective), and after school hours returned
to the little house of the Morrises at Woollahra where I witnessed
the cold family relationships and overheard Mrs. Morris deferring
the demands of dunning tradesmen, and slept at night on a bed
made up on the sofa in the sitting-room. Morris was, however, a
sociable man, and had various interesting friends and visitors;
among these was a family of French Canadians, the Papillons,
and my pleasantest recollections at Woollahra are of Miss
Papillon, a girl a little over my own age. She had all the vivacity
and intelligence and high spirits of her race, together with a complete freedom from sex consciousness. She would play mischievous little tricks on me, always of an inoffensive kind, for she
was eager to be friendly. Once — and the incident was too
characteristic of me — she made frantic and fruitless efforts to
attract my attention from the opposite side of a theatre, reproaching me when we next met for being 'in a brown study.' She would
come behind my chair to fasten her garters, and when I naturally
turned round and detected her remain unabashed. It was she
who asked me to show her my books and when I took some of
them out of my big chest paid me the compliment — more
gratifying than any paid me in that line since — that I had a
better collection of books than any young man she knew. She
treated me with all the frankness and trust of a comrade and
friend; it was precisely such a comrade and friend, making no
appeal to sexual emotion, that I then needed. But I never put
out my hand in response — possibly because May Chapman was

still in my thoughts — and I doubt whether we ever exchanged a single letter. I saw nothing more of her and was too absorbed in my own ideas and my own ideals ever to regret her absence, though now, when I look back and remember what dear and delightful friends I have had in my life who have been of more or less French blood — one above all — I view her with tenderness as the earliest of them.

In all these respects I manifested that passivity which has never ceased entirely to be an element of my character, though it seems most pronounced at this adolescent age. It was not merely receptive, it was more often resistant. I always seemed to lie sensitively open to those influences of Nature which were sympathetic, and I would curl up closely at once against all those influences, and they were many, which were antipathetic. But there was no impulse of active response in the first case or of active aggression in the second. It was the slow and massive attitude as of a tree. Intellectually I may possibly possess the plastic hand of the potter moulding his clay. But in most matters my temperament seems rather that of the clay, moulded by the plastic hand of Nature, with this peculiarity, that while I can bear forever the shape thus imposed upon me, I can also withdraw at will and become impenetrable to every moulding influence which is not akin to my own substance. I am a child of Nature, but she has to be a careful artist in what she seeks to make of me, there are so many ends I am unfit for.

When the casual course of my training at Fort Street was over, I had to give a test lesson to a class to show how I shaped as a teacher and to pass an informal examination by a Scotchman called Forbes, who asked me a few questions and gave me, if I remember, an easy passage in Latin to translate, while he improved the occasion — it was midsummer — by eating an orange. Then I had one or two interviews with Mr. Wilkins, the secretary and directing force of the Council of Education, and shortly after received an appointment as teacher at the half-time schools at

Sparkes Creek and Junction Creek, with instructions to proceed thither almost at once.

The appointment might seem a humble one for the late head master of the grammar school of the city of Grafton, yet it was a good post to offer a youth of eighteen, and much more profitable than that I had left. I had a fixed salary of one hundred and eight pounds a year, together with small fees I was entitled to charge the scholars' parents; I had an allowance of twelve pounds a year for a horse, whether or not I chose to keep a horse (I considered it unnecessary), and I had a schoolhouse to live in rent free. This was equal altogether to nearly two hundred pounds a year. Moreover, living in the bush was cheap; my own demands (except in the matter of books) were still abstemious, almost ascetic, and there was little possibility of spending money even if one were tempted to extravagance. During the year I was in the service of the New South Wales Council of Education I was really better off — with more freedom from anxiety and less pressure of work — than I ever was again for some thirty years. Not that my income was not often (not always) larger during these years, but my needs were greater and the responsibilities I incurred made demands on me unknown at Sparkes Creek. It was not, indeed, until some years after marriage that I again had a banking account of my own (in the earlier years of marriage my wife was my banker), and often and often I have reflected, perhaps with some bitterness, when I have had to worry over pence, that with a reputation that was extending round the world my financial position was less satisfactory than when I was quietly earning my living as an unknown boy in the Australian bush. I know well enough, and I knew all along, that my post at Sparkes Creek was merely a temporary and necessary stage in the plan of my life, and that the attainment of a comfortable position, or the making of money, was for me an altogether secondary aim in life.

The entry on my new duties was not altogether auspicious. It was easy to go by rail to Scone — some hundred miles —

where, I was told, I would receive all necessary information about my final destination. I went at once to see the clergyman at Scone, Shaw by name, a large, fair, placid, kindly man who lived with his sister in a comfortable parsonage where he invited me to spend the night. He had some sort of official position in connection with my schools, but he knew almost nothing about them, and had seldom visited them. (I cannot remember that he ever came out while I was there.) So he took me to see the Scone schoolmaster, a dark, vivacious little Welshman. Roberts, as his name was, proved a hearty and helpful colleague; he told me what little he knew of my post from previous teachers (taking me to see my immediate predecessor, a lanky, dispirited Australian with no qualifications) and he offered to lend me a horse and the guidance of his son to take me out to the place, eighteen miles in the bush. Soon after breakfast at the parsonage — its comfortable bed dwelt in my memory, for it was long before I was to know another such — the kind and hospitable clergyman bade me good-bye, and I mounted the horse supplied by the schoolmaster, who was evidently suspicious of my horsemanship, for he carefully pointed out to me which side to mount, and I set out on my journey to Sparkes Creek, accompanied by the youth, who had evidently been warned that I was probably not a first-class horseman, and we proceeded leisurely, so leisurely that it was well on in the afternoon before we reached the farm of old Ashford, the chief settler near my school, where I had been told that it would be easy for me to find lodging. It turned out to be far from easy, for the wiry little old man, dried up by hard pioneering work, who had been the first to settle in this valley — giving it a name derived from the old home near Birmingham whence he had come in youth — had a large family and no room to spare. But he agreed to make up a bed for me on the settee in the living-room, and my friendly young guide returned home with the spare horse, covering the ground, I am sure, in far less time than we had spent in coming. I passed, I think, two nights in these close and uncomfortable quarters, making acquaintance in the daytime with my schoolhouse and with the two other settlers in the valley, brothers of the name of Barwick, originally coming from English Kent, and each with a young family. Then old Ashford came to me, and said, in his rough way which was not unkindly meant, that I could stay in his house no longer, he had a sick daughter in the next room — I never perceived any sign of her — and my presence was inconvenient; I must go and live in the schoolhouse. I saw for myself that there was no alternative. So I put on my tall silk hat and took up my little bag — one of the Barwick brothers brought out my big box of clothes and books in due course — and went my lonely way to the schoolhouse. I felt very forlorn. Now at last I was completely adrift, altogether, it seemed, cut off from civilisation. I felt like a lost child, and my eyes, as I walked, smarted painfully with unshed tears.

There was no need to shed tears and as a matter of fact I never shed them. If I had known it, I might have seen in imagination such a railing of gold around the little spot I was approaching as Rousseau desired to erect round the spot at Annecy where he first met Madame de Warens. I met no woman there, or man either, who meant anything to me, but I was to find there one who must mean more than any person: I found there myself. This year 1878 was to be in all exterior relationships the loneliest, the most isolated, of my life. But it was also to be for my interior development the most fateful, the most decisive, of all my years.

The schoolhouse, surrounded by a rail fence of the usual Australian bush sort, was situated a hundred yards or so on the slope above the creek — which was most often a mere string of pools, though sometimes a raging torrent — at the point where the path crossed it leading to Ashford's farm. It was built of rough-hewn slabs, letting in the air at places, and had a shingled roof, through the chinks of which at night I could see the stars pass across. The house consisted of two rooms — each, however, having a small portion partitioned off at its back part — with

Sparkes Creek

Taken by Marjorie Ross. An enlargement of this picture stood on
Ellis's table the last years of his life

separate doors on to a veranda in front. The room on the right was the schoolroom; it contained the usual large open fireplace with a broad chimney; and it was supplied with a table and rough school forms and desks. The other room was for the teacher's use and contained nothing but a makeshift bed, formed by a framework of four poles supporting two sacks and resting on four legs which were so insecurely attached that occasionally the whole structure would collapse during the night. Otherwise I found no cause for complaint in it, and used it during the whole of my time at Sparkes Creek, not only at night, but to rest on during the day, as there was no chair in the place, and in the schoolroom I sat on a form at the table. I think there was a little bench to support a tin bowl to wash in with water obtained from the creek, though for drinking-water I would take a bucket to the well on the land of the nearest Barwick family, a few minutes' walk away. Otherwise there were no necessaries or conveniences whatever, beyond a little shed outside for a privy. After the first plunge, however, I cannot recall that I felt any discontent. I certainly made no attempt to add to the furniture of my establishment, beyond a minimum of cooking- and eating-utensils, for the rest being content with the most casual makeshifts. I was more interested in the furniture of my mind than of my body, and if my house was but a fragile shelter against the sky, the sky itself made a delicious house for me.

The first night, certainly, was wretched. I was desolate, not happy on my rickety couch, and in the large chimney I heard wild beasts of some kind noisily scampering up and down, while in the morning I found that a bandicoot or some such small marsupial had evidently made a comfortable nest in my silk hat, leaving some of his hairs behind. Strangely enough, that first night, so far as I can recall, was the only night I was ever disturbed by such visitors. A more usual disturbance was caused by the huge moths which would enter by the skylight above the door and dash noisily against the walls.

In a few days I was peacefully settled in my schoolhouse. The material basis of my new existence was swiftly established. It was, indeed, the easier by virtue of that vein of asceticism — sometimes perhaps a more aesthetic asceticism — which the life at Sparkes Creek doubtless confirmed in my disposition. Under the ordinary conditions of civilised life it might have remained forever latent. My natural timidity with regard to taking the initiative in material matters, so altogether unrelated to my attitude in spiritual affairs, would probably have always held me back. But for my everlasting good fortune I was flung into the wide sea of Australian bush alone, to sink or to swim. Naturally I swam.

It was not a long list of simple material requirements that I made out, and I engaged one of the Barwick brothers for the day to go into Scone and obtain them from the Chinese dealer in everything there, one Charles Trogg. The Chinese was equal to all my demands, and throughout my stay at Sparkes Creek I never had occasion to buy anything from anyone else at Scone. For the rest, my bread and milk were supplied from the household whence I had been ejected and brought every morning by one of the daughters, my pupil, a gentle, silent girl, who also sometimes brought me a present from her mother of a peach pie or the like dish. I had meat sometimes procured from one of my neighbours. Thus was settled, very easily and quickly settled, the physical basis of my life.

On this basis soon began the routine of my professional duties. That also was established with as little trouble as the physical mechanism of board and shelter. It was indeed the only phase of my uncongenial career as a school-teacher that I controlled without effort, almost without thought. The instruction was of the most elementary kind, and its nature and methods were at every stage prescribed by the Council of Education. There was nothing left for me but to follow the simple routine in which I had been trained at Fort Street. The children, moreover, gave me no trouble. The girls, who were perhaps in the majority, were fault-

less. My predecessor told me he had some difficulty with the
biggest one; but I had none; nor ever have had in dealing with
girls; it was with the boys I was apt to fail.

My walks over the hills, several times a week, brought fresh
delicious insights into Nature, such as now came to me for almost
the first time in my life. The fauna of this region was new and
strange, more abundant than I had elsewhere seen. Round Carcoar I had chiefly observed snakes of various kinds and many
birds, including flocks of cockatoos and families of parakeets.
Here there were few snakes (the snake I chiefly recall, long and
tawny, lived, I believe, beneath my veranda, for I once saw him
lying on it), and not many birds. But there were many creatures
of other kinds, huge jew lizards that lay motionless along branches
of trees, and native bears that moved away slowly, very slowly,
if I approached them, and, above all, there were great kangaroos
that I was never able to approach, though I gazed at them with
fascinated and admiring eyes as they would descend the hill-slopes
in large, slow, gracious bounds. It is one of the most beautiful
modes of progression in Nature, and no one has seen a kangaroo
who has only seen a captive kangaroo. The picture has always
lingered in my memory with an intimate and peculiar charm. Of
late I have wondered whether that charm may not lie in a resemblance of my own mental mode of progression to the slow, deliberate curves of those resilient bounds which seemed to me so
gracious and so appealing. Like a kangaroo, too, it may be that I
live among a population of jew lizards and native bears who find
my movements more fearsome or more impressive than they seem
to myself. It was possibly Shelley who first helped me to inspire
the exhilarating air which stimulated such a mode of intellectual
movement. But Shelley was a poet and soared over men's heads.
I am not a poet, but a dreamer who is also a naturalist and a
realist, and like the kangaroo, however vast the bounds I delight
in, I can only achieve them by planting my feet firmly on the solid
earth. A critic of my earliest book, *The New Spirit*, disparagingly

said that its chief characteristic was a calm and matter-of-fact way of making daring revolutionary statements; I had never myself noted this, but the remark seemed to me acute. Now, when I look back, I am pleased to imagine a significance in the intimate appeal to me of those large, silent bounds, so serene and so daring, of the kangaroo.

On the days when I went to my other school — two days of one week and three days of the next, for my time had to be divided equally between them — after I had had my breakfast of porridge and perhaps placed a saucepan containing meat and rice over the smouldering wood fire in the hope it might be done (it was sometimes burnt) when I returned in the evening, and put in my pockets some biscuits and a flask of tea for lunch, I started on my walk across the range of hills which separated me from Junction Creek. The aspects of Nature were my only source of interest beyond my own thoughts, for there was no human dwelling within sight all the way and I cannot recall ever having met a single person during all my year's walks. Yet it was a varied and delightful walk of which I never grew tired, and, while I was often absorbed in my thoughts, I was also always alive to the visions of beauty that were spread before my gaze. Several aspects of that walk still flash before my inner eye. There was the clump of apple gums with the delicious soft grey trunks so subtly in harmony with my mood as I passed them. There were again the twin hills, rounded with large, gracious curves between them, which appealed to me because they looked like the two breasts of a recumbent earth goddess. In my hut I was almost beneath the shadow of another hill, indeed a real mountain, which imparted no such pleasing emotions; gloomy and menacing, at night it seemed to be pressing and crushing me down, and I may perhaps trace to it the repulsion I feel towards mountains. It was on the slopes of this mountain, I believe, that a cedar forest grew which I used to hear of from my older pupils and their parents as a beautiful and wonderful place. It was suggested that one of the boys should some day take me there for a day's excursion. But my shy diffidence or my procrastination stood in the way; I never took the necessary initiative for that excursion and I have regretted it ever since. Yet I need not complain, for my life was never so rich in new impressions, or in fresh stimulation from old impressions for the first time really absorbed. As I sat at my table on stormy evenings, all my nerves were stirred by the prolonged rhythmic curves of gathered-up winds that rolled and tumbled and crashed through the trees among the hills like an ocean let loose. And once, on my return in the evening from Junction Creek, as I approached my hut and saw the blossoming roses that climbed the veranda posts, with their crimson splashes on the green background, a thrill of rapture went through me, and I saw roses as I had never seen them before, as I shall never see them again.

When in the morning I rose from my primitive couch and stood on my veranda — 'en pissant vers les cieux,' as Rimbaud expresses it — the sense of Sabbath peace, the contact of the pure sunny air, would fill me with exhilaration. It was an admirable climate, seldom too hot or too cold. I could not have led a more healthy life, and I had probably never before been so well. My habits were simple, as I have said, my physical needs few; I was perfectly content with the primitive food I prepared in so casual a manner, for I was not then so accomplished a cook as in some respects I am now, though I was taking the first most important step. There was no milk or butter to be had at the season when I arrived. I drank tea, and I recall that when, in hot summer days, returning exhausted from Junction Creek, I desired a cooler and more refreshing drink, I devised a mixture of vinegar, sugar, and water which proved satisfactory. At the same time my spiritual discontent and my emotional cravings attained a degree of calm I had not before known. Religious depression, such as I had sometimes experienced at Carcoar, had already left me at Grafton. But here at Sparkes Creek I was also comparatively free from definite emotional cravings. I was not within sight of any woman who could arouse the impulse of desire, and the memory of May Chapman was fading into a beautiful dream. Certainly I would feel at times the craving for love and the sense of my own unfitness to arouse it. I was, it seemed to me, so unattractive a person; I would sometimes look into the window-pane which served me as looking-glass and wonder what sweet, gracious woman, such as I desired, could ever love the image that met my sight. (I was not vain, it will be seen, and I am not vain now nearly fifty years afterwards, when I think of the supremely sweet and gracious women who have loved me or offered me their love, and wonder still.) One warm evening, I remember, though I think only one, the craving came on me overwhelmingly, and I wandered around my hut at random, my thoughts full of desire — of idealistic rather than physical desire — and tore off eucalyptus leaves as I passed, crushing them between my unconscious fingers till they were soaked in strong aroma.

The craving for love was for me, at Sparkes Creek, so far as I consciously knew, an ideal need. When I took my bucket to the Barwicks' well, to obtain drinking-water purer than the creek yielded, and hoisted up the cool bright liquid, the lines of Swinburne I had lately learnt to know would come deliciously into my mind:

> 'Nothing is better, I well think,
> Than love; the hidden well water
> Is not so delicate to drink.'

I had brought over Swinburne's *Songs Before Sunrise* from England and read it on the voyage with enjoyment. More recently I had picked up the first series of *Poems and Ballads* at Skinner's second-hand bookshop. (I well recall Skinner, hard and pockmarked, a man of the bush, it seemed, rather than of books, very unlike the only other second-hand bookseller, Lindsay of Castlereagh Street, whose shop I haunted more profitably, a large, gentle old man who would sometimes go off angling.) At Sparkes Creek I revelled for a time in *Poems and Ballads* more than in any other

book, for its magnificent exuberance, its imaginative extravagance, seemed the adequate expression of my expanding self, and
as I paced up and down my little patch of enclosed ground I
would shout aloud the stanzas of 'The Masque of Bersabe.' The
splendour of Swinburne's cerebral excitation at that time sufficed,
as never later, to express my youthful desires.

Of physical desire I was as yet scarcely aware in any definite
way except during sleep. That physical efflorescence of sex had
begun with me early and often, as I have already told, at first usually without dreams, and it worried me because of the traces left
behind. In time I understood what these manifestations meant
and accepted them, methodically noting their occurrences in my
pocket diary.[1] I endeavoured so far as possible to avoid anything
likely to evoke them when asleep, and never, by any physical or
mental procedure, sought consciously to produce them when
awake. They had occurred, indeed, so frequently asleep that
there was not much temptation to produce them when awake.
But at Sparkes Creek, where my life, far from any kind of sexual
stimulation, was simple and healthy and regular, these nocturnal
eruptions probably ceased to give complete relief. At all events,
it was at Sparkes Creek that for the first time in my life I experienced the orgasm when awake. I was lying down on my simple
bed, one warm pleasant day, reading something which evidently
had in it for me some touch of erotic stimulation — I believe it was
the *Dames Galantes* of Brantôme — and suddenly I became aware
that the agreeable emotion aroused by the book, without any will
or any action of my own, was becoming physically translated and
fulfilled. I realised what had happened and felt no alarm; evidently there was nothing in the occurrence that was not natural
and beautiful, though it was of course easy to imagine circumstances under which it would have been yet more natural and

---

[1] I have set forth and discussed the resulting record as that of W. K. in the first
volume of my *Studies*, almost the only occasion on which I have used in my books
observations made on myself.

beautiful. It was not until after this event that I ever became definitely conscious of any stirring of physical excitement at the thought or the proximity of an attractive woman.

In this year of my solitary life, as never before or since, there was an immense thirst deep down in my youthful soul, a thirst of my whole being, though scarcely at all of my physical sex nature, for the revelation, in body and spirit, of a divinely glorious woman. My demand was large. There was no one anywhere who corresponded to it, who even more than faintly suggested it, not even among the women who had so far attracted me. And even if there had been, I should have felt myself completely unworthy of a boon so great that it would in my eyes at some moments have outweighed the whole world in the balance. I disdained the women who were within reach; the women I desired, hopelessly it seemed, were women I had never seen or known. How inconceivable a miracle that life was indeed to bring me close to some of the noblest women in the world! Now, when I grow old, sweet and gracious women come to me unsought and are ready to pour out the treasures of their loveliness and their devotion. Then, when their coming might have meant so much, they never came. Still, it is my happiness that for me sex was never cheap. Whatever powers of love and tendernesses I have acquired, whatever aptitude for delight in the bodies and souls of women, was all generated in those days of solitude.

Yet, I am well aware, the desire of love, the physical manifestations of sex, were both alike only rare interludes in my active and sunny life at Sparkes Creek. They were sufficiently acute, at all events the thirst for love, to represent in memory vivid moments of my life, but those moments were few. My desire for knowledge, if less acute, was more massive than my desire for love, and it was omnipresent. Moreover, it was a desire within my power to gratify. So I gratified it, freely and copiously, by means of books, books of all kinds, in English and French and German and Latin: poems, novels, theology, religion, subjects of almost every class, science, strange as it must seem, occupying the smallest place, if indeed any place at all, but in that phase I was eager to grasp the whole rather than the parts; it was synthesis I was drawn to rather than analysis. Though I bought every book I wanted, my books were selected carefully and deliberately. My mind was ranging freely, everywhere with a new power to grasp what it seized and to revel in its acquisitions. I had acquired the power of seeing the world freshly, and seeing it directly, with my own eyes, not through the dulling or disturbing medium of tradition and convention.

It was at Sparkes Creek that I discovered the Bible. Since the loss of my early piety, and my boyish devotion to the New Testament, I had ceased to feel interest in the Bible and no longer looked at it. But now by some unknown spontaneous impulse I turned to it again, and, as art, I saw it altogether afresh, indifferent to its departed religious significance, but full of delight in its splendour. Sometimes at night, with rapturous pleasure, I would read it aloud by the light of my solitary candle, and once, as I afterwards learnt, some of the Ashford family, when riding home, heard me and concluded that teacher was frightened at the solitude, a supposition that had in it no touch of truth, for my solitude was too absolute, too far from any possibility of being broken, to be anything else but perpetual peace and joy.

My activities were, however, by no means merely receptive; for the first time they were becoming genuinely active. I was at the end of the period of adolescence; my physical and mental development — not of course my intellectual development — was completed. I was at the threshold of the creative period of manhood. The sexual efflorescence, of which I now first became conscious, was the physical side of the creative artistic force of which now also I became conscious. At Sparkes Creek I first began to write that prose which has been the medium of all my work in life.

Before I was twelve I had spontaneously begun to write a

sort of prose; before I was fifteen I had begun to write a sort of
verse; but the one and the other were completely lacking in any
note of personal style. At seventeen I was beginning to write
sonnets and these were distinctly more personal in substance,
although not definitely original in form. At eighteen I was
deliberately studying the technique of verse in Tennyson's *In
Memoriam* and that most technically instructive of lyrics, 'Break,
break, break.' But all these years I gave no thought to prose and
indeed wrote none, save, without much conscious care, in some
translations. Now at nineteen I opened a manuscript book and
filled it gradually with a dozen different notes of observation,
criticism, or comment, written carefully and deliberately, in a
way that was alike in substance and in form personal, and
traceably the early expression of my native self, my first *Impressions and Comments*.

Writing for me was of the nature of a natural instinct. I never
at any time set myself deliberately to learn how to write prose,
after the manner of a writer who in my time still enjoyed considerable reputation, Robert Louis Stevenson, so making the
writer's art an accomplishment such as those taught in the ancient
Academies for Young Ladies. When I have studied the art of
writing, it has been as a critic rather than as a practitioner. Still
less have I ever deliberately sought to imitate the methods of
some admired master; that would have been an impulse outside
my temperament, for I have never wanted to be anyone but
myself. I abhor the doctrine of those who teach that a writer's
style must be moulded on the style of other writers. A man's
style must be moulded on himself; it is himself. I wrote simply
because I had something to say, and my ultimate deep, even if
unconscious, impulse was to attain self-expression. But it is
inevitable that we should be unconsciously imitative before we
become complete masters of our natural methods of expression;
and I am sure that, however little I may have been aware of it,
I could not have escaped that necessity. When in recent years

I have looked back, from as it were outside, on my own origins, it has seemed to me that the master by whose style I was most influenced unconsciously when at Sparkes Creek I first began, in the real sense, to write, was Newman. At Burwood, two years earlier, I had bought a lately published volume of selections from Newman, why I cannot tell except that I was impartially interested in every aspect of humanity that was in its own manner good, for Newman was as alien to me then as he has ever been. I read the book with the deliberate care with which in those days I always read books, and for the most part I found little of interest in it; before long I parted with the volume. But I remember that there were several passages in it that seemed to me of an enchanting melody. That seductive and insinuating music acted upon me, as I now believe, more potently than I knew. It is not obtrusive, it is only now and then that it comes into his writing, and it comes without forethought, seemingly without consciousness; it is the style that is the man, the man in the most intimate fibres of his racial ancestry, for one detects through it the instinctive artist in style which we associate with France. To me that artist has always been fascinating. So it may have come about that, when at Sparkes Creek I began to write out of myself, my way of writing at first unconsciously tended to fall into the strains of a music which the fibres of my nerves had learnt from Newman — 'one of the greatest masters of quietly exquisite prose,' he has been called by a sound judge, 'that the world has seen.' In all my earliest writings, then and for some years later, my instinctive ideal of style was delicate, allusive, musical, with more care for sweetness of melody than for choice of jewelled or emphatic words. The *New Spirit*, my first book, represented the end of this stage. Afterwards I rebelled to some extent against this way of writing; it seemed to me a little too refined, and I knew that some people — unliterary people, it is true — were impatient with it and found it obscure. A change took place in my method. Music was no longer its ruling motive, and I wrote in a more masculine way. Whether the change was really due to discontent with my earlier way or whether that discontent was merely the outward sign of a deep and instinctive movement of personal development, I cannot now say. In the spiritual world it is not always easy to distinguish the cart from the horse. In any case my style became more vigorous and more pungent. I was more deliberately careful to select the just and effective word. I sought to avoid all literary allusiveness except when it was urgently necessary for my purpose and could be made clear even to an unliterary reader of intelligence. I supplemented my already acquired tendency — doubtless the outcome of my medical training — to use technical and precise words by a complementary tendency to use also simple and figurative words from vulgar speech, and my imagery became more homely. *Affirmations* represents this second stage in the development of my manner of writing. In this stage, however, the robust vigour which had developed by reaction from the sensitive delicacy of the earlier stage, tended sometimes to take on an air of rather self-conscious bravado which, I found, was a little repellent to one or two who loved me and my work, especially my wife, and was not sympathetic to my own most genuine tastes. It was then that I entered on the third, the most characteristic and I suppose the final stage in the growth of my literary style. I left behind a gusto of rankness which might possibly be detected in the second phase and conciliated what was left with the more delicate and musical first manner. It was then that I wrote, and continue to write, *Impressions and Comments*, certainly at once the most intimately personal, the most spontaneous and the most deliberately moulded, of my writings.

I wrote the notes in that first little black manuscript book with care and with enjoyment, all of them, I think, at Sparkes Creek, but without any special absorption or any realisation that they opened a new era in my mental life. It seemed only one of many new energies of which my life was so full, so buoyant and so glad, exhilarated by sunlight and fresh air. In this wide expansion of the soul there was no time to concentrate intensively or to stand back to study the significance of my own mental movements. I was, however, at the threshold of the most vital movement of all.

It was on board the *Surrey*, on my way to the new world of the South, that, leaving Europe and my childhood's home behind me, I left also behind me my childhood's faith and the old traditional creed of Europe. At Carcoar I meditated on the prosaic vision of the universe, so alien to my own temperament, complacently revealed by Friedrich Strauss in his *Old Faith and New*, as a factory filled with the mechanical whirr of lifeless wheels. Moods of deep melancholy passed over me and were blended with thoughts of sexual origin when I read in the *Elements of Social Science* of the dangerously devitalising effects of nocturnal seminal emissions and feared I might be impotent, a possibility which in youth is not accepted philosophically. So a personal gloom deepened for me the gloom of an empty and mechanical world. At Grafton these moods had fallen into the background, if they had not been dispelled, and I lived a more cheerfully sociable life among companionable people of both sexes and my own age; I was seldom alone; and I was, moreover, waking up to new literary interests. At Sparkes Creek, by another turn of the kaleidoscope, a new mental activity greater than that of Grafton was coupled with a solitude deeper than that of Carcoar, in a physical atmosphere which was for me that of joy. Now evidently, though I could not have known it beforehand, was the moment for the discord in my spiritual life to be at last resolved in harmony.

In those eager days of developing mind my eyes were open for every significant manifestation of the intellectual life yet unknown to me. In this way it would seem that I somewhere (probably in the *Literary World*) read a review of Hinton's books, or of the then lately published biography by Ellice Hopkins, and

had a desire to know more of him, why I do not know. The book
I sent to England for was — fortunately, since it was the book
I needed, and also, I still think, his best — *Life in Nature*. I read
it calmly, with no undue expectation of personal profit; then, if
I remember rightly, I read it a second time, this time more significantly. And then, as I read, I became conscious of what I can
only call, in the precise and full sense of the word, a revelation.
The clash in my inner life was due to what had come to seem to
me the hopeless discrepancy of two different conceptions of the
universe. On the one hand was the divine vision of life and beauty
which for me had been associated with a religion I had lost. On
the other was the scientific conception of an evolutionary world
which might be marvellous in its mechanism, but was completely
alien to the individual soul and quite inapt to attract love. The
great revelation brought to me by Hinton — a man of science
who was also, though he made no definite claim to the name, a
mystic — was that these two conflicting attitudes are really but
harmonious though different aspects of the same unity. And he
presented the matter so simply, so clearly, so persuasively, with
so complete an absence of passion or propagandism and yet with
a profound and passionate reverence for Nature to which my
own temperament instinctively responded, that I was convinced
immediately and completely without effort or struggle. I had
reached the point at which it sufficed for the situation to be presented to me in a beautiful and adequate form, and my response
could only be at once that it must be so. In an instant, as it
seemed, the universe was changed for me. I trod on air; I moved
in light.

An immense inner transformation had been effected, as it
seemed, in a moment. Before long I was able to recognise that
this transformation was what religious people had been accustomed to call 'conversion.' But this conversion was totally unlike any that I had then ever heard of. It was a change in what
is traditionally called the 'soul,' and a change in the soul's attitude

towards the universe, as we generally term the not-soul. But it
was not a change that could be formulated in precise rational
terms, or that involved an act of faith in any creed; it was a
profound change that yet had no intellectual content. Religion,
as I had come to experience it for the first time in a shape really
personal to myself, was in that respect like love, to which indeed,
on another plane, it closely corresponded, and just as love confers
no power to make a single precise statement about the loved
person, so religion confers no power to make a single precise
statement about the universe, and asks nothing either from
metaphysics or theology. I was as far as ever from any faith in
Christianity, in God, in immortality; all my definitely formulated
convictions on separate points remained unchanged. Yet I was
myself changed, and the whole universe — that is to say, my
attitude towards it — was changed. What had happened could
only be expressed by metaphors and similes. It was as though
there had been developing within me, with a painful sense of
strain and division, two diverse streams of tendency which had
now suddenly come together, each entering into the other to form
a fresh stream of a new potency wherein the qualities of the two
original streams were at length harmoniously blended. Or, to
put it in a more psychological way, a gradual process of development, which had been slowly working out beneath the surface of
consciousness, had now, at the chance, but at this moment fitting,
touch of Hinton's book, been suddenly brought to the surface
and consciously realised in all its bearings. For it was only a
chance touch which, because it came at the right moment, had
thus in an instant thrown all my psychic elements into another
state of crystallisation. I never imagined, even at the moment
when I was thus seemingly transformed, that the wand which
effected the transformation possessed any abstract sacred effi-
ciency. I became interested in Hinton, it is true — for a time
perhaps, owing to various circumstances, unduly interested —
but I soon completely gained in relation to him that aloof and

critical independence which marks even my sympathies. On the book itself, which had so shaken me, I bestowed no further notice and never even troubled to retain my copy of it. I have not read it again to this day. Its work was done, once and forever, in a moment.

I have been accustomed to call this experience, by analogy with that common in religious sects, 'conversion.' It is clear, however, that it differs from the kind of experience most usually connoted by the term. 'Conversion,' as it generally occurs, is a social phenomenon, the outcome of emotional excitement, generated from outside, by which a ferment disguised as a doctrine or a creed is violently injected into the youthful organism, and in most cases, though not always, runs its course and exhausts itself, the attack of a sort of spiritual measles. But with me the experience had been the outcome of a slow inward growth, the result of an inevitable inner necessity, and the element of external stimulus was of the slightest kind. Of social contagion, moreover, there was nothing. It seemed, indeed, of the essence of the whole process that there should be solitude and silence, the vast and sunny expanse of Nature, so that the flower of the soul might germinate and bud under the most favourable conditions. And half a century later the flower still blooms.

In those days the phenomenon of religious conversion had not been studied. I speedily realised, however, the significance of my own experience. I was enabled to grasp by actual demonstration the great fact that religion is a natural manifestation, a process that takes place spontaneously in the individual soul. In face of that central fact all the religious creeds of the world, however systematised they may be and however infallible they may claim to be, fall back into insignificance. They are merely the empty husks of that vital process which I had experienced within myself. The whole religious life of the world, the most extravagant utterances of the most ecstatic mystics, became simple and natural to me in the light of what I now knew in the only way in which anything could certainly be known.

During the next year or two I drew up a questionnaire on religious experience; I never used or published it, but it was the unknown prototype of a method of exploring religious phenomena much used in later years. I prepared it in connection with a book on religion which I planned and indeed began to write about the year 1879. Then I laid it aside, not because I had lost interest in the matter, but because I saw that the question of sex came before the question of religion in degree of urgency. It will be better, I said to myself, to deal with the sex problem first and with the religious problem later. So I devoted some thirty, if not indeed fifty, years to the sex problem, which I had already some years earlier set as a main task for my activities in life. Now the religious problem seems less urgent, since so many workers have taken it up along lines similar to those I had planned to follow, though they have not, I think, usually placed the question so definitely as I can on personal experience.[1]

The religious process that took place in me at the age of nineteen was effected in a moment. But it was effected forever. One is suspicious, and rightly enough, of such sudden 'conversions.' Yet what happened to me was of a nature that could not possibly be undone. More than forty years have passed since then. Yet there has never been a moment when the foundation and background of my life had not been marked by the impress they received at Sparkes Creek. Many earthly affairs have caused me vexation, pain, even anguish. Yet beyond that distress of the earth there has always been an inner sphere of my soul, filled with joy and the serenity of Heaven. I have always been conscious that beyond the clamour of the world, below the agitated surface of my life, there brooded a peace that nothing could ever take away. I have worked for the world: I have been very indif-

---

[1] In the *Atlantic Monthly* for June, 1913, I published an article on 'Science and Mysticism' in which I briefly set forth my standpoint and my experience; this was revised and enlarged before taking its assigned place in the *Dance of Life* published in 1923. The narrative above was written independently at an intermediate date; I have not compared the two versions.

ferent to any good or evil the world could do me. I smile alike at
its blessings and its curses.

The problem of my spiritual life was now forever solved. The
problem of my practical life remained. Ever since I had left
school — and even before — I had never had the slightest idea
how to gain my living. I never felt the faintest real vocation for
any course of life. If asked what I would like to be, I could only
have answered as Diderot answered in youth, 'Mais rien, mais
rien du tout.' With me, as with Diderot, a creature of super-
abundant energy, this was far from meaning laziness or indifference. It was merely the mark of one whose temperament is too
obstinately aboriginal to be fitted into one of the existing frame-
works of life. I was most anxious and worried over the matter.
My mother had once suggested that being fond of books, I might
be a bookseller, but that idea had not the slightest attraction for
me; indeed, none of the families I proceeded from, except the
Olivers, had ever been drawn to business, or made any success in
business, and in books as books, moreover, I never took an interest. It might possibly be said that it was by an unconscious
atavistic impulse — I knew nothing then of my remote ecclesiastical ancestry — that the first profession I ever thought of
entering, when about the age of fifteen, was the Church. The idea
was, in fact, most likely the natural outcome of my own religious
attitude and environment, and the fact that my friend Mackay
was at that time preparing to become a clergyman. But it was
a career for which I was in every respect singularly unsuited, and
the idea, which never took deep root, was soon effaced when
shortly afterwards I lost my early faith in Christianity. The
occupation of teaching which I had fallen into on reaching
Australia was as unsuitable for me as the Church, and from the
first I merely adopted it as a temporary resource. I never had
any wish to devote myself to teaching and I have always been
rather sceptical about what is falsely called 'education.' At some
time in Australia I believe that the idea of a legal career floated

passingly across my mind, but for me it was as absurd as any of the others. My future career in life remained a puzzling and painful problem to which I could never see any solution.

The question was still in that position when, a few weeks after the experience I have just told, I began to read the *Life and Letters of James Hinton* by Ellice Hopkins, and by a strange chance Hinton was fated to have as decisive an influence on my practical work in life as already on my spiritual welfare. I was still in the first chapter of the book, reading as I lay — it was sometimes my position when tired after the day's work — full length on the hard bench in my schoolroom, on which I usually sat in the absence of a chair; a position more or less horizontal is always with me the most favourable to mental activity. As I read, in a completely calm and disinterested manner, I came to that point in the narrative where it is stated that on the advice of the family doctor it was decided that young James should enter the medical profession, as giving the necessary scope to his mental activity, and was accordingly placed at Saint Bartholomew's Hospital Medical School, having just reached his twentieth year, the age I had myself then almost reached. Suddenly I leapt to my feet as though I had been shot. 'I will become a doctor!' a voice within me seemed to say. Therewith, in that instant, the question that had worried me for so many years was once and for all decided. On the conscious plane, difficult problems, especially if of a practical nature, are only settled in my mind with the greatest hesitation and much swaying back and forth between the arguments on this side and on that, and even to the end I remain uncertain, although, when once the decision is made, I doubt no more and never turn back. But now, in settling the greatest practical question of life, I settled it in an instant, without even any deliberation at all — for the idea of becoming a doctor had never before so much as entered my head — and settled it so finally that I never once called my decision in question.

How it was that, against all the apparent tendencies of my mental constitution, I reached so instantaneous a decision of a problem I had so long hesitated over, I never tried to understand. When I now look back on it I seem to see that the process was analogous to that which brought about a little earlier the spiritual revolution. It was, that is to say, due to the sudden combination of separate tendencies, slowly elaborated in the subconscious region, and emerging into consciousness, when thus brought into union, with a generation of dynamic energy. I had never thought of being a doctor, yet for years I had been interested in the human body and its processes and had already begun to concern myself with anthropometry. Deeper than this was my interest, alike personal and impersonal, in the questions of sex which, though mostly in abeyance at Sparkes Creek, was slowly and steadily becoming formulated into a main life-study. There was again my more general humanitarian interest in health questions; the only charitable or philanthropic contribution to any funds that I can recall sending home from Australia was in connection with some health scheme, I forget precisely what. Finally there was the underlying persistent recognition of the need for a practical career in life. It was these various impulses which were at this moment suddenly welded into one powerful whole.

It was as well that the process was effected without deliberation. For, if I had carefully considered it, there were many reasons why I should not become a doctor, even apart from the fact that I had no idea how the expenses of the long preliminary training were to be covered. Professionalism of any kind — the professional attitude of mind and the professional manner — is quite alien to me, however valuable for inspiring confidence in the general public. Then my tendency to nervous apprehension and intellectual doubt, however admirable as an aid in difficult diagnosis or any other complicated problem, is not favourable to swift decision or ruthless action. Moreover, practice must be the medical practitioner's main business, and since I have too much faith in Nature to be enthusiastic about practising on her, I hardly seemed to possess the qualities required to pursue a brilliant medical career. Some of the qualities left over — a patient kindness, human sympathy, a certain amount of insight — might be helpful, and have indeed proved helpful in my limited professional experience, but they do not cover a large part of the field of medical practice today.

Yet the sudden inspiration that struck me as by lightning when I lay on the bench that evening in my little schoolroom was absolutely justified. It was as completely right as my spiritual conversion of a few weeks earlier. I have never for an instant doubted either. The two convictions in my life that were on the surface the most sudden and revolutionary were also the most firmly and irremovably based.

I quickly realised that the career of an ordinary medical practitioner had no attractions for me. As soon as I began to reflect on the meaning of that sudden conviction, I saw that the main reason why I wanted to be a doctor was not because I wanted a doctor's life, but because I needed a doctor's education. A doctor's career was not my career, but a doctor's training was the necessary portal to my career. Therein I was entirely right. I might have been tempted to say, like some clever and brilliant people I can think of, that of the things I wanted to know medicine had little to teach and that I could best work in complete independence of traditional investigation. I was fortunately saved from that fate by a primitive trait of my mental constitution. My most revolutionary impulses are combined with an equally strong impulse to reverence tradition and seek out its bases. Just as I could not undertake to study the revolutionary Rabelais without investigating the whole history of the fifteenth century, so I could not reach my own new conception of sex without studying the established conventions of medical science. It has been fortunate for me that it is so. If I had not studied medicine from the beginning, if I had not been a duly accredited practitioner in medicine, surgery, and midwifery, I could never have gained a confident grasp of the problems of sex, I could never have set forth my own personal investigations and results in the volumes of my *Studies*, and I could never have found a decent firm to publish them. I should have spent my days in an almost helpless struggle, and my life-blood would have been drunk by the thirsty sands of time. I should have dropped and left no mark. By adopting the medical profession I acquired the only foundation on which I could build my own work.

In thus regarding medical education merely as training, as the portal to some other career still undefined, or merely, as it often seemed to me, as part of a necessary apprenticeship to life — 'life' being here the development in the world of my own personality — I was thus not really solving the difficult problem of bread-earning but only postponing it. Over this, however, it scarcely seemed that I worried. One step at a time, I seemed now to think, was enough. Therein, as it proved, I was wise. It is true that not until some twenty years later was my own chosen life-work to bring in any sort of pecuniary return. But before I had completed even my course as a medical student I was earning money by my literary work, and I had scarcely obtained my medical diploma before I had abandoned forever the ordinary medical practitioner's career. I had at last reached the long-sought life-course it was so hard to find, a path that was absolutely my own and entirely new. I have never departed from it.

Sparkes Creek had now done its seminal work. The most eventful year of my life was almost spent. What remained of it is a blank in memory. From little notes I made, it appears that in October, Mr. Shaw, who was officially connected with the school, paid a brief perfunctory visit, and his name in the Visitors' Book was the first entered for eight years. It was in October I discovered the brown snake, four or five feet long, basking on my veranda, and that Ashford, when I met him once, told me the place suited me I looked so well, and that it would take a big lump of a horse to carry me. But I now only recall that a few weeks later, it may have been November, the inspector, a quiet, black-bearded, not unfriendly man, came in his buggy to pay the brief official visit. He was almost the only person who came to me from the outside world during the whole twelve months, and that is why I recall him, for we exchanged but few words and he had no fault to find. By this time, I think, the question of my return to England must have been under consideration. Before long my father, whose own ship had chanced never to be chartered to Australia during the years I had been there, wrote out to me that he was making arrangements with Captain Wagstaff of the *La Hogue*, an old and well-known ship in the Australian trade, to bring me back to London as a second-class passenger. Whether the question of my return was first raised by me or by my mother, I no longer recall. But my mother was now becoming anxious to see me and I — who had so far been content to stay in Australia now had a new motive for returning to England. My training for life was opening out before me, though how I supposed I was to find the means for my medical course it is impossible for me now to guess. Perhaps my new faith in the world extended unconsciously even to this practical point. If so, it was to be justified in the most incalculable way. It is, maybe, a simple and instinctive faith in miracles that effects miracles; and my life was full of them.

So the last weeks of that wonderful year slipped out quietly and have left no traces in memory. The most eventful year of my life was over, the year in which I had discovered the universe, and discovered myself and my art and my science; and I left, easily, cheerfully, without a pang so far as I can recall, the sacred spot beneath the Southern Cross I may never see again where all these things were revealed to me. I remember spending an hour or so in Scone before the train left, paying my bills, taking my money out of the bank, saying good-bye to Roberts the schoolmaster, and how he commended me for my pluck in spending twelve months in such an awful hole as Sparkes Creek — how little he knew! — and told me how surprised Shaw the clergyman had been at my courage and tenacity, and how Johnson the inspector had told him I ought never to have been sent to such a spot.

How little they all knew of the gateways to Heaven!

In Australia I gained health of body; I attained peace of soul; my life-task was revealed to me; I was able to decide on a professional vocation; I became an artist in literature. So far as my own individual effort is concerned, apart from other personal influences, these five points covered the whole activity of my life in the world. Some of them I should doubtless have reached without the aid of the Australian environment, scarcely all, and most of them I could never have achieved so completely if chance had not cast me into the solitude of the Liverpool Range.

Part V

V

The passage home was uneventful. There
were on board a number of varied figures, pleasant and unpleasant, which remain vividly etched on the plates of memory. But
none of them touched my life and I need not attempt to revive
them. One attracted me, an Irishwoman, some thirty-five years
of age, the wife of a quiet back-country publican. She had a
beautiful well-cut Irish face and a splendidly held erect figure
(I surprised her by saying I knew she had once been accustomed
to carry burdens on her head), a pure heart and a gay free tongue
which, she confessed, she sometimes wished she had bitten off
before it spoke. The man I associated most with was also, it
chanced, Irish, a priest, on a visit home to Tipperary, after many
years' activity in Australia, the Bishop's official licence in his
pocket. We walked up and down the deck discussing theology,
and he lent me Balmes as well as a volume of Montalembert's
fascinating *Monks of the West*. He was the only passenger I
arranged to meet after reaching London, and I showed him a

few of the London sights, but never saw or heard of him later, or of any other of my shipmates of the *La Hogue*.

After four years' absence I was once more at home, which was now, and for several years remained, 24 Thornsett Road, Anerley, a southern suburb of London, within a walk of the Crystal Palace. There followed a seemingly uneventful interval in my life. I was on the right road, but I was standing still, uncertain of the next step, and yet strangely free from anxiety; for I felt young, I saw no need for haste, the path in front seemed endless. It was not, indeed, until I was nearly forty that I suddenly realised that I was no longer young and that the road ahead could scarcely be as long as the road I had left behind.

My sisters had been children when I went to Australia (the eldest being nearly four years my junior) and the two elder were now grown girls, developed and tall. It was like becoming acquainted with people I had not before known, and the sense of intimacy which thus arose with young women who were strangers and yet my own sisters was delightful to me who all my life had so far known no real intimacy with women. The most vivacious and intelligent of them, Louie, was specially sympathetic to me, and with her I formed an intimate friendship which at first was touched by sexual emotion. This could not have arisen if the long absence during which she grew into womanhood had not destroyed that familiarity which inhibits the development of sexual interest. This little experience was valuable to me, apart from the permanent deeper tenderness which it brought into our relationship.[1]

[1] I rewrite this passage just six months after my sister Louie died in December, 1928. Nothing ever destroyed the harmony of our relationship or spoilt our enjoyment in innumerable subjects of common interest, although there were various circumstances which might easily have made our relations difficult. She was actively occupied as a court dressmaker (after an apprenticeship with Mrs. Nettleship, a daughter of Hinton's) until the Great War broke up her business, but retained a vivid and highly intelligent interest in many subjects and possessed a large circle of devoted friends. During the last years of her life she was crippled by rheumatoid arthritis and suffered much pain, but she preserved her unruffled cheerfulness and gaiety of spirit until the end, of the approach of which she was fully conscious. One of her friends remarked of her that the Ellises knew how to die, and another wrote that she might truly be called a saint.

It enabled me to understand from personal knowledge how it is that, as a rule, sexual emotion fails to spring up between close relatives or people living together from before puberty, and under what circumstances — by no means of such rare occurrence as is usually believed — it may spring up. I was thereby enabled in later years to give clear precision to my conception of the psychological foundation of exogamy.

My mind was made up that I was to go through a doctor's training, but I knew nothing as to how the money to do this was to be acquired. My mother was willing to help me as far as she could by devoting to my medical education the sum of one hundred pounds, which was half of the little sum she had received by the will of her old friend Miss Johnston, who had died while I was away; but that was of course insufficient. In the meanwhile the natural course was to go on teaching, and so I went as assistant master to a school at Smethwick, in the suburbs of Birmingham.

The routine of my life here was completely without interest and I can recall very few of its circumstances. Only one or two points stand out. The head master, who was a self-important and scarcely attractive personality, had a commonplace little wife of some thirty years of age. I never paid her the slightest attention beyond ordinary politeness, but one day, when her husband was out and I was alone in the schoolroom, she came to me in a tearful mood and vaguely confided her married troubles. I was far too shy and awkward and inexperienced to offer her even the most innocent consolation, and even today I am uncertain what kind of consolation she desired or expected. She never came again. That was the first time in my life such an incident had happened to me; it was far from being the last. I also remember that on Sundays it was my duty to take the boys to church, and that we sometimes went to Saint Augustine's at Edgbaston; the service here was at that time most beautifully conducted by a clergyman called Hodges, and there was a noted and accomplished organist, Gaule by name. In the services at this church there was something deliciously serene and even aesthetically satisfying, although they had not the slightest religious significance for me. I have never experienced any of the Rationalist's austere horror of religious observances, and at Saint Augustine's I was still able to feel something of the same enjoyment I used to receive five or six years earlier in Merton Church. It was the last time, however, that I ever had occasion to experience that pleasure. After leaving Smethwick it was seldom that I entered an English church during service, though I can never resist the temptation to linger in and around an old church at other times and find fresh delight in each.

I had not, meanwhile, lost interest in Hinton. I had grown curious to learn more of his unpublished manuscripts mysteriously referred to in the *Life and Letters*. It was, I think, before I went to Birmingham — and perhaps even before I left Australia — that I wrote to his biographer, Miss Ellice Hopkins, to inquire as to the prospects of their publication. She forwarded my letter to Mrs. Hinton, who wrote to me most kindly and invited me to come and see her and her sister Miss Caroline Haddon, an intelligent and enthusiastic disciple of Hinton and his doctrines. I was soon on friendly terms with the whole family, who took me into their inner circle and interested themselves in all my affairs. In later years Mrs. Hinton told my future wife that in some respects I much resembled Hinton, adding, however, some remark to the effect that such resemblance was no recommendation as a husband. (Several people at that time made remarks to my future wife not flattering to me as a prospective husband, and it was characteristic of her steadfast and independent mind that they made no impression on her, though she duly reported them to me.) But the chief bond was, of course, my youthfully keen interest in Hinton's work, especially his unpublished work. Mrs. Hinton presented to me the four large volumes of his earlier privately printed but unpublished manuscripts and lent me endless bundles of later unprinted manuscripts which I zealously read, making many extracts. I wrote an article on Hinton for a liberal religious magazine, the *Modern Review* (1881), consisting mainly of quotations from the printed volumes of manuscripts; I assisted Miss Haddon in editing a volume of selections from the same source; and I stimulated Mrs. Hinton to publish a volume of extracts from the later manuscripts under the title of *The Lawbreaker*. This, though Mrs. Hinton was nominally responsible for it, was really edited by me; I wrote a little Introduction and it was published in 1884. I also wrote a careful and sympathetically appreciative, though not uncritical article, on 'Hinton's Later Thought' which Croom Robertson accepted for *Mind*, where it appeared in the same year. I have never reprinted it because, although I still accept it in the main, I feel that it concentrates on Hinton the thinker a degree of attention which he has long since ceased to occupy in my mind. Some who have known me well hold that his influence on me has been great. To me, when I look back, this seems doubtful. Except at some definite points where I gladly recognise such influence, his mental disposition was so alien to mine, his clinging adhesion to some of the ideas of orthodox religion placed such an intellectual abyss in the way, and his vague confused thought so persistently aroused the critical instincts of my 'Latin mind' — as it has sometimes, I do not say justly, been called — that the possibility of real general influence seems excluded. Nevertheless, so impervious have I been on the whole to influences, whether directly personal or through books, that Hinton remains at all events the most disturbing figure in the history of my spiritual course.

The Hinton family, I have said, took a friendly interest in my private affairs. They certainly knew that I wished to be a doctor and they probably knew that my financial condition would not enable me to obtain a medical education. I had spent a few days with Howard Hinton and his wife at Uppingham where he was science master at the school. It was through Howard that an offer came to me from Miss Caroline Haddon to lend two hundred pounds, to enable me to pursue my medical studies. I appreciated the generous kindness of this offer, and it opened for me the way I wanted to go, which, without that offer, might have been forever closed, and my whole life-course altered. It happened thus, as it had happened before, as it has happened since, throughout my whole life, that, at the right moment, the gift of Heaven, without any effort of mine, fell miraculously upon me. I suppose it is so also for others. And that is why we speak of 'Heaven' and 'miracles.' That is why we try to account for the unaccountable by picturing a fairy-tale God in the skies, who watches over his children and gives them all that they need.

I hesitated to accept such an obligation until I had thought over it, and I asked the advice of my friend Mackay. To his opinion I attached value because I knew that he held money obligations in horror. But he heartily advised me to accept, and as that was also my own feeling the matter was therewith concluded. My life was insured for the amount of the loan should I die before repayment. Some time later, however, Miss Haddon told me that she had no wish for me to return the money. That, as it turned out, was fortunate; it was not till long after her death that I could have repaid the loan. The obligation always a little weighed on me, though by no fault of Caroline Haddon, who entered into a course of affectionate correspondence with me. She was a charming letter-writer and always regarded me as her 'dear camerado,' in Whitman's phrase. On my part, I was ready and eager to fulfil what I felt to be my part in aiding her in all that concerned the maintenance of Hinton's reputation and the publication of his manuscripts. I always felt, however, that my return was inadequate. It has not been until forty years have passed, and then not directly by me, but, through another gift of Heaven, the spontaneous resolve of my wife, that I was able to feel that Caroline Haddon's long-cherished wish for the complete presentation of Hinton's esoteric doctrines is at length fulfilled, that the debt has been repaid and that I am at rest.[1] Moreover, although no part of the loan was ever returned in money to my generous friend, it has been passed on in ways that I am sure would please her. We can seldom return to others the most needed gifts we receive, but we can pass them on to others, and as the years have gone by I know that, even in the form of money, I have given to others who needed it at least as much as I have myself received from others.

To the two hundred pounds from Miss Haddon my mother added the promised one hundred pounds out of the legacy. As I was to live at home during my medical course, without any question of payment for board and lodging, my medical training was provided for, and I had been treated very generously considering my parents' position in life, more generously perhaps than I then realised.

The next question was the choice of a medical school. On this point we were completely ignorant. My mother took me to Doctor Alfred Carpenter, who had been present at my birth and was now a prominent public man, later, indeed, described as the foremost private practitioner in England. He belonged to Saint Thomas's where until shortly before he had lectured on his own special subject, Public Health. (It was the last time I saw him, but forty years later I found his son staying at a favourite hotel of mine in Saffron Walden, The Rose and Crown.) Naturally, he strongly recommended his own Hospital School, but I think he was right. At all events, I have never regretted the choice of Saint Thomas's. Even apart from its sound teaching equipment, it was incomparably the best London school for spacious and beautiful situation, on the banks of the Thames, opposite the Houses of Parliament and close to Lambeth Palace. During the prolonged

[1] *James Hinton: A Sketch*, by Mrs. Havelock Ellis, with a Preface by Havelock Ellis, was completed by my wife just before her death, though, owing to delay caused by the Great War, it was not published until 1918. The whole of what Hinton regarded as his special message to the world was here frankly and fairly, though not uncritically, set forth.

seven years' course of my medical training I saw that beautiful spot under every aspect of day and night, and the river and the Parliament buildings, alike delightfully varied from different points of view and under changing lights. Incidentally, I caught glimpses of many notable personages. I passed Gladstone walking along Whitehall, vigorous, alert, well-set, even in old age; Parnell near the same spot, a tall slender man with curiously shifty, self-conscious, timid eyes; the blind Fawcett being led across Westminster Bridge. On the other side of the bridge I once met Archbishop Benson, and noted his eyes, blue, self-conscious, and shy; I had earlier seen his predecessor a few yards farther away, the grave, statesmanlike Tait, stopping outside Westminster Bridge Station to read the newspaper placards; and on the platform of that station I once saw the dark-eyed Huxley waiting for the train. Across the bridge I recall once by chance seeing King Edward in his carriage, sitting up stiffly, trying to look every inch a king, for he was a king who always, as they used to say, 'played the game.'

The mere practical difficulties of my student days were much greater than they would be now. More than two hours a day had to be spent in going to and from the Hospital, partly by train, partly walking, so that I was at a considerable disadvantage compared to the students who occupied lodgings within a few yards. Another difficulty — incredible as it may now seem — was the impossibility of obtaining a light midday meal, even at Charing Cross. A heavy meal, then as always, was bad for my work, and at that time also bad for my purse; I usually had to fall back on the pastry-cook shops and eat sausage-rolls which soon became nauseating and I have never been able to touch them since. My chief obstacles, however, were mental rather than physical. No doubt the idea still remained at the back of my mind that the main object of my medical education was the education itself, the training for life in the broad sense, a method of obtaining a more complete grasp of the world than would otherwise be possible, in the preparation for my own special work. But, at the same time, I thought that, incidentally, medicine must be my way of earning a living, and so I wished to take it seriously and aimed at the highest qualifications. There were two great hindrances to this aim, both lying in my own nature: in the first place, the expanding and many-sided activities of my mind, hitherto shut in on themselves by the conditions of my life in Australia, but now afforded ample means of satisfaction at the moment of most vigorous expansion; and in the second place, my own mental characteristics. For whatever powers I may chance to possess, they are slow and limited and amply blended with the stupidity of which I find so much around me in other people. Then my memory, while excellent for the things that interest me, has always been unreliable for everything else, so that I have never trusted it and always made notes of everything I might desire some day to recall. There was here a combination of qualities — emphasised by my caution and hesitation — fatal to success in examinations of any kind. That I speedily discovered. I entered for matriculation at the University of London, but failed in several subjects, so that I felt no encouragement to make a second attempt, but fell back on my Sydney matriculation as an entrance in arts to the medical profession. After I abandoned the attempt to become a graduate of London, I proposed to myself the joint qualifications of the London Colleges of Physicians and Surgeons and passed some of their examinations; but failing at the final surgery I was content in the end with the licence of the Society of Apothecaries, which had then recently become a full and adequate qualification in medicine, surgery, and midwifery, though it lacks prestige and is always a little unintelligible for even the most intelligent foreigner, as I have sometimes observed.

But the long course of preparation for examinations, which I sometimes passed and sometimes failed to pass, involved an immense amount of drudgery and wasted time during the most active years of my life. Probably there was some benefit to me in the earlier stages of this training, as there certainly was in the later and more definitely medical stage, and I have never failed to realise that it was all indispensable for my work in life; but the hours spent in tedious attempts to memorise the details of anatomy and pharmacology and similar for me dead subjects, swiftly sliding from my mind which had to be perpetually burdening itself with them anew, seem as fruitless to me now as they seemed then. Comparative anatomy and physiology were more attractive, and in practical chemistry, which has something of the same deductive charm as Euclid, I was a good pupil. But this long, worrying, and uncongenial course of preparation for examinations constituted an element of strain through seven years of my life. It was inevitable, it was worth while, for it forged a necessary link in the chain of my life's work. But otherwise it was simply a prolonged period of anxiety in a field mostly alien to my temper of mind. I recall how, when at last the hour for an examination arrived, I would throw aside my books and notebooks with a desperate joy, inwardly exclaiming: *Jacta est alea!* Then I stumbled nervously, with a damaging self-distrust, through the *viva voce* examination, usually after doing rather better in the written papers, and anxiety would recur until the day came for the announcement of the results. I remember going up to the board in the hall of the College of Physicians one day, and on finding my name there walking swiftly and briskly away. I should have failed to notice, as I passed them, two unknown youths with slow dragging steps if I had not heard one of them remark: 'He's through!' Evidently their psychological insight was sounder than their medical knowledge.

When I consider not only my intrinsic disabilities in medical study but the manifold extrinsic impediments to these studies, my wonder is that I ever secured an honourable medical qualification at all. I was a youth of the largest intellectual and emotional appetites, practically fresh to London and altogether fresh to life. I was eager and receptive for all that life could offer, for all the

Havelock Ellis

At the time he began his study of medicine

finest pleasures of the senses, for arts and for sciences, for philosophy and for ethics, not least for love. Moreover, I had not the slightest idea, and even if I had the idea I doubt if I had the power, of sacrificing any of these appetites to the mere necessity for professional study. Life, after all, I had always instinctively felt, was my business, and a professional education was merely a rather dull and narrow channel to life. So I soaked myself in all the delights — save the merely coarse and sensual delights for me without appeal — which London could offer to my adventurous spirit. It is a marvel to me now, when I try imperfectly to recall the immense range of my interests and activities in those years from 1881 to 1889, how I could possibly have found time or opportunity or strength to squeeze my medical studies anywhere into the course of my life. Yet I know that I was faithful in my attendance at lectures, no laggard in the dissecting room, and not behind the average student in the amount of time I spent at the Hospital. A part of the secret, no doubt, was that I never wasted a moment over the superstition of games, and that I had no recreations beyond those that might have seemed to most students work. My interests in life were so varied and so vivid that they amply sufficed to supply me with physical exercise and mental recreation. Then, as always, I never knew what was play and what was work. No play is interesting to me unless it effects work, and no work is possible to me unless it possesses the amusement of play. So that the whole of life has always had for me the seriousness which for most people only their games possess, and their games have for me no existence because they seem to me to be outside life. Throughout life people have told me how they marvelled at the amount of work I accomplish. I have been tempted to reply: But I never work at all!

To literature, in the wide sense, no doubt, whether in the form of writing or of reading, I instinctively gave a foremost place. I suppose that, directly I came home from Australia, and while still a teacher, with no prospect, so far as I knew, of carrying out my scheme of medical study, I began to write a little, only a little, and very slowly, for if I am, according to the Goethean maxim, 'without rest,' I have certainly always been 'without haste.' Writing as an art had at first meant for me verse. That was so even before I left England in the *Surrey*, but it was more definitely so in Australia. For a few years after I returned to England I still wrote sonnets, and wrote them better; but I gradually ceased to write them, not by deliberate resolve but by the force of events. They needed calm and leisure, and my life had become crowded with manifold activities. Moreover, the growth of my intellectual life for a while submerging my emotional life, I began to feel the need of prose, the vigour of scientific expression, and for the first time I realised definitely that prose also is art. At Sparkes Creek I had indeed initiated my own personal prose writing, but, though carefully, yet instinctively, seeking to express myself with precision, I was hardly yet, I think, conscious of prose as a medium of art.

The first paper I recall writing in England and the first of mine ever printed (in an obscure literary journal, the *Pen*) was a review of a book on Rubens. The choice of subject indicated that I had a living interest in that master. Rubens was indeed the first great artist — though by no means the last — whom I discovered for myself. After an early period of repulsion for what seemed to an idealistic boy — accepting without question the Madonnas and Saints of Raphael — his ugliness and coarseness, I had suddenly in a flash, before one of his most swiftly painted sketches in the National Gallery, received the revelation of the miracle of his genius, and so acquired an interest in his personality and work. Another paper I published a little later, though slight, was more characteristic and personal: 'What is Pureness?' A rather well-known woman writer of that time had written an article entitled 'The Sanction of Pureness.' It presented fairly conventional views, but in my little comment, which was not a direct attack, I suggested — herein more or less inspired by Hin-

ton — that we may have to remould our ideas as to what 'pureness' means; in plainer words, that pureness does not necessarily
mean sexual continence. Therein I had already taken a tiny step
on the path along which my life-work was to lie and I expounded
the same conception of 'pureness' more clearly and elaborately
in my *Little Essays of Love and Virtue* forty years later. The
author of the original article published 'A Rejoinder,' beginning
with a reference to Pilate's question, 'What is truth?' as though
my attitude had been sceptical, which showed that she had entirely failed to grasp what I was driving at. I realised that I had
not yet learnt how to make my meaning clear. My little paper
had been written in a way that was delicate, musical, suggestive,
to the point as I thought, though without insistence and without
emphasis. It was, in short, the way of writing, which, as I now
suspect, may have been unconsciously influenced by Newman,
though I do not wish to imply that Newman could not make his
meaning clear.

After that, there may certainly have begun, though very
slowly, the change in my style which during the next fifteen years
was to render it more vigorous, positive, and masculine. My
first elaborate essay, however, was written, and with much care,
before this change became manifest. It was on 'Thomas Hardy's
Novels,' and I expect it was the most comprehensive and thoughtful little essay that had so far been written on that subject. My
friend Mackay, as I have told, brought to me *Far from the Madding Crowd* on its appearance when I was a schoolboy, and it was
my first taste of Hardy. But there followed a phase of enthusiastic admiration for George Eliot, and it was not till after my return to England that a deep appreciation of Hardy developed in
my mind. Then I set myself to read everything of his that had
yet appeared, so far as I could ascertain. Merely to read all that
an author has written never seemed to me, however, even at that
age when I was making my first attempt at criticism, an adequate
preparation to write about him. To me it was a matter of course

to investigate his environment. I accordingly planned an Easter holiday in Dorset and speedily carried out this plan, selecting Weymouth as my centre. It was in the spring of 1881, and I remember that whenever I walked into the Public Library I saw in the papers the accounts of Lord Beaconsfield lying near death at Hughenden Manor, the house that thirty years later I was so often to be driven past on the road that now has for me its poignant memories. But at Weymouth I spent a most pleasant time, so pleasant a time that I have never ventured to attempt repeating it. I revelled in the lovely atmospheric effects on the heights of Portland; I walked to Dorchester and various other places; I wandered along the characteristic Dorset 'white roads up athirt the hills,' as Barnes calls them, and by a happy supererogatory chance I came upon Barnes's dialect poems in my lodging-house sitting-room and was so enabled to gain a better knowledge of the poet of the land of which Hardy was the novelist.

I now felt I had a grip of Hardy's environment. But the next step, to see him or even to write, I made no attempt to take; I was far too modest and retiring for such a notion even to enter my head, apart from the fact that meeting people has rarely indeed presented itself to me as a desirable end to seek. When later I met Hardy it was he who proposed it, not I.

I dwell on this essay because it has its place in my development. It was in writing it that I learnt to write. The opening sentence was a problem of great difficulty to me; I know that I spent days, if not indeed weeks, over it, though it emerged simple enough in the end. All the rest was written, if with less hesitation, with not less care and deliberation.

Probably I sent my essay to some of the chief reviews, which speedily returned it; I do not remember. In any case it found its way before long, in a rather abbreviated form, to the hands of Doctor Chapman, the editor for many previous years of the old *Westminster Review*, which, although it had fallen from the high place it occupied a quarter of a century earlier, still held a respectable position as the review of intellectual Radicalism, though even here the *Fortnightly* overshadowed it. An amiable letter soon arrived from Chapman asking to see the full version of my essay; that he accepted and published in April, 1883. Almost immediately there came to me a letter from Hardy in which he expressed in the most charming manner possible his appreciation of my effort: 'I consider the essay a remarkable paper in many ways, and can truly say that the writing itself, with its charm of style, and variety of allusion, occupied my mind when first reading it far more than the fact that my own unmethodical books were its subject-matter.' And towards the end of the letter he added that he hoped 'to read some more of your critical writings in the future, and believe I shall discover them without a mark.'

Nothing more delightful could happen to a young writer, on publishing his first essay, than such a letter as this from a master in literature. It may be discounted as a compliment felt to be due under the circumstances; but there is a genuine note in it not usually to be heard in letters of this kind, and Hardy really showed an interest in my later critical writings. I have always been fairly indifferent to opinions on my work, and was never tempted to subscribe to press-cutting agencies, but that letter of Hardy's has always remained to me a source of pleasure.

In the effort of writing this article I completed my apprenticeship in the art of writing and really deserved a word of approval. The essay has never been reprinted; after some hesitation I resolved not to include it, six years later, in *The New Spirit*. The mark of apprenticeship still seemed to cling to it, and, moreover, I was moving away from the rather refined, delicate, and allusive manner of that little study.

The same manner still marked, however, the sketch I wrote in story form in the years that followed — that is to say, the middle eighties — entitled *Kanga Creek: An Australian Idyll*. It is the only thing I have written in story form, though I have planned and even begun others. Really it is modified autobiography, and it was the stress of a personal impulse, the desire to give some sort of expression, however imperfect, to the memory of what I already felt, as I still feel, to have been the most seminal and even the most ideal year of my life, the year I spent at Sparkes Creek. But I found I could only encompass the expression by throwing it into a form of art. So I left out nearly all the really significant events of my life during that memorable year — the events that I have now tried to record here — and simply selected little details of my daily life, some of the sensory impressions that struck on me, and a few of my emotional expressions, as truthfully as I could render them. The hero was not wholly myself, and the heroine never had any real existence at all. But the background was exact, for the most part, though I placed my Creek in an impossible part of New South Wales, not on the road that led to the Liverpool Range, but on that to Carcoar (whence also I borrowed a few details), and all the minor figures of my tale were portraits. That was the main reason — but also the fact that there was much in the idyll that was personal — why I never made, or wished to make, any attempt to publish it until some forty years later. But I showed it to a few friends who all expressed interest, especially Olive Schreiner, who encouraged me to complete it. Arthur Symons, one of the earliest and most careful readers, told me it belonged to the same class as Flaubert's *Trois Contes*. I knew, however, as he certainly knew, that it had nothing of the fine solidity that marked even Flaubert's short stories; indeed, although I have always felt for Flaubert and his work an admiration bordering on worship, I do not regard myself as even remotely of the same type, and my qualities as a writer are scarcely of his kind.

During the acute period of my mental development in Australia, I had already, I believe, begun to take a slight interest in philosophy, proceeding no doubt out of my religious struggle, and it was, I think, in Australia, that I procured Schwegler's *History*

of Philosophy, not an inspiring book or one that gave me any enjoyment, though I read it faithfully. Only after Hinton had entered the course of my psychic life was I able to take a really
vivid interest in any philosophic problems. Hinton himself was
a philosopher of too vague a sort to push me in any definite direction. When, however, my article on Hinton appeared in *Mind*,
Croom Robertson, the editor, seems to have approved of it, for
he asked me to review books and send further contributions, which
I occasionally did, and Thomas Davidson, who read the article
with care, pronounced it 'judicial,' I think with a certain admiration, for that was a quality beyond the reach of his own fervid and
emotional temperament. I now subscribed to *Mind* and faithfully read it, as well as a number of books in the field of philosophy and comparative religions, European and Oriental, especially those dealing with Buddhism, a religion which appealed
to me because of its absence of dogma and freedom from theology.

My reading in this department was furthered by a chance that
put me in charge, for a year or two, of the theological and religious
reviewing department of the *Westminster Review*. Soon after the
Hardy article appeared, Doctor Chapman expressed a wish to
meet me during one of his visits to London from his Paris home,
and later he also came to my Earlswood home to see me; he evidently felt for me a considerable degree of personal regard. He
asked me to contribute further to the *Review* (here was published
my essay on Diderot), and a little later, in 1886, when Mr. Philip
Wickstead resigned the 'Theology' (religion and philosophy) reviewing work, he invited me — a most incompetent successor to
one so accomplished — to take his place; it was a post to which a
small salary was attached and I gladly accepted. Chapman was
at this time attempting to put the *Review* on a better financial
base and to give it a more modern form. Had he succeeded, he
told me, he would have offered me the post of sub-editor. I expect
I could have imparted new life to the concern; I have often
thought I should make a good editor for an advanced review; but

Chapman's scheme aborted and no other chance ever came my way.

After Chapman's death, a few years later, the *Westminster Review* gradually faded away. He was a large and handsome man of imposing appearance, which suggested, no doubt unjustly, a touch of the apostolic charlatan, while in early life, it is said, he was equally striking and nicknamed 'Byron' by his friends. He was really a man of quiet, solid ability, genuinely advanced in his ideas, once a courageous pioneer in various fields, and gifted with an insight that enabled him to recognise and assist some of the most daring and distinguished thinkers of his time. He could have written a remarkable book about them and himself, as I once at least suggested to him, but he was always very reserved and never talked of his own interesting experiences. I used to go to see him when in Paris, both at his professional rooms in the Rue de Rivoli and his handsome apartment in the Avenue Kléber, where notable Frenchmen were to be met. The last time I saw him, he said sadly, though he seemed in excellent health, that he was tired of living. Soon afterwards, during our honeymoon in Paris, he sent a messenger, before we were out of bed on the morning of departure, to invite us to his home. Three years later he died. There was some mystery, I slowly divined, in his domestic life. Mrs. Chapman had a defiant air which suggested an uncertainty of position. The two nieces who lived permanently with them seemed to me probably his daughters, and later I found reason to conclude that I was right. The elder girl, charming and beautiful, became a journalist in Fleet Street and soon after died as the result of an illegal operation. The younger, nearly twenty years after I had lost all touch with the family, appeared unannounced at my house at West Drayton and borrowed money; she said she was engaged to be married, and she asked me to make out the cheque to her in the name of Chapman. I never heard from her again, nor expected to. Still later, I saw in the papers that Mrs. Chapman, who for a while had attempted to carry on the *Review*, had been rescued from the workhouse into which she had drifted; shortly afterwards she died. She had, immediately after Chapman's death, announced an intention to write his biography, and such a work would have been of much interest. Now it would be difficult to do, for his papers were abandoned to chance and scattered. Many years later two of his private diaries were picked up for a trifle in Nottingham (which happens to be his birthplace), and fortunately they came into good hands. A few extracts were published in *The Times Literary Supplement* of September 11, 1930. Some of them were of much interest to me. I had somehow guessed that George Eliot, before she knew Lewes, had been in love with Chapman, undoubtedly an attractive and sympathetic man for such a woman; nothing he himself said to me suggested this; his answers to any questions about her were vague and reserved, and it is noteworthy that, notwithstanding his long and close association with her, living in the same house and acting as her editor and publisher, he contributed nothing to her biographies. But entries in the diaries confirmed my intuition, if so it may be termed.

More fruitful in the end than my association with Doctor Chapman was the still earlier association with Foulger, the friendly printer, editor, and publisher of *Modern Thought*. He was a pleasant and intelligent little man, without culture, but in touch, not only with men of letters, but with radicals of the old school and young socialists of a new school which had still hardly come into being. I used often to look in at his office in Paternoster Row, and we would sometimes go out for tea together to the Cyprus, a teashop on a first floor at the end of the Row, overlooking Cheapside. I was not always Foulger's only companion on these occasions, for his dingy little office was the resort of all the leaders in the new political and socialist movement. He was now publishing and editing *Today*, a monthly magazine to which brilliant representatives of the new social movements, shut out from other avenues to publicity, were always welcomed. In *Today* (where a few small things of mine were printed) Ibsen's later work first reached the English public in Miss Lord's translation; Bernard Shaw's work in fiction first appeared; and the advocates of socialism and land nationalisation had a free field.

As Foulger was printer and publisher as well as editor, all sorts of people destined to become more or less famous gravitated to 13 Paternoster Row. I am not sure that it was here I first met Hyndman, then beginning his heroic attempt to acclimatise in England an unanglicised Marxism, though I well remember the last time when dining with my wife at Professor Herron's rooms in London, and how, when Mrs. Herron, a real musician, was at the piano, Hyndman would attempt to hum in time with the music to my wife's scarcely concealed disgust. Here I certainly began a friendly relationship with Belfort Bax, a daring adventurer in theoretical fields, but, as Foulger observed with amusement, too timid to walk down the Lisson Grove slum by himself. Here used to come Morrison Davidson, a popular orator and journalist among the working class, and the brother of Thomas Davidson, but a totally different sort of person: he was too fond of beer, and I best remember him sitting asleep in Foulger's office with head resting on arms on a table. Champion and Frost, two amiable and noble-spirited young men, both propagandising advocates of land nationalisation and both of good family, though neither destined to become a great leader, were often here. Champion's devotion to the cause of the people was ardent and disinterested, but eventually he seems to have fallen into disfavour — perhaps the workingman found him too obviously a 'gentleman' to be congenial; his health also was affected by veneral disease and he went to Australia, where he took a moderately active part in Labour movements and there ultimately died. Frost was large and solid and quiet, a country parson's son, clearly also an honest and simple-minded gentleman; his career ended more swiftly. He went to the north of Scotland to propagandise among the restless crofters; there he fell in with a clever adventuress professing to be on a similar mission, a washerwoman's daughter who posed as a great lady among the crofters and solemnly presented to them what she said was her grandfather's sword, telling them that it was for 'defence and not for offence.' She captured Frost, who fell hopelessly in love with her and joined his fate with hers. The washerwoman's daughter was soon convicted and sent to prison for all sorts of frauds and vulgar criminal tricks, and Frost was shipped off by his family to America; I never heard more of him. A demagogic leader of a more typical sort also came to Foulger's, a workingman destined to become famous later, John Burns, afterwards a Right Honourable member of the Privy Council of the Realm; but I best recall him on the day that he came out of prison direct to Foulger, to tell us in a quiet, subdued way at the Cyprus tea-table of his prison experiences.

These casual meetings had no special influence. Political movements, especially of a demagogic nature, were not calculated to appeal to my temperament. Foulger, moreover, through whom I came into contact with these people and their ideas, was himself, though alert, inquisitive, and sympathetic, often critical, and his own advocacy of a progressive educated democracy, based on the radicalism of the immediate past, fitted in fairly well with my own ideas at that time. When, therefore, Foulger, to whose home in Maida Vale I would sometimes go on Sundays to dinner, proposed to establish a 'Progressive Association' to further these views, primarily by holding Sunday evening meetings with lectures, but with further schemes in the background, for the promotion of all sorts of large progressive movements, I willingly joined. Foulger was able to induce several distinguished Radicals of the old school, like Holyoake, the co-operative pioneer, to join the committee; some accomplished people connected with the South Place ethical movement, a useful contingent, were willing to assist; and a few prim and stolid freethinkers of Nonconformist mind and habit, mostly of shopkeeping class, gave stability to the society. I was the youngest and probably the most enthusiastic adherent, and so it fell to me to become the secretary. My self-sacrificing zeal amuses me now, but it was genuine, and although in more recent years I have frequently denied the idea of 'Progress,' I by no means condemn the practical activities of the Progressive Association. I never appeared prominently at the meetings, and never once spoke a word in public; but I had a considerable hand in the conduct of the Association and in the selection and invitation of the lecturers, who included men of high distinction. We had taken a hall on Islington Green for our meetings, a place, we learnt afterwards, where the Parnellite members of Parliament were also accustomed to meet in secret conclave to discuss their sometimes rather conspiratory policies. Every Sunday evening, whatever the weather, I set out from my home at Anerley on the dreary journey across London to Islington. It was characteristic of my mother's tolerant attitude that she accepted without any protests this unconventional missionary activity of my Sunday evenings, perhaps recognising it to be, as it was, a transformation of her own religious spirit. Sometimes I would go with Foulger into the streets near the hall beforehand, to distribute the handbills of the meeting. While it was being held, I sat by the draughty door, to give information, receive subscriptions, and sell the literature. Incidentally, I thus acquired a susceptibility to sore throats and colds which pursued me nearly all through life. In addition to other activities on behalf of the Association, in order to supplement the instrumental music at our meetings and to bring out our ethical spirit, I compiled a little book of *Hymns of Progress*, which was published by the Association. This was a task to my taste, and the book may indeed be said to be notable, not only by its literary level, but as the first congregational hymnbook, so far as I knew, definitely disengaged from religious creeds, and without any theological or even theistic tinge. I wrote for it a little hymn of my own,

'Onward, brothers, march still onward,'

which has since been introduced into many Socialist and other songbooks, and when my friends have sneered at it, and at the whole affair, I have sometimes playfully declared that it is by this that my name will be remembered.

To the Progressive came, a little later, as an active member, Percival Chubb, destined to be an important link in my life-story, especially the clue that later led me to the discovery of my wife whose name I first heard from his lips. Chubb, at that time a clerk in the Local Government Board Department at Whitehall, was an ardent young idealist, indifferent to science, not then keenly interested in art except to some extent in literature, but with a wider and more eager receptivity than mine for the new philosophical, ethical, and social movements of the day. He was sociable and entered various circles, so that he knew more of these movements and came more closely in touch with their representatives than was easy for me with my reserved and retiring nature. He was without the originality and the force which place a man in conflict with his own time, but happily endowed with abilities and accomplishments which, combined with his really fine qualities of character, fitted him for good work in the ethical movements of the United States to which a few years later he migrated, and there remains, after forty years, still active. I soon fell into friendly relations with him, as we were both interested in so many of the same subjects and were pursuing them in the same honest and ingenuous manner. Before long Chubb became joint secretary with me of the Progressive Association and was able to take a more public part.

It was easy for me to meet Chubb, as Saint Thomas's is within a few minutes' walk of Whitehall, whither indeed I frequently went to obtain my slight lunch at a pastry-cook's. Sometimes as we walked together he would speak of a man for whom he had great admiration, a man of world-wide reputation, it appeared, though I had not heard of him, an original philosopher, a marvellously learned scholar, a great ethical leader who sought to renew the life of society on a loftier plane, one Thomas Davidson. It seemed

that Davidson loved to gather young men round him and inspire
them with his ideas; Chubb, though he retained a certain independence of judgment, was such a disciple, and had indeed once
gone over to Italy — Davidson wandered much about the world,
and was especially attracted to Italy where one heard of him as a
guest in a Rosminian monastery or renting a house in Capri or
staying in the centre of Rome — in order to spend a few weeks
with the Master at Domodossola. One day he told me that Davidson was shortly coming to London and wanted to meet a few
young men likely to be sympathetic to advanced philosophical
and ethical views of life. He duly arrived, took rooms in Chelsea,
and shortly afterwards I met him, first, I think, at rooms shared
by Chubb with his friend Roland Estcourt, somewhere on the
Thames Embankment.

Thomas Davidson was really a remarkable man; that was clear
to me even on a first meeting; he was alive, intensely and warmly
alive, as even his complexion and colouring seemed to show; here
was the perfervid emotional Scottish temperament carried almost
or quite to the point of genius. At the same time here was clearly
a man who had lived a rich and varied life in many lands, acquiring at once a wide experience of men and a deep knowledge of literature and philosophy, while retaining a fresh and ardent interest in both. I came away feeling that this was the most remarkable man, the most intensely alive man, I had ever met; I am not
at all sure that I should not say so still.[1] It may have been this
same evening that William Clarke was present, also meeting
Davidson for the first time, and similarly impressed. (On Davidson's death in 1900, Clarke wrote in the *Spectator* an article on 'A
Modern Wandering Scholar' which, even if not entirely accurate,
was perhaps the best appreciation of this imperfectly appreciated

---

[1] My impressions of Davidson are recorded in a letter quoted by Professor William
Knight in his book on Davidson. But Knight was mistaken in describing me as an
'intimate friend' of Davidson's. I was never that, and Davidson still remains for
me an unsolved enigma. He was, as Knight once told me, an illegitimate child, and
perhaps that may have had something to do with it.

man.) Clarke was a prominent journalist, a leader writer in the *Daily Chronicle*, then the most advanced London Liberal newspaper, an admirable journalist of a rare type, ardent and upright, a genuinely convinced democrat, inspired by the ideals of Whitman about whom he wrote a book; withal something of a thinker, expert in economics, and widely interested in life and literature. He and I walked away along the Embankment together, and from about that time he became interested in me also, being indeed my earliest outspoken friend in the press, and the writer (in the *Echo*), some seven years later, of the first article about me, as distinct from mere book reviews.

During the weeks that followed I often saw Davidson. I talked to him frankly of the things that then interested me, especially of Hinton's doctrines. He always listened with genuine interest, as though I were telling him something he had long been anxious to hear, and I introduced him to Mrs. Hinton and Miss Haddon. He was much readier to enter sympathetically into my interests and ideas than to claim attention for his own, so that it was only by degrees that I realised the wide extent of his interests and his knowledge. But at times, and especially when several of us were together, he would grow eloquent in setting forth his own philosophic conceptions. I remember that immortality seemed just then a favourite idea of his, and he regarded Tennyson's *In Memoriam* as a philosophic and convincing argument for that idea, while to me *In Memoriam*, which I had studied so carefully in Australia, was just a poem, a beautiful poem, but as an argument not worth a moment's consideration. I quoted Emerson against him on this question of immortality, and he — remarking he had himself re-read Emerson's statement that same morning — retorted by quoting Goethe against me. In the end his last resort was always the unction of his own fervent conviction, but that was an argument which for me carried not a feather's weight. He would complain that I seemed to listen sympathetically and to be carried entirely along with him, and yet next day he would find that I had been moved not at all. It was quite true; it is always my impulse to listen and to absorb sympathetically; agreement is another matter. Such an attitude seems to me the only reasonable attitude. The people who think they can judge even only a dinner by a mere sniff seem to me people of no account. A mere sniff, whether of a dinner or a philosophy, can tell us but little; we must take it in to judge of its quality. This difference continued between us by letter, after Davidson had gone on from London to Rome. It was too much for him before long; he had rarely been attracted to anyone so much as to me, he wrote (in a letter which has now gone astray); but he could not stand this perpetual obstinate criticism; he ceased to write. I was content to make no effort to continue the correspondence. Much as Davidson had impressed me, I had never felt any response to his warm friendship. We exchanged a few friendly letters in later years. What was perhaps the last, in response to one from me, was written from America in 1888, and contained numerous suggestions (one or two of which I adopted) for volumes in the Contemporary Science Series I was then projecting. 'Why don't you write to me sometimes?' he added.

But he had done me a great service, a service which was the last he would have desired to do: he had cut me adrift forever, not indeed from philosophy, but from the philosophers. He had convinced me that his own philosophy was a purely personal matter to which there was no need to ask anyone else to subscribe. I passed on to realise that the same might be said of every philosopher. Incidentally, I was thus warned that I must not allow myself to be caught in the web of Hinton's philosophy. Every man must be his own philosopher. It was Davidson, little as he desired to do it, who taught me that. When in later years I wrote a passage to that effect, in an essay on Nietzsche in my *Affirmations*, it was Davidson I had in mind.

Meanwhile, Davidson had set in action a movement which continued to grow and gather strength, though by no means altogether on his lines, after he left London. The earliest group of us, some half-dozen in number, have not for the most part made any great name in the world. The Fellowship of the New Life was founded (I believe I had a considerable finger in writing its manifesto) to promote the general social renovation of the world on the broadest and highest lines, seeking inspiration in its Goethean motto: 'Im Ganzen, Guten, Schönen resolut zu leben.' A little later, as it grew, the Fabian Society, with a more practical and political programme, broke off from it, and with the aid of men who have since attained fame, notably Sidney Webb and Bernard Shaw, it played the leading part in permeating England with an anglicised form of Socialism. It is in accordance with the irony of human affairs that 'Fabianism' should indirectly have been produced by a man so alien to its spirit as Thomas Davidson. I, who had no political interests, while sympathetic with the Fabians, decided to remain with the parent body, though as I came to realise the inevitable limitations of the movement, my more active participation diminished and ceased, Edith Lees — my wife to be — who had been introduced by Chubb simultaneously becoming its chief organiser and guiding spirit. It continued its quietly influential existence for some years (publishing a little paper called *Seedtime* and holding meetings) until after Edith Lees' marriage when it peacefully expired.

It was at one of the meetings of the New Fellowship that I first saw Edward Carpenter, who was naturally more in sympathy with its ideals than with those of the more political Fabians, though he was later regarded as furnishing the ideal inspiration of the Labour movement. We were in the midst of a meeting at Williams's Library (then in Gower Street) and Nicholas Tchaikowsky — at one moment many years later conspicuous in Russian affairs — was, I remember, with us; many of the Russian exiles, indeed, and notably the saintly Frey, were our friends, for our ideals were not unlike those of the anarchists, though we did not give ourselves that name. I was sitting with my back to the door and hearing someone gently open it I turned round for a moment and saw two brightly gleaming eyes out of the background of a quietly humorous face. In that first swift glance, as will sometimes happen, I gained a more vivid picture of Edward Carpenter's characteristic face than in all the long years I knew him afterwards. It had been through the New Fellowship that I first heard Carpenter's name. At one of the earlier meetings a youth sat beside me who chanced to be in touch with various new things, and he put into my hands a small book, just published, entitled *Towards Democracy*. I opened it, glanced at a few pages, and returned it with the remark: 'Whitman and water.' A little later I saw a new second-hand copy in a box of books at a few pence each in Booksellers' Row, as the long since vanished Holywell Street in the Strand was called. I thought it might be worth while to rescue it, and I soon found that *Towards Democracy* was something much more than Whitman and water; that Carpenter was a person of altogether different temperament from Whitman, and had here written a genuinely original book full of inspiring and beautiful and consoling things, a book, indeed, that before long was to become for some people a kind of Bible. I wrote to him to express my appreciation and at the same time told him something of my own difficulties in life. He replied with words of sympathy and encouragement. It was the beginning of a friendship which lasted till his death, some forty-five years later,[1] fortified on his side when he discovered in me a champion of the sexual invert's right to existence and on mine by the fact that my wife admired him almost more than any other man, learning to know him better than I did, and being indeed almost his disciple, so far as she could be the disciple of anyone, though towards the end

---

[1] I am writing now three months after his death in 1929. In 1927, I think, he came to spend a day or two with me in the country. But he was beginning to fail mentally and physically. He ceased to write and I was disinclined to see him in that state, content to know he was well cared for and fairly cheerful. But I was not forgotten by him, though he had forgotten so many people he knew. He mentioned my name not long before the end and expressed a wish to see me. Before I had made up my mind to go, he was dead.

she seemed to detect some weak points in his, on some sides, rather feminine nature. I had been in correspondence with him but a short time when he came down to our little home at Earlswood to spend the night; my mother always had family prayers after breakfast and I still remember that Carpenter (who had once been a clergyman) sat bravely and patiently through the prayers while we all knelt, for by habit and affection I always completely acquiesced in this family ceremony. At that period I had no knowledge of Carpenter's personal temperament, though that, when I learnt it, caused me no shock and made no difference to me. Personally, I never once came across the least evidence of it, though I heard much from others.

It was indirectly through Percival Chubb and the New Fellowship that I was put on my literary path, Chapman and the *Westminster Review* proving a blind alley. Two of Chubb's nearest friends were Ernest Rhys and Will Dircks, both of whom had become connected with the Walter Scott Publishing Company, Rhys as editor of the Camelot Series (later of the more extensive Everyman Series, with another publisher) and Dircks in the publishing office. This business had just been taken over as a bad debt by a great building contractor of that time, afterwards made a baronet, Walter Scott, an ignorant and uncultivated man, but with an insight into business ability, and he had chosen a manager and given him fairly full powers. This manager, Gordon, of little education, but whom Dircks once described to me as 'a Napoleon of business,' quickly made the publishing house of Walter Scott a great success; he flooded the whole country with good cheap editions of the English classics in prose and verse and was at the same time ready to encourage new ability whenever he could find it, publishing the early works of several writers who later became famous. It naturally happened that I met both Rhys and Dircks on some of the New Fellowship country excursions — as later it naturally happened that on such an excursion I first met my future wife — and before long I was editing numerous volumes for the

Camelot Series. The first (1886) was a selection of Landor's *Imaginary Conversations*, for which I continued — and still continue — to experience an admiration which began when I was seventeen in the Public Library of Sydney. Landor is, for me, a kind of English Flaubert, though I would doubtless place Flaubert first and have given more attention to him. There followed next year a volume of Heine's *Prose Writings*, a volume which still finds friends, for it perhaps remains the best English selection of Heine's prose; some of the translations were my own, especially the *Florentine Nights*, which I had done for my own instruction when I was learning German out of Heine at Grafton, and I am not ashamed of it even yet. Then, in 1888, came Ibsen's *Pillars of Society and Other Plays* (which were *Ghosts* and *An Enemy of Society*), a volume which played a notable part in its time, for it was practically the first attempt to bring Ibsen in his most characteristic aspect before the English public, and it arrived at the right moment, exactly when the advanced party in England were ready and eager to receive Ibsen.

Meanwhile (in 1884) I also made my first attempt to write for the leading reviews, having already published several articles in the *Westminster* and other reviews which were not quite in the first line. The subject of my article was 'The Present Position of English Criticism,' and I sent it to the *Fortnightly Review*, where it was accepted by the editor, Escott, to my great satisfaction. But a day or two later, under some unintelligible pretext, it was sent back rejected. What made the editor so swiftly change his mind I could not ascertain, but I expect it was ill-health, for which reason, not long after, he ceased to be editor; his successor, Courtney, accepted nearly every contribution I sent him, while Sir James Knowles of the *Nineteenth Century* and Sir Percy Bunting of the *Contemporary Review*, although I never made any attempt to approach any of them personally, became my most friendly and appreciative editors until their deaths. The article on Criticism, though a competent survey of the subject, overestimated J. A. Symonds, whose work on the Renaissance I had just been reading with profit and delight, and underestimated Pater, who was perhaps not ethical enough for my frame of mind at that time. It was printed in 1885 in a magazine called *Time* and never reprinted; with the papers on Hardy and Hinton I regarded it as belonging to my 'prentice period. After that date — I was then twenty-five — my judgment, as well as my manner of writing, became more mature; I no longer outgrew my opinions, though naturally I might sometimes modify them. I was nevertheless still firmly convinced that when one is young one is always liable to outgrow one's work, and was determined that I, at all events, would not fall into the error of neglecting this natural development and putting forth in a permanent form work that I might subsequently wish to disavow. I cannot remember at what age it was that I resolved not to publish a book until I was thirty, but I was never tempted to move from that resolution and never had occasion to regret it. At the age of thirty I punctually published my first book, *The New Spirit*, and followed it up in the same year by my second and quite different book, *The Criminal*, thus inaugurating my double public career at the same time. As I look back it would seem that I planned my life from the outset largely and spaciously, with the calm assumption that I should live long enough to carry out my extensive plan at leisure. That confident assumption has in the event been justified, and my chief life-work, the *Sex Studies*, from its first dim inception to the publication of its final volume, was spread over more than fifty years. So I am glad I made that assumption; even though now, as I rewrite these lines after the age of seventy, I have the sad experience of seeing my early friends, some of them younger than myself, passing out of life before me.

My determination to go slowly was by no means an excuse for laziness; if I was without haste, I was also without rest. It was not even prompted, as it might legitimately have been, by the claims of my medical education. I was full of active literary

schemes. The first on any considerable scale was conceived suddenly, without premeditation, and put into execution with much
promptitude and complete success. I had long been interested
in the old English dramatists. On my way to and from school at
Mitcham I used often to buy one or another of the extensive series
of old plays then being published in small type at a penny each by
Dick. Marlowe, as well of course as Shakespeare, I had long possessed and loved. Of late I had been reading the other great Elizabethan dramatists in the British Museum, especially Ford. But
it was an inconvenient way of reading them; it seemed to me that
the best of these plays ought to be made generally accessible, and
in such a way that the finest of all were not omitted for the sake of
some absurd prudery. I could not for instance have tolerated an
edition of Ford from which was excluded the master's chief play,
'Tis Pity She's a Whore. I would have a sound and true edition
of these great Elizabethans or none at all.

At that time (in 1886) it happened that a London publisher,
Henry Vizetelly, was conspicuous by the way in which he had
published fairly literal translations of the chief contemporary
French novelists. My friend Eleanor Marx Aveling had translated *Madame Bovary* for him, and he had issued translations —
it is true by no means always literal — of a large number of Zola's
novels. He had himself been a distinguished journalist in earlier
days, he was familiar with France, and he was really engaged on a
quite honourable and useful work. It occurred to me that a series
of volumes of the best plays, unexpurgated, of the Elizabethan
dramatists — for which I devised at the suggestion of Beaumont's
poem the name 'Mermaid Series' — would be an excellent
scheme for Vizetelly to undertake. I had no idea of proposing
myself for editor, and indeed could hardly feel competent for the
post. I wrote to Vizetelly putting the scheme before him, and
almost by return of post he replied accepting it, asking me to
undertake the work of general editor, and inquiring what remuner-
ation I would wish to receive. Such a proposal seemed too tempt-

ing for a young unknown man to put aside, whatever his disabilities, and even though he was in the midst of training for an arduous profession. I accepted with alacrity, and speedily repaired, so far as I could, my incompetence. I knew nothing as to what fees a general editor was entitled, and the sum I asked (three guineas per volume) was, no doubt, too small. But though I am fairly careful of money, I have never at any time worried over money arrangements or gone out of my way to get good terms; I would far rather receive little than haggle to obtain much. Vizetelly was a capable, intelligent, and honest man; I never had reason to complain of him; he himself took an active and valuable part in elaborating the details of production of the series, while he left the whole literary organisation to me. I selected the dramatists, the space to be devoted to each, and I chose the editors, co-operating in their work, besides myself editing Marlowe, Middleton, Ford, and Porter. I enjoyed the task and cannot recall that I ever found it toilsome. Nor have I ever felt any need to be ashamed of my enterprise, in spite of an incident at the outset which I suppose may be considered characteristic. In the appendix to the Marlowe volume with which the series opened, I printed for the first time in full from the original manuscript in the British Museum the scandalously blasphemous and immoral charges brought against Marlowe by an informer shortly before his death. I accepted the information as a crude and ignorant version of what Marlowe really held, and I justified these acute and audacious utterances as now 'substantially held more or less widely, by students of science and of the Bible in our own days.' Many people were shocked, including even Swinburne and J. A. Symonds, who were both taking part in my scheme, and they both wrote to tell me of their disapproval, while Vizetelly, without even consulting me, swiftly mutilated my appendix, so that only in the early copies did it appear as I had sent it out.[1] At that time, and

---

[1] Swinburne wrote how happy he was to note the suppression of 'the horrible and disgusting passages in your appendix,' and 'I greatly regretted to find these monstrous abominations made public.'

for more than thirty years afterwards, the scurrilous informer's statements were generally ignored or contemptuously dismissed by students of Marlowe. Even today the reasonable view I put forward is not openly accepted, and the latest editions of Marlowe, so far as I have observed, avoid referring to my statement or mentioning my name. Not that I wish to claim any credit, but I am sorry Marlowe should so often fall into the hands of feeble folk unworthy to approach his bright spirit. Even as I write now, however, I am at length justified, and in *The Times Literary Supplement* (June 2, 1921) is printed a newly discovered document which confirms my opinion.

The Mermaid Series was at once well received, and much appreciated both by scholars in English literature and by the literary public. Yet in the midst of its career it was suddenly taken out of my hands and brought to a lame conclusion. Vizetelly was made the victim of a foolish prosecution for obscenity on the ground of his Zola translations and sent to prison; and soon after he died. His business was destroyed. The Mermaid Series was taken over, without any consultation with me, by Fisher Unwin, a successful publisher of that time. He removed my name from the volumes, without any word of explanation or apology to me, or any word of protest from me, though I do not flatter myself he knew that my silence was contempt. I was well aware that for a publisher the editor of a series is an insignificant figure, even though he may be altogether responsible for its conception, mainly responsible for its production, and largely responsible for its success. I had, of course, arranged for volumes ahead, many of them nearly ready for publication; the editors of these were equally disregarded by the new publisher and mostly accepted this treatment with a better grace than it deserved.[1]

The Mermaid Series swiftly passed away so far as I was concerned, and languished to death after it was taken out of my

[1] Fisher Unwin was a successful publisher with wide relationships, and, whatever my opinion of his methods might be, I had later to come into touch with him.

hands. But it was not superseded. I am pleased to be assured — as I revise these lines some forty years later, a paper on 'Havelock Ellis and the English Drama' comes to hand, written by a devoted student of the drama, Montague Summers — that 'the Mermaid Series remains a magnificent service rendered to the English drama, a pioneer work, a work that demanded courage, scholarship, and enthusiasm.'

It was, incidentally, a work that gained for me at least one prolonged and memorable friendship. About the time I was organising the series I chanced to read one day at the Guildhall Library, where I would go to see the current periodicals, an article in the *National Review* on Mistral by a young unknown writer, one Arthur Symons. I was so delighted with the fresh charm of its style that, on discovering later that the writer was then editing some plays of Shakespeare, I wrote to invite him to undertake Massinger for the Mermaid Series. He accepted, a correspondence began, and before long he proposed that on his next visit to London — he was then living at home at Coventry where his father was a Wesleyan minister — we should meet at the National Gallery. That was the first of many meetings, and a long and close friendship which was still continuing forty years later, though contacts were becoming rare.

So much for literature. In science I was mostly content with the practical studies my medical course compelled me to undertake, but I read many scientific books, though at first fewer perhaps than in philosophy. I slowly became interested in psychology; my first interest in anthropology had dated from early in my Australian life, but it was not until 1889, when I started the Contemporary Science Series, that I became a Fellow of the Anthropological Institute (as I am today more than forty years later) as well as of the Berlin similar society, and so came into touch with the science and its leading exponents in England, Galton and Beddowe and Haddon and Tylor, who were all great pioneers.

I may here bring in the origin of the Science Series which occupied me so largely during the twenty-five most active years of my life. When in 1888 the Mermaid Series passed out of my hands, I felt I had now grown experienced in editorial work and I conceived the idea of replacing that series by another and more ambitious series on lines really congenial with my own special work in life. Perhaps, also, I had already begun to realise that literature, in some form or another, was more likely to furnish me with bread and butter than medicine, while at the same time, journalism, the easiest form of literature, fitted neither with my tastes nor with my aptitudes. Editorial work, which demanded a wide outlook and judgment, with the supervision of writing rather than a large actual amount of writing, suited me, as I had already found, much better than work so hasty, so superficial, and therefore, I was inclined to feel, so immoral, as journalism.

It had sometimes occurred to me, with my growing interest in science, that the old International Scientific Series, in which once such memorable books appeared, had now reached its stage of senility. A new series on more modern lines was needed, with more attention to those sciences, and those aspects of science, which were now coming to the front. I projected a series to be called the Contemporary Science Series, and sent in my proposal, this time definitely with myself as editor, to Gordon, Walter Scott's manager, who, as I knew, regarded me favourably. When I look back, I am appalled at my audacity, not only in planning so big a scheme with my slender scientific equipment, but in putting it forth at the moment when, it would seem, all my energies should be concentrated on my approaching final examinations in medicine and surgery. Yet, imprudent as it seems, I now know that I was taking absolutely the right step and taking it at the right moment, while my medical qualification was, nevertheless, obtained at the appointed time a few months later.

My proposal was accepted as promptly and as readily as had been my scheme for the Mermaid Series. Gordon informed me, indeed, that this was exactly the kind of series he had been wishing to start, but had not so far known where to find a suitable editor. Being himself completely ignorant of science, he left me as free to organise as I had been with the Mermaid Series. So all preliminaries were soon arranged, the prospectus was printed, and I set to work at once. Next year the first volume was published. It was characteristic, as well as indicative of my main work in life, that this book was *The Evolution of Sex*, by Professor Patrick Geddes and J. Arthur Thomson, both of them since well known in the world. To place such a subject at the forefront of the scheme seemed daring to many people, but Gordon had made no objection, while the book was well received and soon acquired high reputation and many readers. It was at first planned to issue a new volume every month, but such rapidity soon appeared impracticable with scientific books. We went at a slower pace, but we went steadily for twenty-five years until the Great War. The series was then languishing and the war killed it. But during all the intervening years it had been for me a main source of support, though it involved much work, for scientific men are often poor writers and incompetent proof-readers, while sometimes, of course, my judgment went astray in choosing my writers. In one form or another I had to go through each volume several times, I usually made the index, and several of the foreign volumes I wholly or in part translated. The volume which had the largest sale, strangely enough, was a translation, and of a most stolidly written book, Moll's *Hypnotism*, hardly a subject which would now attract so large an audience. Although there were nearly fifty volumes, I saw the end of the series in 1915 without regret. By that date I was independent of it; the reputation of my work was growing, and my time was becoming too valuable to spend on the tedious routine of editing.

I return to my student days. The only person of any scientific accomplishment and genuinely scientific mind with whom I then came into close and friendly contact, and that from shortly after

I entered the Medical School, was my fellow-student, John Barker Smith. He entered at the same time as I did, but was more than ten years older, and had already occupied himself much with natural science, especially with advanced analytic chemistry (later he became on original lines a recognised expert in several branches of this, especially urinary analysis, in the problems of which he took absorbing interest), winning numerous gold medals in these departments and also being an enthusiastic field botanist. He had, in addition, already published a manual of instruction in pharmacology, and various pamphlets, notably on new advances in agricultural chemistry. (I am even as I now write carrying out a suggestion he made me of using Epsom Salts as a fertiliser for fruit trees and with successful results.) He was thus, when he came to Saint Thomas's, already more than a mere student of medicine. Since of me also — though in a different sense and though I had as yet no achievement to my credit — much the same might be said, it was doubtless natural that we should come together among the crowd of comparatively raw students by whom we were surrounded.

Barker Smith was at the same time a man of sensitive and nervous temperament, whence, before his medical training was completed, a serious mental breakdown with paranoiac symptoms, perhaps to be connected with his birth, which was illegitimate, though both his parents were sound and healthy. He possessed an even poetic sensibility, though of essentially virile temperament, and a rare originality of mind, so that though he might at times by some be thought a bore, his speech was often marked by a memorable seal of his own personality. He never, however, became an effective writer, though he developed into an impressive speaker.

On innumerable little adventures in search of knowledge along widely divergent paths, Barker Smith was pleased to be my sympathetic and intelligent companion, often ready to enter, even more searchingly than I who had suggested the exploration, into the subject before us. Today, nearly forty years since we first met, we remain excellent friends in spite of the breakdown early in his career from which he never completely recovered, and in constant touch with each other.[1] It is possible that one reason why we have always found this easy is that — though my explorations in the genealogical field only began some ten years after my student life was over — we were of allied racial composition; Barker Smith by birth and ancestry belonged to Castle Hedingham, only a few miles away from Sudbury in Suffolk, the town which, as I later found, was my chief ancestral centre. It was Smith who discovered the altar-tomb of the Reverend William Powle in the churchyard of Great Waldingfield whither he had accompanied me in search of possible clues. After that discovery we had many delightful expeditions and long walks together in Suffolk and Essex, in search of our ancestral homes, during many years.

The earlier adventures together of our student days were mainly in London, to museums and lectures and the meetings of scientific societies. There was, of course, the instructive museum of our own school at Saint Thomas's which we studied together; there was the British Museum, especially the galleries devoted to the anthropoid apes; roaming still farther afield from the paths of medicine, there was the fascinating Geological Museum in Jermyn Street. There were lectures, some by eminent physicians and surgeons, but also others, and I recall the gracious figure of Doctor Anna Kingsford (whose brother, Doctor Bonus, also a remarkable

[1] When I rewrite this page it is nearly fifty years since our friendship began, and Barker Smith has been dead for a year past. As he bade me farewell on his death-bed, a few days before the end, he clasped my hand long and tenderly. Until a few weeks before, his step remained brisk, his mind alert; he remained a clever and appreciated medical practitioner. Two months earlier he accompanied me on a visit of a few days to Ipswich — which we had often visited before — to view the Gainsborough Centenary Show, and his mental freshness to new impressions as well as his physical activity had seemed unimpaired, though he fell ill immediately afterwards. His affectionate sympathy and emotional sensitiveness were combined with an acute intellect, notwithstanding the eccentricity left over from the early mental breakdown, and a masculine character. I lost in him a precious friend, and with that loss many things have for me lost their savour.

person in his way, many years later became my friend); and it must have been in my student days that I went, but this time alone, to some of the series of lectures given in London by Renan, who spoke seated in a chair, and I still vividly recall his large round luminous head set loosely, as it seemed, in the socket of his great round unwieldy body. Later there were international congresses — but here Smith never accompanied me — of medicine and of psychology in London and other cities of Europe. Sometimes, too, my scientific curiosity carried me, again with Smith as my companion — before they had become popular — to the foreign restaurants of Soho, whither most of my dearest friends in the world have later now and then accompanied me, and here we would try strange dishes and unfamiliar wines, usually cheap and unwholesome, for it was not till afterwards that I gained a more extensive knowledge and a finer taste in this difficult field. With Smith's aid, also, I made some experiments in fabricating liqueurs.

We frequently went together to the Architectural Museum in Westminster. It was conveniently near to the Hospital and to me full of interest. Herewith I am leaving the field of science for that of art, though my youthful instinct of curiosity scarcely made any distinction of this kind. The earliest indication of my interest in architecture I cannot definitely place, and I am not sure that it was not first manifested in a disgust of the architecture which at that period prevailed in London, with its feeble construction and its profuse false ornamentation — the London architecture of 1929 is often a realisation of my early ideals; but I regard it as a native East Anglian trait and I sometimes also please myself by imagining that it is a relic of my ecclesiastical ancestry, my parson ancestors in the long course of their parish duties having used up all the interest in congregations, leaving only a love for the empty structures. It was doubtless in the Westminster Museum and with the aid of one or two textbooks that I began to cultivate my taste in architecture, and I have developed it in all my numerous excursions over Europe. It has been to me an endless source of enjoyment, but while my tastes have not been entirely ecclesiastical, it is no doubt the Gothic of France, the Catalan of Spain, and the endless variety of English parish churches which have been my chief sources of interest and delight. The hours I have spent in churches have been among the happiest in my life. I trust that the parsons who were my ancestors could have said the same.

But, as was natural, I had first been attracted to pictures. That began when I was a child, and, after the manner, I suppose, of most children, I loved my paint-box, though I achieved little with it; the peculiar penetrating impression of the colours of the paints on a child's virginal sensitivity of retina, never to be recaptured later, still remains in memory.

I took no pleasure, even in my earliest student days, in looking at the contemporary Victorian pictures at the Academy, which I soon ceased to visit; I have only been there once since, in forty years, and then merely to see how a bust of myself was placed, next to another man from Suffolk, Lord Kitchener.[1] But I zealously frequented the Grafton Gallery where the Pre-Raphaelites ruled, for they appealed to me, and especially Burne-Jones, ever since the revelation that the Merlin and Vivien etching was to me when I came across it in the Public Library at Sydney. The old masters I took every opportunity of seeing. Sometimes in the sale-rooms of Christie and Manson's, and always in the special and delightful Winter Exhibitions of Old Masters at Burlington House. I began the habit, I have not yet discontinued, of preserving picture catalogues, sometimes annotating them, and of carrying abroad notebooks to record my impressions of the pictures and other objects that chiefly impressed me in foreign cities. These notebooks briefly record some of the happiest hours of my life.

[1] I never came in touch with him, but a friend once told me that, when he was glancing through her album of autographs and quotations, he paused at my quotation (from my writings) and remarked: 'That is what I like!' I do not mind arousing a smile by the comment that I put this down to racial affinity.

Here, perhaps, I may mention the earliest of those independently planned visits to Continental Europe which have given me so much enjoyment and so wide a scope for my tastes in these directions. My wanderings about the world formed a large part of my lifelong education. I cannot imagine what I should have been without them. So far as the European Continent is concerned, they began (for I omit my visit to Antwerp in childhood) in 1881, while the latest and perhaps the last — for I have at length lost my zest for travel — was in 1925 with Arthur Symons to Paris and Burgundy.

My sister Louie actively shared my attraction to pictures and other forms of art, including some to which I gave little attention, and after much discussion we agreed that we could pay a visit to Belgium, at that time the country which young English people usually first thought of visiting as the easiest, cheapest, and most interesting tour available (for Rossetti on whom that first tour was so memorably influential it remained the last), and we were to be accompanied by a friend of hers, Lottie Bugler. I had been discussing the matter with Mackay, who had never been out of England, and he also was inspired to arrange an exactly similar party with his sister and a girl friend of hers; so the two little parties went over, in more or less close association, by boat from Harwich to Antwerp, the route I had traversed as a child with my father. The Belgium of those days, half a century ago, was not the Belgium of today. In its general aspect one might rather compare it to the more remote provinces of Spain. Bruges was then really a dead city, a fascinating dead city, more like the Segovia of today than like the busy, enterprising, thickly populated, and tourist-haunted Bruges I saw on my latest visit. At Ghent, though we were an unobtrusive little party, people came to their doors and windows to gaze at us, and at the hotel we were amused to find that the chambermaid had taken for granted that we would all three sleep in the same room. At Bruges we put up, opposite the Belfry, at the Panier d'Or, then a simple quiet cheap little place, and in Antwerp at the Fleur d'Or, a charming little Old-World inn situated in a narrow street beneath the cathedral towers, whence all day long and all night long the carillon above us floated down those languid tunes which, however feeble as music, always impart to Belgium for me a haunting fragrance. With these three cities and Brussels, our slender funds were exhausted. But the tour of less than a fortnight had brought so much delight and revelation that I returned home with eager desire for more such excursions in days to come.

During all my student years, however, my means were small and my time fully occupied, so that I made only one other foreign excursion, but that was to Paris, and the first of a long series I have never counted. It was arranged with Mackay and took place in 1883. We stayed at a quiet hotel just off the Boulevard des Italiens. It was a visit that should have been memorable, since it brought the new vision of numberless things of beauty and wonder which grew familiar during the half-century which has passed since. Yet my first impressions seem vague, much more so than those of Belgium, and as I had not yet begun to carry about the notebooks which usually accompanied me in later expeditions, I am unable to say what these first impressions were.

I best recall the dreary and comfortless passage on the deck of the night boat to Dieppe, and my awkwardness in having to adjust myself to Parisian ways. On the return journey we stopped at Rouen for a day or two. On leaving Rouen we missed the evening boat train through not understanding the French custom of announcing train departures, and it seemed we should have to wait I know not how long for the next boat. Mackay fell into a state of wild exasperation and raged at random. I was unmoved, took up the Baedeker and decided it would be a splendid opportunity to spend a day at Dieppe. At once, and instinctively, I sought to turn our bad fortune into good fortune, and it seems to me now a characteristic impulse. Again and again throughout life, in the largest matters as in small matters, I have built my success on a foundation of failure. I do not protest, I accept, but I create afresh. We proceeded at once to Dieppe, put up at the old Hôtel de la Poste (I recall the long table d'hôte), opposite the interesting old church, and the day spent there remains the clearest and pleasantest memory of the whole expedition. It was not until 1890, when I had obtained my medical qualification, that my longest visit to Paris, the most fruitful and memorable, took place in company with Arthur Symons and, for a part of the time, my sister Louie.

The theatre took, and has always taken, a place in my thoughts far below the arts of design. Louie, who was much more attached to the theatre, as later was my wife, usually accompanied me at this time when I went to see a play. Henry Irving and Ellen Terry, then indeed the most brilliant figures on the stage, appealed to us most, and that chiefly in Shakespeare: *Hamlet* and *The Merchant of Venice* remain in my mind associated with the figures of these two players; the tall, slender, gracious, dignified Ellen Terry seems to me naturally Portia, and the nervous, high-strung, distraught Irving naturally Hamlet. I went to see great dramatic artists whenever they came my way, Salvini as Othello, and later Duse on many of her visits. Sarah Bernhardt I must have seen first soon after I went to Saint Thomas's, though even before I ever saw her the dramatic critics said she had lost her golden voice of earlier years. Whether it was because she had already passed her prime, or more probably through not being congenial with my own sensibilities, she made no deep impression on me; Arthur Symons found her adorable, but I was far from that point even at the first, and still farther in later years, when I saw her again and again in London and in Paris. Ristori and Duse both appealed to me as greater; and even dramatic artists of much smaller reputation have given me more satisfaction and more pleasure, especially in France, for the art of the stage seems to me to be above all the art of France. The music-hall is a more genuinely English institution, and on this matter I was more at one with Symons, though this also belongs to a rather later period.

It was music rather than the theatre that drew me, and in old age I can still say the same. As a boy, I have said already, to be able to play, however badly, the sonatas of Beethoven, had been to me an invaluable mode of emotional expression, though, after I reached Grafton where music was at hand, I do not think I ever touched the piano again. Now that I was a student in London I had opportunities of hearing the best programmes and the best orchestras available. My first step was to subscribe to the Crystal Palace Saturday Concerts, where Manns, with the willing help of Sir George Grove, was then giving concerts of a quality which can scarcely be equalled even now. (I heard there, for instance, the whole series of Schubert's symphonies which I have never had an opportunity of hearing since.) So every Saturday, when my morning's work at the Hospital was done, I set off for the Crystal Palace, walking down the hill to my home at Anerley afterwards. Olive Schreiner, lonely and unhappy, was then (1881) for a short term living close by the Palace, and also coming to these concerts, though that, had I known it, would at the time have meant nothing to me. And then, a little later, another little woman, who was one day to become my wife, was also living close by and still unknown, eagerly absorbing knowledge and ideas at the Palace School of Science and Art and even herself already giving lectures there.

Here I touch the most intimately personal side of my life. To complete the outline of my multifarious activities of spirit during the seven years of my medical studentship — though the outline will not even then be really complete as I shall show later — I must describe this intimate side.

When I entered Saint Thomas's Hospital I was a fully developed young man, five feet ten and a half inches in height and weighing almost as much as I ever weighed. After middle-age my weight tended to decline, especially after 1916, the year of my wife's death, and oscillated around one hundred and fifty pounds. I was in good health, at my best, thanks to the four years

I had spent in Australia. The attacks of what I regard as a kind of periodic appendicitis, after lasting for six or seven years, had ceased entirely in 1897, the time when I went to Grafton and entered on the healthiest period of my life. My digestion was probably in a more satisfactory condition than at any time of my life. The sore throats and colds generated at Islington Hall remained a frequent worry in London, though not when away by the sea, and during the years of the Great War, when for the first time after a long period I spent the winter in London, a bronchitic tendency developed, though this disappeared when I ceased to winter in London. My teeth, which I had strangely neglected in Australia, I grew careful over when I became a medical student. (It was at the age of forty that I had to resort to artificial teeth and at about the same age to eye-glasses.) At the coming of manhood, I had begun to shave, but I quickly dropped that practice for the simpler plan of allowing my beard to grow. I took to parting my hair in the middle, as it was too thick to lie well when parted at the side, though with the approach of old age I returned to the more usual custom.

The chief trouble of health I recall in early student days was a slight tendency to nervous excitability, associated with my mental activity at this period, but that, on a physician's advice, was sufficiently subdued by a simple tonic of nux vomica which often later proved useful. At first I found my head tending to become especially active in the evening and I would at that time begin writing down the ideas seething in my brain. The result was that I could not sleep. I find that in November, 1884, I was complaining of singing in the ears. I obtained a mixture of bromide and chloral. But I speedily abandoned its use. I realised that it was foolish to allow my mind to work too actively in the evening. I made it a rule never to occupy myself in the evening with any mental work which might excite my brain. To that rule I have adhered ever since, and the result has been that, except under the stress of some circumstance for which I was not responsible, I have never suffered from real sleeplessness: I go to bed early and I get up early. I have never had any faith in night work, for it seems to me that out in the open air — where most often my work since marriage has been done — is the only right and wholesome place for mental work, and now in later years it is only in the morning that I care to work, or can work well, though I have never, as my wife liked to do, begun work at four in bed. Early breakfast and then out in the open — that has been my ideal and so far as possible my practice, and I hope that others may feel, as I do, the breath of free air over all my work. Whether out-of-doors or in, I have never cared to crouch over a desk to write; I always lean or lie back, whether on a hillside or a couch, and that may be the reason why I have remained erect and never acquired a bent or stooping aspect, to the surprise, I am told, of some who met me and remarked that I failed to present the typical aspect of a literary man.

Mental excitement and sleeplessness and bromide might suggest sexual excitability. But in that form — for there is more to say on the wider question — sex seems little to have troubled me. The only form of auto-erotism which I had up till then experienced — for a little later, when a dear friend told me that she had done so at times from the age of eighteen, I was tempted to experiment with the more active form — was in sleep, for the most part dreamless sleep, beginning, as I have told, at school at Mitcham and continuing at frequent intervals with no pronounced change but a general diminution. I kept a record of the phenomena, and summarised them, as those of W. K. in the first volume of my *Studies*. For though I would never have attempted to put into my books any 'case' or 'history' of myself, to record a mere series of measurable data seemed to me entirely legitimate. If I had written my own 'history,' it would doubtless have been a surprise, to those who could have recognised it, to find how small my experience was and how temperate my estimate of the sexual act. I am regarded as an authority on sex, a fact which has sometimes amused one or two (though not all) of my more intimate women friends. But, after all, it is the spectator who sees most of the game, and it remains true that my experience of sex has been, at all events, ample enough to help me to attain a great experience of love. And it must be a hard task for the sexual athlete to become a great lover.

Certainly, erotic thoughts sometimes played, even insistently, in my waking mind, but even in the solitude of Sparkes Creek there had I think only once been an occasion (it is truly narrated in *Kanga Creek*) when such an impulse, still remaining emotional rather than sensual, was fiercely urgent; and now in London my mind was usually too full of work and of manifold intellectual adventures in every direction for such volcanic eruptions. Yet undoubtedly there were fairly frequent periods of voluptuous revery with prolonged unrelieved erethism, which I now regard as unwholesome, if not enfeebling in their after-effects on my sexual life. Now that I am no longer young, I know sweet and lovely women for whom it would be a joy for me to do what I would with them. If I had known one of them in adolescence, I have sometimes thought, perhaps erroneously, the benefit might have been incalculable.

As for any cheap satisfaction of desire, I had no occasion to consider it, for no impulse in such a direction ever entered my head. If I were a little more easily sociable, I should no doubt have taken opportunities now and then of talking with girls of the street over a drink as some of my serious fellow-students were wont to do without going further. That would have interested me. There was, however, only one occasion at this time when I talked to a prostitute about her life. I was going home after my day's work at the Hospital when near London Bridge Station a woman at a street-corner accosted me. She was not attractive, scarcely young, and I had no wish to have anything to do with her. But I asked her questions about herself and she answered with simplicity and evident truthfulness. As we walked together talking, she led me, without my being aware of what she was doing, down a deserted side-turning. Then, thinking she knew what I desired, she placed her hand on my trousers at the point with which she was professionally concerned. I instinctively started back, realised the situation, and turned towards the main road, while she gently and soothingly apologised.[1] Then I gave her a shilling and went on my way towards the station, as I did so passing a policeman posted under the railway arch who stepped meaningly a yard or two towards me, as much as to say that he knew what I had been up to. I am sure that nothing could have persuaded him that he was mistaken, and that he could in all honesty have testified against me in a police-court, for the mentality of the police is not always that of the public. The incident has more than once come back to my mind when I have read in the newspapers of men of position haled before a magistrate on a charge of public indecency. I took no notice whatever of the policeman. But I had secured, not only an interesting little history, but a valuable experience, and I never placed myself in such a situation again.

Much of what I have been saying refers to the whole period of my studentship. But now I must start afresh in the year 1883. At that time, although at the most arduous period of my medical work, I seem to have had no compunction in continuing to subscribe to the best general lending library available and constantly taking out large serious works as well as novels and the chief current reviews. It thus came about that I read in the *Fortnightly* an article on recent novels by a clever young journalist of most versatile accomplishments, then lately come back to England from an American university, and in later years prominent for a time in business and politics as Sir Henry Norman, Bart. In this article an attractive account was given of a new novel,

---

[1] Not so very much later a woman I loved once touched me, as we were walking along a country lane together, in what was, physically, exactly the same way. I often thought afterwards how well this illustrated the fact that two things may seem the same thing, and yet be a whole universe apart.

The Story of an African Farm, by Ralph Iron, which no doubt
I had heard of already, but certainly here first saw described as
the kind of book which I must read. I proceeded to take the book
out of the library and duly read it. *The African Farm* was not to
me, then or ever, what it seems to have been to many, a revelation,
a new gospel; nor was I able to accept it at all points either as
fine art or as sound doctrine. I had followed my own path both
in art and in religion. When, a little later, I wrote of *The African
Farm*, together with some other books, in the *Indian Review*,
Olive Schreiner disliked my account of her book. She said it reminded her of a man in South Africa with a horse for sale, who,
after admitting a long list of appalling defects in the animal —
and these she enumerated in her vigorous racy way — wound up
by declaring emphatically: 'But it's a damned fine horse!' I accepted the description of my method of criticism and with equa-
nimity all Olive's subsequent teasing about my 'damned fine
horse.' It seems to me that a critic who is not keenly aware of
all the defects of a lovely thing that ravishes him is but a crude
critic, whose opinion hardly counts. My attitude is the same
even in love. The women whom I have loved, and almost worshipped, are women of whose defects I have been precisely and
poignantly aware. The lover who is not thus aware seems to me
a crude sort of lover, scarcely even a lover at all, merely the victim
of a delusion, of which to rob him would be to rob him of his 'love.'
I feel contempt for the 'love' that is blind; to me there is no love
without clear vision, and perhaps, also, no vision in the absence of
love.

What delighted me in *The African Farm* was, in part, the
touch of genius, the freshness of its outlook, the firm splendour of
its style, the penetration of its insight into the core of things; in
part, my own personal sympathy with the mental evolution
described, all the more since it had taken place, as largely had
my own, in the solitude of a remote southern land. I resolved
to write to the author. To this I was moved — though my letter

contained many criticisms — partly by my admiration and sympathy, partly also because it seemed to me that the book had attracted almost no attention and that its fine quality had remained unappreciated. That was no doubt true so far as public expression was concerned, though, as in England will often happen when a book is so unconventional and heterodox that people are shy of speaking of it openly, more attention than I knew had privately been given to *The African Farm.*

This impulse of kindness, I may note — an impulse as natural as any other, as natural as the sexual impulse — has more than once furnished the occasion to bring me near to the women I have been destined to know intimately. A little act of kindly sympathy has come back to me eventually as a precious gift of love to enrich my whole life. I could say — without denying that to convert a natural impulse into a policy would be to stultify it — that the road of unselfishness may be the surest way to the ends of selfishness. My life — I cannot too often repeat — has been full of miracles, and it may well be, I see now, that the wand which effected some, though by no means all of them, was wielded by my own hands.

After an interval the reply came in what I afterwards knew to be her best and neatest hand, for she most often used, even when writing to important persons, a hasty and careless scrawl, sent off without being read, though when she was writing a book she found it as hard as Flaubert to please herself.

St. Leonards-on-Sea, 25th. Feb. 1884.

My dear Sir, On my return from a visit to London I found your letter which my publisher had forwarded here. Had I received it sooner I should earlier have written to tell you of the pleasure your expression of sympathy with the little book *An African Farm* gave me. Thank you for having written.[1]

So began what was, if not the longest, the largest correspondence of my life, and it continued, with scarcely a break, for thirty-six years.

[1] The rest of the letter is printed in *The Letters of Olive Schreiner*, chap. 2.

That first letter clearly opened the way to further correspondence, and two months later, when she came to London in May,
a meeting naturally followed. She evidently expected much from
that meeting. She told me sometime later that at first actually
seeing me, her disappointment was so acute that on going into
her bedroom to put on her hat — for she was to accompany me
to one of the Progressive Association meetings — she burst into
tears. On my side there was neither depression nor exaltation.
But I still recall the first vision of her in the little sitting-room of
the South Kensington lodging-house: the short sturdy vigorous
body in loose shapeless clothes, sitting on the couch, with hands
spread on thighs, and, above, the beautiful head with the large
dark eyes, at once so expressive and so observant.

The disappointment must have been transient, for a few days
later she wrote to say how glad she would be, and what a help
it would be to her, if I would come again. Indeed, from that first
day, though without any immediate obvious ardour on either
side, there seems to have been an instinctive movement of approach on both sides. Before the month was out, she had settled
in Fitzroy Street close to where her chief friend at that time,
Eleanor Marx (Karl Marx's daughter), was living with Doctor
Aveling, and, by one of those coincidences of which my life has
been full, that street chances to be next to Doughty Street where
a few years later my future wife was living when first I learnt
to know her. I had already come in touch with Eleanor Marx
through the Progressive Association and was soon to know her
better; she was just then only beginning to form her fatal relationship with Edward Aveling and full of radiant physical and
intellectual vigour. Olive and I were soon meeting frequently
and going about together to meetings and other places of interest.
At one of the first Progressive Association meetings we attended
I was able to introduce her in person to Henry Norman, who had
by his *Fortnightly* article virtually introduced her to me. By the
time she left London, little over a month after our first meeting,

Olive Schreiner, 1879

Olive and I were on terms of friendship so close that she could write of me as 'the person who is like part of me.' We had found ourselves akin in all sorts of essential matters, with common interests and ideals in the social as well as the intellectual aspects of life, and each was at many points able to initiate the other. She, indeed, was four years older and had had deeper experience of life than I had. But in general she had lived much in solitude and isolation, finding out things for herself in an uncongenial South African environment, so that there were all sorts of things she was eager to know and understand which I could introduce to her or help to explain. Moreover, she had never possessed a friend able to combine personal devotion and helpfulness in practical matters with a wide sympathetic comprehension in deeper matters based on many experiences in common. It meant much to her. She loved in those early days to call me her 'other self.'

She meant even more to me. She was in some respects the most wonderful woman of her time, as well as its chief woman-artist in language, and that such a woman should be the first woman in the world I was to know by intimate revelation was an overwhelming fact. It might well have disturbed my mental balance, and for a while I was almost intoxicated by the experience.

But I have always been of temperament not easily or completely aroused; not merely that it takes me long to act on my impulses after they are formed, but that they have been slow to form. So it has scarcely ever happened to me, either in early or later life, to be repulsed by a woman, not because I have found women unduly yielding or unduly impetuous — I have known women of widely varying temperaments — but because I have myself so often, though with pronounced exceptions, been excessively slow. So at least it certainly was on this first occasion.

I missed no opportunity of writing to her and seeing her; she must already have largely filled my thoughts; but I had no impulse to make any advances. It was a decisive moment of complete trust, almost unique in her life, when at Fitzroy Street, one day in June, she suddenly confided to me the exact cause of the great emotional crisis from which at that time she was slowly recovering, I without doubt being a main factor in that recovery. Memory often links great things with small things: what I vividly recall is that she had just filled my plate with my favourite dish of strawberries and cream and that it remained untouched. It was about the same time that as I left her one evening to return home she raised her face up to me as we shook hands. I hesitated to realise the significance of the gesture, and we parted. But on my next visit, when the moment to part arrived, the gesture was more significantly repeated: she put her arms round me and from that moment our relationship became one of intimate and affectionate friendship. I hasten to add that it scarcely passed beyond that stage.

It is necessary to be precise. She possessed a powerfully and physically passionate temperament which craved an answering impulse and might even under other circumstances — for of this I could have no personal experience — be capable of carrying her beyond the creed of right and wrong which she herself fiercely held and preached; while, as she once remarked, if I were ever to do a bad action it would be really bad because it would be deliberate. For a brief period at this early stage of our relationship there passed before her the possibility of a relationship with me such as her own temperament demanded. But she swiftly realised that I was not fitted to play the part in such a relationship which her elementary primitive nature craved. I on my side recognised that she realised this and knew that the thought of marriage between us, which for one brief instant floated before my eyes, must be put aside. I have had no reason to regret that inevitable conclusion. We were not what can be technically, or even ordinarily, called lovers. But the relationship of affectionate friendship which was really established meant more for both of us, and was really even more intimate, than is often the relationship between those who technically and ordinarily are lovers. It is not surprising that some among our friends assumed that we were engaged.

At the end of June, Olive left London for the country, and a few weeks later she went to a small cottage at Bole Hill in Derbyshire, below Matlock, drawn there by Eleanor Marx, who was staying a few miles away with Aveling. After she left London we remained in daily correspondence, and in August I joined her for a week or so at Bole Hill, staying in the same cottage. Our relationship continued on this level during the years that followed. We wrote to each other almost daily; we met whenever it was conveniently possible, either in London or in the country, but not outside England, except in 1888 when I went across to spend a week with her in Paris, whither she was returning from Alassio.

If I think of that time — the later years of my student life when through my varied external activities the thoughts of my heart were so close to Olive — all sorts of pictures come to mind, standing out vividly from a dim background. I see us, for instance, returning at midnight from the Lyceum Theatre where we had been for some Shakespearean performance of Henry Irving and Ellen Terry, walking joyously, hand in hand, along the Strand, oblivious of the world; I see us again, walking in the country, with Eleanor Marx and Aveling, when Olive for a moment dropped behind those two to put her arm caressingly round me and Aveling cast a sharp glance back; I see her on yet another walk when for some reason I was unwilling to go along the road she preferred, and she softly sang to herself, 'I have a donkey and he won't go'; I see her coming suddenly and quite naked out of the bathroom in the house where she was staying into the sitting-room where I was waiting for her, to expound to me at once some idea which had just occurred to her, apparently unconscious of all else; I see her, on leaving rooms where she had been lodging, presented at the last moment with an extravagantly priced laundry bill, and she began to read out in wrathful tones the items of underlinen, for her vivid comic sense sometimes deserted her when carried away by strong

feeling, especially of injustice; I see her similarly in the upper floor
of the Louvre where the bronze vessels are displayed, talking to
me with grave earnestness of the handicaps by which women are
impeded in life: 'A woman,' she said solemnly, 'is a ship with two
holes in her bottom,' at which I irreverently laughed and she
smiled, and we probably stopped to look at the bronzes; again I
see her at her rooms at Hastings where I had come to spend the
week-end with her, bringing at her desire my student's micro-
scope, for she wished to observe living spermatozoa, which there
was no trouble in obtaining to place under the cover glass for her
inspection, and I see her interest in their vigorous motility. The
pictures are endless that I hold in memory — glad or comic or
poignant pictures — until 1889, when she returned to South
Africa for a stay, only once broken and that in its earliest period,
of twenty-five years during which we corresponded faithfully at
about weekly intervals, neither my marriage nor hers, which
shortly followed mine, making any difference in our relationship,
beyond that inevitably due to distance, neither my wife nor her
husband in the slightest degree disturbing its harmony.

The record of the relationship was contained in her letters
which, until she returned to South Africa in 1889, constituted
a continuous diary, day by day, though after that only at longer
intervals, until her death in 1920, so that they amounted in number to several thousands, all of which (except a few she had asked
me to destroy immediately) I carefully preserved, arranged in
bundles and duly numbered. But in 1917 she conceived the idea
that her friends should destroy or return all the letters she had
ever written to them. With this request, which gave me much
pain, I at first refused to comply. I valued those letters. I felt,
as James Martineau felt when his sister Harriet made a similar
request, that I preferred the certain benefits of the past to the uncertain benefits of the future. I was able to assure her that her
letters would not leave my hands and that I had arranged for
their disposal at my death, while they could not in any case be

legally published without her permission or that of her representatives. She still insisted, even with tears. It was the only quarrel we had ever had. In the end I burnt a vast number, belonging to the later period which, for I do not know what reason, she chiefly wanted destroyed, but painfully, feeling I was guilty of a sacrilege, and for nearly a year we ceased to see each other or to write. Then she resumed writing, without referring to the real cause of the interruption, and we met and wrote as if no breach had occurred. She never again referred to the letters.

But a vast quantity of these letters still remained, including most of those belonging to the early years when we were in closest relationship. In 1923, when it had been planned to publish a volume of her letters, edited by her husband, as a necessary complement to the *Life*, it became clear that such a volume could only be constituted by relying on the correspondence in my hands. I therefore went through all the letters that remained, copying those passages which to me seemed suitable for publication and likely to be of interest as illustrating her life, character, and opinions. I omitted, on the one hand, all that was certainly too intimate for publication, and, on the other, all that was too trivial or of too passing reference to be any longer of interest to anyone. The extracts thus made (and not the original letters themselves) I submitted to Cronwright Schreiner for his editorial supervision, and he made a number of small omissions of passages which it seemed to him undesirable to publish. Even the siftings thus finally obtained, though but a fraction of the original correspondence, constitute the largest part of the volume of *Letters of Olive Schreiner*, 1876–1920, as published in 1925.

Some of Olive's friends, I know, feel that she would never herself have agreed to the publication of these personal letters. I am not prepared to deny this. But neither am I prepared to regret my decision. The possibility of the future publication of a portion of the correspondence was always present to my mind. It seems to me that the writer who is no longer among the living, and whose sensitiveness can no longer be hurt, is not the fit arbiter of what should or should not be published. That arbitration best rests with those who love and reverence the dead writer and who recognise that the dead can feel no modesty and no reserve, however much we may respect those sensibilities in the living. That is the rule I would observe with others, and the rule I am willing to submit to myself.

Nearly all the original letters, at the suggestion of Olive's husband, have now been destroyed. A certain proportion I still preserve and cherish. My letters to her during the early years she carefully treasured; she once told Arthur Symons (rather to his surprise and indeed to mine) that I was the best letter-writer she knew; she fastened them together with thread sometimes, making a number of little booklets. When she went to South Africa in 1889, she sent them back to me to take care of for her; she never asked for them again. When they arrived, they were stuffed into a large overfilled cardboard case; I never examined them; most of them have at one time or another somehow been lost or accidentally destroyed; only a few seem still to remain; it would not be easy to arrange them in chronological order owing to my bad habit of not dating intimate letters. What happened to the letters I wrote to her during the following thirty years I do not know; I have not seen or heard of a single one, except the last which arrived after her death and was returned to me unopened. I suppose she destroyed them as received, or on her removal from place to place.

Now, thirty-three years after they were returned to me, I have been looking through the few letters of mine that still remain, mostly belonging, it is clear, to the years 1885 or 1886. But the very earliest, when I still felt her to be almost a stranger, I rewrote and preserved the first rough drafts, which I still possess. These were largely concerned with the comparison of our early solitary lives in South Africa and Australia and our early intellectual adventures in books. I also wrote of my current literary interests, of Hardy or of Hinton. I quote from one of these rough drafts, certainly of early March, 1884:

> I am sorry you find the world 'empty.' If one finds a thing empty, it seems to me, from my own experience, that one hasn't been looking rightly, hasn't been asking that 'right question' which is the 'half of knowledge.' To me, as I seem to begin to know the world, it seems so full — so much to live and care for. I went to New South Wales eight years ago and stayed there four years. During that time I went through that experience so many of us have to go through who find the error of the beliefs we are brought up in, and which you have described in Waldo. During part of that time I was quite alone among the hills, not at all caring about the outside world, but alone with my own thoughts and books and what, I suppose, one must call 'Communion with Nature' — a very real thing indeed. I have never been able to have that since. I can't get a solitude big enough, and even having to go and look for it spoils it. But at least one *knows*.

To return to the actual letters of late date: they are all undated save by day of the week, but it seems clear that Olive had preserved them in their chronological order. Very hastily scrawled, in a large hand, and evidently not always read over before sending, mostly very short, sometimes two or three in one day, few of them seem of the slightest interest now. They are all full of affection, sometimes of longing, always of tender solicitude. I may quote from two or three which tell of moods and ideas I have almost or quite forgotten; the date seems 1885:

> To-morrow is Olive's my birthday! [*sic.*] I feel happy: I want to come and love her; is she happy too? ... I like and agree with that letter of Mrs. Walters'. One sentence especially I feel with. I am sorry it is rare for women to feel such elementary things. I should think they only want educating — that all women must feel like that in their hearts. But if they don't, we'll dig our claws into them, Lion, and torture them deliciously till they do. It was funny that your gentle hesitating sentence, saying that that was how you felt but you didn't know if it was right or wrong (as if there could be any doubt!), made me feel just as I used to

feel years ago. I used to get into such fierce rages all by myself.
I was amused this evening, after your letter came, when I found
myself rolling about on the bed and grinding my teeth, because
always now I feel so very cocksure, so that the opposition of all
the world seems a very little thing, a thing I can well afford to be
magnanimous about. But I have the other feeling underneath
still, and I wouldn't have the least objection to being martyred. ...
I sent you my old Shelley. I thought you might perhaps like to
have it because it is almost the most precious book I have; it is
like a piece of myself. It was to me, to a considerable extent, like
both what Emerson and Goethe were to you. It was always near
to me the whole time I was in Australia. (But I didn't read it
much when I was at Sparkes Creek.) The only time I read it in
England was that week I spent at Weymouth the day or two
before you came to England. When I was at Carcoar and felt so
miserable sometimes because the world seemed so strange and
empty, and used to think I would throw myself from the cliffs at
Sydney, I always used to fancy that that Shelley would have to
come with me. I've got the very best edition of Shelley now, but
I don't *love* it at all. You must keep it and love it a little bit
though it is so old and ugly. [She soon lost it.] I think I'm writing
more than usual — it's because it's her birthday! I mean to look
forward now to coming to see you, and to be at Pevensey if we
can find a nice, cheap place, but we must be very economical.
Pevensey is country, isn't it? and it is nearly spring. Now I am
going to bed and to think about my Olive in bed. Good night,
Sweetheart.

The next letter refers to the time (about 1881) when we each
used to go to the Crystal Palace Saturday Concerts:

I am going to the last Crystal Palace Concert this afternoon
with Louie and Laura, according to an old promise. I think it
will make me rather sad. Do you know that the very last concert
I went to at the Crystal Palace was that one nearly three years ago,
when we both went and heard the Choral Symphony and it did
us good? I wanted so much that we should go again; and be
together. ... I feel so tenderly and lovingly of all this time that I
was with you, more than ever before, I think. Louie sends her love.

Next day:

> We went to the concert. It was very good. I kept feeling as if
> you were there somewhere. They had my favourite Unfinished
> Symphony of Schubert (that I had a sonnet about in *Academy*)
> and part of Wagner's *Parsifal* — the part the Philistines object
> to so strongly because it is a kind of ideal representation of the
> Sacrament. I liked it. Before Louie and Laura came, I found
> your favourite statue — the Death with the outstretched wings
> and bent, covered head. I understand how you felt about it. . . .
> I've just finished writing out that little Australian chapter and
> am sending it. I feel that it is intensely uninteresting, but it is a
> necessary introduction to my idyll [*Kanga Creek*]. If I ever get
> to the end I will revise and shorten it. Send it back. I meant
> whatever charm it had to lie in the harmony between a certain
> emotional relationship and a certain aspect of Nature, but I see
> the Nature part will become little more than background and
> whatever interest it has be chiefly psychological. The young
> schoolmaster is like I was, but only a part of me, like Waldo of
> you. As I now send this chapter, it is scarcely at all revised and
> the style is often very bad — I find it so difficult to give names
> that satisfy me to people and places. I've just read Roden Noel's
> *Thalatta* again to see if your impression that it was crowded with
> similes was right or mine that it wasn't. I find there are only *three*
> or at most four similes, not one of them applied to the sea. The
> fault of the poem is a bewildering profusion of metaphors. His
> poems are best when he reads them himself; he reads splendidly;
> get him to when you see him again. I hope the landlady has got
> back to her normal state of mind now that I've gone.

(This letter was evidently written soon after a visit to Hastings
in April, 1885.)

And in the letter of the following day:

> It is such a wonderfully sweet letter that came just now. I
> haven't been sad, my darling, since I came home. I am quite
> passive, not restless. It was only the half-hour at Croydon that
> I was so miserable; and that wasn't any personal pain that you,
> or anyone, could have taken away, but just everything — my
> life and your life and everything. . . . You were like Psyche who

brought her lamp and looked at her Cupid when he was asleep. But he never came again. [This refers to an incident at Hastings.] Your Soul's wifie must have that letter in bed close to her tonight. It is so sweet. Goodnight, you darling!

Next morning:

How is that throat? I thought it was getting well. Of course I did not think you a coward about it. . . . I think Roden Noel only writes like that because he wants to see you a good deal. Didn't you say he used to call every day? Get strong, my sweet Lion!

Her reply is dated April 26, 1885, and in it she writes:

You oughtn't to have been sad then at Croydon. You were so sweet and loving to me and made such little things so beautiful by being so loving about them.

And in a second letter later the same day:

Just going to bed, my darling, my darling, you aren't going to be sad to-night, are you? I want to comfort you. Oh, if there were nothing to divide us! If we might be all in all to each other! If it were possible for one human being to make another human being *quite, quite quite* happy! Then you would always be so happy.

And next day she wrote:

My Soul's wifie, what are you doing tonight? Was the concert nice yesterday? All day I have lain still, feeling spent, but this morning I worked a little. I am going to bed now. You looked so sweet on Thursday night, so beautiful. Don't you think you're getting more beautiful than you need to be?

All these actions and reactions of emotion in youth, they seem foolish from afar, but they spring from the depth and they leave an impress which only death can efface.

Though in the published volume of Olive's *Letters*, many extracts from those to me are given, I may perhaps now give a few further fragments, early and late, having a more intimately personal reference to myself. Even before the end of 1884 we were living in an atmosphere of familiar nearness, and in November of that year, when ill in bed, she wrote: 'I am not sure as to where you begin and I end.' A little later, when she had been reading my Australian diary in which I had put down that perhaps some-one some day would read it, and understand it, and love me (Olive is still, more than half a century after it was written, the only person who has read it), she writes:

> And then I was living just like you on a lonely farm, and at night when my work was over going out to walk under the willow trees or on the dam walls and I used to think: 'One day I *must* find him.'

And again, after reading some of my early sonnets:

> I think it is the peculiarity of yourself and of all that belongs to you, that you unfold on acquaintance; it unfolds; voice, manner, everything unfolds, and shows more than one ever thought of. You are a kind of sweet surprise. Take great care of the sonnets. All I have seen ought to be published [forty years later they appeared as a volume], except 'Life and Love.' That isn't like you and has not the strength which nothing else of you lacks, the strength shewn most in your critical power and in your tenderness. I think you are strongest where you are tenderest.

A year later we had grown very close to each other. On the 19th June, 1885, she wrote:

> My Havelock, I want you, I *need you*. In some ways I need you more than ever before. You are my family to me and fill up that deep part of my heart that if it were empty would make life all sad. Only what saddens me is that I feel as if you wanted what it's not in my power to give anyone now, something so much less precious than what I give you. If I were in your place I should feel just as you do. But I shouldn't be so sweet and glorious as you are.

And three days later: 'My darling, darling comrade, what would I do without you?' Yet again three days afterwards: 'I feel so clingingly tender to you — the one soul that meets mine and touches it. [George] Moore came after Philip [Marston] and Mackenzie [later Lord Amulree] were gone. Oh, Henry, how much closer you are to me than anyone!'

After a leap of four years and after much emotional turmoil in which several men and women were mingled, when about to return to South Africa, she still writes (Sept. 3, 1889): 'Fancy, when I think of leaving England the thing I mind most leaving is you. Isn't human affection a funny thing!'

A year later she ends a letter about Dürer from her cottage in Matjesfontein: 'I wish I could see you, my brother, my dear one, who has loved me more truly and faithfully than anyone.'

And in January, 1906, some fifteen years after we were both married, she wrote from South Africa: 'I believe if I heard you were dangerously ill, I should start off to England at once, if I had to borrow the money and know I should likely die on the way.'

Part VI

VI

I<small>T WAS</small> about the year 1887 that I first met
Edith Lees. The Fellowship of the New Life had then been in
existence three or four years. Percival Chubb was still its leading
spirit in Thomas Davidson's absence, but my active participation
had diminished. I had come to realise the inevitable limitations
of the movement, though my interest and my sympathy remained. When I met Chubb from time to time in the luncheon
hour, and walked back along Whitehall with him to his room at
the Local Government Board, he would tell me of the Fellowship's
movements. Of late he had frequently mentioned with much satisfaction the name of Edith Lees, which I thus heard for the first
time, as a helpful and active assistant in the secretarial work. He
had met her, as I later understood, at Stopford Brooke's house,
and had speedily interested her in the ideas of the Fellowship, for
which she was prepared by recent practical work in the London
slums with her friends, Stopford Brooke's daughters.

I still went to the Fellowship's meetings from time to time and

I rarely failed to join in its occasional excursions into the country. It was on one of these that I first saw Edith Lees. She, it appears, asked Chubb who that man was. 'That is Havelock Ellis,' he replied impressively. But she was not impressed; it seemed to her that my clothes were ill-made, and that was a point on which she always remained sensitive. We were, however, introduced and walked along together for a few minutes, talking of indifferent subjects. She was a small, compact, active person, scarcely five feet in height, with a fine skin, a singularly well-shaped head with curly hair, square powerful hands, very small feet, and — her most conspicuous feature on a first view — large, rather pale blue eyes. I cannot say that the impression she made on me on that occasion was specially sympathetic; it so happens that the dominating feature of her face, the pale blue eyes, is not one that appeals to me, for to me green or grey eyes (I believe because one is drawn to those of one's own type) are the congenial eyes, and I never grew really to admire them, though to many they were peculiarly beautiful and fascinating, 'pools of bluebells,' as one friend wrote after her death, 'between the gold of the furze in flower.' It was always her beautiful voice that most appealed to me, and when I came to know her more intimately, the lovely expressiveness of her eloquent underlip, as I used to call it. On her side, as I say, the impression was also not specially favourable, if not indeed unfavourable. It so happened that, in the course of our walk through a remote district, we came upon a little chapel which we entered. In a playful mood I began to toll the bell. This, it appears, rather jarred on her serious humour — more serious than in later life — and she regarded it as a feeble joke in bad taste. We had no further conversation that I recall. Indeed, during the next two or three years I came little in personal contact with her. I remember once going up to shake hands with her just before a meeting of the Fellowship of which she became the secretary in 1889, but nothing more. No doubt I was drifting farther and farther away from the Fellowship.

Probably I should never have come into close touch with her if it had not been for one of those strange coincidences which sometimes determine the whole current of our lives.

Early in 1890, my first book, *The New Spirit*, then just published, was presented to Edith by a man (Lawrence), a friend of hers who was in the publisher's office, and had a hand in securing its publication, though not personally known to me. She read it when staying on the Norfolk Broads. (I have the copy now, well-worn and much marked, with 'Edith M. O. Lees, March, 1890,' written on the fly-leaf, as she had preserved it during more than a quarter of a century.) She enjoyed it immensely. It seemed a book after her own heart. Only a few weeks before her death, I find that some notes, written to preface a semi-public reading of passages from my books, began with the declaration: 'When many years ago, about twenty-eight, I first read *The New Spirit*, I knew I loved the man who wrote it.' That declaration, and the words of 'eternal comradeship' that follow, are precious to me now, for it enables me to realise how, beneath the failing health, the mental confusion, and sometimes the apparent alienation of these last weeks, her heart still remained unshaken.

In that same year 1890, in late July or early August — and unknown to me, as I was not in touch with her — she started with her faithful servant Ellen Taylor for a walking tour in Cornwall, her first visit to a land in which, it so happened, she was destined to spend part of every year, willingly or unwillingly, for the whole of the rest of her life — almost the half of it. In the course of their walk, after leaving Penzance, on the 13th of August they reached Lamorna, where lived Miss Agnes Jones, who had been in correspondence with Edith, I believe, concerning the Fellowship; Edith called to see her, and was invited to stay for the night.

Now it so happened that that same year, and about the same time, though of course unknown to Edith, I also left London for my first visit to Cornwall. It was not a holiday visit; I had, a year earlier, obtained my medical qualification, and I was now

going to a week's work as *locum tenens* for Doctor Bonar of Probus, near Truro. But I had planned a holiday to follow, and my
old friend, Miss Agnes Jones, who lived at lonely and beautiful
Lamorna, occupying indeed the only good-sized house (built in
part with a view to serve as a chapel) at that spot, had invited me
to spend ten days with her from the 13th of August.

On that fateful 13th of August, shortly after Edith had accepted the invitation to spend the night at Lamorna and had been
shown her room, Miss Jones casually mentioned that she was
expecting Havelock Ellis that afternoon. Thereupon Edith
wavered in her decision to stay. Evidently, notwithstanding *The
New Spirit*, so impressionable was she then and ever since by
directly personal things, the badly tailored and tactless person at
the picnic still outweighed the revelation of the book. She retired
to her room for a quiet consultation with Ellen. A man was coming (so, she used to tell me, she said) whom she disliked, and
would prefer not to meet. Should they push on that same day to
Land's End? It was Ellen who decided the matter. Her feet
were already sore with much walking; she pleaded for a quiet rest
in that comfortable house. Edith agreed, the more readily as it
was not easy to reject the accepted invitation. *Jacta est alea.* A
servant's sore feet changed the whole course of my life.

Late that afternoon, Edith saw a figure in a professional silk
hat, bag in hand, and wearing (so at least she always asserted) a
torn mackintosh, walk up the path to the house after following
her own track from Penzance. My recollection of the evening,
though pleasant, is vague. I only know that we speedily fell into
a tone of sincerity and intimacy. That was certainly Edith's doing. She always penetrated swiftly to realities, and was herself so
real, and her sincerity so transparent, that those she spoke with,
men or women, seldom failed to respond, and often uttered the
thing that they had never confided to any before. What we talked
of I cannot remember, but evidently among other things Edith
told of her old physician, Doctor Birch, and of her trust in his in-

sight, for the one remark of the evening I can recall came from Miss Jones, with whom I sat alone for a short time after Edith had gone to her room. 'What an extraordinary faith,' she remarked with a whimsical smile, 'some people have in their doctors!'

My memories are just as vague, as pleasantly vague, concerning the next day. With Miss Jones I accompanied the two walking tourists as far as Miss Jones's strength permitted, along the coast-guards' path as it winds through the varied and lovely little bays, towards Land's End. No fragment of the conversation remains, only the reminiscence of a pleasant feeling of association, the germs of comradeship were beginning to arise. The lithe and sturdy little figure passed on with knapsack on back, and the stout staff, as long as herself ('the little lady with the big stick,' the people called her), she long afterwards used. I now wandered about alone in the exquisite atmosphere of Lamorna, so suggestive of Turner, who must surely have known it. I lay on the cliffs and sometimes saw the young foxes playing together not far off. At night in bed in the loft of the house I could look over at sea as far as the twinkling light of Eddystone. But no more definite memories remain of that week. One picture alone stands out, not of Lamorna, against the background.

I had gone across the Cornish peninsula, for the day, on my first visit to Saint Ives. On the same day Edith also chanced to reach for the first time the town with which we were destined to be associated through so many years. I can no longer recall whether we had appointed a meeting at Saint Ives. It is possible. It is also possible that I had reckoned on the chance of meeting her there on that day. But so far as memory serves, perhaps rightly serves, the meeting which actually took place was the joyous outcome of unexpected good fortune. I was passing through the narrow old street which leads to the ocean side of the town at Porthmeor when her quick eyes caught sight of me from the recesses of a cobbler's little shop. She had gone in to have her boots mended on the spot — a characteristic proceeding — and was waiting in her stockinged feet. She ran out instantly in stockinged feet and I heard behind me her clear, eager, beautiful voice — the voice which, as more than one friend noted with astonishment, retained all its qualities, through ill-health and exhaustion, to the end. We entered the shop together and waited for the cobbler to finish. Then we rambled on to Porthmeor and along the beach. Our conversation, though impersonal, was now more intimate; at Lamorna Miss Jones had nearly always been of the party, and here we were alone together, for Ellen could be left to trudge in our wake. We exchanged views on marriage and they proved congenial. I can no longer remember what I said, but I know that in her mind some of the things then said always remained. We were beginning to be friends.

I accompanied her along the Carbis Bay and Lelant coast as far as the Hayle Ferry, for she was going on to spend the night at Gwithian, finding lodgings in a little cottage occupied by two old sisters of whose quaint proceedings she ever after delighted to tell. I stood desolately alone and watched the ferryboat cross, and the two figures receding in the distance over the towans. It is strange, but, through all the years I have lived so close to that ferry, I never once passed across it to Hayle. Only at last, less than a year ago, have I watched the ferryboat from the Hayle side, with tender thoughts of the old days at my heart, while Edith lay grievously ill in the Hayle Hospital. I shall never cross the ferry to Hayle.

Therewith ended the fateful adventure which might have meant so little and in the end meant so much. Nothing definite had happened. But each of us had come in contact with a real person who seemed to possess the makings of a comrade and friend. Each of us had drawn aside and disregarded that exterior veil over the other, which at first had seemed repellent, and found an attractive person beneath. It was a real and true discovery on each part. Yet, it may well be, our exteriors are also real, and not to be disregarded with impunity. Neither of us ever lost that interior vision of the other; on the contrary, it grew deeper and more fixed with the years. Yet, when the first glow of the new discovery had slowly passed, and intimacy rendered the trivial circumstance of exterior personality more insistent, for both of us the first impression was apt to recur, no one could ever foresee at what moment, to produce again and again a discordant jar with the inner vision, impulsively uttered on the one side, more silently endured on the other. Her ideal man, surprising in a woman so unconventional, and not, in reality, an ideal with which she had the slightest inner congruence, seems always to have been the correct and conventional man of the world, certainly often a charming type. But the type was obviously not realised in me, and again and again when she recognised this fact she resented it. For my part, always a dreamer, reserved and diffident and sensitive, the swift impulsiveness of her actions, her incalculable nervous irritability, caused me often to repeat to myself the saying of Alphonse Daudet, concerning his own charming and accomplished wife, that a literary man's wife should be like a feather bed. But no one could be less like a feather bed than Edith; I was sometimes made to feel that she was more like a little porcupine. That perpetually recurrent external discordance made always a thread of tragedy running through the love of two people who at heart remained, always, lovers and comrades, united in an intimacy of confidence that can be but rarely attained. It must also be said that even the divergence of temperament that in the acute degree jarred was at less degrees of tension even an advantage. Her ever fresh and eager vivacity then became an unalloyed joy to me, and my quiet and tender sympathy brought ease and rest to her. Even during the last terrible winter, when her mind had grown so distracted and she lay in the Convent Home at Hayle, I had but to lie beside her, outside the bedclothes, with my arm across her, and she would slowly and peacefully sink to sleep. 'I am his champagne,' she was in the habit of saying playfully to friends, 'and he is my opium.'

She proceeded on her leisurely walk up the coast to Tintagil and settled for a few weeks at Condoldon near Camelford, in the farmhouse of a Mrs. Cobbledick. She soon found out that there was a slaughterhouse attached to the farm and that the landlady's son was the butcher. She always had a horror of slaughterhouses — even though later she kept pigs, had them killed in the yard, and cut them up herself — and so it seemed a little incongruous when the young butcher made a proposal of marriage to the bright and friendly visitor. When she left, she invited Mrs. Cobbledick and her daughter to stay with her in London. This visit came off not very long after, and some ten years later she narrated its chief incidents, almost exactly as they occurred, in a story included in *My Cornish Neighbours*. She even retained Mrs. Cobbledick's real name in the first version of the story, feeling that it was impossible to improve on it, but this she altered later on my suggestion. It is perhaps the only story in the volume that may be regarded as literally true, though, for that very reason, it is a little too farcical for art.

It was from Condoldon, two or three days after leaving Saint Ives, that Edith first wrote to me. I had not so far written to her. In the little note to 'Dear Mr. Ellis' from 'Yours in haste,' she told me of her whereabouts and added: 'Make your way here if you come, as it is cheap and comfortable and ye fashionable corners are stocked.' Slight as the note was, I carefully preserved it, possibly with some vague premonition of all that the writer of it was one day to become to me. She also — as I have found when examining her private papers since her death — had on her part carefully preserved what may well have been my first letter to her. This was more remarkable, for throughout life it was always her habit to destroy all letters, even with undue haste, on receipt, immediately they had been dealt with. Exceptions to this rule were only made in the case of three or four rare and special people very close to her heart, of whom I was the only man. This note addressed to 'Dear Edith Lees,' is dated the 15th of October, when she had returned to town, and invites her to visit me and my sister: 'Will you not come some day, before long — when Satan can find no worse mischief for your energetic feet to do — and narrate what women can do at Tintagil, and the rest? ('What women can do' was the title of a lecture she was giving in these days.) But of this first meeting in London I have no recollection.

At that time, as I have told, I was living a full, active, and varied life to an extent I had never before lived and rarely since. My meeting with Edith was the climax of many new, absorbing, and sometimes agitating experiences, though at the time it seemed a calm and peaceful climax, scarcely indeed as yet a climax at all. It was in September of that year, soon after the return from Lamorna, that my sister Louie and I left Redhill, where my mother had died, and took a house in Saint Mary's Terrace, Paddington, where I had a large sitting-room of my own, to use as a study and for the reception of visitors. It was the first time I had lived in so central a part of London and my active interests in life were thus fostered and increased. My heart remained free, though perhaps not altogether contentedly free. Olive Schreiner, whom I had loved and worshipped for seven years, was now in South Africa and I had become resigned to the fact, I had long known, that we were never to be more than affectionate friends.

Edith used to run into my rooms from time to time — usually, no doubt, by arrangement — in her swift, impulsive way, always very busy, generally in a hurry, yet often staying much longer than she had declared it possible for her to stay. I never went to her rooms in Wigmore Street. But on rare occasions we would meet in town, usually to go to a concert or a music-hall together. There was, at first, no approach towards intimacy, and I cannot recall that any thought of love arose. The relation was one of pleasant comradeship with an energetic and much-alive woman who, as I soon began to realise, had a sort of genius for friendship. She was constantly referring to dear friends by their Christian names, in a casual and familiar way, and there were so many of them that it was long before I could distinguish them and fit them in their right places.

The first approach to real confidence came from her side. One day she burst into my study, and for no obvious reason and with few preliminaries, told me how she was, or had been, in love with one of the leading spirits of the New Fellowship, a friend of my own, who had, however, shown no recognition of this attraction, or experienced any corresponding attraction, and had now passed out of her life, having left England altogether. This man, I may note, was the only man she had ever experienced any such attraction to. There were several men in love with her, for some of whom she felt real friendship, and she had had numerous offers of marriage, but her own feelings were not involved. Whatever passionate attractions she had experienced were for women. How I responded to that confidence I am unable to recall. But gradually a certain degree of intimacy developed, without any ardour of absorption, and, so far at all events as I am concerned, no conscious anticipation of deeper love ahead. It seemed simply the natural growth of a sympathetic comradeship.

She often referred to various episodes of her past life. She was honest and frank, there was nothing she sought to withhold. But I scarcely think that then, or indeed ever, I showed much inquisitive eagerness to question her. When I first began to know Olive Schreiner, I had carefully formed with her help a complete and orderly picture of her earlier life. I never at any time felt a similar impulse in regard to Edith. Perhaps the very fact that she told me, and was ready to tell me, so much made me feel that here was an open book ever before me which I could turn to when I wished with no need to read it through in order. The result is that it is not possible to me, even today, to narrate accurately the connected course of her life before I knew her, though she has often talked of its phases and vividly narrated various incidents. The only note I ever made was of her remarkable ancestry.

The main facts are clear. Edith Mary Oldham, as she was

christened, was born on the 9th of March, 1861, at Newton in Cheshire, the only child of Samuel Oldham Lees, landed propri- etor, and Mary Laetitia Bancroft, his wife. The Lees family were thoroughly Lancashire in type and character; the Bancrofts, who belonged to Mottram in Cheshire, were different. It was through the Bancrofts that Edith acquired those vivacious qualities which made so many people regard her as Celtic. She was frequently supposed to be Irish, which always pleased her (she used to say her soul was Irish), but I would playfully tell her that if she was Celtic she must be Welsh, and that always displeased her. There is commonly supposed, however, to be much ancient Celtic blood in Cheshire, mixed with Anglo-Frisian (Beddoes states), and this must have been the source of temperamental traits which were distinct from the Lancashire type, and still more from that of the average Anglo-Saxon. The ancestral traits which the child of these stocks inherited were her destiny. Her mother, who died shortly after the birth of her only child, was, as all who knew her declared, a woman of singular sweetness and charm, greatly loved. I can well believe it, for her sister remains today in old age a charmingly fresh and delightful person, and has always been much attached to the child of the beloved Mary. The young wife met with an accident to her head during pregnancy and, whether or not on this account, her little daughter was born prematurely at seven months. It was doubtless a fact of much significance, for she remained in some degree undeveloped, in temperament as well as physically something of a child, and with the undue nervous sensitiveness and susceptibility of one whose textures had never had the chance of acquiring completely normal powers of resist- ance to noxious influences. Her organism always reacted too quickly and for the most part excessively; like a child she re- sponded to very small doses of most drugs; she was apt to catch any disease that was about and to suffer from it severely; at the same time she had marvellous powers of recuperation and nearly always recovered more rapidly than her doctors expected; even in her last illness she seemed to be rallying wonderfully almost to the sudden end. Notwithstanding her delicacy she was not only muscularly strong ('a pocket Hercules,' an old friend once called her), but there were sturdy elements in her, derived from the robust, big, long-lived yeomen of Cheshire which the Bancrofts seem to have been, though several of her uncles — children of an austere father — were regarded as ne'er-do-wells. She used to speak of the peasant's blood in her — though I judge the Bancrofts to have been of a well-to-do class — and one felt that there was an element of that kind, a beneficial element in relation to the other elements at the basis of her constitution. Her mother, whom she had never known, she worshipped throughout her life, and to the end there was always a large portrait of her mother over her desk.

In 1898, Edith met a lady who had known her mother: 'She says I'm like my mother in eyes and hair and wit and jollity, and you should see her face when she speaks of her! Everyone loved that woman.' Towards her father her feelings were much more like hate, although with the years she had learnt to understand him better. The Lees family of Ashton-under-Lyne in Lancashire scarcely possessed the calm solidity which seems to have marked the Bancrofts, but possessed extraordinary vigour and energy. Edith's great-grandfather, Oldham Lees, was evidently a remarkable man, self-made, miserly, hard, tyrannical, but very kind to animals, so that he would think nothing of sitting up all night with a sick horse! He acquired much wealth, leaving thirty thousand pounds to charities and public purposes, and twenty thousand pounds to his grandson, Samuel, Edith's father. Silas, his son and Edith's grandfather, was, she told me, a drunken collier who would chase his wife round the room with a carving-knife.

His son Samuel, Edith's father, who inherited much of his grandfather's money, failed to inherit the energy his father had recklessly flung away. He was sent to the University and acquired intellectual tastes with the love of books. He had no ability to make money, and though he plunged into various business schemes they were disastrous failures. It seems to have been in connection with some such scheme that he ultimately went to America, where he died, a fate his daughter narrowly escaped forty years later. The germs of morbidity in the father and the grandfather became intensified in the son. He was highly eccentric in some of his ways and habits, of angular disposition, nervous, hypochondriacal, fastidious, irritable, cruel, one of those tortured persons who cannot help torturing others. It was in this way that he tortured his daughter. He seems to have been quite unable to understand children, especially such a peculiar, sensitive, high-spirited child as his own. He tried to break her spirit by force and punishment, but the very opposite effect was produced. Her individuality was heightened by opposition.

At the same time he aroused in her a deep resentment, not only against himself, but to some extent against all men, which persisted through the greater part of life, so that the mere appearance of harshness towards her in a man, the faintest approach to the exercise of any control, never ceased to arouse in her quite automatically the fiercest revolt. ('Do meet me at Euston,' I find in a note written seven years after marriage, 'for I long for a sight of you — a man who has never bossed me. I should *kill* a man who ordered my body and soul about as if it were a soup ladle.') She always wished to write about the wrongs done to children, and in her last imaginative book, *Love-Acre*, she at length introduced some of her own early feelings.

It is probable that she was not altogether just to her father's memory; she had suffered too much to be just. But her suffering was not due entirely, and not even chiefly, to her father. He had married again. This second wife was apparently a woman of quite ordinary intelligence and character, but she was just as unable as her husband to be lovable or to love and comfort the wayward and sensitive child entrusted to her care. She fell into the traditional part of the stepmother. The violence of the father was supplemented by the still more cutting sneers of the stepmother. She died only a few years before Edith herself, but during all our married life they only met once, and then only by chance. Her stepmother on this occasion expressed a wish for a reconciliation, but to this approach, Edith, though she had long ceased to feel hostility, could only imperfectly respond. She was throughout life the first to seek to make up a quarrel, and the fact that even after the lapse of forty years she was still unable to take up a friendly relationship with her stepmother shows how deeply the sufferings of her childhood had entered into her soul.

Yet I am not prepared to say that her sufferings were all due to her father and her stepmother, lamentable as was their lack of comprehending love, and pathetic as it was that a child so rarely fitted to experience both joy and pain should have had so little of the one and so much of the other. Edith herself possessed not only an element of the beautiful charm and sweetness of her mother, but also something of the tortured and torturing nature of her father, while her power of cutting and reckless sarcasm, when roused, probably far exceeded her stepmother's. In childhood, as often in later life, suffering, and even tragedy, lay for her inevitably in her own nature and the equally inevitable reactions of that nature to the external world.

The child seems to have been sent for considerable periods to relatives, especially a grandmother, but here also, I gather, she received little love or tenderness, and suffered from neglect, even from improper and insufficient food. At about the age of twelve her father put her into a convent-school at Manchester. The nuns were gentle and kind; the ardent and wistful child gained her first glimpse of peace and joy. Of course the natural result followed: she wanted to become a Catholic and be a nun. She told her father so. The agnostic disciple of Tyndall was horrified at this logical result of his own action, and hastened to remove his daughter from the convent at once. The wish to be a Catholic speedily died out, but Edith retained an affection for nuns, and she always regarded the Roman Catholic Church as the only possible form of Christianity; when towards the end of her life it was necessary to take her, a little against her will, to a hospital, the only one available chanced to be attached to a convent, and I always remember how warmly and sweetly she greeted the sisters who admitted her.

To avoid making the same mistake again, her father now placed her in a school near London kept by a German lady of freethinking opinions, a Madame Thesma, clever, though not specially judicious. Here Edith made two or three good friends, for life, but the education was mostly of the ordinary perfunctory sort then accorded to middle-class girls, and, quick and clever as she was, I do not suppose that she took the slightest interest in it. If she acquired anything at school it was a love of literature, for in that the German schoolmistress was an enthusiast, and Edith was an apt pupil. Her much-scored copy of Shakespeare, which I now cherish, dates from those days. Madame Thesma seems also to have encouraged the attempts of her pupils to act Shakespeare, especially *Romeo and Juliet*. Here Edith, with her strong aptitude for drama and mimicry, seems to have been the leader, playing the chief male parts while the chief female parts were taken by a schoolfellow who afterwards became a successful and rather noted actress, Aida Jenoure. At this period, also, she had an enthusiastic admiration for Byron, and was much pleased to be thought to resemble him in appearance. Whatever her proficiency in ordinary school tasks — and I cannot believe that it was considerable — Edith's personality and ability much impressed her schoolmistress who vaguely prophesied a great future.

I think that it was not till some years after the time when Edith left school that her father died, on a visit to America, in Salt Lake City. She lived with her grandmother, going out daily to teach pupils, and leading a rather hard and energetic life with no home comforts. It must have been about that time, however, that a young local doctor fell in love with her and wished to marry her. Nothing came of this, I forget why, but the young doctor was the first of a series of admirers, who met with no success.

I believe that it was at the age of twenty-one that a sum of money — one hundred pounds, I think — fell due to her. It seemed to her an inexhaustible sum, and with her large ideas and lavish generosity she planned expensive presents for everybody, so that in a very short time the money was more than all expended. That was characteristic of an attitude towards money which she never quite outgrew, and in the end, indeed, it was exhibited afresh on a larger scale. She could scarcely have been much older when she left the North to come to London to start a girl's school at Sydenham. I have a copy of the very correct and businesslike prospectus of this school. I know nothing of her life as a schoolmistress — a position in which it is not easy to imagine her unless one remembers that in early life she was much more severely strenuous and austere than on the surface she seemed in later life; for it somehow happened that she talked little about it, although casually she often referred familiarly to 'Girton House.' In some respects I think she was more of a success than I had been when circumstances thrust me into the position of youthful headmaster of a so-called grammar school, and I know that on one at least of her pupils, who has achieved high success in her own special line, she had a lifelong and gratefully remembered influence. But the final outcome seems in her case to have been more disastrous. I imagine that she plunged into this new scheme — as she plunged into every new scheme to the end — with a sanguine enthusiasm, a reckless expenditure of energy, a lavish thoroughness, which anticipated speedy and complete success. Evidently she had an arduous struggle with worries, anxieties, and overwork, while at the same time her mind was developing a restless intellectual activity. In 1884, when at Girton House she took out her ticket (which she preserved and used to the end) for the British Museum Reading Room, and was giving lectures at the Crystal Palace School of Art on Mrs. Browning's *Aurora Leigh,* and similar subjects.

Finally, after two or three years, I suppose, she found herself hopelessly in debt and she suffered a serious nervous breakdown. Then two friends arose to save her, friends whom she ever after tenderly and reverently loved. The first was a sweet and motherly old lady of means, living at Forest Hill, Mrs. Drake, who heard of Edith's troubles and spontaneously came forward to tide her over the period of financial anxiety. Edith came to speak of Mrs. Drake as a 'second mother,' always referring to her as 'the mother,' and to regard her with affection until the old lady died at an advanced age only a year or two before herself. The other friend was Honor Brooke, the eldest daughter of the Reverend Stopford Brooke. I do not know how they met, but I know that Miss Brooke, with a self-sacrificing devotion and skill that called out Edith's deep love, nursed her back to health, brought her into cheerful and cultured society — opening to her the charming refinements of the Brookes' house in Manchester Square, a notable intellectual centre — and turned her renascent energies into channels of social work in the slums.

But recovery was not speedy, even with the aid of the wise old Harley Street physician, Birch, who understood her so well, and Edith often referred to the tortures she endured when occupying a little garret near Manchester Square. In that breakdown she suffered much from a horror of being alone, especially at night — she desired someone within call, though not in the same room — a horror which she felt, indeed, in more or less degree all through life, and when ill or rundown she was always liable to fits of nervous terror in the early morning when it was imperative for her to have some loved person to whom she could cling convulsively and be unashamed of her weakness; she specially dreaded my absence at such times, for I was the person with whom she could be most completely herself. There were some people to whom she seemed to be as brave as a lion. But that appearance covered an abyss of terrors of all kinds. She learnt to take life gaily, but life was often a great struggle. 'Courage is a habit,' she would say aloud, as an injunction to herself when faced by some difficult duty. How often have I heard her! It was a saying she had learnt from Stopford Brooke.

Stopford Brooke's house in Manchester Square, I have said, was now freely open to her. Her work in the slums was here supplemented by the enlarging and refining influence of contact with the stream of notable personages in art and literature, prominent politicians, active social reformers, which entered this genial and liberal-minded preacher's door. It was to her not only a house of comfort, of physical and spiritual edification; it was here, as already mentioned, that she met Percival Chubb and so was put onto the path which henceforth she followed to the end.

To return to my narrative: We had begun to feel a personal, though not yet clearly defined, relationship growing up between us. It grew up the more easily and imperceptibly because, while she had no intimate men friends, I had no intimate women friends, now that Olive Schreiner was in South Africa, scarcely indeed any woman friend who was more than an acquaintance. It was natural, therefore, that we should go together to attractions that drew us both, notably to concerts, music-halls, and to Ibsen's plays which were just beginning to be performed in London; less often, I think, to see pictures — in which she was always less eagerly interested than I was, although ever deeply moved by the beauty of the actual world — and never, I am quite sure, to scientific meetings. Occasionally we went to a restaurant together. One of the earliest of these occasions she never forgot, for she used to say, half playfully, that I had broken down her resistance to luxury by giving her lager beer at lunch in a restaurant near Oxford Circus and then taking her to Bussard's for an ice. She was also half serious, however absurd it may appear.

I was myself too absorbed in other interests, not to say too destitute of means, ever to lead either myself or anyone else into paths of luxury, but I was not altogether indifferent. Edith had hitherto been both austere and indifferent with regard to eating and drinking. The early hardness of her life had been succeeded by a long period of idealistic endeavour which left no thought for such needs as other than mere necessities. When at last her attention was called to the subject in the early Fellowship days, especially when in close touch with a group of ascetic Russian idealists, the noble Frey and others, she was led to adopt a vegetarian diet with a predominance of fruit and nuts; it was a diet at that time favoured by many ardent social reformers, and she preached it to her friends with all her characteristic conviction. She had largely given it up before I began to know her well, but she used to tell how some years later she found a friend practising it and asked her who had persuaded her to adopt such a diet. 'Why, you did!' replied her aggrieved friend. But a change slowly came over Edith's tastes in this matter. As time went on, though still able to live simply, she cared more for good food, for wines and liqueurs, more than was at any time the case with me; when she travelled, especially in France, she would note methods of cooking that appealed to her, she would learn from accomplished friends, and she slowly trained Priscilla, the Cornish maid who was with us longest, into an admirable cook. It was by no means merely a matter of luxury. With her energetic yet nervous and easily exhausted constitution, nothing made so much difference as food and wine. This was so even in illness and, sometimes against medical advice, rump steak and a glass of Burgundy proved more beneficial than slops; and a lobster salad, as she used herself to say, was always more digestible than milk. But in our early days together the influence of the old habit was still strong and we were little concerned with these things of the table.

Our talk was much more of the fundamental problems of mar-

riage. Concerning the economic basis of the relations between
men and women, we had, I think, already begun to speak as we
walked along the beach at Porthmeor. Our opinions on that
point were from the first identical. We both alike firmly believed
that the social equality of men and women should involve an
economic equality in marriage, each partner thus preserving independence. Practically, moreover, in our own case, should the
question of marriage arise, we found that this was the only basis
possible, for we each had an income of about the same size —
in my case earned, in hers unearned — and sufficient only for one
person in our own walk of life, so that it would not have been
possible for me to support her. We were prepared, in a playful
yet serious spirit — in which she took the initiative — to be most
exact and thorough in our division of expenses, and she used to
declare, whether or not with truth, that we divided the cost of
the wedding-ring, which we went together to Hatton Garden to
buy. That ring she wore to the end, even when we seemed to be
separated. To the end also, as throughout, she insisted on her
freedom and independence, sometimes indeed exaggerating it,
alike in fact and in statement. The principle seems a sound one,
and I should hesitate to admit that my faith in it has wavered.
Yet I cannot say that in our case it proved a success. In practice
it gave greater scope to her than to me, because of her greater
practical energy, of her more impetuous impulse and swifter decision. It enabled her to live out her own life in great freedom, and
therein I often benefited, but it also led her into many mistakes
from which I also, and sometimes chiefly, suffered. Again and
again, it would happen that, on her own initiative, with all the
ardent precipitancy of her nature, she would take up a new
scheme, without waiting even a day to consult me, and I could
scarcely refuse, even when she left me free to refuse, to take up
my share of all the burden, which sometimes proved grievous, for
she was ever sanguine and never able to count all the cost of any
undertaking.

Edith Lees

A photograph taken a few months before her marriage to Havelock Ellis

The result was that during the whole of our married life we were rarely free from some degree of worry over money, and the fact that we were both honourable and scrupulous in money affairs, and both belonged to families which had always lived within their means, made this still less easy to bear. During the first half or more of our life together the strain was about fairly divided, though it was she rather than I who determined the level of our expenses. But during later years not only were her frequent serious illnesses a source of expense, but after she had given up farming and lecturing, novels and plays seemed to be holding out promises of success, and, with her usual eager confidence, she anticipated and outran these prospects, so that while her income increased her expenses still more increased. Thus it came about that all the unused balance of my income, which was also beginning to increase, was always transferred to her, and my share of the expenses was henceforth constantly supplemented by gifts and, in every emergency, a loan. These loans were always increasing to the end, and she always meant to repay; I am sure, indeed, that there was never a moment — for death came too suddenly for her to realise it — when she doubted she would and could repay them. She never realised that all she left behind her would not even suffice to settle the current bills of tradesmen she had left unpaid, to say nothing of loans. In these ways it came about that throughout our life together she was able in perfect good faith to declare emphatically that we were living in accordance with the principle of complete economic independence of husband and wife, while yet the reality was quite otherwise, and though, as I continue to affirm, the principle holds good, in our particular case a more old-fashioned principle would have worked out more happily.

At the same time it must not be supposed that the financial difficulties which so often worried us were due to any careless or even, one may say, unbusinesslike habits in Edith's way of carrying out the joint functions she so largely arrogated. She was a good household manager and organiser; by family tradition, as she would say, 'house-proud' — no one could make a room look charming with less expenditure of money or efforts or in a shorter space of time — and she was wonderfully successful in the difficult task of drawing the best out of servants and often of winning their attachment; her quick and alert mind was singularly apt to drive a good bargain, though she would often give more than she promised; she never failed in doing well whatever she took in hand, so long as will and strength remained to carry it through; she impressed even business people as a singularly good woman of business. She was careful and methodical in her accounts, always balanced the results of each undertaking separately, to show profits and losses, and for many years kept a minute daily record of the smallest expenses — a task I have never once in my life attempted. The fatal lack seems to have been in the eager impulsiveness of spirit which could seldom see more than one side of a project and failed in the foresight necessary to measure the path to the desired goal. Therein I could have been helpful, had she been willing — which was rarely, as she had no faith in my business qualities — to accept a more cautious estimate of possibilities.

There was another essential point we discussed: the legal form and ceremony of marriage. On that point also we were at one, after we had adjusted our slightly different points of view. We neither of us felt any personal need for an ecclesiastical sanction of marriage. That was a standpoint, common to both of us, which we took for granted. I do not even know how or when she had reached it, but I think it may be regarded as implicitly assumed, although not explicitly stated, in the principles of the New Fellowship. It is true that, at the moment when our friendship began to become more intimate than mere friendship, she was for a short time troubled at the possibility of a too cheap or merely temporary relationship and that (as I find by our correspondence)

I had at first said that I thought marriage good neither for her nor for me. I never repeated the remark. We both regarded marriage as sacred and inviolable, but as the primary concern of the two persons who entered on that union, though also (as she at the time specially insisted) a matter that concerned the State. But it is one thing to cherish faith in an abstract social creed, and quite another to propose to carry it into immediate practice. On that point also we were, from the first, at one. I had never proposed to myself a free marriage union as a practical possibility, and I certainly should not have proposed it to her. The alternative could only be between an entirely private intimacy — then a form of sexual union opposed to her feelings and ideas — and a recognised legal union. We were both in relation of friendship — though quite independently — with Karl Marx's brilliant and attractive daughter, Eleanor, who had formed a free and open union with Doctor Aveling, and I expect that that union, which later on ended tragically, hardly seemed to us an enticing example to follow. In any case, we accepted, without dispute on either side, the practical necessity of marriage. At the same time our convictions on marriage were by no means merely platonic. Edith was always prepared to uphold those who thought it right to reject the legal form of marriage. A woman, indeed, who became one of her chief friends and mine, had maintained this position, in spite of her husband's entreaties to make the union legal, although, it is true, without admitting the facts to the world. In our own case, also, we both felt, as the years went on, with increasing conviction, that the difficult path of life might have been in some ways easier to us if we had refrained from placing on ourselves the arbitrary fetters of law which it is now so hard for those who love each other tenderly to have struck off, even when there may be good reasons for legal independence.

As our resolve to marry thus began to take definite shape, there was another yet more intimate question to discuss: the question of parentage. This also was a question over which I cannot recall that we had the slightest dispute, though considerable discussion, for we were at first much in doubt. At that time the problems of eugenics had hardly come to the front, and I had taken no active interest in them. But (as my book on the criminal shows) I regarded heredity as a matter of serious concern and fully realised the responsibilities of parenthood, while at the same time I had no keen anxiety for parentage, even apart from the fact that I scarcely felt myself in the economic position to become a father. Edith also, at that time, although always sensitive to the beauty of motherhood, seems to have had no overpowering desire for a child. We were, therefore, able to discuss the matter with fair impartiality, as a question of her health and ancestry, since my heredity was as nearly as possible perfect, and my health — with due allowance for an intellectual worker's nervous hyperæsthesia — would pass all ordinary tests. In resolving this difficulty we were both much influenced by the opinion of her Harley Street physician, Doctor Birch. None had ever studied her so thoroughly and so minutely, or understood her so well as this clever old doctor. Up to her death she would still take at times, and with benefit, a drug he had prescribed. I believe that she first came into his hands after her breakdown at Sydenham a few years before I met her, and it was then that his very thorough examination took place. 'I study you,' he said, 'as I study the Bible,' and he was a religious old man. Although there was evidently no hint of indecorum, there was (before psychoanalytic days) something rather unconventional in such minute study of a patient; and that he realised this I judge by a question he asked her about my attitude to him when she told him of her approaching marriage. She had not gone to consult him about the advisability of marriage; he had told her his opinion on that point before any question of marriage had arisen.

That opinion was that she ought not to marry, but that if she should marry she certainly ought not to have children. At the same time he had told her that he believed she would never find

her way to the lunatic asylum, but that if she were ever to enter
it she would never come out again. That saying was often sadly
in my mind during the last tragic months of her life. So also was
a remark made earlier by Mrs. James Hinton's daughter, Margaret, who sometimes went to Bethlem Hospital to play the piano
to the women patients, and when asked what they were like replied that some of them were 'like that Miss Lees.' Those words,
which I never repeated, clung to my mind, and some thirty years
later there actually was, at one moment, a question whether
'that Miss Lees' should be taken to Bethlem.

We decided to accept Birch's advice against children, and there
was no protest on Edith's part. But, it must be added, she always disliked the idea of any kind of what seemed to her unnatural union, and that dislike soon became stronger and had a
significant bearing on our relationship. Many years later, when
it was too late to reverse the decision against maternity without
grave risks, she sometimes regretted it. But, much as I have
sometimes wished that it had seemed possible to risk parentage, I
have not wavered in my belief that the wisest decision was made.
Even if she were physically apt for maternity, and in most respects she certainly was, her inherited nervous instability would
have involved serious risks to herself, and possibly still more to
the child to whom it was passed on, perhaps in an exaggerated
form, through my contribution of nervous excess. Moreover,
while she possessed many maternal aptitudes I doubt whether
she was adapted to be a good mother unless perchance the discipline of maternity trained the abrupt irregularity of her moods.
Much as she liked children, she could not endure them for long,
and it was a sore trial to her to stay long with friends who had
young children; it was only with animals that her patience was
inexhaustible. So that, much as there always is in life to regret, I
am thankful still to feel that, in this matter at all events, what
seemed best to do was done.

That I am here fairly representing the spirit of reasonableness in which I approached marriage is confirmed by a letter which I received in this year of our union from my oldest and nearest friend, Angus Mackay, to whom I had, perhaps first of all, confided my approaching marriage. He had himself married happily a few years earlier. 'I am sure,' he wrote, 'from your account of the matter, that you are making your choice on wise principles — principles too seldom taken into account, and hence the marriages which are failures and the marriages which are humdrum and commonplace. Add the unions founded merely on passion to those made for money or position, and who can wonder at the great and bitter cry of married men and women? Their fate is the outcome of laws which never shall be broken, and the whip with which they are scourged is of their own making.'

It is in my temperament, however passionate beneath the surface — and as Edith used to say 'restless underneath' — to be reasonable and cautious, hesitant in action, not apt to be moved by impulse or to reveal the impulse I feel. But on this or other accounts, I should perhaps say here, there were many to whom I scarcely seemed a desirable husband. Some of Edith's friends, and even of mine, when she announced to them her approaching marriage, exclaimed, actually or in effect: 'That man!' One or two, not indeed speaking from any definite knowledge of me, warned her against the marriage. This must have been a little disconcerting to her. But she was far too true and deep, too independent as well, to be moved by these protests, though, later on, there were moods in which she recalled to me the warnings she had once received.

There was another discovery, I may here remark, which she made in the course of these announcements of her marriage: one or two men friends, with whom she had been good comrades without being in the least in love, had apparently been in love with her. This seems to have been so with William Clarke, the finest journalist of that day in the advanced liberal and democratic camp and a Fabian economist as well. He had been interested almost from the first in the New Fellowship, though he never actually joined it. He knew and admired Thomas Davidson, and when Davidson died he wrote one of his best articles in the *Spectator* (later included in the posthumous volume of his miscellaneous writings) on 'A Modern Wandering Scholar.' I had met him and known him from the day of his first meeting with Davidson when I walked away from the house with him afterwards. From that time he took much interest in me and in my work; in the *Echo*, a few years later, after my first book appeared, he published an article on me as one of the men of the day, the first of that sort I ever received. I, on my side, had invited him to contribute a book on economics to the Contemporary Science Series, though, being a busy journalist, he eventually had to hand this over to his friend, J. A. Hobson. Edith doubtless began to know him when she became secretary of the Fellowship.

Clarke was nearly ten years older, a man of neurotic temperament somewhat like her own; a creature of moods, of profound depressions, of frequent illnesses, with an organism full of toxins, probably with high blood pressure such as she later showed, and dying ultimately of the same disease of diabetes. Their social ideals and aspirations were singularly alike, and held with a like fervour and sincerity. But her temperament was much more buoyant, inspiring, and genial in personal intercourse. It was therefore natural that he should often come and spend hours in her rooms, frequently arriving in the deepest dejection and going away a totally different man. There was no suggestion of love; into her mind at all events the idea had never entered. But when one day she met him in Gray's Inn and gaily announced her approaching marriage, he suddenly changed countenance, she told me, and seemed to have been struck a great blow. From that moment he ceased to seek to meet her, and he avoided me: I believe I never saw and scarcely heard from him again, and he no longer took any friendly interest in my books, though it is not likely that my later books would in any case have appealed to him. Edith heard indirectly, a little later on, that he had been suffering from 'an emotional shock.' He never married, and died ten years later.

It may seem to some that the spirit in which we approached marriage was not that passionate and irresistible spirit of absolute acceptance which seems to them the ideal. Yet we both cherished ideals, and we seriously strove to mould our marriage as near to the ideal as our own natures and the circumstances permitted. It was certainly not a union of unrestrainable passion; I, though I failed yet clearly to realise why, was conscious of no inevitably passionate sexual attraction to her, and she, also without yet clearly realising why, had never felt genuinely passionate sexual attraction for any man. Such preliminary conditions may seem unfavourable in a romantic aspect. Yet in the end they proved, as so many conventionally unpromising conditions in my life have proved, of inestimable value, and I can never be too thankful that I escaped a marriage of romantic illusions. Certainly, I was not a likely subject to fall victim to such a marriage.

The union was thus fundamentally at the outset, what later it became consciously, a union of affectionate comradeship, in which the specific emotions of sex had the smallest part, yet a union, as I was later to learn by experience, able to attain even on that basis a passionate intensity of love. It was scarcely so at the outset, although my letters to her in the early years are full of yearning love and tender solicitude. We were neither of us in our first youth. I was able to look on marriage as an experiment which might, or might not, turn out well. On her part it was, and remained to the end, a unique and profound experience which she never outgrew. Yet, had anything happened to prevent the marriage, it is not likely that either of us would then have suffered from a broken heart. The most passionate letters I wrote her were, as she realised, not written until some years after marriage. I can honestly say that, by a gradual process of increased knowledge and accumulated emotional experience, I am far more in love with her today than twenty-five years ago.

Yet to both of us our marriage seemed then a serious affair, and with the passing of the years it became even more tremendously serious. She, at heart distrustful of her own powers of attraction, would from time to time be assailed by doubts — though such doubts were in conflict with her more rooted convictions — that she was not my fit mate, that I realised this, and that it might be best if we separated in order to enable me to marry someone else. This was never at any moment my desire. Much as each of us suffered through marriage I have never been convinced that our marriage was a mistake. Even if in some respects it might seem a mistake, it has been my belief, deepened rather than diminished, that in the greatest matters of life we cannot safely withdraw from a mistake, but are, rather, called upon to conquer it, and to retrieve that mistake in a yet greater development of life. It would be a sort of blasphemy against life to speak of a relationship which like ours aided great ends as a mistake, even if, after all, it should in a sense prove true that we both died of it at last. Each of us exhibited a constant process of spiritual and intellectual development during the whole of that quarter of a century of close intimacy. My own work in life had been more or less definitely planned before I knew her, yet it was altogether carried out, and to a more triumphant conclusion than at the outset I had ever imagined, during my fellowship with her.

She on her part was developing during all that period, and she only attained the complete adult maturity of her spiritual and intellectual powers a year or two before the end. Though I failed at first to perceive that she was the most difficult woman in the world to marry, I always knew that she was unique, and though there were other qualities I craved from a woman which she could not give, yet those other qualities had their chief value, I always well knew, in supplementing hers and could never replace what

she had to give. She was far more to me than a 'liberal education' to enrich, she was also a constant discipline to fortify. The
presence of her naked and vital spirit moved my more dreaming
and aloof spirit to a realisation of the fundamental facts of living
which has been beyond all estimation. In some respects I am
what she has made of me.

On her part, again, although she, too, craved qualities which
I could not give and which I never grudged her finding in others,
she yet always affirmed, and never denied, that I was the one
person in the world who understood her, and it was on me that
in all moments of difficulty or terror she instinctively called.
That she altogether realised how entirely in this matter my
attitude was the counterpart of her own I do not positively
affirm, nor even that I made great efforts to explain my attitude,
for in such matters I have always held that protestations are
suspect, and even worthless, and that what cannot be divined
must be left. Moreover, in matters of love I have ever been shy
of promises, always so facile, always so meaningless; I can honestly say that my performances excelled my promises. Certainly
it was so in the deep sense with marriage. At the outset it seemed
to me — though never, I think, to her — as possibly only an
experiment. It was an experiment to such an extent that to
many if not most people it might seem no marriage at all. Yet it
was a relationship so deep and so binding, so gripping the heart
by its tenderness, and so compelling the whole being by the
intensity of its spiritual passion, that the thought of any second
relationship of the same kind seemed a sort of sacrilege. It is
probable, however, that this feeling largely rests on the ritual
formality which surrounds marriage and sets it apart, making it
appear a unique relationship. It is always possible for me to
imagine a more or less sexual relationship with another woman
which sprang from a scarcely less deep root, for the varieties of
relationships are infinite. But to repeat in exact detail a relationship, the closest of all, which had seemed and remained unique, to

repeat publicly to another person the old formula of binding words, to place on another hand the same kind of ring, to confer on another the same right to bear the precisely same name before the world — all that, however tenderly I might love the new person, seems to arouse within me a deep repulsion. It may be an artificial feeling, not lying in the essence of things, but only in conventions. Yet it remains.

When I turn to my pocket diary for 1891 and to the letters we wrote to each other at that time — for, unknown to each other, we both preserved probably all of these early letters, though later letters were by both more often destroyed — I can reconstruct much that took place during the months preceding our formal marriage. The letters are fairly numerous, for she went down several times for a few weeks to the little cottage at Carbis Bay (she had taken it in the autumn from a woman artist friend) which later became our first Cornish home, while I during the spring was away for a month with Arthur Symons in Provence and on to Spain, the first of many visits to that country, entering by Barcelona and emerging by San Sebastian. My letters indeed were not usually dated except by the day of the week, and she never preserved the envelopes which might have proved the date; but hers were nearly always carefully dated, as well as sealed when specially private, for, with some ground, she was suspicious of country post offices. I always preserved the envelopes, so that on the whole the letters present a fairly clear and continuous record.

It is with the opening of 1891 that they become increasingly numerous. At first just frank and friendly, she sometimes signed 'Your little comrade Edith,' not dealing with matters of special intimacy, and showing a certain quiet reserve and restraint. As our relations slowly grew closer, this diminished. Notwithstanding her idealistic and high-pitched temperament, with that union of opposites which is found in complex natures there is nothing high-flown or extravagant in these letters. She realises

the grave and serious changes that are going on within her, there
is no overrating either of me or of herself, and she warns me
repeatedly of her 'moods and morbidities,' of which yet indeed I
had seen little. Then, and ever, she felt humbly about herself at
heart, however arrogant and domineering she could be on the
surface, far too proud to let the world guess her humility. In
reply I assured her that I could bear with the morbid — having
perhaps a trace of it in myself — better than with the commonplace.

In June a crisis occurred. During the previous month, while
still signing herself my 'comrade,' marriage already seemed to
be glimmering in the distance, for in that month she wrote
happily to me from Carbis, where she was staying with her perhaps dearest friend of those days, Flo Kneller, a school friend, a
woman of fine intelligence and serious character, happily married, who died not long after in India to Edith's great grief,
'In the long years we shall be able to know each other in trust
and love'; and she added that her idea of marriage was 'the
deepest sympathy possible with all chance for each individual to
remain an individuality.' 'It is the deep cool wells of life that
bring real peace,' she had written in May, 'and I'm glad I've
found you. It is much more likely, Havelock, that you will
sigh one day when your little comrade is in one of her erratic
moods. I'm a queer-grained creature and you are a different
cast of soul — please know how wicked and cross and surly I
am, and like me in spite of it.'

But in June there was for a moment what seemed on the surface
a revulsion. Evidently an inner conflict had been going on, though
I had seen no signs of it. She felt herself drifting into a relationship such as she had never in her life known before; she felt it was
threatening to affect her freedom and independence; she felt, at
the same time, that it was not clear to her whether I viewed that
relationship as seriously and sacredly as she viewed it. So, for
the first time, she wrote me a courageously straightforward

letter in which she set forth her own nature and needs, her inability to accept symbols in place of realities, or a part in place of the whole, and her own ideal of a complete and permanent union of body and soul. She declared that that was the ideal she must remain true to, however romantic and visionary it might possibly seem to me, and that, much as the relationship with me meant, she must renounce it if I was not at one with her on this fundamental point. I was a little hurt at the abrupt and hostile shape assumed by the suppressed conflict which thus suddenly appeared at the surface. At this she was much grieved, and the very next day she wrote me a tender and beautiful letter to explain, and to assure me how near she was: 'I rest in you deep down, but the strangeness and the wonder of things is on me.'

Evidently there really was a certain difference of attitude towards this vital question. I held that an intimate personal relationship need not necessarily be open to the world, that the State was only concerned with it when the question of children arose, and that the formality of marriage should consecrate an existing relationship rather than be set up irrevocably before it could ever be ascertained that a real relationship was possible. She, as she admitted in another letter of about the same date, was in this, as well as in some other matters of belief, more 'old-fashioned.' But the difference was not fundamental. She, with increased knowledge and experience, became less and less 'old-fashioned'; I, while not changing my convictions, became, with the growth of years, more and more tolerant of the 'old-fashioned' view. In a few years' time there was not the slightest difference between our views of marriage. The approximation began and ended with this very letter, and, as I now look back, it seems to me that the letter was in part the dying protest of outgrown traditions, the loss of which still caused her some alarm. The letter from which I now quote was, I believe, called out by her attitude at this time, and was perhaps the most difficult and deliberate letter I ever addressed to her; this is even indicated by the fact that I carefully dated it: June 13, 1891.

We have never needed any explanations before, and that has always seemed so beautiful to me, that we seemed to understand instinctively. And that is why I've never explained things that perhaps needed explaining. This is specially so about Olive. I have never known anyone who was so beautiful and wonderful, or with whom I could be so much myself, and it is true enough that for years to be married to her seemed to me the one thing in the world that I longed for, but that is years ago. We are sweet friends now and always will be; but to speak in the way you do of a 'vital relationship' to her sounds to me very cruel. Because one has loved somebody who did not love one enough to make the deepest human relationship possible — is that a reason why one must always be left alone? I only explain this to show that I am really free in every sense — perhaps freer than you — and that I haven't been so unfair to you as you seem to think. The thing I wanted to tell you about that has been bothering me was this. I had to decide whether it was possible for me to return the passionate love of someone whom I felt a good deal of sympathy with, and even a little passionate towards. She would have left me absolutely free, and it hurt me to have to torture her. But I had no difficulty in deciding; the real, deep, and mutual understanding, which to me is more than passion, wasn't there, and the thought I had constantly in my mind was that my feeling towards you, although I do not feel passionate towards you (as I thought you understood), was one that made any other relationship impossible. — I wonder if you will understand that.

Now I've got to explain what I feel about our relationship to each other — and that will be all! Perhaps the only thing that needs explaining is about the absence of passionate feeling. I have always told you that I felt so restful and content with you that the restless, tormenting passionate feeling wasn't there; and I have seen that you didn't feel passionate towards me, but have said over and over again that you didn't believe in passion. So we are quite equal, and why should we quarrel about it? Let us just be natural with each other — leaving the other feeling to grow up or not, as it will. It is possible to me to come near you and to show you my heart, and it is possible to you to come near me; and (to me at least) that is something so deep and so rare that it makes personal tenderness natural and inevitable — or at all events right.

In reference to marriage: I said (or meant) that I did not think either you or I were the kind of people who could safely tie ourselves legally to anyone; true marriage, as I understand it, is a union of soul and body so close and so firmly established that one feels it will last as long as life lasts. For people to whom that has come to exist as an everyday fact of their lives, then the legal tie may safely follow; but it cannot come beforehand. I have seen so much of unhappy marriages — which all started happily — and I do not think anything on earth could induce me to tie myself legally to anyone with whom I had not — perhaps for years — been so united in body and soul that separation would be intolerable. Surely, Edith, you, too, understand that you *can't* promise to give away your soul for life, that you can't promise to love forever *beforehand*. Haven't you learnt this from your own experience?

I don't think I've anything more to explain. Now it's your turn, and then we'll have a rest from explaining. I've told you simply and honestly how I stand towards you. I took it for granted before that everything I have said was what you could have said too. Tell me where you don't feel with me, and tell me quite honestly, as I have told you, how you feel towards me. We aren't so young that we need fear to face the naked facts of life simply and frankly. You know how much you are to me — exactly how much. Putting aside Olive, I have never loved anyone so deeply and truly, and with the kind of love that seemed to make everything possible and pure, and even my relationship to Olive has not seemed so beautiful and unalloyed as my relationship to you. It has seemed to me that we might perhaps go on becoming nearer and nearer, and dearer and dearer, to each other as time went on. My nature isn't of the passionately impetuous kind (though it's very sensuous), and my affections grow slowly, and die hard, if at all. Even as it is, we shall be dear comrades as long as we live. You have hurt me rather, but I don't mind because there mustn't be anything false, and our relationship is strong enough to bear a good deal of tugging.

HAVELOCK

Hardly a conventional love-letter, perhaps, but with far more truth in it than such letters usually hold; and when I read it once

more long years afterwards I know its truth far more deeply
than I possibly could when I wrote it.

The letter which perhaps embodied my first reaction to her
letter of doubt and questioning is that which now follows, and
I give it in full because it was also one of the most serious letters
I ever addressed to her, and its effect seems to have been decisive.
It begins abruptly:

Monday night

I have been trying to work, but I can only think of that letter
you wrote this morning. It's not exactly what you say about
marriage; I am not quite clear (on reading it carefully) what your
point is there, nor whether we really differ: and as to dreams, you
must surely know that I am at *least* as much of a dreamer as you;
but it's the heartless, antagonistic way you write. I thought I
understood you, but this I don't understand: how you could
write *that* letter on Saturday night and then — before we have
even seen each other — *this* on Monday morning. I feel as though
I had given my heart to a thoughtless, petulant child to play with.

You are a child, Edith — much more of a child than even I am.
I will be comrades with you as much as you like, and talk as
frankly with you as you like, about marriage or anything else,
but it seems to me now that until you have won, *for yourself,* a
real knowledge and experience of life and of love, and realise how
serious a thing love is, that it goes far deeper than our theories
and our dreams — until then, it seems to me now, there cannot
be between us any possibility of a deeper relationship than comradeship. Your instincts have always seemed to me so true and
sound that I thought they could teach you everything; but nothing does instead of life itself.

An ordinary woman can become the reflection of any man she
comes near to; but you are not an ordinary woman, and if you
were I should be absolutely indifferent to you.

Oh, if you had only gained the insight which would enable you
to understand! How is it that you seem to come so near to me,
and that then directly afterwards I find you so far off? But you
are growing, you *will* grow; and by the time you can understand
the love I give you, you will deserve far more than I can give.

But, however this may be, I still love you the same — love you enough to be content to be merely a step to help you toward the experience that you need.

H.

I know you didn't mean it, Edith; it's only that you've somehow failed to sympathise and understand.

That letter represents my natural and fundamental reactions to her recurring sudden and extreme transitions of mood, though now I scarcely recognize myself in it. At a later period I should have written more tenderly and could not have set the matter forth with such self-possessed precision. But the letter had its effect. She seems to have carried it about with her; it is well-worn, as is also that previously quoted, and long after, once or twice at least, she referred humbly to the remarks about the 'step,' and said that if I were only a step it was indeed a golden stairway. Her faith was reassured; her doubts were removed. Henceforth a new tone appears in her letters. The old reserve for ever disappeared, to give place not to any reckless abandonment, but to a deep and restful trust. From this time on, although no change had taken place in our relations, she now and then addressed me as 'My Husband,' or signed herself, 'Your Wifie.' 'I will never leave you — I know you will never leave me,' she wrote in a letter of this period. It was a true intuition, and during the quarter of a century that followed, it never ceased to be true, though she herself may sometimes have doubted it, and the faith of both of us was sorely tried.

The two following letters from me, each written on a Sunday, seem to come soon after the foregoing:

Thank you for your true, beautiful letter which is good for me. Now I think we understand each other. Let us always be perfectly frank; it is best, even if a little hard at first. We shall grow slowly to know each other perfectly. There is no need to be in a hurry: that only spoils it. No human relationship is perfect: one human being can't give another quite everything that it craves for, but you and I can give each other what is most precious to

us, and that is a great central fact; it makes us belong to each
other. Life doesn't happen according to our dreams; it happens
quite differently, but it's often much more beautiful and wonderful. I sometimes fear that you are a little too enthusiastic — too
romantic (shall I say?) You mustn't be, dear; it may hide the
real beauty of things.

And in the next:

It was so lovely to have you today, and it's left a sweet, joyous
feeling behind. It's good to lie close and restful and feel the
clinging tendrils that grow up slowly from one to another and
are always binding one closer. Do you have that sort of feeling? —
But it's rather horrible about the other people; I'm so afraid
that I make it awkward and unhappy for you. It's very pathetic,
when one thinks of it, that people think it wrong and unnatural
for two persons to learn to know each other before they think
of binding themselves together forever. — Marry *first*, and then
you may be free to find out that you've chosen the wrong person!
One realises how that sort of pressure works on weak young
creatures and leads to so much misery.

You must really find a spare hour for us to finish our lesson of
anatomy and physiology. I'm alarmed at your ignorance! —
can't rest till you have a few *elementary* ideas about the chief
facts of human life!'

I proceed to propose a meeting for this purpose, and in the same
sentence — characteristically it may be — a visit to a picture
gallery afterwards.

I may here quote a disconnected letter of hers I happen to
possess, because chronologically it comes in at this point, when
we had at last reached mutual understanding. It is addressed to
Olive Schreiner and dated the 7th of July. Before knowing me
she had had a prejudice against Olive Schreiner owing to absurd
rumours unsympathetically repeated to her by a man for whose
opinion she had great respect. I speedily brought her to a better
knowledge and she felt repentant for her prejudice; it was a
lesson, which she never forgot and always acted on, never to
heed rumours about people, but only to judge them from per-

sonal knowledge. It was thus that with her unquenchable faith in human nature and her strong impulse to befriend the friendless, she many times suffered grievous disappointment in her self-denying efforts to help those unfortunate weak-willed, but often plausible persons who sooner or later collapse again abjectly and betray the trust put in them.

> *Dear Olive Schreiner*, I wish you were here — I want to take your hands and I should like you to kiss me. I have grown to love you, though, long ago, this would have made me smile to think of. I feel you are very beautiful and true and that is why I am writing to you. It is strange, and yet natural too, that you should even care a little for me. I looked up at you once at Chenies Street Chambers and you looked down upon me — do you remember it? We both smiled and went away. I wish you were here.
> Yours in sincerity
>   E. M. O. L.

From that time her admiration and affection for Olive remained untouched till her death. There was never the faintest touch of jealousy for my enduring love and regard for Olive; it seemed to her, on the contrary, that that was something sacred which she should rather seek to cherish. Olive on her part was equally loyal and tender to the end; she was one of the small group which followed Edith at last to the crematorium. She regarded her as a fine and lovable personality rather than as a significant artist and thinker, but that was characteristic of her peculiarly high standard for measuring achievement (which yet had its lapses); I do not think that she ranked me high, either, in any category but that of personality.

I do not seem to have Olive's reply to this letter, but in a letter of Olive's to me from Matjesfontein, dated November 22, 1890, I find a reference to the same incident that Edith mentions: 'I saw her once a long way off and liked her very much; felt she was true. Dear, if I could be jealous of anyone,' she continues, 'it would be of you, you seem so much mine, how could you love

anyone else? And yet I want you to marry. No one would be so
glad as I, dear, if anything beautiful came to you. If ever you
have a little child, you must get your wife to call her after me!'

I have quoted my own letters less often and with less assurance
than Edith's because though she preserved so many, and often
what is evidently in the right order, I am unable to fit them in
confidently owing to my unfortunate habit of dating them merely
by the day of the week. It is no longer clear what the letter of
mine which follows refers to, but it certainly belongs to the
period shortly before marriage.

> *My own darling,* You must not be hurt at what I said. I know
> how proud and self-reliant you are; that is just one of the things
> that I love so much in you and is so beautiful to me. But I am
> sure you must feel, really, that it is good and sweet for us to share
> our worries as well as everything else. There is a very lovely little
> chapter about love in the *Imitation of Christ.* I must send you a
> translation I made of it years ago if I can find it. Love ought to
> make everything lighter for us. You mustn't quarrel with me,
> sweet one, for not liking you to be selfish and keep all the worries
> to yourself.

I quote this passage because she always remembered and cherished that little chapter on Love, and twenty years later used
part of it in her *Lover's Calendar.* When I translated those say-
ings of the old mystic I knew nothing by experience of their
profound truth. It was meet that they should have been
cherished so tenderly by the woman who was to arouse in me
whatever possibilities I held of becoming in that mystical and
transcendent sense a Lover.

At this time she was still the secretary of the New Fellowship,
and with the chief burden of the care and anxieties of that Fellowship House at 29 Doughty Street in which she lived with a miscellaneous assortment of people; it was an experience which afterwards led her to parody a saying of William Morris's and to
declare that 'Fellowship is Hell.' Ramsay MacDonald, the

Labour leader of later years and still more recently Prime Minister, was her chief associate in establishing this household, I think the year before. In a novel, *Attainment*, she later wrote a playful and more or less disguised account of some of the adventures and worries here experienced, though she resisted the temptation to introduce actual portraits of any inmates of the Fellowship, except her devoted servant Ellen Taylor ('Ann'). Nor, I am sure, though she had no wish to repeat it, would she condemn the experiment. But, as she makes Rachel, who stands for herself, say: 'The people there were such miles beyond their preaching. All the most beautiful things that happened there were quite unconscious.'

The inmates were certainly a miscellaneous crew. The oldest was Lespinasse, a journalist and man of letters of note in a small way, who in early days had known Carlyle and other famous men and he had written various biographies of literary notabilities. There was Captain P-foundes, also elderly, a quixotic figure of a man, who knew and loved Japan, and went about lecturing on that subject, apparently his sole interest, so I do not know how he came into the Fellowship. The others were all of a younger generation. There was Miss Agnes Henry, an active anarchist, who was frequently visited by the most famous Italian and international anarchist of that day, Malatesta, who, as I write now, forty-three years afterwards, has recently died as a humble labourer in Rome; there was a young Polish actress; there was a young man, I believe a clerk in a City house, whom later the actress married; there may have been one or two others whom I do not recall. Like-minded friends used to come to the house; I remember the simple and saintly Russian anarchist who went by the name of Frey, and was held in high regard, even veneration, by Edith; he had set up a little printing establishment and produced the Fellowship's organ, *Seedtime*: in Russia he had been an aristocrat and a general, but had sacrificed everything for the sake of his convictions. I also remember a tall, quiet, grave man who was Mr. (now Lord) Olivier. There was, besides, a fairly constant stream of strangers to interview the secretary concerning the aims of the Fellowship, while cranks and faddists of various kinds haunted the place. Few people, even in the Fellowship itself, could realise how significant a centre it was, though it endured for so short a period, and was dissolved very soon after Edith left it.

She (seconded by Ellen Taylor) had, indeed, borne the brunt of the work in which all were supposed to take a part, though Mac-Donald also accepted a considerable amount of responsibility. No one suspected how big a figure he was to become in the world. His humble origins were known, and it was recognised to his credit that he had risen to become private secretary to a member of Parliament (Lough) and an increasingly active exponent of political Socialism. But he had already planned his ambitious life-course. Edith told me how he had just declared his intention of some day becoming Prime Minister. That, be it noted, was some thirty-five years before the goal was actually reached, and in later years MacDonald has disclaimed any anticipation of the high post to which he had been called; yet this early ambition, to which I can bear witness, is altogether to the credit of his pertinacious and justified self-confidence. Though his ability was recognised, this ambition was not too seriously viewed in the Fellowship — which upheld ideals not greatly concerned with worldly advancement — and when in some moment of misplaced irritation MacDonald once told Edith that she was trying to reach success by clinging to his coat-tails, she received the accusation with mixed feelings: it had never occurred to her that that was a road to success, and, if it had, she was of much too proud and independent a spirit to choose such a road. She did not, however, resent this remark, though her admiration for him was qualified, and she was shocked when she found that at this time he, a declared Socialist, had written for the *Scottish Review* a pseudonymous article on Socialism which, though not exactly an attack, was a skilfully elaborated warning, from an assumed height of lofty superiority, against the risks and dangers of Socialism, perhaps an early anticipation of the attitude he was long after to assume as leader of a National Government. They were in friendly and helpful co-operation without either being warmly attracted to the other; she would look after him when he was ill; apply liniments to his back when he had lumbago; and so forth. But a certain ungraciousness, noted in later years by his nearest colleagues, already marked MacDonald and marred his undoubted qualities. He never, then or later, showed any recognition of his once close and friendly relations with this colleague, the secretary of the New Fellowship, and when once in later years, following her natural impulse, Edith wrote him a letter of sympathy in a time of his distress, no word or sign was vouchsafed to her in response.

Part VII

VII

We were now at one in all essentials and our future life in common was beginning to open out before us. We resolved to inaugurate it by spending a few days alone together in the country. There was, however, nothing violently indecorous in our plans. It seemed most beautiful to both of us that our first days together should be spent at the same ravishing spot where our first real meeting had taken place. I arranged to stay several weeks at Lamorna when Miss Jones was away and her housekeeper in charge, and Edith arranged to come down a little later, to spend a week with me at Miss Jones's house and then to go on to her own cottage at Carbis.

I wrote her from Lamorna:

It's very lovely here — so delicious to lie in the sun and hear nothing except an occasional insect or bird, and to know that our dear brother men are at a safe distance. Burton the fisherman and his wife have pleasant recollections of the clever little female

who spent a day here with her lady's-maid, and they were glad
to hear that she is coming again. (That's the result of kissing
the dirty babies!) But they won't be so glad as I will. — I've
taken a little house (rent free) made of granite and bracken and
honeysuckle. It's a lovely little house, hidden away from the
world; the pillars of it are two huge foxglove stems which tower
up above you against the sky when you lie down in it. I've got
room in my house for a little wife — but she must be small —
I've also got a nest in the rock right over the sea — and a very,
very tiny sweet bird might nestle in close beside me there. — I've
also got an ordinary rock, the same I had last year, where I lie
and bask in the sun and read or dream.

The programme was carried out as arranged. (I may now add,
many years later when Agnes Jones and the husband she later
married are both dead, that it was sweet on her part to be so
hospitable on such an occasion. Some years earlier, when I was
in frequent touch with her and receiving long letters in which she
told me about Hinton whom she had known and idolised, she
mistook my interest in Hinton for a personal interest in herself
which I was far from feeling; since for me she was simply an
invalidish woman of a rather older generation who could communicate to me many interesting facts. Hence arose a painful
and embarrassing situation which she bravely succeeded in over-
coming.) Edith arrived on the 18th of July. I met her at Penzance Station and we walked to Lamorna; that walk remains in
my recollection for the prosaic reason that I was carrying her
heavy hold-all and had a severe struggle with the steep Paul
Hill.

We always regarded this week together as our honeymoon and
always looked back to it with pleasure, though we had many
later little 'honeymoons,' as she liked to call them, in the years
that followed. She loved Lamorna ever after, and went there
from time to time to stay for a day or two with some dear friend
at the same house which, after Agnes Jones gave it up, became an
hotel. This always happened when I was away, for that was the

season when, in my absence, friends came to stay with her; we planned to go together more than once, but we made these plans in the unseasonable time of winter and they never came off. Lamorna remains to me the memory of a Paradise I never entered again. It is much changed now, I am told, but for me the wild beauty of that bridal place can never be changed.[1]

Yet the memory is dim save at a few points. I know that we would spend the whole of the days together, wandering along the cliffs or the rocks, finding sweet nooks over the sea, or lying together on fragrant mounds of heather and thyme, talking of all the problems of life and all our plans for the future. It seems strange even to myself, but I recall absolutely nothing of our life within-doors. A few days after she had left for Carbis, as I find by my pocket diary, I went over to her there, but I cannot clearly recall the visit. It is all to me a mist, but, as the mists of Cornwall may be, a mist of beauty.

During the next few weeks, when she was at Carbis and I was back in London, we wrote to each other constantly, and more intimately than before. I quote from two letters of mine which clearly belong to this period.

> *My wifie*, I lay on my couch this morning so happy reading over and over my letter that was so full of love. You mustn't have too good an opinion of me, darling, but you may be quite sure I have the merit of loving you! And it's rooted very deep down and I don't know what could tear it up. I don't think you need fear, Edith, that I should ever try to sap your independence; because, you know, I take quite a selfish delight in your independence; it somehow appeals to the woman element in me — and I think to the man part too. I can't imagine myself with a wife who was just my shadow without any character or will of her own. — No one who liked dependent women would come in your direction!

---

[1] I am not astray in speaking of the beauty of Lamorna in those days, however now spoilt. Even some years later, a true poet, W. H. Davies, in a charming little poem, 'Lamorna Cove,' wrote: 'Who ever saw more beauty under the sun?'

That letter, and still more the next, which may have been written before the other, bear witness to her hypersensitive independence, and the dread lest the smallest piece of advice, the most innocently loving anxiety to know all her little doings of the day, might be evidence of a desire to dominate her. That fear was always ready to wake up, and was manifested even on the very last day that I saw her conscious. I cannot recall what was the trifling annoyance referred to in the following letter; it may have been nothing more serious than the advice I gave her about this time to 'read a little French every day' — an excellent piece of advice which she would quote to me teasingly from time to time during all the years that followed.

> I was so eager for my letter this morning; you thought it would hurt me, but it is *very* beautiful to me. I don't think you quite realise how much absolute truth and sincerity are to me — 'the value and magnanimity of truth,' as Thoreau says. It is very easy — to me at least — to be silent; one can get a cheap reputation for many noble qualities in that way, and in ordinary friendship I think it is quite right. But it is different in the nearest relation of all; and if the time ever came when I had to keep back *any* thought, however horrid and disloyal — or that you had to — then I should feel that we were very far away. Surely, my Edith, you feel that too? It is the union and freedom of the soul that is so precious, and we cannot give that up. *To be oneself* is just the most precious thing that one can give to another soul. I gave you one of my moods, and I gave it you as a mood, or rather it was something much less than a mood, that had never for one instant taken possession of me, but only passed across me; and there was nothing in it that was not sweet and flattering (that isn't the word!) to you — and then, you see, you think that I am a rather contemptible creature, though still your husband! But I should have had a feeling of untrueness if I had done anything else — though doing it has made me feel very humble indeed ever since. As long as I am strong enough to do that, you may be quite sure I am utterly yours. And you will learn to understand, and you will always do so too? Will we not, sweetest? ... I'll try not to ask you how the lecture and the French are going

on if it hurts you, dearest. I hadn't the least idea it did. Once you seemed to like it. I need very much to see you and then you will tell me all the little things I am so hungry for. . . . I must just tear this open to put in one little word of good-bye before I rush to the post. You do not feel hurt now, my own wife? You will let me feel always that I can say whatever I must, and that you won't be hurt or misunderstand? And you too? I want you so much: I want to come and put my head on your breast and be your child.

Thus we each jealously guarded, and both of us succeeded in retaining, our independent spiritual lives. It was certainly and obviously so with her. It was equally so with me. From the time at the age of seven my intelligent independence began to develop and I sought out in the library case of my father's cabin on the *Empress* the books that suited my individual taste, my mind developed on its own lines in a many-sided interest in the world, absorbing all that suited it from others and never itself absorbed. But that in no way impaired our intimate emotional life, but far otherwise.

I have sometimes seen in marriages of devoted couples who are never separated that when one of them dies the survivor, beneath a real grief, experiences a current of relief, able at last to go freely his or her own way without the perpetual burden of little constraints. In our relationship we were only dependent on each other for a peculiar comradeship and affection, a special mutual understanding. The things we gave each other were the unique things that no other person can ever give.

Edith only returned to London from Carbis at the end of September. She was much occupied at this time in preparing a lecture of Socialist tendency she was to give to the Ancoats Brotherhood [1] in Manchester in November: 'The Masses and

[1] It so chances that as I revise these pages in September, 1933, the death of Charles Rowley ('Rowley of Ancoats'), the founder and director of that famous Brotherhood, is announced in the London *Times*, at the age of ninety-four. He was the champion of the poor of Manchester and influential in obtaining for them the best higher educational opportunities, notably by the Sunday afternoon lectures given

the Classes: A Plea.' This may not have been her first important lecture to a large audience; but it was certainly the first of her writings to be printed separately. She duly went North to deliver it, and wrote to tell me of the enthusiasm with which the working-men at Ancoats had received it, and how at the end she announced to the audience her approaching marriage to a man who felt about these things as she herself felt. After spending a few days with various relatives in the neighbourhood of Manchester, she returned to the Fellowship House, and then, on our wedding eve, a month later, we corrected the proofs of the lecture.

We had decided in favour of a marriage at a registry office. I was living in Paddington and the Paddington office was se-lected. Hither on Saturday, the 19th of December, I walked, accompanied by my sister Louie, who was to be my witness, and a few minutes later we met Edith accompanied by her friends, Evelyn and Sybil Brooke. The simple ceremony is quickly and easily accomplished. But Edith was a little overcome by the occasion, rather timid and quiet. She said afterwards that she was alarmed at the firm and decided tones in which I had re-peated the words of the assigned formula. There came on her that ever-recurring horror, dating from her childish experiences, of any masculine domination or even the faintest indication of it. Then we each returned to our respective bachelor homes. I suppose we neither of us ever expected or desired to visit the Paddington Registry Office again, and shortly afterwards I ceased to live in Paddington where neither of us lived again for twenty-five years. But then, it so happened, Edith took by her-self and spent the last weeks of her life in a flat which turned out to be in Paddington. So it came about that, after a quarter of a century, I set out once more to walk to that same registry office, alone now, to announce her death where before I had announced

by many famous men and women. In old age, it is said, he would declare that 'no one else has ever led such a distinguished and varied procession across one stage.' Edith was much appreciated at Ancoats and always spoke of Rowley with the most friendly regard.

her intended marriage. She never knew that the fate which brought her to Paddington for her wedding was at last to bring her back for her funeral.

There was no wedding breakfast. Edith used to say that her only wedding breakfast was of porridge. For the afternoon, however, she had invited all her numerous friends in town to an At Home at the Fellowship House. It was necessary for me to appear at this function, but she mercifully arranged for me to arrive late, so that my discomfort might be of brief duration. Next morning we started for Paris.

It had been my suggestion, and by her gladly accepted, that we should go to Paris. I knew Paris well and I longed to show her its familiar beauties and to initiate her in its charming ways of living. But I feared she might not be comfortable at my own old and still purely French hotel, the Corneille, and took her to a rather more English and more central hotel I knew of, the Hôtel d'Oxford et Cambridge in the Rue d'Alger. It was practically her first journey abroad, for she had previously only crossed the Channel for a brief, uneventful visit with the Stopford Brookes to Switzerland and it had not brought her in contact with that Continental life which meant much more to her than scenery. She drank in all the new impressions eagerly and joyously; from that moment dated her love of the French, her enjoyment of French ways, and her delight in Paris. Here at once all the child in her would spring unrepressed to the surface. I recall her loud demonstration of pleasure as she called my attention to the fact that the cabmen wore white top hats, and my instant attempt to quieten her demonstration which I thought would arouse the amusement of onlookers. She rather resented this, and would afterwards remind me of the attempt to subdue her; but she had her revenge, for a street photographer invited me to have 'the leetle miss's' portrait taken, and she professed to believe, and would playfully tell our friends, that in Paris I had been mistaken for her grandfather. It was quite true that while there was only a difference of less than two years separating us, I looked older than my years, while she looked much younger, and always enjoyed asking strangers to guess her age, whereupon she would triumphantly announce her much higher real age — until the time came at last when people no longer underestimated her age. We duly visited churches and museums. Of course also she was attracted by the restaurants which, though of the ordinary sort, were something of a revelation to her and furnished many ideas she profitably developed at home. She specially liked the large Duval establishment in the Rue Montesquieu, where, then and on later visits, we would sit in the gallery overlooking the hall below. Often and often, when far away, she would recall that pleasant memory, and exclaim: 'Versez, galerie!'

There is one memory, more solemnly beautiful, which ever remains in my mind, as it also remained in hers, from that first visit to Paris together. We went to the Sunday afternoon concert at the Châtelet Theatre to hear Beethoven's Ninth Symphony with the chorus. On this occasion, much as Edith loved music, the emotion was mine even more than hers, though I was not hearing the symphony for the first time. I shall never forget, and never know again, the rapture which I experienced in that little side box at the Châtelet. In the exaltation of that solemn hymn to Joy my own new personal life seemed to blend harmoniously with the vision of my mission of work in the world. This realisation shone radiantly out of my eyes, and in much later days Edith would still sometimes describe my face as she saw it then. I have heard the Ninth Symphony since, but I never again recaptured the rapture of that moment.

Yet I enjoyed many memorable concerts with Edith by my side, and nowadays nothing brings me so much consolation as music or so many poignant memories. Edith also, from first to last, always found joy and refreshment in music. Without any technical knowledge she had acquired a good taste in music. It so happened, indeed, that perhaps her favourite symphony was

Tchaikovsky's *Pathétique*, which has little appeal for me (I preferred his Fifth); but we had no dispute on the matter, for I understood her deep temperamental sympathy with the com-
poser who here so well expressed himself. During later years she
took an ever-growing pleasure and interest in the theatre, but in
this was mixed a kind of professional study, for she was ambitious to write for the stage. She never, however, craved for the
theatre when away from it, genuine as was the enjoyment it gave
her. During our long months together in remote Cornwall the
one absent delight she longed for was always music. Nowadays
I am often sad to think that the gramophone, which brings to my
country solitude the most beautiful music in the world, was not
in existence then to soothe her spirit on wintry evenings in our
storm-beaten cottage. I but imperfectly shared her interest in the
theatre, so that she seldom expected me to accompany her (though
she easily obtained seats), except on great occasions as when a
play of her own was to be produced. But in music our enjoyment
was equal and our tastes usually alike. So that we were always
ready to go to a concert together; in that respect she was unchanged even in the mental distraction and suspicion of the last
months of her life. Perhaps our happiest and most exalted moments were in listening to music, side by side. Always music
was as it were the sacrament of our spiritual union.

Early in January we returned to London. I went back to my
rooms at Paddington and Edith to the Fellowship House. She
had sent in her resignation as secretary of the Fellowship as soon
as our marriage arrangements were completed, but the resignation only took effect some weeks later, when the members in appreciation of her work presented her with a complete edition of
Emerson's Works which was handed to her by Edward Carpenter. In the meanwhile we were constantly meeting and quietly
planning our future lives together. She was also devoting her attention to lecturing for Socialist and other societies and to writing. About this time she printed a lecture on *Democracy in the*

Kitchen, and, a year later, a pamphlet embodying her own ideas and experience, entitled *A Novitiate for Marriage*. Of the latter she characteristically ordered a thousand copies to be printed, and as only a small proportion of these could be sold or even given away, in spite of her efforts, there was always a large and heavy box of them in every house-removal, until after her death what remained were mostly destroyed. (The essay, in the form in which she later revised it, was included in the volume of her papers, *The New Horizon in Love and Life*, published after her death.) But the opportunities to lecture were not frequent, though she was always a good lecturer, and she was still a slow and deliberate writer, so that the period following marriage was probably the easiest and least strenuous of her life, and this was no doubt how she came to turn her thoughts to farming. Her activities steadily gained in momentum throughout her married life until in the end she may be said to have been hopelessly carried away by them.

These early days of marriage were not only the least strenuous, they were probably the most quietly happy of her life, the least alloyed by mental or emotional worry and strain. Marriage brought no ecstasy, but it brought a certain liberation, a greater freedom to be her real self, a relaxation of that high-strung ethical tension which she came to regard as a little priggish. As I read again the letters she wrote to me during the twelve months following that crisis in June, when our hearts first came truly together, never again in the deepest sense to part, I can see how they follow a slow *crescendo* course. At first grave and quiet, to a degree impressive in one naturally so eager and impulsive, new notes of deep tenderness are from time to time struck; and then, gradually, tones of careless freedom, moments of reckless expansion come in, though never, then or ever, any trace of sentimentality or of adoration; from that she was always saved by her crisp sense of humour, her shrewd and mischievous wit. 'You rest every fibre in me and suit me, sir,' she wrote soon after our return from Paris, 'and I crow like a wee child at the breast, and I'm happy, happy in you, my true Heart.' Thus, even in these early days she fell into that attitude towards me, as of a child to its mother, which she had never known for a real mother and which always appealed to me so deeply. It is an attitude again and again reflected in her letters. Thus, in 1896, when unwell and in bed, she wrote: 'I'm so woefully depressed. Oh! my Boy, my Boy! I wish you were here with your loving arms to help me and to comfort me. I'm like a weak tired child and want my mammy.' It was an attitude she never abandoned until the mental disarray of her last months on earth, the attitude which in my heart she never ceased to take. Indeed, this sort of maternal feeling which I felt continued to grow in intensity throughout the whole period of our lives together. It was fostered not only by my realisation that her temperament was that of the eternal child, but still more, no doubt, by the fact that, as the years went on, frequent acute and prolonged illnesses, as well as later the insidious progress of organic disease, not to mention her tendency to impulsive rashness, perpetually placed her in a helpless condition needing at my hands all sorts of little cares and attentions, and thereby developing even to an acute degree of aching tenderness, however awkward I might be in manifesting them, all the femininely maternal impulses that may chance to be latent within me. I well remember how, less than a year before her death, we sat one day in the garden of the cottage we were occupying at Speen, and rising she stumbled on the rough lawn and fell, spraining an ankle (her feet were very small), not for the first time. At her sudden cry of pain, I ran towards her, exclaiming, it seems, for I was not conscious of it, 'My Baby!' But she heard me and was much touched by the involuntary manifestation. Even today, when I am told by friends who were near her towards the end of some little incident, maybe the result of her own imprudence, which caused her distress, I feel that same aching tenderness, the same impulse to run to her side as though she were still alive.

Yet it must not be forgotten that the 'child' was at the same time a woman, and even more than a woman in her staunchness and capacity, admirable in emergency, and, if need be, as fearless as a lion. Almost equally early in her letters appeared the reverse feeling which never forsook her, the feeling that I was a child and she my mother. 'I'm ever so much more a woman than I used to be,' she wrote in March when occupied with a lecture (which to my regret later went astray and was lost) on 'Latterday Puritanism.' 'I long to be really well and to write. I feel the power in me to do a lot somehow. Good night, my own darling, sleep in your old bachelor bed. I feel so like your mother tonight, as if I could rock my sweet babe to sleep on my breast and kiss away every gloomy thought he has ever had. Sweetheart — come soon.' (And I pause to brood over these words of loving care out of the far past, tonight, when I am alone, with my eyes resting on my 'bachelor bed,' while, outside, police cars rush about with notices of an air-raid and searchlights probe the sky with their great shafts.) A little later, in a letter from Carbis, for the first time, in a mood of wild ecstasy, she exclaims: 'I could lift the world by one arm and carry it to God!'

Two or three months later, on the 17th of July, she wrote from Haslemere to Probus, where I was then again doing medical work for a short time:

> My love, do you know that by the day of the week this is the day a year ago when you and I went to our little house with the foxglove towers and gave ourselves to ourselves? I look back and it seems years and years ago. I was shy and frightened and cried over my wee babe that was never to be, and you! — you made me think of how beautiful men could be. So long ago and yet only a year, it seems as if every phase of life has gone on in me and I'm years and years older. I think when I'm dying I shall see that house and smell the fern-roots and look into that blue sky and see the gulls and feel as near the heart of a great mystery as I did then. I've been reserved, more than is my nature to be, with you and have come to you inch by inch, but I shall never

go back, and if you ever leave me, I shall try the other mystery. Talk of miracles! I look into my heart and wonder I can breathe. As the years speed on, I shall be nearer and nearer to you. I say to you far far less than I feel, and somehow, when you are with me, I seem to be able to say nothing at times. I wonder what you feel as you look back over the year? I wonder do you regret when you see my quaint moods? And yet, in spite of it all, you must know I'm best for you of all you know. Yet I get so weary of struggling with my nature sometimes. Well, good night. Bless you, my darling one — make me sweeter for you and keep me always close to your heart.

The 'quaint moods' were hard to bear sometimes, though doubtless I had my part in provoking them. Less than a month later there is a record of one of them in a letter which I doubtless preserved for the sake of that which immediately followed. One of our little difficulties — though we sought to adjust it by mutual concessions — arose from the conflict between the demands of her sociable nature and my unsociable nature. She had an expansive temperament, a brilliant personality, a widely sympathetic disposition, troops of friends; when we were living near London she liked to have a succession of visitors. I was shy, awkward, reserved, a literary man who worked slowly, and though not unduly sensitive to noise or disturbance (much less so, indeed, than Edith became as a writer), I needed much peace and solitude. In some respects she might be termed extrovert and I introvert. It would appear that this summer Edith was inviting one friend after another, old and new, to spend the day or stay with us, not exclusively friends of her own, but also friends and relatives of mine. An old friend and devoted admirer was visiting us, to be followed by Bernard Shaw, and then an old friend of mine. During a few days in London it seems that I had uttered a protest, and she had replied with what she called 'stupid naughty words,' for on the 12th of August she wrote in a state of despair, 'almost on the verge of brain-fever,' at my silence and cruelty and her disappointment with me and my dis-

appointment with her and the general irony of life. But the very
next day she wrote this letter:

> *My Husband*, After a night's sleep and with your patient letters
> in my hands, I'm utterly ashamed of my wild, stormy nature, and
> its moods, and yet — it is me too. Love me for my faults, and
> not my virtues, Dear, and then I shall never disappoint you!
> Poor sweet old love, I wish I had your dear head here now, and I'd
> bury it in my wee breast and kiss the poor brain where I have
> kicked (the description is excellent, and I seemed to writhe as
> I heard the squelch of the white brain matter gurgling). Poor
> dear Havelock — and yet, paradoxical as it seems, if I did not
> love you I could not kick you. However, I can only promise to
> try. Love can do much, and to know you really love me will
> probably work miracles. You see now why I have to be quiet and
> not overwork or worry; it is an inheritance, and I fear me will
> forever make your *utter* reverence for me impossible. I seem to
> want you very badly. I think I can pour in the oil and wine now,
> if you'll let me.

Then she explains how she will readjust the visitors, and ends:
'Just kiss me, sweetheart, and know that these things do not
hinder but deepen love really,' and in a postscript: 'I open this
again to rock you to me, darling. I *do* love you, Havelock, and
need you with my whole woman heart.' This episode was typical
of many that occurred from time to time, and sometimes at frequent intervals. They were usually, in large part, due, as she
hints, to fatigue or nervous exhaustion, and though the effect
on her of such a nervous explosion was more often than not beneficial, the effect on me was truly described in the image she re-
peats from my letter. It remained true to the end. For these
episodes occurred to the end. Only at the end they were not immediately followed by the reaction of tender love. And that was
part of the sorrowful evidence that a process of mental disintegra-
tion had begun.

But the letters just quoted belong to a slightly later date. I
may go back a little to quote from two letters of mine (it is not

necessary to reproduce all the little details) which were written from Paddington shortly after our marriage when we were still at the stage of arranging our coming life together, and my old habits were not yet outgrown. The first is dated March 9, 1892:

> *My Wifie*, A word to give my love and kisses on your birthday. So glad to get your long letter. . . . . I hasten to enclose your seal. Also a photograph (amateur) of Olive just arrived in her old costume which I thought was worn out long ago. Please send it carefully back, at once. Isn't she sweet? It's snowing here; [Barker] Smith and his daughter coming this morning; also Miss Bradley and Edith Cooper [Michael Field]. I hardly think we need a studio — at all events at present; I'm not such a devotee of silence as that — provided I can have a solitary place in the open air. You hadn't time to look at the lovely platinotype photos the railway company have put up at Paddington — a hundred of 'em. When I go there to get my *Pall Mall* I can almost look at you at Saint Ives and Tregenna and all the other places. To-night I'm going with Symons to the Empire — some wonderful Bedouin Arabs. . . . I want to go to Haslemere next week; please give me directions; I suppose there's no need to give anyone notice.
> Your   HAVELOCK

This was written just after she had gone down to Carbis to re-arrange the little cottage for us together there, and we see how, from the very first, she was anxious that I should have a quiet place for work. I repeatedly told her I had been accustomed to work anywhere. But she adhered to her excellent design and it proved a great boon to me. We see, also, how with her prompt executive ability she had practically secured the Haslemere bungalow before I had even seen it, and there could have been no happier plan.

The other letter from Paddington was evidently written in the following June:

> *My Darling*, I'm expecting Doctor Louis Robinson — the Darwinism in the Nursery man — to talk over a book for the [Contemporary Science] Series. Went last night to Wagner's *Tristan and Isolde*; it's wonderful beyond words — a sustained

ecstasy of love that never flags or grows monotonous. Almost the greatest thing in the realm of music. Performance perfect, immense enthusiasm. Went this morning to the Anthropological Library, but didn't get anything out for you this time.[1] Shall have to send you two pairs of socks; the light pair got two big holes in one day! My *Pall Mall* cheque was £1.18.6. I read Olive's letter to you before even knowing it was yours. . . . I felt very loving to you at the Opera last night; wished so much you were there. (Vernon Lee says that at *Tristan* you feel that if any great temptation presented itself, you wouldn't be able to resist it; unfortunately none did present itself). . . . Louie and Symons came to the conclusion the other day that I had not been at all spoilt by marriage; you'd hardly know, Symons said to her, that I was married. Rhys, on the other hand, they decided, had been spoilt. Although better groomed than formerly (or perhaps because!), he looks pale and depressed, and has no spirit for anything; always has to be with his wife. . . . When are you going to get to your lectures? Good-bye for the present, dearest.

Your Husband

A fortnight after Edith went down to Carbis in March to prepare the cottage, I joined her there. We remained two months, then returned to London, and a few days later settled for the summer in the little Haslemere bungalow on the slopes of Hindhead in the grounds of the Honourable Rollo Russell (son of the famous Lord John Russell), whose wife, the daughter of a distinguished musician, Joachim, had for some years been a friend of Edith's. We furnished the bungalow which Rollo Russell had only recently set up, adding what was necessary to Edith's things brought from the Fellowship House, our most important acquisition being a big double bed. This we sold on leaving, as it would not have fitted into the little Cornish cottage and we never replaced it, as we preferred two small beds if possible side by side, and ulti-

[1] I had become a Fellow of the Anthropological Institute in, I think, 1889, and (except for an interval of some years when I could not afford the subscription) I am so still, nearly forty-five years later. About the same time I joined the Berlin Anthropological Society, and also subscribed to numerous scientific journals (anthropological, psychological, medical, etc.) in French, German, and Italian.

mately we usually had separate rooms. We rented the bungalow for several summers. It was an ideal summer residence for students and writers, entirely shut off from the world, the haunt of a singular and sometimes embarrassing profusion of birds and small mammals and insects. After we left, it was for a time occupied by Rollo Russell's nephew, the famous philosopher, Bertrand Russell. We were here all the summer, I going up to London for a few days every week or two. In November we shut up the bungalow and went down for the winter to the Cornish cottage.

This was the general pattern of our life: the winters together in Cornwall, and the summers in a looser association either in London or in some country place near London, while Edith was mostly in Carbis busily occupied with her cottage-letting season. During 1892, we spent about twenty-six weeks, or rather more than half the year, under the same roof; but during the early months of the year we possessed no common roof in town, though constantly meeting. I found her writing at the end of May, 1891, when the question of our marriage was still in an indefinite shape: 'I believe in folk separating at intervals, don't you? Yes, I know you do. How I should loathe a creature I was *always* near!' She always declared that the beauty and intimacy of our relationship was largely founded on this independence and the frequent separations. She would tell to near friends the story of some people who once travelled down to Cornwall in the same carriage with us and wondered who we were. They chanced to inquire of friends of our own, and, being told, one of them exclaimed: 'Oh, they could not have been married! They were so interested in each other, and he was so attentive!'

But I may add that during all the later years she became, in practice, less reconciled to these separations. She would begin to dread the announcement of my departure as soon as I arrived at Carbis for the winter; it would sometimes happen that she was ill on the morning fixed for me to leave and that I lingered on in consequence. She was never tired of urging me to accompany her on her visits (in 1914) to America. She would ask why we should be apart when we had perhaps so short a time, as indeed it proved, to be together. Even during the last weeks, with mind growing unbalanced and almost regarding me as an enemy, she was still flying in unexpectedly to make sure I was well.

I am bound to say that, while we were actually, perhaps, more together in the later years, and that this fully accorded with my own wishes, I yet felt at times a need, which she seemed not to feel about me in any marked degree, to leave her in order to seek rest and peace. She used to declare that I was myself, though so serene outside, a very restless person inside, and that may have been true. But she was a restless person both outside and inside. From early morning until after dinner, when she was soon ready to lay her head on the tiny pillow she always carried about (I still preserve it), and fall immediately asleep like a child, she was so radiantly energetic in mind and body, so full of her own joy or her own grief, yet so alive to everything and everyone about her, overflowing with fun sometimes, yet so unexpectedly apt to fall into nervous irritability, evoking either laughter or tears around her, that there was little rest or peace where she was. Many of her friends, much as they loved her, found that this radiating and incalculable energy, however stimulating, sometimes became exhausting. It is not surprising that I, who have scarcely found anyone whose continuous presence is congenial, should have felt, in spite of all the depth of my affection and comprehension, a recurring need for solitude and silence, a need stronger than the sense of all the risks thus involved.

During the first two years there were various absences not due to any wish to be apart. I twice again went to Probus as *locum tenens* for Doctor Bonar, in July, 1892, for several weeks and in January, 1893, that being the last time I ever undertook any ordinary medical practice, and she went North once or twice to lecture. From Probus in 1892 I find the following letter which she had preserved (I omit various trivial details):

My Darling, No letter today — but I've not yet exhausted the sweet letter of yesterday.... Very few patients today, but proofs have come in to correct.... When I get back shall be busy for a day or two getting *Nationalisation of Health* ready to send off. Should like to come down to Haslemere about 10th of August to stay for some weeks at least, working at my *Man and Woman* book (if I'm not frightened back to London by visitors!). I expect Mackay will be in London soon and should like him to come to Haslemere for a day or two. When you see Mary Cameron don't forget to ask her if the Dyers at Saint Ives were my friends in Paris — C. Gifford Dyer, American artist, with one daughter, Stella. I shan't be able to go to the Alhambra with Symons or to meet Signorina Legnani (the most delightful of all ballet dancers) on Tuesday! I'm afraid that I'm not altogether sorry that I shan't be able to go with you on Sunday. Somehow or other the very thought of it made me feel ill and helpless. Now I feel quite happy! And then I don't at all like to feel that you are at all dependent upon me in any way except of love. I don't feel dependent on you in those things and I'm sure I could never have loved you if I hadn't felt that you were strong and independent. You are *really,* my sweetheart, are you not? — I can't bear to think that you are ever such a tiny bit like those wives who hang round their husbands' necks like millstones. I'm sure you aren't *really....* Just had a letter from Olive. Is doubtful about coming to England next year, but may. Would like to see you; doesn't much want to see me. But I am the only man-friend she corresponds with regularly; she sends me a pound to buy something for myself to wear. What shall I get? What a long letter this is for me! Quite time I started on those proofs. Good-bye, my own, own wifie.

Your own Husband

That letter sounds rather strange to me in places now, both as regards substance and tone. She was swiftly reconciled to my failure to feel able to accompany her on social and other visits, and was anxious to spare me, so far as could be conveniently arranged, from such visits to our home as I might consider an infliction. On my side I ceased to employ inconsiderate protests. Our mutual independence was harmoniously adjusted.

Thus it is that, however much I may be tempted to regret the hours when we might have been together and were not, I recognise that things were better as they were, and am content. In the spiritual world the part is sometimes greater than the whole.

The beauty and intimacy of our relationship, I have said, was built on our separations, separations without which the relationship might perhaps have dissolved. Yet — and herein we may see the irony of life — out of these same separations also sprang some of its tragedy, and that even during the early period of marriage. I had remained in London while she was in Carbis revelling in her newfound felicity. And in the climax of her felicity my felicity received a jar which affected, directly and indirectly, the whole course of our subsequent relations. Being alone, Edith was joined by an old friend of nearly her own age whom she had known from girlhood, a woman brought up in a luxurious home, but of simple, wholesome, hearty nature, affectionate but unsentimental, made to be a staunch friend rather than a lover either of man or woman. But in the fermentation now working in Edith to a new experience of freedom and joy her heart went out with exuberant emotion to the friend whom chance had thrown close to her. I knew, for she had told me everything, of the sentimental and sometimes passionate attraction which from early school-life up to a few years before marriage she had experienced for girl friends. I knew that when a schoolgirl the resulting relationships had sometimes possessed a slight but definite sensuous character, though it had not found that experience in later adult friendships with women. I knew that such feelings were common in young girls. But at that time I had no real practical knowledge of inborn sexual inversion of character. In the essay I had written on Walt Whitman in *The New Spirit* I had passed over the homosexual strain in Whitman, in a deprecatory footnote, as negligible. I am sure that if I ever asked myself whether there was a homosexual strain in Edith, I answered it similarly. I was not yet able to detect all those subtle traits of an opposite sexual temperament as surely planted in her from the beginning as in Whitman, and really the roots not only of the disharmonies which tortured her, but of much of the beauty and strength of her character. The masculine traits were, indeed, not obvious in Edith any more than the feminine traits in Whitman; most people, I believe, failed to see them, and I cannot too often repeat that she was not really man at all in any degree, but always woman, boy, and child, and these three, it seemed, in almost equal measure.

As soon as she perceived this new emotional outflow towards her old friend Claire (as I will call her), she wrote to tell me of it with all her native trustful confidence, simple, direct, and spontaneous. If I remember right, she wrote with a misgiving hesitation at first. There was, as I now look back, a pathetic wonder and beauty in that appeal to my comprehending love, as though addressed to a divine being superior to the weaknesses of a human husband. The response, as her letters show, was the response she desired and expected. But it by no means came from a god-head, but from a human and suffering heart. It is true that — though I cannot now be sure — I do not think my pain was immediate. My emotions work slowly. I think the first effort at self-conquest seemed successful, but was less successful than it seemed, and that it was not till the spring of next year that, as I still vividly recall, I restlessly paced up and down my study at Paddington with heart aching over letters from Carbis. It was not so much the mere fact — for I had no prejudices and I well knew she could be guilty of nothing ugly or ignoble — but the realisation, as rightly or wrongly it seemed to me, that this new absorption in another person was leading unconsciously to a diminution in the signs of tenderness in her love towards me. Still I conquered my pain and gave no sign that I had even felt any.

On the 8th of March I wrote:

> *My own Wife*, My letter was very lovely this morning; I read it over ever so many times. Yes, nothing in the world or out of it will tear you away from my breast-bone — unless you want to

go. I am perfectly happy that you should be so close to Claire. I feel very tender to her. Give her my sweetest love.

I had the reward of my self-conquest, then and thereafter — I may honestly say to the very end — in a deep and tender gratitude. A little later, in June, 1892, Edith wrote to me: 'I dreamt you died last night, and the loneliness was horrible. I shivered in my sleep with the intensity of the feeling that I was in a world where no one understood me.' That refrain concerning 'the one person in the world who really understands me' occurs again and again in her letters through all the years that followed.

I had tried to conquer, and given little or no sign that the conquest was not complete, or even that there had been any need of conquest. But, after all, I was human. There remained beneath the surface the consciousness of a flaw in the ideal of married love I had so far cherished, and a secret wound of the heart, 'not so deep as a well nor so wide as a church door,' but enough to kill that conception of mutual devotion in marriage which all my purely intellectual interest in Hinton's doctrines had never destroyed as a personal aim. We were destined to work out a larger and deeper conception of love, but that beautiful conventional conception had for us been killed. Even my strong sense of justice could scarcely have long tolerated so one-sided a sexual freedom in marriage. It might be true that I was exclusively heterosexual and she was not, and that therefore there was no demand on me to go outside marriage for love. But it was also true that the very qualities in her nature which made her largely homosexual were qualities which, fortifying as they might be to our comradeship, were inimical to the purely feminine qualities of sweetness and repose which a man seeks in a woman, and therefore opposed in our case to a strict conjugal fidelity. And so it proved.

In after years, when I no longer concealed the feelings I had then experienced, Edith would say that this early attraction was really slight, and that in any case I should not have left her so much alone. It is true that this relationship only had a fleeting and shallow sexual colouring and soon merged into normal friend-ship, as her letters clearly show, although a joy and help to her while it lasted. Whatever I might think in hours of depression, it never interfered with her larger and deeper love for me, and Claire was also my true and affectionate friend. As to my ab-sences, I have already noted that at the beginning, and always in theory, Edith was as warm an advocate of independence and fre-quent separation as I was. There was really no need of excuses on either side. All that happened was the natural and inevitable result of our temperaments and our circumstances. We neither of us needed apologies, for we bravely faced our difficulties to-gether, and out of them we won a new harmony and reached pro-founder depths of love.

This growth and development may be illustrated by a selection of passages from the letters she sent to me during 1893. On the 14th of February she wrote: 'I told Claire you would be trusted with all and she smiled, "You *are* two odd people!"' It is her purity and sweetness which have made me love her; she is so childlike and unprudish, and gives me like a child a love which has rested and comforted and strengthened me in a way that amazes me.' On the 11th of March, just after her birthday, she wrote to me at Paddington from Carbis where she was with Claire: 'It is so wonderful to have married a man who leaves a woman her soul. I'm utterly satisfied in you, Havelock. It passes all my comprehension, though, why you love me.' But at this very time the crisis of my pain in my own emotions clearly de-scribed, the only crisis of the kind I ever experienced with Edith, was already approaching. A few days after writing the letter just quoted, she went with Claire to Manchester.

The next passage is from a letter I wrote from High Stoatley Cottage, the bungalow in Rollo Russell's garden, apparently early in the year 1893 (though I do not feel absolutely sure I place it right) when she had gone up to Manchester to lecture at Ancoats for the first time since her marriage.

My Love, just a word to say good night before I go to bed. I've been wondering how you got on and feeling awful loving to you. It's getting very cold.

Your own H.

Monday

I got your letter midday.... I've had no money, but have wanted none. Mrs. Russell has sent a partridge which we've had for dinner today. Mrs. Upfold [the cook char] insisted on making an apple-tart; you had given orders, so she was bound to; started it today. I expect to have about finished my book [this would be *The Nationalisation of Health*] by tomorrow night, and thought of going away about Thursday. It's very good of Symons to let me use his rooms; he is always doing things for me — I never do anything for him.... I enjoy your letter ever so much and like to think of my little wifie going about the world and helping people and stimulating them and making new friends and getting new experiences, while her old husband is coiled up in his shell at home. He is quite comfie. You mustn't expect me to write letters like when you were at Carbis and I in London; I only write like that when I'm *very* miserable and suicidal, and now I'm quite happy and awfully loving to my little darling. I hope it was a bigger audience in the evening when they discovered it was the right person; you ought to be careful to keep 'Lees Ellis' for Manchester.

She was staying with people who were almost strangers and she was lecturing, both things that strained her, so that she needed all the messages of comfort and love I could send. But, though I was not acting with deliberate cruelty, I was for the time completely obsessed by the idea that Edith was finding joy and happiness in another person, and, while I had not the slightest feeling of jealousy against Claire, it seemed to me that I was myself becoming a secondary object in Edith's affections. It was not jealousy, for I had never grudged the love Claire received, but even been glad of it, but the feeling that there was at this time what Edith herself called a 'philosophic' tone in her letters to me evidently hurt. Probably this was one of the unfortunate results, not the only one that ever occurred, of our prolonged absences; without absence love tends to fall into commonplace routine, but it must always be accepted that, if absence keeps love alive, it necessarily keeps alive the tragedy which is inherent in love. Now suddenly my letters began to show — in reaction against the letter that hurt me — an obscure restless discontent and unhappiness. I was ashamed to explain precisely what I felt, but it was only too clear that I was suffering, and Edith could not fail to detect the cause. She never kept these letters. It was evidently her habit only to keep those letters of mine which seemed to her beautiful, worthy some day to be re-read; and certainly a large number have thus survived. Unknown to each other, this was the practice of both of us, though I kept some letters in which she had expressed what seemed to me a just resentment or grief. It is thus that I have the letter in which she showed how completely overcome she was by the blow my letters had dealt her. She had merely stumbled through her lectures; her distress was so great that she couldn't conceal it from the people she was staying with, who realised it had something to do with me; she became ill; she wanted to see me at once. At the same time she was stung to bitter resentment. There was no doubt about the suffering I had caused her. In that realisation my obsession was dissipated, at once and forever. I became completely repentant. I showered letters of remorseful tenderness on her by every post.

These letters, as I find today, Edith had carefully kept together and I should perhaps quote a few sentences from them.

My Sweet Heart, I am so pained at your letter, that I have hurt you so — and when it was only out of my love. It makes me hate myself. But you say *exactly* the things that I have been feeling. Only your letter isn't like a 'philosophic' lover's, you know. And in that, although it pains me you are hurt, it takes a great load off me somehow. You know I have all these weeks been loving you *so* much, and seeming never to be able to think of anything else but you, and I was so glad about Claire — and I think I

got into a morbidly sensitive state, and that is why your philosophy hurt me so. I feel so angry and ashamed with myself I let
you see it; I tried not to. And yet I can't love and *not* tell you
what I feel.... That letter needn't have pained you so. It only
showed that I love you a great deal more than is wise. It is funny
that only a little while ago I was writing to Olive such an enthusiastic letter about how I love you, and about how at last I had
got to that exalted state in which mere loving itself is sufficient
and one doesn't crave so much about the amount of the return —
and it isn't true at all! (I mean about the return!) I do wish it
wasn't my nature to love so intensely. All my life long I have
been trying to be philosophical, but I haven't succeeded. And
now I know I never shall succeed. You see if I could love you
quite moderately and peacefully, you would be quite happy and
undisturbed! Please do not imagine that I felt miserable before
a week ago and was hiding it. Or that it was because of your love
to Claire — but I know you won't suspect me about that. Love
is funny and I am funny. It needs its wifie's little breasties every
two hours like a baby, and if they seem far off — it do shrike!
(But you know, my Love, when the mother hears her baby, and
knows she has that within her to soothe it, she doesn't feel that
she must yell too!)

Your own troublesome and unphilosophic but absurdly loving
                                                              Husband

A line before I post just to give you my latest love, you dearest
thing in the world. I am distressed till I get my letter tomorrow
saying you are. — I long to comfort the injured little wifie as is
plagued with a husband what's madly in love with her.... You
will have realised now how terribly you misunderstood, and I
need not say very much. All these weeks my whole body has been
like a bundle of sensitive nerves throbbing with love of you, every
tiniest act of the day has seemed mixed up with love of you, I
have had no thought and written no word that wasn't love of
you — and you calmly refer to my 'satirical letters.' Good God,
are you blind — or what?... Do you know that the fact that I
can still love you after that letter and feel perfectly sweet is about
the most precious proof I could ever give that I am indeed hopelessly in love with you? I fold my arms round you. I seem to be
almost grateful to you for enabling me to give you such a proof of

my love. I seem to be a mother, and you my fretful babe that
I fold and smother in my breast. I do not mind the 'philosophical
love,' or anything. I only know that I love my babe and am
satisfied with loving. But, oh, my Love, my own Love, how could
you think such things?... Good-bye, my own Sweetheart. Be
rested. Have no more unloving thoughts of the heart that is entirely yours. And do not be hurt that you misunderstood a little,
for you couldn't help it, and the wounds you gave have all turned
to sweetness; there is no bitter at all. Lie still, my own, and rest
beside me, and grow strong.

Always your   HAVELOCK

Soon she was herself again.

> Your three soothing letters have come [she wrote on March 22,]
> and now I *know* you are hurt over my letter yesterday, but I was
> almost mad with horror and illness. I felt you'd gone somehow
> and it frenzied me. It tastes glorious to me that you love me like
> this; and you must know me well enough to know that it is the
> very need of my woman's nature to be and to love like that.
> Forgive me, my Sweet — nothing matters if we belong, and the
> very thought of you being away from me made me feel like a
> suicide. What I said yesterday only came out of a wearied hurt
> heart — a blank horror that the great corner-stone had slipped
> from my house. I should go stark raving mad if you left me, and
> yet — so long as you love me I don't mind a scrap who else you
> love. My sweet Sweetheart, I will take you into my arms and
> cradle you ——

It is too sacredly beautiful to quote more. A day or two later she
wrote:

> Your letters make me glow that you love me so. You know, in
> your ear, this is how I wanted you to love me — with passion and
> force — and I know now you were not *quite* in love with me when
> we went to the registrar's. I am not 'far away' but in your very
> bowels and heart. I believe I have an exceptional power of loving.
> What has hurt you? I don't think you can ever guess what this
> deep great love of you is to me, and your love — and Claire's too.
> I live and I bathe in love, and you must not grudge it me. *Nothing*
> can make me 'far off' for you — it is impossible.

That was the first and last time in our life together that any
cloud arose from doubt on my part as to her love. I had not been
in the faintest degree jealous of Claire, but, rightly or wrongly, as
I have said, I had felt that Edith's love for Claire involved a
diminished tenderness for me. If it was so, my outburst had itself
restored my position. I never repeated it, or felt the slightest
impulse to repeat it. Thereafter Edith had a succession of intimate women friends, at least one of whom meant very much indeed to her. I never grudged the devotion, though it was sometimes great, which she expended on them, for I knew that it satisfied a deep and ineradicable need of her nature. The only test I
applied to them was how far they were good for her. If they
suited her — and her first intuitions were not always quite sound
— I was not only content but glad. I never had a quarrel with
one of them, and some of them have been — now more than ever
in our community of loss — my own dear friends. It must not,
however, for a moment be supposed that these special friends
with whom she had had for a time an intimate relationship such
as one side of her nature craved were more than few in number.
There was a succession of them, but each relationship was exclusive while it lasted, which was usually for years, and would
have been permanent had circumstances allowed. She was always relentlessly true to her ideals; she loathed promiscuity; she
was attracted to purity of character, though by no means to
puritanism; any touch of coarseness or of vice was fatal, and produced in her a revulsion of feeling which nipped in the bud one or
two relationships.[1] The few friends with whom there was ever
any question of such relationship at all were but a small proportion of the army of her friends, most of whom never guessed the
special and sacred attraction which she had felt for a few. I never

---

[1] It is notable, notwithstanding her sensitive and quickly inflamed temperament,
and her extraordinary skill on occasion in hurling crushing language at the heads of
those who offended her, I never once heard her use even one of the coarse vulgarisms
or common swear-words in which it is so easy for the nervously irritable woman to
indulge.

knew anyone who had so many friends. She had a passion for friendship. They were people of all kinds and classes, from Ranees and duchesses down. That made no difference. She was equally natural and herself with all of them, equally full of sympathy and tender solicitude. Her longest, staunchest, and least interrupted friendships were with people of the highest character living in the conventional world, though she herself remained unconventional, and was quite capable of making a friendly remark to the butler at dinner — and being forgiven for doing so. But at the other end of the social scale she was equally attached to people of the humblest position and even won the devotion of downright rapscallions, such as the light-hearted and glib-tongued Cornish gaol-bird who on one occasion, to do her honour, declared to various people that she had given him five shillings when in reality she had given him nothing.

I have said that my delayed outburst in the spring of 1893 was never repeated, and that henceforth there was no shade of personal pain in my feelings towards Edith's affection for any of her friends, unless when I felt that her own interests were concerned. But there was before long another cause at work to prevent that feeling ever again arising in my breast. For we were almost immediately to become equal in this matter. Towards the end of May in this same year 1893, at Haslemere, it so chanced that for a time Edith had no servant sleeping in the bungalow, and therefore desired a companion for the occasions when I was away. There was no friend of her own available, and in all innocence I suggested a young lady, an acquaintance of my own, whom I will call Amy. She was found free to come, and she came. Amy, whom I had known from her childhood, was at this time twenty-four. I had never paid any special attention to her; with my idealistic and intellectual preoccupations I had overlooked the gentle, quiet girl who, on her side, had cherished admiration for me from a distance. But in the narrow limits of the bungalow I began to become aware of her sweet, soothing, unselfish qualities.

I began to discern a personality, a yet unobtrusive personality, singularly unlike Edith's, indeed, but yet attractive. One day I went for a walk with her to a pine wood near Hindhead; there we sat side by side on a fallen trunk, and there I gave her a kiss. It was but a single simple kiss, and for months, even years, afterwards there was little further progress in intimacy, for with me relationships developed with extreme slowness, and Amy was much too inexperienced to make, or to invite, any advances.

Yet from the day of that first kiss I hid nothing from Edith; there was never, then or later, the slightest deception, and never a stolen interview. Any such lack of openness towards the woman in the world who was nearest to me would have been impossible; it would in any case have been unpardonable when she was absolutely open to me. Whatever the difficulties might be, we met them squarely, both Edith and I, and conquered them as well as we could.

Edith scarcely made the way easy to me. Her high-strung emotional nature at once came into play. It never occurred to her that in essentials she was not called upon to face more than I had been called upon to face in her relationship to Claire. It seemed to her, at first and for long after, merely the influence of what she was accustomed to call a 'femininity.' The explosions of her nervous temperament led to some painful and humiliating scenes. Amy, whose character and personality were still shy and undeveloped, remained quiet and gentle, without taking any steps to solve the situation. The situation might have solved itself if left alone, and the difficulty melted away into nothingness, for at that time I was drawn to Amy, so far as I can judge, by no strong deep impulse. Edith's first indignant resentment had two results — neither of which, I think, she ever clearly realised. In the first place, the injustice of her attitude aroused an opposing sense of justice in me and stimulated a firmness the emotional impulse itself might have been too weak to attain. In the second place, the original impulse was fortified by the attention which, through

Edith's attitude, I concentrated on it, whereas in a calm and free atmosphere it might soon have withered. As it was, that one kiss became a germ that slowly grew more vital during many years that followed.

The problem was not yet solved, but the storm swiftly died down. Amy stayed the appointed time, leaving early in August, though henceforth there was a grievance that in moments of irritability might be brought up against me. That, however, was merely on the surface. Through both these dangerous adventures, hers with Claire and mine with Amy, it might be true that the original and largely conventional ideals of love with which we had both, scarcely more than a year earlier, come together, had been undermined, but we were struggling towards ideals which would be truer to the nature of each of us, and our deeper union, far from being destroyed, was being consolidated.

I will again quote from her letters. In September, shortly after Amy had left, during one of my brief absences in London, Edith wrote: 'I shall always fly to your breast and tell you *everything* — you *are* me, I *am* you, and not gods or devils can tear us from each other.' The words were true, and I think she would have admitted this truth, though perhaps not have repeated them, even to the very end. For me they have always been true.

On the 13th of September she wrote from Manchester, where she was lecturing:

> I don't know what on earth is the matter with me, but I feel a nearness and sweetness, strength and depth, about you that is like the rush of the sea or a mountain ridge. I seem to have lived years and years, and that tiny misery and problem about Amy has helped me so in helping others. . . . I shall always tell you everything, and lie on your heart. I am surged with love of you and nothing in the world could make me not bear what you may bring to me, for men and women *seemingly* must hurt those they love. . . . Think of me and know that in your arms and on your breast is my one complete home.

A week later, when staying at the home of Claire, she wrote:

> I wish you were having so good a holiday. I am simply full
> of life, my eyes clear, my skin rosy, and my spirit like a girl's.
> Mr. X [her host] says he never saw a woman keep her youth so
> in his life, he cannot realise I am married at all. Well — I am,
> and *desperately* in love with my husband. I want to be bigger and
> nobler and broader just to rest and strengthen you.

It was not a momentary attitude, but recurs perpetually.
More than a year later, I find her writing:

> I long to see you and talk to you, and then croon into your
> strong true arms and hush and bless myself with your love and
> faithfulness. I never was more truly and deeply in love with you,
> and I find myself setting folk on to praise you with a kind of in-
> ordinate lustful feeling, just to hear them say true and sweet
> things of you.

Through all these incidents, alike at Haslemere and at Carbis,
the ordinary business of life had steadily to be pursued, and for
me that was studying and writing. Edith's activities, outside
housekeeping, were at this time probably less than at any time
before or after. She had, indeed, written and privately published
her pamphlet, *A Novitiate for Marriage*; she was writing, and
from time to time delivering, outspoken lectures on various advanced social and moral questions. In these ways and by her
magnetic personal qualities she had already impressed and influenced many. I recall how one woman friend, herself of some
intellectual distinction, had enthusiastically declared that Edith
was 'the light and hope of our future civilisation,' and often afterwards we would playfully bandy about that saying between ourselves. But her more public activities were just now leisurely and
intermittent, for she realised her new duties and responsibilities
as a wife and devoted much more time and attention than was
possible or necessary, when later her own activities again increased, to establishing the best conditions, not only for my
domestic comfort but for my work.

At an early stage she had rightly seen that the Cot, as she had named the little cottage at Carbis Bay she had already taken on lease before the question of marriage had arisen, would not be suitable for me to work in, and that I must therefore have a place for work outside. It was she who discovered and arranged on my behalf the tenancy of a studio at Hawkes Point. This was not merely the only possible place in the immediate neighbour-hood, it was the ideal place, for my work. Within about fifteen minutes' walk, situated on the point in the middle of the Bay, on the sea side of the railway line, this rough little building had once been a mining shed at the head of a small now disused shaft. It was a convenient and yet solitary and isolated spot from whence I could look down on Lelant sands, in the distance see Saint Ives on its peninsula to the left, and to the right the more deserted dunes stretching towards Godrevy lighthouse, but no nearer habitation was visible. Edward Carpenter, who knew England well, declared, when he came down to visit us, that my hermitage had one of the finest outlooks on the whole English coast.

In front of the low buildings placed against the hollowed hill-side, half a boat had been set on end, and there in this little ivy-covered shelter facing the sea, I would sit writing or reading when-ever the weather allowed, which in the mild Cornish climate is sometimes more or less during the whole of the winter. But inside the studio various changes were effected for my comfort, under Edith's supervision, and here through the winters of more than ten years — until, indeed, I was turned out by my landlady who decided to put the place to other uses — I was able to work in complete freedom and under conditions which suited me per-fectly. If I owed nothing more to Edith than the opportunity to obtain and to preserve these conditions in the happiest manner possible, my debt to her would still be immense. Soon after breakfast I would start off with such papers or books as I might need — for I maintained my studio in an almost bare condition and kept few or no books there — and after three hours' work would return for lunch, though once or twice a week during the earlier years I would walk along the coast-guard path to Saint Ives to join Edith for lunch at the little restaurant kept by Miss Kevern as a resort for artists, or occasionally, later, to suit Edith's convenience, I would take my lunch with me to the studio. During the afternoon I made my own tea; and when the day's work was done, I returned to the cottage to spend the evenings alone with Edith. It was a quiet unbroken routine, completely to my liking, though Edith would go out now and then to spend an hour or two with any friend who happened to be living in the neighbourhood, and occasionally friends at Saint Ives or Lelant would be invited to lunch or dinner. That long remained the usual course of our life together.

During these early years, however, the evenings were sometimes devoted to joint work. This was especially the case when in February, 1894, I undertook, with Edith's help as amanuensis, to make a complete, unexpurgated translation of Zola's *Germinal* for private publication. We executed the whole of this together during the evenings of a few months at the Cot. I dictated the translation while she wrote the whole — a laborious task, as the book is long — in her swift, clear handwriting, without weariness or complaint, now and then bettering my translation of dialogue with some more idiomatic phrase. I had arranged to do this work for fifty pounds, simply to enlarge our little income, and we shared the sum between us. In a somewhat similar way Edith took a share — with her pen, for we were then only at the threshold of the typewriting age — in the mechanical work of some of the translations which I made, partly or entirely, for the Contemporary Science Series, such as Ribot's *Psychology of the Emotions*, and would also copy papers for me, until in the course of a few years her own work developed and she no longer had the time or energy to render assistance of this kind. Thenceforward I accomplished all my literary work by myself with my own pen, sending it away when finished, if necessary, to be professionally typewritten.

At Haslemere our movements were freer and less subject to routine, while our lives generally were less strenuous. I would go up to London for a few days every week or two to work at the British Museum, to see friends, or to enjoy concerts, theatres, music-halls, pictures, scientific meetings, and all the other manifold things which interested me, while Edith, with her innumerable friends, was able to gratify her warm social instincts. Still, even at Haslemere I accomplished much work in my pleasant little study, ill-adapted for literary purposes as was a room in a small bungalow compared to my Cornish studio. I remember writing at *Man and Woman* here, and it was here, walking up and down on the grass in the twilight, that I thought out the General Preface to my *Sex Studies*.

I had already found out that my work must be done, especially when it involved any original effort, in the open air. I have not, indeed, so much thought out my work in the open air — I have done that anywhere and everywhere — but actually written it in the open, to an extent probably which few writers have equalled, always in spacious and preferably rather bare spots, on the moor or among the rocks — I could not write in a forest or a cave — where there is sun and air and a large prospect of land or sea. Many have remarked that they wonder how it is possible to write under such conditions. It is natural to me, a naturalness which may be part of my nearness to Nature, that quality of the faun and the satyr which some of my friends see in me. It is under such conditions that my best inspirations have come. It is, moreover, only by living under such conditions that I have escaped the feverish and nervous irritability which so often overcomes those writers who work within four walls. Perhaps also it is this habit, or this temperament, which caused people to remark with surprise to me or to Edith that I had nothing of the appearance of a literary man. The ease with which I long retained an erect figure may be connected with the fact that I have been in the habit of reclining to write instead of stooping over a desk and the suggestion of 'some great god Pan' which Edward Carpenter found in me may possibly be due to much living with Nature in the open.

During these first quiet winters of our life together in the little Cot at Carbis Bay, various interests that were later to absorb much of Edith's time and energy were initiated in their small beginnings. Important among these was her first dog, Jock. She used later to say that her little farm had originated with Jock. He was a large dog of mixed breed, but a dog of great vigour, character, independence, and intelligence. She had first known him as the most cherished possession of an old woman in the neighbourhood, and would occasionally bring him a bone. Old Mrs. Glasson was attached to him because he had been devoted to her husband and had jealously guarded the old man's body when he fell dead in a field; Edith used to say that forever afterwards Jock would stand still and look expectantly at any old man in the distance who resembled Glasson. (It is I now who, as I pass along the street, sometimes catching a glimpse of some firm little figure like one I once so well knew, cannot help looking vaguely at the woman's face it belongs to — and am reminded of Jock.) The old woman, shortly before her own death, begged Edith to take charge of the dog. Jock understood this, or at all events made a similar arrangement for his future, and the very night his old mistress died he ran to the Cot and installed himself there. He was large for so small a place, but he had always been accustomed to live indoors, and he was accepted without demur. Jock was the first of a long series of dogs and cats — sometimes two or three of each at the same time — on whom Edith expended much solicitude and trouble. But none of them possessed so much individuality, caused so much anxiety one way and another, or — as a result, no doubt — absorbed so much of our affection as Jock. He was a dog of tremendous spirit, almost neurotically energetic, absolutely fearless, and more affectionate than obedient — in many ways, indeed, rather like his mistress in temperament. Sometimes, also, he seemed uncannily intelligent. I recall, for instance, how one day when a tedious visitor made an interminable afternoon call at the Cot, Jock finally solved the situation by taking up the visitor's gloves from a chair and solemnly placing them on her lap. I was attached to him, in spite of all the trouble he caused us, as I never was to any of his successors, and he had an affection for me which dated more especially from a sad accident that once befell him. I was taking him for a walk along the cliff to Hawkes Point when, dashing along with his impetuous energy, he fell over the edge down onto the rocks in the sea. With excellent pluck and judgment he swam to the Point and was able to climb onto the dry rocks before his strength was completely spent. I ran on to send for assistance from the houses above, and then descended to stay with him and comfort him till help arrived. Legs and ribs were broken, and it was long before he recovered, but from that moment, for some mysterious reason, he was almost as devoted to me as to his mistress. In old age he became diseased and irritable, and Edith decided to have him shot; this was done swiftly and painlessly by our farm man in my presence, while Edith went away into Saint Ives, and that evening there were tears in the eyes of both of us.

It was partly, though of course not entirely, to give exercise to Jock that Edith, while still at the Cot, set up a dogcart and bought a pony. The pony, like the dog, though a vigorous little animal, had never been properly broken in. Edith enjoyed mastering Dolly, but, as was wont to happen, she took far more risks than was desirable. One evening, when I was sitting alone in the Cot, awaiting her delayed return, she arrived, escorted by a stranger, after an accident which might easily have been fatal. Dolly was being carelessly led out of the market-garden on Lelant Hill by a man when she suddenly broke away and dashed round the corner: before Edith had time to gain control, the dogcart was completely overturned and she was underneath. It might have been worse if a passing young lady with fine presence of mind had not immediately sat on the pony's head. As it was, Edith's head was hurt and an injury to the nose was liable to produce trouble for years afterwards. Dolly was disposed of, though not immediately, but she had involved the hire of a stable and a field next door to the Cot, and that had suggested the idea of a little farm.

That was the first though not the last time that Edith met with injury, which on at least two subsequent occasions might also easily have proved fatal. It was in the Cot also that she had her first attack of pneumonia. This was a slight attack and she recovered with fair ease, but later there were two other attacks which proved more serious, with difficult recovery, and finally it was from pneumonia that she died. It may be said that during these early years of our life together at the Cot all the main influences of her later life were established.

One day she came in and announced to me that she had taken the Count House. I had received not the slightest intimation of this beforehand, but I now knew her impulsive decision, her confident self-reliance in practical matters that she regarded as within her own sphere, and I cannot recall that I was greatly surprised. But certainly the Count House, as it then appeared, would never have commended itself to me as a possible home. Built some forty years earlier, as the official business headquarters of the mine, the Count House had been found of no use when the mine stopped working, except as a brief summer resort for a Saint Ives family. With windows blocked up all the winter by boards, and never built for a home, it had looked to me a peculiarly dreary, dilapidated, God-forsaken building. But Edith always had an eye for the possibilities of a place; the artist in her delighted to develop these possibilities. Her artistic instincts in the domestic sphere were always right, although her calculations as to the cost of her creative activities were apt to be wrong. But on the whole it went well with the Count House, though the repairs needed were considerable. It had a beautiful outlook over sea and moor to start with, and it became a fairly comfortable home. Its external bareness was relieved by creepers; there was a passion-flower to please Edith, and an Australian eucalyptus, which soon sprang up higher than the roof, to please me.[1] We lived there for some twelve years. Much later it has become the home of Mr. Bernard Leach, perhaps the chief art-potter of our time, and he has effected various improvements in the house. He told me lately that a prehistoric hut-dwelling had been discovered just below the garden wall, and I was annoyed that I had not had the skill to discover it, for it would have been a source of much delight.

The justification for the move to the Count House was not only the imperative need for a more spacious home than the miniature Cot, but Edith's new impulse to farming, which might, it seemed, alike benefit her health and assist her finances, while it certainly seemed to gratify her native instincts for practical activity and close contact with Nature and earth. There were two or three small fields (to which Edith later added others) attached to the Count House as well as a stable, and the farm began with one cow. Miranda was a gentle and beautiful animal, so named by the farmer near-by who had reared her, a cousin of Sir Henry Irving, who named all his cows after Shakespearean heroines. Several cows were later added, some born on the premises; there were two donkeys; pig-breeding became a speciality; there were a large number of pigs and fowls and ducks. My place in the farm, from the first, was nowhere, though I might occasionally be called upon to kill a fowl. A man was kept; there was a dairy-woman from outside, and two servants in the house; cook and housemaid, who sometimes helped with the farmwork. But Edith herself liked to be able to do everything, even to plough, and really took an active part. She had known nothing of farming and little of country life

[1] This was given me by my interesting friend, Doctor Bonus, part of a consignment he had received from his old friend in Sydney, Doctor Creed, who, it so chanced, had been the doctor at Scone when I was there, though I never met him, but came to know him when later he spent a long period in England. He was a man of vigorous personality and much mental activity, who became a member of the New South Wales Legislative Council, wrote a book on his experiences, and died at a very advanced age nearly half a century after the Scone days. The tree, being too near the house, was cut down after we left.

before settling in Cornwall, but her keen interest, her vivid, alert
intelligence, and the familiarity which it was so easy for her to
establish with labouring and farming people, enabled her to master
the mysteries of the art with wonderful rapidity, and she never
made serious mistakes. The fowls were from the first almost entirely in her own hands, and they absorbed much time, labour,
and thought; she used incubators and was careful to secure the
best breeds and to adopt the best methods and foods, though she
found in the end, as others have found, that her sanguine expecta-
tions of ultimate profit in this department were scarcely fulfilled.
She bred pigs diligently, and from time to time a butcher was sent
for to kill one; on these occasions she would go round beforehand
to friends and neighbours to obtain orders; then she would spend
a long and arduous morning in cutting up the carcass herself into
the required joints (on one of these occasions being discovered by
a cultured West End friend of her half-brother who unexpectedly arrived), and afterwards carry some of them round in a basket to the purchasers. A considerable amount of hay was made
to stack or sell; but crops were on a very small scale, though she
cultivated flowers and vegetables. She had indeed a deep congenial love of the earth and its creative energies. I shall never
forget how, one morning after dressing, I wandered to the window
of her study and came suddenly on the vision of her below, spade
in hand, vigorously digging up potatoes, with almost a fever of
exhilaration, her face radiantly beautiful in its animated joy.

From the first there was another practical activity associated
with the farm, the letting of furnished cottages. The Cot was
not given up when we moved into the Count House, but was let
furnished. Three other cottages in the neighbourhood were successively taken, usually in the same quiet, prompt, decisive way
as the Count House, so that I seldom knew anything of the matter
until it was virtually settled. They were 'artistically furnished'
as the prospectus stated, for Edith loved to pick up pretty things
at sales and in cottages, finally completing the operation with a

copious supply of fabrics from the best London shops, Liberty's especially, to make curtains and hangings. Then with business-like activity she successfully set herself to find tenants for the cottages, in all of which, also, we lived ourselves, at one time or another, for a longer or shorter period as the Count House was occasionally let.

It was her aim, indeed her instinctive impulse, to do everything she undertook thoroughly and well. Sometimes, when a cottage had to be prepared at short notice for an incoming tenant, this involved an undue strain on her strength; while, in the end, perhaps, the little place she had spent so much trouble and skill in making charming and cosy would be greeted with contemptuous disapproval by some vulgar London suburbian. She had, indeed, a strange series of experiences — painful, entertaining, delightful — with these cottages. The most extraordinarily varied people drifted into them. Amid the sprinkling of stodgy suburbians there were exquisite artists, noted men of letters, soldiers and diplomats, eccentric foreign scholars, runaway unwedded couples, people with obscure Continental titles, victims of alcohol and of morphia, on two occasions mysterious and clever adventuresses who of course escaped, even when their true character had been discovered, without paying rent.[1] But there were charming and lovely people among them, and some of them became Edith's devoted friends and still cherish her memory.

The cottage industry proved fairly remunerative in Edith's skilful hands, and it worked in with the farm which supplied the tenants with farm produce. But the farm began to flag after some ten years or so. For this there were several reasons. It had never been really profitable. Good management and even good prices were not enough to make up for smallness of scale and the heavy

[1] The list — as I recall a few names at random — included Henry Bishop, later A.R.A., a painter of distinction who became a lasting friend; Somerset Maugham, dramatist and novelist; Lutoslavski, the eminent Platonist scholar; E. V. Lucas, one of the most prolific and versatile of authors; Edward Garret, well-known South African editor; Major Pratt, a pioneer in pacifism.

charges for labour, while during a long and serious illness of
Edith's with neuritis involving later for a time the use of crutches
— the most prolonged illness she had had since marriage and my
time and thought largely absorbed in nursing her — careless
servants ran up expenses unchecked, and serious losses made
retrenchment necessary. The increasing uncertainty of her
health itself made the strains and stresses of farm life undesirable.
Moreover, as the farm began to become a toilsome routine, it also
began to lose interest for one whose alert and active mind was ever
eager for the novelty of new conquests. A fresh field was, indeed,
opening before her in the sphere of art, with her increasing impulse
to write novels, which was scarcely compatible with the constant
and urgent demands of farm life, and to produce plays, which involved much time in London. There was yet another reason why
she was becoming alienated from farm life: she had always had a
horror of the slaughter of animals; in the ardour with which she
adopted the farming spirit, that horror had been temporarily suppressed; but it began to reassert itself more strongly than ever,
and her pronounced love of animals, her uncontrollably fierce
hatred for all cruelty to animals, were never so developed as during the latter years of her life.

The farm might, however, have lingered on some years longer
if it had not been brought to an end by what was really a stroke
of luck. An ingenious speculator had devised the scheme of
reopening the mine to which the Count House was attached, and
a company was formed. The building was required for its original purpose, but Edith was firmly secured with a long lease. The
company offered ten pounds to clear us out, but Edith demanded,
I think, two hundred pounds and held out until it was paid. The
company soon abandoned its mining efforts and failed. We used
playfully to say that it had only been formed to enable the farm
to be brought to an end. For there was no more farming; two
animals only (except dogs and cats) were left, an old horse and a
donkey of charming disposition (his one weakness a fondness for

cigarettes) born on the farm and the horse's inseparable companion; nothing would induce Edith to sell them or separate them;
she took a stable and a field for them, and afterwards brought
them up near London; they were a source of trouble and expense
until a year before her own death. When they were growing old
and diseased, she had them mercifully killed, I watching the operation on her behalf, as when Jock had been shot more than fifteen
years earlier.

It seems surprising to me that in thus narrating the chief events
of these years I never refer to my work, although I was all the time
living in it; with scarcely a day's intermission, and with complete
absence of all those recreations, amusements, social engagements,
etc., with which it is usual to space out 'work.' The reason seems
to be that for me 'work' in the usual sense has scarcely ever existed. I have always said that I have no aptitude for 'work'; that
I can only play. What would be called work was for me simply
the atmosphere in which I lived, and there is nothing to say about
it because it was omnipresent. The imagery of the bee collecting
nectar, transforming it into honey and storing it in cells, to furnish
sweetness and light for mankind, has always been attractive to
me, as it seems to have been to Swift. I suppose the reason is that
it really expresses what might be considered the unconscious ideal
of my own activities in life, and such activities are so natural and
spontaneous that there is little to say about them. In 1916,
Doctor Davenport wrote to me from the American Station of
Experimental Evolution: 'You seem to me about the only English
writer with whom I am acquainted who uses the facts of social
behaviour as facts of natural history to be discussed as any other
biological facts.' I had not been definitely conscious of such an
attitude, but the remark interested and pleased me. It seemed
to indicate the kind of natural-history atmosphere in which I
spontaneously move. I should be inclined to attribute it to that
natural-history temper which certainly marks the East Anglian
people from whom I so largely spring.

Early in 1894 my sister had given up the house at Saint Mary's
Terrace, Paddington, and I had joined Arthur Symons at Foun-
tain Court in the Temple, moving there my small possessions at
Paddington, in order to retain a little foothold in London, where
I could stay for a few days or weeks at a time to work at the
British Museum, or to see friends and interview people on literary
business, especially in connection with my Contemporary Science
Series which was at this time in active progress and my chief
source of income. In the autumn of the same year, Edith and I
gave up the delicious summer bungalow in Rollo Russell's grounds
at Haslemere and sold the furniture. There was, however, no
question of her sharing my little foothold at Fountain Court; it
was too small and she had not the slightest wish to live in London.
After spending so much of her life in London, and enduring so
many painful or tedious experiences there, she was at this period
of her life athirst for the free and beautiful life of Nature in the
country and had grown in love with Cornwall. When she wanted
to come to London, she would spend a few days with friends, and
once or twice we stayed together for a night or two at an hotel
near the Strand. Carbis, where a new life seemed to be opening
out, remained her sole home for a number of years, and during
those same years was my headquarters. Now and then, though
seldom in the winter, I would run up to London for a fortnight or
so, and every year or two I would go with Symons for some six
weeks of wandering abroad, which it was always a joy for me to
plan carefully long beforehand, Symons being content that I
should organise, though in smaller details and on the actual journey, he was often the leader.

In the spring of 1894 I had indeed gone by myself (for Symons
was then making a prolonged stay in Venice) to Italy on what I
always regard as the most glorious of all my foreign tours, full
throughout of unalloyed delight, and favoured by perfect weather.
It was in connection with the International Medical Congress in
Rome. On my arrival I was visited at my hotel by Lombroso and

Tamburini; and they appointed me a secretary of the Psychiatric Section (an honour due to my book, *The Criminal*), where I met Ferri, Marro, and others whose names and work were familiar to me, including Doctor Kurella who later became the friendly translator of my *Sex Studies* and finally died during the Great War. But I took my duties lightly. I spent nearly all my time in rambling, in ecstasy and at random, about the great city I had all my life desired to see, and found — an almost unique experience — that it even surpassed my anticipations. It is only in Rome, as I still continue to feel, that one realises what it means to belong to the human species. It was the classic Rome that absorbed me, and to such an extent that the memory of Shelley never once entered my head, though in earlier years the pyramid of Cestius near where his ashes repose had seemed to me the most sacred spot in Rome. Then I went on to Naples and visited Capri, where I found the famous Blue Grotto disappointing, spent a memorable day at Pompeii, and revelled among the treasures of the delightful Naples Museum. On the way back I joined Symons for a few days in Venice, though I stayed in the house on the Zattere of the hospitable scholar, Horatio Brown, J. A. Symonds's friend and literary executor, who met me in true Venetian fashion at the railway station in his gondola and conveyed me to his door on the canal.

Three years later I went to the next International Medical Congress in Moscow, and on this occasion Symons was with me all the time. We fitted in a visit to Munich and Bayreuth for *Parsifal* on the way, as well as to Warsaw, and took Saint Petersburg (as it then was), Prague, Budapest, Vienna, and the Rhine on the return journey. This expedition, full of deep interest, was alloyed by various discomforts, especially by the tedious journeys and the extreme (quite unusual) heat of Moscow. In both expeditions medical objects played the smallest part in my aims. I had by this time altogether abandoned any thought I might once have had of general medical practice and saw the last of it in 1894, when

once more I went as *locum tenens* to Probus, and felt on leaving
that such work was not for me. (When again in demand for the
year following at Probus, I introduced Barker Smith in my place,
and for many years after he was my appreciated successor there.)
But I have never ceased to be to some degree in touch with general medical work, and have remained throughout a member of
the British Medical Association, for which, at my election, as I
am always pleased to remember, I had two such distinguished
sponsors as Hack Tuke and Augustus Waller.

Fountain Court, with the two little rooms which I rented from
Symons, until he gave up the chambers on his marriage in 1901,
was for my purposes absolutely ideal. The chambers consisted
of four rooms at the top of the building, two overlooking the
Court and occupied by Symons, two of smaller size overlooking
Essex Street which were mine. A narrow passage joined Symons's
rooms to mine, but there were two separate doors onto the landing (double doors so that when we wished, it was possible for each
of us separately to 'sport the oak' and exclude importunate call-
ers), and each of us with his visitors was completely shut off and
independent of the other, while yet we were in close touch whenever we so desired. It was part of the arrangement that Symons
should be free to put anyone else in my rooms when I was away
in Cornwall; I do not recall that he ever made use of this freedom
except during one season for W. B. Yeats the poet, and again to
install Verlaine during his brief visit to London. On that occasion
Verlaine wrote a little poem about the 'Coin exquis dece coin
délicat.'

That, indeed, is how it appeared to me and how it will always
remain in memory. It was an oasis of silence and beauty in the
midst of the City desert. I still think with pleasure of the Court
bordered on one side by the ancient Middle Temple Hall rich in
memorable associations, of the fountain gently plashing, of the
tree beside it with the seat on which on summer nights, when the
Temple gates were closed, Symons and I would sometimes come

out to sit in the silent Court, now become as a Court of the Alhambra, marvellous in its deep peace only broken by the gentle plash of the water.

It was pleasant, too, to have at hand so agreeable and congenial a companion always so delightfully fresh, so vivaciously Celtic, in his sensitive appreciation of the beauty of things. It was pleasant, again, when one grew tired of talking of art or of life, to lie back on his lounge and listen as he played the piano, or to accompany him to music-halls, for as music-hall critic to the *Star* he had the entry to all, and they were then at their finest and most distinctive period of evolution.[1] It was pleasant, also, to be able to wander down onto the Embankment in the twilight on every evening, and walk up and down between Blackfriars Bridge and Westminster Bridge, ravished by this, at that hour, loveliest scene that I know in any city of the world. It was in those years I discovered that loveliness and I cherish it still. Now, indeed (I write in war-time), this magic beauty has attained an exquisite height it never touched before. For of old there were always crude glares one had to overlook: they are all gone now, and for the first time, and perhaps the last, we see all the undesigned magnificence of that mysterious dream which Nature and Man have wrought together on the evening waters of the Thames. When at last Symons gave up his chambers, I was not there to bid that loved spot farewell. I have never felt able to enter Fountain Court since, often as I have passed its gates. But it amuses me to think that I accidentally retained the key to my rooms on that

---

[1] In the *British Journal of Medical Psychology*, vol. XII, part IV (1932), appeared an elaborate article by an American medical writer entitled 'The Case of Arthur Symons: The Psychopathology of a Man of Letters.' This study is, throughout, incorrect and misleading. The writer, though familiar with Symons's writings and aware of his insanity in later life (of which Symons himself published a version), had never met him, had failed to understand his temperament, and wrongly diagnosed his mental disorder. His 'facts' are frequently perverted or imaginary, his conception of Symons's character opposed to the reality, his deductions astray, and his interpretation of the books he quotes unreliable. The editors of the *Journal* (who had not known that Symons was still living) much regretted the publication, but decided that nothing could be done to mend matters.

upper floor and could enter them by stealth this evening if I so wished.

The foothold of those little rooms not only enabled me to go easily about London by day and by night, but was convenient for seeing friends and acquaintances. It was here that my relationship with Amy slowly ripened into intimacy, for her home was in the suburbs within easy reach. Nothing was concealed from Edith. But there were difficulties of various kinds, and even for years I was not happy over the relationship, for all the peace and refreshment it brought me. Especially it troubled me that Edith, often obscurely and sometimes definitely, resented it, notwithstanding that she herself exercised, and had initiated, a freedom which I regarded as identical. There arose, moreover, entanglements on Amy's side which I need not explain — though there would be no discredit for any of us in explaining them — which led to incidents painful alike to Amy and me and to Edith. I had not desired, I may say, that Amy should in any way whatever bind herself to me; I told her that I could not answer for my affection, that very likely it would not last, and that she must regard herself as perfectly free.

At one time I felt that the situation was intolerable. I resolved to terminate the relationship and to cease seeing or corresponding with Amy, while she on her side, willing to second what seemed to me best, took a situation on the Continent and remained there for several years. But on my side the resolution was a complete failure. As soon as I felt completely cut off from Amy, my dejection became so obvious that Edith clearly saw it was useless to expect me to be able to persist in the effort. After only a few weeks, I was again in correspondence with Amy. Still much had been achieved even by this failure. It enabled me to realise that, whether or not this relationship was to be a big thing in my life, I could not destroy it by a mere exercise of will power. It enabled Edith to see that I had, at all events, been willing to make an effort, though in vain, and that the situation must be accepted.

Then the whole problem was thrust into the background during three years when Amy was abroad and I was unable to see her except on her rare visits to England, or when I chanced in the course of a Continental tour to contrive a meeting of a few hours. Thus, in the end Edith and I conquered a difficulty which might well have been fatal to our union. I should say that she never at any time felt any personal dislike for Amy, who was indeed of a sweet and generous nature which attracted the affection of all, men and women alike, who knew her. As the years passed, Edith placed more and more confidence in Amy and it became a genuine satisfaction to her to know that in her own absence Amy was near me. On her part, Amy had never shown the slightest sign, even in the most intimate moments with me, of animosity against Edith: it would have been unreasonable, indeed, but in such matters people are not reasonable, women least of all, and therefore it is worth noting that we never discussed together Edith's attitude or temperament. That would to me have been an impossible disloyalty, and Amy instinctively respected my feelings. Edith sometimes found this a little difficult to believe; but it was true. She had a horror of being 'talked over.' It was also a torture to her to think that anyone would feel 'sorry' for her. That remained a trouble when all other trouble in the matter had passed. She was reconciled to the facts, but when she knew or suspected that they might be a subject of scandal among people who would be 'sorry for her,' she felt the situation intolerable.

It was a long time before there was complete and permanent reconcilement in her mind. 'Life is so funny,' she wrote me in August, 1895, 'but really nothing matters but love, and I love you dearly and truly for always.' That was her fundamental faith. Yet during many many years there would be occasional revulsions and outbursts of bitterness. She would sometimes say that what she felt (though I could have said the same of most of the women to whom she was herself intimately attracted) was that Amy lacked the strength of character and mental force which could alone make it safe and fitting for her to enter our lives. But Edith herself possessed fully all the power of mind and character which I needed in an intimate soul comrade. They are precious qualities, but are not necessarily accompanied by other precious qualities of sweetness and gentleness which I also craved and found in Amy. I felt, and I still feel now that all is over, that I could do no other; that under all the circumstances my attitude was not unreasonable, and that even if by a great effort I could have thrust away from me forever that beautiful influence which soothed my life, I should merely have succeeded in crushing my own spirit, with whatever possibilities for use in the world it possessed. Yet also at the same time I well understood how Edith, too, with her special temperament, could be no other than she was; that her moments of wounded pride for herself, and even for me, were inevitable; and I could not resent her resentment, for I knew that with her pride the deep springs of her love also gushed forth. So I shared her pain, even if I sometimes rose in rebellion against it, as well as endured my own.

I find traces of those revulsions of hers in letters written a few years ahead. In March, 1898, both Claire and Amy notwithstanding, she could end up a letter: 'I miss you terribly, my own Love, who are woman and man. Your own child Wifie.' A year later she had gone in June to stay with a friend in London, leaving me at Carbis to keep an eye on the animals and the servants. It so chanced that just then Amy was staying not far away in Cornwall and she proposed to come over for a few hours one day to my studio. I mentioned this to Edith. In her next letter, in which she tries to comfort me in the loneliness of which I had complained, she writes: 'Do cheer up, sweetheart, and if you *must* spoil Carbis Bay for me, why do, for after all she can never rob me of all the best and sweetest memories of my life which laugh in the blue sea and will never be stolen by a mere player at life's realities.' I had not the faintest wish to spoil Carbis Bay, but it scarcely seemed to me that Amy's little visit — which I could

In his studio

At Hawkes Point, Carbis Bay, December, 1897

hardly have forbidden even if I had wished to — could possibly do that. It duly took place — though I was careful not to accompany her when she went to see Saint Ives and in my scrupulosity never showed her even the outside of the Count House — and left a benediction of lovely memory which soothed me for long afterwards.

Edith, as was often the case, reacted from her sudden outburst. Ten days later I find her writing from Claire's home to which she had moved on:

> *My Love*, Your letter is indeed a veritable epistle of Saint John, and it has done me more good than all the heart exercises and drugs in London. I only have realised lately how much more I love you than I ever did, or you could not make me suffer so hideously. And though I may not yet comprehend you, you also don't quite see why I feel things; but all is sure to come right, for love carries folk through everything in the end.... I'll soon be back and nestle you close to my silly heart and see if that will do it good.

A little later she wrote to me from Carbis:

> The demand that when we love that love should be true to *us* and to our share in it is all anyone who lives and thinks can ask: to *demand* more is to court deception, estrangement, and misery. I've arrived at this conclusion after *intense* suffering about Amy, but I shall never suffer again. Do what you will — be what you will and don't feel you must ever *make* me understand. I shall ask no questions; but we will be both free in the real sense of the word — free to respect and love the love of others, free to *trust* our own love in the face of everything.... This is the best of me, so I give it to you as a gift from the woman who loves you.

It was probably about this time (as usual my letter is undated) that I wrote to her from Carbis where she had left me in charge:

> I am well and peaceful and working — but always with a yearning, unsatisfied ache of love to you in my heart. There is no news; everything goes on quite well and the hirelings seem to be always working — an immense lot of painting and tarring done by Robert last week. Your letter is gentle. But I can see

you do not understand, even the tiniest bit. I wish that in love people could see straight into each other's hearts and that it was not necessary to try to put things into words which are always inadequate. I may do things that hurt you on the surface and for the time, because I am a person who must love in my own way and my love would be poisoned if it were forced; but if you could only *see*, you would know that right deep down I belong, and always must belong, wholly to you, and that I could never do anything that would *really* hurt you when you understood exactly what it meant. Human beings are very complex things, and no one can have a human being constituted *exactly* as he would like — probably we shouldn't like it even then — but it is a very great deal to have the fundamentals right.

Again she wrote to me from London (after describing the physical exercises which by the physician's advice she was learning, under a good teacher, in order to improve the condition of her heart and to reduce the tendency she was now showing to put on fat):

I am feeling ever so much happier and very close and sweet to you: your last letters have made me feel and know things that are lovelier to know than if events had never come to produce them. I am much more terribly in love with you than I have ever been; but you, too, must have patience with my way of doing things and seeing things. To feel close to you and sweet is the best cure for my heart — of that I am sure. I love to feel you my child, but I get 'uppish' when the man of science is too rampant; the best thing we can all be is to be little children. I'm getting sicker and wearier than ever of complex things and modern things. — Your letter has just come and I smiled: if *you* could see into *my* heart you'd see I'm ashamed at my want of faith (an inherited vice), and that I hate confessing I'm wrong, but I believe I've been making a huge mistake — so there! Chuckle over that, but try and go on loving me, for to me 'Thee art the one man i' all the world as I do love!' God knows I ache to hold you to my breast at last.

The fluctuations continued when any jar, real or imagined, occurred to cause them. Six weeks later I left her peacefully happy in Carbis with the old lady, Mrs. Drake, whom she always called 'the Mother.' On the 3d of August she wrote:

> I think of you and love you and wonder! — wonder much in the mother part of me and in the wife part, too. You are as free as air — choose whichever way seems the sweetest and best to you, for I am sure to bind is to lose and to fetter is to destroy [words she again applied to love, nearly twenty years later, in her book on Hinton]. I shall never leave you nor forsake you: the only thing that can happen is a shadow, but that may disappear in time. I am more complex than you have ever guessed: you are more impenetrative in some ways than I ever knew. I am a devil, you are a saint — the complexities that arise are manifold. But love solves more than this. I am growing strong now to live, and it is best, for I'd hate to leave you in the silence where you could never explain and I could never understand. As it is — all is bound to be well in the end.

A week later she wrote:

> *My own sweet Baby,* Eh! mon! thee ought not to go far from your mammy's apron-strings, for thee wants thy bottle sadly! I wish I had kept that letter of yours, but if you *meant* nothing against me, well, I am sorry I read it as such. You never realise what a proud devil I am, and how I eat my heart and soul out rather than stoop to the one I love best i' all the world. I ran to send a wire to comfort you, darling, and I trust it will, for I long to put my arms round you and cheer you.... Try and be happy and know I am always *really* in love with you, but I fear I'm a woeful proud crittur. My heart is not quite right yet somehow, but a real loving letter from you will soon set it so.
>
> Your own Sweetheart

It is not to be supposed that these episodes are of frequent occurrence in the letters which during all these years — never more so than between 1895 and 1900 — are for the most part full of sweetness and tenderness, of playful banter, of all the little intimacies of daily life. It is only at intervals that there occurs such a letter as — a few months later than the last quoted — the following:

My poor Boy, My heart is aching and aching for you, and my eyes (not boy's eyes but woman's eyes) keep filling at the thought of you. Oh! dear, oh, dear! *why* have you and I to keep making one another miserable, when no other person could ever be really as much to the other as you and I are? Try and be cheered a wee, for it *must* all come right in time and we may be ever so much nearer through it. I feel an intense desire to see you, and am sad and tired, and want you to realise I want to make you happy, but like you I can't do it at the expense of all my personality.... Come home, dear, dear child, and you shall be fed and hushed and comforted by your wifie.

It was probably somewhere about this time that she wrote out and sent me Emily Dickinson's poem 'Proof,' on the tests of love, ending:

> 'This dost thou doubt, sweet?
> Then have I
>
> Nothing to show
> But Calvary.'

The path of love may well have sometimes seemed to each of us the path of Calvary. But, as all Christendom has testified, the path of Calvary is not the path of failure.

Thus we slowly achieved the conquest of a great difficulty. But it must be added that in the process our marital relationship in the narrow sense was permanently brought to an end. This happened on Edith's proposal, I no longer know in what year and in our letters there is not the slightest change by which it might be detected. I made not the slightest objection. On her side, in addition to any feeling she had regarding my relationship to Amy, she had experienced from the outset a dislike to the mechanical contraceptive preliminaries of intercourse. On my side, I felt that in this respect we were relatively unsuited to each other; that relations were incomplete and unsatisfactory, too liable to jar on one or other of the partners. The loss was in our case a gain. We had secured all that that 'golden key' to the 'deepest secrets of intimacy' has to give and we could now develop our relationship better without it. In all other respects our physical intimacy remained the same, and nearly to the end we would find consolation in lying or sleeping together, a nearness she sometimes deeply craved. Some years after the period I am here concerned with, it happened once that — whether by deliberate resolve or sudden impulse I never knew — Edith proposed to me that we should go back to our early relations and henceforth suffice to each other. I allowed the proposal to drop without discussion and she never brought it forward again. The whole matter seemed entirely to pass from our minds; so much remained that it seemed to leave no blank.

It is, I know, not uncommon, almost indeed the rule, after some years of married life for the passion with which it may have begun to die down into calm friendship or cool indifference, or worse. With us the real love — it was scarcely passion — gave place to none of these things. On the contrary, it grew; it grew into passion, and this more than a spiritual passion, since the yearning tenderness of the body was not excluded. Only one thing was left out, a real and definite thing, yet so small in comparison to all that was left that we scarcely missed it. Even years after her death and all was in seeming over, I would find myself exclaiming inwardly: My sweetheart!

The greatest of all the revelations which my life with Edith brought me was this discovery that not only affection but the deepest passion of love can exist and develop continuously even when the relationship of sex in the narrow sense has ceased to exist. That it may require some such relationship for its foundation, I believe. But what I have learnt is that passionate love — that is to say a love deeper and more intimately moving than simple affection — may continue forever in its absence and stir the heart long years after the woman who inspired it is dead. I know by experience that love can last as long as we last. I know how it is that in old days, when they expected to live again, they said that love is 'eternal.' I can understand that threefold sigh of joy over a dead lover: *Amavimus, Amamus, Amabimus.*

Part VIII

VIII

I⊤ ⲓѕ time to refer to an event of a more
external nature which made a mark on the lives of both of
us, and for my own work in the world was of far-reaching significance: the prosecution of the first published volumes of my
Sex Studies for 'obscenity.' This took place in 1898. But first
I must touch on Edith's literary activities which on a serious scale began in this year and chanced to be connected with
my *Studies*. I have indicated that the early years of marriage
were for her a time of comparative repose and freedom and
expansion. But her energetic nature soon began to manifest
itself. The practical details of domesticity, the occasional help
she at first gave to me as an amanuensis, the progress of her
continuously developing career as a lecturer and speaker, the
pressure of intimate emotional struggles and those duties of
friendship which she always took so seriously, the ever-increasing
activities of the little farm — all these were not enough to absorb

her. She also found herself as an artist (which she slowly came to feel her chief function) and wrote her first and most powerful novel, *Kit's Woman,* or, as it was entitled in the first edition, *Seaweed.* This was begun even before we moved into the Count House, and was completed by 1898. I call it her first novel, for she herself attached no importance to the story called *Love and Honour* which she wrote at about the age of eighteen, to run through numerous numbers of the *Manchester Magazine,* though it was never ever completed. *Kit's Woman* was a real work of art, well planned and well balanced, original and daring, the genuinely personal outcome of its author, alike in its humour and its firm deep grip of the great sexual problems it is concerned with, centring around the relations of a wife to a husband who by an accident has become impotent. I say it was 'genuinely personal,' but it is not, I now add, till long after I wrote those words that it has seemed to me that the story was consciously or unconsciously inspired by her own relations with me and of course completely transformed by the artist's hand into a new shape. In that shape it splendidly presents exactly what I have attempted to present in the preceding pages: the triumph of a deeper passionate love over physical passion.

The bold sincerity of the book's outlook and the occasional unconventional freedom of its language caused it to be banned sometimes by prudish people, and offensively classed by coarse-minded people. But there should have been no doubt about the real natural purity and lofty idealism which inspired the book, and still less concerning its splendid assertion of the spiritual supremacy of love. It received the warm commendation, even the enthusiastic admiration, of many excellent judges: in my opinion, which may be prejudiced, it is a book too good to be allowed to die. But it was too outspoken a book to find a publisher easily, and it thus came about that it was accepted by the unconventional publisher who had already just arranged to issue my *Studies.*

For many years I had been slowly working my way towards those *Studies* which I regarded as my chief life-work. In 1894 I had published *Man and Woman: A Study of Human Secondary Sexual Characters*, which constituted the prolegomena to the *Studies*, in the sense that it was a book to be studied and read in order to clear the ground for the study of sex in the central sense in which I was chiefly concerned with it. *Man and Woman*, primarily undertaken for my own edification, had itself been developing from very small beginnings during some ten years. It embodied not only much careful thinking and balanced generalisation, but far more tedious labour in the collection, sifting, and classification of data than appear on the surface. It received almost no attention at all from reviewers, who had given so much attention to my first two books four years before, in part perhaps because of the very various aspect of the subject it presented, in part possibly because it included a chapter on menstruation which alarmed modest editors. But it had a large and continuous sale through several revised editions (the eighth and last in 1934) and in various languages; it stimulated workers in several fields to initiate new and fruitful investigation; it received privately the high commendation of authorities of different kinds. I was especially pleased when Doctor Beddoe, then the chief English anthropologist, always kind and helpful to me as to many others, wrote pleasantly to me that it was 'a great little book.'

That task being completed, I turned to the *Studies* themselves. The volume I resolved to put into shape first was *Sexual Inversion*. That resolve was a mistake. It was, indeed, a kind of accident. Homosexuality was an aspect of sex which up to a few years before had interested me less than any, and I had known very little about it. But during those few years I had become interested in it. Partly I had found that some of my own most highly esteemed friends were more or less homosexual (like Edward Carpenter, not to mention Edith), and partly I had come into touch through correspondence with John Addington Symonds, for whose work

I had once had an admiration which somewhat decreased with years. He had already printed privately two small books on the subject, one on Greek paiderastia, and another, more novel, but of less value, on the modern aspects of the question. He was feeling his way towards the open publication of a comprehensive work on the subject. He now proposed to join forces with me. I agreed, and I drew up a scheme of the book with the parts I proposed to be assigned to each author. He accepted my scheme, remarking that I had assigned the most important chapters to myself, but making no demur. I had no wish to take the chief share, but it seemed clear to me that it was on the scholarly and historical side alone that Symonds could properly come into the book. He set to work on his share of the collaboration and he sent me a collection of 'histories' he had been able to collect among friends; these were duly included in the work I eventually published. But before we could make any progress or even meet, Symonds died, suddenly, during an epidemic of influenza, in Rome.

Thus our attempt at collaboration came to naught. I do not regret it. A highly individual writer cannot write in association with another writer, all the less if they are both highly individual. In the early days of my friendship with Olive Schreiner we planned to write a paper together, but speedily realised that it was impossible. Arthur Symons and I planned to write a volume of essays on Spain together, and that plan also was eventually abandoned as impracticable. The collaboration with Symonds would have been still more unfortunate, not only because of incongruity of style, but because the significance of a book on inversion would have been greatly discounted by the fact that one of the writers was known to many as personally concerned in the question of homosexuality. But I loyally attempted, though already rather doubtful of their value, to use as much as possible of Symonds's booklets and other fragments, and in this I had the consent of his literary executor, Horatio Brown. For the first

version of the book, with the joint authorship declared on the
title-page, I succeeded through my good friend and translator,
Doctor Hans Kurella, in finding (in 1896) a German publisher
before I had found one in England. Kurella entitled it for the
German public (though this title was not one I approved of) *Das
Konträre Geschlechtsgefühl*. It was never published in English,
for at the last moment, when the English edition was already
bound and on the eve of publication, the Symonds family seem
to have taken alarm and Brown bought up the edition, though
numerous copies nevertheless (not, of course, by my connivance
nor to my benefit) succeeded in getting into circulation.

That was in 1898. I go back to the interval after the German
publication when my thoughts were occupied with the question of
a suitable English publisher. I selected Williams and Norgate as
a small firm who issued quietly some serious scientific books,
and thus seemed fitting publishers for mine. It so happened that
they submitted my manuscript to the judgment of a dear and
highly valued friend of mine, a distinguished alienist, Doctor
Hack Tuke. He had for nearly ten years previously, as editor of
the *Journal of Mental Science* and in other ways, been helpful to
me, and had a high opinion of my co-operation; the relationship
had taken on a friendly character and he had invited me to his
country house and introduced me to his wife.[1] Hack Tuke was
not prudish or illiberal, but he was a Quaker brought up in an old-
fashioned school which could not possibly view sympathetically
any detailed approach to the problems of sex. He advised
Williams and Norgate against publication. At the same time,
with characteristic loyalty, he told me of the advice he had been

[1] It is a small world, and long years after her death, I learnt that I had an interesting link with Mrs. Hack Tuke. I possess a fine miniature, handed down from my
maternal grandmother, of Mrs. Stickney, who was the mother of Mrs. William Ellis,
no relation of mine, but a famous and prolific author in her time. Both mother and
daughter (who in early life had lived in Suffolk) were friends of my grandmother's,
my mother told us, and I had long wanted to know more of the Stickneys. When
I found that Mrs. Hack Tuke was by birth a Stickney, and closely related to the
attractive Mrs. Stickney of my miniature, I was much annoyed that the discovery
came too late.

asked and had given, and explained his position: as a book for specialists he had nothing to say against my study, but he felt that a book could never be confined to specialists, and so might exert a demoralising influence. 'There are always,' he said, 'the compositors!' I had not the slightest resentment at his attitude, which I accepted as inevitable, and his regard for me remained unchanged: our friendly relations continued, as before, until his death which followed not very long after, and before the book was published.

Then I heard, through an able scientific friend whose own original work received but little recognition, F. H. Perry-Coste (later he wrote it 'Perrycoste'), of what seemed a most promising opening for publication. A man of some wealth, he told me, interested in scientific and philosophic subjects which made no appeal to the larger public, was about to set up a small printing and publishing house for the unostentatious issue of a few such works. This seemed exactly the sort of publisher I wanted. He was a certain 'Mr. J. Astor Singer,' and his agent in London was his brother-in-law, a certain 'Dr. Roland de Villiers.' The former was always in the background and never visible, but I was soon in the presence of the latter, undoubtedly a German, probably of the Rhine, though familiar with English, a large, gentle, fleshy man with something of the aspect and the stealthy tread of a cat. The publication was speedily and easily arranged on a financial basis which, under all the circumstances, I regarded as satisfactory. From that point of view, indeed, I had no serious complaint against De Villiers; he fulfilled his pecuniary engagement with me and it is quite possible under the circumstances that the author obtained more money from the book than the publisher. Nor could I seriously complain of the other volumes which he proceeded to arrange to bring out in conjunction with mine. They were, indeed, not all scientific or sociological, for they included Edith's novel, *Seaweed*, but they were serious and original books, and when they dealt with sex it was in a manner which I regarded as entirely proper. But as I learnt to know more about De Villiers various puzzling and rather disquieting traits began to become clear. He was tricky. After first giving the publishing firm a name which suggested connection with one of the most famous London publishing houses, he finally fixed on another name, the Watford University Press, which was even more objectionable, since there was not the faintest ground for dragging in the word 'University.' He had, indeed, it appeared, a perverse love of mystification even for its own sake. The mysterious 'Mr. Singer,' the supposed wealthy principal in the concern, of whom De Villiers would speak with reverential awe, was always out of reach; sometimes he was staying on the Riviera; if much wanted he was travelling in Mexico; clearly he was a creation of De Villiers's brain. There was, however, 'Mrs. Singer' living in the same fine house with De Villiers, ostensibly his sister-in-law, but really, I was in time given to understand, his wife; the money employed in the transactions was largely in her name. It began to appear that 'Dr. de Villiers' himself was largely a fiction.

The fact was that Perrycoste, who thought to do me a service by telling me of this opening for publication, really knew nothing of De Villiers; he was misled by Mr. (later the Right Hon.) J. M. Robertson, who, in his turn, had himself been misled to the extent of publishing two or three books with De Villiers, and transferring to him the magazine he had previously edited himself. We were all misled. None of us had the slightest idea who 'De Villiers' was. Only the police knew, and at first even they were ignorant. So far as I am concerned, I never knew the details of De Villiers's career even twenty years afterwards, until, literally, yesterday, when at length I had the curiosity to read the history of the prosecution of my book as contained in a volume of reminiscences entitled *At Scotland Yard*, written by Mr. John Sweeney and published six years after the trial. Sweeney was the detective charged by Scotland Yard to work up the case. His account of the whole affair is clear and intelligent, even amusing, and, allow-

ing for the fact that it naturally takes for granted the police point
of view — quite fairly accurate wherever I can check it. He states
that the real name of 'Dr. Roland de Villiers' was Georg Ferdi-
nand Springmuhl von Weissenfeld, born in Germany and the son
of an eminent judge; he was educated at Giessen where he obtained high honours in science, medicine, and literature, and
married a German lady of good family. By his dubious conduct,
however, he became estranged from his father, and at length, after
forging cheques, he fled from Germany and settled in England in
1880.

Here he lived as a swindler and was once sentenced to
twelve months' hard labour for forgery and other offences. He
practised all sorts of frauds. Once he established a Brandy
Distillery Company, Ltd., which consisted only of himself, and
by circulating prospectuses containing photographs of vineyards,
none of which belonged to him, he secured capital to the amount
of about £60,000, out of which he paid a dividend of ten per cent.
He accumulated innumerable aliases, and to avoid confusing the
identity of the various characters he had invented he kept a
register in which he entered each alias with its own specific signature. He and his wife, also, had thirty distinct banking accounts
in London under different names. Even his servants were used to
aid his mystifications, and housemaids, cooks, and nurses would
at times pose in the drawing-room, robed in excessively smart
gowns, as the wives and daughters of statesmen, ambassadors, and
other celebrities. There are also tales of his unscrupulous sexual
depravity. Sweeney, who speaks with authority on this matter,
calls him 'a fascinating criminal,' even 'the most extraordinary
criminal of modern times.' Of all this I knew nothing whatever.
The whole man, however, it eventually became clear to me, was
a mass of mystification. I never regarded him as a criminal; even
now it seems to me that he was essentially a man afflicted by
a peculiar mental trait which it would have been psychologically
interesting to investigate. He was always seeking to mystify

others, even in the smallest matters. But he was himself the chief victim of his mystifications and died of them at last.

Sexual Inversion appeared with no undue delay. The Watford University Press had laid down expensive linotype printing plant, and the appearance of the volume was unexceptionable. It was issued quietly, as I had desired, only announced by prospectuses posted to doctors and others, and sent for review to a few medical and scientific journals. Not many reviews appeared, but they were respectful and appreciative without being enthusiastic. This was all I had expected or desired.

But suddenly things altogether ceased to be as I expected or desired.

There happened in those days to be in London a little society called the Legitimation League for the advocacy of unconventional ideas on marriage and parenthood, upholding a formal acknowledgement of union in preference to legal marriage, and seeking to raise the position of the illegitimate child. The League published an equally unconventional periodical called *The Adult*, a vigorous little paper edited by George Bedborough, who was also the secretary of the League. I had no connection whatever with the League or *The Adult*. But the League was in touch with De Villiers and it stocked a few copies of my book, without, however, exposing it or announcing it for sale. At that time a society of this kind was regarded as rather alarming and even anti-social. It thus happened that anarchists would attend the League's meetings, although its members had no sympathy with anarchism. In this way the League attracted the interest of the police, and so also it came about that the Bedborough prosecution was engineered by the anarchist section of Scotland Yard under Chief Inspector Melville, whose death, it so chances, was reported only a day or two ago as I write. Continuing to be worried over this movement, the police at length excogitated the brilliant idea that they could crush the Legitimation League and *The Adult* by identifying them with my *Sexual Inversion*, obviously, from their point of view, an 'obscene' book. Sweeney, who had much experience of anarchists, regularly attended the League's meetings in his capacity as detective, was treated as a friend of the movement, and won the confidence of the honest and unsuspicious Bedborough. When the police had completed their case, Sweeney came one day to the Society's office and purchased of Bedborough a copy of my book. Two or three days later, on the 31st of May, 1898, he arrested Bedborough. That same day at Carbis Bay, I received a telegram informing me of the arrest from a lady personally unknown to me — Lillian Harman, daughter of the American Moses Harman, a great pioneer of sex movements in his day — who then happened to be on a visit to London and in Bedborough's company at the time, and soon after I heard to the same effect from De Villiers, who added that he had been privately informed that I also was to be arrested. From that moment he himself timidly disappeared (ostensibly to Cologne, though it is quite possible that he remained all the time in his own house at Cambridge, for he was an adept in secret passages and concealed cupboards), after authorising me to obtain legal representation and undertaking to defray the expenses, an obligation he duly fulfilled.

I went up to London on the 6th of June to make arrangements for the defence in so far as De Villiers and myself were concerned, which was not directly, and the Legitimation League saw to the defence of Bedborough. Never having been in such a position before, I was at a loss to know what lawyers I should entrust with the defence, though my rooms were at the centre of Law, so I called upon W. M. Mackenzie, a young barrister in the Temple and the only lawyer with whom at that time I was in touch (introduced by Olive Schreiner), and who, indeed, I had formerly, in his early days of struggle, endeavoured to help by giving him to edit for the Mermaid Series the plays of Rowley, though that scheme, with many others, was brought to nought when the Mermaid Series was wrested out of my hands. He advised me to go to Messrs. Humphreys at Holborn Viaduct, which I accordingly did, and found Mr. Humphreys a kind, capable, and reliable adviser through all the difficult circumstances of the case.

I was alone at Carbis when the news of Bedborough's arrest reached me. Some days earlier, Edith had gone to London to stay for a week or so with Miss Ellen Dakin at Wetherby Gardens. Miss Dakin was an old and dear friend: they had first met when Edith was lecturing at William Morris's at Kelmscott House on 'What Women can do,' probably somewhere about 1888, and was much impressed by Edith's personality and the skilful way she answered the numerous questions addressed to her. It was the beginning of a friendship which lasted without a cloud until Edith's death. Miss Dakin, whose father had been a Lord Mayor of London, moved in a conventional social world which might seem altogether alien to Edith's habits and tastes, yet she always enjoyed it, always remained her unconventional self in it, and her tender affection and admiration for Miss Dakin's beautiful and unspoilt character in a conventional environment was profound. On the 24th of May she wrote:

My Love, What a time I'm having! Nelly is superhumanly kind. Yesterday was a heavenly blue day, warmth and sun enough to waken the dead. In the morning I went with Nelly and bought me a Paris silk blouse. Then I went on to Doctor Birch's and met Emmeline Pethick [afterwards Mrs. Lawrence] there for a moment. Was with Birch two hours; heart much more irritable and weaker; but he says it is the result of influenza poison, and guarantees I will be all right if I have no strain and no worries!! Examined me well and says I am as good as a doctor, and put some funny thing in my mouth which in an hour took all the pain out of my back and made me feel so different — he thought it would, but was not sure. Well, then I went alone to the Circus Restaurant and had stewed beef, new potatoes, asparagus, a glass of claret and coffee. Then I drove on to Emmeline's and spent one and a half hours with her. She looks very sweet and nice and gazed with great toleration at my clothes! Then on to Woodhouse [the dentist] (Sir W. Richmond, who had just come up from sketching Gladstone, was there in his Court dress and stars; he had such lovely legs; I told Woodhouse I'd love to have legs like that.) Well — tell Henry [the farm man] that I had a big double tooth out and a bad tooth filled and was one and a half hours in the dentist's chair and never uttered so much as a groan. He said if I did not have the tooth out at once it might mean serious inflammation. I looked at him with very grave blue eyes: 'Now — without gas?' I said, and the thrush flapped its wings. 'Yes,' he said very firmly and got the devilish thing in his hand. I threw down my glove and, after feeling as if my head had knocked at the golden gate, I heard: 'Good brave girl!' and he had my hand in his. He is more a darling than ever and told me a lot about himself. He wants to see your photo, so I'm going this morning to show it to him and to let him take the pack out of my toothless gum, as he put it in so that I could go to the Richter Concert. We went and I sat next to an old old foreigner who had played for years in the orchestra and comes always. He begged me to stay in London for a month and go to all the concerts, for 'I see you are a musician — you can sit for hours at home — just start the melodies on the piano and then — you are in Heaven, for dey all come floating in de brain.' I laughed so merrily he laughed too, though at what he never guessed. I told him skylarks were my musicians, and ducks and hens, etc.! — but it is curious how I find out instinctively what is good in music — what comes from a man's soul or only from his violin. Oh! I *was* happy, and a month of it would do me worlds of good. This morning we shop, and this afternoon De Villiers [about *Seaweed* which he was publishing] and Honor [Brooke] come, and tonight we go to *The Liars*. I feel like a child, am cared for and spoilt right and left, and it does suit me down to the ground. Next year I shall be in London all June and feast on civilisation. I'm sorry to say I've no wish to come home, but I feel lovingly sweet to you and I wish we could hear all these things together. We *must* go to Bayreuth! — I'm Wagner-hungry [in later years she quite lost her taste for Wagner] and Oh! I've not had half enough music yet. We go to Knightsbridge tomorrow morning, to *The Little Minister* in the afternoon, and then I pack in the evening. Tell Henry on a wet day to paint the inside of my study windows and tell Janey before I come home to scrub my couch. The bliss of having trained servants about is lovely, and Crisp [the butler] is back again, having married the cook. [She would always insist on treating the butler as a human being, even in the dining-room!] I'm lying in bed, waiting for my silver tray, silver egg-cup, etc., and I'm supremely restful and content — and at last out of pain in my back and heart. I suppose I shall be homesick some day, but now I think with horror of that house and its cares — only you and Jock stand in it as things I ever want to see again. I'm thinking sweetly, too, of the Sundts [dear friends up to the end].

Ever your Wifie

Next day she wrote:

My Love, I shopped all the morning yesterday and bought me real pretty things; then we had a late lunch at home and went to Dale's, and the fitter was killing; he said he *could* not believe the measurer and was thankful to see me. I gave one of my roars and asked him if I was the only woman with a proper breathing apparatus he had ever fitted. 'Well, madam, ladies nowadays lengthen their backs and take in their waists so much.' I told him when I saw men doing that I would perhaps begin. Then we came home and rested in Nelly's boudoir, but neither Honor nor De Villiers came. Then dinner and *The Liars* which I enjoyed immensely. I had Alice's [a servant at Carbis] dirty-looking note, saying the white cock was dead, which Crisp brought on a silver salver — all I wished was that they were all dead. I'm getting anxious — I could stay here a month without a qualm and I'm generally very homesick. This morning I am tired, but I'm in bed always till ten, and then we are going to have a long, long time with the pictures and a late lunch, and then Miss Dakin [Miss Ellen Dakin's sister] is going to drive me two hours in the Park with her two bays, her tiger, and her jolly carriage, as we can't get seats for *The Little Minister.* Claire writes to say that when I get there I shall never go! But, sweetheart, one day you will see me back, and now you realise what a bad time *I* have when you are away. Tell them to send on Friday 1 lb. butter and 4 doz. eggs to B., and to ask Mrs. F. if she wants any butter. I found I had more cash in the bank than I thought and it is a great relief; can send you some if you like. I dread that long journey tomorrow. This *is* a lovely house to stay in, and Nelly is *so* good and seems so happy to have me. Emmeline sees me off tomorrow. You sweet old love, you don't know how I appreciate the way you are giving me my holiday in peace by looking after things.

I expect it will do me a world of good. I went again to Woodhouse and he says I am sound for a year he thinks. *Wasn't* I brave? I nearly wired to tell you. You won't get such long letters after today for two reasons — I shall never be alone and there won't be much to tell, and, as you know, what there will be will be difficult to write. I've felt most spiritual in London somehow — like my old soaring self without the ethics, a person of aspirations and ideals. I wonder if it is the good dinners or what? Candidly I believe Alice drives me mad; these quiet well-trained servants rest my soul and body like hymns, and they've never told me yet they are 'sweating like mud!' I look and am an utterly different person, and I'm beginning to think I'm more at home in London than in Cornwall. But it will pass, I suppose, and I shall long for the wind and the dairy and the dogs, but now — no!! The weather is very warm, and today rather dark, but the lovely peace of the streets, the absence of cobblestones, the delicious thud of omnibuses, the picturesque grouping of hundreds of keen faces, the delicious dresses and flowers soothe me so, and make me think of all these clodhoppers with fatigue. Of course — as the wife of a scientist — I realise that it is a mere swing of the pendulum, but never again will I stay so long in that climate: I could never do the work I mean to do without the touch now and again of a complex world with its art, its music, its dancing, and its more graceful way of sinning. Good-bye, sweetheart — I hear the clock striking nine, so my breakfast will soon be here.

Your own Wifie

Such a sad letter from Miss G. — evidently another in a trap — Eh, but, mon, we're pretty well off — Eh?

I reproduce these self-revealing letters almost in full, for they are characteristic of her in those too rare moments when she was — even though ill — free from the irritation of strains and worries, and they show how her wonderful buoyancy of spirit could, under favourable conditions, even surmount ill-health. I could not, indeed, easily match them from later letters for un-alloyed light-hearted cheerfulness. As the years went on, indeed, anxieties and the physical distress of chronic ill-health tended to form a background even to her brightest moments. She might well put two exclamation marks after the physician's advice to avoid worries. Even as she wrote, the new blow was impending.

It fell, as I have said, on the 31st of May, a day or two after Edith had reached Claire's home in the North. I wrote at once to tell her. It is probable she replied with a telegram, but in any case she replied by letter on the 2d of June:

> *My Love*, I'm just starting off on my way to you — you poor old Love. Never mind, I'll stick to you and help you, and I'm at last *glad* to come home to you and cheer you and love you and comfort you. We'll live in England and spit at them, and two together can pull a boat that would else sink. If I get a wire to-night I shall be off tomorrow to you as fast as civilisation can bring me. Claire sends love and hopes all will be well.
>
> Your own Wifie
>
> Here is cheque for £2.

None was ever more staunch in emergencies, so prompt, so resourceful, so consoling. She whose physical temperament made her apt to fall into nervous terrors over mere nothings, whose health was always uncertain, who had just been told that the condition of her heart was worse and that she must avoid all worry, simply and as a matter of course flung all such considerations aside when a real trouble faced one whom she loved, and revealed, as Froissart said of the Countess of Montfort, the heart of a lion. Through all those trying and vexatious days — and by repeated delays they were spun out for nearly six months — she was as often as possible by my side, always bright and cheery, always helpful; it was, more especially, by her exertion among friends that perhaps the largest part of the Bedborough defence fund was raised. She made little of the misfortune which thus overtook her own book, by ill-luck only just published (the special copy she had bound in leather for me is dated May) and at first carried off by the police in their indiscriminate raid, so that until reissued some years later in a completely new edition, under the title of *Kit's Woman*, it had no real circulation.

I quote a few passages from her letters to me during this June:

> The indescribable tenderness I have towards you because of
> this attack is like being 'under conviction.' You sweet old love,
> I'll feed 'ee love 'ee and tend 'ee. I never knew I loved you so
> *terribly* — it has taken ever so much out of me, but in a way I'm
> glad it has been, for I know a lot now and we shall soon be together
> again. . . . Never doubt I love you, for I feel sure it would *kill*
> me if anything awful happened to you. I wish for many things
> I could be there. I'm so afraid folk may imagine your wife is
> either antagonistic or thinks you an invert, and it is good for the
> cause that people who are one should face these things together.
> Years ago I told you I'd rather you'd do this than love me, and
> today, if all England were against you, and you in prison, I'd
> repeat it. I'm very restless and can settle to nothing, longing to
> be with you in London. If the case still goes on, I think I shall
> run up next week for a few days. . . . I am much comforted with
> your sweet note; it made my heart bump on another side for love
> of 'ee. De Villiers is a coward; if *you* had gone to Cologne there
> would have been no need for you ever to come to Carbis again.
> I think there is something funny about him. . . . An unutterable
> tenderness is over me: I feel as if I'd like to take you and carry
> you far away from all this respectability to a fair land where it is
> warm and full of flowers. I'm terribly depressed today, one of
> those warm close Cornish days. I wish you were here — wish
> you could get down and come to my arms. I've a wild wish to
> suckle you almost, and when I got your letter it made me set my
> teeth for fear they hurt you, but never mind, if they make England
> impossible for us we'll sell all and go abroad on what I have and
> live our lives as friends and lovers and dreamers. I'm not a bit
> the money-loving beastie I appear — love is all to me and I love
> you more than ever, for I've never found you fail in essentials.
> You can no more get free of me than you can of your own guts,
> as Janet [in *Kit's Woman*] says. Send me a wire if anything new
> turns up, and of course I'll do anything any time. Good night,
> my sweetheart. Oh! dear! *what* a thing it is to love your man a
> thousand times more six years after marriage than before!

The whole course of the case — in which I had no legal standing, although my book was the ostensible subject of it, and no

power over the decisive steps of the defence — was profoundly unsatisfactory. There was little but confusion, muddle, disappointment, even rascality, from first to last, and in the end the issue was never, after all, fought, because Bedborough decided, and under all the circumstances I have never blamed him, to plead guilty. In the forefront of the indictment, *Regina v. Bedborough*, was placed as the 'first count' the charge that Bedborough, who really had no connection at all with the production of the book, had 'sold and uttered a certain lewd wicked bawdy scandalous and obscene libel in the form of a book entitled *Studies in the Psychology of Sex: Sexual Inversion.*' But the other counts dealt with the publications of the Legitimation League, which had no claim to be scientific, and with which I had no connection, just as the Legitimation League had no connection with my book.

The issue was thus, perhaps deliberately, confused, for it was possible to uphold my book and to disapprove of the League's publications, or to uphold the League and disapprove of my book. On this and no doubt other accounts not a single prominent scientific or medical person came publicly forward for the defence, and though I received, with permission to use them, the most handsome testimonials from the leading authorities in the medico-psychological sphere, foreigners as well as British, the writers were not prepared to go into the witness box on behalf of the book. I was not even prepared to go myself, for I could not possibly give proofs of the reality of the confidential cases reported in my book, which my solicitors thought it very desirable to do, and I knew also that those same defects which have always prevented me from attempting any kind of public speech would make me a bad witness, while I could not claim any recognised position in the medical world which would give authority to my evidence.

It thus came about that the defence was from the first made mainly a question of 'freedom of the press,' and a 'Free Press Defence Committee' was set up, consisting, for the most part, of the most variegated assortment of secularists, anarchists, radicals, and unconventional literary free-lances. The secretary, Henry Seymour, was an anarchist, I had never heard of him before, though he was prominent in the small anarchist party of London, but he wrote to me immediately on Bedborough's arrest, and thenceforth this admirable little man took the leading part in the defence, as staunch as Edith, and even more unwearied and self-less, for he had no personal concern in the matter and yet was willing to sacrifice his own time and labour and business interests in this impersonal cause. When the trial was over, he was the one person in the new crowd the case had brought me in contact with that I was able to look back on with pleasure and I continued to meet him at intervals for some years afterwards.[1] The variegated committee certainly included many sound and more than a few brilliant people. Such were Grant Allen, Belfort Bax, Robert Buchanan, Herbert Burrows, Mrs. Mona Caird, Edward Carpenter, Walter Crane, Mrs. Despard, A. E. Fletcher, G. W. Foote, Frank Harris (who brought the *Saturday Review*, which he then edited, to the side of the cause), G. J. Holyoake, H. M. Hyndman, George Moore, Frank Podmore, H. Quelch, J. M. Robertson (who wrote vigorously about the case), Henry S. Salt, William Sharp, Bernard Shaw (who was helpful in journalistic quarters), H. M. Thompson (editor of *Reynolds'*, which devoted much sympathetic attention to the case), John Trevor, etc.[2] But there was not a single doctor of position among them and the official men of science deliberately stood aloof.

The perils of the defence arose, not only from defective and rather compromising support from without, but still more fatally from failure within, the solicitor for Bedborough's defence was

[1] He became prominent in the gramophone industry, wrote a technical book on the manufacture, and invented a widely approved sound-box. His activity for anarchism diminished, but in late life he developed an enthusiasm for the Baconian theory of Shakespeare, edited *Baconiana*, and threw into the cause his characteristic energy.

[2] W. T. Stead, though not on the committee, was sympathetic and spoke up plainly in his *Review of Reviews*; later he became a friendly and admiring reader of the *Studies*.

chosen by a prominent member of the League from among his own acquaintances. How anyone could have chosen a solicitor who bore his character so clearly marked on his limp, shady, and shabby figure, it is not easy to understand. He was unsatisfactory from the first, inattentive to the case, not to be found when wanted and scarcely helpful when found. But we rested our hopes on the counsel who had been selected with care and judgment to champion the cause of freedom and science. This was Mr. Avory, later a judge, but then a rising barrister who had not yet been given any great occasion for distinguishing himself.[1] He espoused the cause with an even personal ardour and believed that it furnished the great occasion for which he had long been looking. I am convinced he would have made a splendid defence. But it was not to be.

The case lingered on for nearly six months before coming to trial. Then, as later appeared, Bedborough went to Scotland Yard to see the Police Commissioner in charge of the case (quite probably by invitation from the Commissioner, who thought it might be better to compromise matters) and it was arranged that he should plead guilty to the chief counts of the charge and the case be dismissed or the sentence 'deferred.' How this arrangement affected the solicitor's conduct has never been clear to me. It all seems a muddle. But at all events, although the solicitor had two hundred pounds in hand wherewith to fee counsel he never paid over the fee, and the etiquette of the Bar made it impossible for Avory to appear. So that when the case was called, Bedborough was not represented and my book not defended. After the trial was over, the solicitor's conduct in the matter and his appropriation of the fee was investigated by the Law Society (in which my solicitor happened to occupy an important official position) and his name was struck off the rolls. But that was but

---

[1] He amply distinguished himself in later years and died as recently as 1935, unquestionably, it was said by *The Times*, the ablest as well as the oldest criminal judge on the bench.

a sorry consolation for us. For in ruining himself he had also ruined our defence.

During the first agitated weeks I had had to go up and down frequently between London and Carbis, with or without Edith. The autumn months we spent together in Carbis waiting for the postponed trial to come off, and when the date was finally fixed, we went up together toward the end of October. It took place at the Old Bailey on the thirty-first of that month. De Villiers, of course, remained in mysterious concealment. Humphreys, my solicitor, considered that the judge might possibly call for me. So, accompanied by Edith, I remained in a room off the court — undisturbed, for my name and the book were not even definitely mentioned in the proceedings — and then at length Humphreys came to tell me the result. It fairly corresponded to what we had been led to expect. The defendant, having pleaded guilty, was released on his own recognisances.

The Recorder of London, Sir Charles Hall (formerly attorney-general to the Prince of Wales, afterwards Edward VII, and, I am told, personally a capable and amiable man), was sitting as Judge. He addressed to the defendant the following remarks (taken down by a shorthand writer employed by the defence): 'You might at the outset perhaps have been gulled into the belief that somebody might say that this was a scientific book. But it is impossible for anybody with a head on his shoulders to open the book without seeing that it is a pretence and a sham, and that it is merely entered into for the purpose of selling this filthy publication.' That elegant sentence caused me more amusement than resentment even at the time — for I knew too well what the official judgments of the world are worth — and I still take a mischievous pleasure in reproducing it. I cannot recall how we received the news of the outcome of the trial, but I think our chief feeling was one of relief that the strain was at last over.[1]

[1] How promptly we were organising our next step is shown by a note written by Edith two days later on the train when returning to Carbis: 'My love, I've just

I remember that I went from the court to the office of the *Daily Chronicle* to see Massingham, the editor, who had been preparing to take up the question of the scientific value of the book when the trial was over, but he had evidently been deeply impressed by the judge's dictum; he merely sent his secretary out to me to make a few non-committal remarks, and next morning the *Chronicle* published a leader which was a beautiful counterpart to the judge's observations. Ostentatiously following the court's example by refraining from mentioning the names of author or book, the writer is good enough to give me credit for 'scientific intentions,' but 'the courts of the law and the criticisms of the press are the responsible organs of public opinion in such matters,' and 'we cannot take the view that the book has any scientific value whatever'; on the contrary, 'in the discharge of our duty to the public we feel bound to say that the book in question ought never to have been written or printed'; for it is 'a highly morbid production,' and 'worthless as science even if the science it professes to advance were worth studying.' In later years Massingham became more appreciative of my work, and sought me out as a contributor to the *Nation.* Yet it is worth while to quote this characteristic example of the high journalistic temper to match the high judicial temper. Law and the Press were indeed well matched, and between them they thought that they had dismissed me and my book from the world. Yet I — rather the spirit of Man I chanced to embody — have overcome the world. My 'filthy' and 'worthless' and 'morbid' book has been translated into all the great living languages to reach people who could not say what a recorder is, nor read the *Daily Chronicle* even if they ever saw it. Unto this day it continues to bring me

bought the *Sketch* and you are in it with such a decent defence of you — I only hope that old puzzle-headed Recorder will see it and sneeze. Mind he has a pamphlet too. Get the tickets and we'll leave this pure country for the sunshine and do come home on Saturday. I shall sleep at Maudie's till you do — never slept after 2 this morning, heart very bad again. Get a pound and a quarter of Cooper's tea to bring home, as we shall need some abroad. Take care, my Beloved old Pal. — I *hate* your libellers like parsnips.' (That was her favourite symbol for repulsive things.)

from many lands the reverent and grateful words of strangers whose praise keeps me humble in face of the supreme mystery of life.

For, look, how the world is made. See what happens to those who, as the men of old days put it, fight against God. They blindly achieve the exact opposite of that which they vainly imagine they have accomplished. Here was I, a shy, solitary, insignificant student who chanced, a little before his fellows, to feel and to see and patiently to work out a problem which would soon visibly concern all men. But meanwhile what he had done was a crime for which no descriptive terms were too opprobrious, no language of abuse too strong. The mighty engines of Social Order and Respectability were set in motion to crush this infamous thing. What they really accomplished was to enable that infamous thing to crush them. I had modestly chosen to issue my book in the quietest way I could find, almost privately. Order and Respectability killed, not the book, but the method of publication (incidentally also the publisher), and I immediately turned to the United States and placed my *Studies* in the hands of an active medical publishing house with a high reputation and an army of travellers. By the method which Order and Respectability closed to me, my books would perhaps have sold by the dozen; by the method Order and Respectability compelled me to adopt they have sold, and continue today to sell steadily, on a far larger scale, in an ever-increasing circle round the world. The creatures who were the puppets of this show began to fall to pieces when it was scarcely over. The judge died first, suddenly, still in the prime of life, so swiftly after the trial that one might well believe the home truths he could not fail to hear concerning his part in it had struck him to the heart, many of the others soon followed, and Doctor Roland de Villiers, that fantastic figure from an alien underworld strangely associated with books whose mission concerned him so little, was destined to end tragically within a few years.

I may, indeed, here go forward a little to round off the story of the whole episode. Directly after the trial, I completed (and De Villiers's press privately printed) *A Note on the Bedborough Trial*, in which, without directly defending my book or answering any criticism I calmly set forth my position and stated my resolve to continue my own work in my own way, but no more to publish it in England. Then I at once proceeded to complete Volume II (now Volume I). Although De Villiers had been invisible from the time of Bedborough's arrest until the trial was well over, I was still unaware of the grounds for his extreme caution and altogether ignorant of his past; he had backed me up throughout the case and supplied promptly all the financial aid needed for the joint representation of himself and me, leaving me a free hand to control the defence. I felt rather bound to him on this account alone, and on the ground that he had suffered through my book. I had nothing to bring against him except his unpleasant passion for mystification and his seemingly excessive timidity over the case. So that I agreed without hesitation to place the publication of the next volume in his hands. I stipulated firmly, in accordance with my declared resolution, that it should not be published in England, and De Villiers readily proposed to issue it only from Leipzig. I knew that he was connected with Germany, and I believed that he would be in a position to carry out his proposal in this matter. A year later the book duly appeared as published, according to the title-page, at Leipzig by 'The University Press' and at Philadelphia by the F. A. Davis Company, who copyrighted it in America. The book was sold as quietly and unobtrusively as I desired. But before long I discovered that it was stocked in England and I found reason to suspect that the supposed publication at Leipzig was merely one of those mystifications in which, as I well knew, De Villiers was so great an adept. The situation worried me; I felt that, in view of my declaration after the issue of the Bedborough trial, I was being put into a false and unpleasant position. I was in doubt what course to take, the more in doubt because De Villiers continued to treat me with all consideration, and I had no definite complaint to make concerning his methods of handling the book.

The problem was solved without any action on my part or indeed any knowledge beforehand. The police, who had at length established the identity of De Villiers, and worked out his history, were again on his track. One day in January, 1902, a strong force of detectives, having first guarded all the exits, entered the large and luxurious house in the best quarter of Cambridge, where, it appeared, my publisher and his wife were then living under the names of Doctor Sinclair Roland and Mrs. Ella Roland. There was an elaborate system here of concealed cupboards and passages to hide in or escape by. But all precautions had been taken, a systematic search was made, and a secret panel at last discovered revealing a passage into which one of the detectives entered and flung himself on the haggard fugitive found there with a loaded revolver which was speedily struck out of his hands. De Villiers was handcuffed. A few minutes later he appeared strangely agitated and called for a glass of water which was brought by a servant. He took a few drops, gasped, and fell dead. The coroner's jury decided that the cause of death was apoplexy. It seems possible. But Sweeney states that he was at the time wearing a ring which a few years before he had boasted to contain behind the seal a poison to kill a man and leave no trace behind.[1]

That was the tragic end of the first publisher of my *Studies* and of the first edition itself. Several thousand copies were stated to have been found in the house at Cambridge and were ordered to be destroyed. There was nothing left for me to do but to declare,

[1] I am quoting from the reminiscences of John Sweeney, the detective who at an early stage was set to watch the activities of the Legitimation League, *At Scotland Yard* (1904). It is no doubt a fairly reliable account of the whole affair from the police standpoint, and Sweeney regards De Villiers as the most amazing criminal of modern times. He admits that he wrote largely from memory, and many of his statements and opinions concerning the Bedborough case are to my knowledge incorrect.

as I promptly did, that I had no objection to offer to this course, since the agreement entered into with me had been violated by the method of issue.

Thereupon I at once entered into an agreement with the F. A. Davis Company of Philadelphia for a new, revised, and enlarged edition of the two volumes, issued in the reverse order in which they now stand, and followed during the next ten years by four other volumes, and finally, after a long interval, a supplementary seventh. The F. A. Davis Company remained the sole publishers of the *Studies* in English until 1936, when difficulties with that company having arisen, they were transferred to Random House of New York and reissued in a cheaper and more compact form, and the sale no longer restricted, as hitherto, to professional readers.

A few days after the Bedborough trial, Edith and I had returned to Carbis, where we found that some of our poorer neighbours were under the impression that I was in prison, though I am not aware that they therefore thought any the worse of me. Exactly three weeks later we embarked at Plymouth on an Orient liner on the way to Gibraltar for Tangier. After six months of wearing suspense and constant absorption in some new phase of the prosecution and the repeatedly postponed trial, and after this compulsory acquaintance with some of the least pleasant traits of our national character — its narrow puritanism, its intellectual timidity, its hypocritical conventionality — we both felt the imperative need to escape from England for a while, and Islamic Africa seemed a fascinating change. 'It is an old story now, but it aged us both,' Edith wrote in a lecture fifteen years later. On her side, moreover, there was the ill-health and increasing cardiac trouble already mentioned in her letters. It was largely on her account that Tangier had suggested itself to me as likely to be a beneficial winter resort. A little while before, the editor of the *British Medical Journal* had been to Tangier in search of health and written about his visit an interesting series of articles. It seemed to me both an attractive place to visit and a health resort likely to benefit Edith. On the first point I proved entirely right, but less right on the second. Edith, for her part, eagerly accepted my proposal; adventure always appealed to her and she never lacked spirit to meet it. The difficulties and discomforts — though no serious complaint came from her, full of keen enjoyment in her novel and instructive experience — were greater than I anticipated, and I never again attempted to lure her from the safe and beaten paths of tourist travel.

In abandoning England for a while, I was by no means abandoning or even postponing my work. The second (now the first) volume of the *Studies* was to appear as soon as possible. I was completing it, with a more feverish activity than I ever applied to any other of the volumes, almost up to the day of leaving England. It so happened that a girl secretary, Miss Bacon, formerly with W. T. Stead, had in his office conceived an admiration for me and my work as well as for Edith, and had agreed to come down to Carbis, occupy our cottage, take charge of Jock, and generally overlook things in our absence. (She died, in a little cottage of her own close by, only last winter, twenty years later.) She was an expert shorthand writer and typist and I dictated to her from notes the whole of my *Study of Periodicity*, and was thus enabled to make rapid progress. It was the only occasion on which I have ever adopted this method.

I regard the Bedborough case, which filled for me the greater part of 1898, as the turning-point of my life. It was not the opening of a new chapter as was my return from Australia at the age of twenty, or the publication of my first books speedily followed by marriage about the age of thirty. I was now in the midst of the long period of active and sustained work which lasted until the *Studies* were completed in 1910, and may even be said to have been maintained until 1915, when, partly although not entirely through anxiety and depression over Edith's steadily failing health, I began to be conscious of a permanent even though not pronounced failure in my own physical and mental vigour. In 1898 I had not even reached the most mature period of mental power, for the prosecuted first edition of *Sexual Inversion* was distinctly inferior in many respects to the later volumes of the *Studies*, although in a subsequent edition (1914) it was fully brought up to their level, and I do not suppose that I have ever thought better or written better than in the *Impressions and Comments* which date from 1912 to 1923.

Yet none the less, the year of the Bedborough case was in my interior life a turning-point, even the chief turning-point I have ever encountered. It was the end of the upward climb of life, and, as we never seem to be standing still, it was the beginning of what I felt to be the descent. Until then, although I always looked older than my age, I had retained an instinctive feeling of youthfulness. It seemed to me that I was young and that life was all ahead. I believe that I always had an inner feeling of deference towards an adult, as though I had not quite realised that I was myself an adult, and I know that it was always with a certain surprise that I heard that anyone prominent in the world was not so old as I was. But now, somehow, this instinctive feeling was suddenly and forever killed. I realised that I was no longer young. This realisation, which was mainly due to that ageing effect of the prosecution to which Edith alluded, was confirmed by the appearance, about the same time, of various signs which we associate with old age. My hair began to turn grey at the temples, and the process continued, until now, twenty years later, it will soon cease even to be grey and be all snowy white. I knew that this sign is of no great significance: my friend Mackay never became grey, yet he died younger than I am now, while my father, who was always more robust and healthy than I have ever been, began to turn grey at thirty; so that I might accept as true the consoling remark which Celine, the charming waitress at the Boulant Restaurant in the Latin Quarter I had frequented many years earlier, made to me when, a year or two after this period,

I found her still the same and still at her old post while I, as I re-marked, was growing grey: 'Les cheveux ne comptent pas.' Yet, when one knows that one's hair is turning grey, one can no longer retain the instinctive feeling that one is still a youth.

A few months later, also, at the age of forty, I had to adopt eye-glasses for reading and really needed them earlier. My eyesight had been most excellent in early life, as befitted the son and grand-son of sailors, and still remained so for far sight. But with the appearance of grey hairs I had to use glasses, and the youthful assistant at the optician's as he handed me the glasses, and I ex-pressed regret at the necessity for using them, responded lightly that it was merely the usual accompaniment of old age. Then, also about the same time, I found it desirable to wear artificial teeth. I had had very fine teeth, as my father had, though mine began to decay comparatively early and his remained all sound in old age; a few years earlier an admiring charwoman had asked Edith if my teeth were my own; henceforth it would no longer be possible to answer a question of that kind so satisfactorily, though even today only one incisor has gone, for I have long since endeavoured to make up for that early dental neglect which most people of my generation suffered from in early life.

All probably within the same twelve months, these various signs came to me to show that I was no longer, as I had hitherto supposed, on the upward path of life, but on the downward path. My work, however, still lay mostly ahead, and this new view of life made no change in my calm and steady attitude towards that work, which I still continued to pursue, without rest, but also without haste. That there was no general recognition of it troubled me not at all. From the first a few people whose good opinion was worth having had known and admired my books, and therewith I seem to have been content. Some years before the period I have now reached, Remy de Gourmont, a penetrating critic who was also severe, had said to a friend of mine that I was 'the most advanced person in England.' But it was not till some ten years later that I first saw myself in a *Times* review casually included among 'celebrities.' And it was probably about this same time that I heard that an artist I knew at Carbis, a good painter with little recognition, had remarked to another that I was among the 'arrived.' It interested me, I remember, to hear this, for it was a point on which I had no assurance of my own. Not that I was worried over the matter. I suspect that below the surface there may have been a serene confidence that I stood for something the world could neither give nor take away, and that there was no need to worry. But I am not certain even about that. I am only certain that from first to last I have never had any ambition in the world beyond the deep instinct to attain self-expression, which instinct was accompanied by the conviction that thereby only could I fulfil the desire of my heart to help others. Fame, for one who is by temperament and taste a recluse, could be nothing but an embarrassing superfluity.

We spent one night — more than enough — at Gibraltar in the Royal Hotel, and next day crossed to Tangier. I recall that, as we sat on deck together in the midst of the Straits, Edith found that one of her teeth required the dentist's attention, and we realised for the first time that we had left Europe and civilisation behind. There was no doubt about that when we entered the harbour and Tangier made an ineffaceable impression on both of us. It was still Eastern in character, more Eastern than any other spot in the western Mediterranean. Here one could learn to feel and to understand not only the spirit and the aspect of Islam; one was also plunged back into the atmosphere of the Old Testament and helped to understand that of the New, while at the same time, to my surprise, I found that I was also brought near to the classic antiquity of Greece and Rome. No purely visual experience anywhere in the world has ever been so helpfully instructive to me. Edith on her side entered into the novel experience of this adventure with all the eager enjoyment of her alert and sympathetic temperament, and began at once, as usual, to make friends in various directions, the first of these being Dukali, the picturesque and good-looking young Moor assigned to us at the hotel (Villa de France), who came down to the wharf to rescue us from difficulties on arrival and was henceforth our agreeable guide and companion on every little expedition. In a different sphere we made friends with Doctor Alexander Hill, at that time Vice-Chancellor of Cambridge University and Master of Downing College, with whom I had been in touch through correspondence over a book on the brain which he had at one time agreed to write for my Contemporary Science Series, and who was at this time spending a short time in Tangier with his wife. Another figure I recall was that of the Shereefa of Wazan with whom we once or twice spent an afternoon, amused by the lively description of her experiences in Morocco, as the English wife of the most sacred Islamic figure in the land, a difficult position in which she had maintained her part as the sensible, practical English woman, very conscious of an Englishwoman's traditions and rights. Some years later she published the narrative of these experiences.

Once we arranged to pay an afternoon call on the outskirts of the city. Edith had an introduction to an American artist and his wife who had settled a mile or two out, and they had invited us to come and see them. Edith rode on a donkey, I walked, and we were accompanied by Dukali and another Moorish attendant who professed complete knowledge of the house we wished to visit. At last we entered a beautiful estate and were finally asked into a drawing-room quietly furnished in the best Old-World English manner. A lady entered, with whom Edith entered into conversation. As this conversation developed, I, who as usual took but a small part in it, began to realise that Edith and the courteous hostess were playing at cross-purposes. Edith herself had no perception of this; while she had an incomparably keener vision than I for the external surface of life, and would often banter me on my lack of observation, I was more sensitive to influences that are below the surface and less perceptible to people of strong and dominating personality. At last I intervened, and then it was revealed that we were visiting Miss Drummond Hay, daughter of a famous diplomatist who had once been much associated with Morocco. She graciously assured us that we had really done quite the right thing in calling on her, as we apologetically withdrew and at length found the American artist in his studio.

While the spectacle of Tangier was full of delight and instruction for both of us, it was less beneficial for Edith's health than I had expected. She seemed indeed improved, and could not fail to be since she was always so greatly influenced by mental impressions, but the climate and the conditions were evidently not specially favourable for heart troubles, nor was an expensive and pretentious hotel, not too well provided with luxuries or even the comforts which in Europe would be a matter of course, altogether conducive to well-being. After spending three weeks at the Villa de France, we moved down to a Spanish hotel of more modest and homely character, on the beach; it was the hotel at which R. B. Cunninghame Graham, one of the most original and fantastic personalities of my time, was wont to stay from time to time; he was not there at that time, and I was sorry, for he was a man I should like to meet; I have since heard from a common friend that he would like to meet me; but the meeting has never come about.[1] We stayed only a week at the Spanish hotel. Here we were fully exposed to the three-day spells of the *levante* wind which had on us, on me especially, an abjectly depressing influence; perhaps, too, we began to rebel against the exotic atmosphere, however fascinating to watch, of this un-European world. We found at our new hotel a homely Californian of Lancashire origin with his wife, Davis by name, an orange-grower bound on a mission in connection with the European orange-growing industry. They were about to visit Malaga on this business. We resolved to accompany them, and finally left Tangier at the end of December.

[1] It is now too late. It chances that, as I revise these pages (in March, 1936), he died a few days ago in Buenos Aires at the age of eighty-four.

It was an exquisitely bright, warm, and calm Mediterranean day which we spent reclining on deck on the passage of the Hall Line boat from Gibraltar to Malaga, where we arrived just too late to enter the harbour that evening. Next morning we explored the city for an hotel. But while Malaga ostentatiously proclaims its really magnificent claims on the health-seeker, there was not, then at all events, a single hotel in the city which could even on the surface be acceptable as a livable residence for any but hurried business men. In this dilemma an excellent and serviceable little English-speaking Spaniard in the Hall Line's office, who later was often helpful to us, came to the rescue and told us of the Hotel Hernan Cortez in the pleasant suburb of Caleta, conveniently situated on the tramline. Even this hotel was mainly a restaurant, the favourite evening resort of well-to-do Malagans, and the elect place for banquets which occasionally disturbed our nights with the sounds of revelry. But even with this drawback, which was on one side an advantage, it suited us admirably. (It has since been completely rebuilt in the modern manner, and some thirty years later I even saw it advertising itself in the London *Times*.)

The spectacle of Andalusian life in its most characteristic aspects was constantly before our eyes. To Edith it was a perpetual source of delight, and with all her ignorance of Spanish she came into touch with it, being viewed with evident favour by all the Spaniards of various degree with whom she thus formed an imperfect acquaintance. She even persuaded an old woman, one of the servants at the hotel, to agree to come as servant in our Cornish cottage, though eventually I convinced her, as she would have realised in time for herself, that it would be unwise and unkind to remove the old woman from the Andalusian home she had never left to so uncongenial and alien a clime.

Our most prized Spanish acquaintance was a most beautiful, distinguished, and accomplished Sevillean dancing girl, Dolores. Our good Spanish friend at the shipping office, Manuelito, had conducted us one night to an obscure Old-World dancing place so hidden away we should never have discovered it for ourselves, the Chinitas, and not long afterwards altogether abolished. I regard it as one of the best of the old unspoilt haunts of Spanish dancing. Dolores was the chief dancer there at this time; when Manuelito introduced us between the dances and we all drank little glasses of Manzanilla together, we found her to be a sweet and gracious woman as well as a fine dancer. The Chinitas became a favourite haunt, and sometimes special dances were performed for our benefit on the table in a side-room at the expense of numerous bottles of Manzanilla. One day we went to see Dolores and her father, a courteous old bull-fighter, at their home, while her fiancé eyed us jealously from the background, and later Dolores and her sister (a dressmaker) lunched with us at our hotel. Arthur Symons, who had come after a winter in Seville to stay with us for a few weeks, shared in some of these delightful experiences. For Edith they were a revelation as well as an unforgettable delight; later in the year she wrote a story inspired by Dolores, whose photograph, given by the dancer, always remained a cherished possession.

One evening I found seated next to me at dinner a gaunt, dour Scotsman who was obviously ill. He addressed me, recalling that we had met at lunch some years before. It was J. F. Nisbet, the dramatic critic of *The Times* and author of a then oft-quoted book on *The Insanity of Genius*; at this time he was correcting the proofs of his last and most reflective book, *The Human Machine*. In a dying state, as he doubtless knew, he had yet left his family to come to Malaga alone. A remarkable personality, an able and busy journalist, a vigorous and independent thinker, he was also a man who had sought, in his own sardonic fashion, to live, so burning the candle at both ends. It was to Symons that he talked most frankly of himself and of his experiences with women: 'I like to drive them three abreast.' He returned to England almost immediately after we left, though it was still March, and died in London a week or two later.

We found the winter climate of Malaga during January and February almost perfect. We could usually lunch in the garden under a lemon tree, and the sun on our south room, from which we could sometimes see the African coast, was so hot that at times it almost hindered sleep at night. At the end of February, the weather began to be less settled and delightful, for March is a disturbed month even in Malaga. The time had come to bid farewell to everyone, for Edith had by this time made many friends and acquaintances, including the highly intelligent English consul, who had proposed that Symons and I should accompany him on an expedition, which unfortunately was prevented by weather conditions, to open out an unexplored cavern in the neighbourhood; Doctor Visick, the kind and shrewd old English doctor, whose advice Edith had once or twice required; and Mr. Johnson, an Englishman who spent every winter at the Hernan Cortez and had various playful little encounters with Edith, who used to banter him on the two charming young Spanish *comadres*, godmothers as she would call them, who came every week with castanets to spend an afternoon in his room; he duly carried out a promise she extracted from him, to liberate secretly on the morning of his departure a fettered canary kept by the landlord's children.

We started for Cordova, accompanied by Arthur Symons, and after a few days there went on to Seville for a week; here we parted from Symons, and after a day or two in Ronda, settled in Algeciras for a week to await the P. and O. liner at Gibraltar for our return home. There were no good hotels in that pleasant little old town in those days, and ours, the Cuatro Naciones, was dirty and uncomfortable, with a flea-bitten little maid to wait on us; Edith, with her good housewifery instincts, always looked back on the Four Nations as a nightmare. It was, indeed, the only drab spot in her joyous memories of Spain, which she always desired to revisit, though circumstances never again permitted; whenever I went to Spain afterwards it was alone.

Part IX

IX

We arrived at Plymouth on the 26th of March, Palm Sunday morning. There were a few hours to wait for the train to Carbis Bay. It was a wintry and cheerless day; we wandered disconsolately through the dreary and lifeless streets of an unbeautiful English town on a dead Sunday morning. Edith felt poignantly the contrast to the warm and beautiful and living land with its friendly people that we had left behind. It was a contrast she always felt on returning to England from the Continent or America, though it never seemed quite so keen to her as on that Sunday morning in Plymouth. She was at heart thoroughly English, and her home was English, and so were nearly all her chief friends. But in external manifestations she was not English; the cold, formal, prudish, conventional, undemocratic Englishwoman was absolutely alien to her. Every stranger, of any class or of none, was to her a possible friend. She knew of no class distinctions, whether of superior or inferior;

wherever she might be, it was natural to her to give help, when it seemed to be needed, or to ask help, with the spontaneous directness of a child. Naturally, she was sometimes rebuffed, and would feel the rebuff, though it never made any difference to her. But this was not apt to happen outside England. Foreigners responded more sympathetically, and were delighted to find an Englishwoman to whom it was so easy to respond. She was democratic, she loved beauty, she was full of vivid interest in life, and so it happened that, closely as she was bound to England and great as was the devotion that held her to her English friends, she still felt at times an alien in England, and never quite abandoned the dream that it might some day be possible to settle in some more congenial land.

We soon fell again into the routine of our old life, however, and I was glad to greet the early Cornish spring with blood already filled and invigorated by the sunshine of the warmest winter I had ever spent since leaving Australia. I had completely outlived the troubles of the prosecution, and with fresh and restored mind I sat down in my boat summer-house at Hawkes Point to write swiftly and without premeditation a little book, *The Nineteenth Century: A Dialogue in Utopia*. This book, suddenly prompted by the extravagance of the one-sided eulogies of the nineteenth century then appearing at its close, I poured out from the exuberance of a refreshed spirit and published in the same year. I recognise that it may not be completely achieved, and it was never meant as an adequate estimate, but it sets forth many of the beliefs which have ever been parts of my personal creed.

We spent the greater part of the year quietly at Carbis Bay, going up to London, separately or together, for a few weeks now and then, and in November, Edith, already eager to be abroad again, crossed over to Brussels to stay for a week or two with staunch and lifelong friends, the Sundts, who had been originally, like some other faithful friends, tenants of one of the Cornish cottages. At Brussels, as usually happened when she went abroad, she was able to write to me that she was 'supremely content.' After Morocco and Spain, a Continental visit no longer seemed formidable to her and occurred from time to time during the next sixteen years. Eight years at farming had exhausted the ardour with which she had at marriage turned from London and ethics and the Fellowship House to the natural earth and its primitive products. Not yet ready to abandon them altogether, she was now thirsting for a wider vision of the world, for beauty and for art. 'I find I'm anything but a real ethical person nowadays,' she wrote to me in this year, 'and am rather wondering how I am to get my artistic needs satisfied in my brief life.'

In health she had been benefited by the winter in the South, but the heart trouble remained, and in May (never a good month for her in Cornwall) she was suffering much from this cause. In June she began to consult an old physician, a distinguished heart specialist, Doctor Sansom, who treated her with much kindness and consideration, without fee, as the generous manner of doctors is with the wives of doctors. At the first interview he said she had evidently had shocks, and before she left, suddenly asking if he should put her character into one word, he smilingly wrote 'Militant.' (It was in the days before that term meant a violent suffragette.) Sansom gave her much wise and helpful advice up to his death some years later.

It was in this year also that, as I look back, I think I can begin to trace an attraction which became of almost supreme importance in Edith's spiritual life, affording satisfaction, not only to her deep affectional impulsion towards women, but also to the artistic cravings now becoming prominent. During the long winter interruption in the South her love for Claire seems to have fallen back to its old level of friendly appreciation, on which it calmly remained for the rest of her life. But there was always a place in Edith's heart, a sacred and beautiful place, only to be filled by a woman who must be more than a friend in the conventional sense, a woman on whom she could expend a love which was

like passion, even if an etherealised passion, and lavish those
tender refinements and protective cares of which she so well knew
the secrets. It was Lily who occupied this place in her heart,
during the brief period she knew her, more securely than any
other woman before or after, and at her death was worshipped
as Edith never worshipped anyone else, not even her mother, who
had never been a real living person for her.

Lily was a Saint Ives artist who lived, with an elder sister by
whom she was jealously tended and guarded, in a little home of
refined culture. She had studied in Paris without, however, being
touched by the Bohemian life of the Latin Quarter, and as the
sisters had private means she was not dependent on her art for a
living. The family was of Scotch-Irish origin from Ulster, and
Edith, who made no distinction between different kinds of Irish,
regarded Lily as the exquisite flower of the typical Irish spirit and
for her sake adored everything Irish all the rest of her life. In any
case, Lily was certainly quite unlike the homely and kindly family she belonged to. She was a creature of fascinating charm that
was felt alike by men and women, by rich and poor. She possessed, moreover, that artistic temperament which at this time so
appealed to Edith. Much as Edith always admired the clean,
honest, reliable Englishwoman, there was yet, as I have already
indicated, something in that type that was apt to jar on her in
intimate intercourse; she craved something more gracious, less
prudish, pure by natural instinct rather than by moral principle.
In Lily she found the ideal embodiment of all her cravings. Lily
was not, indeed, an artist of original achievement: her work in
painting (though I doubt if Edith would have admitted this)
never rose above respectable mediocrity, however much trouble
she spent on it, and she achieved nothing in any other field. Yet
there was in her the temperament of the artist, and the atmosphere of art and beauty was always around her. She loved poetry,
she was an amateur actress on occasion. She was genuinely musical and played Chopin and Grieg with delicate skill. The key

to her nature lay, I think, largely in her fragile constitution. There was always something delicate and ethereal about her; she was a sprite rather than a human spirit; fastidiousness with her took the place of morality, yet leaving her fancy free to roam without restraint; she had no strength of character, always inclined to follow the path of least resistance, and she was dreadfully afraid of being bored. I think it was that last trait which counted much in the attraction, certainly real, she felt for Edith, although a nature such as hers could scarcely fail to respond to one so rich and strong and impulsive, with a vigorous earthly vitality such as she herself never possessed. A year or two after Edith came to know her well, Bright's disease was diagnosed, and a little later she was dead, at about the age of thirty-six.

Edith and Lily only came to know each other slowly. Circumstances — especially the circumstance of the elder sister, who ever watched over Lily like a mother — seldom permitted more than occasional and difficult private meetings. Sometimes these were stolen and took place in a quiet little wood between Saint Ives and Carbis. But they often met more openly in Lily's studio at Porthminster. On one occasion I gave up my studio at Hawkes Point for the day, to enable them to picnic quietly there. It was but rarely, indeed, that they could spend the night together and that Lily would hurry to Carbis with her little nightdress at a late hour when she had almost been given up. Of all those meetings there was only one which stood forever after in Edith's memory in a halo of beauty, an October night which always lingered in her memory. In what the special beauty of that night lay it was not for her to tell, or for me to ask, only to divine, but I know that she always recalled the anniversary of it as one of the sacred days of her life. She was indefatigable, as she always was, in her devotion and endlessly inventive in a lover's attentions. At such times she had all the air and spirit of an eager boy, even the deliberate poses and gestures of a boy, never of a man, and on one side of her, deeply woman-hearted as she was, it was more than a pose, with her restless activity and her mischievousness and her merry, ringing laugh, which suited so well with her well-shaped, compact head and her short, curly hair. To Lily this boyish ardour was certainly delightful, as delightful as was Lily's ethereal fragility to Edith. For notwithstanding that element of wholesome grossness in her love of the earth and even sometimes in her humour, Edith felt an intense repugnance to all grossness in love; even a trace of its presence, or a suggestion of viciousness, more than once brought to nought her nascent attraction to a woman. Lily's purity, with its brightness and its reserve — a reserve that seemed to both of them deeper than the more superficial reserve of the English — and its flashes of audacity, together with her charming wit, and the touch of the instinctive artist in all her actions, suited Edith perfectly. Throughout her life she had numerous intimate relationships with women, but no woman, before or after, ever appealed to her so deeply, or satisfied her so utterly, as Lily. I think she more or less clearly realised that fragility which was a note of Lily's character as well as of her physical constitution, and knew that they could never be mates in soul, for Lily had no soul; but she knew also that there is a sphere of love in which that counts for nothing (there was doubtless the thought of Lily in her mind when many years later she wrote a little play called *The Pixy*), and it was precisely because Lily embodied something that was entirely unlike and outside herself that the fascination she exerted was so strong. They were never sufficiently long together for Lily's weakness of character to grow into a barrier between them.

I can see that after she began to know Lily there was in Edith's love for me a subtle change which had not been produced by her affection for Claire. She no longer called me 'sweetheart' or said that I was both woman and man to her. I remained her 'boy,' her 'child,' always her 'comrade,' and 'the one person in the world who understands me.' I am sure she realised that Lily was not only ethereal but fragile, the last person in the world to rely upon. I never felt the slightest tinge of jealousy, for Lily so clearly represented something with which I could not compete. I would as soon have been jealous of the beauty of a star. Lily was for Edith a star, a star to which for all the rest of her life the chariot of her spirit was attached.

It was in June, 1903, that Lily faded swiftly, gently away, after a few months' illness. During those months Edith's keen desire to be at her side was rarely gratified. She was seldom admitted to see her, scarcely ever alone. It was not even evident that Lily desired to see her. The rumour reached us that Lily had made fun of her and had no wish to see her. (There was a light, irresponsible, unconsciously cruel attitude in her behaviour where I was concerned, for though she was always nice to me, and I was always friendly to her, I knew that she had sometimes spoken slightingly of me and of my love for Edith, in this unlike any other intimate friend of Edith's, before or after.) I sought to soothe her pained heart by saying, quite honestly, that in the languour of illness the supreme desire is for peace and that she was not strong enough to resist the influences by which she was constantly surrounded. This view probably proved acceptable, and these painful experiences seem to have been effaced from Edith's memory.

The figure of Lily, immutably radiant and unstained, became forever fixed in her mind. Simply and slowly, she dedicated to her a kind of worship which increased rather than lessened as the years went by. Lily's portrait was ever on her desk or by her bedside, closer even than mine, and carried about in all her journeyings. Every little present that Lily had ever given her was cherished, constantly used, indeed, but guarded with anxious care: Lily's cushion, Lily's looking-glass, Lily's cup, Lily's tablecloth, most of which I now possess, and Lily's brooch, which was always on her and was cremated with her at last. The books she had given Lily — especially one or two of mine and Swinburne's *Tristram of Lyonesse* which they had read together — were secured and treasured. (It is I who treasure them now.) Edith had found out — what Lily at first characteristically neglected to mention — that she already had an intimate woman friend belonging to an earlier period, and though this friend lived far away in America, Edith succeeded in coming into touch with her, exercising all her skill and patience to overcome prejudices, and securing at last her regard and friendship. She was a frequent pilgrim to Lily's grave at Lelant, with tributes of flowers, long after the spot became neglected by all others who had loved her; and during all the remaining years at Carbis when worried or depressed she would drive off to Lily's grave, to linger alone there for an hour or so and find rest and consolation. She had even, in the first abandonment of grief, purchased the neighbouring plot as a grave for herself, though before finally leaving Carbis, and when she had decided in favour of cremation, she gave it up.

Moreover, the whole conception and working-out of a beautiful anthology of love poems, *The Lover's Calendar*, was really, in her own mind, dedicated to Lily. I cannot quite recall when the idea first occurred to her, but I think it was when Lily was still alive. When the volume was at length published, in 1912, she wrote in the Preface that she had compiled it during the past twelve years. But it certainly was not until some time after Lily's death that it took definite form and that she was able to see that the lover's calendar included not only the seasons of love, but that, as she says, 'death also, and the union of spirits after death, may make a claim on the reader's desire for romance and adventure as powerful as the passionate love of those who are still on earth; and these two facts must enter into the calendar if the cycle of Love is to be complete.' It was only thus that the anthology could become for her, as she called it, the 'epitome of a love-history.' Although its compilation was never her sole occupation, it was always during those years much in her thoughts, and it really involved much labour and correspondence, more trouble, indeed, than any of her original books, except only the *James Hinton*.

Yet it always remained a cheerful task of love. It was the only one of her books in which I took any active part beyond criticism and discussion, yet only in small part. Most of the writers she selected from she discovered for herself, and all the selections she independently made for herself in accordance with her own standards. I am sure that every passage was tested by what seemed to be its suitability to the case of Lily and herself and its congruence with what seemed to her the spirit of Lily. It is in this way that the anthology attained a fine, beautiful, and exalted harmony, though anthologies are so numerous that I am not aware that its qualities were ever widely appreciated and its sale was small. She was, however, perfectly content. The book was not made for fame or profit. It was her monument to Lily, an exquisite shrine at which she could carry on a kind of worship of Lily. I might, indeed, say that, unlike as many of the circumstances were, Lily came to occupy in Edith's mind and heart much the same place as, with better reason no doubt, Edith came to occupy in mine.

But Edith went further in cultivating a relationship with Lily after death. Lily not only lived a glorified and sanctified life in her mind and heart, but came to be regarded as a still living personality capable of coming into touch with her, of guiding her and consoling her. It is probable that Edith had never definitely and decisively abandoned the traditional belief in the persistence of individual spiritual life after death. But it had not been a vital or influential faith. Much as she loved her mother, whom she had never known, she never at any time regarded her as a continuously living personality with whom she could come in contact, though latterly she imagined her as a beautiful spirit in 'Love-Acre.' When a dear friend from school days, Flo, a lovely and gracious personality I well recall, died in India soon after our marriage, Edith received a great shock, but the possibility of still entering into communication never crossed her mind.

It was only as regards Lily that this idea arose, and Edith seemed to have little wish or impulse to extend it to other persons. She was never the adept of any methodical system of spiritism. She was led naturally and slowly by her own inner and outer experiences, so that I can scarcely say how or when the movement began. I remember — though this was scarcely the beginning of it — how once, when she was standing in the main road at Carbis near the Count House with a friend (I mention this circumstance as in the absence of any witness one might possibly suspect hallucination), a lady, a complete stranger spending a few days at Saint Ives, walked up to her, desired to see some ornament she was wearing, and, rejecting everything else, fixed on Lily's brooch, and said she had been sent to bring a message of consolation from the friend associated with that brooch. The strange lady was never seen again and her message remained a mystery, but it left its impress. I think this may have occurred before Edith came into touch with a medium of high repute whom she saw at intervals during the remaining fourteen years of her life, and whom she seems to have first met within twelve months of Lily's death, I think in Cornwall. Swedenborg professed to come to her through the medium, and not once only, though she had never taken any interest in Swedenborg, and never at any later time made more than rather perfunctory attempts to investigate his doctrines. This medium, who refused to practise for money, claimed to have been consulted by high personages and was considered notably successful. Edith had much regard for her, and she seems to have had much regard for Edith, so that a friendly relationship arose. Long after Edith's death I saw in the papers that she and her husband had committed suicide together.

It must be said that in these experiences Edith by no means displayed abject superstition or lost her shrewd powers of estimating human nature. Not only was she without any taste for spiritualism in general — which, she wrote in the last months of her life, is 'often as unspiritual as prostitution is in regard to love, and merely materialism on another plane' — but she was usually suspicious of mediums, especially those who practised for money, and inclined to regard mediumship as a dangerous and even demoralising activity. Some persons assured her that she would herself make an excellent medium, but, though she thought this possible, she refused absolutely to make the attempt. Her experiences with her medium were certainly remarkable, even though one sought to explain them, as I sought, by thought-transference. Lily would speak to her through the medium in what seemed her own natural voice in life, talk of familiar things, foretell the future, give advice which was usually good, and utter words of love and encouragement and comfort. These spirit interviews were consoling and helpful to Edith. They never led her astray; she was, indeed, always prepared to believe that they might be deceptive, though at the same time willing to fortify her own resolutions by Lily's approval. Thus she was encouraged in her plan of a lecturing tour to America, for it was communicated to her that this would be successful and prosperous, as up to a point it was. Some years before her death it was foretold to her that she would live to publish eight books, and this proved exactly true, for though she handed over the ninth (on James Hinton) to her publishers, she never lived to see it published (that has come about only this week, two years later, as I write). Not long before her death she told me it was said to her that she would either die very soon or live seven years longer; yet she never hastened to carry out an intention of modifying her will, and actually died before that was done. All such prophecies, indeed, she took, not indeed sceptically, but without the slightest attempt to make herself their accomplice. I think she attached more importance to the vague and general admonitions she received, such as one she often repeated: 'What seems an impediment is a star.' What she found in her 'spiritualism' was not a method of discovering events, but, as she said in the paper already quoted: 'To reach true spirituality one must be able to forge the lost with the found, and wed the words of life and death, a new birth not only in civilisation but in humour and joy.' It was a special personal religion which she had created for herself, with Lily as its supreme deity, and her special medium as its sole priestess.

In addition to communications of this mediumistic order, Edith also believed, from a fairly early period, that she had occasional visitations from Lily's spirit apart from intermediary aid. At rare moments, without definite sensory manifestations, usually in her own room at Carbis, she would become conscious for a while of Lily's presence. (She would sometimes say that at these times her favourite cat behaved strangely as though some mysterious presence pervaded the room.) These experiences never became definitely sensory, but she found them consolatory.

I have said that all this was to her a kind of religion, but a private and esoteric religion. She would naturally tell me, for there was nothing that concerned her she hid from me, and she would speak of it to a few special friends, but always quietly and with restraint, as something too sacred and intimate for expansiveness. She made no attempt at propaganda, and was incapable of exploiting her experiences in self-glorification. To spiritualism of any kind she never referred in her books. It was only towards the end that this attitude was modified. Her last novel, *Love-Acre*, published in 1914, is faintly tinged by her religious outlook, especially the Epilogue with its reference to 'Emanuel,' though few readers would recognise that this meant Emanuel Swedenborg. During the last few months of her life, when with increasing disease and failing mental power her natural restraint and reticence diminished, she wrote, indeed, a lecture, which she delivered to small audiences, on 'Communication between Worlds.' Here she openly declared her faith, and spoke of her own personal experience, even obscurely alluding to 'the Lily of Heaven.' She proposed to include this in the book she had planned, *The New Horizon* (posthumously published), but it is so slight, so uncharacteristically stuffed with quotations, that, after some hesitation and with the support of a sympathetic friend, I decided that it would be inadvisable to publish it.

In all this I took no active part. It may seem, indeed, altogether alien to my temper and habits of mind. Yet I never adopted, and was never even tempted to adopt, any attitude of ridicule or contempt. There was never the slightest trace of that element of discord which arose between Robert Browning and his wife when she became attracted to spiritualism. Edith regarded me as very scientific and she was pleased that I, most genuinely, admitted that my mind was always open and that I could not pretend to offer any scientific explanation of her experiences. Then, sometimes, she would playfully remark that after she was dead she would come and pull my hair to see what I would say. (She never has been manifested to me, gladly as I would encounter that manifestation, and however I might explain it.) I, on my part, recognised that her head was not turned by her experiences, that she devoted no undue thought and attention to them, but (until near the end) remained her shrewd and sensible self. I am always tolerant to what is natural and sincere. But in this matter my attitude was more than that of toleration; it was nearer to reverence. I realised that in this revelation of Lily as a source of spiritual succour Edith was making her nearest approach to the consoling power of mysticism. She was not naturally possessed of the mystical temper, much less so than I am. To me it had come in youth through a natural interior development, with no strong impulse from without. She was rebellious to such development. Her egoism was too strong, her sensibilities too acute, her temper too dominant and energetic for the mystical spirit to be natural or easy to her. It could only come through the crushing shock of love swiftly passing to loss, and even then she was never entirely subdued to it. But such as it was, it was her religion, the only real religion she ever

had, the true Heaven of her soul, and there was nothing for me to
feel but reverence.

I have run far ahead. I must return to Lily's death, long before
any suggestion of 'spiritualism' had arisen.

This summer of 1902 at Carbis was a sad and depressing time
for Edith. She kept up and worked, but she felt it hard to live
and sometimes doubted if she would live. It was a cold, wet,
and wintry summer, bad for her health, which was poor, the
heart more than ever troubling and the darting pains in her knee,
which later were to develop into severe neuritis, now beginning.
Her favourite dog, Jock's son, who had always been delicate, had
to be shot after a distressing illness; the only cow on the farm
fell ill and died; we both of us were at this time suffering from
lack of money. She had, moreover, the strain of a very busy
season, letting cottages and catering for a number of people,
though this was beneficial in so far as it occupied her thoughts
and helped to relieve the financial situation. For literary work
she had lost all spirit and inspiration.

It was evident that a real change and some form of effective
medical treatment were becoming imperative. At this point
Doctor Sansom's advice proved of the greatest help. He told
Edith she must go to Aix-les-Bains, not merely for the sake of
the treatment, but because the air and situation would suit her
case, and he gave us an introduction to his old friend, Doctor
Blanc, the leading physician at Aix. This was not a place that
would ever have occurred to me. I have always had the greatest
horror of fashionable health resorts, notwithstanding my pleasant
experience of Harrogate, the only place of the kind I had had an
opportunity of really knowing, and I have never even yet so much
as passed through the Riviera.[1] As my choice of Tangier on the
previous occasion indicated, something a little unusual and
adventurous more appeals to me, even in the matter of health

[1] This is no longer true. In 1923, with my dear friend of later years, Françoise,
I spent two summer weeks at various spots on the French Riviera, which was then
only beginning to become a summer resort.

resorts. But the wise old physician showed an admirably sane judgment. Edith accepted his decision, and I at once fell in with it and promised to accompany her.

It was decided that we should go rather late in the season, in October, when prices at Aix would be more moderate and when, also, Edith's own summer cottage-letting season would be over. I left ten days in advance, passing through Belgium, in order to spend a few hours with Amy, and remained in Paris until Edith joined me and we started for Aix. Of Belgium and Paris on this visit I can recall no definite memories. My recollections begin when the train stopped at Dijon and the varied and attractive contents of the luncheon basket we there secured called out Edith's always vivid interest in novelties; at this point, also, we fell into conversation with a young fellow-traveller who was a member of an archaeological exploring party in Egypt and, it turned out, a student at Toronto of a friend of mine, Professor Mavor.

On arriving at Aix we went to an hotel (the Germain) we had chosen beforehand as being inexpensive, but which proved not to our taste, for it was situated in a cramped position, low down in the town, and crowded with visitors, while the small room assigned to us, with its tiny washing basin in the old French manner, altogether repelled Edith. So next day when we called upon Doctor Blanc he kindly took us to the Hôtel d'Albion, where his influence, my position as a doctor, and the advance of the season enabled us to secure rooms fairly within our means. This hotel — pleasant and comfortable and in every respect well equipped and managed without being luxurious — suited us perfectly. We could not have been better situated. We had two good rooms, leading into each other and with a fine view, which had not long before been occupied by the Duke of Norfolk when on a pilgrimage to Rome, and before that, during a succession of years, by a fashionable and famous French portrait painter, Carolus Duran.

Edith, always so swift to react to a new favourable environment so long as she had any vitality left, was delighted
with everything, and her restoration, on the psychic side at least,
was almost immediate. It was, I think, on the third day after
our arrival that she awoke in the early morning and was inspired
to begin writing a humorous Cornish story. It was the first
time she had been able to write since Lily died. This little story
initiated a series which she now continued with a new ease and
skill. She discovered that she was an artist in the short story as
well as in the novel, and she revealed a new development of the
Cornish humour she had already shown in *Seaweed*; it was now
brighter and more sparkling, the artist's hand lighter, and the
ability to utter profound things playfully more accomplished.
Most of the stories were based on some slight real experiences,
though one, purely imaginary, *The Subjection of Kezia*, was a
complete success, as the public recognised when, after she had
transformed it into a playlet, it had a long run on the stage of
several London theatres. Yet even Kezia was a transformation
of reality, for I am sure that in drawing Kezia she was thinking
of herself and objectively studying all that moody contradictoriness which she well knew that she herself was apt to display in her intimate domestic life. These stories were sent to
Mr. Pethick Lawrence, who had become the husband of our
friend, Emmeline Pethick, and was at this time editor of a London
evening paper, the *Echo*. He approved of them and they appeared,
one every week, in the *Echo*, and eventually (1906), in a volume,
My Cornish Neighbours, which was dedicated 'To Havelock.'
It was a book which met with the warm commendation of good
judges, and the appreciative enjoyment of a considerable public.

Our month's stay at Aix, so far as I recall it, was of unalloyed
though peaceful enjoyment. It was so to me — though in the
first place Edith's health had been my sole guiding motive —
scarcely less than to Edith. She would take her prescribed bath,
be carried back to bed in a sedan chair according to the custom of

Aix (I have a photograph I took of her on one such occasion as she
looks out laughingly from the curtains), and when she had rested,
we would explore the neighbourhood, inhaling the clear and calm
air of this high valley, delightful even in late autumn, sit beside
the beautiful Lake of Bourget, and enjoy the variegated spectacle
of the ever-shifting stream of cosmopolitan visitors.

Occasionally we would go for a longer excursion. The most
memorable of these was to Chambéry, whither we went chiefly in
order to walk out to the home of Madame de Warens and young
Rousseau at Les Charmettes. That day, the 24th of October,
remains memorable in my life. I was impelled to visit Les Charmettes by no enthusiasm. It had indeed happened that Rousseau's *Rêveries,* found among my grandmother's books, had perhaps been the first book in French I had ever read for my own
pleasure, and its gracious music had impressed me; I had, moreover, read the *Confessions* at eighteen and been mightily interested. But Diderot was my hero, not Rousseau. Les Charmettes merely seemed a pleasant and easy little excursion. It
was, indeed, an agreeable rural walk to the seemingly deserted
little villa. Few visitors, it seemed, ever came. We tugged the
rusty iron bell-pull and the bell rang out loudly, but there was no
response, and we wandered around until we found at last the
woman in charge, who admitted us and showed us about the
empty and solitary building. It was a revelation of what can be
achieved by a happy blending of chance and neglect with a fine
artistry in veneration. Here was a little museum of sacred relics.
Yet the prevailing impression was that of a small country house
lived in more than a century ago and untouched since it was left.
Of any attempt at renovation or restoration, which the energetic
Anglo-Saxon could not have resisted, there seemed to be none,
and so the ancient charm still adhered to these ancient decora-
tions, to these bed coverlets now falling to rags. The very air that
Rousseau and his *maman* once breathed seemed still here. The
aspect of decay and death became the very evocation of life. I

have never by any external environment seemed brought so close to the hearts and bodies of people who died more than a century before.

When we looked out together from Madame's (as we supposed it to be) bedroom window at sunset and saw the delicate colours painted on the distant mountains, and when, as we walked back with lingering feet to Chambéry from that spot enchanted by memories of the past, I felt that a new interest had come into my life, and henceforth Rousseau, no longer the merely extinct volcano he had once seemed to me, had become a living and fascinating human creature with an inexhaustible complexity I can never completely unravel. That visit has always been hallowed with beauty in my memory, and it has taken on a new beauty since the companion of my heart who shared it with me has now, like Rousseau, become an enchanted memory.

We left Aix early in November with regret, for it had been a time of new inspiration and vigour as well as of keen enjoyment for Edith, and for me of unalloyed happiness. It is usual after the course of baths to go to some other health resort for a brief rest before returning to the ordinary routine of life. Doctor Blanc recommended Montreux on the Lake of Geneva. On the way there we spent a night at Annecy, associated with more memories of Rousseau and Madame de Warens, and at Montreux, with Clarens close by, we were again in their atmosphere. But Montreux itself left little impression on us — the Castle of Chillon is its best memory — and as the grip of winter was now tightening on Switzerland, we were glad to leave for Paris, whence Edith returned direct to London while I again went through Belgium to miss no chance of a glimpse of Amy. A few days after reaching London, we were again at Carbis for the winter.

For both of us Aix remained a beautiful dream, a dream that we always hoped some day to realise again. The proposal would come up from time to time, especially after some serious illness of Edith's, but there were always difficulties in the way, usually

of money, and it remained a dream to the end. In the very last
year of Edith's life, after her return in shattered health from
America, it seemed on the point of realisation; it was a final hope
to which I clung, with memories of what had happened before,
and I wrote to Doctor Blanc to ask if he would advise me to
bring her under the new conditions of disease. He was still alive
(he died a few months later) and replied kindly, recommending
a visit at once. But the difficulties of travelling for an invalid
under war conditions, as well as the usual financial impediment,
proved decisive, and I shall never know what promises of restoration were unfulfilled in Aix.

It was doubtless the delightful experiences of Aix which led
Edith the very next year (1903) to another stay in France, this
time as an independent housekeeper. She arranged with the artist
Cayley Robinson, to take his flat in an ancient house on the Quai
Bourbon in the Île Saint Louis in Paris for the month of June.
We were accompanied by Priscilla, the housemaid, who had now
become, as she remained till she left us nearly ten years later to
join her sister in Australia, a companion and friend equally liked
and appreciated by both of us, wayward and trying as she was for
all her charming qualities. Edith had found her some years earlier
in a characteristic manner. She always naturally and instinctively entered into conversation with the people near her on a
railway journey and in this way one day met a nursemaid who
was out of work and looking for a place. She liked her appearance,
and Priscilla was engaged immediately as housemaid; not long
after, her sister became our cook and her brother our farm-man
and gardener, a stolid, reliable, and faithful fellow who stayed on
as long as there was any work to do. (He came to see me in
London only a few days ago.) But Priscilla, in whom there had
from infancy been a fragile and morbid strain (she died at thirty-
six), was different from the others, with a refinement and good
taste, an unaffected love of Nature and of art, which were doubtless in large part the fine flower of her delicate and sensitive

temperament. A friend of Edith's, who could speak with knowledge on such matters, once remarked that Priscilla was a real lady. I, who at all events knew Priscilla better, could say the same; the gracious impulses of fine breeding seemed to come to her instinctively. Exasperating she could often be, but she was really devoted to both of us (with for me sometimes a tender recognition of intimate insight) and we both appreciated her. She suggested to Edith some of the traits of the housemaid, Wilmot, described in her novel *Attainment*, who was 'more like a blackbird than a girl,' or of the race of mermaids, seeming to have the subconscious impulses of a creature whose nature it was to fly or to swim.

Our month in the Île Saint Louis was not so memorable as the stay at Aix, but it was full of novelty and exciting interest to Edith, who enjoyed this attempt at French housekeeping and the triumphant efforts, through imperfect French and much gesture, to wrestle with marketing problems. It was pleasant to me also to guide her into an enlarged knowledge of Paris and things Parisian including the Opera, which before I had always religiously avoided as merely conventional, but where I now enjoyed with Edith Rameau and Dukas and Debussy, and once at the Trocadero my beloved Gluck. To Priscilla it was a unique and never repeated experience.

In these middle years of our life few experiences stand out. The strands of our existence were being more intimately twisted together and outwardly a certain routine was established. After the marriage of Symons and his departure from Fountain Court, I had in 1901 taken a small flat in Rectory Chambers, Church Street, near the old Chelsea church. Here, although quarters were cramped, it was possible for Edith to come when she wished, and even for Priscilla to sleep on a bed-couch in my study. (That simple little couch has been in use for nearly forty years and I recline on it now in the revolving sun-hut of my country garden.) From time to time I went abroad, usually alone now that Symons was married, and there were occasional interesting little excursions with Barker Smith to ancient haunts of my family in Suffolk. But most of the time I was in Cornwall at the Count House.

There was, indeed, one episode (belonging, I think, to about this time) which I cannot altogether pass over, since it was perhaps the most painful that came to us from the outside. A new admirer of Amy's, who considered himself aggrieved, sought revenge by an attack on my domestic peace. It is unnecessary to describe the circumstances, which were not directly due to Edith or to Amy or to me, and, rightly understood, reflected no discredit on us, while they caused acute pain to all three. A manuscript reached Edith by post one day, containing the story, under a transparent disguise, of my relations with Amy. There were, of course, no essential facts here of which Edith was ignorant, but the sting of the attack lay in its vulgarity and in the diabolical ingenuity with which plausible suggestions and perversions of truth were woven with real facts, in the manner most likely to make me appear ridiculous and to wound a wife of Edith's proud spirit. Nothing more malicious could be devised. When Edith read it in her study, she fell to the floor. But deeply as she was wounded, and even though she could scarcely help feeling that there was some truth in the perverse falsifications the narrative insinuated, her unfailing loyalty was proof against so despicable an attack. She treated it with the contempt it invited from one of her temper, and acknowledged it with a brief and dignified reply.

There was one little element in this episode which has left a comic memory. The writer of the letter, in his aggrieved malevolence, had, it appeared, at some time previously employed a detective agency to watch my movements. There was little, indeed, in my usual studious routine of life in London, and almost daily visits to the British Museum, to satisfy a detective. But it so happened that, during the period when I was thus unconsciously subjected to observation, there fell a day which of all days in my life I might mischievously have selected as most fitted to worry a detective. Edith came to town with Priscilla, to spend the night at the Euston Railway Station Hotel and leave early next morning to lecture in Manchester. Priscilla had never really seen anything of London, and Edith arranged that I should employ the day in showing her the sights of London she most wanted to see.

Priscilla was eager and indefatigable, and it was a pleasure for me to enjoy her enjoyment and the reaction of her sometimes sensitively fine taste. I have never in any city had so extensive a round of sight-seeing, because for myself I prefer a more parsimonious reception of new impressions, and I cannot recall all the places we visited. We went to Westminster Abbey, I remember, and the National Gallery, and the British Museum, and then to a restaurant in Soho, where we had with our meal a well-deserved bottle of French wine, and then to Saint Paul's, where we climbed to the Whispering Gallery and then up to the deserted top of the dome (this incidentally enabled the hitherto shy Priscilla to release on the stones a copious stream) in order to view London from a height, and then to my rooms in the Temple for tea, and thence to Charing Cross footbridge to see the Thames at dusk, before the at length satisfied and happy Priscilla was sent off to Paddington where she was to catch the night train home. For a poor detective there could not be a more tedious and unprofitable day's work. I should have liked to see that detective's report. All that I heard of it was that it contained the statement that we had gone to an hotel in Fleet Street, which indeed we passed, though I was ignorant even of its name, and that I was 'leading a very immoral life with women.' Since then I have been suspicious of the absolute reliability of private detectives.

I here introduce the cheerful letter I received from Edith, staying at the Midland Hotel, Manchester, a day or two after she left Euston (April 17, 1904):

> *My darling Boy*, All is well over — it was a most intelligent audience, a good debate, and I had to defend my own mysticism.

One man said he thought Carpenter was my disciple. Gallichan was there and spoke to me afterwards. My stepmother was the first to come, and looked very staggered when I held out my hand and spoke nicely to her. My brother had left a note last night saying that she and he were dining with friends at the hotel, but I never saw them, and *she* said that Job [the nickname for Edith's half-brother Arthur] was so terrified of a scene that he never came to the dinner and was in bed in a rage that she was going to hear me as it would upset me; but it did not a bit. I hear Nelly [Dakin] has written saying I looked *lovely!* She says I *must* go on lecturing. This is such a glorious playhouse of an hotel, I'm revelling in it, and could telephone all over England from my bedroom if I wanted. My father's lawyer heard I was here and came to see me, and millions of relations come tomorrow morning. A. is here and very sweet. Post just going, so I close. I love you always.

The finally hurled missile recoiled on the head of him who discharged it, and thereby ensured his complete exclusion from Amy's life. Our relations remained the same. The wound in Edith's heart, however, would from time to time rankle. At intervals, at long intervals it might be, during all the years that followed, she would refer to 'that manuscript.' In a sense it never made any difference; yet it was a blow that had come to her, as reasonably enough she could not help feeling, through me. Love that lives is fed by pain as well as by joy, and alike in her experience and in mine that was found true.

It so happened, however, that throughout the ten years that followed this humiliating episode, whatever troubles we might have to traverse, no shadow from within or from without, real or imaginary, fell across our love together. Edith followed the shifting and sometimes disturbed path of her own intimate friendships with women, always with me for her closest confidant. I remained quietly devoted to Amy of whose society I gradually secured more without any anxieties and with Edith's slowly increasing approval. Edith and I entered upon the long period which most surely and firmly rooted our deep affections in a soil from which no power in or out of the world could ever tear them up.

So far as I am concerned, I am sure, as I look back, that this process was intensified by Edith's state of health and her now frequent and severe illnesses. I was myself never ill, although my constitution was not robust; I was liable to minor ailments, but I seldom needed to spend a day in bed, and I never once required real nursing during the whole quarter of a century of my married life. I was always the nurse and not the patient. I will not say that I am sorry the parts were not sometimes reversed, for I know the care which Edith was prepared to spend at the slightest signs of illness in me, and the anxiety she experienced when the smallest shadow of risk seemed to be over me. But I realise how acutely one's love is sharpened and deepened when the thing one loves is the perpetual object of one's tender care. In all Edith's real illnesses I was never her doctor; I never desired that responsibility and she never professed any faith in my medical skill, while for slight disorders she was a skilful doctor to herself. But I was invariably her nurse, and as such she always accepted me, not only as a matter of course and of necessity — for our circumstances and the size of our dwelling would usually not have admitted a professional nurse — but to her entire contentment and satisfaction. She was always peculiarly sensitive in regard to intimate contacts with strangers and it was a trial to her that anyone but me should be present to assist her in the intimacies of the sick-room. During all the years I knew her, and through all her illnesses, I cannot recall that she once had a nurse (except for massage and similar special treatments) until the last year or two of her life when circumstances had changed. I was always her nurse, by day and by night, if need be, though Priscilla might help from time to time, and kind friends would come in to sit with her for an hour or two while I went out for a walk or lay down to rest. Under such conditions my work could only be done at odd moments or not at all, and sometimes weeks passed in this way, once at least a whole month.

The earliest of the more serious illnesses at this time was in 1905. In that year I had given up my little flat at Chelsea in order to share with Edith a larger flat near Battersea Park which she had taken over from acquaintances who were unable to complete their term of occupation. She would come here from Cornwall from time to time, bringing up Priscilla to do the work, and I cannot recall being there by myself. In the spring I had gone away alone on one of my numerous visits to Spain. I mention it because it was one of the most memorable. Barcelona, as often before, was to be the chief centre. I stopped at Nîmes on the way, and at Gerona, and I also spent a few delightful days in Majorca. But, above all, I made my first and unforgettable visit to Montserrat. The two perfect May days I spent in the clear air of that serene and lovely height mark the most prolonged period of sustained and almost ecstatic exaltation I have ever reached. For a moment, for an hour, possibly for a day, I have sometimes attained such inner joy before, and even, though of this I am less sure, since, but never, unless possibly at Sparkes Creek, has the experience of joyous exaltation been so prolonged, while with that economy of joy, that fear of reaching the dregs of the cup of pleasure which I must regard as one of my traits, I left when I might still have spent a day there. In my *Soul of Spain* I have tried to give some record of that visit. A few years later I went again. I was wise enough to know that I could not repeat the experience, but I was seeking to obtain material for a more elaborate study of Montserrat I wished to write, though now I know it will never be written. The days of that second visit were sad days. My mood had changed; my vigour had diminished, so that I had to abandon the fascinating climb up to San Jeronimo I sought to repeat; the place itself, beginning to be vulgarised, had changed forever.

We spent the summer at Carbis, and Edith was in the midst of

her busy summer season when she was attacked — not for the
first time or the last — by pneumonia. We were in the Count
House, but the end of July was approaching when the house had
been let to a large family. The date was postponed a little, but
could not be further postponed. Edith was slowly recovering,
nothing was needed but that she should continue to rest peacefully
at the Count House. The agitation of moving, of transforming
the house for tenants, of travelling to London, of settling in the
sordid environment of Battersea, was all clearly undesirable and
risky. But there seemed nothing else to do and it was done. The
lungs healed, but the strain on the exhausted nervous system
was too much. She fell into a state of listless depression and
melancholy, incapable of physical activity or mental interests.
As I now recognise, she was suffering from the same condition
which, again as a result of the exhaustion of disease, overcame
her, in a more serious form, ten years later, the reaction of an
organism normally active and alert even to excess. Nothing
seemed to avail. Priscilla was helpful and friends were kind.
I remember especially that Conrad Noel (son of my old friend
Ruden Noel), at this time a curate in the north of London, would
find time to come across London, a troublesome journey then,
several times a week to cheer and interest her, and succeeded
better than most. Her London doctor at the time was an able
man, himself of neurotic temperament, and energetic in his
methods, he made every attempt to stimulate her to activity,
but with no brilliant results. I remember that on one occasion
he told her to exercise her will resolutely and walk round the lake
in Battersea Park. She was docile enough to obey. I accompanied
her and she succeeded in achieving the feat, but only with immense effort.

Salvation came at length in the way it most often came to
her, with a change to new air and scenery and the stimulation of a fresh interest. I persuaded her to come with me to
Reigate where my sister Louie kept a little foothold of two

rooms; these I arranged to take for a fortnight or so. Priscilla came with us and slept on a couch in the sitting-room. It was a complete success. Here within a few days, in the bright autumn air of this height, in the pleasant little pine wood close by, Edith swiftly began to revive. This revival was considerably aided by the attractive and fantastic figure of a woman who also haunted the wood. Of course, Edith soon made her acquaintance, and found her to be an accomplished person of musical training and moving among artists, so that an immediate and seemingly mutual interest arose. No real friendship, however, developed, for it appeared before long that the fascinating dryad of the wood was in practical life a morbid, mischief-making creature with a constitutional lack of veracity. So the acquaintance was ultimately dropped. But so long as she remained the bright-haired dryad, she performed a useful function. Edith was soon completely restored. When we returned to Battersea, I lose for a time the thread of memory.

The other chief illness of that period was more prolonged and even more distressing. She had been complaining, even for years, of occasional darting pains in the knee. Now, I think with the onset of winter, this knee began to become seriously bad, and extremely painful. Our good friend, Doctor Nichols of Saint Ives — for whom Edith always had much friendly regard, though without great faith in his medical skill — was kind and attentive, as he always was, and treated her in the orthodox manner for rheumatism, with a prolonged course of salicylates and later by immobilising the joint. I came later to regard the neurotic element as most prominent in the condition. Day after day, week after week, month after month, she was confined to her bed — which was at the Count House at this time side by side with mine — and I was seldom far away so as to give all my best attention to nursing her. The evening and early night were to me the most trying time, for then she would be delirious — a condition largely due, no doubt, to the salicylate, for she was always susceptible to drugs — referring to the people and the things of her girlhood, and struggling to get out of bed and go out on the moor, so that, sometimes with Priscilla's aid, it might be necessary to hold her down. With the passing of the winter the acute stage passed, but the immobilised limb had become helpless; she was lame, unable to walk, and, still confined to bed, only able to move across the room on crutches.

It was at this time as she lay in bed that with my camera I took a series of pictures which, among all the innumerable snap-shots I had at one time or another taken of her, remain my favourites. One, indeed, suggests her to me at once more beauti-fully and more truthfully than any portrait I have of her before or since. She reclines on the pillows in a posture of complete repose reading a book, with the usual vase of flowers on the little table between her bed and mine, dimly visible in the background, and on the wall the Saint Ursula of Carpaccio, given her by Stopford Brooke before we had ever met, which still hangs near my bed (and there it still hangs, now thirty years afterwards). In this position of restful repose all sense of strain has passed from her face; the full, half-closed eyelids, the eloquently expres-sive underlip, the softly rounded chin, speak only of a happy yet still vitally alive calm, so often absent, so lovely and so satisfying to me when present. One sees in her face, what was indeed the fact, that this illness, distressing as it had been to me and painful to herself, had not left her nervously exhausted, like the attack of pneumonia.

Her spirit was as ardent as ever. Soon she was downstairs, and with too eager a delight in her new method of locomotion she fell with her crutches in front of the house, and learned to be more careful. Much trouble was needed to bring motion back to the joint. When that was almost achieved, she hastened to London, though still rather helpless, and the crutches were soon thrown aside and forgotten; vigorous treatment by heat and light baths and similar methods completely restored her power of motion.

It was such illnesses that bound me to her with new cords of attachment vibrating in my heart with an anxiety perpetually stirred by the mischances which her temperament and her adventurousness induced, and never henceforth allayed until the end. She accepted my care for her with a matter-of-course air, just because it was her nature to give all for love as a matter of course and to expect the same from those who loved her. She was hurt if she suspected that I ever spoke of it. She delighted to have me within call and ready to render any little service she needed. Sometimes she would snub me in the presence of friends, and if they protested she would reply: 'It's good for him!' She had the idea that I was becoming successful and exposed to the demoralising influence of adulation which it was her business to counteract. I understood this; there was no shadow of protest on my part when she treated me as a child who needs sharp correction in the small details of domestic life. I accepted this attitude calmly, even when it was a trifle embarrassing. 'Nobody contradicts me now,' wrote Queen Victoria after her husband's death, 'and the salt has gone out of my life.' I am sure that Queen Victoria hated to be contradicted, and I sometimes resented being scolded like a child, but no one treats me like a child now, and the savour has gone out of my life. (It is nearly twenty years since I so wrote and it is no longer true, for I have happily spent a large part of that interval with a beloved friend whose attitude towards me has been in many respects like that of Edith.)

Little things, little joys and little worries, and the routine of work, broken from time to time by Edith's illness, seem to have made the whole web of our lives during this period. There were no great external troubles and no intimate conflicts to rend us apart and bring us back with a clash of reunion. The nervous irritability of Edith's temperament was still there, but I fully understood it now, and indeed preferred it to fall on me rather than on others, when it was apt to cause trouble. She used to

repeat with amusement the remark concerning her of a neighbouring farmer, an excellent man with whom she had various
dealings: 'Not a better little woman in the world,' so it was
repeated to her, he had declared, 'but, my God! tread on her
toes, and you'll know it.'

It was perhaps owing to the comparative calm of our life
together at this time, and also to briefer separations — in 1905,
for instance, I find that we were together in Cornwall and London
for all but nine weeks of the whole year — that for a period of
some seven years after 1902 I find to my astonishment that I
have preserved almost none of her letters. I had no notion that
such an immense hiatus existed. There must have been a large
number of letters written during this period, for we were never
absent without writing daily. I imagine that they were concerned merely to assure each other of our welfare, to record
briefly the day's doings, and make arrangements for the future.
That this was so is confirmed by one or two of her notes which
have been accidentally preserved because I used them, as was
my custom with odd scraps of paper, to make notes on. The
extraordinary thing is that this hiatus exists not only in the series
of her letters to me, but also of mine to her. She seems to have
preserved even the slightest note of mine — in flagrant opposition
to her lifelong habit of destroying all letters immediately —
written during the first years of our marriage, and the larger
number of those written during the last years. I preserved most
of those she wrote during the early years and nearly all written
during the last years. But both of us, unknown to each other,
systematically rejected as unimportant all the letters of the
middle period. It seems to be evidence of a curious kind of
pre-established harmony.

The chief events during these years were various little holidays
and visits abroad. We usually took them separately. On her
part there were friends abroad with whom she could stay, or
others on holiday whom she desired to join. On my part, though

it was always a pleasure to go about with her, I had become nervous, on account of her health, of taking her abroad or to any strange place by myself. Yet, wherever I went, even with Amy, she was constantly in my thoughts, and I was making mental notes of beautiful spots or comfortable hotels to which I might bring her. She was, I think, sometimes doubtful of my anxiety to do this. From time to time, however, we went away together, especially to Suffolk, which I was beginning to know well, and made pleasant visits to favourite resorts of mine, to Ipswich and Lavenham and Clare.

I do not seem to have spoken as I should of those visits to Suffolk which, once or twice or thrice a year, formed so pleasant an interlude during more than twenty of the busiest years of my life. They constituted an essential part of what has formed the chief hobby I have pursued in my career: the study of the families from which I spring. I was not on any snobbish search for noble ancestors, and I was not surprised to discover that my ancestry has been persistently middle-class as far back as I can go, even though on various middle-class levels. Until I was near the age of forty, I knew nothing whatever about my forefathers more than two or three generations back and had never felt the faintest desire to know. But then my father handed over to my keeping a few old documents and letters which he had received from his father. One among these specially aroused my interest: the will on parchment of William Powle, who had died at Great Waldingfield in Suffolk in 1727. What he was I had no idea (for I strangely overlooked that he described himself as a clerk in holy orders), but I knew he was an ancestor, for I had an Uncle Powle who had been named, I knew, from a family back in our history.

I resolved to go to Great Waldingfield to find if any Powles lived there. It was natural I should consult my friend and old fellow-student, Barker Smith, on the matter, for he had been born at Castle Hedingham, only a few miles away from

Great Waldingfield. That village is within a walk of Sudbury, so we planned to spend a few days at Sudbury and explore. At Sudbury we set up at the Rose and Crown, a fine old inn with a courtyard, close to the church — an inn we stayed at more than once on subsequent visits — and next day set out for the village. We soon discovered that the name Powle was unknown at Great Waldingfield, so we proceeded to the churchyard to investigate the gravestones, I taking one section and Smith another. Before long Smith announced that he had discovered an altar-tomb with a long Latin inscription, well preserved since it was inscribed in slate, recording the virtues of the rector of the parish, the Reverend William Powle. From that moment I was embarked on a research which I followed up eagerly and persistently in leisure hours during the years that followed, constantly adding to my store of family history. It may not have been on this occasion that we called on the rector, Canon Stokes, who had published a little ecclesiastical history of the church; he was kind and helpful and took no fee for supplying me with Powle entries from the register. I can say the same of other Suffolk rectors whose help I needed in my research.

But it was a research which demanded far more than visits to churches and rectors, though all that could be done in that way I accomplished, visiting the churches or homes, all in Suffolk (save one at Dartford in Kent), of some half-dozen old parsons from whom I was doubly descended by the cousinship of my parents. I found valuable material in the Manuscript Room at the British Museum (as well, of course, as in the Library itself), among the old wills at Somerset House, as well as in the local Suffolk Probate Registry, in the Record Office, and also in the Suffolk Archidiaconal Archives, where I was shut up alone to do my worst in a little room piled up with old documents. I also came into friendly touch with the two chief Suffolk antiquaries of that day, Mr. Edgar Powell and Mr. Muskett. The former, in an appendix to his book on the Powell family, had sought and set forth the genealogy of my Powle family (quite distinct from his main subject) in a most helpful way, and the latter had not only published many essential documents concerning my Kebles, but he possessed and later presented to the British Museum the interesting diary of Adam Winthrop (father of the famous founder of Massachusetts), who had therein furnished glimpses of the activities of his neighbour, Paul Powle, the ecclesiastically troublesome grandfather of the excellent William Powle.

I write this reminiscence in 1937, and I tell of experiences which are now in a dim past. But as I look back, I am impressed by the time and energy, and I think I may add skill, which I expended in selecting and following up clues in so unfamiliar a field. Evidently I was here exercising in a new field the same qualities of flair and judgment and persistence which I had already long been developing in a totally different field of research. It was a research always full of pleasurable excitement. But the most delightful memories that remain with me are the walks planned with my dear and quaint old friend, Barker Smith, to some remote church or village, with rests by the wayside, when Smith, as an enthusiastic field naturalist, would perhaps discourse on flowers he had plucked, with lunch on bread and cheese and ale at an inn, and at length, our mission for the day accomplished, the simple meal in the evening, perhaps on delicious Suffolk ham, at the hotel where we had put up.

The outcome of my research, which took many years to complete, was the gratification of my curiosity concerning the chief families I was descended from for as far back — about the fifteenth century — as I could go with certainty. Altogether the mass of information was considerable, and I could make an interesting book — which I no longer expect to make — concerning English middle-class people, often parsons, and the families they intermarried with — Kebles and Powles and Peppens and Ellises and Olivers and Grays and Wheatleys and Havelocks — a pleasant picture on the whole, though, unfortunately, the man I know most about, and who was not a parson, Paul Powle, came to be justly described by Archbishop Laud as 'very troublesome.' Laud would have said the same of me, though not on similar grounds, and I have been so regarded by the judicial successors of the old ecclesiastical courts.

It was, indeed, an interesting and unexpected result of my ancestral explorations to find out how strangely I had, without knowing it, combined and reproduced special marked traits of my forefathers. Speaking broadly, I may say that my own character and activities blend the two temperaments most pronounced on both sides of my ancestry: the adventurous temperament of the sailor and the spiritual attitude of the good parson. That is true even though I knew too much of the sea ever to want to be a sailor, and that a brief thought of entering the Church, long before I had ever heard of any parson ancestors, was already dispelled before I sailed for Australia. But even in more detailed traits, however we may choose to figure to ourselves the nature and course of hereditary genes, it was remarkable to find a distinct resemblance to this, that, or the other ancestral family or some definite ancestor: persistence, fidelity to a principle against one's own interests, a calm indifference to opposition, a tendency to place responsibility on women, a spontaneous and unconventional mysticism, a natural temper of moderation — these are not matter-of-course traits and I knew nothing of their existence among my ancestors when they were already developed in myself and in my attitude to life, even though freshly constellated.

For the most part, however — though Edith's agile mind and impulsive disposition often led to new adventures which were apt to become new worries — I recall these years as mainly lived in what for me was a routine of steady work, apart by myself at my studio at Hawkes Point all the mornings and afternoons, while she always had her hands full of a number of things (and at one time had a studio of her own in Saint Ives), even though sometimes it seemed to her that I left her alone too much. I was sorry, but my work made it inevitable; and while I had not in Cornwall a single friend or a single distraction other than work to take me away from her, she had many friends to occupy her lonely hours. I usually returned for lunch, and would bring with me to please her any rare or beautiful thing I had found on the way, some late honeysuckle or gorgeous autumn leaves or January gorse, or those feathery 'palm' sprigs which always rejoiced us as the earliest sign of spring. She was never without flowers, even in winter and the Cornish violets she so loved might generally be had from Lelant all through the winter. Fresh flowers on the table and in the rooms were a luxury she found it hard to be without, however scarce money might be. She would certainly have agreed with Mahomet when he said that, if a man finds himself with bread in both hands, he should exchange one loaf for some flowers, since the loaf feeds the body indeed, but the flowers feed the soul. There were, too, always a few to be sent to some dear friend in London, and she never failed to place some in my bedroom, though sometimes — suspicious, and not always without reason, of my swift observation — she would later ask me if I had noticed them. Every May, in due season, I found by my bedside a little vase of the delicate *Stellaria* or stitchwort, which is my favourite wild flower, and on rare occasions she gave me the white roses to which she attached a deep and special significance. In June of 1891 she had written to me: 'The white roses brought you a message. Did they give it, I wonder?' and a quarter of a century later, a few weeks before her death, she bought in the street and gave me a white rose, that same or the following day writing (for a little meeting at which she was giving readings from my books): 'When many years ago — about twenty-eight — I first read the *New Spirit* I knew I loved the man who wrote it. Today, in reading *Impressions and Comments*, I realise that the man who has written both books is worthy of love and forgiveness and eternal comradeship.' Now,

more than twenty years still later, I watch in my garden a
lovely white rose of June — Snow Queen or Swansdown —
slowly unfolding, and my thoughts go tenderly back, still wondering over the message they were to bring.

It was I think in 1906 that we left the Count House. Tin had
for the moment gone up and a certain smart little man succeeded
in engineering a company for the plausible purpose of opening up
the old Chy-an-Wheal Mine to which the Count House belonged.
The house was accordingly required and the company offered a
few pounds as compensation. Edith stood out for a more sub-
stantial sum and eventually obtained it, though the mining
scheme, as might have been foreseen, was a failure, and slowly
died out after the shareholders' money had been wasted. The
little farm was thus brought completely to an end and we moved
into the Moor Cottages, which Edith had long rented in order to
let furnished.

The two Moor Cottages, in a single building, stood inland at an
isolated and awkwardly situated spot behind the mine and off
the road, only approached by rough paths. It was a beautifully
peaceful place, with no houses in sight, facing the south, the
grounds running down to a little streamlet near to a well. This
position, so admirably suited for two writers, to some extent
compensated for the inconveniences of the cottages. They were
two small plain ordinary labourers' cottages containing altogether four small and four very small rooms. The two upper
front rooms were the best and with the pleasantest outlook.
That in the right-hand cottage became Edith's study and bedroom, that on the left mine. We had proposed to put in a door
joining the two rooms, but the landlord refused permission to
knock the two cottages into one.[1] That refusal caused me
many moments of acute anxiety at times. When Edith's health

---

[1] They have since been united by a little porch. Many years later, an artist
friend, Mr. Bernard Sleigh of Birmingham, when staying at Saint Ives, painted,
and kindly presented to me, a little sketch of the cottages which now (1936) hangs
in my country bedroom.

was uncertain, as it often was during the period at Moor Cottages,
I vividly recall how sometimes at night I would press my ear to
the thick wall in the endeavour to reassure myself, but not daring
to enter the cottage and so probably cause unnecessary disturbance. Indeed, this would not have been easy, for when we
became settled it was arranged that Priscilla — who usually
slept in Edith's cottage and only when some friend was staying
with us in mine — should lock me up at night so as to be able in
the morning without disturbing me to enter and light my fire.
This locking me up at nights was often a joke with Edith.

So long as there were no upsetting disturbances the lives of
both of us went on comfortably in Moor Cottages. I have said
that we were now two writers. The forcible disruption of the
farm — though several fields and animals and a stable, with
Bert, Priscilla's brother, to look after all, were still retained —
had definitely determined that literary vocation, germinal in her
youth, towards which, through all her farming activities, Edith
had been slowly tending. The revulsion from ethics and the
conventionalities of London life which she experienced on marriage, the enthusiasm for Nature, the delight in farming and
gardening, constituted a necessary phase in her development, a
necessary fertilising process in her spiritual life, but their work
was done, and in her uncertain state of health a rough natural
life had become even harmful. She was now acquiring the habit
she retained occasionally for the rest of her life of spending the
early hours of the morning writing in bed, sometimes as early as
four o'clock, for she was always fresh in the morning, and thus,
moreover, escaped the household noises and interruptions to
which she was more sensitive than I have ever been. On well-in-
spired days she would prop herself up in bed with cushions, so
that she could enjoy the pleasant prospect from the window and
with her bed-table before her — the bed-table specially made for
her which now rests in my bedroom for my eyes to fall on tenderly — and a cat or a dog or both lying on the bed, she would

do most of her work, having breakfast in bed, and then, perhaps, if the impulse persisted, writing on till towards lunch-time when she would have her bath and dress, the day's literary work finished.

I also had breakfast by myself in bed, and before that meal I would read, never having been able to write before breakfast. I had given up my studio at Hawkes Point, and Edith had two large plain summer-houses made and set up in the grounds of the cottages, a few yards apart from each other, one for me to work in and the other for herself. They were, though fixed, of the same size and type, with one side unenclosed, as the revolving shelters which we knew nothing about then but learnt to know later, and I recline now (1937) in one of them in my Sussex garden. It was here that much of the last volume of my *Sex Studies* was written, and here in good weather Priscilla would lay lunch. In the afternoon Bert would bring the trap round and Edith would go for a drive, perhaps to Saint Ives, usually by herself, for I never cared for driving (or later for motoring), while I went for a walk. In the evening after dinner we would each go to our separate rooms and beds, she to fall asleep instantly and I to read for a while. That was our usual way of life, and at Moor Cottages, where so few external influences could enter to cause disturbance, it became an almost stereotyped routine.

The only disturbances came from within and were chiefly due to Edith's health. For the rest, our life together would have been at this period singularly peaceful and happy. I can recall no incident that marred our quiet harmony at Moor Cottages, although one may be sure that there were sometimes the little nervous storms that Edith's temperament rendered inevitable. She was happy in her creative work — novels and short stories and lectures to be written and occasional articles in the *Daily Chronicle* — and as soon as her morning's work was done she was impatient till she could read it to me: 'When can I read you what I have written this morning?' After lunch or shortly before dinner usually suited me best, and she was eager for my opinions and criticisms, not always pleased with them at first, but disappointed if there were none. After the publication of her first book, she had little or no difficulty in finding a publisher except for *The Lover's Calendar*. The admirable little volume of humorous stories, begun at Aix, *My Cornish Neighbours*, appeared in 1906, dedicated 'To Havelock.' Next year came the considerably revised and rewritten version of *Seaweed*, now entitled *Kit's Woman: A Cornish Idyll*, and dedicated 'To All My Loyal Friends.'

In 1909 followed a novel, *Attainment*. This book, which we talked over beforehand more than over any other of her books except *James Hinton*, arose out of the idea, which had occurred to her many years earlier, of embroidering a novel around some of her own experiences in the Fellowship House. It was to be a free and artistic version of those experiences and to represent some of the successive phases of her own development. The idea appeared to me excellent and I warmly encouraged her to carry it out. The heroine is an intentionally vague image of herself, the servants introduced are more exact pictures of servants of her own, and the hero was in part suggested by me and one or two friends. She introduced three characters suggested by Stopford Brooke, William Morris, and Thomas Davidson, whom she realised quite fairly well, though she had not known him. The book seems to me well done, yet it is scarcely a success, for, with her usual impatience and her anxiety to complete and publish, she brought it to a premature end with the heroine's marriage. The idea was thus suggested that marriage was attainment, though that was far from her intention and rendered the story more feeble and futile than if she had carried out her intention of carrying the heroine's development further. Well written as it was, I thus count it the least satisfactory of her books. In sending it to me on publication, for I chanced to be away in London, she wrote from Moor Cottages:

> *My Boy,* Here is your *Attainment* with my best and truest love.
> But for you it would never have been written, and but for you
> probably never given to the world in this very nice way: I wish
> you were here to let me hug you and then tell you you had ashes
> on your waistcoat! I feel very near to you and I *do* love you.
>
> Your own Wifie.

A few months later, she wrote concerning her next book:

> *My Darling Boy,* I'm glad you like the Preface. Why do I feel
> so near to you? I told Olive in my letter that nothing could divide
> you and me. It couldn't, could it? D. [her dearest friend during
> those years and a sweet unselfish woman] really comes tonight.
> Love to Amy.

The Preface was that to *Three Modern Seers,* revised lectures
on Hinton, Edward Carpenter, and Nietzsche, which appeared
in the following year, 1910, with the words: 'This book is dedicated to my husband, Havelock Ellis, whose help in my work
has been its greatest stimulus.' She had herself been a little
doubtful about the success of this book, which was entirely
different in character from her previous books, but I had always
had faith in it. This faith was justified, for the book found, and
still finds, numerous and appreciative readers.

This work was all done in a struggle with physical disabilities.
She was always suffering, or liable to suffer under any stress
or strain of fatigue or worry, from her heart and circulation.
There was cardiac hypertrophy and dilatation and a tendency
to pseudo-angina pains. She was stouter in body at this period
than in early years when she was quite slender, and this increased
weight, which diminished again in later years, added to difficulties
further increased by the hilly Cornish district and the boisterous
climate. It was imperative that she should always guard against
these risks, she with her eager and sudden impulses, her disregard
of self, her helpfulness, her generosity of spirit, her pride which
disdained any confession of weakness. So it was that I, who had
come to know her so well, slowly acquired a perpetual emotional

undertone of anxious apprehension such as I had not known in the earlier years of our life together, when I had too easily entered into her reckless spirit of adventure. Now my love grew mixed with fear, and fear made my love more sensitive while love sharpened my fear. When I knew that she was safely tucked up in bed writing on her little bed-table, I was at rest. My worst moments were when her afternoon drives in the pony trap, mostly alone, were unusually prolonged, for I would recall the dangerous accident that had once happened to her on such a drive. She would be impatient if I asked her when she would be back; any sense of compulsion was intolerable to her, and there was no saying what matter of interest might not arise to cause delay. So when I thought she was due to return, I would leave my papers and come down to pace the garden path, with a grow-ing and as I knew unreasoning nervous apprehension in the deep-ening dusk if her return was delayed, as it sometimes was, for an hour or more. Then at last, and long before the trap appeared in sight, I would hear from the curves of the steeply undulating path the welcome tinkling of the little Spanish bells, brought from Malaga and fastened to the pony's harness, and I was at the gar-den gate to greet her. Anxious or not, I was always there to meet her on her return, and a friend spending a few days with us, who once accompanied her on the drive, still recalls what she describes as the radiant love on my face when I lifted Edith down from the trap.

Nevertheless, I went to London as usual, though at longer in-tervals, and when arrangements with Edith allowed, sometimes, as she may have thought, only too readily. But if the tender and devoted D. was able to be at Moor Cottages, I was even more at rest regarding Edith's welfare than when I was there myself. 'I am happy so long as I know you are all right,' I would say to her. 'Then you would be happy if I were dead?' she would answer, in a puzzled way. But, as I tried to explain, my happiness in ab-sence from her was bound up with the feeling that she was always within reach, and that we were each threading a path that would soon bring us together again. Nor was it true that I was at peace away from her. The undercurrent of apprehension was ever beneath the surface of my mind. It was always acutely stirred when a telegram reached me in London. I would tear it open with feverish haste. It was, indeed, oftener than not from her, not necessarily to convey any serious news, but to send a word of cheer or tell of a change in arrangements. The terrible telegram I dreaded was long in coming, yet it came at last, and was the more terrible because I was not there to receive it in time. Now, when I take a telegram into my hand, I may smile sadly to myself, and open it leisurely, assured that it cannot be terrible.

There was a serious illness one winter at Moor Cottages, apart from the more constant strain of the heart trouble, a prolonged attack of broncho-pneumonia. I felt acutely at this time the separation in different cottages. I was her sole nurse with Priscilla's assistance. So for some time I spent the nights in my dressing-gown on a narrow couch near her bed, and found this a great mental relief during a period of anxiety. The illness was prolonged, and necessarily slow. But her mental activity asserted itself at an early stage. In the course of two or three mornings she dramatised in one act a little story, 'The Subjection of Kezia,' in *My Cornish Neighbours*. Kezia was a living figure into which Edith had wrought, no doubt consciously, traits of her own nervous irritability, and the story dramatised admirably, with a real knot simply and cleverly unravelled. I warned her how hard it was for an unknown dramatist to receive even consideration at the hands of managers, but, swift as usual in thought and act, she sent it off at once to Mr. Otho Stuart, who was then producing some remarkable plays at the Court Theatre. Almost by return of post, to our delight, he replied accepting the play and stating that he wished to produce it immediately. Edith's joy was tempered by the consideration that she was still too ill to go to London to oversee the production, and a little later, while she was yet confined to her bed, the playlet was put on. I sat by her bed while this great event was in progress and one of her most valued friends, Mr. Frank Fowks, of the South Kensington Museum, had the good inspiration to send a telegram to assure her it was a real success.

So it turned out. As a curtain-raiser *The Subjection of Kezia* was played for many weeks at various leading London theatres, as well as in the provinces. It was, indeed, Edith's one unqualified popular success on the stage, and a year or two later, when she sold her rights in it, she had, for those few hours' work on a sick-bed, received a hundred pounds. It also brought her into personal touch with leading actor-managers, who were ready and anxious for any promising idea for a play, and incidentally it gave her a free entry to the theatres, now not only her chief recreation, but an opportunity to study the methods of the stage. At the same time her large circle of friends and acquaintances began to include a contingent of actors and actresses, often of course on the pounce for good parts.

This new stimulus in her life, which remained active to the end, reinforced the influences which were already at work to effect a change in the current of her existence and mine. The removal from the Count House had brought to an end the already waning attraction of farm life. The recent illness and the condition of her heart had made it clearer than ever that the climate of Cornwall, as Doctor Sansom had told her long before, was not the most favourable, while here also she was cut off from good medical advice and help. Her new mental activities, moreover, called for her frequent presence in London, although, after the earlier break on marriage, she never again wished to live there entirely shut off from the country life she had come to love. Now there was a new motive. The first and immediate step was to give up the Moor Cottages, too cramped and uncomfortable, as well as too isolated for one so sociable as Edith and also so liable to be an invalid. She resolved to make Rose Cottage on the main road, now the only cottage left to her, the one Cornish foothold. She had had this cottage on long leases over many years, and it had proved profitable for letting purposes. Once we had lived in it for a few weeks, but had not found it homelike. Gradually, however, with her usual ingenuity, Edith had introduced a number of improvements; it had become as pleasant and comfortable as one can expect an old Cornish cottage to be. Henceforth it was our Cornish home whenever we were at Carbis during the remaining six years of her life. Now it is more heavily burdened with memories, sweet or sad, than any home we ever lived in together. She had put my name into the lease so that on her death what she regarded as a valuable source of profit might benefit me. But I have never seen it since; I transferred it with the furniture, for a trifling consideration, to one of her friends. It is still often in my thoughts, and Carbis Bay is now to me a Paradise from which, by my own resolve, I am forever excluded.

I will go back a little to give some extracts from Edith's letters (which I again began to preserve in 1909), serving to show how life was dealing with both of us. I had resolved to take a larger flat than the small three-roomed one I occupied at the top of a little building near the Tate Library in Brixton, very inconvenient if ever Edith stayed with me. For the advantage of us both, I selected a more commodious flat (on the first floor, as it was still not easy for Edith to mount many stairs) in the Canterbury Road, not far away, opposite the police station. It was a solid and well-constructed building, erected some thirty years earlier and considered a notable achievement when flats were still a novelty. It proved to be my London home for twenty years, during most of that time, indeed, my only home. On the 7th of September, 1909, Edith wrote from the Moor Cottages:

> *My Darling Boy*, I think that the flat idea sounds splendid. Offer them £46 at first and let me one room for £10. Be in it before I come up and I will bring a bed and a few things with me.

I should not disturb you a bit, as I can always — as I do at the Club [the Lyceum where she sometimes stayed] — cook my own breakfast, etc., and I should be *so* glad to have one room I could lock up and go to whenever I wanted. If you think £15 fairer, I could perhaps manage that, or £12, whichever you think. [I agreed to the £10 and I always prepared her breakfast, which she had in bed.] I shall be very anxious to know if you do this. If there is a vile paper, it could be papered later, and I prefer a stained floor as you know. They began the *Kezia* week in Manchester last night. Wish I could have afforded to be there. I have had to have the Hinton lectures retyped, as they are scribbled all over and no publisher would look at them. I've read the new Nietzsche Life and I don't see I can say much more unless I put in another person's thoughts, and in my book [*Three Modern Seers*] Nietzsche is the least important 'seer.' D. sends her love. We are both sitting in the garden in the sun, but there is a sharp wind. We go to Prussia Cove tomorrow for the day, and Gertrude Russell [Honourable Mrs. Rollo Russell] who is at the Lizard, may come over on Thursday; they are selling Dunrozel [the Hindhead estate, where we had occupied the charming bungalow]. Don't say you would not like me to have a room in your flat — I wouldn't disturb you. I'm used to seeing to myself lately.

We evidently settled in before September was over, but two months later, when leaving London for the winter, I let the flat for a time to Mrs. Montefiore, a friend who was at that time a prominent feminist and suffragette. She is referred to in a letter of the 21st of November from the Moor Cottages:

My Darling Boy, I am very anxious to know how you are. It is very cold, but gloriously sunny. . . . Do take care and stay in one room, use mine if you like, and get Amy to nurse you and come whenever you want. I hope you have just said Mrs. Montefiore is a lecturer and social worker. I expect it is only prostitutes they don't want, though in these days how one is to know t'other from which, Heaven knows. The place looks perfectly sweet and all newly done up. . . . I love you very, very much, and though you try me a bit at times, I know I try you ever so much more; but we *do* love one another, and nothing and no one will ever alter it.

The next letter I have preserved is written in the early spring (March, 1910) and is in the same tone. After practical details, she concludes:

> I do trust you will be all right. I hate to think what a poor time you have had lately, but all shall be sweet for you when you come back. I love you *very* deeply, and nothing could ever make me unlove you. Like Tryphena, the worst of me is in my tongue. God bless you!

And a few days later:

> Bitterly cold here. I don't feel a bit vital — sort of worm, and neither man, woman, nor kid. Do take care, for it is madness to be in London now. I shall be delighted to see you back, for nice and sweet as N. [the dear friend then staying with her] is, I can't concentrate on my work the same and I want to get new work done. My photo is coming out in the *Bookman*. Glad Symons is so much better.

Early in May she went over to Paris, to see special friends, and notably for the first time the American woman W., who had earlier been the chief friend of Lily, and a fellow-artist, though it was only gradually, owing to Lily's silence, that Edith heard of her existence. So that relations had been difficult. But Edith skilfully overcame the difficulties and the two became genuine friends in their joint affection for the dead Lily. Letters or cards came to me nearly every day.

> Safe and well and happy. Lovely crossing. I do hope you are enjoying your brief period of peace. Shall I never disturb it again? ... W. is charming. I am feeling quite different, and we talked sweetly of Lily and of the future. I think of you always.

And on the corner of the card in D.'s hand, 'Love from D.'

> ... I've just heard the King [Edward VII] is dead, and there is no news from you. I do trust you are all right. All here so sweet to me, and my little D. is adorable, but we wish you were here. My heart yearns to you, and yours to me, I know. This is a dreadful thing for us — I liked my king, and the new one will

be no use in all the crisis. D. sends a big kiss and I send more
than you ever realise. Take care, dear, and write sweetly to

Your Wifie.

She was in France again for a short time at the end of August,
and it was arranged that I should come over to Normandy for a
day or two before going to see Amy in Belgium.

> *My Darling Boy* [she wrote on the 24th of August from the
> Hôtel du Prince le Galles in Paris]. All is well. I'm a different
> person at once in this land of sparkle. It is like being at home.
> Same room, hotel deliciously comfie. I have my café at 9, and
> no lunch — only a biscuit any time I feel like it. W. and I are
> like splendid men pals. She talks easily about L. and has had
> her new friend for five years, a singer and as tall as herself, so I
> look like a hyphen between two big American words. W. is
> changed, a quiet resignation on her. She seems quite to have ac-
> cepted what I struggled to make clear years ago — that L. was
> sick of me and only waiting to see her. Thank God, she thinks
> no evil of her — that is what L. would have wished, and no one
> can take away from me my own memories. I walked about Paris
> all alone yesterday, did several miles, I fancy. I had on my new
> hat with a lovely ruffle D. has sent me, which has turned me at
> once into a *chic* Frenchwoman. I travelled with a charming
> American girl musician and gave her the roses Montefiore brought
> me. She declared I was not English: 'The Englishwomen are
> dead — dead. You — oh! you are alive — My! so alive.' When
> I told her my age, she did laugh! They all spoil me here. W.
> kissed me once on the lips and pushed her hands through my
> curls; 'I expect L. rather liked your curls,' she said. Yesterday
> a funny little look came on her face and she said: 'Do you know,
> sometimes you have L's identical intonation and, a little, her smile?'
> It seems to be so natural to be with her somehow and there is not
> an atom of strain.... We start on Saturday for *le bon Dieu* knows
> where, but I'll let you know; anyhow, I fancy we shall stay a
> night or two with Montefiore's friend at Duclaire near Rouen.
> I feel as lethargic as a cat and as alert as a snake and a dragonfly
> in one body.

A few days later, she wrote from Duclaire:

The holiday of my life! We are having everything splendid here, with Monte's friend, for five shillings a day. Tomorrow we settle in Caudebec. Get a new hat before you come and reach us on Sunday at latest.

I duly arrived on Sunday (4th of September, 1910) to meet the little party at Lillebonne, going on shortly after to Belgium, visiting Louvain, and spending days or nights at Malines (where I heard a memorable recitation on the Cathedral Carillon), Brussels, Antwerp, and familiar Bruges. Both Edith and I were back in London a week or so later.

I may seem, these letters suggest, to have overemphasised Edith's illnesses and my anxieties at the Moor Cottages. She was by no means always ill there, nor I always anxious. In the good season of the year especially, it was a place of delight and of joyous work for both of us. I remember how I would walk up and down the narrow paths on one side or the other, between the potato rows, or near the sweetpeas, dreaming or thinking out my work, glancing up now and again to perhaps catch her bright face at the window. (She loved sweetpeas, growing them in quantities, and one year this was rather a sore point with me, for she put up a notice, that they were for sale. Proud as she was in some respects, she had none of the foolish conventional pride from which I could not quite free myself, and she would sell a pennyworth of flowers with the radiant delight of a child over the transaction.) It was in the summer-house she had set up for me in these grounds that I had at length brought to a conclusion the task of my *Studies*.

That work, the task of my life, had been in my mind for more than thirty years. It had first glimmered vaguely before me, as I have already told, in Australia, while I was pacing up and down the avenue at Burwood after my school duties for the day were over. It began to grow stronger, though still formless when, three years later, at Sparkes Creek, the inspiration flashed upon me that I must have a medical education or my work could not be done. A year or two later, on my return to England, I had begun in a small way the collection, which I have never since ceased to carry on, of data, notes and memoranda. Then, during the years of study at the Hospital, the scheme of *Man and Woman* slowly grew, as a preliminary study to clear the ground for the investigation of the sexual impulse itself; I anticipated it would not be more than a pamphlet, but in the ten years that passed before I had completed it for publication, in 1894, it had become a good-sized book, and it continued to grow until it reached its final eighth edition in 1934. Meanwhile, the *Studies* themselves were slowly, very slowly, taking shape in my mind. It was, as my nature is, a natural growth. I never at any stage drew up a systematic outline beforehand. I never knew far ahead what shape it would take. I was only very sure that it was there, and would grow.

It was intertwined with all sorts of other work. I never feel able to work at one subject long at a time — for my work is play and play demands freshness; but always I knew that the *Studies* were my main work, and whatever else I might be doing I was always consciously or subconsciously furthering the progress of that work. When I see myself praised, as sometimes happens, for my erudition, I smile, for I am not a scholar who lives surrounded by books, but a dreamer lying in the sunshine, and erudition is the smallest qualification for the work that I have done. The supreme qualification has doubtless been a deep inner sympathy and an ever closer personal touch with other human beings, combined with an artist's power of expression. It happened at the same time that I am interested in many things, and that at every moment I have at once instinctively felt the bearings of every fact I encountered on the main interest I had at heart, noting it down accordingly. It was thus that during long years I acquired a vast amount of miscellaneous material to be woven into my *Studies*, and incidentally acquired the undeserved reputation of immense encyclopaedic erudition, whereas it is the artistic skill and critical judgment expended in using the material rather than its mere accumulation for which credit should be assigned, if credit is due.

The first volume was published in German in 1896, in English shortly afterwards, and the others slowly followed at intervals during the next fourteen years. Sometimes, as I felt myself growing older the fear of death would come over me, but if I shuddered, it was solely at the thought that I should leave my work unfinished. That thought never had the slightest influence in hastening it; to me it was natural to work, if without rest, still, after the Goethean maxim, without haste. So, finally, the last, the longest and most important volume,[1] was brought to an end in the summer-house that Edith had made for me — as she had made so many of the conditions that favoured my work — on that quiet southern slope at the Moor Cottages. In my pocket diary for the year 1909, at the date of the seventh of August, I find pencilled the entry — and in the whole series of diaries it is the only entry that is not a bald statement — in the words of the great Elizabethan, George Chapman: 'The work that I was born to do is done.'

A deep, calm joy possessed me, a serene exultation. I could enter into the emotion that stirred Gibbon when he wrote the last words of his *History* in the summer-house at Lausanne. Certainly I had not, like him, achieved an immortal work of scientific art. My work, I knew, must in the nature of it be always crumbling and every day grow a little more out of date. I have myself had to rewrite parts of it.[2] Nevertheless, I felt that my satisfaction was justified. I had not created a great work of art. But I had done mankind a service which mankind needed, and which, it seemed, I alone was fitted to do. I had helped to make the world, and to make the world in the only way that it can be made, the

[1] I mean volume VI, *Sex in Relation to Society*. Many years later (in 1928), I published a large volume of supplementary *Studies*.

[2] Now as I revise these pages, in the summer of 1937, I have just completed a new and for me final edition of the chief volume, *Sex in Relation to Society*, for publication at length in England. Again I am reclining in a summer-house, this time the revolving shed in the quiet garden of the Sussex cottage where I mostly live, surrounded by the loving care and devotion of the dear companion of my last years.

interior way, by liberating the human spirit. The gratitude of men, and of women, has made me humble. I have sometimes felt that the taunt might be flung at me which was flung at Jesus: 'He saved others, himself he could not save.' Yet, I am well assured, with as little truth in the one case as in the other. For I have never sought any salvation for myself. I have been well content to be a Knight of the Holy Ghost. As I write these words, I recall that Edith's pet euphemism for the male sex organ was 'the Holy Ghost.' Well, be it so! For I have always instinctively desired to spiritualise the things that have been counted low and material, if not disgusting; and where others have seen all things secular, I have seen all things sacred.

Part X

X

It was by chance, and not by design, that the conclusion of my *Studies* almost coincided with the change in our external life which severed many of the links with Cornwall. It was an innovation when in 1909 I took the larger London flat which contained a room for Edith. Previously, when spending a few weeks in London, she had taken the furnished flat of some friend, as mine was too small for more than a few days' visit, though we had on occasion fitted Priscilla into a small couch in my study. But pleased as Edith was with the new arrangement, it had to be modified in a year or two.

As her activities in London increased, Edith found the journey to Brixton, especially at night, too fatiguing; it was also rather disturbing to my regular habits and early hours which were the same for me in London as for both of us at Carbis. It thus came about that in 1912 she took a flat at the top of a doctor's house in Harley Street, the doctor (Doctor Jensen) being a friend whose patient she had shortly before been. Here she was comfortably and centrally situated; here I could go to see her, and she could come from time to time to spend a few days at my flat, no longer as a tenant, but as a welcome guest. This was an arrangement that suited us both. It was always a joy to me to make her as happy as I could, to provide all the little comforts she needed and appreciated, to think of the things she most liked to eat, to bring her breakfast in bed, to prepare her bath, to serve her and wait upon her in all things — for we were now nearly always alone — with more skill, no doubt, than in the earlier days when she had been my sweetheart in a more conventional sense than she had now become in a deeper sense.

We were nearly always alone because Priscilla had now left us. This happened, suddenly in the end, at Rose Cottage, in 1911. She had been ill, a prolonged and persistent feverish attack, and Edith sent for a Doctor Hamilton at Hayle, a kind and sensible Scotchman in whom she had acquired confidence, to attend her. But convalescence was slow and Priscilla remained weak and ir- ritable. She had latterly manifested something of that inde- pendence and self-will which old servants — she had been with us ten years — usually assume, but which Edith in her uncertain health sometimes found intolerable. An incompatibility of moods thus arose, and one morning this culminated in a determination on Priscilla's part to go home at once. So Edith drove her to the station and we never saw her or heard from her again, although her brother, the devoted Bert, remained with us a year or two longer, and has in recent years come to see me. Edith felt the loss and was hurt, for she had come to look on Priscilla almost as her child. From time to time she would propose writing to ask her to come back. That, I easily persuaded her, would have been a mis- take, nor would Priscilla, I knew, ever come back. She looked upon Edith as she looked upon her mother. But, as happens to people of limited and morbid nervous energy, she was a philos- opher. She sought to guard her sensibilities. You must forget, she would say to me, what you can't have. It was part of this philosophy, having cut herself off from us for whom she cared more than for any other people in the world, to make the cut complete. So she never again gave a single sign. It was not indifference but the reverse. She went out to Queensland to join her married sister, who had once been our cook, with her set up a shop, and died from complications of influenza just a year before Edith.

The immediate cause of this shifting of our centre of gravity to London was, however, the success of *Kezia*. As soon as possible, Edith came to London and before long was on friendly terms with all concerned in the production of her playlet, especially the actress, Beryl Faber (Mrs. Cosmo Hamilton), who in the chief part had largely contributed to its success. One day Edith went down to the pleasant house and grounds which Beryl and her husband occupied at the village of West Drayton, thirteen miles from London. Now Edith and I, since realising that Cornwall could not be our permanent home, had often talked of taking conjointly some little house with a large patch of ground, not too far from London, where we might peacefully enjoy our old age together. On coming to Beryl's, Edith exclaimed that that was the kind of place she would like, and her hostess immediately told her that the adjoining piece of ground with a clump of cottages in the middle was at that moment to let. They went across to view it. Woodpecker Farm, as it was called, consisted of a piece of land ten acres in extent, with a compact half-timbered building used as three cottages and a large solid old barn with stables. The building was ancient, with much rough-hewn oak, dating back at least three centuries, I suppose, but altogether out of repair, ruinous in places, infested with vermin, occupied by the lowest characters in the village, gaol-birds and the like, who seldom paid their rent. Edith was enthusiastic; with that keen vision for the possibilities of a place which had been tested before, she knew how much could be made of Woodpecker. She went to interview the landlady at once; and before she came away, as her impetuous manner was, she had almost committed herself and me to take the place on the longest lease possible.

When she broke this news to me, that day or the following, I was, naturally enough, dubious, and not less dubious when a little later I accompanied her to view our future estate. There was no doubt about the possibilities, but to convert them into actualities the fifty pounds of the builder's estimate would, I knew, go but a little way, and I caught the smile on the face of the landlady's business agent who accompanied us round. But Edith brushed away my caution. Difficulties were always a stimulus to her; she was fortified by opposition. She declared that it was too late to go back honourably, and that if I refused to share the responsibility she would find someone else. That would hardly have been feasible, as I knew. But I yielded, and even entered into the spirit of the adventure, subduing any hurt feelings over the manner — so natural to her temperament though so alien to mine — in which I had been drawn into it. At the same time I spent sleepless hours at night over the burden we were assuming that neither of us was really able to bear.

The first blow to Edith's satisfaction over Woodpecker came soon after the lease was signed and long before the place was ready for us to enter. Beryl Faber, whose presence as a friendly neighbour had been one of the chief attractions of the place, announced that in consequence of a disagreement with her landlord she was leaving West Drayton immediately. It was not the first time that Edith, who never found it easy to learn by experience, had encountered a similar experience. She had, in the early years of our marriage, taken a little cottage in Cumberland on a long lease to be near an old school-fellow friend whose family shortly afterwards was obliged to give up their estate, and that cottage had been a source of much worry. Woodpecker, however (after a preliminary fumigation to dispel the vermin), was progressing favourably. Edith, always fertile in excellent ideas, was making the place ever more convenient and more agreeable, and so of course piling up the financial indebtedness of both of us, while there was always some new and unexpected expense to meet. Priscilla, too, who was part of the original scheme, had left us before we actually entered into possession, and for some time the servant difficulty was a source of worry; but after one or two unfortunate experiments a devoted young woman arrived whom Edith had befriended because she was about to have an illegitimate baby, and she remained with us, always full of gratitude, until a year or two later she married. There was, however, for a time the faithful Bert, who duly came up together with the pony and the donkey, and most of the Cornish furniture. Edith had a telephone, which (unlike me) she henceforth regarded as essential, brought across the grounds and set up at her bedside, and finally in 1911 we settled in Woodpecker.

It had become a charming spot nor had our difficulties yet dispelled Edith's sanguine hopes for the future, while I, too, was happy to live in summer under the great walnut tree where when possible we would have our meals, being both at one in the instinct to live out-of-doors, she even more than I. In winter, however, difficulties became pronounced. To try to meet the serious expenses Edith occasionally took a paying guest from among her acquaintances, not a proceeding that was really agreeable to either of us. It helped to arouse in Edith a distaste for Woodpecker. At last she realised that the cost of the place was more than we could bear, and that any prospect she had earlier cherished of its paying for itself was remote. After we had been there two years, a wealthy American lady who had lately entered the circle of Edith's friends and become highly esteemed by her, paid a visit to Woodpecker, fell in love with the place, and offered to take it over from us with all it contained. The offer was on a liberal scale, covering much of the outlay, and was soon accepted. Of my share of the purchase money indeed I saw little, for Edith argued characteristically that her debts were urgent and I could wait, so my repayment was postponed to a time that never arrived. With strangers honourable and generous in money matters beyond the wont of women, Edith was willing to let friends wait, though always with sanguine confidence that all debts would ultimately be repaid. So ended our attempt to set up house together on an equal basis. We had planned other attempts, but circumstances never permitted us to make them.

That settlement at West Drayton in August, 1911, the first for nearly twenty years within a few miles of London, marked, I have already indicated, a new stage in Edith's development. She was now easily able to go up to London every day if she liked (I went more rarely) driving to and from the station. Now she was able to exercise her personal magnetic influence as well as her social qualities, heightened by the intellectual vigour slowly matured through the inner and outer experiences of her active life in Cornwall. She was already an effective lecturer when I first knew her; as a speaker as well as a personality she sometimes aroused enthusiasm; it was soon after our marriage that a friend had declared to her that she was 'the light and hope of our future civilisation,' a saying that I would later sometimes playfully recall to her. But in the early years she was also a little crude, narrow, and inexperienced, apt to be overserious and too highstrung. A touch of exaltation for good or for evil was no doubt often present to the last; though blended with compensating elements, it was a part of her temperament. But there was also at the core a solid structure of firm fibre, needing long to mellow but susceptible of much refinement. Now, approaching the age of fifty, but still youthful in mind and spirit, though her hair was soon to be touched with grey, she had gained both insight and breadth, for she had probed life deeply and become tolerant, her seriousness blended with a swift humour, often daring but never belittling what it touched. She could grasp sympathetically the character of the most various people she met and say the word that unlocked the heart of each.[1] As a public speaker she had gained in power and range and was easily able, on occasions either grave or gay, to speak extemporally; though, always desirous to do everything well, she would if possible think out every speech beforehand.

The centre of her social activities henceforward was the women's literary and artistic club in Piccadilly, the Lyceum — the house happened to have once been that of her early idol Byron — and here she could transact business, meet friends, and largely increase her already large circle of friends and acquaintances. Here she found the medium in which her long repressed social activities might harmoniously expand. She was, I believe, the chief founder and organiser of a poetry circle which offered hospitality to various prominent writers of the day; she was congenially active in arranging the dinners in connection with this circle, and a much appreciated speaker at these functions. I was never present, for they were alien to my tastes, but I heard the rumour of them. She seems to have been popular and a general favourite at the club, whatever jealousy and dislike may possibly have been felt by a few. Her winning simplicity and directness of manner, her humanity, her ready wit, with an occasional mischievous sting disarmed by the small woman's genuinely childlike disposition, overcame the shock in so respectable an environment of outspokenness and unconventionality. She never hesitated to

[1] For illustration I quote from two letters she left behind, one from a man, one from a married woman, each of whom she had met only once or twice. The man wrote: 'I feel I must tell you how much I valued your kindness today. It is such a wonderful thing to find someone who understands without condemning or consoling too much. "Broadminded" people do harm by exaggerated tolerance, and yet I cannot tell you what it means to find someone who keeps a sense of proportion. I wish I had met you ten years ago.' The woman writes: 'I wish I could tell you how all you said at the Club that day remains with me. The vitality and the vividness was so impelling, and the strange thing was that you were speaking directly to me as an individual soul. I shall carry a wonderful memory of you to make into a reality in my life. The width of the world is in your sympathy. I wonder if you know how you touch us who only draw near for a moment in a lifetime. Courage inspires courage, and after I had been with you I felt I could do anything that had to be done and in the right way.' There must have been many who wrote to her, or could have written, as these two persons wrote.

express vigorously her opinion of any proceeding in the club management of which she disapproved, and the democratic attitude
long cultivated in her Cornish farmyard remained unimpaired in
Piccadilly. Thus she took a human interest in the head porter, a
Frenchman of rather superior type, once or twice even took him
to the theatre, without making any secret of the matter. I doubt
whether any other member of the club would have dared to be so
outspoken or so unconventional, or could have been so with such
impunity.

While she was luxuriating in these metropolitan activities, it
must not be supposed that troubles were absent. They could
never be long absent from one of her equally adventurous and sensitive temper. Her health, indeed, was fortified by various beneficial courses of treatment. But the efflorescent excitement of her
life was compensated by an underlying sombreness of outlook, a
deeper grip of the fundamental tragic verities of life and death.
This largely dated from an episode which belonged to the early
part of this period.

Her successive intimate relationships with women usually ran
a fairly natural course. If they once or twice ended in disappointment, it was an end in which she acquiesced, an end which was
merged in ordinary friendship. A strong compelling attachment
had never drawn her to a person who failed to respond. That,
however, was what now happened. A woman of high character
and considerable distinction as a doctor fascinated Edith's love
and seemed at first to respond to that love in the same spirit. But
she quickly realised that there was in it what she felt to be an abnormal element alien to her own nature and traditions, and became cold to all further advances. Gradually a genuine ordinary
friendship grew up between them of precious quality with, on
Edith's side, a beautiful element in it of affectionate tenderness.[1]
But meanwhile for many months — most of the time in Cornwall
— Edith passed through a period of almost melancholic depres-

[1] The friend died, unmarried, a few years after Edith, still in early middle life.

sion and desolation, constantly apt to brood over the love she had missed, or seeking how she might gain it. I had never before seen her in this mental state, since it was unlike the natural grief and dejection over the death of Lily. Doubtless it was some relief to her that my sympathetic ears, to which she ever simply and spontaneously at once brought every trouble, were near her at this time, though there was little help I could give. As I look back, it seems to me that the state into which she had thus fallen was an early manifestation of the more serious state of cyclothymic depression which more or less clouded her intelligence in the last winter of her life. But this time the cloud passed when her trouble was resolved by its transformation into a calm and mutual friendship.

It was during this period that she wrote most of the stories, all more or less coloured by the thought of death, collected under the title of *The Imperishable Wing*, a title I had suggested from Rossetti's line — 'The Wind of Death's imperishable Wing.' These mostly sombre stories never became so popular as the earlier collection, *My Cornish Neighbours*, but they bore witness to a real advance in art. There is a deeper insight, a firmer touch, a more virile grasp of the last essential verities of life, and while the humour is less gay and reckless, it is more finely subdued to the ends of art, and attains at times an almost Shakespearean quality in its nearness to tragedy. In one of these stories, scarcely one of the best, 'Clouds,' she symbolised her own state during this period of dejection, but transmuting her emotion, as she was always able to do, into art, and embodying it, as her way was, in a masculine form. It was, I believe, the same episode in her life that partly inspired another of her writings of about the same date (included in Ishill's privately printed posthumous volume of her *Stories*), *Heaven's Jester, or the Message of the White Rose*, though there is also in it the influence of Lily. In form and style it shows that she had begun to be interested in Oscar Wilde's prose stories. It is unlike anything else she wrote; its interpretation was not quite

clear to me, and, as ever, I never asked her to explain it, though it
is a beautiful and intimate thing. 'Heaven's Jester,' I gathered —
for I do not remember that she ever told me so — was a name
Lily had playfully given her, or, as she put it, so inscribed in the
register of Heaven, and thus given her the part she was henceforth
to play on earth.

In this poignant legend she expresses, once and for all, her love
and reverent worship for women, body and spirit, and the melancholy underlying the gaiety with which she could shake her cap
and bells, an attitude associated with Lily's death, 'Thy soul,
after her passing from earth, had barely gained thy body again
before the cap and bells were donned by thee'; that is to say, it
was just after Lily's death that her humour matured and that she
wrote *My Cornish Neighbours*. The Jester is represented as giving
his cap and bells to a deformed beggar who had asked for them,
and his precious instruments to his cold-hearted lady who could
draw no music from them, and in the morning he is found dead
with the faded petals of the white rose she had given him on his
breast. 'Maker of men,' he had prayed, 'pour into a Fool's heart
the understanding of higher joy and pain. Make my spirit at one
with the great order.' She had written, or completed, *Heaven's
Jester* when on a visit to Normandy with an earlier friend of Lily's
in August of 1910, and I imagine that it may have been that companionship which made more vivid to her the nature of her relationship to Lily and helped to inspire *Heaven's Jester*. 'When
Death claims thee, and thy cap and bells are laid aside, God's
Jester shall sleep with a white rose on his breast. "Dead," they
will say, but no! At last thou shalt hear the eternal song of the
souls of women and be satisfied.' There is, however, more in
Heaven's Jester than an allegory of her love of women. On every
page it contains in brief sentences some statement of her deeper
experiences and beliefs concerning Life and Love and Death. As
I now read and re-read this little allegory, it seems to embody the
only statement she ever made of her own secret feelings concern-

ing her nature and function as an artist. 'Nothing can take from
me what the sun made of me through his shining,' the white rose
says to the Fool. 'Even as I die, the fragrance remains. Nothing
can rob thee of the hours when all things seemed possible because
of thy hopes and her vows. Love is pain, but over-love is peace.
Turn thy tears into help and pity for those who dwell in dungeons
and are not yet registered in Heaven as wise or foolish. . . . On thy
knees, then, and pray for strength and courage, with thy cap and
bells in readiness by thy side, and joy within thy heart.'

Heaven's Jester is so intimately personal and impressive that I
now lovingly seek to penetrate its meaning. But when she gave
it to me to read for the first time, the impartial criticism with
which I always read her work the first time — and it was so she
desired me to read it — led me to form a not altogether favourable opinion. I thought that, notwithstanding its beauty, it was
a little obscure and imperfectly achieved. That seems to have
been the judgment also of the editors to whom it was successively
submitted, only to be rejected. It was not published until Edith
visited America when it appeared in *The Little Review* in 1914.
Before that date she had written another paper, 'The Philosophy
of Happiness,' more simple and direct in form, if less intimately
personal, which was a final statement of much she had sought to
set down in *Heaven's Jester*, and is quite free from the melancholy
which fills *Heaven's Jester*. 'The Philosophy of Happiness' —
which was published in the English *Everyman* and the American
Forum, as well as sometimes given as a lecture — was perhaps
Edith's best piece of prose and certainly the most mature and the
most serene statement of her experience of life.

Before leaving *The Imperishable Wing*, I may refer to a story in
it called 'The Idealist.' It is notable as the only story Edith ever
wrote dealing with the problem of inversion, and the tragedy of the
invert's position in the world. Yet on the surface it contains not
the faintest reference to inversion. With her artist's instinct she
transformed the situation; she merged this special problem in the

general problem of the abnormal and symbolised it in another anomaly of which she had only an imaginative insight, making her hero — clearly suggested by a local ne'er-do-well of her acquaintance famed for the zest and skill with which he discovered the bodies of the drowned — a fisherman with a kind of necrophilic attraction to corpses. So she transformed her deep feelings on this problem into a little work of art. The transformation was not the result of timidity. She also vaguely planned, or sometimes talked to me about, a long novel which was to deal more openly with the same subject. Had she lived I have little doubt this scheme would have matured. She was slow in approaching a subject, but when she had fully come up to it and grappled with it and mastered it, she never lacked courage to declare what she had found. During twenty years in which this problem had been more or less clearly present to her, she had never written about it or discussed it with strangers, but now at length her mind was made up. At the same time that she wrote 'The Idealist,' she was also preparing two lectures, sometimes more or less combined in one — 'Eugenics and Spiritual Parenthood,' 'Abnormality and the Spiritual Outlook' — in which she set forth paths of useful social activity and high spiritual function which remain open to the invert notwithstanding all his disabilities. She was thus able to help many who suffered from homosexual disabilities, though doubtless there were others whom her attitude and her plain-speaking shocked. The first time she gave one of these lectures was to the Eugenics Education Society (later the Eugenics Society), but they never again invited her to lecture. She delivered the lectures, however, on various occasions, both in England and America. It was at this period that, with her growing maturity of outlook and increased confidence, she became more impressive than ever before in personal intercourse. This was felt even by those who made no demand for sympathy or help. A woman friend, a fine artist of recognised ability, who had known her from her teens though not intimately, has attempted to describe this impression in a letter I received but a day or two ago: 'One couldn't analyse the attraction — it was just the radiation of her personality, not what she said but just the absence of barriers. One has to climb so hard to get over the walls with most people — but she was just *there*. It is impossible to forget her.' Her intimate personality had, with the slow progress of her development and the ripening of her experience, become more and more expressed in all her activities, public and private. She was already a good lecturer and speaker when I first knew her, exerting influence by the persuasive power of her personality and speech, by no means only on cultured people, for she was able to arouse real enthusiasm among the working-class audiences she addressed in early years in the North at Ancoats. But she was constantly making herself a better speaker. As she had never learnt elocution, practised speakers were puzzled at her method of voice production and its success. They were simple and natural methods, and, with her beautiful, ringing, honest voice, the expression of her whole personality. On the platform, as everywhere else, she sought to do her best, to dress and look her best, to speak as well as she could, simply, with conviction, persuasively. For many years she carefully practised her lectures beforehand in private, and spoke with the paper before her even when she almost knew the lecture by heart. She had no flights of eloquence, but the slow, grave, simple, convinced tones with which she uttered the things that seemed to her the most worth while in life were more impressive than any arts of the orator. With growing experience she attained greater freedom and, except for her more important lectures, she learnt to speak without notes, especially at formal dinners as of the Lyceum Club, and here she seems to have achieved much success, so that her help was frequently sought. She was always nervous beforehand, though all her special qualities of temperament and training fitted her for this part.

But the same qualities came out just as vividly in her personal

private life where I was myself best able to know them. They
came out not only in her ready wit and quick repartee, in her
swift impulse of helpfulness towards everyone who seemed to need
help wherever she might be, but in every spontaneous gesture.
Her movements responded unconsciously and immediately to her
emotion. Well I remember how it would happen during the latter
years that, recovering from an illness, when some dear friend,
woman or man, entered the door, she would sit up in bed, fling
wide her extended arms as in the instinctive first movement of an
embrace, perhaps without a word, with an eager expression I can
not describe, but can never forget. Nothing could be more
natural, more beautiful, more pathetic. Her whole organism
was the expression of herself.

The appreciation in which she was held by the members of the
Lyceum Club of which she was so active a member well came out
on an occasion (July 20, 1912) when she invited the whole of the
members of the Club Poetry Circle, with which she was specially
associated, to spend the day at West Drayton. They formed a
large party, not entirely confined to members of the club. It was
the only occasion on which she ever invited a large party to our
house, not merely because of my dislike of such functions, but
because, sociable as she was, she preferred at most two or three
friends at a time. The member of this party I was most pleased to
greet was Henry W. Nevinson, the only time I have met him, a
man for whom I have a high regard, while on his side he has
frequently written of my work with sympathetic admiration. It
was he, indeed, at a much later date who was to preside at a dinner to be given in my honour in celebration of my seventieth
birthday. But such functions are not to my taste and I declined
the honour. On this occasion at West Drayton my part was subordinate and I was able to realise the affection and admiration
felt for Edith. It was clearly expressed afterwards in various
poems written in description of the visit, and notably one by
Miss Close, too long to reproduce but charmingly telling of the

hostess's 'right royal welcome,' adding that it was 'echoed by the Philosopher within,' of Edith's familiarity with the pigeons, and of the 'loaded boards' in the lovely cottage that 'groaned 'neath the bounteous cheer and sparkling wine.'

It was during those years that most of my associations of her with London were formed. During earlier years, we had seldom been in London together except to pass through. The times I had spent in London were usually the times when she was most busily occupied in Cornwall, and when she came to London it was generally my part to keep watch at Carbis. But now during these years in London, even though we were often living under separate roofs, there were frequent and sometimes daily meetings appointed at places that might suit the convenience of one or other of us; at railway stations, at restaurants, at concerts, at the British Museum Reading Room. Railway stations, especially, were always peculiarly associated with her, for during our life together, it was constantly my part on her numerous excursions to see her off or to meet her on her return, and, especially during the later years, to go up to town with her, when we would separate for the day or longer and meet again at the station for the return journey to our country home, I nearly always arriving first at the station, but she never failing to appear at least a minute or two before the train was due to leave. There grew, indeed, to be countless other places where we would meet or visit together, scattered about the main thoroughfares of London. Whenever nowadays I go about London on my business or my recreation, I constantly come upon them: here she stood; here we met; here we once sat together; just as, even in places where she never went, I come upon some object, however trifling, which leads, by a tenuous thread of suggestion, to her. So that it sometimes seems to me that at every step of my feet, and at every movement of my thought, I see before me something which speaks of her, and my heart grows suddenly tender and my lips murmur involuntarily, 'My Darling!' Thus the streets of London, even when I walk

them carelessly beside some unheeding friend, have a new poignancy to me, sometimes 'Stations of the Cross' on the way to
Calvary, sometimes the starry arch of a Milky Way.

A frequent meeting-place at this time was the Down Street
Tube Station, just round the corner from the Lyceum Club in
Piccadilly. Knowing my unsociable dislike of coming to the club,
she had thoughtfully fixed this conveniently near but retired spot,
where we could meet to go together for lunch or dinner, or just
to see each other for a brief space and talk over any plans of
mutual interest. But of all our meetings here, which her bright
presence made starry, the one meeting which stands out in
memory makes of that obscure little station a Station of the
Cross on the way to her and my Calvary. For it was here one
autumn day in 1913 that she came to tell me that she had just
been found to be affected by the disease that was in a few years to
kill her. Some years earlier she had insured her life for two
hundred pounds and, in spite of her heart trouble, our good
medical friends at Saint Ives, and even the insurance company's
medical examiner, took a cheerful view of her health, a justified
view indeed, since the cardiac conditions improved. That two
hundred pounds was pledged to cover a loan in case of her death.
Now she wished to repeat this performance, for there was again
another loan and a large bill for a special course of medical treatment into which she had slipped without quite realising what it
involved and felt that she must pay off even if it meant another
loan. The sum was far too large for me to advance and hence the
scheme of the insurance to serve as security. But medical examination revealed the presence of glycosuria, possibly a permanent
diabetes, with the impossibility of effecting an insurance on her
life, and it was this discovery, just made, that she imparted to me
with a grave face that evening when we met in Down Street.
Long and long we slowly paced in serious communion up and
down that little street, surveying the new aspect of our future
lives thus suddenly revealed, for there had been so far not the

slightest symptom in her general health to indicate the disease. At her age, as she knew, it was not speedily or necessarily fatal, as it would have been in a younger person. It was a disease in her family, however, and she knew its serious character, though never taking it — for that was not her way — too seriously, adopting the dietetic treatment at that time regarded as necessary so far as seemed practicable, but not with punctilious rigidity, while the medical aspects of the disease became to me a subject of acutely painful interest. It was not, I may remark, until just after Edith's death that the discovery of the insulin treatment made so great a change in the diabetic patient's outlook.

As I look back, it seems to me that from that time dated a new and more realised depth of tenderness in our love for each other. That is not to imply that love had grown cold. On the contrary, during all these middle years we had been growing closer in communion, there had long ceased to be any serious shadow of disturbance over the harmony of our lives together, and even our absences — though these had never been due to any desire for separation — had become very brief, however frequent, as they remained till the end, except for her visits to America. But this very smoothness of our lives in all essentials may have diminished the need for the expression of love. It is a curious fact that about this time — though, it must be said, about a year before, and not after, the discovery of the glycosuria — after having by a common and unrevealed impulse failed to preserve each other's letters for so many years, each of us, still unknown to the other, began to preserve letters again and so continued until almost the end. I can only suppose that we found that they were now better worth keeping. She realised more than before that she might soon have to leave me; I, who had long felt the shadow of her loss in front, now knew that there was a more definite reason than before to justify that feeling.

I have been telling nothing of our varied external movements. But from 1912 I can record some of them from her own letters. In that year, while we still possessed the Drayton cottage, Edith, after having for several years shared with me the rent of the Brixton flat, began to feel that, in a state of health which demanded a long course of treatment in central London, the strain of travelling to and from Brixton was too great, while she also became a little prejudiced against the flat, since she had discovered (which I had not) a slaughterhouse concealed close by, having on one occasion heard the cries of animals in the early morning after which she constantly imagined that she could hear them as she lay in bed. She wrote to me from Drayton in August:

My darling Boy, The awful woe lifted a bit when I got home and found your sweet letters. I had felt you needed me no more and I felt I *must* die. I was very ill all Friday and when I got to the Ranee's [the Ranee of Sarawak] she poured champagne down me. You see it is a whirl and readjustment for me as well as you and such thousands of things to see to. The tenants have fled from Rose Cottage, say it is damp and stuffy. I shall have to go down when I get from here. Will you care to come with me? I thought everything over when I was at the Ranee's (I only just got home when I sent you wire) and came to the conclusion I could only be an awful strain on you and not feel free either, and with the slaughterhouse and the long distance I made up my mind to ask Jensen to have me as a tenant, and have taken a large and lovely unfurnished room at the top of the house for £50 a year. It has gas fire, electric light and all I could ever want in the world. I told J. that as I was having treatment and must be near my Club, and as you and I *had* to be quiet and unstrained, conventions must go to the winds. You see he has others there as tenants, so I don't see it is so unusual. I'm dead beat and D. and A. came today. C. goes tonight, so I shall be alone when you come. I love you ever — nothing and no one could ever replace you. When I got your dear letters I felt steel and iron had been cut from my heart. We are *both* strange and trying folk, but we love one another and under this new arrangement we shall meet and love in peace. Jensen does not mind my having my cat a bit.

Your own loving Wifie

One feels in this letter, as in some others of the same period, a certain overexcitability of strain and nervous exhaustion in an enfeebled state of health. Her varied mental, emotional, and physical activities, her vivid interests, her consuming energies could not be restrained, especially in the feverish atmosphere of London where she now felt her life mainly to be, but they were often more than her constitution could well bear. The seeds of the diabetic poison were being planted.

I do not think it could have been prevented. The long seclusion of Cornwall had been highly favourable to her development. But she had exhausted the possibilities. She hungered for a full environment in which to expand her new powers. Excess of energy, both physical and spiritual, was in her temperament. She responded to all the stimuli of a rich social atmosphere, not taking her colour from it but, rather, giving it her colour. 'The Road of Excess leads to the Palace of Wisdom,' said Blake. I do not deny it, but it is a dangerous road, and if the only road I, at all events, shall never reach that palace. My instinctive tendency has always been to temperance as hers was to excess. If she drank two glasses of wine when exhausted and felt better, she would propose to drink a third glass. I also found two glasses good, but I knew by experience that two are more than three and had not even a desire for the third. I claim no moral superiority; our differing instincts were matters of temperament and heredity. At the same time her instinct of excess never led her into any vice. There also she was safeguarded, perhaps by instinct, and certainly by deep conviction.

I went down to Cornwall with her in September as she had proposed, and we stayed there peaceably nearly three weeks. On the day after our return to London she wrote to me from Harley Street:

> *Oh! my Boy!* This strange world after Carbis! I've never regretted leaving anywhere so much. I miss you horribly. Now isn't that strange? But it is true. I will be at the Queen's Hall

entrance tomorrow and will get the tickets this morning on my
way to the Club. Have tea with me after, as I've heaps to tell you.
Havelock — I think it is *because* I love you that I get so frenzied,
or else I'm best dead. I seem never to have had quiet for years
and last night what passed between J. and me made me feel
dreadful. I got a horrid pain in my heart and felt I must run
back to Cornwall. Of course by this morning I just feel nothing
and realise that he is strained. But I will tell you when I see you.
I feel I want to see you so badly and to kiss you well after my
jig-jags. Please try and help me not to be like that. It is your
apparent callousness to me sometimes that makes me want to
put pins in you. Anyhow, of one thing I am sure and that is that
I love you and love you more than you can guess.

She was no doubt right about that appearance of callousness.
I have always been conscious of it. Thirty years afterwards in
my later life, I suspect it may be that same 'apparent callousness'
that has sometimes made it difficult for my dear Françoise to
realise how much I love her. Partly it is that my affections tend
to be deep and equable and calm; when love is established, it
never occurs to me either to give or to ask any declarations of
love, while for Edith (as perhaps for women generally) love never
seemed sure without visible proof; it might vanish at any moment, so that the continual evidence of its existence was necessary, and its realisation an ever fresh, vivid, and joyful experience.
Partly, also, I am not demonstrative even when the sense of love
is urgent, and I feel an instinctive and unconquerable repugnance
to furnish any expected and, as it were, conventional response.
At such times it seems to me that silence is more than all speech.
Priscilla, with whom I had something in common, when once
charged with indifference, replied: 'One is always saying "Thank
you" for trifles, so how can one say "Thank you" for real things?'
Edith at least knew how I felt, and in writing of me she recalled
a saying of mine to the effect that I wished I had a tail like a dog
that I could wag. But, all the same, it was something that she
craved and missed.

Two days later, Edith wrote to me from Harley Street to Clare, where I was spending a day or two near Amy:

> Your dear letter just come. I went to the theatre alone; saw the Lawrences there and the Ranee, etc. Came home and made cocoa and my cats loved me, and I slept almost philosophically and woke quite so. Wrote a short letter to *Chronicle* on play, and about twenty others, and am going to have my breakfast and bath and then to Drayton and dining with Miss C. tonight at Kensington. Do have a good time with Amy and tell her to love you up and comfort you. I wish I could, but I seem no good to anyone really. Be prepared to settle down in Drayton on 21st. It will be very nice and I shall just take a first-class season again in the cold weather.
>
> Much tender and lasting love from   Your Wifie

We went down to Drayton together for our last winter there. We had, indeed, completely given up the place, but returned by the kind proposal of the new proprietor. She had gone to India and suggested that we should occupy Oldmeadows (as she had renamed the place since Americans regard the woodpecker as unlucky) to look after it during her absence. Except that it was winter, so that we could not live out-of-doors under the big walnut tree, this was probably the pleasantest part of our whole occupation. The place had been much improved and made more luxurious since we left, while we were relieved of the burden of anxiety and responsibility which the undertaking had placed upon us, and Edith no longer felt called upon (as she sometimes had during our tenancy) to invite some friend or acquaintance to stay as a paying guest. In November she went down to Carbis with a friend, Mrs. M., for a week or so to put Rose Cottage in order for new tenants, leaving me at Drayton. Thence she wrote:

> *My darling Boy,* I'm in heaven — the glorious sea and sky and clouds as never anywhere but here. I'm trying to knock Mrs. M.'s ethics into a cocked hat. Don't expect letters — I want to read and dream and forget pens and paper.

But the Cornish climate is capricious. Two days later she wrote:

> The sight of you writing this morning almost made me weep. I had a fearful dream and woke at two unable to sleep again. I dreamt you were dead. I felt I should have to get out in the drenching rain and wind and come to you. Then I fell asleep at five and dreamt that Beryl [the actress friend who induced her to take Woodpecker and had since died] was there and said: 'Curls, we shall soon be together again.' It is cold and stormy and terribly wet here now.... I hate you to be lonely and of course you must not stay there if you hate it.
> My eternal love to you.
>
> W.

It is a perpetual source of amusement and wonder to me to think how from the first, separately and together, she and I had cherished ideals of freedom and independence, both in theory and in practice, and cast contempt on the narrow self-absorption of domestic love, and, as it would seem, had done everything to make such love difficult or even impossible. And yet the love we achieved during a quarter of a century seems to lie beyond even the imagination of those conventional couples who proclaim the duty and the beauty of mutual devotion, never leave each other's side, loathe the ideals of freedom and independence — and in their hearts loathe each other.

Just after writing that letter, Edith foolishly took a long walk while the gale was still raging, to please the friend staying with her, and with consequences that might be anticipated.

> *My Darling One* [she wrote two days later], I've had a very severe angina attack, but slept at last last night and am staying in bed all day; so I shall be *quite* well tomorrow; no lung trouble. Thank God you love me — I love you and know that neither of us could live long without one another.... Doctor Rice came in yesterday, says I had better stay in bed today and sees I know myself best. All are quite kind and good and my room is sweet. Don't worry *a bit* — you know I always come out all right. No

sun here — only shrieking wind and fearful rain and hail at intervals. You would have hated it if you had been here.

Bless you, your own   Wifie

'I know that neither of us could live long without one another.' I had forgotten she said it, yet I have always known that, in a sense, it is true. That she had found me was from the outset, I knew, beneath all her turbulent independence and deep reserve and playful mischief and agitating moods, and at times something that was almost contempt — it was always, I knew, though not in her nature to say so, nothing less than a miracle. The realisation of it remained unobliterated even in the final decay of body and mind. No one could take, in the smallest part, my place; she could not admit more than one person to the inmost springs of her being. (I recall how, when she would speak of what I would or should do after her death, I once said I hoped I would die first and she replied, gravely and quietly, that that was selfish.) I felt, as I watched her dying and saw, after an interval, her last sighing breath softly rise and fall away forever, that life for me was over. I might go on living, cheerful and content, working more assiduously than ever, always ready to help when my help was needed, even loving and beloved, yet realising, perhaps rather sadly, that there was little I any longer really needed. The whole world seemed an insubstantial and evanescent dream. My thoughts were instinctively with Prospero on his island. I might not be a magician — though that is what a dear friend, who was also her friend likes to call me — but Prospero's vision of the world was becoming my vision.

I felt that my real life had come to an end. And in a sense it was true. My main life-work had been completed at her side and with her constant support. I saw nothing that greatly mattered awaiting me in the future. But for me also a miracle was possible. Gradually in my slowly developing emotional life it was achieved. For I have of late always felt that, while the memory of all that Edith meant is forever alive within me — even today almost to a

day twenty-two years after her death — the years I have since
spent with my dear Françoise, who so often recalls to me Edith,
are nothing less than a miracle, for they include the years of most
unalloyed happiness I have ever known.

To resume. In a few days Edith was back with me at West
Drayton, and for some months there were no letters, since I never
cared to leave home in winter, except for a day or two in town
about once a week, and she had no further occasion to go away
except for frequent long days in town. We often went up together
separating on arrival in London, though we would sometimes
meet again during the day, and it is noted in my pocket diary that,
on the 12th of February, 1913, repeating the experience of more
than twenty years earlier, we went together to hear Beethoven's
Ninth Symphony. On the 31st of March we finally left Woodpecker, and during the summer Edith's headquarters were at the
Harley Street rooms and mine at the flat, where she also came
occasionally to sleep, though meetings in town were easy and
frequent. Early in the summer Edith went with two friends to
spend a fortnight at Bruges and Ostend.

> *My darling Boy* [she wrote from the Hotel Marion at Ostend],
> I am really having a wonderful time of rest and peace and loveli-
> ness. This air is superb and we all three get on splendidly and
> are already planning heaps of tours in Spain and Italy and all
> sorts together. I'm sleeping beautifully, drinking beer, and
> feeling cold water paradise as in Spain. I wish you were here.
> I love you more and more, and my hopes are you will soon have a
> long rest too.

She found rest and peace at last. When I go to that quiet
garden at Golders Green, over which her ashes were scattered, and
sit in silence — as she would sit by Lily's grave and come back
refreshed and would surely so have sat by mine — while the
laburnums let fall their gold and the hawthorns are covered with
their thick rich pink blossoms and the roses begin to burst their
buds and the birds gently sing, my heart too is at rest. For I know

it would please her well that all of her that was mortal should rise again into this life of peace,

> Where, like an infant's smile, over the dew,
> A light of laughing flowers along the grass is spread.

She went on to Lausanne for a short time to stay with an old friend there. It proved to be, little as she guessed it, her last visit to the Continent. Soon after her return I went on what may perhaps have been the last of my numerous visits to Spain, and I well remember Edith coming to see me off at Victoria Station and expressing approval, rare from her, of the new light tourist suit I was wearing. That suit was perhaps not auspicious and this tour was altogether the least happy of all my visits to Spain. I started happily, indeed, on a day of exquisite loveliness and spent the night in Paris, leaving for Spain the following morning. On reaching Toulouse I felt so fresh and eager that I determined not to waste the night there, but to push on to Barcelona by the train that left a few hours later. Part of the time I occupied over a good dinner in the excellent and handsome station restaurant, and walked up and down the platform until the train was due. Evidently I gave the impression of a foolish and well-to-do English tourist, for as I climbed up into the carriage a youth pushed in front of me, turned round facing me, and called out, 'Où est l'homme avec le bagage?' while behind me an elderly man pressed on, with 'Passez, monsieur, passez!' Then they vanished, I gave them no thought and settled down comfortably and semi-somnolently, after my good dinner, into a corner seat.

It was not until I entered my room at the familiar Barcelona hotel that I found that my pocketbook — entirely my own unusual negligence, for tailors had not yet adopted the useful practice of furnishing the breast-pocket with a button — had disappeared, and then I recalled the significance of the unremarked incident at Toulouse. I record this as the only episode of the kind that has ever happened to me during all my wanderings. It deprived me of part of the money I had brought for my holiday, together with various precious little objects that were of far more concern to me, and, though I seek to worry as little as possible over the irreparable, it spoilt the charm of my holiday at the outset.

Barcelona, also, I found, had changed since I was there last, and grown more commonplace. A wave of municipal reform had passed over it, shortly before my arrival, for the correction of what was regarded as licence. The free and racy spirit of the soil had been banished from its amusements leaving a tame vacuity only too familiar at home. I left Barcelona to spend a day or two at Ripoll and then by the road to France over the Pyrenees I had long promised myself the pleasure of traversing, and found it full of delight. Hence I went slowly on to the French Catalan city of Perpignan, a revelation to me more than twenty years previously and now at length revisited. As I wandered about its streets reviving old memories, I became conscious that I was feeling out of sorts, so I sat down outside a café and ordered a vermouth, my usual resource in a foreign city under such circumstances. But no refreshing effect followed and, being a fairly good judge of the significance of my own sensations, I realised I was in a state of fever. Returning to the hotel, I found I had a temperature of 102° and that, for the first time in my life when alone and far from home, I had fallen ill. What exactly was the matter I could not be certain, though later I came to the conclusion that I had been attacked by the intestinal form of influenza. It was naturally aggravated by the conditions and the impossibility of resting in peace. I could scarcely touch the elaborate hotel meals and the simple dishes I sought to order instead could not be provided. My mind remained receptive, and I was never prostrated: I was able to spend part of the time wandering about the new cities I visited on my slow and painful progress towards home — such notes as I wrote have their place in my *Impressions and Comments* — but during all those days my life was a nightmare. I had planned to meet Amy at Granville for a week's tour in

Normandy, and at the appointed date I was able to be there on the quay to receive her. But for several days longer my condition remained the same, with an inevitable consequent exhaustion. The turning-point occurred at Étretat. It was the first place I had reached at all touched by the sometimes despised English influence, and as we passed along one of its streets I spied an attractive little shop where 'English Tea' was announced. We entered the cosy deserted little room. I have never anywhere, even in Moscow, found tea, or indeed any other beverage, so delicious. It seemed a real elixir of life. I came out feeling strong and cheerful, and before long appetite began to come back. When we reached England, I was almost my normal self again.

Even this is not the whole story of this accumulation of little misadventures. Directly after seeing me off, Edith had sent a card to my hotel at Barcelona: 'My heart misgave me as I saw you go. I would have given *anything* to be going with you. Do take care. :.. I am *really* with you in heart if not in body.' It was a premonition of loving insight, but two or three days before I fell ill in Perpignan, she also was attacked in London by precisely the same kind of illness, aggravated by anxiety when she heard from me of my illness, though she was relieved to know that Amy would soon be with me. She was in the midst of the turmoil of moving from Harley Street, and the final misadventure of this series occurred when, in the course of dealing with my correspondence while I was abroad, amid this outer disorder and mental confusion of illness, she was unable to account for a cheque sent from America, on which I had been relying. She felt sure she had put it in a 'safe place' and was more distressed than I was at her inability to find it, 'the one thing I have failed you in,' she wrote, and it was her high pride never to fail in the tasks of love. However, that final mischance of this unfortunate holiday was put right when we discovered that she had by oversight returned the cheque to America with the receipt. To console me, so far as possible, for the loss of my pocketbook with its precious souvenirs, she now gave me another, inserting into it a little card on which she had written: 'To my precious Comrade and Boy and all sorts of other people a life of twenty-two years together.' Now that pocketbook will have its place among my sacred possessions together with the last similar pocketbook my mother also gave me not long before her death.

I have detailed this accumulation of petty troubles around my last visit to Spain because they were unique and present a contrast to the otherwise delightful series of my visits to foreign lands. For a time the charm seemed broken; and in fact I have never planned another visit to Spain. But, as I could not know when I first wrote this record, to France — at all events, Touraine and the Pyrenees and the Riviera — other expeditions as delightful as any that went before, still lay ahead in the lovely society of my Françoise.

Edith had been spending an active, agitated, and worried time; it was under such circumstances that she often succumbed to illness. She was preparing to make a new turn in life; 'I am resigning all Committees [at the Lyceum Club], even the Poetry, so that I can at last live as an artist.' She was giving up her room in Harley Street and setting up a tiny cottage in a friend's grounds at Stanwell; she was winding up all sorts of affairs, with the inevitable result that she was encountering all sorts of urgent expenses which she was unable to meet. This spurred on her literary activities and led to still further overwork. At the same time she was actively organising a big Swinburne memorial dinner wherewith to end up her more prominent functions in the Lyceum Club. It was in the midst of this whirl that she was knocked over by the influenza attack so strangely like mine. Before hearing of mine, she wrote to me at the Normandy address I had given her on the 28th of June, which happened to be one of my worst days at Nantes, though she had not yet heard of my illness:

> *My Darling One*, I am very ill. Cannot get right at all — somehow. Heart worse than it has ever been in a way, and had fever,

and have been in hell. I'm wretchedly weak and sleepless. Don't come home, as I may pull round, but I feel the smash-up I have dreaded for years has come at last. It is the Swinburne Dinner on Monday and Heaven knows what will happen. Try not to let it spoil your holiday, but God only knows what it will be to see you again. Letters are pouring in for you and I don't feel fit to cope with them, for my own are beyond me. I dread it all — and if I die I shall leave all in confusion, and what can I do? I may be better and could not bear you to come home for me.

Two days later the Swinburne Dinner took place and her spirit was equal to the occasion as it always was; then, two days later, after hearing that I also was ill, she wrote:

My Darling One, I've been in an awful state of agitation about you. I felt you were very ill and *I* have been too — could digest nothing for days. However, the rest at Granny's [an old friend, Mrs. Fowke] did the trick to a certain extent, and though I *felt* very inadequate, everyone said I was wonderful. It was a magnificent evening. I sat between Robert Ross [Oscar Wilde's literary executor] and Lord Dunsany. The latter I just loved. He took a huge fancy to ―― and I thought as they stood together — he towering over her — what a marriage it might have been. He is a real poet and such a dear, and he liked me too. Such a child! I never got to bed till three, but, do you know, at the end of the dinner they all rose with one accord and said what a dear I was and sang 'He's a jolly good fellow' till I thought the roof would come off. I nearly cried and could only say, 'Oh! you dears!' Right and left I was told of my *charm!* and May Sinclair was so nice to me.... Today and tomorrow I pack up and put everything in the Stanwell cottage till I leave. Rest is my one craving. Do take care and tell me how you are and when you come home. If before the 15th, I will wait for you. I love you ever and thank God Amy is there to take care of you. Kiss her for me.

I returned to London earlier than she expected, but, as she received no notice beforehand of my arrival, she had already left London, as arranged, to spend a few weeks with her dear friend of that period. In many ways it was a good change for her, but it failed to give all the rest she desired and needed. She was still ill, and worried over various troubles including demands for payment of old debts (though I was helping beyond the usual household allowance to the utmost of my ability) and she was stimulated to literary activities beyond her strength. At the same time she was in a social atmosphere she found trying. I quote a few sentences from letters written when staying with her special dear friend:

> My poor heart and brain are bad indeed, the eternal frontal headache making me wonder how to go on. I've been terribly worried all the time.... It's no use upbraiding me, I should only get desperate. These awful headaches and melancholy keep me sleepless, and I try to hide it all from —— who gets bored if she is not gay, and I do what I can, but I feel so strangely alone. If only you and I had a central place together or I saw more of you in peace (not snatches of days), or I felt I could die somewhere in peace, I should feel better, I think — and if *only* we'd money. I've done all I can and I'm writing *hard*, and rewriting *Kit's Woman* [in the dramatic version]. I've written a fine new First Act and we are going to dramatise *Evensong* as a first piece while we work out the *Jester* play. But it all wants a clear head and strong heart, and I've neither. All this eternal chatter threatens our peace, and being weak, it worries me. I miss the treatment; don't believe I shall ever be strong, and but for my debts want to die badly.... Oh! Havelock, my own darling one, can you tell what I suffer? I pray you are better. Write and tell me you love me and don't want always to be away from me. I feel that I'm not wanted anywhere and yet I have such love.
> Your own Wifie who longs and longs to see you.
> —— is so sweet, but cannot realise, the darling, that it is so difficult to work with a head like this.... I feel a sort of awful hopelessness about everything. I shall see you and that seems the only thing that gives me life. These women round —— make me despair, and I feel I can't do anything but leave her to them, as it all worries her so. Oh! Havelock, don't feel you don't want me. I let myself drift into thinking you only want Amy and not me, and my poor brain is tired and suffering and worrying over money.... Your letters are like miracles. All sorts of horrors

have happened here. I fell iller than before and my heart is pretty bad. All I feel I want in the world is to get into your arms and be told you want me to live. Be prepared for a wire and meet me if you are able, for I shall be fit for nothing. My one great longing is to see your dear face. ... I arrive at Euston at 3. I just want to go to bed and rest and rest. It is all sad, sad, and I feel in utter despair, but surely you will comfort me. Do love me and tell me I'm not an utterly impossible human being as I'm beginning to think.

During the next nine months we were mostly together, not separated for more than a few days at a time, so for this period there are no letters. But those that I have quoted reveal the strains to which she was subjected and make clear the devastation in her health that was soon to be revealed. That happened in the autumn, a few months later, as I have already told.

Our lives had, however, become more equable again, and even the recognition of the diabetic disorder, while it caused some anxiety, was a useful injunction to a quiet life. At the little cottage at Stanwell, indeed, where much of our time in the late summer of 1913 was spent, we were necessarily already quiet. Stanwell is a small Middlesex village some miles from any railway station, and the cottage — probably the smallest of all the small dwellings we ever occupied — was a tiny modern three-roomed building, intended for servants, in the stable-yard of a large house belonging to friends of Edith's, who had offered to rent it to her. She had snatched at the chance, as it was at no great distance from West Drayton, and it not only enabled her to find a convenient shelter for herself and her things from Harley Street, but settled a greater difficulty by offering a comfortable home for the horse and donkey now displaced from West Drayton. On the whole, however, though we made the best of it, this was a makeshift arrangement not altogether agreeable or comfortable for either of us. I expect we were pleased when the time came to go to Cornwall, although it was a trial to Edith to leave her animals behind even in good hands, and awkward to be deprived of her trap. We went to Cornwall for a month in September, back to Stanwell and occasionally to my flat, then to Cornwall together in November to remain there until March. All this time we were never separated save now and then for a few days.

During the autumn the dramatic version of *Kit's Woman* was performed by one of the best stage societies of that day. It was well played, received with applause, and the author called before the curtain at the close. But one felt that the larger and more conventional section of the audience had been puzzled and even shocked. No manager, however friendly, was inclined to give the play a run. Edith never realised, not only that a good novel will not necessarily make a good play, but that the accepted limitations of the stage less easily lend themselves to a writer who is daringly and instinctively unconventional.

It was during this long period, when there was no occasion or need to discuss serious questions in letters, that the idea of a visit to the United States germed and developed in Edith's adventurous mind. She was over fifty years of age and, though in some respects her health had improved, it was deeply undermined. Yet her spirit was as high as ever and her energies as fresh; so, indeed, they remained until the end. No adventure daunted her and risks stimulated her.

Various factors entered the inception of the American enterprise. Her friendship with the two American friends of Lily had been consolidated during their visit to Europe and they had invited her to stay with them in New York. She was beginning to form other connections with the United States, partly through the Lyceum Club, partly through her writings, which were bringing her into touch with American editors and publishers. It seemed to her that, as other schemes for financial retrievement had failed to remove money troubles, perhaps an American lecturing tour would achieve that result, and there were many to encourage that idea. Then, too, it seemed to her that the beloved spirit of Lily was also waving her on in that direction; from time to time she was now seeing a medium, of remarkable powers and high repute, able to evoke — however the manifestations may be explained — the seeming spirit of Lily with wonderful vividness and truth, and messages came encouraging her to go to America and foretelling great success there. It was true; but at what a cost the message failed to tell. By March the scheme had taken definite shape. Some rather vague proposals had come from America for one or two lectures which would probably lead to more, and it was arranged that she should sail in the early spring.

In preparing her lectures for this American visit the idea occurred to her — spontaneously, I believe — to write a lecture on Havelock Ellis. She at once proceeded to do so — I can no longer recall where or when, but evidently about this time. I offered no active opposition to the idea, but I scarcely liked it, for it seemed to me rather too intimate a thing to do. When it was completed, I accepted it as satisfactory, perhaps still a little coolly, and it was duly delivered on various occasions in the States. Since her death, I have to confess, my attitude to that lecture has altogether changed. Instead of being a little ashamed of her frank discussion of my personality and career, I am profoundly grateful to her. It is now to me among the most precious things she ever wrote. I am for the first time able to appreciate it, in an almost impersonal manner; I realise how discriminating, how forbearing, how just, how manysided it is, and with how deep and sympathetic an insight into the central parts of my nature. It is written by the person who knew me best and longest, and nothing that anyone else has written about me can be put beside it. She wrote it, moreover, at the moment when we had at length reached the summit of the long and difficult path of life we had climbed together, and when she was herself at the point of complete development, so that it is easy to believe that, as some think, it is one of the best things, outside her artistic work, she ever

wrote. It was first published, after her death, in the New York
Bookman for July, 1918, and later (1924) appeared in the volume
of *Essays* by Mrs. Havelock Ellis, privately printed by Joseph
Ishill at Berkeley Heights, New Jersey.

In January of this year 1914, my old friend Olive Schreiner had
come from South Africa to England after an absence of many
years, and I had run up from Carbis to London for a few days to
greet her. She had soon gone on to Italy and, undergoing a
special treatment, settled in Florence whence she wrote complaining of her loneliness and saying how pleasant it would be if
I could come out to Italy. I was not at that moment anxious to
go, but Edith, though never eager for me to leave her, urged that
I owed it to so old and dear a friend not to neglect her wishes.
Olive in a later letter wrote: 'Dear Havelock Boy, don't come for
my sake. I'm so sick and faint all the time it will be no pleasure
to you. Unless, indeed, the joy of seeing you makes me better.'
I agreed to go in March. It was an easy and pleasant tour and I
never regretted it. Indeed, when a few months later the Great
War unexpectedly broke out, I was thankful that I had gone.

I went up to London a few days before Edith, who followed and
stayed with me for a week at the flat which she arranged to occupy
with the devoted servant Annie during my absence. Just before
she left Carbis to join me, she wrote in the only letter I have for
that period since the previous summer:

> *My darling Boy*, so thankful to get your wire. Awful gales and
> sheets of rain last night. I was demented with people all day....
> Get in plenty of firewood and coal, please, and leave us any odds
> you have. I've still that horrid pain, but quite normal, thank
> goodness. I think it is all neuralgic run-down pains now, and
> that I shall be better away from here.... All I've to do is to keep
> alive and lecturing. It's a big thing, but worth it. I hope we
> won't be an awful nuisance, but it is a joy to be able to kiss you
> again before you go. I feel sure you would regret it terribly if
> anything happened to Olive and you had not gone, but if *you*
> are not all right, I shall never forgive myself either. Now I must

away to thousands of poddles.[1] You are deep in my innermost heart, and no man, woman, or child could ever uproot you.

I know that that constant refrain of her letters was the utterance of her deepest self, and whatever happened when disease began to undermine that self, I have never ceased to know it.

In referring to this as the only letter written during that period, I have deliberately left out of account a special letter of altogether unique character. From an early period she had realised the likelihood that she would die before me and been anxious to leave everything in order and spare me all unnecessary trouble. With this object she wrote a letter of instructions for me to keep at hand, but only to open immediately on her death. One or more such letters she had withdrawn as the circumstances altered, and replaced by another. In February of this year 1914, in view of her visit to America, when we were at Carbis Bay together, she wrote the last, inscribed 'In case of my death,' which she never expressed any wish to reclaim. It remained in my pocketbook for more than two years before the time came to read it, but I introduce it at the time when it was written. In addition to her wishes in regard to cremation, to instructions regarding business affairs, debts, and souvenirs for friends, the envelope contained this letter, the most measured and deliberate statement of her attitude towards me and towards life. In previous years, at moments of exhaustion or exasperation, which may or may not have been justified, she had sometimes spoken to me bitter words which seemed to be uttered with intense conviction. In the last year, when her mental integrity was enfeebled by disease, she sometimes spoke, not only to me but of me, in ways that were altogether without justification. But in this year 1914 her mind was not only completely intact, but she had at length reached the full growth in character and intellect of her slowly developed personality.

[1] This was her favourite word for all the little odd necessary tasks that are outside the regular ordinary routine of life. It seems a good word, but I do not know where she got it from, and the dictionary affords no help; possibly it is connected with the verb 'potter.'

The words she wrote at this moment in secret, knowing that they would only reach me as a voice from the grave, I can now read with a solemn joy which there is nothing to impair.

> *My Precious Boy* [the letter opens], When you read this I shall be in beauty and rest at last and no one is to fret a moment. If it is possible I shall help you more than I ever could here because of the illnesses I've had to fight. There is no death for real love and we love one another for always. I hate to feel I've ever been a hurt and a strain, but no one can understand better than you why this has been and why I've been such an impossible creature — born too soon and dead too late. Just *try* to do all the things I'm putting down on enclosed if you can. Bless you for all the love and care you've given me always.
>
> Your own Wifie

The Italian journey was uneventful. I went direct to Florence and joined Olive in a large dull cosmopolitan hotel, of a type I should never have chosen myself. I found her in fair health and spent ten days there. Then I went on alone for a few days at Ravenna and Bologna. I had planned to stay at Rheims, Laon, and Saint Quentin, none of which cities I had seen before, on the way home. In the end I omitted Saint Quentin, for it happened, as it had often happened to me before, that as I approached home I speeded up my journey. I have often wished since that the intuition, if such I may term it, which led me to visit for the first time that part of France at that moment had not drawn me to other neighbouring places since ruined. But I am endlessly thankful that I was among the last persons to see the original Rheims intact. The cathedral, above all, to me singularly lovely and its windows glorious, remains enshrined, however faintly, in my memory forever.

I came back to the flat at Brixton where Edith stayed on with me for a week when she had to join her boat at Southampton, the *Minneapolis* of the American Transport Line, with, characteristically, only ten pounds in her pocket to meet expenses in

America. With tender solicitude — the tenderness of our love on both sides was never greater than at this period — she affectionately commended me to Amy's care, and arranged a little code by which she could inform me by wireless on nearing New York how she had fared. I was not accompanying her to Southampton; the brief stay there she had reserved for the dear woman friend whom I have before alluded to, but her last evening in London was devoted to me. We went for dinner to one of our favourite resorts near her club (where she was spending the night for convenience), the Popular Café in Piccadilly. A kind of sad exaltation filled both our hearts and seemed to find external expression when the band began playing Tschaikovsky's *Chanson sans Paroles*, one of the things that Lily used to play. The beautiful memory of this time together often came to me during the weeks that followed, and to her also, for she referred more than once to the tender look which, she said, then shone on my face.

During the two days or less that elapsed between bidding me farewell and finally losing touch with England, I had six letters full of love and cheer and last instructions, in case she never returned.

> *My Sweet Boy* [she wrote], I felt I must fling out of the train into your dear arms. . . . I am sure to *feel* how you are and you must just rest on my breast and know I am ever your Wifie. . . . At last I've realised some of the awfulness of this separation, but I mean to do the game — out and out. I was so dead beat we scarcely spoke and went each to our rooms. I'd have slept long but my cough was so bad. . . . Do, do take care. You are more to me than you have ever known: it is a strange world and grows stranger day by day. I wish you were here. I see you now with your dear eyes all gone in, getting your breakfast, but you are not alone. I am there every inch of the way. I broke down when you'd gone and was so thankful no one was in the carriage. . . . At last I am off. Such letters and wires and wonderful love, to send me, like Whittington, to my fortune, though Annie has my cat who has now three tabby kittens. A lovely day and I am sure, in Lily's gentle hands, all will be well. My

heart aches at going and yet I know it is the *only* way. Even if
I fail I shall have done all I can. I trust you and Amy are closer
again. I can't *bear* you to be hurt. Just use my love and everlasting tenderness. The temper is the mere growl of a dog too
stupid to know how else to show he is ready to die for what he
loves. Soon now I'll be back.

Then, when the ship was losing touch with England, came the
final message by wire:

ALL WELL   DELICIOUS WEATHER   LOVE   WIFIE

Yet even that was not the end of her loving messages. She was
ever inventive in the art of loving, full of tender solicitude, not
only for me, but for all who were dear to her, and on the eve of
leaving London, when spending the night at the club and full of
business, she found time to write three more letters which she
secretly left with her friend the club porter to post at intervals
during the following week so that there might be little break in
her communications to me during the voyage. These letters
reached me at regular intervals with a glad surprise and they
arrived in what was evidently the order in which they were written
and intended to arrive and yet with no apparent numbering on
the envelopes. But tonight, nearly six years after they were written, it occurs to me to remove the stamps and I find — with an
ache of the heart at this last fresh sign of her tender care I may
ever discover — beneath each stamp, in her hand, the date when
the letter was to be posted, to which dates the postmarks duly
correspond. It is a little thing, but the thoughtful care behind
such little things is of the essence of the art of love, and it was
altogether characteristic of her that even at this moment of high
pressure, in the early dawn of the day of her departure, she could
not fail therein.

> *My sweet Boy* [she wrote in the first], I shall always see your
> deep-set eyes wherever I am. Somehow, after all these years, I
> want to bring some of the depth and loveliness your mother
> brought you. I am always with you — always loving — and it

is not so very long before I come back to you and the new home.
I feel Amy will perhaps yet be more to you than ever before.
Try and put yourself into the 'dangerous age' as you put yourself
into my tantrums. I can't bear you to not have letters so, you
see, through Pottier, I *can* get at you! This with my eternal love.

Wifie

My darling One [the second ran], Just a wee line of cheer.
By this time I shall be just looking forward to coming home.
I mean to be victorious in all sorts of ways and understand more
and more. Take care of my precious baby for me, for that you are.
All these days of disappointment my very bowels have yearned
over you. She has not *meant* to leave you, for she loves you and
she has been a sweeter woman than I for you and that is why
I want to get you close again. Cheer up and eat slowly and good
nourishing food. All will be well or Lily would not have told me
to go. I kiss you tenderly and love you ever.

Your Wifie

She was here troubled over some temporary misunderstanding
with Amy to whose care she had commended me during her
absence. The 'eat slowly' was a frequent injunction of hers,
vainly, I fear, for it was natural to me to eat quickly. It is an
injunction which now, twenty years later, comes with a sad smile,
for it is no longer needed. With a troublesome throat affection of
which I cannot see the termination I am unable to eat except
slowly.

The last, timed for Friday, is short:

This, my Sweet, is to wish you a happy week-end. Get into
the sun with Amy and forget all dull and painful things and be
happy, for life will be full for us when I come home. Everything
points to it. Take care, take care.

Your own Wifie

I've been writing since four to get all done.

And the wonder of it was that all this love and tenderness and
passion on a sea of adventures, apart or together, then and
throughout, was on both sides without, in the narrow physical
sense, any elements of sexual emotion! We neither of us thought

of that aspect of it at the time. When one loves one cannot analyse love. But now, as I look back, I feel all the novelty and the fascination of it as well as its instructiveness.

In due course the wireless came. It signified that all was well. From that time to her return early in July, a little over two months later, she took every opportunity to write so that I have some twenty-five letters covering the period, and can follow all her movements. Moreover, I think for the only time in her life, she kept a private diary, in a leather-bound volume furnished with a lock, partly for my benefit and partly to aid her own memory. My letters to her were not preserved, and my life during this time is almost a blank in memory, though it has left a few traces in *Impressions and Comments*. I was living and working quietly in my flat, never out of London but once. That break is all that stands out from the darkness. I went in June for a fortnight's ramble with Amy, in the country and by the sea in East Anglia. There had been during the earlier part of the year a cloud of misunderstanding (referred to by Edith), almost the only one that ever arose and which soon dispersed. This little tour at the best season of the year was probably the most beautiful, and almost the last, that we ever enjoyed together. She had now reached middle age and had really begun, however late, to feel the confidence of being complete mistress of her own actions, while I, equally late, had finally conquered an element of misgiving, latent and concealed, which had sometimes marred the joy of our relations. Now we felt a careless and joyous freedom as we went about openly, two independent persons occupying our separate rooms, not ashamed to enjoy each other's society, and indifferent to the speculations of other people. It is one of the compensations which alleviate the burden of increasing years. I recall all that bright interval. For the rest I was vegetating in my rooms, writing, and looking forward to Edith's letters. She was living for both of us.

On board the *Minneapolis* she wrote a letter to me from time to time:

She is a lovely boat and though I have felt queer now and again I've not missed a meal. M. [a friend who was crossing in the same ship] is very sweet and I sleep nearly all day and night and feel much better already, though my cough has not gone yet. ... I nearly cried for you last night, the big black waves were so dark and the sky so grey, and I began to wonder if I had not been a big little fool, but I know it is all for the best. ... I'm as brown as a berry. I've been drefful homesick for you again and do pray all is well. One word *Come* and I shall beg, borrow, or steal and come back. People have spotted me and I've been reading to them all this afternoon. I see you so plainly, my Darling and love you so much. It seems intolerable not to have a word from you — I feel I can't bear it and yet I've just got to. ... They are all so sweet to me. I chose our seats at table near a groom and some very ordinary folk, but it has been no use. They all say the usual thing and tell me I shall take the States by storm. I feel very humble. It is love I love, all your love and that of my friends seems to help me day by day. The cough still persists a little and the pain in my side, but it will go, I know. ... The ex-Attorney-General of Philadelphia prophesies great things for me and has given me a lot of hints. I am sure this was the one thing to do to save me in health and purse. The only thing is the awful silence of these days and not knowing how you are. ... We are nearing now. I sent a wireless yesterday. I fold you close, and am your loving

Wifie

Her arrival might well have been disconcerting and even overwhelming. The last days of the passage were the worst, and the ship reached New York through a thick fog. Here, plunged suddenly into the deafening whirl of what seemed to her a strange and terrific city, she learnt immediately that the season was so late she could only give a few lectures and that, moreover, the friend she expected to stay with had suddenly been called away to Europe to the bedside of a dying relative. But she had no time to be dismayed; her diary and her first letter plunge at once into the stream of exciting events, and she realised almost immediately that there was no need for dismay. The beautiful hospitality,

the unfailing cordiality, the simple helpfulness of Americans —
for which her warm gratitude and admiration never ceased —
surrounded her from the first moment. She was taken into the
house of Doctor and Mrs. (also Doctor) McLean, and their un-
bounded kindness and high social position were of the greatest
aid to her throughout the visit. There were half a dozen interviewers awaiting her, and, great as had been her horror of interviewing up to this time, she felt, as she said, that she must
enter into the game, and played it exultantly, indeed with a frankness and good humour scarcely common even in America. A large
number of the most prominent women in New York were brought
to be introduced to her, she was made a member of some of the
best social clubs, and a round of visits to important people and
interesting sights began at once. No wonder that on the third day
she wrote: 'I was *so* tired yesterday I could scarcely crawl about.'
But that, one understands is America, and that mainly is why all
the persistent pressure brought on me by Edith and by others has
never sufficed to carry me there.

'I've just fallen right on my feet; things are opening wonderfully,' she wrote in this same first letter. Even in her second letter
she wrote that it was arranged she was to come over to America
again on the first of November, and her lecture agent began at
once to arrange a tour for that future visit.

> I am the woman of the moment and it is *so* funny. They all
> seem to love me, and I am fascinated with these terrific youthful
> faces here. This afternoon fourteen of the most prominent women
> in New York are coming here to meet me, and yesterday I was at
> the house of a wonderfully beautiful woman as a *lioness*. It is
> all to me a strange experience. I am getting a little used to the
> expressions. So much is so very French. I am being taken *such*
> care of, and am keeping very well on the whole, but this *vitality*
> in the air is tremendous.

A week after her arrival, on the 5th of May, she wrote:

> *My Beloved Boy*, Your letter has come at last and has taken
> a fortnight!... Everything is opening, and Mrs. Maclean says

more has opened for me in a week than for most in years. Every
day we motor to glorious country and every impression I had of
America is fading. It is *wonderful*, and so rarely refined in the
corner I have crept into. I'm reading three times this week, and,
as you know, I go to Chicago (a thousand miles further from you)
on Monday.... Oh! my sweet! Every bit of me rejoiced to see
your writing this morning. It just seems years since I left you.
This sorrow to you [the passing trouble in regard to Amy] has
been shared and I love you more and more. Perhaps I have never
fully realised the union and love between us until this separation.
I am growing stronger day by day — getting the old throw-back
of my head. This dry sunny climate, the delicate food and ways —
all so French and beyond it — the love I'm getting and the understanding and the surety of success, simply is curing me. Mrs.
Maclean says she can't let me go back. There's even a cat and
dog in the house! They have put me as a temporary member in
the three best clubs here, and I tell you your wifie is just spoilt to
death. Oh! Lily, Lily, how well you knew and how wonderful it
all is!... With the deepest tenderest love a woman can feel for
a man,

Your Wifie

All this time her diary and her letters continued to be mainly
the swift and summary record of crowded and delightful days:
meetings with distinguished and interesting people, visits to
attractive resorts and great hospitable houses, receptions in her
honour, her reading of her plays and stories and her speeches,
interviews with journalists, arrangements for future lectures and
articles. (At one of these readings, as she notes in her diary, she
was introduced by Ernest Seton Thompson as 'a prophetess from
the wilderness, neither wholly woman nor wholly man, but wholly
human.') It is an animated and attractive record, but it has little
interest for anyone but me now. She was revelling in the environment that most completely suited her, and she was organising the
future, an occupation in which she always delighted, and which
had not in it the tiring strain of actual execution. There is never
once in her swift, enthusiastic letters the faintest jar to the music

of love and tenderness that sounds throughout them, and that was always the sign that all was well with her in health of body as well as of spirit.

> We have passed the Rubicon [she wrote on the 9th of May] I've given all this fortnight to details and experiences and we've won. I am the rage. It shows how I have been hurt that it is just nothing to me except that it is a joy to realise the wonder of this new civilisation. You simply *must* come with me in November and then we'll go to Bermuda or somewhere for the winter. It will heal you and me too. I am an utterly different creature already in this dry, stimulating climate. I went to the Robert Ingersolls the other night, and the first person I saw was little Dorothy C. you and I held years ago in our arms — a girl of twenty. It knocked me over somehow. . . . I read at the Cosmopolitan Club to 250 of the picked women of New York, expert actresses, etc. They just adored me, but I felt terribly nervous. They speak so sweetly of you. . . . We motored down the Hudson to a lovely club house among the magnolia trees, and twelve of the leaders of society were invited and I was again the guest of honour. Mrs. D., the great actress, was there and had heard me read the day before. She said I had magnetism and a voice which would hold any audience spellbound. It is *all* here now. I wonder why people love me so. They do, you know, quite genuinely, and if I could only believe a little of what they say I think it would help, but the knocks have been too great. I *long* so to see you, sweetheart, and if all the women leave you I am with you and love you deeply and truly and forever and ever, as a mother her babe and a woman her comrade.

She duly went to Chicago for a week, staying at Hull House, where Jane Addams sweetly gave up her own room to Edith and swiftly won her most heartfelt admiration. There was again the constant round of interviews, receptions, luncheons, dinners, readings of plays and stories, lectures, speeches, and sight-seeing, especially of all that concerned social reform in this vividly alive and progressive city. Again also she was everywhere met with the same warm hearty enthusiasm, both for her own sake, and, as she recognised, for mine. 'It is just as if I had died and woke to real understanding. . . . They said things about you I thought would choke me. God knows what I said — I felt there was at last the realisation of all my struggles. I said I would drag you over the ocean and the land by your beard if you would come no other way. I've never realised such enthusiasm.' Every day or two she wrote me swift, loving letters full of her joy and wonder, though now and then there would be a touch of sadness. 'I am again the woman of the hour or week, but I must have died last summer — I realise so many things now.' It was a reference to emotional experiences touched on in letters of that period already quoted in their place. Again she refers to 'what I felt last year at —— I shall never quite get over that, I know. I am always near and close to you and I am getting on well. Everyone says I look well and happy, but really I've grown more philosophic.' As she writes, however, a little later, summing up her visit: 'I've had the great adventure and *the* time of my life. I just never can be grateful enough to America for understanding what you and I stand for.'

At this stage, near the end of her visit, there appeared in her letters the sole little cloud on the sunny tenderness of her affection. I had been a little worried and hurt by the frankness with which she had spoken to interviewers of me and of our relations. She, who had always viewed interviewing with contempt, who had once reproached me for giving a quite impersonal little interview, was now publicly entering into details of our private relationship. Some of the statements she made even admitted of total misunderstanding and were duly garbled into absurdity when copied into the newspapers. I knew that she had been animated by the desire to clear up misunderstandings, the extent of which she doubtless exaggerated, and the mere existence of which was to me in any case a matter of indifference, and that she felt she was only entering into the American spirit and method of emphasising at once both our mutual independence and our unity. But some of our English friends were a little shocked, and I knew that even some American friends smiled. I wrote several times in succession to convey my own feelings on this matter. Whether, as may be possible, too emphatically, I do not know, for she preserved none of these letters. Instead of soothing my ruffled sentiments, she became herself irritated and showed it in the letters she wrote during the week or two that followed the reception of mine. Then the cloud passed. But, as I look back, I see its significance. It foreshadowed the greater cloud which, in the heightened exaltation and nervous exhaustion of her second American visit, appeared unexpectedly and more persistently in our sky.

On the 21st of May she wrote: 'I told Mitchell Kennerley you were distressed at the personal interviews, but he says they are inevitable, and *I knew it.* You see it dissipates all idea you and I are not at one, and if you don't say some things they make them up.' In a following letter she says: 'You have hurt me badly.' Later, on the 7th of June, the feeling was nearly past.

Yes, I've conquered, and however much you may hate some of the interviews, they were inevitable. I'm booked well for the autumn; I mean to be here on November 1st, and want you to venture. I can protect you easily, and the sun and warm places would do you good. No more English winters for me. I will tell you all when I come. I happen to have 'caught on' for some reason. Even your name would never have done it alone and most of the women have never heard of you. Now — the men declare — they realise why you have done what you have! They just love me. It is very funny. I ought to lose my head, but it is scarcely touching me, though the feeling that all our worries will be over is a great sedative. I expect I'll just live to pay my debts and fling out to a greater America. ... Aren't you proud of me? It was a bit plucky, you know, to do Whittington and win, but then if I failed you ought to have loved me more. I *long* to see you, but don't worry me about those interviews. If you were here, you would realise how little it really matters except to open a way for publicity at the start. I've been to see Ella Wheeler Wilcox twice in her lovely home, and she wants me to stay there. She called on me and amused me awfully. She has had to write against my theories on love. I am thankful you and Amy are drawing closer again. Our best theories don't comfort us if they are carried out on our aching hearts, I find.

Love to you ever.

But even a week later, my objection to the interviews still stuck in her mind. 'Somehow I can't get over the things you said about these interviews. If I am a free individual, I have a right to do what is best, and in this case it was best for us both.' But that was the last of it, and in the letters that follow she is tenderly looking forward to our meeting and hoping that we should go direct to Clare, a place for which she had an affection, for a few first days together. That proposal for some reason, however, failed to prove convenient.

Everything had opened out for her wonderfully in America, as she wrote in her last letter before leaving: complete social success and new friends on every hand, so that much as she had moved about she had never once stayed at an hotel; several of her books accepted by publishers, plays likely to be produced, articles wanted by leading journals, lectures successfully arranged for the winter. She felt gladly confident that she would live to pay off all debts and obligations. But she was evidently becoming a little tired after all the activities and excitements of this great reception so unexampled in her experience. Her health was no longer satisfactory. She wrote tenderly in these last letters, but there was in them once or twice a shadow of doubt concerning the love of those loved ones she had left in England for 'the poor fool who is here worshipped as a divinity.' There were numerous references in those letters to fatigue and headaches and bad nights, though her last words were of cheer. She needed the refreshment of the voyage across the Atlantic to home.

That voyage proved entirely beneficial and restorative. It was the good season of the year, the passage was throughout pleasant and uneventful, she could rest quietly with the comfortable assurance that her quest had been achieved. At the same time she made, as she made always, some delightful friends. I think it was on this passage that with her quick discernment she detected that there was an understanding between the captain and a lady passenger. They were secretly engaged, she was travelling across simply to enjoy his society, but they had arranged that no one was to know. Edith's penetration of the secret made both of them, who shortly after were married, her good friends until the end. In whatever society she might be, her vividly alert and sympathetic nature could always find elements of joy and interest. When she arrived in London at the beginning of July, she was in excellent health and all signs of diabetes, clearly marked just before she left New York, had disappeared.

She came to see me at the flat for a few days, and then we went down to the little cottage at Stanwell, where the pony and donkey had been well tended during her absence. Here we spent two months peacefully and happily, seldom apart, except when now and then we went up to London for a day or two, and we usually went up together and came down together. That cottage was the most absurdly small cottage we had ever lived in together. But we had seldom had a more harmoniously serene time in any of them. Fortunately it was a rarely beautiful summer, that summer in which the Great War was to break out. Near-by there was an old park, of which the house was uninhabited, and by arrangement with the caretaker we spent a considerable part of every day here in preference to the grounds in which the cottage stood. After breakfast, while Edith settled the little household affairs — in which I also had taken a share — I would go across to the park carrying her rug and the bed-table on which she wrote, together with my own papers, and settle down to work beneath a large tree in that peaceful and beautiful retreat. (I remember writing there a paper on 'Masculinism and Feminism' which Edith was to deliver as a lecture in America on my behalf, and I wrote with a special regard to her delivery of it.) An hour or so later, she would arrive with her papers and settle down to work beneath the same tree a few feet away; we had seldom found it possible to work together in the same room, but here in the open it was easy. Then she would return to prepare our simple lunch and I would shortly follow. In the afternoon we would again be in the park and then after a cup of tea we usually went for a drive, for, though in Cornish days I rarely cared to go with her driving, when the conditions were changed and we were both in an unfamiliar district I was content to accompany her. It was rather a strange equipage, for, since the pony was growing old, Edith ran him together with the donkey who was ever willing and well-paced. Then home to dinner, usually cooked for us by the gardener's wife in the cottage opposite, and early to bed — she in the large room above and I in the little room below — where our rest was sometimes disturbed by the loud clatter of horses' hoofs along the adjoining road.

As I looked back on those summer weeks for some years afterwards, and before I knew how much of my life still lay ahead, they seemed to me the lovely and peaceful sunset of the long working-day of my life. It also came to seem tragic, since we never knew how fateful a war was approaching nor how fatally her health and life were about to be crushed. Yet it has always seemed beautiful. No period of our life together remains more vivid in memory, and none happier. It was a honeymoon at the end of our life together, yet of a rarer kind, for love had grown deeper and more tender than at that first Lamorna honeymoon. This, too, was in a delightful though unlike spot, and there could be no more splendid summer weather. She was also in better health and spirits after the sea-voyage than for years past, fairly free from worries, and looking forward to her lecturing tour, while the thought of leaving me filled her with an unaccustomed gentleness which now seems like an unconscious premonition of the end. We were both in the fullness of our mental power to work for the world, and could lie down through the day under the great beech tree working together, while the doves were softly cooing, and the doom of war was still concealed in the future.

Part XI

XI

Bᴜᴛ now we were in August and the Great War was beginning. Even in this little village remote from the railway we felt its presence. (And, so it chances, today, twenty-four years later, in another remote little village, again a great war seemed approaching, and gas-masks only a few days ago were officially issued to us.) Indeed, the landlord of the public-house near-by where we would go for our supply of ginger beer had once been a personal servant of Kitchener, in whom he was full of admiring trust, and we would look in to hear the latest news or to exchange opinions about the situation. Then the great Metropolitan reservoir which happened to be situated just outside the village had to be guarded by pickets, and so there were many men in khaki about. One day, as we walked along the road, we met a young officer, and Edith, in her characteristic way, cheerily asked him as he passed how things were going. 'Oh!' he replied, still more cheerfully,

'we'll soon cut up the Germans like pork.' Edith made no response, but she had had experience in cutting up pork and in the
years that followed she more than once referred to the remark
which the brutality of war had evoked from that wholesome
pleasant boy.

Her attitude towards the war was spontaneously, and not as
the result of any discussion or argument, identical with mine.
She had friends in every camp, most of them, of course, zealous
patriots, many of them pacifists and conscientious objectors, one
of her dearest friends a German living in London. Her relations
with all of them remained unaffected. She was, as she always had
been, absolutely opposed to war. At the same time she believed
that England had played an honourable and justifiable part in
entering the war, though she was far from sharing the cant current at the time concerning the wonderful results to ensue. But
she maintained a singularly disinterested and aloof attitude, aided
in this, no doubt, by the fact that none near and dear to her were
actively engaged. She was never disturbed by any war-scares, nor
was she ever moved to take the smallest part in any of those
various kinds of 'war-work' into which the women around her
were feverishly plunging; not that she cherished any rigid pacifist
principles against so doing, but simply, I think, because the whole
operation of war was so alien to her that she could not interest
herself in assisting it. Later, in America, which had not yet
entered the war, she was careful to maintain a correct attitude, as
a foreigner, by refraining from discussing the merits of the war or
championing the cause of her own country, though she privately
hoped that the 'war fanatics' would not draw America in. This
attitude of courtesy was misinterpreted by the German propa-
gandists in the States and she was approached by an emissary
from the German Embassy with a large financial offer which,
needless to say, she rejected with indignant surprise. After her
return to England, the war was beginning to touch London
nearer, but she remained calm and indifferent even in the face of

risks, for those nervous persons who may be terrified by imaginary dangers are often courageous in the face of real danger. It was while watching a Zeppelin raid, in which she showed not the slightest fear, that she caught her fatal illness.

During these months, I have said, we were seldom apart. Now at last, in August, I have a letter from her. She had gone to spend a day or two with an old friend who had recently taken a house at Speen, a small village, some miles away from the railway, in Buckinghamshire. Thence she wrote:

> *My darling Boy,* so glad of your dear letter. I've a lovely scheme for you and me if you can fall in with it. Daphne has a furnished cottage close by this one and will lend it to us for two or three weeks in September early. I shall pay a girl to come in and do for us, and of course provide meals. It is ideal, a revolving shelter in the garden, *absolute* quiet and not a soul near, fine woods, and air like Suffolk. Don't fix up anything else, but come and let us for once be in peace together as we were in Condon's garden. [She is referring to a happy fortnight we had spent years earlier when, escaping from the constant demands on her of farming and domestic life, we took rooms in the house of a farmer's daughters, at Carbis Bay, close to our own place, but in peace.] This air and quiet is superb.
>
> Till we meet, and always, your tender old
>
> Wifie

This was entirely characteristic of her swift impulses and decisions and her aptitude for organisation. It all took place exactly as she had planned, and it was all as she described, though even more delightful. The cottage, now pulled down, was very ancient. 'The Old House' it was named, and it belonged to a refined invalid lady of old family who had gone to America and never returned until the war was over. She had made it comfortable and furnished it with taste, so that we found there all that we needed. Speen is in the Chiltern Hills, and the clear, exhilarating air — though for me less invigorating than that of Suffolk — the little woods of beech or pine into which we could freely wander without meeting a soul, those tree-covered heights which became glorious in tint as autumn approached, were a joy to us both. We were both able to work in the little garden, she in the revolving shelter (such as I lie in at this moment nearly twenty-five years later in Suffolk) and I reclining in a hammock chair close-by, usually just out of her sight, so that I might the better concentrate my thoughts, though this was a disposition not altogether to her taste, for she liked to be able to see me. In the early morning, Elsie, the girl who waited on us, would come in time to prepare our baths and the breakfast, and then, having done the morning's house-work and laid our cold lunch, returned home; we ate the lunch by ourselves, first sometimes, after due consideration, going to the village inn with a jug for some ale. In the late afternoon, Elsie would return to prepare the dinner, and when the heat of the day was over, and our work, we would often go for a walk, less often for a drive, as the walks were pleasanter. One, I well remember and repeated more than once, through the fields and up the hill as the colours of sunset began to tint the sky and the slopes, in which we would share a communion of bliss. Under such conditions I was able to write well and easily. It was then, I remember, that, among other things I wrote, and without an effort, an article published in the *Edinburgh Review* (and intended for expansion into a long chapter of a book on the genius of Europe, which will ever remain unfinished) on the psychology of the English people. It was animated by a patriotic enthusiasm, aroused by the war, which I had never felt before. I may add that I have never felt it since.

The delightful month at Speen was soon over. Before it was over, it became necessary for Edith to make frequent visits to London. She was becoming oppressed by all the preparations necessary for this long and important visit to the United States. It was not merely the preparation for the lectures, which had gone on satisfactorily, but an equipment in dresses and other necessaries, for it was not her way to embark on any enterprise without careful organisation. There were also many affairs to wind up in

England. This meant, again, a worrying financial strain, and to it was added a failure in health. The fresh vigour with which she had returned from the voyage in June was lost and the diabetic symptoms had returned. She never ceased, and with insistence, to urge me to accompany her. But on that point I was adamant. Indeed, I have always rejected the most tempting offer to go to America, and if she could not persuade me certainly no one else ever could. Once, when she and Olive and I were lunching together, she returned to this point, but Olive took my side and declared that I must be left free to decide for myself. Still her indomitable energy, and the hope that animated her for the future, surmounted all difficulties, and the preparations for the venture were completed as planned.

Early in October she took away her dear friend of those days for a quiet farewell visit to a seaside resort in Suffolk I had recommended to her, having myself once stayed there enjoyably with Amy. This visit was the occasion of the next letter I have, and it is a letter which well reveals the climax of the relationship which had grown up between us and the mutual comprehension it involved:

My Darling Boy, How sweet you are! X is tender and more sweet than ever before, and looks at me as I never thought possible for her nature. We are very comfie here, and in spite of the extravagance it was the only way. [Not being able to get into the hotel I recommended, which had closed for the season, they had gone into another more expensive one near-by.] Beautiful food, huge fires in our rooms, lovely beds, perfect weather. I've just wakened from seven hours' perfect sleep and am a new creature. I believe I should have smashed entirely. Thank you for all the relief about the money. I shall get through now, I believe, but it *has* been a strain. I keep thinking of you and dwelling in your heart. Yes, I had seen the papers. Now it is my turn to ask why fabrications get into the papers. Funny! That I have helped you in *Man and Woman!* I guess I have, but not in the way they think. My brain has ease at last and I can think. We went to the lovely harbour of —— or wherever it is yesterday and sat in a sheltered sunny spot from 11 to 3.30, and no lunch, as we have big breakfasts and dinners. We may go to —— tomorrow. We do as the moment prompts, and we went to the Ritz Theatre here last night.

My love ever, my precious one that no one can separate from me. Love to Amy.

W

The last days passed rapidly in a whirl of preparations so that I can no longer recall any details. I smile sadly as I realise how blind we both were to Fate, how little intimation either of us had of the significance of those days. With tender affection on both sides, there was less of the solicitude we had felt before her first plunge into adventure across the mysterious unknown Atlantic. We both felt, I imagine, that it was no longer mysterious and unknown. She was merely repeating an experience that had proved altogether successful, the only difference was that this time a still greater success awaited her. There seemed no occasion for anxiety. I failed, as much as she failed, to realise that this separation was to be for a much longer period, that far greater strain would be incurred, that she was going at the most trying season of the year, and that she was in a bad state of health. As I look back, I seem to see us standing at length on the final height of our life's course together, more at one than we had ever been before, and from that moment I was to remain there rooted for-ever to the spot where we had been entirely at one, while she was to slide, slowly or rapidly, down a terrible slope, beneath my eyes, and no power on earth could give strength enough to my arms to hold her still within my grasp and against my heart. And if I had accompanied her, it might have been so different!

Yet one moment remains, and will ever remain, vividly in memory, and that was the last. The night before she had spent at the club to be near her dear woman friend, and thence she wrote:

My precious Lamb, This is just a sweet good night. Our bodies are apart only as they are when you are in Brixton and I in this club. Nothing and no one can ever separate our spirits. After this no more homelessness, for we will make one home possible for us both. Just try and think I'll soon be back, and if either of us crosses over to fairy-land and rest, we know or should know that it is well worth while and be ready for our next job. I just hold you close and love you.

W

The last hours this time were to be given to me alone. I went down with her from Fenchurch Street to Tilbury Docks where her ship, the *Minnetonka*, lay, and she was anxious I should see the cabin in which she was to pass the voyage. But the official fear of enemy activities had by this time increased, the regulations were strict, only passengers could be allowed on board, and there was no one who could give me a permit to enter the ship. We lingered on the hither side of the narrow gangway while the crowd of passengers drifted across. At last I handed over her dressing-bag, a wedding present which had accompanied her on all journeys throughout our life together, and she too passed across. We stood gazing at each other, while the crowd now more eagerly surged on board. Long and sadly I gazed as though I knew that I should never see quite that same woman again. Only a few feet of gangway, but it stood over an abyss which would never be completely bridged.

Then at last, when the tension could no longer be borne, I moved away, waving my hand as I disappeared among the crowd, and the vision passed from my eyes. I recall restlessly pacing up and down the desolate railway platform while at the hour of noon hungry workmen swarmed across the line to dinner. After that there is a long blank in my memory.

There was, however, one more letter next day, written as the ship passed down the river:

My Beloved Boy [she wrote], I thought I had blood in my tight throat when that awful moment came. I caught myself moaning while I was trying to laugh and joke. Never mind — it is already

so many hours to the time we meet again. I hate to go, but it is
the only way. I wish you were here lying peacefully in the sun.
I shall soon be back and no distance can part our love. I've my
job to do and I'll do it. A pathetic note from X; she is feeling it
badly. Take care, my own, take care, and write often and in love.
The pilot takes this soon. It will be long before I hear, but my
thoughts are always with you.

Your own Wifie

What I experienced with this woman — I feel now many years
after her death — was *life*. She was the instrument that brought
out all those tones which the older I grow I feel to be of the very
essence of life, tones of joy sometimes, but oftener of anguish, not
happiness. I smile when I find people cheerfully talking of
'happiness' as something to be desired in life. I do not know what
happiness may be, but it is not life. I have lived. And this
woman, by her peculiar temperament, by her acute sensibility, by
her energy of impulse, by her deep hold of my most sensitive
fibres, struck out the notes of joy and anguish which are love and
which also are life. For love as I have known it is a passion more
of what we call the soul than of the body; unlike the passion that
is alone of the flesh, it is a flame that continues to burn even long
years after the body that may seem to have inspired it is turned
to dust. But it is because I have known love that I have lived
and that my life and my work in the world have been one. My
work, I am often told, is cool and serene, entirely reasonable and
free of passion, but without that devouring passion of the soul my
work would have been nothing.

I speak of a flame. Yet when I inhale the scent of a flower this
woman loved, or gaze on a picture or a book that meant much
to her, I am wrapped away from the world and caught up into
another sky. I realise what are the only things in life that have
any value for us, and I know — what all our science as well as our
art has so often asserted — that the so-called 'realities' are
nothing, that it is the things that are made of space and time, out

of emptiness, our symbols and our pictures, that are alone the eternal things.

I continued my narrative. The day before she left I had sent a little letter to New York:

> This is a line to meet you, I hope, when you arrive, and to tell you how I am with you in the spirit all the time and thinking of you and loving you and praying that all goes well with you — as I still have faith that it will. I am always looking forward to your safe return (with or without money!) and to the prospect of our settling down peacefully for a time in Speen or Carbis, if possible without any worries. In the meanwhile I shall be shut up in my flat, safe, no doubt, though rather dreary, and trying to work hard. I shall be writing to you twice a week at least — though you mustn't be worried at delays for the mails seem so uncertain in length of passage — and, anyhow, alive or dead, I shall always be loving you.

The following day I wrote:

> I have just got back from Tilbury and am feeling very desolate without you. I always seem to see your sweet face, and am sorry I could not see your cabin so as to picture you there. . . . I always seem to love you more and more and your last absence doesn't make this one any easier. . . . Your lovely and unexpected letter just comes as I was going out to post this. Thank you, Darling — it is a great help to me and I shall read it over and over again till I hear from you.

That was Saturday, and on the following Tuesday I wrote:

> On Saturday evening when I was undressing, thinking of you, and feeling very lonely and sad, your unexpected wire came. I have felt much cheered ever since, though still low and sad, Amy thinks, and doesn't know what to do with me; she came to take me to dinner on Sunday, but I preferred to be alone with thoughts of you; went by myself to concert in the afternoon. I am quite well and working fairly, and shall no doubt get along all right. . . . It is nice to feel that in less than a week you will be in New York and I shall have word from you.

In due course, when the *Minnetonka* was nearing New York there came the little wireless message, this time not so absolutely reassuring as after her first voyage. Meanwhile, a week after leaving London, she had written on board a letter to send me from New York. Here is the greater part of it:

> *My own darling Boy,* Never shall I forget your beloved face as I left it. I tried to smile to the end, but it was as if I had blood in my throat. It was *awful*, and the whole journey has been awful, but I shall feel better if only I hear you are safe, and that you are not missing me as I miss you. This silence for all those days seems to make it a year! It is the worst of the whole thing. I've been eaten up with remorse at coming and yet I see no other way to freedom. It has been a horrible voyage — thank God you were not here to endure it. I've been ill more or less all the time, but I've never stayed in my cabin more than half a day. Now I am better, but have had no heart to write till now. I've a nice cabin and my stewardess is a dear, but that is all. The ship is demoralised over the war. There is scarcely any cargo, so that it is not steady: they've been chased once, the captain was ill at the beginning, and Karl Schneider, the chief engineer, in charge of the ship. Everyone half in panic and the war gloom is everywhere. Mrs. Ryan [a friend who chanced to be crossing in the same ship] has been ill all the time, but it's been a comfort to know someone. I've not been able to work at all; there are ten children near me, my heart has been very weak, my head bad, and the weather horrible except for a few days. One awful gale made me feel I wanted to die and get it over. We *hope* to get in Tuesday morning, but who can tell? I feel I shall *hate* America and wonder if I shall even get through, but I expect it will be different when once I am in New York. The war news seems pretty awful. Turkey in now and I suppose Italy will follow. The whole atmosphere reeks of despair. My heart is in England, and oh, my Boy, my Boy, I hope you have not heard the cries I've called you with. I feel already ten years older, but I've the sense to realise that the voyage is the worst part, as when I get your letters I shall feel better. Thinking has been impossible. I gave it up at last in despair and just sat in my deck-chair and watched that awful sea. I keep wondering and wondering how you are and the Pater.

[My father was dying when she left.] I shall come back the moment I see myself pretty clear of debt. This is the only way. Nevertheless, I dread it all because I am not strong. I'll never again cross in a boat I do not know well. My Darling, go away with Amy to the sea some fine days, do anything and everything to make you happy, and when once I come back I'll see to it we are together and at rest at last. *If* the Germans win we must live in California — Eh? I'm dying and longing to get your dear letters. Love is a terrific thing. It was like sawing my bowels out when I left you. Never again must you see me off. All the time I've pictured your grey dear face which I love more and more and forever and ever. God bless and keep you. Love to Amy.

'Together and at rest at last.' I smile sadly as, after an interval of nearly six years, I read once more that expression of her constant desire which now can only be fulfilled when one day my ashes are scattered where hers already lie. But deeper than smiles or tears is the love that rings out in such letters as these. I have never attempted to disguise how keenly I sometimes suffered, how at moments all my nervous system was jarred by the temperament at once tortured, fierce, and tender, of my life's comrade, but when it is realised — and I myself never failed to realise it — how I received for a quarter of a century the deepest love of this woman who had such a genius for loving combined with her acute and shrewd intelligence and whose nature went so eagerly into manifold affections, it cannot seem surprising that the stamp of that flaming love, long purified of earthly stain, has been burnt so profoundly into me that all other love that comes to me now often seems only a kind of play, even if a heavenly play, and I remain forever hers.

Now, when, sixteen years later, I read these words, I leave them standing. I could not tell when I wrote them that deep love and comradeship in life were not over for me. Yet deep as is the love and comradeship which binds me to the cherished companion of my later years, deeper than ever after the many years it has lasted, some of them bringing me more unalloyed happiness

than I ever knew before, nothing can ever efface the stamp made
on my being during the most active period of my career by Edith.

When she reached New York, as Edith had herself anticipated,
the gloom of the voyage was quickly dispelled by the sunny
stimulating climate and the warm welcome of sympathetic
friends. She wrote on the 6th of November from the National
Arts Club:

> *My Precious Boy,* Oh! the loveliness of getting a letter from
> you after that *awful* voyage. They won't let codes go now and I
> felt eight shillings was well spent to save you anxiety, as I feared
> you might see in the papers what an escape we had and the
> *Olympic.* I never felt so horrible in my life as when I felt I might
> leave you all those debts to face. E. and M. and his wife and the
> Ks. met me, and oh! how kind, and Miss Tarbell here had all ready
> for me. A lovely large room and every comfort. The houses are
> so wonderful, and oh! the love I left here to find again. I lecture
> on you next Thursday at the Court Theatre and that is my chal-
> lenge to New York. The inevitable section is awake on you and
> me — our 'decadence,' etc. Who cares? I sent you *Love-Acre*
> yesterday with my deepest and tenderest love. Oh! God! Have-
> lock, never think I don't love you. It is awful the homesickness
> and longing for you, and I've had no English letters yet but the
> one you wrote before I left and I love it so. Yes — in life and
> death, my Sweet.... Those darling Ks. have taken a flat under
> theirs, furnished it and put their secretary to sleep there, and told
> me I am to have it as my headquarters always and leave my
> things and wander where I will. He declares I have saved him
> and he says nothing material he can do is more than a ripple.
> I've accepted. Why not? It is my turn now to be taken care
> of or I'll die.... I will write regularly every Tuesday and Friday
> and Sunday. I shall risk that horrible Atlantic to come back.
> I just fold you to my heart and long, long, long for a letter.

The same notes recur in the letters that followed, the homesickness, the longing for my presence if only I could face the cost
and the journey, gratitude to her loving and generous friends,
meeting with distinguished people, a whirl of social receptions,

public speeches, business arrangements. And, amid it all, references I now find so significant to her health, and how easily she
was exhausted. She had not been in New York a fortnight before
she was knocked over by an attack of influenza specially affecting
her throat, though dispersed by skilful and heroic treatment. She
wrote on 13th of November:

> Of all miracles I've ever had, the fact that your lecture was
> ever given is one — the day before I got the grippe, here taking
> the form of tonsillitis. My! how sick I was; had to leave the
> luncheon table, worse than any sea-sickness. Then that Mrs.
> F. pestered me for hours with her mental healing and stayed
> till 10 and I thought I should never survive, but a dear thing
> here by name of Mary Austin massaged me till nearly one, and
> the wonderful Mitchell [Kennerley] sent me a wonderful gargle
> and by power of will I went with help to the Court Theatre and
> you see the result in the papers. The last ten minutes my voice
> broke, but the applause was great. They all loved it and you.
> It was a crowded theatre and I was told that everywhere there
> was the greatest enthusiasm. General Gordon's daughter and
> Ingersoll's daughter were emphatic in their praise and love.
> They are all so dear and sweet to me. I am relaxing at last.
> Don't worry a wee bit, my sweet Love, I shall be all right in a
> day or two. Everything that can be done will be done, and I
> love you every second and for all time and all eternity. — I've
> had four letters from you, Darling, and only one from ——.

At the end of this long letter she mentions that Mrs. McLean
is sending her a nurse who can do wonders with ice-packs and so
on, and in the next letter she writes: 'Nurse G., who only takes
very special people, has given me three nights' treatment and
only took three dollars a treatment. "Your husband turned me
from a savage to a human being," she said.' But, as she mentions
in a later letter, this attack left behind much exhaustion and
a severe cough.

In the letters I wrote to her between the 23d and the 30th of
November I find:

It is not possible for me to come out, but even if it were possible I fear I should be a worry to you and I should certainly be wretched. I shall rejoice to see you again, but you must not feel homesick or come back before you are quite ready. If you were here now I really do not quite know what we should do, without money and with no Rose Cottage [which was let]; London is not very attractive, even in an ordinary winter. The weather seems to have jumped suddenly from September to January, and it is very cold. But I am quite well, though not very strong. One still feels the war all the time, though nothing is going wrong and I hear the War Office is cheerful just now as to the situation. I quite believe there may be a Zeppelin raid and possibly an attempt at invasion. But we are prepared for them and they may do good by making people realise what war is like. I seldom go anywhere except now and then to the Museum and an occasional Sunday concert. There is little temptation to go to the seaside this weather, and with troops swarming everywhere. Amy also has no wish to go — and is busy with house full of Belgian refugee friends, etc. — but I am planning to go a long walk in the country with her some day. Olive came to lunch and I have just had a card that she enjoyed her visit and that I am looking 'much better.' ... I am always loving you and praying that all goes well with you. I often think how sweet it would be alone with you, away from cities, as in the Rose Cottage dining-room — even with the door wide open! [An allusion to her rather excessive love of fresh air, as I thought, in the winter at Carbis.] ... Tomorrow I have to go down to Folkestone over Pater's affairs. There is to be just a stone kerb with simple inscription round the grave at Folkestone (where Miss C. will plant roses) and his name will be added (according to his wish) on my mother's tombstone at Redhill. ... The war goes on steadily, but so slowly that one is now settling down to it and it does not weigh on one so much. Most of the best things said about the war seem to come from America. But one is always aching for the poor Belgians and it is terrible how all the charming old things are being destroyed there. The Belgian doctors are in a state of great destitution. I've sent my case of surgical instruments, dating from student days, as an anonymous contribution. ... So many poddles always — literary, probate of will, correspondence, household, etc. — that little time is left for real work. But there is always time to love you, and I am constantly thinking tenderly and anxiously of you. Now that you are well advanced, I feel that I can begin to look forward to your return.

She wrote to me from New York on the 21st of November:

> *My Precious Boy*, I was so glad to get your letter. I am staying with E. and H. [her old friends, associated with Lily] and got it as I was coming from my bath. I am having a lovely time at last. This drastic treatment and tonic have pulled me through: I've only hoarseness and a desperate night cough. Things are opening up, and I'm to lecture in West Virginia, Milwaukee, Buffalo, and courses in drawing-rooms, etc., and on Thanksgiving Day I take the night train to Chicago. . . . I've never imagined such kindness as these folks show — all alike. . . . Dear old Pater! how sweet he is. I wish I could see him once more before he boards the greater *Winifred* [the last ship my father commanded]. I am always with you, loving you more and more. People do so love you here. I must bring you once; you can hide as easily as possible. . . . Write to Chicago when you get this. I've taken a studio and bathroom close to the Maurice Browns and there I cater for myself while I work like a black for three weeks. Some of the worry poison is at last escaping out of me. England nearly killed me. Here it is like Speen air, only more so, and brilliant sun. Take care, my little Havelock. Oh! if I could just kiss you, my Havelock.

I do not need to rely solely on her own letters as evidence of the enthusiastic cordiality of her reception in America. Apart from her letters and the reports of the newspaper interviewers, letters reached me from American correspondents, then and later, testifying to the same effect. A new woman friend, who occupied an adjoining room at the New York National Arts Club, and saw much of her during her serious illness, wrote to me even more than ten years later: 'I shall always see her as she was here at first, so interested in everybody and everything, and herself so interesting, and her beautiful nature, so warm and kind she was.' She adds in connection with the illness: 'I realised how worried she was, so many times she said to me, "I do not want Havelock to know how ill I am, he would be so worried."' Again, Huneker, the noted musical critic with whom I had long been in friendly touch, wrote to me also some years later: 'I had met Mrs. Ellis here, we talked of you, she worshipped you. A glorious intelligence, hers, and a noble woman. My wife and I sympathize with you — no mere lip-service this.'

A few days later she wrote:

> I go to Chicago tomorrow, but, alas! I can't get my studio till October 1st, so must go all alone for three nights to an hotel. The war news scares me for England, but it is a time when we must all face *anything*. This is only a wee line to reassure you. I'm being just adored and everything is being made as easy as it can be, but my strength is so limited, alas!
>
> Oh! my Boy! I'd give anything to fold you close. Take care, and know I am your own Wifie.

She wrote next day in the train (I give but brief passages from this long series of letters full of details of her doings):

> Here I am speeding my 1000 miles to Chicago with less trouble than in going from the club to Brixton. I've had a wonderful few days, but my cold has been troublesome.... I went to the Opera and for five hours I heard *Parsifal*. Oh! if only you had been there. War seemed an impossibility. Then I slept at the Kehlers and Kehler saw to everything. They are all waiting on me hand and foot in the train.... The war has made people save as they are doing at home and everyone says I am lucky to have got any work at all. I speak first on Sunday night on Edward Carpenter. *Love-Acre* has already made me some real friends. You *must* come over one time. There are things you would love here. You are always in my thoughts, my precious one.

And she wrote on arriving at the Auditorium Hotel in Chicago:

> Here I am, my Boy, safe and sound and easier in the throat. I just rarely spoke for twenty-four hours and rubbed in things. I've a lovely room and bath in this huge hotel leading into the Little Theatre building, and I shall cook in my room, having everything I want in my boxes.

On December 1st:

> *My Precious Boy,* Your letter has just come telling me of the
> Pater's funeral, but I've not had one telling of his death. Dear,
> dear old Pater. I wish I had seen him once more, for I've a very
> tender spot for the dear old thing. I hate to have been away
> when this happened, and yet it was the only way. Here I am in
> Chicago, the wealthiest city, and Lily is doing her work. I met
> Hamlin Garland, the novelist, at the Setons' and he has given me
> wonderful invitations. Everything is opening and you will see I
> am on my job. The Carpenter was a great success, though it was
> a pouring night. I'm staying here. I *dare* not run risks. I cook
> for myself when I'm not invited out, which is nearly always, and
> in bad weather I need not go out at all. It is economy, as I have
> to guard my throat, and this address opens up my possibilities.
> Doctor Kiernan comes; he looks well and has given me something
> to help the stuffiness in my nose. He thinks I look pretty well.
> I'm still weak, but otherwise getting on. Oh! if only you were
> here! I know I could protect you and there are such interesting
> things going on. My plays are in rehearsal. I am sure some great
> things will open out. Emmeline Lawrence is staying at Hull
> House for a few days and I go there to dine tonight. I'm having
> daily birthdays with presents, from gold pens to electric reading-
> lamps. If only you were here I'd enjoy it as well as learn and
> earn from it. I was laughing to myself last night. Imagine *me*
> years ago, in Chicago, not knowing anyone the first few nights,
> sleeping alone in a huge hotel! I go to Milwaukee for the day to
> lecture on Carpenter. Do take care and I will earn a new home
> at last.

That idea constantly recurs. She was upborne by it through the
incessant fatigue of this — as it really was for her sensitive and
fragile nature — heroic adventure. But the new home she was
earning was not in this world.

> I expect I will have a lot to tell you in my next letter. I can't
> get away from that telephone which brings me new chances
> ever and anon. If only I had more strength, and money to buy
> really nourishing food. Here a sixpenny breakfast costs a dollar.
> God keep you, my precious Havelock, and soon now my face will
> be turning homewards.

I quote largely from her long and frequent letters because they were a chief interest in my own life at this time. There is little worth quoting from my own letters. I was living as quietly as possible, only anxious for the end of this solitary uncongenial winter in the London climate — unfamiliar to me at this season for many years past — not inclined to do much work, not seeing many people. Even of Amy I saw little, as she was at this time almost entirely absorbed by various home duties. My letters are filled with the small details of my life and of the little items of business I was transacting on Edith's behalf, such as the payment of old bills, all interspersed with affectionate solicitude for her welfare. On the 3d of December I wrote:

> I went down to Folkestone for five hours on Tuesday, the whole time taken up in arranging the Pater's little affairs. He left everything as clear as possible, but it still means a number of things to do. The war will change all my immediate literary plans. But somehow I find no time for work and am doing very little — there seem so many small things to do. I have not yet been able to finish off the new edition of *Inversion*. You will know more about the war than I do. There is much dissatisfaction here at the way the news of naval disasters is being stupidly held back, although published at full length in the American papers.... I have no news and go on quietly as usual. My only dissipation is an occasional Sunday concert. I am always thinking of you with love. I shall rejoice to see you again, but am not specially anxious you should come back in the bad weather or into the gloom of war, and of course shall be glad if you can fulfil your purpose and make money.

Next day another letter followed:

> I wrote to you this morning to Chicago and am now sending this to New York by another mail going a few hours later. We are having a tremendous storm and I have rather a bad cold in head and throat — but I expect that in London this time of year. I only trust that your throat and cough are better. I've sent you the *Times Literary Supplement*. I don't know any paper which takes a larger and more reasonable view of the war. So free from bitterness.... Your letters are always so lovely.

And on the 7th of December I wrote:

> I was glad to get your letter this morning, though a little troubled that you do not feel strong. I trust that by now you have been examined to see how the diabetes is, and I do pray that you are doing everything wise and sensible. All is well with me; today has turned wet and mild like Cornwall, and at once I breathe easily as if by magic. My time, however, is much taken up by poddles, especially winding up the Pater's little affairs, which involve endless red tape; I had to spend the whole morning at Somerset House today and am not near the end of it yet. Poor Amy is very much worried and has to spend all her time nursing her mother. So my proposed day in the country is indefinitely postponed. I have written an article on 'Kultur' for *The New Statesman,* but that is all the literary work I have found time to do lately. Fisher Unwin has asked me to write a book on the Psychology of European Nations. It happens, curiously, that that is *exactly* what I intend my next book to be; I've had it in my head and partly written for years, but I do not intend to give it to Fisher Unwin. [Six years later, however, the book still remained unfinished. Now, twenty-three years later, I must still say the same.] You needn't be scared about the war so far as England is concerned. The Germans are making no progress and not likely to. And if they *do* make any desperate attempts, we've now had ample time to prepare. . . . I am always so thankful that people are so sweet and helpful to you. That is what reconciles me to your being in America. I am constantly thinking of you. I fold you close in my arms and look forward to your safe return as soon as ever you have done all there is to do.

On the 5th of December she had written from Chicago:

> *My Sweetheart Boy,* So much happens here every minute I scarcely find time or energy to write letters; but life is so wonderfully organised, everything without effort or disturbance. I never see a servant in my room, and yet it seems as if I had six clean towels and two clean sheets every time I went out for a walk. My cough is rather hacking, this Lake is so damp and cold and windy, but here is the money and here I stay till the 22d at least. This hotel loves me, and I'm treated out so much I simply take cocoa and rusks in between. 'Porky's Cissy' [the last Cornish

story she ever wrote] was loved by the men yesterday, and to-morrow I lecture on you. I get a *fearful* longing for you at times. I just love you, and in life or death I am closer to you than ever you can know. Take care, my Pet.

Four days later:

My beloved Boy [she wrote], this silence is awful, I've only had one letter since I came here and I just feel I can't go on. I feel so weak, but a wonderful doctor woman is examining me today. She lost her great friend in March, and I can help her and she comes to all my lectures. She gave me electricity last night, which did me good, as I'm so weak and this awful cough and cold still linger.... I'm struggling with the war articles. My room is very quiet and I am a lot alone and that saves me. The lecture on you was a great success, heaps of men and the theatre crowded; they loved it. It will nearly be Christmas when you get this, my darling, and my heart will ache and ache. I feel it is years since I saw you. We must go to California next year. I can protect you and I can't stand another winter without you. My eternal love to you.

So much is happening [she wrote on the 13th of December], I do not know where to begin. Thank Heaven for three letters from you this week and that all goes well. It must be our last winter apart and never again a winter in England. The waste of energy and joy is too much. You must come to California with me next year. My success is now assured. One has to work hard, but my success is assured. I am getting over the flu. Doctor ——, one of the medical wonders of Chicago, gives me electricity often. She tells me I am magnificent and will put all her skill to get rid of the evil which she thinks will all go and that I shall live till I'm 100! The women doctors have taken the Orchestral Hall which holds just on 3000; have invited me to give the 'The Abnormal in Eugenics' for women only, and they guarantee no worry and no expense and a cheque on all left after expenses. They just love us — you and me — and this is one of their ways of showing it. Three times in a day I was asked to speak and did it as if I loved it, but the society part is as terrible to me as to you.

She goes on to tell of all she was doing and of the interesting people she was meeting. 'Oh, my Loved One, that you were here and I could fold you to me and wish you a happy New Year. Love to Amy and bless her for looking after you.'

Next day, for she was writing now nearly every day, so much was there to tell, she wrote:

> This is another letter to beg you to do something for us both. This is going to be a huge coup for me on February 4th under the Medical Women's wings. Nothing would so add to it as if you sent me a paper to read with my own. The title of the whole thing is 'Sex and Eugenics,' or how to combine sane eugenics with a fine spirituality. I shall include my 'Abnormal' article and, of course, say other things I feel strongly about, but I want you to send, to meet me in New York, on or about January 9th a paper I can read as from you and also any odd scraps and suggestions on my own side. My lecture on 'The Loves of Tomorrow' was heard by a most intelligent audience; thirty people were sent away from my lecture and seats were put in every spot. Men come to my lectures and women doctors. They do love you so, in a genuine sense, so write a nice and fine and glowing thing, chiefly for women. There's a tendency here to pass laws on every blessed thing. Now I must finish the *Craftsman* article which baffles me.

It was, I think, in response to this appeal that I revised and completed the paper on 'Feminism and Masculinism,'[1] begun when we were writing together under the beech tree at Stanwell, with a special eye to its effectiveness when spoken by Edith. It was duly sent out in time, proved, I believe, to be what was wanted, and was eventually published (1916) in my *Essays in War-Time*.

> Your three welcome letters are here, one by one [she wrote on the 17th of December], and what a relief they are! The war news yesterday made me feel very bad; four thousand miles is an

---

[1] 'Masculinism' was, if I am not mistaken, one of the numerous words which I devised (like auto-erotism) and introduced into the language and which later became a part of more or less current English.

awful way and I just feel I ought never to have left. Do be careful for my sake. God knows how anxious I shall be. It is horrible. I am terribly overdone, as I simply can't afford to spend what I ought to have in food to keep me going at this pace. Those awful interviewers wake me up at eleven at night and early morning. On the whole, they are not so bad and of course it is getting me notoriety (alas!) and work. I can't move out now but some-one knows me. I've earned £110, which is not bad in these war-times and other things are to follow. The big coup is the medical paper. Send me as your share to last at least twenty minutes and give the scientific side of eugenics and sex. I'm lecturing, writing, and rehearsing for the plays in February. I think of you till I ache and ache to see you. Oh! Havelock, go and stay with Amy if there is a bit of risk, so that at any rate you will be together or with someone. It is indeed hard to keep hate out of one's heart. ... It has been bitterly cold here, snow always about, and below zero, but one does not feel it like the English damp and cold. We must be in California for next winter. Your *Impressions* is very much loved here and so are you.

And she goes on to tell of her lectures and journeys:

I return here to read my plays before the Drama League of America, and the big lecture on February 4th. So far that is all that is booked and if no more comes I shall start for home, but if more comes I shall stay longer. I just long, long, long to see you, my Precious One, and I love you always.

My sweetest Boy [she writes three days later], it is a horrible thing to be separated; the war news here seems dreadful. A cable will bring me back at once, if it is possible to come, if anything is wrong. There is bound to be an invasion, I am sure, and they will do their worst. I should feel happier if you were with Amy. I can only pray and wait and I seem to get a lovely lot of letters from you. The miracle is happening with me. I can scarcely find time to cope with all the wonders that are befalling me. This medical affair on 4th February is to be a tremendous thing. I begin by explaining Eugenics as the science of good breeding in more than one way: it must include kindness and consideration for those unfit who are *here*, etc.; leading from this to responsibility of mothers and teachers to teach *truth* about sex, etc. Yours will come in then on the social and scientific need for eugenics, etc., and I shall move on to abnormality and general laws of spirituality about sex and eugenics, etc. There are one hundred prominent women on the Committee. My photo (Genthe's) is to be posted everywhere (thank goodness I shall be away for a time), and it is hugely advertised. It will lead to far more work than I can do, but will book me up for another time. I am splendid so far. Dear Doctor —— I told you of is giving me electricity whenever I can get time to walk over to her office and she says I'm splendid. I am eating well now, as I was getting very weak with doing so much and not eating. Doctor Lobdell and Miss Cook (who are getting up this thing) come in often and drag me down to dinner — cocktails and steaks and laughter. 'Mystics must be fed,' they say. I love my quiet room, but shall be glad to see the real country again.

And she goes on at length to tell cheerfully of her movements and the people she is meeting.

In the letters that immediately follow — I give but a few sentences, for they are long and full of her constant movements, her plans, her impressions of people — she is approaching the climax of this American tour, and overflowing with the exuberance of her delight in all the beautiful new experiences that were coming to her. But one feels gradually creeping on — and I see the significance of it better now — the morbid excitement of the high-tensioned life around her: it was difficult even for her energy and her delight in this new world to keep up with it; the whirl was growing vertiginous, and her rapidly written letters, with occasional almost unconscious repetitions, seem to reflect that whirl.

She wrote on the 26th of December ('17 below zero and sun like midsummer') from Wyoming:

My darling Boy, How *did* you manage to get me two long letters on Christmas Eve when I arrived, and two more yesterday morning? It was a strange journey of 25 hours — Madame Schwimmer and I; she is so like Olive and we are having wondrous talks. This is a *wonderful* house. I've never imagined anything in the world like it. It is all new life to me in the midst of all this horrible war and lust of killing. Well — Lily was right — it is all opening. I stay here till the 1st, when my dear Mrs. Ward takes me to a huge charity ball at Buffalo, and the next day I go back to Chicago, the kind and wonderful, to give my lecture (which I have rewritten) on the 4th on Olive.... Oh, Havelock, my darling — this sun — this life — this *new* world. I pray the fanatics may not induce war. Thank you, my Love, for all your letters. They are such a relief when one gets all this war news in the papers. Now I am off to my bath and to dress and go in the snow. God bless you, my sweet.

On the last day of the year she wrote:

This has been a lovely restful week for my body, but oh! what heaps and heaps I've had to do. I ought to rejoice as so many people can find no work, but I can't keep up. I am feeling very anxious over the war news. They are all *mad*. I do pray you will take care. Tonight at seven will be your New Year and I pray all will be well. Anyway, I am earning money at last.... I shall soon be out of debt at this rate, but of course the expenses are pretty big. They have mended me up here and they say it is always to be my home. It is the simplest and most informal and yet dignified house I have ever been in. I am keeping pretty well, but I run no risks. This climate suits me so much better than England.... I hope to send you something nice for your birthday. I rarely buy anything. My one idea is to make and not spend, but I found I was getting very weak for want of good food, so I am careful of that now. I have been writing since five.... It is so wonderful to *never* feel an alien — always to be taken for what one has tried to be.

New Year's Eve had ever been one of her great anniversaries, full of tender and precious memories, but mails were uncertain and no messages came from any loved ones.

From Buffalo she wrote on the 2d of January, amid the busy details of her doings and her plans:

I never had such an attack of homesickness as on New Year's Eve. I am praying that after my long night journey tonight to Chicago I shall find several letters there. I am indeed in full swing now, three lectures this next week and four long journeys.

This awful news of the *Formidable* is here this morning, and I am feeling I cannot bear the suspense of what is happening day by day. Would you like me to throw up everything and come home or will you come out? It makes me sick unto death.

Four days later, she wrote en route to Buffalo whither she was returning from Chicago to lecture:

Here I am on the train to Buffalo. Oh! the rest to be away from people. I've been nearly demented over you. Since Christmas Day to *yesterday* I've not had a single line. I began to lose my poise at last, as I had letters from other people by different mails. The relief made me just sit down and hold my breath, and when I read about the little baby Havelock curl it was almost more than I could bear. [This memento of my infancy, a little brown curl cut from my head at the age of fourteen days by my mother and found in my father's desk at his death, I had forgotten in the stress of the last six years, and Edith forgot it too, but on searching in the desk I find it there still.] You know in spite of work and being spoilt and all the rest, fits of *awful* homesickness come over me at times — the longing to be utterly myself and not be in the public eye. This is the relief of being in the train, but even there now I am not quite safe. When I arrived in Chicago Sunday morning, I found heaps to do and all the afternoon I had rehearsals, and who should speak to me through the telephone but —— [a man who had meant much to her more than twenty-five years before]. It quite agitated me, especially when he informed me he had nearly been killed that morning in a railway accident. The next day he came to see me, and it was the funniest feeling — a sort of conjuring trick — the old and the young, smiling and struggling so differently. Of course I made myself very nice and it was a long time before he was himself. We compared many notes. He never mentioned you, though I spoke of you in and out. . . . My three plays will be very beautifully done. The bathos of life! Chicago to be the place to make me after all! If this lecture is a success they are going to offer me about £600 a year to speak once a week there for forty weeks in the year, going where I like: so that we could live in a lovely little house about forty minutes away. But don't hold your hair! I shall make no answer till I've been to you and England. . . . It is a mighty strenuous life, I was at it from five yesterday morning till

I got on the train at night at eleven, but it is all under weigh now. I go to New York Friday night (the night-train saves me hotel bill, and I love the rest and freedom)....No copies of your *Impressions* to be got now in Chicago, so you see what I've done! But you hamper me, I find, as much as help me. People are afraid to have me at the clubs. I lectured on Olive to a crowded house on Monday and they said it was 'the sanest lecture on the woman question they had ever had.' I am giving E's brother the £5 she lent me, so you see I am getting things shipshape a bit. Tickets are going like fire for the 4th and one hundred of the finest women in Chicago, including Jane Addams, will be on the platform. They say so much about my 'light and help.' Funny, I'm only a babe. The woman doctor gives me electricity, and I'm off and on, but ignore symptoms whenever possible. Money freedom I am determined to have. You may imagine I am busy, but I love you and will give you a splendid time yet. Keep my baby curl. I love it and you.

From New York, where she had arrived into a whirl of excitement and confusion, she wrote, after a disturbed night, in a rapid and occasionally rather incoherent letter: 'It is now four in the morning and the only chance of quiet I see. I am really alone at last. I am very busy, but am told I look very well. If only I had money to stay in an hotel here, but that will come.' Then she speaks of a surprise party of a hundred people to meet her, including Ruben Dario ('a celebrated Spanish poet who knows you: he stammered all sorts of compliments often: said I was the best interpreter he had ever had'); he, too, was lecturing and was also to fall ill and die the following year.

Thank you for all your dear letters and advice. My correspondence is now enormous. Oh! the joy of being away for a few quiet hours from the American voice, and yet how kind they are.... Now, good morning, my sweet Boy. I am desperately homesick at times. I could never do all this in Europe.

This letter, like the others, is full of her doings, the lectures she was giving, the people she was meeting, the articles she was writing. Two days later:

My word! Things are indeed coming at last. I can't keep pace with them. I need to lie in a quiet field for weeks to cool my head. ... Madame —— wrote and asked me to go with her in her box to hear Christabel [Pankhurst] speak on Wednesday. I went out of curiosity. It was all buttering of the Americans and a vilifying of the Kaiser. Madame —— shouted from the box; and I had hard work to keep my tongue, but I did, when I heard people all round me call her Joan of Arc. Yesterday Madame —— was at my lecture and called me aside. I had been spotted in that box with her by some men from the German Embassy here. My God! Havelock, they sent her to me to offer me huge sums of money to follow Christabel and in discussions oppose her — 'the only woman who would be fair to both sides.' I went deadly quiet — it made me see how wretchedly poor people get caught. When I refused, she tried other arguments. I said: 'What I want to say will be because I've an unpaid mouth and because condemnation on either side is to me as low as war itself.' She'll try again, but I won't see her more than I can help. She is dangerous, I fancy, but beautiful and intellectual. I think it abominable to come to a neutral country and make strife.

By this time the little paper, 'Masculinism and Feminism,' I had written for her to read at her great Chicago meeting, came to hand. She had been eagerly expecting its arrival, and was delighted with it, especially (as I knew she would be) with the words I had contrived to introduce: 'To Hell with your laws!' At the same time, also, amid all her wild press of activities and excitements, she found time to spend some trouble in seeing newspaper editors and getting better terms than the agent could for a little article I had written on the war; 'with my dearest love,' she said, 'and glad to do you this good turn.'

Letter swiftly followed letter, all full as ever of unalloyed tenderness, of affectionate anxiety, the desire to fly home when she heard of air-raids, swift notes of her journeys, of her delight in Washington and her horror in Indianapolis, of constant lectures and readings and interviews and meetings, of the interesting and enthusiastic people she was constantly seeing, of her continuous hard work, sometimes, in addition to all else, dictating for six hours a day, and of her joy in it all and her hope of financial success. Then, suddenly, on February the 4th, the day of the great occasion in the Orchestra Hall in Chicago, to which she had so long been looking forward, there was a change; the beautiful tenderness, undisturbed for so many months, I might say so many years, was ruffled into irritability and querulousness and resentment.

Part XII

XII

No doubt such a break was bound to come on the nervous side, even if it had not been followed by a break on the physical side. It had even occurred, as I have duly set forth, on her previous visit, when the strain had been incomparably less, but a slight break that time and quickly repaired and not the precursor of any physical breakdown. Now the strain was in every way immensely greater and more prolonged while the power of resistance was diminished. It was marvellous that she had proved so equal to it, that the energy of her spirit could carry through so triumphantly her frail nervous system and her delicate constitution, still further debilitated by the slow progress of disease.

Yet I have no wish to disguise the fact that, great as was this accumulating burden, it was I who, innocently as I supposed, added the last straw, if indeed it may not be considered a whole bundle.

From the time that Edith left I had been living in retirement and loneliness in my Brixton flat through the uncongenial London winter climate, deprived not only of her society, but, save for occasional visits, also of Amy's, who was then fully occupied with her own affairs. Here, it so chanced, there came to see me towards the end of December, duly furnished with an introductory letter, an American woman, a stranger alone in London for the first time in consequence of trouble. I need not here describe her. She was not unknown in her own country, but her name was quite unknown to me, though my books had been an influence and an inspiration in her own work. To me as a person she had never given a thought, but the author, it appeared, at once affected her as favourably as his books. On me this first meeting simply left a pleasant impression which, aided by sympathy with her lonely situation in a strange city far from husband and children, induced me to invite her to come again. The second visit sufficed to bring us into a relationship of friendship, I may say of affectionate friendship, later combined with admiration and gratitude, which has on both sides continued to subsist during the following six years to the present (now over twenty years), though during the greater part of that time we have seldom met. An American of Irish origin, she attractively united the good points of both nationalities. They are not my English traits; she was quicker, more daring and impulsive, than it is my nature to be. But we soon found that, both in emotional attitude and mental outlook, we had much in common and never jarred on each other. I had rarely known a more charming and congenial companion and I had never found one so swiftly.

The relationship — I speak more especially concerning my own attitude in it and she showed herself beautifully willing to accept my attitude — was one of calm friendship, even though there was a sweet touch of intimacy about it. There was thus no trace of guilty consciousness to spoil its delight. It was not my habit to practise deceit, but here I never even felt the need of secrecy. Yet it was some weeks before I mentioned my new friend in my letters to Edith. The reason was that I wished to feel sure first about my new friendship. To form a friendship so quickly was such a novel experience in my life, to form any new friendship had indeed so rarely, if at all, happened during the previous twenty years of steady emotional equilibrium, that I needed to know first exactly where I stood. That this new friendship could prove a shock to Edith, who herself was constantly forming vivid new friendships, I innocently failed to recognise even as a possibility. It had come so naturally, so charmingly, so unsought, at a moment when in my loneliness I needed it so much without even realising that I needed it, and it had come by so strange a chance in the person of one who combined the qualities of two lands both so congenial to Edith, that it seemed to me that I was forming a new bond with her rather than breaking an old one. It thus came about that when I once began to write about my new friend, I wrote about her in every letter, so that it seemed to Edith my letters were all full of this new friend. That was the way in which in some degree — to what degree it is not possible to unravel — I innocently contributed to the tragic procession of events which filled the following eighteen months, and beautiful as my new friend was to me and continues to be to this day, I have sometimes been tempted to wish that I had not met her.

My honest stupidity was the result of absence. I have always been in favour of frequent absences in love, and I even think that a deep and real and vital love is scarcely otherwise possible. I think so still. But we had never before been subjected to so long an absence and one so complicated by distance. With people of calm and solid character, like my father and mother, the constant absences of nine months' duration, through over thirty years of married life, led to no difficulties, but I and still more Edith were of different temperament. It had indeed often before happened that a letter on one side or the other had, from impulse or accident, contained a thorn, but a succeeding letter or telegram had removed the thorn which never remained to rankle. But three weeks must pass before I could know the result of that letter and in the meanwhile I had sent at least six more letters each with its thorn and the wounds had grown too poisonous when at last I realised and put forth my best efforts to cure them. It would have been easy had I known at once; when at last I knew, it was too late.

By ill fortune it happened that the first letter reached Edith just before the great day, so long anticipated, of her most important lecture, and the reading of my paper, at the Orchestral Hall in Chicago on the 4th of February, precisely at the moment when the accumulating physical strains and nervous exaltation of her tour were at the climax. Her sense of deep love for me and of spiritual communion in life and in death had never been so firm and so unalloyed as during these months, and on this mood my letter broke with a shattering blow. 'If I lost Havelock,' she had said, with large-eyed seriousness, I have lately heard, to a woman friend in Cornwall some twenty years before, 'the earth would rock.' It was absurd that my letters, which came from a heart so devoted to her, should produce an earthquake, but in the exalted state into which she had been wound up it now seemed to her that the earth rocked. She said to me later in the year, using the words of Oscar Wilde, that 'every man kills the thing he loves,' and that she had been killed in March, referring, I suppose, to these letters, though it was in February that she received them, March, however, being the month in which, owing to additional physical strain, her health really began to break down.

But all that month I was innocently continuing to pour poison instead of balm into the wound I had without knowing it made. I lived alone in my flat with my chief thoughts eagerly fixed on the days when the American mail arrived, and my chief consoling distraction lay in the occasional little excursions, usually to a concert, with my new friend. To me a deep love which had grown ever stronger through a quarter of a century of trials and proofs was something far too solid ever to be shaken. My love was sure, and I knew it was sure, just as I knew hers to be sure. But it was not her nature ever to feel sure. She had a natural vein of suspicion, and an intense self-distrust which it seemed to her that past experience had justified. So that when in letter after letter with simple frank abandonment, such as I had always used to her, I poured out the praises of my new friend, having nothing else of interest to communicate, Edith was bewildered; her natural tendency to doubt was fortified by the undoubted fact that such a sudden new friendship was a novelty in my life; her own friendships had often been just as sudden and warm, and I had never felt any need for doubt or fear; but my nature, she probably felt, was different. She took indeed the precaution of checking her own judgment by the unusual course of showing some of my letters to the only intimate friend she had in America — the friend who had been Lily's friend — who remarked, as Edith later told me, that they were 'strange.' That they may well have seemed to an outsider, as often also Edith's own letters would have seemed to an outsider; we each wrote only for the other's eye. Unfortunately none of these letters are extant to quote. It happened a few weeks later when Edith was staying in an American house that the police came on some mission; it had nothing to do with her, but in her nervous high-strung condition and with all the incalculable results of war conditions in her mind, she hastily destroyed some personal letters, including mine, which she thought too intimate for strangers to see. She regretted this later, when I told her she must be exaggerating the character of my letters, and I also regret it. But I am well aware that she was right in the main, for I wrote with freedom, strong in the security of a sense of loyalty, though — such is the ingenuity of self-torture — that it was for Edith the very fact that my new comradeship was of the soul rather than of the body that made her feel she had been dispossessed in my heart. I have not, and never had, any thought of blaming her, nor even of suggesting that her

impulse was morbid — though it was certainly in part the result
of her nervous high tension and physical exhaustion — for Amy
also felt in much the same way, and with equal unreason. So
many applications are there of that oft-invoked saying of Pascal's
that 'the heart has its reasons which reason knows nothing of.'

My unfortunate letters, as I have said, began to reach her on
the eve of her great day. I had so little anticipated any evil effect
of them that I had not thought to guard against this. Indeed, at
first they seemed to have no evil effect. She wrote me a long and
sweet letter of six large pages on the morning of the 4th of February, a little sadly but with no bitterness:

> *My Darling Boy,* Here on the great day of my public life I
> awake at five and write my English letters, for never am I alone
> now. I got all three of your letters and read them when resting
> after my Turkish bath. Of course I got a fearful jump when I
> realised there is another ——. If it makes you happy I am glad,
> but somehow it is a kind of strange realisation which makes it
> still easier for me to die. I *want* to die, and yet I am at my
> zenith, and if I can only live two more months I shall not die in
> debt. Everything is opening, as Lily said — everything, but oh!
> the reporters and the chatter is so very trying. Yesterday I spoke
> at a banquet of 600 men — such fine men — at the Chamber of
> Commerce. It was a unique experience. It is curious how I have
> felt a strange feeling about you for some time — a realisation how
> it is a law of life that a vacuum fills. Thank God someone has put
> life and joy into your sad face.... Be careful, for I realise so
> much here how hero-worshipping is like drug-taking. I've had to
> cope with it, and even sometimes had to be brutal, in a way, as it
> is mawkish. A curious aloofness from the world makes me feel
> sure that at last I am nearer leaving it than I thought. Houghton
> Mifflin will soon publish my plays. They are sweetly acted at
> the Little Theatre and *The Pixie* is fine. Of course I'm pretty
> tired. I've never worked so unrelentingly night and day as now.
> I've never time even to put a button on or to think, but it is
> telling at last. I lectured on Olive at the smartest club here on
> Tuesday and they went crazy over me; they have given me the
> run of their beautiful club: it is close-by here and a great rest....

I am terrified of tonight. It is a huge hall, but my voice carries, even in a whisper, almost all over it. They are all crazy over my voice. Isn't it dear of these medical women? Doctor Lobdell takes the chair. . . . I wonder how you spent your birthday, Dear One? Which of the —— came, or did they come in relays? Now I must have my bath and my breakfast, go through my lecture, and then dictate to my typist. After lunch I mean to cut off the telephone and sleep. People say I look splendid. With my dearest love and all tender hope for your happiness,

Your Wifie

P.S. I drank to you and your new —— in a cocktail last night.

The lecture seems to have been an immense success. She gave me no account of it, but sent the newspaper reports, as she always did of all her doings and her interviews. She had bravely wound herself up to this greatest effort of her great adventure, but she was evidently already showing signs of fatigue, for she told me once how Doctor Lobdell had seen her beforehand, told her she needed a good dinner, and took her off and gave it her. Directly after the lecture, over a bottle of champagne half a dozen prominent people who were present wrote me kind greetings with loving and admiring words about Edith on a single sheet of paper to which Edith also put her name and a few words to her 'sweetheart boy' (she was apparently going to write 'baby'). She signed last, using, by a strange mistake which she never observed, her usual maiden signature, 'E. M. O. Lees,' which she had not used for over twenty years. It was a revealing little indication of the nervous disturbance which this life of high strain was producing.

She wrote, enclosing this sheet, three days later. In the meanwhile more letters had come from me which seem somewhat to have irritated her. These new letters were probably in the same key as those that immediately preceded; they could have contained nothing fresh about my American friend, for there was nothing more to tell, then or later, and any wish to cause irritation was never farther from my heart than at this time. The long letter she had written in the early morning of her great day was a little

excessive in its reference to a desire for death, but it was always
natural to her to be a little excessive, and for the rest it was simply
sincere, affectionate, natural, with a touch of mischievousness,
altogether characteristic of her normal level. The effort of this
lecture, however, had evidently produced a profound reaction,
and the elasticity with which she was wont to recover from such
reactions could no longer be discerned. There is a note of exhaustion and weariness now in her letters, a rather querulous,
irritable tone, for the first time since she left England, something
more than the old passing moods. In this letter of the 7th of February, she dreads — a foolish fear, as she might have known —
that her secrets will be given to another woman; all the old apprehensions and anxieties that accompanied, by no one's fault, the
coming of Amy, recur to her mind and she recalls them because it
seems to her that perhaps they are coming over again.

A few days later she had regained much of her poise and saw
things in a juster perspective, though the details she gives of her
life showed how severe a strain she was putting on her already
overstrained constitution:

> *My darling Boy* [she wrote on the 19th with the old tenderness],
> I fear my last letter was not very bright. I had a stupid feeling,
> in spite of all they say here, that those who love me best are better
> without me so long as I am a money-earning machine: you know
> it is a long time to be away from the old country and you all,
> and often my heart gets very sore and sick: you see I am not
> *really* strong enough to work like I am doing. Outside the feasts
> people ask me to, I live more or less on things that I cook for
> myself and that costs very little — my big room and bath are my
> only extravagances. Well — the lecture came out for me just
> £51 when all expenses were paid. You see the hall and advertise-
> ments and things cost just on a hundred, but it was a fine adver-
> tisement and has led to many other lectures. I have opened a
> little account in a bank here (if anything happens to me Doctor
> Effie Lobdell will see to everything for you) [and she goes on to
> give particulars of the various little accounts she was settling in
> England]. I am doing all I can and need no upbraiding. [But

there was never a touch of upbraiding nor any occasion for it.]
I am deciding not to come back yet. I vowed I'd get out of
debt, and I will; up till after Easter there are always openings
here, and now they just adore me, so I had better make the best
of it while it lasts. They are all wonderful to me. I spoke to 500
women at the dramatic luncheon the other day, and last night to
200 nurses at the biggest hospital here, and tomorrow I speak in
the drawing-room of the tinned-meat millionaire; I sat next the
President at the dramatic luncheon and next but one to Christabel
Pankhurst: they go crazy over my voice. So you see I am hard
at it all the time. The intimate loneliness is pretty 'fierce' as
they say over here, but I mean to die in peace over debts. Sebastian Hinton [grandson of James Hinton] dines with me on
Friday and goes to the plays. They are only on for a fortnight,
but will lead to other things; *The Pixie* is perfection, and the
men adore it. I have made several inquiries about M. [my new
friend]. Some like her very much and some say she needs balance.
Greet her from me and say I hope she will stay, and cheer and
comfort you till I get back. I am just eating bread and Bovril
as I write, and I've been writing since five. I've had to have a
typist several days and have dictated six hours at a time. It
cost me twenty-seven dollars, but it could not be helped....
Now I must stop. The home letters are *so* welcome, but they
seem to come so rarely. God bless and keep you, my precious Boy.
I think I am growing up at last. Chicago is a terror of a place,
but so wonderful too.

But three days later she writes sadly, feeling her loneliness in
the midst of the crowd, longing for the presence of 'someone who
cares,' and it seemed to her that I had ceased to care.

I'm terribly busy — never so much in my life. I am determined
to stay till I am out of debt. The fact that I can see you do not
really need me is of course not making me feel I shall hurry; but
I just take a day at a time.... The plays end tonight — there
was not standing room last night. Tomorrow I give a little dinner
here to my company.... I am very sad and lonely, but I mean to
do my job, and when all my debts are paid surely the Jester can
rest. I always speak nicely of you, but I shall cease saying some
things as I've no wish to pose in America as a deluded *wife*. I

am almost beginning to hate my popularity. It is the real beautiful intimate love I am craving, and every expression of wonder
and adoration here makes me long to go to Lily. I feel so strange
to be always impersonal. I feel sort of stunned as if the 'belonging' between you and me had got its deathblow. I only want to
die because I feel in human nature there is nothing for me any
more — only in Nature and music.

The depression of that letter was in part due to an interval
without letters, for although they were sent with unfailing regu-
larity the mails were becoming irregular. Two days later she
wrote cheerfully once more:

My darling Boy, Your two letters are here at last. I was
beginning to have a sort of feeling I was dead and not buried
somehow. It takes so long to hear and I am so dreadfully lonely
in spite of all the worship here. I'm never in bed till 12 and at it
at 6.30, so ought not to feel lonely. I could not do one quarter
I do here in England. I love all you say and perhaps I have
exaggerated the situation with M. You see I'm a Tobias-Jester
and have been so badly hurt I am only longing always to die....
No, dear one, I did not want anything for placing the article —
on the contrary, shall I send you something for the use of the
'Feminism and Masculinism'? I thought I would use it again,
and then, if you like, place it here for you.... I gave a little dinner
last night to my theatre company, as the plays are over, and they
loved it, and it was Valentine's Day and I felt very homesick.
I think sweetly and tenderly of you, and I love you as no one
else can do more. I envy you an Irishwoman.

The strain of this exacting life was telling on her constitution.

My Precious Boy [she wrote on the 24th of February, enclosing
a medical report of her condition], I am afraid you will be a little
troubled at enclosed report, but I am sure I shall be better when
I get out of this terrible noise and rush. You see I've been doing
enough for seven folk, but I saw no other way nor do I yet. I'm
not here to sit and think about things, but to do them. Thank
God — if anything happens, slowly and surely from here results
will come to you, and these wonderful people who really care will

help you. I have been very troubled over conditions of the war, and somehow just terribly lonely in spite of all. I am glad you are happy, I see it is all for the best and my only prayer for so long has been to pay my debts and go. But I don't suppose I'll go. I never do, do I? ... Dear Mrs. Ward and Miss Westcott are coming to Buffalo to take care of me, so you see I am in good hands. The sun and fresh air will revive me at once. In this cheap room I never see light all day. I just feel done. I am now going to keep any money in Express notes, instead of in the bank, so that if anything happened you could get it at once. ... I'm only writing this just to ease you in case I'm very ill. I've not known how to sit up some days, but it's all right. Your letters have been so welcome. I don't want you to worry. I do hope M. is out of trouble. People say she is deep and sweet and good, and that is beautiful. Tell her from me to take care of you always, and Amy too. ... *Later.* Having had my bath, eaten my breakfast, and read my mass of letters I feel a warrior again in a way. The letters have partly done it. Someone has told them in Washington that in an interview I said I was not married. I wish I'd brought those 'marriage lines' to upset them! Oh! I'm *so* tired and feel, once I get somewhere beautiful and quiet, I'll die as a sheer luxury. Of course my success has brought on petty jealousies, and I'm confronted with such absurdities all the time. ... Speen I shall see about later. But will you care for it? I wonder? God keep and bless you always.

From Buffalo she continued to write me two long and tender letters every week, as she had never failed to do however overcome she might be by work and exhaustion.

She was a little easier at Buffalo, with more quiet and sunshine. But there is a pathetic note continually being sounded through all these brave and loving letters. She feels how serious is the state of her health, she is not sure she will live to return home, 'the worship and understanding amongst all these people make me almost want to live to repay it, but Tobias and the Jester long to die'; the continual strain, the almost constant society, and yet no one with whom she could be her own natural unconstrained self, the long hours and late nights — for one who loved freedom

and was accustomed to much solitude and liked to go to bed as
early as a child — could not fail to be destructive. 'Oh! God!
how I pine for solitude!' she breaks out. 'Interviews and journalism, and incessant voices that clip-clap all day long: they are the
dearest people and the most generous in the world, but they never
think you want to be alone.' She was being forced, moreover, to
temper the childlike unadulterated enthusiasm of her first impressions of America. She was beginning to realise that her success aroused jealousies and evoked injurious rumours and stimulated 'the eternal thirst for thrills in newspapers.' She was a little
disturbed at the foolish report that she was not legally married,
as it seemed to be injuring her work, and, again, when an advanced young journalistic woman whom she had befriended, but
who thought she had not sufficiently shocked the public, published
an article on 'Mrs. Ellis's Failure.' She was beginning to feel
lonely amid the crowd, and longing for home and for love, and yet
tempted to feel that she had no home to go to and no lover. It
seemed to her that I was well content and happy without her, and
she scarcely realised that my willingness that she should stay on
in America as she herself proposed was based in part on the glowing reports of her own earlier letters, and in part on my belief that
she was better there than in the war-disturbed atmosphere of
London. So reasonable an attitude may well have seemed too
temperate. In her impulsive temperament, ever doubting and
self-distrustful, it was not easy to understand how near to her in
heart I remained. 'My darling Boy,' she yet breaks out in the
middle of one of the Buffalo letters, 'don't think I don't understand. I love you always — deeply and more than you can ever
have realised; but more and more I see how I ought never to have
been allowed to be born or to grow up. I'm a waif and an alien.'

The irregularity and long delays of the mails — for my letters,
though always faithfully despatched, now took about a fortnight
to reach her — was constantly unfortunate and almost tragic.
The letter that reached her was never the response to her im-

mediate need and mood, but to some experience of a month before which by this time she had perhaps quite outlived. I realise how sound was the instinct which had led her, in spite of all my obstinacy, to persist in trying to persuade me to accompany her to America. She needed me. My presence would have been a perpetual help and relief to her. Moreover, all the germs of misunderstanding would have been killed at the outset. But I had known well, as I know still, that, even if it had been practicable, the life that she was living in America would for me, with my totally different temperament, have been an impossible life of torture, and that the seclusion which she promised to secure for me would have been absurd in a land where I was so well known by a reputation she was herself helping to make more conspicuous.

The next letter (of the 4th of March from Washington) has had for me a sad significance because I see in a little incident it narrates — a little inevitable incident when travelling among strangers — the last straw bringing breakdown to her exhausted and overstrained organism.

> *My Precious Boy* [she wrote in this long letter — marvellous how her love found time for these long letters, so clearly and neatly written], your two letters yesterday nearly paralysed me. I expect in my tiredness I've hurt you and yet I've never meant to. You know how lonely and mistrustful of myself I always am, and somehow old memories *will* cling when I hear of new women in your life, for women, I'm daily realising, are maniacs over notorieties. I'm pursued by it all here, and it makes me adore Nod and Ricky and Tom [the cat, the donkey, and the horse]. It is all right. I have no earthly right to feel or say a word. I had actually posted you that newspaper where I said about loving the woman one's man loves when, the day after, your letter about M. came. I laughed and cried together. I hear a good bit about her now — all think she is sincere but needs ballast.... I've broken down. That week in Buffalo with Mrs. W. was terrible. We were all in rooms together, and the incessant voices and noise and interviews, as well as five lectures in four days, has just sent me crazy. How I ever got through only Lily knows.... I'm longing, longing

to comfort you and the intolerableness of this dreadful separation
threatens sometimes to break me up altogether. We got here in
the worst blizzard I've ever encountered. Like all millionaires,
Mrs. W. saves pennies and gives pounds and we carried our hand
baggage from one station to another. I refused till she — seventy-
six — began to take it and then, of course, I took up mine. When
I got here, everyone saw I was nearly done, for they put me to
bed where I've been for two days with all my old aches and pains
for the first time in America: but don't worry, as I'm well on the
mend and for two nights I've slept beautifully, but my heart is
pretty bad. I am going to send you a week-end cable for my
birthday treat to tell you I love you more than you have ever
known. I expect to be back the middle of May, but have an
enormous amount to do yet, though I seem to work day and night.
There is to be a big house-party tomorrow and I lecture on you!
The clergyman has even announced it from the pulpit. If I can
help M. over here, tell me. I wish you and I could somehow live
in a quiet spot here (and there are gorgeously beautiful spots
within a reasonable distance) and spend half the year here and
half over there. If the Germans win I could never live in Europe.
So much here suits me. Perhaps when M. is back, you will feel
differently about it. I've the offer of a lovely cottage in the
Adirondacs, if Fate keeps me this side, but if so I shall fret myself
to death. . . . Love to A. and tell them all to take care of you. Tell
Olive the moment it is safe to send it I am going to send her a
cheque for her birthday and bless her for me. Mine will be a
queer one this year, but I am glad to be here for it. Now, my
Precious Boy, be comforted. I do not mean to be cross or cruel
or naughty. I am tired and in spite of all very lonely for someone
to hug me tight that I want. It's all very well to be a prophet,
but it's a damned lonely show.

On the 8th of March, the day before her birthday, that anniversary of which she always thought so much, I cabled my greetings and love to her, and at the same time she was characteristically cabling to me, by way of giving herself a birthday treat,
to say that she was better and resting, 'with tenderest love always
and birthday thoughts from me.' At the same time she wrote a
note to tell me that she had really had a bad angina attack at

Buffalo, but was now very busy again with plans and correspondence, though having with her hostess a time of '*comparative* rest;
she is so like me — eternal energy and fuss and kills us all with
plans all day; but she is lovely.'

The next day, her birthday, she wrote a long and more deliberate letter, full of tenderness twined in with business.

> *My Precious Boy*, I wrote a hurried note yesterday, as the sleigh
> was waiting at the door, and now — on my intimately lonely
> birthday — I write again. I've cried a little in the early morning.
> Havelock, I'm really not very well, but I suppose I would be
> worse in England. It is bitterly cold, and that congests me, but
> the dryness is so splendid. The snow lies on the ground and the
> birds are singing and the sun shining, and I am lying in bed
> writing. I am waiting to hear of certain dates for lectures, and
> then I shall know what to do. The mails are terribly uncertain
> — it seems like a new death when I don't hear. I fear you are
> angry with me and yet in my heart I resent nothing. All I can
> say is that I've never felt myself since I realised a new love in
> your life, and yet it is not a bit jealousy. I think it is I am dead
> sick of complications of all kinds, and of hard work and of trying
> to leave you free of debt and also this life is very lonely for the
> lover in me. The two new books and the book of plays will ease
> my mind, as royalties will come in regularly. . . . I shall come back
> — mines or no mines — the moment I've done all I can do. I
> make a new resolve today. After these books — *New Horizon*
> and *Hinton* are off my chest, never more any ethics or propaganda.
> If I live it shall be only drama and artist work — nothing else. . . .
> Your royalties ought to increase. So many say they are buying
> your books after my lectures. I am so busy I feel quite bewildered.
> I think it best to wait here till the hum of everlasting voices and
> cities lull in my brain a bit. I've perpetual headaches, but I'm
> used to those. They say it would be dangerous to cross, but when
> I am ready I am coming, though in many ways I feel you are
> more peaceful without me. *Later.* Miracles and marvels! Your
> lovely cabled message has reached me. I am sure that is M. who
> has taught you how to send it. My! how glad I am to get it. The
> sun is radiant and I shall come home the moment I see a free
> chance. Today I have the proofs of my plays, so they are coming

out quite soon. I've heaps and heaps to do yet. I love you always as you know, and I am struggling to live.

Your own Wifie

On the very next day she wrote again to say that Mrs. Ward had persuaded her to stay on and rest till her next lecture.

> It is good discipline, too, to live more simply than the peasants in Cornwall, and never, even on my birthday, see a small liquor. The servants made a cake and set it covered with little candles; they all love me.

In these letters, brought back to the familiar homely thoughts aroused by her birthday, she seemed almost her old self again. Only a few small points might need to be excepted as the outcome of overstrain. Yet even they were part of her old self: exaggerated fears, exaggerated hopes. More significant in its revelation of the crushing blows — in themselves insignificant — that were now disorganising her sensitive exhausted overstrung nature was the following letter, written from Mrs. Ward's house on Saint Patrick's Day, a great anniversary with her on account of its association with Lily. It is all the more piteous because even beneath its distracted doubts and fears, justified or unjustified, there is clear to see the deep ocean of love. Small points in the letter remain rather obscure to me; it is evident that the sudden realisation of the censorship and the incident (cautiously withheld in this letter) — misunderstood as she later discovered — which alarmed her into destroying the letters had induced considerable reticence:

> *My Darling Boy*, at the end of what was as unlike a lovely Saint Patrick's Day as can well be imagined your five letters all at one time arrived. Thank God. M. [her chief man friend in America] had sent me a lovely little shamrock plant, some whisky in a little flask for my journey (as all in this New Thought house would faint if they saw anyone drink), and a bottle of wonderful Californian water which has already done me good. I have been *very* ill — so ill that I cannot imagine why I did not die. I should

have left here long ago but for that. Everyone seems to have had the grippe, or something. That is why I sent a cable, knowing what the newspapers here are, and not knowing what you might see. I broke in Buffalo, and I've had a lot to bear, as Mrs. Ward, sweet as she is, has obsessions about thrift and is forty times more restless than I am, so that her own family cannot stay here long, and those around her are mostly self-interested. I am very sorry, for I really care for her. I wish you would write her a little note of thanks for all her kindness to me. Yesterday morning when I woke I wrote long letters to you and to Y. and later thought it wiser to burn them and all the letters you both have sent me. The thing I have dreaded ever since you wrote of M. has come. I have never been well since you told me, but thank heaven you did. All the time I have felt forebodings of the Bedborough Case atmosphere. X. sent me enclosed, but thank goodness I casually mentioned M.'s friendship with you when he was here, having also heard about it among the Socialists in Buffalo. [The enclosed was an innocent — but meaningless — little newspaper cutting incidentally mentioning that M. was working with H. E. in London.] When no letters came, all this time I've been so ill, I was frantic, knowing so well what can be made of things here. Then imagine what I felt yesterday when H. [an old American friend in New York] wrote that the Censor had not only forbidden a silly baby-cable for Saint Patrick's Day to Y., but demanded to know its inner meaning. She seemed very agitated and said there was no knowing what they would do. I dragged myself out of bed, dressed, and burnt all your letters, as M.'s name has been in all lately; and I thought it better in case I die — for I've had about enough to kill two of one sort or another — to destroy all letters I had here, not because of anything that mattered, but because of newspaper gossip which will overpower me, I know. I still feel that you do not realise that the adoration of these women must be taken in a different way to what we are used to, but it is all too late and you have probably been hurt at what you think is my jealousy. It is not that — it is soul and heart and body weariness of perpetual everlasting crucifixion. . . . We can have Speen cottage till end of June. I shall want to be with Y. a little while. She is very sweet and beautiful, and if only I could trust anyone or anything maybe I could get joy out of it; but things have hurt too badly, I fear, and like Tobias I only want

Love-Acre. Poor little M., but she can't grumble; she is only paying her price, as we all do. The unbearable loneliness in this illness has been awful. I was amazed at my courage in staying, yet what could I do? When I get to New York I will try to place your various papers. I have at last finished my long article on war and one to give later as a lecture at Washington. I am going to a wonderful doctor in New York at once about my heart — it is so very painful. Here it is bitterly cold and deep snow on the ground. . . . I can't imagine what it will be like to be in an orchard at Speen. . . . You will be missing M. and be very anxious about her. I wish I could say nicer things, but I seem always to say the wrong one. I am going to entirely reorganise my life when I return so that I need never be a burden on you or anyone. Money alone can do this and I must make it. Y. will come over with me if I have to come again, but there are signs this last fortnight that the tide is turning. And now we shall be dubbed 'free lovers.' It does not really matter — nothing does. But in face of my serious condition and exhaustion I shall probably prefer the wilderness and not attempt the impossible against overwhelming odds. I shall probably know next week the dates of my final lectures and book my passage, but I've heaps to do yet. My plays will be published by Mifflin on the 24th of April, under title *Love in Danger*, then there will be the Cornish stories to get into shape and the lecture book too [probably *New Horizon*, not published in her lifetime]. Then I am going to try to get the plays on in New York. Don't think unkindly of me, Dear One. I am sad and terribly spent and want freedom; and money alone will bring it, and I've not health to make and enjoy doing it. Always the fear of breakdown. I shall try now to get a few well paid lectures in England. I just hold you to my heart and love you always, and am sorry if my pride or pain cannot support all things at all times.

Your Wifie

I have reproduced this letter in all its significant passages. It is altogether characteristic of her in times of trouble with its swift transitions of subject and mood and throughout its firm underlying devotion. Here and there it may be a little unjust to me, a little unreasonable. But I am not concerned to justify myself. I only feel her 'unbearable loneliness' which I know that I could have comforted, as so often in times of trouble before. I still do not see how I could have gone to her. But in any case, I have certainly, to use her own phrase, 'paid the price.'

I am bringing forward in detail those more intimate relations on which my private thoughts and feelings were concentrated. But I do not wish to suggest that these were visible to the outsider or even that they interfered with the general course of my literary and other activities in the world. I may say, indeed, that I had never been more busily occupied than I was at this time, nor do I think that at any time my work was of better quality. I was writing essays which were later to take a prominent place in my books, the *Dance of Life* and *From Rousseau to Proust,* and I was writing those *Impressions and Comments* (the First Series was published in 1914) in which my literary style is supposed to have reached its highest point. In a different field it was in this year that the final much-revised and enlarged edition of *Sexual Inversion* was issued. I was also producing a number of mostly short articles suggested by the war in progress and appearing immediately in the best English or American journals (many of them later in two volumes of *Essays in War-Time*), never of a pronounced 'patriotic' character, though on the other hand they could not be considered definitely 'pacifist.'

My correspondence with friends and acquaintances went on, I believe, much as usual, though it is not easy to produce samples in proof. But I may refer to the letters addressed during some forty years to my friendly scientific acquaintance — carefully preserved and docketed by him and returned to me by his son after his death — and I find a few of this date. He was an ardent Rationalist, and various points I now omit in my letter were connected with queries of his, now scarcely intelligible, connected with his own work. My letter is dated January 6, 1915:

> *My dear Perrycoste,* Yours to hand. I have wondered how you are occupied these times and have once or twice been on the point

of writing to you. Somehow I have always been extremely busy
(in spite of the fact that the general depression of course affects
the sales of my books) and of late also private affairs have required
much attention, in consequence of the death of my father, at
eighty-seven, in full possession of all his faculties; I was pleased
to note that he accepted the coming of death quite cheerily,
being willing to go, he said, as he had 'had a good innings.' In
spite of his traditions no humble reliance on the Blood of the
Saviour! In saying that his affairs have taken much time to
settle, I do not mean that there is any 'estate' to speak of, for he
lived on a pension and left five children. . . . I am glad to hear you
are making progress with the *mag. op.* I rapidly read with much
interest the first volume issued, and should like to see the rest.
The difficulty with me is that I can find so little time for reading.
The spirit indeed is willing, but after all the unavoidable work is
accomplished for the day the flesh is weak. . . . Some time ago you
sent me a card asking about Ferrars.[1] I have since had a message
from him indirectly. It appears that the war broke out before he
had left Freiburg where he remains, able, I suppose, at intervals,
to witness the bomb-dropping prowess of the Allies. . . . I was in
the National Gallery this morning. Formidable protection precautions have been adopted there — with timber and water and
sand — not to mention that all the best pictures have been stored
away. . . . My wife is in America lecturing. Notwithstanding the
depression there she is successful and the climate suits her. On
account of her absence I am spending the winter in London, and
am thus able to bear heroically the absence of that anti-cyclonic
weather which is so delightful in Cornwall and so appalling in
London. All such good New Year's wishes as may be possible!

The next letter to Perrycoste is dated April 8, and deals with a
forthcoming book of his which he had sent me in proof and which
I describe as 'vigorous and stimulating':

I am in complete agreement with your main propositions,
though personally I view most of these questions from a slightly
different angle. I should myself be inclined to say that you over-

---

[1] A British government official, retired from Burma and occupying a teaching
post in Freiburg University, who, under the name of 'H. Hamill,' had published
a pioneering book on *The Truth We Owe to Youth.*

rate morality, which I regard as simply conformity to the ever-shifting *mores* of the moment, and underrate the importance of religion, which is the expression of the fundamental emotional nature. The importance of the religious emotions (as of the sexual emotions) may be measured by the obvious magnitude of the harm they incidentally wreak.... I am rather surprised you never mention Salamon Reinach's *Orpheus* which seems to me the best (and most authoritative) history of religion on a free-thought basis. I think Maritt's book on primitive religion quite enlightening. You seem to me to overrate Petrie, who is first-class as an Egyptological explorer, but very lacking in broad and judicial vision when he begins to *discuss* things. I entirely share your admiration for Lecky. But how — oh how? — can you leave out of consideration Westermarck who in his masterly *Origin and Development of the Moral Ideas* has long and carefully documented chapters on 'The Belief in Supernatural Beings,' 'Duties to Gods,' and 'Gods as guardians of morality'!

The next letter of April 18 is largely a continuation of the same discussion:

I rather fear that your distinction between an absolute and eternal morality, which you accept, and the general *mores* of all the world is suspiciously like the religionists' distinction between their own absolute and eternal religion and the religions of all the world. I don't myself admit the existence of any rigidly absolute and eternal morality, but regard all morality as a matter of relationship, as I set forth in an article on the 'Art of Morals' in the *Atlantic* last year.

Then, in response to my correspondent's request for the loan of Ripley's *Races of Europe*, I reply that I should be pleased but can only lend it for a few days as I constantly need to refer to it for its bearing on my next book on European Psychology, which, however, was never completed.

My darling Boy [Edith wrote on the 22d of March], Oh! it is so wonderful to be in New York again and yet and yet — all seems so different now. I travelled from 9 in the morning to 7.20 at night and loved the solitude and the beautiful scenery. Mitchell and Bliss Carman met me and dragged me off to a good dinner,

and I came to the National Arts Club and slept like a child. . . .
I had a nice shock the day before I left Wyoming. A detective
in plain clothes arrived at the house and everyone got very excited. I set my teeth and realised that it was worse I'd burnt
those harmless letters than if I had kept them. He had come to
arrest one of Mrs. Ward's servants about the stealing of a watch!!
But my precious letters have all gone. However, it is best, for
if I died the curiosity in this America would raise my body! The
Socialists have got hold of your helping M., and Mrs. Ward even
asked me if I'd show her just one of your letters. You see, we're
both thought to be free-lovers, and she wanted to see if you really
cared for me!! If, as I shall be, I am badgered by interviewers, I
shall say my work is not in that range and that I believe in free
speech, but I do not believe in defying laws except by trying to
alter bad ones into good ones. They all think I look very changed
— Genthe and Mitchell and Miss Tarbell — but I'm going to do
my best to live. The pain in my heart and rheumatism is more
than I can bear, so I'm going to see a doctor tomorrow. . . . All
the vulgarity of those dreadful old days and the Bedborough case
is coming back. You, shut up in your flat, can't realise what it
is to be trying to do mystical and lovely work, and then to be
faced by things like that where to escape intrusion is impossible.
You did not mean it, and I know would not have done it for
the world — it is only the invariable truth that 'all men kill the
thing they love.' I fear the gossip has done for me. It is as in a
flash this shadow has come, and it is no use saying, 'Why can't
people see?' . . . I will leave details till I come. I have no heart
or strength to write long letters. You see, you don't see *what*
I mean. It is not you have ceased to care — it is — well, just
what it is, and perhaps only a woman knows what that is. . . .
That you cannot see it is the comedy — that I do is the bathos
and the pathos in one. However, love remains, if it is love, whether
it wears a veil or has its finger to its nose. God keep and bless
you in this new thing and may she make up for all our failures.
Your comrade who loves you.

In all the contradictoriness and contrariety of this long pathetic
letter, from which I reproduce a few characteristic passages, one
sees the expression of an organism oversensitive and overwrought

and almost altogether distraught. Forms of terror are evolved from little or nothing. The detective's mission becomes personal to herself, the naïve American inquisitiveness becomes an attack on her character and work, and the pleasant friendship I had so innocently confided to her became a 'new thing' that is to fill all my life to the exclusion of herself and everyone else.

The next letter, written two days later, shows how these hob-goblins of the mind spring from a profoundly injured physical body, and, as ever, she at once began to respond to treatment.

My darling Boy, I am being saved by the skin of my teeth. These lovely New York friends have just seen and realised and not a moment has been lost. I've had an introduction to Doctor Northrop, the oxygen specialist — old Henry Irving took it every day he was acting here, and Julia Marlowe, and all sorts of people have kept well through it. Two treatments have eased me to bear agony in my heart. It has brought life to my face and eyes again. Then the (free) hair and scalp treatment daily — for they say the roots are being killed — by the greatest specialist in the world is a bit restoring it, and doing my awful headache good. 'What does not kill you strengthens you.' I am revaluing once more, and as I do it I get news that another of my great rocks has slipped out to sea. Mrs. Drake [the early friend who had come to the rescue when she broke down as a schoolmistress thirty years before] was dying when they wrote. Somehow I feel what I want most is a little ease from physical torture and mental sadness and I am getting a new strength once more, but I can't travel yet, and anyway I've far too much to wind up and do. ... Everyone here is so good. I am being helped and it is heaven after hell. It has all sobered me and changed my outlook, and I see the way to walk very definitely. Life is one damned thing after another, and one's dreams are one's only realities. ... God bless and keep you and may life give you what you need most. My love ever. Your comrade from beginning to end.

One feels in that letter not only the exhaustion of disease and overstrain, but also the inevitable reaction from the exuberance of the first contact with America to what was, after all, a more

sober attitude in spite of the delusions that had been mixed up
with the process of reaching it.

> *My darling Boy* [she wrote on the 27th of March], I got your
> letter much more rapidly this time. Oh! how much good it did
> me! I had just heard of the beautiful death of the mother and
> it soothed me as nothing but Love-Acre and music can. She said
> good night at six and slept without a struggle or even a murmur.
> It is as if my deepest foundations are passing to newer spheres. . . .
> To me *you* are the amazing revelation. You will be glad to hear
> I am being saved, but it has been a very near thing. Doctor
> Northrop who gives me the oxygen says I must take it without
> fail every day for a month at least. The heart has been in as much
> pain as years ago at Carbis, and the specialists say my poor head-
> scalp was as tight as a billiard ball. No wonder I've had all these
> dreadful headaches. No one will ever know what I have endured
> before I broke, both in mind and body. Work to me is a help
> and a stimulant — it is the other things. . . . About the cottage
> [at Stanwell, which had unexpectedly been required by the owner,
> so that our furniture had to be removed]. I am so sorry you have
> been worried, but my directions were plain with Mrs. Mole's
> place or a safe locked storeroom, but Mrs. Rogers alone knows
> how to move the things, as Lily's picture, etc., must be carefully
> moved. I ought not to have troubled you at all. You need not
> worry over me. Whatever happens I've friends here who will
> nurse me. I am trying to nourish myself, but somehow I seem
> to have lost care, but it will all come back, I guess. The spring
> always tires us all. With my tender love and do not get too en-
> tangled in difficulties, your tired old comrade.

For a long time there have been no letters from me to quote.
Their absence I have already explained. The answer to her letter
of 27th of March is the first she preserved after this gap, and so
it may be brought in here. It is slight, but its tone is that of all
my letters:

> *My darling Wife*, I have been to dinner at Smith [I and Barker
> Smith, who had recently lost his wife, at this period invited each
> other to dinner on alternate Sundays at his home and my flat,
> the meal here being entirely prepared by me] and then by myself

to a Queen's Hall Concert, and now I write a little letter to you, as in the rapid letter I wrote to catch the mail on Friday I had not time to comment on all the points in yours. I was very relieved that you approved of storing the things at Shoolbred's. But why do you think I found it a 'trouble'? I was very glad to arrange it for you, and even if someone else had arranged it I should still have been equally concerned. I had specially told Mrs. Rogers that care has to be taken of the picture. . . . Yesterday was a very fine day, and I went with Amy for three hours into Buckinghamshire for an enjoyable little walk to two charming villages. The sunshine was beautifully warm, but we could not find any primroses in the woods yet. I keep very well (though one is still surrounded by colds and coughs) and always busy. I often lie awake at night thinking of you, and looking forward longingly to your return. I hope to hear you are feeling much better. Take care of yourself, Precious One. I wish you knew how much you mean to me.

Always your loving H.

It is a simple letter and calm, perhaps too calm in face of her pain and agitation. But it had become my part in life always to remain calm in face of her agitation and so to seek to soothe her pain, knowing that that pain was likely to pass swiftly away. I had not yet realised that she was now reaching a point where the strength to throw aside the burdens which her organisation placed on her was itself swiftly passing away.

The four letters that follow were written by Edith during the acute period of a serious attack of throat ulceration, which was not rapidly subdued even by the devoted care of physicians and friends. I note in all these letters that, as so often occurs during an attack of acute physical illness, all her nervous doubts and suspicions disappeared, the old familiar outlook was restored, and there was nothing but love and tender forethought.

My darling Boy [she wrote on the 2d of April], My heart aches and aches to see you. I'm very ill — a dreadful throat with a temperature of 102 and the least exertion makes me worse. We hope I shall be all right in a few days, as this morning I am better

than last night when the ulcers burst.... Somehow I've never
recovered and I'm worried and distracted over the war and you
and all sorts. Of course this is taking my money, and no more
lectures except Chicago are coming in. I sail if all is well on May
7th, but I'm beginning to wonder if I shall ever get back. It has
been too great an adventure, and those shocks and things threw
me back. I need no more discipline.... I can't write more. If
I've hurt you, I'm sorry, for I love you so very much and feel
like you that when we are apart it is like a child alone. I feel
utterly desolate. Bless you always, my own one.

The next three are in the same tone, and detail the course of
the illness. It suffices to quote a few lines from each:

I'm still very ill, so ill they've nearly taken me to a hospital,
but *I* know I'm getting better.... You need not worry. Dear
Mrs. Edward Brown (Miss Margaret Wilson's cousin, through
whom she has come to me) has a room next to mine for day and
night nursing; she is a born mother and nurse and oh! what she
has been to me in these dreadful nights. She says I am a little
warrior, and she will be here till Mary Prendergast takes her
room, to be secretary and nurse. All my plans are at sea, but I
know that probably I shall live to cross over and suffer again and
again. I'll send a cable when I'm out and about, but it will be
some days yet. They say strain and debility has brought it.
Don't worry. No letters from England for nearly a fortnight and
an awful blizzard raged when I was at my worst. If I go to a
hospital I shall tear up all letters and see all is packed up safe,
but I *know* I am to be better again. I love you and will cable at
week-end if possible....

Well, my Boy, the greatest throat specialist in New York has
had to be sent for, after eight days of incessant agony in the
throat; he has been twice and says it is being under par and he
should imagine shock. He cut deep and I bore it bravely at the
times he gave no anaesthetic, but collapsed later and not even
oxygen pulled me round for a long time. He says I must give up
lecturing and journeys for some time.... It is all sad — sad —
and no wonder I half dread coming back to new complications.
I'm as weak as a child, so forgive more. I can't help feeling this
is the finish and almost hope it is. I'm old now and can't start
life all over again....

The worst is over, as I've had an hour's sleep without choking and pain. Now it is a question of convalescence if no collapse comes.... I crawled off to the specialist today and he finds the throat very evil yet, but thinks there may be no more ulcers. Forbids me to speak publicly for ten days, so I've had to give up practically all. I sail on the 8th by the *St. Anne's* or the *Philadelphia*. I don't feel I shall ever reach England, but you know who has charge of my things here. My love ever.

At this point a letter of mine is preserved. It scarcely seems to show an adequate sense of the serious character of her illness, but I was always upheld by the slowly accumulated experiences of her acute illnesses in the past and her swift and wonderful recuperative powers. I had not realised, and never realised even to the end, how these powers were being undermined by disease. Moreover, although my love was doubtless more firmly resistant to the attacks of accident and mood than hers, it was not in my nature, as it was in hers, to feel the acute sudden poignancy of love in emergency, or perhaps even to respond to it adequately when presented to me.

My own darling Wifie [I wrote on the 20th of April], your three letters of the 5th, 8th, and 9th have all arrived during two days, and tell me how bad you have been with that awful throat and that you now seem to be recovering. Of course I still feel very anxious and long to get later news. I do trust you will be able to convalesce nicely, and wish you were leaving earlier, as the rest and peace of the voyage at this lovely time of the year may do much good. And I trust, too, you will have no worries, financial or other. You speak of fearing complications over here, but do not say what they are, not serious, I hope. That blizzard you mention seems to have been a bad one; I hear of it in a letter this morning (from Maine) as one of the worst ever known. We have been having the most lovely spring days lately, but the spring is late; no wild primroses yet out near London or (I hear) in Buckinghamshire yet. Those I enclose [one remains yet in the letter] came from Cornwall. It is so delicious to feel the approach of spring, and all one's cares would melt away entirely if only I felt assured that you were well and flourishing. I am keeping

you company with a bad cold in my head and on my chest, more
bronchitic than any I have ever had (getting old!), but I don't
feel ill in myself, though a little tired, and easily get about. Otherwise I go on quietly as usual, as when you left, except that now
I have the joy of looking forward to you and the spring. I take
out your new photos sometimes to look at, but they make me
long too much to see you and hug you. There is no news at all
here. I have not heard from M. for nearly a fortnight, nor seen
her for nearly two months, but suppose she will be back to London
soon for a little while. Nice if Speen proves possible. I am always
thinking how lovely to be with you there. I am now going to sit
in the Old Garden. Good-bye, my Precious Darling.

Your always loving H.

I always feel so grateful to the dear people who are looking
after you so nicely.

I reproduce this letter in full, for the tone of it, without any
doubt, is that of all the letters that are missing.

On the 15th she had written from the Hotel Flanders:

This, my darling Boy, is only a line. I'm convalescing but I'm
terribly weak. Poor me! I just seem unable to face it all. I'm
moved here to be near the throat specialist for a week or so.
The only thing now is to get strength at a minimum of expense.
Try not to worry. *I* try, but I'm in hell with those old nervous
feelings and the worst weakness possible, and the noise in New
York is *awful*. I'll try and cable, but I've no money now and it
has been a fearful time. I love you ever. . . . Oh! this ghastly war.
. . . I've written for Speen Cottage. Try not to worry. I've done
my best and anyway I feel you are safe. My Dear — I fear I've
hurt you and yet I've suffered so and my heart seems broken.

Your own Wifie

Next day she writes, for once not dating the letter, but the post-
mark is of the 16th:

My Precious One, just a line on receipt of your lovely letter.
Oh! God! have I hurt you and I love you so — such a love and
yet I seem to have hurt you and you me. I'm trying to recover.
If I had had this break on the ocean I should have died. I've
never felt so ill — never — but I'm struggling on. Yes — my

poor brain has been tired and I feel no use in the world. . . . We will pitch our tent together, my Love, and let no one hurt us. Save money and I will come here once more to finish all debts and you perhaps with me. Deep down I am so close that *nothing* can take me away — not even death.

There was nothing more until the 22d, and then she sent a cable from Brookline, Massachusetts — 'Convalescing with Doctor Keisker, tender love' — to which I believe I cabled a reply — and on the same day she wrote:

> *My own Precious Boy,* Oh! Child! — oh! my Darling — I'm aching and aching, but you are suffering and in despair. At last I am with Doctor Laura Keisker and her sisters in their lovely home here. [Doctor Keisker had been a correspondent of mine for some twenty years.] They want you to come, but I know you can't. Get M. and Amy to see to you, and cheer up. I'm trying to get strong. I've had a brutal and horrible attack, and the complications, and I was nearly alone in the hotel at last. Mitchell has been divine. I would have died but for him, and he persuaded me to come here and got me somehow on the train. It was a terrible journey, but I've relaxed and am in bed in a wonderful room and such weather, but I toss over you all the time — lest I've hurt you. My Pet — it was just that eternal belonging which made me feel the foundations of the deep were gone when you seemed to have gone. I love you so, and maybe my illness and tiredness broke me up. I can't write much — I'm terribly weak — terribly. [There is an irregularity in the handwriting of this letter, though it remains clear, never seen before.] There is nothing to do but to lie and sleep and relax and give in. . . . My plays are published here this week — if only I could have borne up to speak at the Dramatic League and Chicago. Oh! Havelock! let us come and live over here one day.

I never took seriously this invitation to go across to America, which also came, I think, in a letter from Doctor Keisker. I regarded it as a kind formality on the part of Edith's hostesses and in my replies I seem not even to have mentioned it. The crisis appeared over, the date of departure was close ahead; so that even if I could overcome the practical difficulties, the journey seemed useless. I never supposed that, though there was no emphasis in the invitation, they really were anxious that I should come over to take the responsibility of bringing the invalid home, an invalid whose convalescence was by no means so advanced as her letters seemed to indicate. Perhaps — in spite of that 'They want you to come, but I know you can't' — perhaps I failed here. And my heart contracts at the thought that if the positions had been reversed she would never have failed me. Long before she would have begged, borrowed, or stolen the necessary money, and flown across to my side. But I know, and she knew, that my nature and my devotion were not of that impulsive kind. Once, once only, on her return, she gently referred to my neglect to respond to that invitation, without any reproach. I made no defence. But I understood then that the issues had seemed graver on that side than I had realised on this side.

It was a week before the next letter, the last from America, was written. It is dated the 29th of April:

> *My darling Boy*, I'm dreadfully weak and ill yet. I shall of course sail on the 8th if able, and you'll get a cable, but I'm not fit to face anything. Dear, send Lily's picture when you can to T. — it is safer there. The things at Shoolbreds will furnish a flat for you and Amy and M. if I die, but I don't suppose I shall. I never do. All this cruel illness has taken my strength and money, and Failure is in my brain and heart. Doctor K. and all are so good, but it is no use — I've endured the unendurable. Oh! Havelock — if stupid interviews are in the papers they are cooked up from last year. All sorts of things are wanted from me next year, but I'm having to let them slip. You will upbraid, but I've done my *uttermost* — every way. Last night was the first real long sleep. The quinsy poison got in me and I was forlorn and lost in New York, as people were afraid of my throat. Hell — hell — hell — it has all been. Mitchell has been divine — just divine — he got me here somehow — will send my forlorn person across to you — for what? Oh! Havelock — Havelock darling — I feel that the foundations of the deep have gone if you are merged

in someone else. I've never recovered it — and yet I'm glad of it in a great way — glad you've someone to help and comfort you. I've done my uttermost.... I've had grippe, quinsy, etc., and *had* to get about too soon. They want me to stay on till I'm better. I don't know anything — I'm too ill to worry and yet I worry all the time. I love you always and belong — if only, only I could see you and be comforted and blest — your own Wifie.

Well, indeed, I knew that attitude, so inconsistent, so wrong, so natural, so childlike. I knew that my arms alone could soothe her to peace, and perhaps have saved her. I knew it was the moment when she needed me most, and the whole ocean lay between us. Well may she have found my eyes sad, sad with a prophetic inextinguishable sadness, when we gazed so long at one another across the gangway at Tilbury.

When this letter reached me the 8th of May had passed and no cable came to tell me of her departure. I grew restless and wrote again. The letter came back following her and only reached her some weeks after her return. She preserved it. Here it is; so few of my letters of this period have survived that it may be well to reproduce it in full:

My ever darling Wifie, I have been restlessly awaiting cable to say you sailed on Saturday, and it has not come, and so I suppose I must conclude that you have not left. I shall be very anxious until I hear from you, but in the meanwhile it is better to chance another letter to New York. The *Lusitania* was a great shock to me, more than anything that has happened in the war, and all the more as the news came on the very day you were to sail. If, however, you were coming on the American Liner it does not mean any real risk to you, and in any case all sorts of precautions will now be taken. However, you will doubtless do what seems best, and I only wish you could have left a little earlier.... I had your sweet and pathetic letter of the 29th yesterday and am so sad that you still feel weak and depressed. Of course you need not feel depressed; you have had great success, not 'failure.' In the same way it is of course quite ridiculous to refer to me as 'merged in someone else'; I can't think what I can have said to put so silly an idea in your head. M. is quite nice and a very pleasant companion, but she has no power to help or comfort me; I should never dream of telling her I *needed* help or comfort. It will make no difference at all to me when she goes away. It takes me years to get really attached to a person. Amy means much more to me. And you know, or you never will know, that only *one* person has really hold of my heart-strings, for good or for evil. I shall never have any peace or happiness till I can put my arms round you once more. You are never out of my thoughts. I long to get away from London after six months here without the smallest break (the sight of the lilacs makes me feel faint), but I couldn't bear to go away with *anyone* but you. I would give anything to know you are on the way back.... *Why* should I 'upbraid' you, my Darling? I cannot think of any reason why, and there is nothing but love for you in my heart.... I wanted my cable to you, 'All well,' to mean a great deal and comfort you a little.

Always your belonging H.

To measure one's feelings towards the people one cares for is never quite pleasant. But I felt called upon to do it under the circumstances, and, having done it, I can recognise still today that as regards Edith every word yet remains true. If there is some modification as regards M. and if I should now speak of her with a greater degree of affection, that is simply in accordance with what I have said in this letter: 'It takes me years to get really attached to a person.'

The cable, which had been left to a friend to despatch, came at last. All the unhappy circumstances of her departure I only learnt later. She had sensibly selected an American boat, the *Philadelphia*, to travel by, as probably safer than an English vessel, since America had not yet entered the war. It so chanced that the news of the torpedoing of the *Lusitania* — one of the most fateful and for most people the most dramatically tragic events of the war — reached New York the day before the *Philadelphia* left. The result was that passengers for England with one consent rushed for greater safety at the last moment on to the *Philadelphia* which thus became overcrowded and excessively uncomfortable. At the best, it was an old boat overrun with vermin and sickening for a sensitive invalid to travel in. Naturally, also, the whole boat was filled with the atmosphere of nervous apprehension and the perpetual expectation of danger. Edith was too brave to be crushed by this atmosphere, but she had her own more abstract nervous terrors, always associated with illness, when she craved for my arms, and the whole voyage seems to have been a nightmare of agony to her, though she fortunately had two kind women acquaintances on board, who were a source of comfort. But the Atlantic voyage, which under better conditions had been a restorative, failed now when she needed it most. There could, indeed, have been no worse experience for a scarcely convalescent invalid. It was one of those mischances which henceforth were so often to befall her.

Part XIII

XIII

The ship was to arrive at Liverpool, and the day before it was due I went up to Liverpool and was careful to select a comfortable hotel, the Saint George, for her reception. The formalities to be gone through next day before I could reach the ship-side were so confusing that the *Philadelphia* was already being moored alongside the wharf when I came up to it. I speedily saw her amid the sea of faces on the ship and she immediately saw me. 'Are you alone?' was almost the first question she asked. It appeared afterwards that a silly journalistic woman acquaintance on board had suggested to her that I would come accompanied by my new friend M. and in her shaken mental condition she had accepted this suggestion as a possibility. But in the delight of seeing her, I overlooked the disconcerting significance of this question. On her side, too, the excitement of seeing me at last had a vivifying effect so that at first I could see little change in her appearance and felt reassured. It was a sweet reunion. When all the formalities of landing were at length accomplished, she came with me to our comfortable hotel and she spent by my side the most restful night she had known for many weeks. But after the prolonged and extreme phase of nervous exhaustion she had passed through, it was far more than one night's rest that she needed. Next morning she was not inclined to get up; she wished to spend a few days quietly at the hotel before moving on to London. I argued against this; it seemed to me awkward and inconvenient for her to spend the day in bed in an hotel; Liverpool was not a pleasant city to stay in; it would be better, and she would be more free, if we went direct to London, to the Brixton flat. So I argued: I knew that in the past if she were firmly convinced of the desirability of staying she would have resisted my arguments and I would have been willing to drop my objections. But after a time she yielded. I failed to understand that she yielded, not because she was convinced, but because she was tired and weak; she had lost her old energy of resolute self-assertion. She dressed and we came to London. But before we reached Brixton, she began to show distressing signs of exhaustion and irritability. I realised that her instinct had been right and that it would have been better to prolong the peaceful and happy period of rest which had begun so beneficently at Liverpool. It was not the last mistake I was to make. During a quarter of a century I had been slowly acquiring knowledge by which I continued to be automatically guided. I could not quickly realise that the conditions had changed and that my knowledge was no longer to the point.

I was, however, soon to receive very definite indications of the profound underlying change that had taken place. There was usually indeed the old affection in her attitude towards me. Soon after her return she wrote a careful letter (keeping a copy as was not usual with her) to the man friend on whose help and kindness she had much relied in America, but whose conduct at the end had seemed to her strange and incomprehensible. In this letter she referred beautifully to my steadfast devotion. I fancy there may have been a feeling at the back of her mind that the qualities, to which she was by no means insensitive, of surface chivalry and gallant attentiveness in her brilliant American friend had for a moment seemed to reveal a lack in me, and it would have been a legitimate feeling. But it must have been soon after her return, at Brixton, when she was in bed one morning, not feeling well, that Amy called. I left them alone for a while, and Amy with kindly intentions, but not happily inspired, spoke of my care and kindness and hoped that would soon help her to get strong. A few minutes later, when I returned to the bedroom after seeing Amy out, I found that during the moments she was left alone she had swallowed a number of morphia tablets. Nothing had happened to worry or upset her, only the visit of Amy for whom she had long had a genuine almost affectionate regard. The act was unpremeditated, inconsequential, a child's act. She quickly told me at once what she had done: she meekly swallowed the simple emetic I hastened to prepare; the tablets were speedily returned and no ill results followed. I think she was rather pleased at the concern I showed. That revealed to me, more clearly than anything else had, that her nature had been undermined and the fibres of her soul as well as her body weakened. For never before, in any mood of depression, had she given evidence of suicidal thoughts, to say nothing of suicidal attempts; they could not enter the cheerful, sanguine, courageous scheme of life, which was in part natural to her and in part slowly built up. But this was not the last incident of the kind in the months that followed, to render even more acute the anxious apprehension with which my thoughts were concentrated upon her.

After a few days at Brixton we went to Speen, according to the plan she had made in America with my full agreement, for the weeks we had spent in the same old house there the autumn before were still a delicious memory. At the same time the horse and pony and trap, which had been left in the care of the Stanwell friend, were also sent to Speen. It turned out a beautifully bright and warm summer: we could not have been more pleasantly and comfortably situated. We had, I know, many calm and happy moments together, and the letters I received during the occasional days when I was away in London bear witness to her affection. But, somehow, it is the more poignant and anguished moments which have cut deepest into my memory, and I know that even the more peaceful hours of my life there that summer had beneath them a perpetual undercurrent of apprehensive solicitude. Certainly, if ever I was at fault before, I know I cannot reproach myself with coming short in love and tenderness at that time. In one way I was better able to help her than ever before because, largely owing to her absence in America, I had been able, by living simply and working, to improve my financial position and so to assist her with greater ease in the little money troubles which, as ever, often beset her. I remember my simple pleasure in being able once, when in the nervous flurry which would easily affect her in these days, she lost two pound notes when taking her ticket at Marylebone, to replace them at once in spite of a protest on her part; I could not always have done that so easily in earlier days when we sometimes had literally to count our pence. It was during this summer that stumbling on the rather rough lawn she fell and sprained her ankle, whereupon I sprang towards her exclaiming unconsciously, and to her pleasure, 'My baby!' It was my business and pleasure, when the foot was getting better, to rub it with embrocation as soon as she was in bed at night; sometimes I gave it a kiss during this operation, and she liked that little token of love and would playfully hold up the foot, like a child, to be kissed when I approached.

But there are more painful memories. I was constantly reminded how, in spite of a show of the old energy, she was really enfeebled in body and mind as never before. The book on James Hinton which she had been working at for years had necessarily been laid aside during the American visit. Sometime before, with her sanguine enthusiasm, she had secured from the publishers a considerable advance on account of royalties — a plan I have always avoided — and now the publishers were worrying and almost threatening her over the long delay. They knew of her activities in America and naturally could not believe that she was not well enough to complete the book. She started toiling at it again, but it was a peculiarly difficult book, not only on account of its subject, but because of the vagueness and repetition of Hinton's copious manuscript. In the morning I would take down her cushion — 'Lily's cushion,' which I cherish yet — and her large despatch box of papers to the revolving shelter on the little lawn, and here she would come to puzzle over her task, arranging the endless slips of notes she had made into order and pinning them on the table before her, while I would recline in my hammock chair with my work near-by, turning the shelter round from time to time in accordance with the sun or wind; if I were not in sight as she worked she would complain, though for me it was rather easier to work when not in sight. I could see she was not strong enough for the mental strain of this tedious task, but it would have worried her more to leave it undone.

Once or twice a week she would go to London for the day, or for a day or two, with or without me, for appointments at her club, and sometimes we would go to Brixton. She would drive to High Wycombe, leaving the horse and trap at the Red Lion. In the evening she would often be exhausted. There was, too, a new and alarming feature about this exhaustion. Often in earlier times she would be tired and irritable after one of these full days into which she put so much activity. But after a good dinner, with a little claret or Burgundy, she would at once become herself again, full of her mischievous cranks and quips. Now there was an ominous change. The dinner was the same, but it no longer had the same effect. It was precisely in the evening after dinner, in the hour or two before bedtime, that she was most depressed.

Evidently her resilient strength was going; she could no longer react normally to the refreshment of food; it was merely an added strain. She would sit before the great fireplace of the Old House, and I near her, in a spirit of complete dejection which nothing would move, and bring forward afresh the grievances which no arguments could touch. The old tenderness had not gone, but it was in abeyance and could not be aroused even when she lay in bed with the doors open between us. Sometimes she could not sleep, and then, I am sure, her melancholy was at its worst. She told me one day that in the early morning she had quietly gone down to the well just below my window with the intention of throwing herself down it, but, she added, had not, at the last moment, the courage to do it. My state of mind became even more apprehensively anxious, and though it was a lovely summer and I had much work, and the little garden was an ideal study, I could not but feel the strain which was upon us both.

There was always some unhappy incident to increase the depression. She had been affectionately attached to the pony she had had for so many years and to the donkey of beautiful disposition born on the farm at Carbis, and had always carefully looked after their welfare and comfort. Now they were both growing old and unhealthy and she felt that the last duty of putting them safely and easily out of life was laid upon her, even though she felt that with their death she was severing one of the last ties that bound her to earth. She arranged that they should be destroyed in accordance with the best humanitarian method. One day we drove into High Wycombe — she had latterly been harnessing pony and donkey together — for the last time. To me was assigned the duty of seeing the deed properly done — as formerly when Jock was shot — while she went into a stable, for though she never lacked courage, there was no need to court unnecessary pain.

After that, when she went to London, she was driven to and

from the station by a local man. In the evening I would walk a mile or so along the peaceful silent road amid the hills to meet her, and hear her clear voice talking to the driver perhaps five minutes before the trap appeared. On other days we would towards evening, if not earlier, take a little walk together into the woods which are so delightful around Speen, and of such walks my memories are happy, for that time at Speen, like every time that ever I spent with her, was not all pain. This I may still see in her letters during this period. They reveal that immense tenderness which had accumulated around us, even though that tenderness became sometimes so poignant that perhaps neither of us knew whether it was joy or pain.

Soon after we went to Speen, her friend Y. joined her there and I stayed in London.

> *My darling Boy* [she wrote immediately after I left] I do pray you are all right. You looked so sweet when you went away and I loved you more than you ever can tell. Y. is utterly dear. She knows how to massage for circulation, but I never slept till four for no reason at all. If you care to go with Amy for your week to Somerset *now*, do, or I can arrange for Y. to return later. Let me know by return.... These motor drives and massage and the realisation of many wonderful aspects of love in you too, and perhaps even in me, may give me the cure here, after all, outside Aix. The back of my head is very bad, but Y. thinks she can help it. We've talked out lots of things. When you come back we can easily have M. here one day. I hope and feel when you see me next I may have turned the corner. I shall think of you with M. tomorrow: say I hope she will come here before she sails. *I mean this.* I've waged it out at last. I miss you and long to hear you are rested. No more, as it makes my head ache.

A little later she wrote in pencil:

> *My darling Boy*, I am feeling very ill — my head and congestion with the cold wind is more than I can bear. Last night was horrible — I just feel I can bear no more. Y. is so sweet, but she must be feeling it a dull time. I long to see you, but I am glad you are free to work and see people.
>
> With my love always, your Wifie

That note, undated, shows how the strain of physical depression sometimes kept her outlook normal; the next, which must have been written very soon after, shows less physical but more emotional depression.

> Alas! I still feel far from well. I had best just sleep away. You have all got those who can be more than I can ever be now. Something has killed me, I know. Y. writes and talks and thinks of her new friend always and you have all you need. I am a mere encumbrance. If all is well, we shall motor up on Tuesday if fine. My longing to see you is very great, but somehow the sadness of worse than death is over me. I know I am very ill and just cannot die. I hope Amy and M. are all right and a comfort. I will wire on Tuesday if we are on our way. Be prepared, darling. I may come on to Brixton.
>
> Your ever loving and despairing Wifie

That letter is characteristic of what I am sure was often her state of mind during the twelve months after the breakdown in America, if not indeed until the end. There had always been moods of self-depreciation — her own inferiority was so brutally hammered into her in childhood — which her sanguine self-assertion, the 'masculine product' as Adler called it, could not entirely crush. But now that brave spirit had been broken by disease, and the self-depreciatory mood was unfettered. So I explain much in her actions at that time. It was not true, it was never less true, that those she loved no longer had need of her. But it had become difficult for her to believe. In another letter a few days later she writes from the Lyceum Club where she often spent the night to avoid the fatigue of coming out late to Brixton:

> Your letter is very beautiful and perhaps you are right in all you say. A young married woman is dying in this club, with two doctors with her now, from an overdose of something. I wonder what maggot got in *her* brain. Y. is very sweet and I am a little easier. I saw E. S. [her friend and doctor] yesterday and she says I must do *no* brain work for two months and have no worry at all.

There are no more letters until a month later; we had been together at Brixton and at Speen. Then, on the 26th of June, I went for a few days to Somerset with Amy — the last time, it chanced, that I ever went away with her — and Edith arranged for Y. to come to Speen the day before. But by one of the mischances that were always befalling us at this time, on that very day Y. had an accident with her motor-cycle and was slightly injured, and Edith waited at the station in vain. Edith wrote next day to tell me of this trouble:

> Tragedy pursues us. . . . We got here at 8.30 and I am glad we did it now. She is fearfully bruised, but sweet and very brave. If I had wired or gone back to you, I should have put you out or worried you and I did not want to do that. So my dream-week of motoring won't be and it is all a big expense, but it can't be helped. . . . I wake every hour, but escaped the worst torture, as I had a big battery treatment yesterday. I do hope you are all right. Why I still live is a puzzle, for I shall always feel in the way, as you know, but I may get to America once more. I am hoping for a wire from you as I write and then I can post this. We've been lying in the sun and I have slept quite a long time. I shall come up on Friday for a long treatment, and then to you at the flat and go straight to bed. Have a lovely time of peace and sunshine, darling.

Next day, still depressed, she writes to me in Somerset:

> I am glad you are having such a nice time and at last recovering from your cold. Y. is much better, but her bruises are pretty bad. Yes — it has been a great disappointment not to motor, but I am at last learning that to live hour by hour as well as one can is the only thing left for me to do. I shall try to see M. on Friday before treatment and then come on to you. I am very sad and feel that now you are going up in health and wealth and I am not — only longing to die and can't. Heigho! My love to you and greetings to Amy.

She refers to Aix. It was natural that at this breakdown in health we should think of the breakdown of ten years earlier

and how swiftly she had risen up, body and spirit, under the
reviving influence of that beautiful valley which had remained a
dream of delight to us both. It is true the illness was not the
same nor were the circumstances of the time the same. So I
wrote to our old friend Doctor Blanc, still the leading physician
of Aix — though he died a few months later — setting forth
Edith's condition and asking whether he thought it would be
benefited by a visit to Aix, and whether war conditions would
admit of such a visit. He replied with friendly kindness, urging
us to come, as he was distinctly of opinion that a visit would be
beneficial, and that war conditions had caused little change at
Aix. But when we examined the matter more closely, it seemed
clear that it was undesirable for an invalid to face the difficulties
and delays of the journey under war conditions, while the expenses
of such an expedition were beyond my means, or hers. So we
were both content to abandon all further thoughts of Aix.

But, in Edith's mind at all events, there were thoughts of our
going together farther afield than Aix-les-Bains. She was already
beginning to look forward to another visit to America, expecting,
with her ever-sanguine spirit, to carry on to a better issue the
success which had been so disastrously interrupted on her last
visit. She had always longed for me to accompany her to America,
and now that cherished idea became more insistent; she never
quite gave it up, even to the end of her life, when she was arranging the details of another American adventure. In October of
this year 1915, writing to her lecture agent, she says: 'Everything is opening before me in quite a wonderful way. The
moment the war is over I shall make arrangements to return to
the States. Probably my husband will come with me, though he
might not stay long in New York.' There were, I imagine,
several elements in her desire for my presence, though she
scarcely formulated them all definitely. There was the real need,
amid the loneliness of an alien crowd, of even the mere physical
comfort of my nearness which always meant so much to her in

moments of depression. There was the desire to make clear to the world that in spite of the doubts which, she nervously imagined, had spread abroad, I stood openly beside her in close association. She would protect me, she said, against the social life which she knew I found so repulsive. But she also once proposed that I should sit on the platform while she lectured about me! I thought, and many of my friends thought, that for anyone who was naturally and habitually such a recluse, the situation would be a little ridiculous. Olive Schreiner took this view and remonstrated to Edith that I must just be left to decide for myself. But Edith could not entirely give way, and finally I made a half-promise that I would perhaps join her in Bermuda or California. It was the only occasion on which we ever had any difference of inclination on any question of an expedition together, big or little.

It was to this that the next letter (July 12) refers, written when she was spending a night, as sometimes happened when she wished to be in town, at the Lyceum Club:

> I also have a headache — partly with the idea that you are 'crushed' about America. Pray don't be. The chances are I'll be much further than that by October; and if not I will not dream of letting you go if you hate it. The people who *love* me are always ready to do what *they* like, but not what will save me! . . . If I can come to you I will wire, but I expect not. Y. was very sweet, but I felt, as I am feeling more and more, that you all just need to feel I'm 'safe' and that to me means dead. Edward [Carpenter] thinks America would do you a lot of good. He thinks I look very strained. . . . I love you and hope you will have a nice time with M.
>
> Your ever loving Wifie

The reference to being 'safe' refers to a remark of mine once that I was content, even though not with her, so long as I knew that she was happy and safe. It was not, I fear, a felicitous thing to say, and she had responded at once: 'Then you would be content if I were dead?' Next day she wrote:

My darling One, I also was feeling dreadfully depressed, but I believe it is this awful war. Child — don't worry. I am trying all I know how to get strong. I cannot bear you to be sad — it *hurts* as mothers are hurt.

Just a good night from her mother to her babe [she wrote two days later from the club]. Bless you, my darling, and give you something more worth while than I am. What will cure me will be the renewing power to help.

This, my Darling Boy, is only a line to say that if you *want* me, I'll come to sleep on Saturday night, and go to Mitcham with you in the morning. M. will tell you what a nice time we had yesterday. I've decided not to say any more about America to you. It is for you to choose, as it is for me to choose. It seems my only way to go, and if I must go alone I must take chances once more. I felt I could never be separated from you so long again or I'd die, but you see I never die, and it is no more selfish of me to leave you than for you not to come with me. Anyway, I feel it is my only throw to get square about money. Life anyway is too sad for words. You have two devotees left with you, and I have only a cursed sense of duty to comfort me. I think of you and love you more than you know and am facing more than I ever did in America. I shall never dread dying because I leave what I had imagined once would miss me.

Then, as still, that difficulty over America was poignant for me, and the consciousness of failure accompanied my profound instinct against going. I note the melancholy touch of desolation at the close of her letter, and next day she wrote: 'I feel — like always when there is anywhere to go with me — you do not really want to go tomorrow.' Yet she had never been so surrounded by devoted friends as at that time, nor, so far as I was concerned, had I ever felt so tenderly near to her. That I was never anxious to go to see strangers was true enough.

The visit to Mitcham, to the house of an artist acquaintance, duly came off. It was almost the last little expedition we ever went together. The artist (Hagborg) utilised the opportunity to make a drawing of me. At that time Jo Davidson, the sculptor, had just modelled my bust, in two sittings, with feverish energy. Edith had come to the studio to see the result and I have elsewhere recorded her remark to the effect that it was not like me, and his retort: 'You have never seen him!' I expect she would have found more like me the vividly alive bust executed twenty years later by the Hungarian sculptor, Strobl.

In her next letter, so chances, she refers to this visit to Davidson's studio: 'The bust gave me a conglomeration of feelings.' I imagine that she was impressed, as I was, by the burden of reflective melancholy the sculptor had found in my face. The bust must, however, have had some resemblance, for some five years later, when I first met Joseph Conrad in a theatre, his first remark was that he had recognised me afar, as he had seen the bust in Davidson's studio. The remark, if I may accept it, was significant of accurate observation in memory.

There is an interval of over a month during most of which we were together at Speen, I busy in writing and sending off articles, mostly to America, and Edith, among other things, struggling with her study of Hinton.

The only letter is this interval was when Y. was staying with her for two or three days and I was in London:

> It always seems as if I was walking on one leg or had lost an arm when you are away. We went to the Coliseum and had a French lunch, but all but three shillings has gone. Y. returns to town by the 6.30, so you will arrive before she leaves and I may want a few shillings to refund which I will return from my cheque. I had my treatment and E. S. says I am much better, but must go slow. I hope you are having a lovely time, my Sweet One, and thinking only of what I feel for you and not of any rough things. I love you ever.

A letter from Whiteley's Stores to Brixton on a morning we had gone up from Speen together runs:

> *My Darling Boy*, Your sad face haunts me. Surely there is enough anguish in the world without people who love one another

as we do adding to it. Have a sweet time with Amy, who will do you good. I shall be rested by myself perhaps and arrive to-morrow at High Wycombe to meet you by your train. I've had a big scrimmage, but got a lot done.... Bless you, my Child — I'll teach you as Duse did her acting lovers — how to be kind to me. You are not to think it is even half your fault.

> Your own loving Wifie

I do not know what that letter referred to, but the note of reaction in it is one that often followed moments of irritable anger or scorn. I never quarrelled with her, but I can well believe my face was sad, for I felt how deeply and perilously disease had touched her.

The next letter (September 17), more than a fortnight later, and the last I possess written to me from London, begins with the same words:

> Your face haunts me, but so does my own.... My heart feels tired and I long to die. However, such is love. I love you and ever shall and while you really need me shall be there. Sleep and rest and bring your dear self safely here tomorrow.

During the weeks that followed, when we were always together at Speen or at Brixton, there were no letters, but I well recall how worried we were as to how we would spend the winter. She was undergoing electrical and other medical treatment in London, coming up for this about twice a week when at Speen, but we neither of us regarded it as desirable to spend the winter in town, where we never had spent it once since our marriage. I saw no alternative to Cornwall, and was even hopeful of benefit there, although I knew that in some respects it was no longer an ideal climate for Edith. After all, our home was still there — a peaceful home in a mild and wholesome air; she had dear friends at Saint Ives and the common people all round regarded her as almost one of themselves. Moreover, the tenancy of the couple to whom she had sublet Rose Cottage was now ended. But Edith displayed a strong repugnance such as she had never shown before, though, it is true, after twenty-five years of work that was sometimes drudgery and worry, Carbis was already losing the attraction it once held for her. But she could give no reason for her repugnance nor put forward any alternative plan. So my proposal conquered, and if, as the result seemed to show, I was wrong, I do not know what else could have been done, and at all events she never reproached me.

When staying at the Lyceum Club, she had been waited on by an American housemaid who was leaving the club. She was drawn, as servants usually were, to Edith, who had found her good and attentive. The girl's family had belonged to Cornwall: she wished to go there herself, and graciously consented to come from this Piccadilly club to our simple little cottage as a general servant. That turned out to be another unfortunate event; there was no end to them now.

After so long an absence and the departure of the tenants, Rose Cottage required much attention. Edith went down before me at the beginning of November to see to this, accompanied by her friend Y., but without the new servant. On the way down she had met in the train a casual acquaintance who told her of Cadgwith at the Lizard and of a pleasant house to stay at there. Meanwhile I was feeling the strain of the summer, though busy with work, and suffering just then from neuralgia and abscess in the mouth. She wrote next day, after referring to money difficulties:

> I would not go to Cadgwith, but I simply am tired to death, and this cottage has only two rooms available as yet and it is all confusion and I can't cope with more difficulties yet. I ran and flew and worked yesterday and walked to Saint Ives for food and then from Carbis Station, and that horrible Doctor —— came in at 8.30 and stayed till 11, our first night. I'm up now at 6 and settling heaps of things. It is really sweet here and you'll love it, but endless little things to do. Y. is quite sweet so far. I keep thinking how strong I'll make you here — we should have a lovely winter. We go today to Cadgwith; I've heard of nice rooms. I think we'll come back Saturday night. I shall try to rest com-

pletely. I am sending you a little cream. Remember after next week I shall be able to put you up, but I shan't be straight, as they've left the place in an awful mess. *Later.* Your letter here. Darling, it distresses me dreadfully. Do take care. Let me hear at Cadgwith. I love you and long for you to be better.

She little knew, and my apprehensive mind never guessed, how sadly the 'lovely winter' would turn out.

But it began well. Her first letters from Cadgwith were the most buoyant and cheerful I had received since her return from America and they were the last that ever were so. It must have been in answer to the first of these, which somehow I do not seem to have, that I wrote the last letter of mine she seems to have preserved, and on that account, and because it is fairly typical of those that are lost, I quote it in full.

> *My darling Wifie,* I was disappointed to have no letter from you this morning, but it has come in the middle of the day, and I am most delighted and relieved to hear that everything seems all right and that you were able to rest in bed. It is still as bad as ever here, howling wind and pouring rain. Do take care and don't do anything silly for Y. or anyone. I enclose a little note as a present — to spend on being careful. When your letter arrived, Smith [my old medical friend] was here and had just dug his knife into me with most beneficial results. I had had another awful night. Now if I avoid cold I hope to be soon all right. Amy looked in this morning and brought me some ox-tail soup, and will probably look in again. I got my *New Republic* article [on Rémy de Gourmont, then lately dead] finished yesterday, in time, but it was an heroic effort. I shan't attempt anything more at present but little poddles. I suppose it is the result of rundownness, etc., as I have no bad tooth. I am quite comfie and all right here, and in my recent condition have been thankful to have no one to inflict myself on.
>
> Always your loving H.

She wrote from Cadgwith on the 7th of November:

> *My Darling Boy,* Really Fate *is* kind — the weather as far as sun goes is like June and this place is gorgeous and cheap and

comfortable. You and I must come some day soon. Yesterday we walked five miles and took our lunch — wonderful sands and valleys and Cornish sweetness. War and wrangles seemed unknown. We go back, alas! tomorrow to secretaries and servants and cleaning. Y. is so dear about it all and is helping me in all kinds of ways. We leave here early tomorrow. I'm drinking absolutely nothing of alcohol in this lovely air. I sleep and eat and walk like a 25 one and am purposely not doing a line of work. ... Today we go to the Lizard in the little pony jingle we can hire and stay out all the time it is light. This coast is very guarded and they are very particular about lights. ... Try not to do too much head work at first when you come, but sleep and enjoy what I shall have ready for you. I shall send off your little box of goodies separately. Well, darling — take care. Your letters make me ache for you, for none of us except M., and she is away, seem much good to you.

She repeated more than once, on her return, the hope of going again with me. But that was not to be. The end was approaching too rapidly. Nothing remained but the wish to go alone and capture the memories of her presence in the spot where she knew the last rays of unclouded brightness that Life was to bring her. But for one reason or another that was not possible until six years later. Then I found Cadgwith even more pleasant than she had reported, and spent three winter months there, together with my old friend Arthur Symons. It was not only a pleasant and wholesome shelter from winter such as I had scarcely before found even in Cornwall, it was a spot rendered beautiful to me with the thought of her, occupying her room and sleeping in her bed, and now, as I write, I am cheered by the thought of going there yet again to commune joyfully once more with that invisible presence. Since these words were written, I have been there peacefully again and again during the winter months, by myself and finally, though not with Edith, with my dear Françoise.

She spoke in that letter of Fate being kind, but, alas! during all that period Fate was never kind to her for more than a moment, and before that same day had ended the sun was over-clouded. She wrote on returning to Carbis Bay:

> A tragedy always has to end my good times. We'd had a perfect few days and on Tuesday in walking on the upper path to Kynance Y. slipped on a high stile and hurt her back badly. I wondered if we should ever get here, but we've managed it. In the middle of the night I had a violent stomach attack, partly as a result of chill and shock. I got through, but was horribly weak yesterday when I had so much to do and nothing ready in this house and Millie [the new servant] arriving at night; but I managed it and am a little better this morning. Y. will be in bed a day or two, but, thank goodness, is easing. Millie is wildly delighted with the 'picture world' and seems cheerful and willing. It won't be ready for a fortnight. I am thankful you are out of this muddle.

Her enfeebled and highly wrought state made her unduly sensitive to minor shocks, though even yet, it seemed, she was able to cope with them successfully; but all those minor strains, I now see, were preparing a further breakdown.

Amid the confusion of the cottage, with workmen painting and distempering, the new servant learning her work, a typist busy, her friend disabled in bed, she wrote (November 10) to me cheerfully:

> However, we are getting on, and if only Y. could get easier it would be better. We had such a lovely holiday, and so far not a horrid time except for confusion and illness. ... I am writing at six in the morning to get done. I feel I shall never get to the *Hinton* again. ... I shall be thankful when you and I are settled in; it will be very comfie and I hope we shall stay a long time. ... Well — my precious, how are you? Give my love to M. and Amy (I am writing to her one day) and love me even as I do you.
>
> Your tired old Wifie

And the next day she wrote with the same spirit, but it was clear the physical strain and domestic worries all day long were becoming too much for her. She ends up:

> Six is the only hour I have to write to you and I feel too weak to do it. Forgive more. When once you are here I do hope we shall

settle for some time. This continual moving is killing me. It seems years since I saw you and I love you and long for you, but not in this confusion. With my love and tenderness.

And the next day it is still the same story:

> *My darling Love,* Oh! it rains and rains and I wish I could see you, I'm feeling like a lonely child and long for you, but not till it is straight. I can't get Y. proper things to eat, and I've no money at all and just long to die, and I've pains and nausea again and no wonder, for I got very wet yesterday. I feel just to see you and hold your hand would be lovely. How are you, I wonder. It seems years since we parted. *Later.* I've worked like a navvy, and there is some semblance of order out of chaos. My pet, are you so weak yet? You shall be taken such care of, and have orderliness and rest. Good-bye.

Little troubles went on accumulating, and a few days later she wrote:

> *My Darling One* — Oh! This awful gale! It has broken a window — uprooted the evergreen tree — turned over one of the sheds [in which we worked] and smashed it — and what with the rush and all I am so weak I don't know what to do. I want you so I feel I'll just be meek and sweet forever and ever! Come directly moment you can. The mere sight of you will revive me. I love you and long for you and belong to you. My pride is all broken. The continual waiting on Y. and the gale and the other things make me wonder what will happen next. Oh! I *want* you so! Say you are coming and Y. will go. We'll have no animals, but just one another. . . . Your letter just come. I feel a hunger for you so intense. I *must* see you, and yet I would not have you come a day before you want to. But I feel just to hear you say you love me and really need me would be heaven. I have a horrible fear one of us will go and the other be left, and then what should we do? Oh! — Havelock — Havelock — I feel like your little lost child who has the hope of seeing you soon. Come to me — come. Come and comfort me. My foot is aching and wants you to kiss it. . . . I fear all sorts of things and want to be reassured as you used to reassure me. Today the chimney smokes to add to things, but the house looks more shipshape. You in it seems to me all it needs.

(And now, as I write, it is Christmas Day more than six years after her ashes were scattered on the grass, and I sit alone in the room at Cadgwith where that 'lovely holiday' was spent, and a soft lullaby strain of music reaches me from a neighbouring room, and my arms are once more gently enfolding her and she lies on my breast, and my kisses and my tears are falling on her curly head.)

In a few days I was to be with her, but during that short period letters continued to come swiftly, sometimes long letters, sometimes two a day, and they were all in the same tone, and all had the same refrain of longing and tenderness. I might seem to detect in them the obscure realisation that there would never be another opportunity and that into these last letters, as in one sense they were, she must crowd the whole of her love.

> *My Darling Love* [she wrote in one] It is only six and I am in pain again. I feel the only thing that matters is to see you. I want you under my care and I don't mind what I give up for it. I want you to come the *moment* you are ready, but I wired yesterday for Tuesday [I have preserved the wire, for I must somehow have felt that everything was now becoming precious] so that you knew you had not to rush or hurry. Y. is less selfish than of old, but I dread Millie giving in, as her weakness is not being treated as a servant, and Y. is the last person to understand this; it makes a great strain. But it is you — you — I want. I've a horrible feeling you are very ill. Olive says you look so ill. Dear Heart — write and say the moment you *want* to come and it can be managed. . . . I shall be all right when we are together and able to lead regular lives. I will take much care of you. It is absurd to long for anyone as I do for you. . . . Your sweet letter has come. I'm just longing for you. Y. is going on Thursday, so come when you can. Oh! to see you. . . . The second post has brought your present of Panopepton. I fear I am confusing you with all these alterations, but it is so difficult to know what to do. I have a terror of this weather for you, and I feel we must be together as soon as possible. . . . Just to feel your hand and hold it — just to know you forgive me the pain I've given you as I do you, though I never meant it. We'll talk and plan a sweet old age to-

gether. . . . I felt last night I should literally drop dead. I don't know how we will get through till Y. goes. Everyone says how tired I look, but I'll be all right directly moment you come. . . . I've had a fearful time seeing Y. away, and my poor heart is very bad, but *don't* worry about me. I must endure and strive. Poor [W. H.] Hudson, who is with the Ranee here, is also broken up and is *so* depressed. She is sweet. I feel broken. I am no use to anyone. I feel a pathetic feeling that you too dread being with me. A new love is born in me — the love born of gratitude and understanding of how you've loved me in the most beautiful sense. Your fur is warming me outside as your love inside. Come when you want. I feel only one thing matters — to see you and hear you say I am worth while.

Next day, and just before I left London to join her, she wrote once more, and it is the last letter I ever had from her which I count as real:

Your wire is a great relief. I felt awful yesterday, and am staying in bed today, as I'm just as if I'd been skinned and peppered all over, and the war news is dreadfully depressing. You seem to think I shall be annoyed with you or something. Child — I'm always suffering and longing to be dead, but I want you more than anything in the whole world. Y. evidently wanted her holiday by the sea in luxury (which for once it could not be) and it will always be so. . . . I am going to try very hard to be all you want and not be a burden. . . . I slept like a log last night and wondered at last if it was coma. [A few months later it was so.] I was horribly lonely and all in me cried out for you. Try and stay down till we've let the place in February, and then we'll have a little time at Mullion before London. I am organising this place to go easily and it will look very nice. As soon as my poor brain and heart have recovered, I must set at the Hinton book. That through, all will be well. [Her death took place almost immediately after it was sent to the publishers.] . . . Pay Wilkinson what you can, Darling. Thank God, at any rate we have a roof over us, and warmth so far, and we 'belong' and have weathered through to a new love and life together. Such loads of horror everywhere. Never mind — you will soon be here and we will help one another to the end. I will be at Saint Erth and have a cab there or at

Carbis Bay.... Come to me soon and know I am just yours in a new and wonderful way.

Your Wifie

I linger over those letters. During the previous six months after her return from America, she had been so often in a morbid mood of depression and suspicion and doubt. But the change to her old home environment by the sea, and all the practical activities it involved, although trying for her physically, had largely restored her mental balance and brought to the surface the deep love which had, through a quarter of a century of life together, become the deepest part of herself, not to be destroyed even by her own destruction. It seemed, indeed, after being so much overclouded in America, to come to the surface in a new birth, and with a pathetic simplicity of expression rarely before manifested, for it was natural to her to be proud, independent even in love, and to veil the intensity of feeling in playfulness and mischief. No doubt it was physical weakness, the outcome of disease, which had broken down that spirit. When at last, a few months later, this phase of tender dependence passed, to yield to an unreal reaction of assumed pride and independence, a more fundamental dissolution was taking place, and the end was not far off.

I returned and all at first went smoothly. It was joy and peace to her to have me quietly at her side and it was a great satisfaction to me to be there. I felt that we were doing the best that under the circumstances was possible. Those recurring moods of melancholic suspicion which had so tortured me at Speen remained absent and she seemed on the road to recovery; I had not realised that what was happening was simply a transition to a different phase of disorder, and one perhaps even more serious. But she was obviously below her old level of health and spirit: the diabetes was active in spite of care, and even the increased dependence on me — so unlike the mischievous bravado of old — was pathetic.

It must have been soon after my arrival that, the long strain of the summer telling on me at last, I experienced a kind of general lassitude of condition which much alarmed her and she wrote (as I long afterwards learnt) to friends that I was seriously ill. She made me stay in bed in the morning and insisted on making and bringing up my breakfast. But in a few days I clearly saw that even this little strain was too much and we brought it to an end. Soon it became my turn always to prepare her breakfast. I overcame my phase of lassitude and was indeed strong enough during the following months — upheld, I am very sure, only by love — to endure the greatest tension I ever had, or ever shall have, to endure.

It was natural that I should be more tender and attentive to her than I had ever been before and that she should appreciate this more than she ever had before. She occupied as a bed-sitting-room the room on the ground floor that had once been the cottage parlour, and in my bedroom over it I was able through the floor to hear any sound and to come at once if needed. I wrote, when indoors, in the dining-room and there we both sat in the evening. Nearly every morning she liked to walk — the only method of progression now left — to Saint Ives to see some of the numerous good and charming friends she possessed there; that was the best relief and diversion for her sociable nature under the gathering physical and mental burden. I would stand at the gate and wave to her till she disappeared in the curve of the road, or often I would accompany her to the verge of the town, then turning to the moor on the left to settle down with my papers and for work.

So things went on as quietly and happily as might be until at least after Christmas. The tragic events of this winter stand out so vividly that the background of ordinary life is dimmed. I remember that Christmas seemed rather sad, but the war alone would suffice to account for that. Just one characteristic little trait dwells in my mind. A dear German Jewess friend in London had been accustomed to send her a Christmas tree of the German brand, with its little candles and other traditional items, and it was always a delight to Edith's childish temper. This Christmas the tree came as usual, though, owing to the troubles of the time, it was very small and of inferior workmanship. But Edith cherished it, and now and then after Christmas she would bring it on the table at dinner-time and light the candles for a few moments and I would note with a quiet sad smile with what patience — for patience was never her strong point — she would over and over again carefully restore the little tree's shaky balance. I doubt if these things any longer brought her joy, but they came to her with the echo of the joy of happier days. On New Year's Eve, also, the last of her life, she was able to carry out a still more old-standing custom, associated in her mind with the beloved Lily whose fascinating personality had once played a leading part in it. This was the annual entertainment of the Saint Ives Artists' Club. She was driven there and back — while I as usual went to bed — and she took the new servant Millie with her, as she had formerly always taken Priscilla, to enjoy the fringe of the festivity.

It was Millie who proved the instrument for striking a decisive blow at Edith's unstable mental poise. She slept next door, so that we could feel freer, though there was a small spare bedroom in the cottage, but she had lunch with us. That was a trait of Edith's democratic feeling, though it had not been usual in our married life, and now not only I but Edith also, in her present state of mind found this uncongenial society very trying. Millie had not the quiet and disarming charm of Priscilla, she was used to American habits, and while she had been drawn to Edith in happier days at the Lyceum Club, she had not had time to know her thoroughly and to balance her sharp tongue and uncertain moods against her warmly human disposition, her boundless generosity and kindness, all the fascination felt by those who really came to know her. Moreover, these were now not so easy to know. So an attitude of instinctive hostility grew up on both

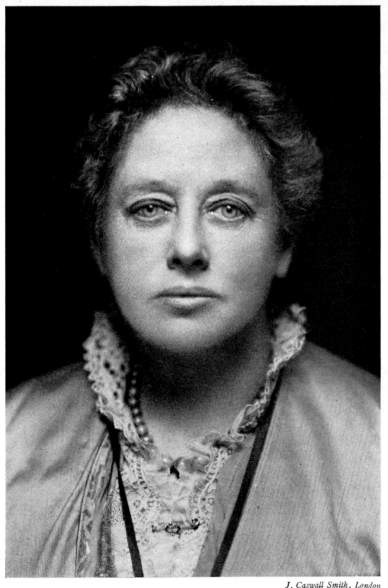

Edith Ellis about 1914

sides, and culminated one day in words of such unrestrained rudeness spoken by the justly or unjustly offended Millie that she had to be told to leave the house at once. As she went out of the front door she called up the stairs that she was very sorry for me, a mark of sympathy which I curtly repelled.

In earlier and happier days that little incident would soon have been outlived. In Edith's tempestuous career there had been many such violent scenes which she quickly forgot or laughed over. But disease had now worn thin the fibres of her nervous system and this insignificant clash sufficed to jangle them all. Millie, quite naturally, stayed on for a while next door until she could find employment, but this greatly disturbed Edith. She felt that here was an enemy close at hand to work against her among the neighbours. Even if this suspicion had been reasonable, it was quite unreasonable to suppose that a stranger could do her harm in a place where she was known so well and so generally liked. But even if in germ the idea was plausible, it sprouted up in her mind during the weeks that followed into imaginations that could scarcely be regarded as within the range of sanity. She felt sure the neighbours were talking against her, especially they were saying that she was a drunkard; so, although entirely against her tastes and habits, for she had always enjoyed a glass of wine at dinner, she firmly refused to touch any alcoholic drink. She even began to suspect that neighbours were planning an attack on the cottage for purposes of robbery, and carried a few of her little treasures to Saint Ives for safe-keeping with friends there. Our doctor neighbour, who was accustomed to look in from time to time to see how Edith was getting on, took these symptoms very seriously — no doubt not unreasonably — and formed the worst prognosis. He was a typical Irishman, a delightful talker and of kindly heart, though of violent speech, himself in delicate health and of pessimistic temperament. His opinion of the case was frankly alarming.

I cannot say that during the weeks that followed I had much

chance of gathering counterbalancing hopes. What changes there were only made her condition more pitiable and my anxiety deeper. In all her ways she became the opposite of her old normal self. She who had always been so full of energy, so fond of organisation, so house-proud, and so jealous of the slightest interference in household management, seemed to have lost all will-power and all self-pride. There was nothing she could do, and the care of the house as well as of her fell into my hands. It was fortunate that the local woman whom she had engaged after Millie's departure to come in every morning to do the housework, although a stolid silent creature without the smallest initiative, was not without a stupid kind of comprehension. She had herself once had some kind of nervous breakdown, and she took her orders from me and went through her work and seemed blind to everything, though Edith, full of vague terrors, would dread her arrival in the morning. It was my only consolation during all those melancholy weeks that she never dreaded me and, indeed, could not bear to be away from me. She never had a harsh word for me, never an unpleasant memory came to the surface, no wilful mood, for her wilfulness had left her with her will; all that defiance and independence, which had once seemed almost a part of her love for me, had disappeared.

I would prepare our breakfast in her little bed-sitting-room while she lay in bed, with the cat sitting up on her bed-table; she never forgot to know how to look after his wants, though she was a little confused and awkward in making the tea. Then the woman would arrive and in due course the hot water was taken up to the little room we called the bathroom. Here I would conduct her and leave her for her bath: there had been nothing she regarded as more indispensable than the morning tub. But now, as I knew, it would be very difficult for her to take it. Sometimes I would go down and walk up and down the garden for half an hour in the hope that, feeling thus abandoned, her will would be stimulated to action. I would come back to find her still standing beside the bath. Then it was equally difficult for her to dress. There was some objection to every garment, and this dress, she said, was too old to wear (it hangs in my cupboard now, eight years later, laden with memories) and that one too good for every day. Then as she came downstairs she would sometimes sit down on the stairs and remain there obstinately, for an indefinitely long time, doing nothing. So with her correspondence; I would suggest to her to send a line to her dear friend Y., and she, the readiest of letter-writers, would sit with her pen in her hand in front of a postcard and be unable to write a word. At mealtime, again, she, who so enjoyed her meals, would sit before the dish I had ordered or (in the evening) myself prepared, and take nothing, until, suddenly and rapidly, she would eat a little. In the afternoon, with less difficulty, I was usually able to persuade her to go for a walk with me, but, so as to avoid the fatigue of going uphill, it was always the same dull flat little walk, to Longstone and then a little way inland. Yet, dull and rather melancholy as they were, those little walks linger in memory as the times which at this period she seemed most nearly like herself. At night I would see her into bed, and tuck her up with the thoroughness she always required, as of old, and leave her with the indispensable good-night kiss. But I knew, as I went to my own room above, through the thin flooring of which I could hear every sound, that that was not likely to be the end. She could sleep but little and was depressed — in this at all events like her old self in nervous moods — by the feeling of loneliness. Worn out by anxiety, I would try, if not to sleep, at all events to rest. But I knew that for her there would not be much rest. I would go down from time to time, unable to resist the appeal of her restlessness. But sometimes, worn out and weary, I would hear her calling and long fail to respond. But, more often, I would come down, and get into the little bed and lie close beside her with my arms around her, and then it was that she had most rest, though for me the only rest was her rest.

A few years earlier I had read and been deeply touched by the

narrative in the third volume of Edmond de Goncourt's *Journal*
of the slow mental decay which preceded the death of his deeply
loved and closely associated brother Jules. In after years I have
sometimes recalled to memory — for I have felt that I could not
bear to read it again — that account of increasing failure of
nervous adjustment to life which seems so like the history of
Edith during these months. But there was another point also
about it as it returns to memory: one feels that the narrative is
the more pathetic because of a scarcely hinted undercurrent of
remorse. Edmond had clearly been irritated by the nervous
awkwardness of his brother as his mental weakness became more
manifest; he had failed to understand, and the realisation of his
failure stung him. It has been a consolation to me to feel that —
however much I may possibly have failed Edith, before then and
after, I do not know — I never failed her, scarcely even from
sheer fatigue, during those weeks at Rose Cottage when she was
relying solely upon my support. I never failed in understanding
or in tenderness or had any desire outside her.

When I first knew Edith, before our marriage, I had sent her
(as I have set down in the proper place) what has ever seemed to
me as deep and true a statement of the meaning of love, in the
essence of its passion, as has ever been made, the greater part of
the fifth chapter of the third book of *De Imitatione Christi*, in the
little translation I had made of it. Edith profoundly appreciated
that sheet of manuscript, from the first and always. She must
often have carried it about with her, for it became worn and
faded: she cherished it to the last and it lies before me now. I
quote a few lines: 'A great thing is love, a great and altogether
good thing; for love alone makes every heavy burden light, and
every unequal burden equal. Because it bears the burden without
being burdened, and makes every bitter thing sweet and delicious.
Like the living and ardent flame of a torch it ever rises and safely
passes through all.' For once in my life, during those last months
at Carbis Bay, it was mine to know the full truth of those

words so strangely inspired to a medieval monk of the Lowlands.

Such, then, is the power of love that I seemed none the worse for the constant strain. It affected my health apparently not at all, certainly less than the weeks at Speen during the previous summer. And I think that the significant difference was that there was something to do, and that something useful and appreciated. My service was accepted and my love was answered. That makes all the difference in the world, even to physical health.

The old friends at Saint Ives would come to cheer her. They were in touch with our doctor neighbour and they could see for themselves how unlike herself she had become. They were naturally concerned, and, although they saw how I had accepted the situation, they seemed almost as much concerned for me as for her. We consulted together as to the best course to take; I suppose it was the first time I had ever consulted over her welfare in her absence. But she seemed to be growing worse rather than better; the time might soon come when further help was absolutely necessary, and there was no proper accommodation to offer a nurse, even had a suitable nurse been within reach.

We thought of Doctor Hamilton of Hayle as the best man to give advice and help. She was fastidious about doctors, knowing how peculiar her constitution was, but she liked Hamilton, and five years earlier, when Priscilla was seriously ill, had called him in rather than any nearer doctor. He was one of those solid, kindly, quiet, reliable men who so often come out of Scotland, in all but kindliness the opposite of our Irish neighbour. He came, was willing to take charge of the case, and proposed that she should go to the Convent Nursing Home at Hayle, conducted by trained nurses, which Hudson had only a few days left. This seemed to us the best possible arrangement under the circumstances and I agreed at once. We anticipated difficulty in persuading Edith to go, for in all her illnesses she had never before been taken away from home, and in fact she was full of nervous terror over the removal; but in the end it proved easier than we expected; her old spirit and will had gone, giving place to a pathetic childlike docility mingled with her nervous fears. Her devoted old friends from Saint Ives, Mrs. Moffatt Lindner and her sister — Gussie and Blue as she always familiarly called them — came and packed her things and accompanied us in the carriage to the convent, and she affectionately greeted Sister Mary Basil, whom she already slightly knew, at the door — it was fortunate that an affection for nuns had persisted from her early days at the convent in Manchester — and was led away to the room I already knew which Hudson had occupied. I took rooms a few minutes' walk away, so as to be within reach if needed. In accordance with Hamilton's quite reasonable line of treatment, she was here to be entirely excluded from her world, not to see any friends, not to receive any letters; I alone was to see her, for a little while every day.

Therewith, little as I or she knew it at the time, my active life with Edith came to an end. We were to plan otherwise, but it was never to be; it was never henceforth vouchsafed to me to be of much use to her. In the following year, ten months after her death, when on a visit to Arthur Symons at his country cottage, feeling rather unwell for some unknown reason, after lunch I lay back in an easy-chair before the large old fireplace and against my usual custom fell asleep. It seemed to me that I was sitting, with Edith beside me, in front of much the sort of fireplace I was actually before, such as we had often known, and in response to some remark of hers I could not recall, I said playfully: 'You don't know how useful I am!' There was no cause for grief present to my sleeping mind, and no idea of her death; but it seemed to me that repressed tears came into my eyes. Then she seemed to rise, to stand behind me, and bending over, without a word, kissed away my tears. That dream was true to the deepest spirit of both of us, even during those last weeks in Cornwall. It was never to be completely true again.

Part XIV

XIV

Now began a period during which I was tortured as I have never before or since been tortured for so long in my life. I was outwardly calm; then and since I confided to no one, yet even today, when all is receding into the past, when nothing matters, it is only with an effort of resolution that I force myself to write of these weeks.

At first, it is true, things may possibly have seemed to me easier, though only in seeming. Every morning, after calling at the Home to inquire about the patient, I would take the train to Carbis Bay, to look after things there, to superintend the woman helper, to attend to my own and Edith's correspondence. Often I would go up the moor to lie there with my papers, as in old days, trying to attain a sense of rest, and it really seemed that there was a decreasing need for anxiety and that in her seclusion from the world Edith was improving. But — unfortunately, it proved — it occurred to me that recovery might be stimulated by allowing her to receive some little sign of affection from her dear friend Y. So, having obtained the permission of doctor and nurses, I wrote to Y. and suggested she should send flowers or fruit, but without any letter, addressed directly to Edith. She did so at once. On the afternoon of the morning on which the parcel arrived, I called as usual at the doctor's, on returning from Carbis Bay, to hear his daily report. He met me with a serious face. It appeared — to combine the information I obtained from various sources — that she seemed as usual that morning and that on receiving the parcel she simply remarked: 'So she has found me, has she?' Hardly an hour later, by means of an ingenious subterfuge, which showed premeditation, she eluded the good nurses who were watching her with care, though they had seen no reason to take precautions, locked herself in the lavatory — having just left it, but making a sudden excuse to return by herself for a moment — and threw herself from the window. She was found on the concrete pavement below moaning: 'My foot, my foot.' She had injured her foot, and also severely cut her head. For some days she lay in bed, only imperfectly conscious. But that incident was a turning-point in her disorder, the melancholic shadow that had more or less hung over her for at least nine months was entirely dissipated.

The precise psychic mechanism of the suicidal act I have never been able to grasp. Her acts were often impulsive and incalculable. But I could always grasp their significance. This act alone continues to puzzle me. It is true it was definitely the act of a disordered person. Still even a disordered mind is moved by motives, however unreasonable they may be. Why should a token of affection from a dear friend, who was associated with no seriously painful memories, have had this potent influence for evil? Moreover, how far was the act consciously planned, how far subconsciously accomplished by a sort of secondary personality? She herself, after she regained full consciousness as well as later, would tell me how puzzled she was over this question. She certainly retained no consciousness — and I knew her too well to doubt her honesty — of any suicidal intention on that morning; it is well known that any sudden shock which abolishes consciousness abolishes also the memory of the immediately preceding events. She could only conclude, although unable to understand, that it was an accident, that she had overbalanced. But it very certainly was not an accident; she herself, by some force which for the moment possessed her, had suddenly and definitely planned the act.

The physical results were not permanent, though she walked lamely many weeks afterwards; the psychic results might even be said to be beneficial. Yet the effects were unfortunate, and perhaps decisively evil. For henceforth the doctors were prejudiced and definitely established a bad diagnosis while the Mother Superior of the convent grew nervous and desired a speedy removal of the patient. So the social environment, otherwise favourable for recovery, was rendered unfavourable. It was not understood that this act was really the climax of self-destructive thoughts which had haunted her since the illness in America. She not only never again made any attempt of the kind, but, so far as I could observe, she never again had any suicidal impulses.

The patient had sought violent death, but, with the usual irony of life, it was the doctor whom sudden death overcame. One Sunday morning, about a week after this incident, that good kind man, seeming in excellent health, arrived to dress the patient's wound and reported good progress. I exchanged a few pleasant remarks with him. Within less than a hour, completing his round in his car, he lighted a cigarette while the chauffeur turned homewards and fell back dead. It was yet another of the tragic mischances which dragged Edith's feet down the slippery path of those last few months. The medical man who came to replace Doctor Hamilton was not helpful.

Meanwhile, she was slowly emerging from the mental confusion which followed the fall. The fact that the almost comatose condition which had first supervened never developed into a fatal

diabetic coma showed how much vitality she even yet possessed.
Her mental condition greatly improved, as so often happens in
association with physical lesion; most of the symptoms which had
disturbed us passed away. She remained pathetically tired and
dependent in spirit, though that, also, was in her unnatural.
Never had she so clung to me for strength and consolation. Every
evening I would spend alone with her, lying close beside her on
the bed, but outside the bedclothes, with my arm across her. This
greatly comforted and soothed her; gradually she would fall
asleep, and then I would try to slip quietly away and out of the
hospital to my own sad rooms. But it was not always easy to do
this. I would have given anything to be able to stay with her, but
the nuns offered no indication of willingness to permit such a
breach of the rules. She would plead with gentle and smiling
Sister Mary Basil that I might be allowed to lie beside her, 'only
like brother and sister,' but it was in vain. I had to go out into
the dark night, quietly closing the hospital door, almost beneath
her window, behind me, and as I walked away in anguish — again
and again it happened — I heard her clear and beautiful voice
penetrating the silence and dying away: 'Havelock! Havelock!
Havelock!'

I would sit down in my alien room and perhaps try to read —
I still have a book I was reading then and have never yet read
more of it — but when I look back at this period, it soothes me to
think that whatever experiences life may yet hold it is only once
that love can call upon us to ascend Calvary.

Yet even when the heart is most wrung some sweetness comes
to ease the pain. When I recalled the previous summer and the
suspicion and alienation then brooding over her mind, there could
not but be a delicious feeling in this tender need of my touch, in
this involuntary cry for my presence. Even though in normal
days she had usually kept a tight rein over that need and veiled
it with mischievous speech, she was at all events more herself than
ever since she sailed for America. Her old self might be outra-

geously impatient or bitter, no doubt often provoked by my awkwardness or stupidity, but swiftly grew tender and apologetic at my pain. So now, it would happen that I had not been an hour in my solitary room after having thus grievously torn myself away, before she had scribbled on any odd fragment of paper a few words of love and consolation and sent it across to me by the special nurse. In the agitation of those days only two of these notes were saved. They show, even in their incoherence, how even the unbalance of her mind threw her the more helplessly into my arms. The first is on a small scrap of an old letter:

> *My Loved One*, I *want* you *so* much at once. You must come, please, and you can go whenever you want — 10.30 or whenever you like, but because I love and want you tell this sister when I may expect you, for I want you.
>
> Wifie

The next is in shape more like her usual letters, though in substance distracted:

> *April* 12, 1916
> *My Beloved*, Don't be hurt. I love you so. Come as early as you can tomorrow and we will map out the near future and the further future if Lily wills. She alone can send me to heaven. I'll do all I can for you and all in this near crisis and would give all tonight for one of you who love me so much to send me to sleep, but you alone I need this moment. Sister is helping me with that ham, and I am loving you. I long for you, but won't upset them and you always understand. Oh! to be with you here, and they want me to go soon and you and I need each other forever. I long to see you and I want you to come early. I'm just as ever yours and you can tell the fifty darlings who love me if I die that all is well. I kiss you, sweetheart, and will help you later and you me. Come soon.
>
> Your own Wifie

An attempt was made to have her received by one or two well-known asylums in and near London. But the suicidal attempt proved an insuperable difficulty. They would not accept her as a voluntary boarder. The question of her certification as a lunatic was raised. But that was more than I could bear, except as a last resort when every other effort had failed. I knew what it would mean to her, and the thought of carrying her off by some ruse, when she was still so alive to everything round her, and leaving her a prisoner in an asylum, was more than I could bear.

Then it was suggested — I think the idea arose in my own mind — that a trained mental nurse should be brought down, so that the patient might have skilful attention and at the same time the Mother Superior be in some degree relieved of responsibility. I agreed at once. Doctor Hamilton communicated with a London mental nursing institution, and in due course the nurse arrived. In this long chain of fatal events she represents a link which I look back on with satisfaction, for she took us safely across a perilous point and there was never any further mention of an asylum after she arrived. By a rare chance she was at once a capable and experienced nurse and a human, youthful, and agreeable person, with no offensively professional airs; we discovered, some while after she came, that she was married. Edith, so sensitive to personality, accepted her at once, and became more soothed, so that, if I remember well, I soon ceased to be tortured by my farewells at night. Nothing happened to disturb her; she was slowly recovering from the fall, and seemed to be more herself mentally. The loss of will-power had gone, as well as the fantastic notions; she was craving for strength and activity; and, while before the nurse came, she could not be persuaded to touch any stimulant, she now begged me to bring her champagne, though she was not allowed to have it.

But although all was going well, the Mother Superior still wished the patient to leave as soon as possible. The nurse suggested and recommended a nursing home in London, specially for convalescent mental and nervous cases, situated near the Crystal Palace. This was an excellent plan; I accepted it, and agreed all the more readily as the home was within a bus drive of my Brixton flat; Edith took it to be a general nursing home, but that involved no difficulty.

At about this period, indeed — while the events of these days are stamped on my mind I cannot always place them in the exact order — Edith asked me, indeed implored me, to take her to the Brixton flat. I could not see my way to do so under all the circumstances. But I am still tortured by the possibility that her impulse was right and that, if I had had her close beside me at that turning-point, her mental health might have been furthered and any alienation from me have been prevented. Her own feeling I understand perfectly. My presence had always meant rest to her, and tender, devoted love. To be with me seemed to her at this time, more than ever before, refreshment and almost salvation. But she had no clear recollection of her own state during the weeks we had just passed through. She knew she had been very ill, and not herself, but it was only a vague dream to her, at most a nightmare. She was unable to realise the tension of my anxiety, or the apprehensions which all around her were feeling. She had forgotten, moreover, that she did not really any longer like living in the flat and that it was not in any case a fit place for an invalid. I would have everything on my hands and often be obliged to leave her alone, so that, should any tragic event occur, I should feel, and others would feel, that the blame fell on me. But she was not in a condition to realise the force of these considerations. Even if she had been, I think she would, in my position, have flung them aside. For years she had loved Swinburne's poem, 'The Leper,' and often read it aloud in her beautiful impressive voice in her public readings even to the end.

It is true that I fancy she was perhaps thinking, when she read it, more of Lily than of me. But I take it to myself now. It is one of the strange things that give unity to my life that at the outset the first verse of that poem should so often have sung itself joyously in my youthful brain as I carried my two buckets of water from the well at Sparkes Creek:

> 'Nothing is better, I well think,
>   Than love; the hidden well-water
>   Is not so delicate to drink.'

That seemed to express my outlook on the threshold of life, though now, as I near the end, it is the last verse that I say over again in my brain:

> 'A scribe's work writ awry and blurred.'

And I wonder whether that may not sum up my experiences of love in the world. For whatever the world may think of me, of good or of evil, of myself I only think as of a lover, very humbly, a lover who has fallen far short of perfection. Nothing in the end really matters but love. For other things are of the individual, but love is of the species. It is Nature, or, as the early Christians said, Love is God.

When we reached Paddington Station, I had the first indication of a change of phase in her mental state, and that the pathetic phase of loss of will-power was at all events over. She went towards the telephone box to arrange to go and see at once her friend Doctor Ettie Sayer. In my nervous apprehension concerning her ability to look after herself, I tried to lead her away and to continue the journey as arranged. But her old spirit of independence revived; she fiercely resented my attempt to control her actions; so I desisted. We went to Ettie Sayer's, had breakfast with her, and then continued the journey to the home at Sydenham.

Here at first everything went well. It was a comfortable and well-managed place, and Edith's native receptiveness of new impressions, her open-hearted impulses of friendliness, came into renewed play, even with a morbid exaggeration, for she only slowly realised that this was exclusively a home for convalescent mental and nervous cases. She was delightfully conscious of her renewed energy, though, as soon became clear, at all events to her friends, this was not her own sane and normal energy. It was arranged that our old friend Doctor Barker Smith, who had from of old given her his advice from time to time, should visit her in his medical capacity during her stay. I well remember his first visit (and he also referred to it lately to me nine years after) when she was lying in bed the second day of her arrival. She sat up as he entered the room, flung her arms wide open as he approached, embraced, and kissed him. She had never done so before, having no close personal affection for him, but I seem to understand the wave of emotion which surged up in her at that moment. She realised the crisis she had passed through, and, on seeing again this old friend out of the past, it seemed to her that she had come home again safe and sound. Possibly, also, she remembered that Barker Smith himself had once had a sad mental breakdown, and a fellow-feeling was part of this impulsive outgoing.

For the time all seemed to be moving in the right direction. She was pleased with the home and noted it down in her address book as a place to be recommended. I came to see her from Brixton nearly every day and my visits were always welcome. There was no shadow between us. But that implacable Fate, which with damnable iteration dragged her apart from me during all those months, again intervened.

An American woman, a stranger but a friend of Edith's dear friends in New York, was passing through London, and Edith invited her to call at the home. She came and was evidently fascinated, as so many were even to the end, by Edith's vivid personality and delightful conversation. She stayed so long that Edith — with the defective sense for the proprieties which now marked her — took on herself the duties of hostess and invited her visitor to spend the night at the home. But there was no vacant room, the superintendent happened to be away that night, and the nurses could not act on their own authority. The visitor seems to have been lacking not merely in tact, but in common sense. But Edith was furious; she had always had the highest sense of a hostess's duty to a guest, whatever her poverty or her weariness, and always succeeded in being a lavish and charming hostess. So that when circumstances baffled that deep-rooted impulse, it was a serious shock in her state of unstable equilibrium. The visitor had no choice but to leave the house, on her way finding an opportunity to send me a vaguely disturbing telegram, to announce Edith's departure at once, which was somehow delivered at my door at four in the morning. I had been too long on the rack of apprehension for any further twist of the screw to produce much effect. I lay quietly in bed until there would be some means of conveyance to the Crystal Palace and arrived before breakfast. She was prepared to leave and received me cheerfully, without much surprise. We had breakfast peacefully together. I settled the account and we left. She had swiftly decided — for her old aptitude for swift decision had now returned — to go to an old friend in the west end of London. For a few weeks she stayed with various old friends, often, I fear, with discomfort to herself, and sometimes, I knew, to the discomfort of her friends, who could not help realising that she was scarcely in a normal condition. I was helpless, and her mood of pathetic dependence on me was changing to a mood, much more painful, of ostentatious independence. She said this was out of consideration for me, in order that she might give me no more trouble, and so much was the quality of her mind changed that I was no longer able to discern clearly whether or not such a notion expressed her genuine feeling and was not a pretext. Certainly the underlying movement was a change in her cyclic mental state — in what later might have been termed her schizoid temperament — from morbid apathy to morbid energy. In this reaction from one extreme to the other, she not only lost all wish to return to my flat, but suddenly and unexpectedly arrived one morning to carry away all her heavy luggage.

She herself rejoiced in this return of energy, unable to realise how factitious it was. She knew she had been nervously and mentally ill, though the details were obscure to her. Her great desire now was to go back to Cornwall, not merely to settle up affairs at the cottage, but especially, I am sure, to demonstrate to friends that she was restored to health and was now again her old self. I knew this visit would be a mistake, and I asked her lawyer and Doctor Ettie Sayer, the two friends in whom she was now putting most trust, to assist me in persuading her not to go, but they professed to be helpless in the matter. I knew that I was now helpless. I talked matters over with Olive Schreiner, knowing her affectionate regard for Edith. Her advice was decisive; she said that in a state of mental instability such as Edith was in people were always liable to turn against those who were nearest and dearest to them; she advised me to go away to Spain for six months. I replied that the more serious Edith's condition the less possible it was for me to go away. I must be on the spot in case of emergency, to be ready when she needed me. All that I would agree to do was to go quietly into the country for a few days. Soon afterwards, I went, in consequence, to Brandon in Norfolk, staying at the White Hart, where I had often stayed before in happier circumstances, and walked about in misery for two or three days while a steady rain fell.

My quiet and brief withdrawal from London without notice to Edith may seem a simple thing. But it was really unique in our life together. Never before had I made any movement without keeping in touch with her. And by the tragic irony of life — which in a novel we would condemn as not lifelike — she also, who had never before gone anywhere without making arrangements with me, she also on that very same day went off to Cornwall without a word to me. Her mind was, I realise, firmly made up to go to Saint Ives to demonstrate her health and sanity to her friends, but she knew I was opposed to her plan, and so for fear I might make it difficult she decided to slip away quietly. She had not gone alone. Besides a faithful little servant, Annie, to help in settling up things at the cottage and packing what she would need for a new home in London, she had also taken down with her an ambiguous youth she had lately met by chance in an omnibus, and finding he had just been left an orphan took him under her protection, called him her 'adopted son,' and as he was almost penniless, though trying to get on the stage, she assisted him with gifts and clothes, though really far from able to afford such generosity. He was a worthless youth, who repaid her kindness with callous indifference, and in later years I was told that he found his way to prison.

The incidents of that sad journey to Cornwall, so eagerly undertaken, I never heard in any coherent shape. She was too deeply wounded, largely, she felt, through me, ever to talk about it, and I only heard little fragments from the reports of friends who felt the matter was too painful to say much to me about. But I knew that she went to her old and really devoted friends, determined to show that all her mental and physical vigour had come back to her, and quite prepared to emphasise it by a little artificial energy and merriment. But when she came away the memory of her that remained was of a gloom that nothing had occurred to change. Our pessimistic friend the Irish doctor had spread about the worst rumours as to her mental state, and when she reappeared he felt it his duty to let her friends know that they must be cautious, for she might be 'dangerous.' So that when she came to them wearing her old radiant air and expecting a joyous welcome, she was received with alarm and reserve, and not even allowed to see the children. Nor was this all; not only was her eager wish to rehabilitate herself dashed to the ground. In that small centre of gossip where she knew nearly everyone of all classes and all knew her, rumours, true and false, could not fail to spread concerning her illness and disappearance. They soon reached her when she was in the midst of them; she heard that she was to be shut up in a lunatic asylum, that I had 'signed papers' to enable this to be done, and even that orders were now out to carry her away. As happens when the mind has lost its normal stability, while she could obstinately refuse to accept reasonable statements, even

from me, she had become easily credulous of unreasonable statements, and ready to believe the worst of these stories. Leaving
Annie to complete arrangements at the cottage so intimately associated with our life together, which she (or I) was never to see
again, she hurriedly returned to London with the boy by the night
train, viewing with alarm everyone who approached the carriage
door. Yet even then, and, as her actions showed, never at any
time after, did she in heart turn against me. Her love — as today,
nearly ten years later, I see more clearly than ever when I look
back — was so deeply founded in the mysterious depths below
consciousness that nothing could upset and no loss of mental stability loosen it. I had acted, it seemed to her, with a treachery she
could not have conceived possible, but it seemed weakness, weakness she must guard against, but deserving of pity and not forfeit-
ing love. When the train reached Paddington in the early morning, and it was not clear to her where to go, the thought of the old
refuge in time of trouble instinctively came back to her: 'We will
go to dear Havelock,' she said. 'Dear Havelock, indeed!' exclaimed the youth (as she told me afterwards), callously remind-
ing her of the rumours they had heard. They came and came in
vain. I was not there to comfort her. I arrived back from Brandon some hours later in equal need of comfort; my heart aches
still.

It is easy to understand that, with thoughts and activities so
tied to Edith at this period, my ordinary public work in literature
was impeded. But it was not entirely arrested. That, indeed, I
could not in any case afford. I was still writing articles — for the
most part more or less round the war — for the chief English
weeklies, the *Nation* and the *New Statesman,* and in the course of
the year I published a miscellaneous collection of these under the
title of *Essays in War-Time.* I was also making occasional *Impressions and Comments* for the Second Series of that work, not,
however, published until five years later, in which I am pleased to

think my art of writing reached its highest point. I was at the same time certainly doing much of the laborious preparatory work for my proposed big volume on the Genius of Europe. A long absence of letters to Perrycoste is an index to the general state of my correspondence at this time. The first letter in 1916 to Perrycoste was written from Brixton in July, to arrange a meeting. I quote a few sentences:

> We can have a little meal somewhere in this neighbourhood and generally discuss our own and the world's affairs. . . . I have had an exceedingly trying time since last autumn owing to the distressing nervous breakdown of my wife, poor health of my own, and general worries due to present circumstances. It is only during recent weeks that I have attained a little peace and been able to resume work.

Next month I had occasion to write to Perrycoste again, and I quote a paragraph:

> I hope your *Usages of War* will get itself published. It seems to me the subject is quite interesting just now, and I should myself have probably found it very helpful in writing some of my *Essays in War-Time* of which the proofs are now coming in. If I have a spare set, and you would care to see them, I should be pleased to send them on.

The next letter to Perrycoste is dated September 6:

> I am now enclosing the rough proofs of my *Essays*, in case you care to glance at them, and then throw them away. I do not expect you will always agree, and they are, also, far too slight and popular for my own state! I hesitated considerably about republishing them at all. I take much more interest in my big book on Europe. . . . Glad to hear that there is some chance of your *Usages of War* appearing. But it ought to be published *at once*. The subject is interesting now, and next year it may be less so. We shall be more interested in peace then.

But I am here in advance of my narrative and close to the fatal end of this phase of my life.

It must, however, have been immediately after Edith's final and unhappy visit to Cornwall that she formed a resolution that was in flagrant contrast to the whole past tenor of her life, and up to now would have been unthinkable to her. Whether, as I now suspect, the idea was put into her head by her lawyer, I shall never know, but she decided that she must have a legal separation from me. It was a legal separation only that she had in mind, not a separation in any other sense, not even a separate domicile. Her deep love remained unshaken; she still realised that we belonged to each other. But she had come to believe — and nothing henceforth shook the belief — that I had been proposing to shut her up in an asylum. She felt, for the first time, that she could not trust me; I had done what, in my place, she could never have done; I had been weak, probably led away by others, but my weakness had amounted to a treachery from which she must in future guard herself. Once, a little later, only once, she spoke to me quite gently about her feeling in this matter. I should have known, she told me, that in those periods of depression all that she needed was to be alone with me and have my loving care and companionship, and she would not fail to come through. But the memory of that time was a vague dream to her; she knew she had been ill, but the details were dim and altogether forgotten. She was never able to see, and I was never to the end able to make clear to her, that she had been having my love and devotion and companionship by day and by night, until the growing difficulties seemed insuperable, and that even then I had not consented to her certification for an asylum, but had successfully eluded that decision by bringing her to the home at Sydenham. It was a simple position, but she could never accept it; she used to say she 'had proof' (which, of course, she could not produce), and, if I seemed to be emphasising my care for her, she would assure me that it should never be necessary again and she would never more be a burden to me. I will not be sure that she was unconscious of the cruelty of her words, for she well knew that in love are no burdens. It was part of her new policy — reversing the habits of a lifetime — never to ask my advice or consult me beforehand. So not until the contract of separation was arranged and drawn out was her lawyer instructed to send it to me for my acceptance. It was a pathetic yet characteristic proof of her tenderness, even over this seemingly hostile action, that she carefully impressed upon the lawyer that the document was to be sent so as to reach me in the morning and not in the evening lest it should worry me and prevent sleep. She was distressed when she heard from me later that he had carelessly disregarded her request. But in my state of tense and prolonged anxiety, the document hardly came as a new trouble, even though it raised a new problem, but almost as a relief. During the next day or two I asked the advice of Olive Schreiner; I think she was the only friend to whom I did confide the matter, as she was the friend of us both; she was not perhaps the wisest of counsellors, but my mind was really made up already. Without hesitation she advised me to accept the proposed arrangement.

I was the more willing to do so because I fully entered into Edith's motives and altogether shared them. I recognised that there was no change in her love and that it was not even a personal separation that she desired, far from it. What she had come in her disturbed mental state to think was that, owing to some strange and altogether unexpected perversity or weakness on my part, I had become a menace to her personal freedom. She had always been the most independent of beings; she had always resented, and from me as much as from anyone, the lightest touch that seemed to be of compulsion; in that respect, at all events, she remained her old self. I delighted in her freedom, and in her impulsiveness, even when it happened to be a little embarrassing, for it is in my nature to feel such delight. I had never applied or desired to apply any compulsion. So that I was glad to give her the proof that this was so — however sad that it seemed to be necessary — and I was even relieved to be assured that I should never even be called upon to apply any compulsion to her, for that possibility had been a source of torture to me during the past months.

This 'Deed of Separation,' as Edith's legal friend (whom I also personally knew) wrote in submitting it to me, was a matter for amicable arrangement, a mutual agreement to be settled 'voluntarily without any pressure.' It set forth that Edith 'may at all times hereafter live separate and apart as if she were sole and unmarried,' and that I should not 'for any purpose whatsoever use any force or restraint to her person or liberty.' That was the essence of the deed, and it merely stated a position which we had both of us accepted and acted on throughout our life together as a matter of course. A clause was added, due to the fear that I might be saddled by her debts, that she would indemnify me against all debts and at all times keep and maintain herself, which also had been a mutual understanding from the first. There was a final clause which was deeply significant and, as I well knew, expressive of her underlying feeling throughout: 'It is expressly agreed and declared that in case the said parties hereto shall at any time temporarily live together as man and wife the same shall not put an end to or render void the separation of any of the covenants herein contained.'

We went one morning to the rooms of the Law Society in Fetter Lane, and, in the presence of two lawyers, duly signed this document. Then we left the lawyers — I wonder what they said to each other — and went away in a taxi to have lunch together, just as though nothing whatever had happened. I cannot, indeed, recall that we ever talked on the subject again. Her mind was now at ease on that point and I had accepted the arrangement once and for all.

It seems a strange deed of separation, perhaps one of the strangest ever drawn up. Yet it meant exactly what it said and it meant no more than it said. It made no change in my love for her, and I am very sure it made no change in her love for me. She showed that in every little way. She still wore her wedding

ring; she still carried round her neck the locket in which she bore
a little portrait of me together with that of her dearest woman
friend (I treasure that locket yet). She still cherished all the
proofs of our love and still continued to manifest her tenderness by
tiny gifts. Most significant of all, when during the next few weeks
she took for herself a flat in the north of London, almost her first
care was to arrange that the room next to her own living-and-bed-
room should be fitted up as a bedroom for me.

That, indeed, sadly revealed that the new arrangement had in
one sense produced a more real separation on my side than on
hers, although no change in my love. I passively co-operated in
all the arrangements for the new flat which was in the same building as that of an old friend of hers, though not one to whom she
felt closely attached. It was more expensive than any place she or
I had ever taken before, but I now felt unable to remonstrate that
it was beyond her means. I accompanied her on all her visits to
agents and upholsterers. It was not until long after that I suspected she had a motive beyond the obvious one in desiring me to
accompany her on these visits. She had always been open as the
day with those she loved, and I failed to realise that the presence
of a husband is a guaranty in business arrangements of this kind.
Scheming had always been foreign to her nature, and it was hard
for me to recognize how disease was subtly changing her mind.
When the room was ready for me, however, I always refused to
come and occupy it. The feeling may have been an unworthy one
— I am willing now to think that it was; but it seemed to me a
little ridiculous for a man to share rooms with a wife who had just
arranged a legal separation from him. So I only occupied the room
once, and that on the night she died. It grieves me now, for she
had always nervously dreaded sleeping when no one was within
reach. Only a few weeks earlier I had been at her side day and
night, a perpetual source of comfort. Now, as I learnt at the end,
the same need was returning and she had to beg friends to come
and stay the night at the flat. Fortunately, wherever she might

be, there were always devoted friends at hand, and at this time I knew there were at least two whose tender sympathy and help meant much for her. After some weeks she converted the room intended for me into a lecture room, with a little platform, and here to scanty audiences, chiefly of friends and acquaintances, she gave lectures and readings at frequent intervals. She was anxious I should come to 'take the chair' at one of the lectures, just to show, she said, that we were not really separated. She well knew that I always refused any kind of public appearance. But I am sure she was disappointed. It would not have been a really public appearance, since often less than half a dozen people came, and perhaps none of them strangers. Now, ten years afterwards, this remains among the things I would gladly do when the chance to do them has passed away forever.

She was now entering into that stage of furious activity which represented the exalted phase of the mental circular state which in its opposite period of helpless depression she had passed through a few months earlier in Cornwall. It seemed to her that she was her normal self again and that large new possibilities of work were opening out in all directions. New friends who had faith in her ideas, as well as new parasites who hoped to profit by them, gathered around her. To me it seemed sadly as though the mainspring of a watch had broken and was swiftly unwinding itself to the final end. A friend who saw her at this time, after a long absence, with clairvoyant eyes, wrote to another friend: 'Mrs. Ellis is dying. What can be done?' But nothing could be done.

The number of plans and schemes with which she actively occupied herself during these last four months seemed almost endless. There were not only the lectures and readings which she gave almost daily at the room in her own flat, sometimes elsewhere, and even planned to give at the Bechstein (now Wigmore) Hall, the owners of which, after giving permission, later withdrew it. She was starting a little publishing business at her flat, which she called The Shamrock Press, employing a firm of printers near-by, who printed off for her, from the plates in her possession, the sheets for a considerable edition of her volume of short stories, *My Cornish Neighbours*; I found several big bales of these sheets at the flat after her death, and not knowing what to do with them in the midst of the Great War or even where to store them, I left them behind to be destroyed. Among other proposed publications was a pamphlet by the popular novelist, Marie Corelli — not a writer who would normally have appealed to her — and she extravagantly motored up to Marie Corelli's house at Stratford-on-Avon where her persuasiveness prevailed upon the novelist, who, however, shortly after, wrote withdrawing her permission, as her agent would not agree, though the letter showed that she had been won by Edith's personality. The hire of the car, by the way, she never paid, but it was a proof of the trust she inspired — and a trust that when she was her real self she never betrayed — that the car-man took her a number of other long journeys which remained unpaid, until, after her death, I gradually settled nearly the whole of the large bill, for he was a poor man, and I carefully selected among her many debts those which seemed to me to mean most to the creditors, though by our separation arrangement I was not responsible for any. She always loved motoring — though she had never before indulged in it by these reckless and dubious methods — and it always stimulated and benefited her. Another scheme was to buy a car and make it pay by hiring it out; she had at her death paid several instalments for its purchase, and they were never refunded by the dishonest sellers. Perhaps more important than any of these schemes was a film-producing company she began to establish in order to assist in raising the level of the screen. She was herself to write some of the scenarios, and she had obtained the co-operation of a film-actress of some promise and a manager of some experience, though I understand that neither of them would have proved quite satisfactory. But her death occurred before the company was really constituted, though money for shares was already being offered and given by friends and sympathisers. At the same time her dramatic and literary interests combined in a plan to take the Little Theatre in Chicago during the coming winter season. She was also studying to write on Swedenborg; she wanted to take one of her secretaries to the British Museum Reading Room, and obtain the use of a private room there; I dissuaded her from making what seemed to me an impossible request; in some matters she was still ready to accept my judgment even to the end, distracted by strange notions as her mind had become. The list of her activities is thus by no means complete: I will only mention one other, not connected with any thought of financial profit, and that was her interest towards the end in the Sufi movement led by Inayat Khan. I hardly think this movement would have appealed to her in earlier days — and it is not clear to me how far its leader was a charlatan — but it appealed to her now as to others whose minds were becoming imperfectly balanced, and she tried to serve its cause and to make it more widely known.

It is not surprising that in this feverish medley of incongruous activities — through which she was receiving high-frequency electrical treatment from her friend Doctor Ettie Sayer who possessed a very special installation — she required two secretaries. It is perhaps also not surprising that, with her original sanguine temperament now running uncontrolled, she believed that schemes which really needed half a dozen guiding brains would swiftly bring in money. Some of them really gave promise of doing so; a certain amount of money came in and she obtained more by borrowing from friends and acquaintances in a way she would never have done in earlier days. (I later repaid various such debts.) But she lavished it so recklessly on herself and others that she was sometimes actually penniless and scarcely able to obtain food. I never knew that till after the end, for she observed her vow of independence from me, or I would have taken means to help her. But I was troubled by her extravagances and I remember gently reproaching her for sending me a telegram when

a postcard would have served. She replied in an almost shy way
which touches me still that a telegram was 'more affectionate.'

In her letters of this time, however, the affection was far from
unmixed, nor was it at our meetings. It was that, perhaps even
more than what seemed to me the embarrassing situation caused
by our legal separation, that held me much aloof. It sometimes
seemed difficult for her to write to me without bringing in ancient
grievances which we had really long outlived, or the new fantastic
charges I had vainly sought to explain. I had come to realise that
explanation was fruitless in her morbid condition. I recall how,
again and again, I wrote to her, gently, almost hopefully, that
there were cobwebs in her brain, and that when these were swept
away all would be well. She kept none of these letters and I find
that I kept none of hers.

But I find one of July I had preserved, and it shows not only
how her feverish activities were wearing her away, but how like
she was to her old self when she forgot these cobwebs, and how
closely, through everything, we remained associated.

> *My Darling Boy*, I'd a lovely day yesterday, ending with a
> long visit from Edward C. [Carpenter] and George. They had
> supper here and Edward was divine. I want so to read his 'Life'
> and I hope he will send me a copy. All the Hinton stuff [manu-
> script of her book] goes in at three on Wednesday, so if you like
> I could come on, with what I don't finish and send today, to the
> British Museum at eleven that day, and bring my secretary with
> typewriter in case of emergency, as she can then take it to be
> mended on her way home, and you can lunch with me if you will.
> I'm full of adventures and there is no doubt whatever about the
> future — none. Whelan is delighted and glories over my success.
> I've heard from Bourchier and Otto Stuart today. *Such* a batch
> of letters from America. Thank you for the photos — just what
> is needed. I am looking forward to asking you to be a shareholder
> in our Company (Cinema). A splendid chance to invest money.
>
> P.S. Cannot get away to Museum, as there is an urgent com-
> mittee here at 11.30, but do come here as soon after nine in the
> morning as you can and look over what I have ready to take at

three. You can be quite alone in my room as the committee is in the lecture room. Stay on while you can. I am giving three speeches on Friday, and Mrs. Wentworth James is paying me to go to her At Home and speak before my lecture on Friday.

Thank you for [reading-lamp] candles just received.

Yours ever, Wifie

When she came to my flat there was always the same uncertainty. She would come now and then, without announcing her visit beforehand, when she happened to be free or anywhere in the neighbourhood, accompanied by a friend (she told me she had been 'warned' not to come alone), always impelled, I am sure, by the loving impulse of her old self, but it nearly always happened that, before she had been long in my room, the new morbid self would come to the surface, and (sometimes first putting the friend in another room) she would cast at me all the now familiar charges of my falsity and my designs on her freedom, of which she had 'positive proof.' I would endure the flood of speech patiently, knowing that she was an ill person against whom all argument was powerless; but it would sadden and leave me crushed. One such visit was typical. She was accompanied by her dear friend Y., who told me afterwards how lovingly Edith had spoken of me in proposing the visit and how pleased she (Y.) was at that disposition. But Edith had not long been in the room when, in Y.'s presence, the old charges were launched again with the old indignation. I bore the invectives gently, with scarce a word. On their way back, as she later told me, Y. reproached Edith for her harshness, and Edith replied: 'But think of the things he said to me!' Y. was rendered speechless.

My visits to her, which I always announced beforehand or made in response to her invitation, went off more easily, though not altogether happily. For I always felt that, though she was genuinely pleased that I should come to her, my good reception was partly also due to my being a guest, for she never lost her impulse of graciousness to a guest. She would busy herself to make me comfortable; she would prepare me a little meal with her old skill, often a very simple meal (and I later knew why), though a glass of wine was never lacking; the familiar accusations were not brought forward. All this time, also, and to the end, she was showing tender thought by sending me little presents, as I to her, and occasionally we would meet for a promenade concert at the Queen's Hall. The last concert she proposed we never went to; it seemed to me that the symphony for that night was uninteresting, and I wrote to her to postpone our concert meeting for a few days. But the concert was postponed forever; the time had arrived for her fatal illness and I do not forgive myself for that postponement. It so chanced that a few days later I went to a promenade concert by myself and sat next to a young woman who in the course of it began to sob bitterly, no doubt having lost some dear one in the war. How often, in the period that followed, a sob was in my own heart at those concerts endeared to me by beautiful memories.

Before that, somewhere towards the end of August, Edith came with a friend on her last visit to Brixton. It is the season when Muscat grapes, a favourite luxury for both of us, are cheap, and I had placed aside a bunch to give or take to her on my next visit. But when she went away she left me, as often before, sad and crushed; that the grapes were forgotten is almost all I can recall of the visit.

Yet her letters were often still touched by the old tenderness that never died. I have one of 28th of August:

> *My Darling Boy*, I have been too utterly busy to write and even now I've no time to do it fully. Come here if possible tomorrow at 12.30, stay to lunch, and I'll explain everything. I've had to go to Stratford-on-Avon from Friday to Monday on business and had a glorious time including an hour alone with Marie Corelli, who has taken a great fancy to me, including the promise to publish her next book through the Shamrock Press. I am in full swing and can soon prove that I am no failure in any way. I hope to find you better, so do come and lunch alone with me here.
>
> Your loving old **Wifie**

A few days later (September 1):

> *My Darling Boy,* I would have gone to the Promenade Concert, but until Tuesday I am very busy. Here is a patent tie thing you put under your tie to keep it nice. Wednesday, if you like, we can go to a concert, but let me know early. I was to have gone to Stratford to Marie Corelli today to see about many things, but so much to do. Do send us more typing when you care to, as we are getting on well at last. With love and hoping you are better, believe me
>
> Yours as ever,   Wifie
>
> Shall we dine together Wednesday and go to concert later?

It was the concert I fatally postponed.

These letters were significant and pathetic. We see the feverish activity and we see what was a key to it. She realised her breakdown of energy and will-power during the winter: 'I can soon prove that I am no failure.' Yet these final letters are in the main just the rapid, simple, spontaneous, businesslike, sympathetic, affectionate letters she had written of old, sometimes with little mistakes, and forgetfulness, the inevitable results of the immense press of affairs she was plunging into.

The end draws near. Sunday, the 3d of September, was the day when the first Zeppelin was brought down in flames to the north of London. She wrote next day:

> *My Darling Boy,* I am sorry you are not well. But who is, with the war, worry, and work? I was at our front door at 3 A.M. on Sunday, watching Zeppelins, etc. I was not a bit afraid, but nearly everyone here was. As you do not seem very keen on seeing me yet, just choose when you can or care to, next week. If you care to come here to lunch at one tomorrow, I shall be alone till 3.30 when I read Swinburne. Do take care and let me see you soon.
>
> Yours as ever,
>
> E. M. O. ELLIS

And next day a card:

> Will be at Museum as near 12.30 tomorrow (Wednesday) as I can. Want to see you. Take care.   **W.**

But on the Wednesday she sent a card:

> I am so sorry not to have lunched with you today, as I am staying in bed with a sort of rheumatic chill, and as I lecture tomorrow I had better remain in the house until it is over.

And on the following day a friend wrote a card for her to say that 'as she has rather high temperature, she cannot go out. She will write as soon as she is able, and sends her love.'

It appears that on the early Sunday morning the inmates of Sandringham Court where she had her flat were awakened from sleep by the rumour of the approaching Zeppelins. Throwing a few garments over her pyjamas, chiefly a cloak, Edith went to stand in the street doorway, with the little group of other inmates doing likewise. One of them, a woman — I do not know who she was — complained of feeling cold. Edith, impulsively and characteristically, removed her own cloak and placed it round the other woman, who selfishly accepted a protection which proved to be at the cost of the giver's life. During the next few days the chill developed. She gave to an interviewer a few words of impression of the scene she had witnessed — the last words she ever gave for publication. It was significant of illness poisoning her brain that she drew several cheques at this time with no money at the bank to meet them, so that they all came back; when she was her normal self she had always had the greatest horror of a dishonoured cheque, and her mental disorganisation could not be more conclusively shown. But I believe that she still continued for a few days longer the series of lectures and readings, which she had planned to extend months ahead, in the spare room at her flat she had converted into a little lecture room. However few the audience, they were a pleasure and a stimulation to herself, and a friend has told me that, though she might look fatigued when she began, she would become her old radiant self, to the last, when delivering a lecture. After her death I found on her desk — seemingly the last thing with which she had been occupied before illness struck her down — on the top sheet of a writing-pad, under the heading 'Readings from Havelock Ellis,' the words: 'When many years ago — about 28 — I first read *The New Spirit*, I knew I loved the man who wrote it. Today, in reading *Impressions and Comments*, I realise that the man who has written both books is worthy of love, forgiveness, and eternal comradeship, as a fine spirit forges into beauty, however long it takes, and that not one of us but many write not with ink but blood.' With her last effort of failing strength she had evidently been setting down the introductory notes for a reading from my books. That writing-pad is now one of my cherished possessions.

For early September I had planned a visit of a couple of days with my old friend Barker Smith to Clare in Suffolk. It was a favourite spot of mine; I had often stayed there before, once with Edith; I never expect to go again, even though, as I can now add twenty years after the event, I spend happily my last days in Suffolk only a short distance from Clare. We were preparing to leave London on Monday the 11th and to return on Tuesday or Wednesday. But after the 7th no further news of Edith reached me, I began to grow anxious at the prolonged delay and on the Saturday made up my mind to go unannounced to her flat early next morning to be assured that all was as well as might be before I left London. I could not possibly have gone away in doubt, and that brief Sunday morning visit still remains a memory, to redeem a little of the misfortunes and stupidities which accompanied me in that period of life.

I found her in bed with a nurse by her side. She was recovering, I was told, from an attack of pleurisy. I could quite believe that she was recovering, for her physical condition seemed satisfactory, while she was bright and cheerful; mentally, indeed, she seemed her old self. It is well known that a physical disorder often has a clarifying effect on a clouded brain, and even in ordinary times I had often noted in Edith that any illness that kept her in bed tended to have a beneficial psychic effect; so that I had often felt more at ease about her when she had to rest in bed than when she was energetically careering over the country. Also, I am sure, my visit gave her pleasure. Once, whenever illness came, her first thought was for my presence. In her new frame of mind, when she had absurdly decided that she was to ask nothing of me, she had refrained from giving news of herself. So that my spontaneous anxiety, and this sudden visit — the first I had paid to her flat without previous arrangement — joyfully reassured her doubts, for she never understood my seeming aloofness. I felt her pulse. I told her to put out her tongue, and she did so, but said directly afterwards, with her mischievous playfulness, remembering our formal separation: 'You know you must not give me orders now!' She assured me — as I seemed also to be able to see for myself, though I ought to have better realised the uncertainties — that she would soon be well. She urged me to go to Clare; it would do me good, she said. I knew that she had dear and attached friends who were caring for her, while her skilful friend, Doctor Ettie Sayer, and a kind local doctor, were medically watching her. It seemed that all was well. I stooped down to kiss her, but she would not let me for fear there might be any infection. So I kissed her hand. It was the last kiss I was ever to give her in life.

We are the idle playthings of Fate and I went away feeling happier and more at rest than I had felt for a long time past.

That same day she asked a friend to send a postcard to reach me on Monday morning before I left London:

> Mrs. Ellis is improving hour by hour and the fever is diminishing. Instead of being as in the beginning 103° it is now only 100°. And all is sure to be well in a few days. She sends her love, and hopes you will have a good time while away.

On Monday from her bedside, in the hand of the same friend came the last words she ever addressed to me:

> Your wife has just got your kind letter and wishes me to say that she is going on well, has no fever now, and the doctor says she is a miracle as usual. She has a mountain of grapes by her bedside! Mrs. Ellis has written to Mrs. Schreiner to ask her to

stay here a few days and sleep in her lecture room. She hopes you will have a lovely time, and says she and Y. thought it the loveliest place they had ever been in.

The letter was awaiting me at breakfast in the Bell Hotel at Clare on Tuesday morning and seemed so reassuring that a half-formed intention — for I was not entirely without anxiety — to return to London that day was changed and with Barker Smith I resolved to stay till Wednesday. But all this stay at Clare, save at one or two points is a dim dream, effaced from memory. On Wednesday I duly returned and on opening the door of my flat at Brixton I found on the floor a telegram with the words:

MRS. ELLIS DYING   COME AT ONCE

It had been sent on Tuesday, by whom I never heard and never inquired. For years, knowing the uncertainty of her health, I had opened telegrams with apprehensive haste as though by a premonition that some day by a telegram the fatal news would reach me. At last it had come and I was not there to receive it. I open telegrams calmly now.

At once I took a taxi and went to Maida Vale. The knocker of the flat was muffled, everything was peaceful and in order, and the nurse was by the bed. Not long before, a nurse who stood very high in her own professional world had learnt to know and admire Edith; she had appeared on the scene and taken superintendence of the nursing arrangements. Doctors and nurses and friends had all been at hand, to do everything that could be done. Only I had been absent. I helped to lift her in the bed, when that was necessary to shift the sheet, all that remained for me to do. I stayed in the room, or in the next room, for the eight hours of feeble life that remained to her. She was comatose; she had entirely lost the power of speech or of recognition a few hours before I arrived. She gave no sign at all. A cylinder of oxygen, such as had helped her during her serious illness in America, made no difference now. After some hours I went and lay down on a bed in the next room, the first and last time I occupied the room she had been so pleased to prepare for me a few months earlier. When the end was approaching, one of the two nurses who remained with her came to call me. Her breathing was shallow, but calm and regular. She who had lived so vividly, so eagerly, often so tempestuously, died in perfect peace. Not the slightest shudder passed over her as her spirit sank to silence, merely the breathing grew slower; then there was a pause, then another breath; then no more forever. The two nurses quietly left the room and left me alone, silently alone beside her silence.

It has often since seemed to me strange that I, who have lived in hospitals and attended the sick, and wandered through so many regions of the world, in the whole of a life that is now little short of seventy years (now, indeed, over eighty), should only have seen two people die, and that those two should be the two women nearest to me in the world, my mother and my wife. I am glad that it has been so and that the two persons whose departing spirits I have been privileged to inhale should be just those.

In the early morning I slipped quietly away from the flat while the nurses rested, and returned in profound melancholy, however undemonstrative, to Brixton. During the next day or two I learnt all that I was ever to know concerning my dead woman's last conscious hours on earth. Her last letter to me, with its note of cheerful optimism, seems to have sprung out of the little flame of vitality which so often ushers the approach of Death. Next day there had been a sudden change for the worse, too sudden, fortunately, for her to realise it clearly. The fever in her lungs was doubtless passing off, but it had used up her small vital force, and the lurking diabetes came to the front to spread its fatal veil of coma over her consciousness. But at first this veil was imperfect. She could still sometimes recognise the persons around her and from time to time, the nurse told me, she would utter names of those dear to her, her friend Y.'s, mine, and, as I would have known if never told, most often, Lily's. One incident of that night is graven forever on my heart. Unable to speak, she pulled at the arm of the drowsy nurse beside her and pointed to the picture of me on the wall in front. What she wished was not clear to the nurse who was too sleepy to try to find out. I can only suppose that she desired me to be sent for. And another thought — another memory from twenty-five years earlier — has often come, even deliciously come, during the years that have passed since that night. We know that in those who have reached the final point of consciousness, as in coming near drowning, the significant picture of the past life may float across the final vision. Twenty-five years earlier, after our brief honeymoon at Lamorna, she had written to me of the little 'house' I had playfully selected for her on the cliff with its foxglove towers: 'You made me think of how beautiful men could be. . . . I think when I'm dying I shall see that house and smell the fern-roots and look into that blue sky and see the gulls and feel as near to the heart of a great mystery as I did then.' And now she was dying, and the memory of me was tugging at the failing heart. I do not feel foolish to believe that the vision she had foreseen passed at the end before her dying eyes. And the old cry for me, now voiceless, rose again within her, and she plucked at the drowsy nurse's sleeve and pointed to the portrait on the wall.

She made no further spontaneous movement, though consciousness was not yet abolished. In the morning when her doctor friend came, she was able, in response to her question, to recognise her by saying 'Ettie!' After that, nothing.

Some time previously, when it became clear that we should henceforth be living little in Cornwall, Edith had given up the grave she had too hastily bought near to Lily's grave in Lelant churchyard. We then decided, after discussing the matter, that the best method of burial is cremation, and of the rightness of that decision I am ever more convinced. The cremation was arranged, accordingly, at Golders Green Crematorium. She had expressed the wish that if any words were spoken they should be by Edward

Carpenter, for whom she had for so many years felt an affection
and admiration, almost a discipleship, such as she experienced for
no one else. Carpenter, no longer in robust health, was unable to
come from his home in the North at such short notice.[1] So we
decided that nothing should take place at the cremation save only
the playing of the organ, in which, at my suggestion, was included
Handel's familiar Largo, a piece which had always given her peculiar joy and satisfaction; I think it somehow served to express
her own large and soaring and confident aspirations.

There seemed to be many persons present — though no formal
notice had been given and many who desired to be present were
thus prevented — but I was scarcely aware of them. I only know
that Olive Schreiner came, though ill, because, as she said, she
knew Edith would have liked her to. When the coffin is to glide
into the great furnace, any special friends who so wish may come
forward to witness the consummation which is otherwise invisible
to the congregation. Algernon West and I went forward, as also
(at his request) Inayat Khan. As I gazed at that beautiful sight,
at that vast and seemingly liquid mass of golden intense heat, in
which the coffin was so swiftly swallowed up, my pain at this last
vision of all that remained of the being, who for all my active life
had been so near to me and so dear, was merged into joy at the
glory of the vision. I realised how fitting it was that one whose
spirit in life, beyond any I ever knew, had been a flame, should
pass from the world in actual flame, a chariot of fire, to rise into
the air, and to become one with the panorama of sky and sea,
with those things on the earth to which she had been so exquisitely sensitive because she herself was of like nature and destined
to join them. So no tear stained my cheek, as none had when the
last breath left her body. It has not been so since. Often, as I
have walked the street, at some memory or some scene, I have felt

---

[1] Shortly afterwards, however, he read a paper about her at the first meeting of
the Edith Ellis Fellowship, a little group which met from time to time during several
years. (This paper was later prefixed to the volume she had planned, entitled *The
New Horizon in Love and Life*.)

tears brimming over my eyes, and even now — when it is ten years but a few days since she left — it is so still.

Three days later I came with two or three friends to the crematorium, to witness the scattering of the ashes over the quiet and beautiful garden. This method of disposal seemed to me far better than preservation in an urn, though it was only later that I learnt from a friend that she once had actually expressed a wish for her ashes to be scattered over the earth or the sea. The attendant with the basket of ashes on his arm walked slowly and gravely about scattering the ashes with his hand as he went. All that was volatile of her body had passed into the air, and I was glad that what remained would continue to live in the roses or even only the grass.

No memorial of this ceremony was set up at the crematorium at the time. I could not have borne the expense even if the wish to put up any memorial had occurred to me. But a few years later it was arranged that tablets might be set up in the clerestory to the memory of friends whose remains had here been cremated. In due course, some seven years afterwards, when able to afford the rather considerable cost, I had a tablet set up in the central position of a bay facing that part of the grounds where the ashes had been scattered. After the arrangement had been made, I agreed to the offer of Algernon West to take a quarter share in the expense, for though I would gladly have taken it all myself, I could not deny this satisfaction to so good a friend who had tendered her his whole-hearted devotion before I had ever met her, and never withdrew it, even after her death assuming all the troublesome duties of executor. The inscription I set up was one of the earliest, by its date apparently much the earliest, for people do not set up memorials to friends who died seven years previously. It ran:

> *The Ashes of Edith the wife and comrade of Havelock Ellis were scattered over this garden on the eighteenth of September 1916*

The formula of this inscription, sometime since imitated, was new when I devised it, the old tombstone formula previously used on crematorium monuments seeming to me unsuitable. I have left a space on the tablet, so that it may one day, I hope, record that I have been able to

> 'Marry my body to that dust
> It so much loves'

Meanwhile, from time to time, when the sun shines, I travel across London to wander for a few minutes at least around that spot, just as she herself, from time to time, used to go from Carbis to the grave of her beloved Lily at Lelant to soothe her nerves with peace, and come back refreshed. There the picture comes back to me of the ashes of what I held so dear slowly scattered, in a sudden gleam of bright sunshine, over the grass and amid the flowers. And I stand once again alone in this lonely and pleasant spot which holds so few memories of the dead and attracts so few of the living. But in the years that have passed, my favourite sister Louie's remains have also been cremated here and in the same bay I have placed a little tablet to her memory, her dearest friend Muriel Brown sharing in this, and still more recently it has been Muriel's turn, and to her memory a tablet has been set up close to Louie's. Sometimes there blows there a strong, exhilarating breeze from the west, such as we knew it to blow in Cornwall, and I meet it with a sad joy as I pass slowly round the garden and recall how Edith wished that her friends should not be sad at her death, but rather make merry in her name. At such moments it is Nature that makes merry in her ashes. The lawn that was smooth to receive those ashes sometimes grows high and wild with various grasses in full flower, and big patches of red sorrel and sheep's parsley here and there, and scattered golden celandines and lady's-slipper, where a little apart is a huge bed of roses, white and red. She ever loved flowers and could never feel content if none were at her side, even of the simplest, while roses were to her the most sacred symbol of love. I know not if any of those who once loved her ever come to this garden. For my part I am glad to hasten year after year to the one spot where her mortal remains are still alive, if only in leaves of grass. It was in flowers that her restless and aspiring spirit sought peace and joy. Now she is among flowers and flowers have become her very flesh.

To bring back my general mental attitude and external activities during the months following Edith's death, I cannot do better than quote from my letters to Perrycoste. The first (November 17) was after an interval of some two months:

> Thank you much for your kind and sympathetic letter. For a long time my wife's health had caused great anxiety and distress; she was much unlike her old self and mental condition impaired with the progress of the disease (diabetes). But just latterly she had seemed more like herself, so that the sudden end was the greater blow. ... As you may imagine, all this has been a source of additional grief to me, although I know that the end (pneumonia leading to diabetic coma) could not have been more merciful and gentle. ... She is constantly in my thoughts, and it is quite true, as you say, that living entirely alone, as I do, one dwells on things more, though I have no wish to recall too much the painful and pathetic memories. I have various invitations to go away (even to Florida), but, as you know, I do not care to stay with friends, though I have just now been staying with one of my sisters at Tunbridge Wells. I am very sorry to be shut out of Carbis Bay, as no place suits me so well in winter, but there are far too many memories there, and I am trying to get rid of the lease of the cottage to a friend. So far, also, I have had little strength or spirits for work, and there are, too, a great many anxious worries to deal with, for of late my wife lost critical judgment and plunged so recklessly in new schemes of activity that the liabilities are considerably more than can be met.

In my next (February 19, 1917) I wrote:

> Thank you much for your sympathetic letter of 21 November. I am getting along as well as I could expect, and though living alone — and through the wretched London winters after so many winters in Cornwall — there is always someone or other to

see. I am also now doing a fair amount of work. Thank you also for returning the *Edinburgh* [with my article on the 'Psychology of the English']. You seem to be right as to sending to France because although the regulations as published referred to enemy and neutral countries, it is also taken to cover *allied* countries. At present I am in correspondence with the War office with regard to a permit to send manuscripts to American magazines and, as several 'References' are required, I have taken the liberty of mentioning your name among others. I trust you will not object, and I do not imagine they will trouble you. It is a completely unnecessary piece of red-tapeism, because, permit or no permit, anything sent is still at the absolute discretion of the Censor. I quite appreciate your criticism of my article: you must remember it is really only an *abstract*. The whole essay is very much longer, and stuffed with facts and references. It will altogether be a big and laborious book. — I wonder what has happened about your war book.

In telling you of the order observed at the cremation at Golders Green, I rather had it in mind to ask you if any suggestions have, to your knowledge, been offered for the use of those who object to religious funerals of the orthodox kind. It is rather an important question now that so many people do object, and often submit merely because they know of no satisfactory substitute, and really it is not easy to compete with the Church's rite, which in its way is very fine and was still finer before the last Elizabethan revision. Speechifying at such a moment is not always attractive, or possible, and I agree with an old seventeenth-century parson among my ancestors who forbade any funeral sermon at his death and gave excellent reasons against the practice. It certainly seems time that suggestions were put forward.

The next is dated August 15:

I am pleased to have your letter. There is another on my table which I have been meaning to thank you for. Just now, however, I am spending a few days with my sisters and will therefore keep to the main point in your last. [It seems to have been an anthropological point connected with left-handedness, and I conclude the passage about it]: The literature is enormous and I have a quantity of cuttings and references; I could look up any special point if you liked. I regard myself as naturally left-handed, though right-handed by education. I was a left-handed bowler at cricket as a boy and cannot throw a stone with my right hand. I regard a certain muscular inaptitude in my case as perhaps due to the conflict between nature and education in this matter.... I am sorry to hear there is little chance of seeing you in London this year. I had a wretched winter with depressed health and strength and no inspiration for work. And I very much miss the winter in Cornwall, though I feel quite unable to go down now; I have been arranging to transfer the remainder of lease of the Carbis Cottage (which we had greatly improved), but so far this has only led to a most worrying muddle. With the warm weather my health, spirits, and power of work considerably revived, and I am now getting along as well as I can hope to, though finding life rather lonely. I work steadily at my psychology of European peoples and write occasional articles for the *New Statesman.* Glad to hear that you have satisfactory news of your son's progress.

It was natural that my first feeling should be that with her my life had ended. In a sense, indeed, that was true. She was an integral part of my life during its period of most intense activity, the long period, that is to say, devoted to the elaboration and publication of the work which I have always regarded as my chief task in life. I had my own world of dreams and should have had even if we had never met. But my most intimate points of contact with the outer world were mainly in her, through her, or, at the least, with her close against my side and sensitive to every movement, so that at first it seemed that she had now entered my dream-world and that the real world had receded.

Grief is one of the greatest mysteries of life. In losing a beloved person one is plunged into sorrow. Yet at the same time one is raised above all doubts and fears and anxieties into a sphere of joy which nothing can henceforth touch. While the loved one lived there is always doubt whether the love will last; there is always fear of giving or receiving hurt; there is always apprehension of harm to the being who is so dear. Now one is raised forever above all doubt and fear and anxiety. One enters the heaven of complete and eternal possession which nothing can henceforth touch. To think of the loved one is now of all pleasures the greatest. What one truly loves is veritably one's own soul, and to lose one's soul, as religion makes clear, is to gain it, for love is, in a certain sense, religion. All the ardours of religious love — even its saints and its relics and its shrines and its holy places — are but the transformations of the simple facts of natural love.

We are bidden not to build ourselves a melancholy prison in old age and shut ourselves up with our memories. I have built no melancholy prison, but rather a Palace of Joy. Its windows and its doors open onto the streets of today where crowds of living figures move, and those figures are scarcely less living to me than the lovely dream-figures within. Today, more than ten years since she died, I have more friends, dearer and more intimate friends, than I have ever had in my life before, and they bring me as sweet a devotion, as unmixed a joy, as have ever been brought to me, or perhaps — I somehow imagine — to any man. So that I can truly say that, while I have lived more deeply in earlier days, I have never at any time lived so happily. I should have been false to all that she thought meet if, when she was gone, I had abandoned myself to melancholy or refused to accept all that life might yet have to give me. Some of my dearest friends today are women who knew her and still think of her with tenderness and admiration, and that is a bond which I always remember and which makes them the dearer to me. One of them, whom I count the dearest, who gives me the name of 'Faun' and who inspired my essay on the 'Play Function of Sex,' wrote to me two years after Edith's death, in French, of 'the fauns, with flutes to their lips, who play behind the bushes, and conquer so easily, Havelock, because all the wisdom and all the light of the world is theirs'; and now, many years later, I know she would still say the same. For to 'play' has become more natural to me than it ever was before, now that the work of life is over and its anxieties done with. But the people who come to see me and who tell afterwards how 'gay'

I was, how 'cordial,' do not know that inner life from which those qualities spring, the fount of joy, so often touched with melancholy, the presence of influences out of the past.

And when I speak of 'play' in connection with Françoise, I must make clear — especially now (in 1939) that I write more than twenty years since our relationship began — that the 'play' has in course of years sometimes merged in phases so serious that they might seem tragic. The pure 'play' belonged to the earlier years, more conspicuously during periods of summer holiday, such as her profession at that time as a teacher made possible, in various parts of France, at Saint Cloud (in the house of my old friend Marguerite Tracy), on the summer Riviera (only beginning to be sought and I had always kept aloof from the winter Riviera), the Pyrenees, the only mountains I love, and notably Touraine, a stay which later remained in our memories as a sort of honeymoon.

During the ten years and more after Edith's death the Brixton flat remained my headquarters, with an ever-increasing store of books and papers, but I would take a charming little cottage at Frieth in Buckinghamshire for the six summer months, living alone and delighting to receive for beautiful and intimate visits my more special friends, while in winter I would go for three months to Cadgwith in Cornwall or somewhere on the south coast. But at last Brixton seemed in various ways to have become impossible and at the same time Françoise found too severe the strain of teaching, so we in a large measure combined our domestic lives, partly in a house at Herne Hill and partly in a country house with large garden at Wivelsfield Green in Sussex, and she gave me some aid with secretarial work and domestic organisation, also understanding work as a translator, while our relationship became closer and more complex, all the more so through illnesses of hers and later of mine, when she was my most devoted and capable nurse.

Finally, after some ten years of occupation it seemed necessary to give up also these two houses. I was too ill to go in search of another. Françoise went on my behalf. Finding nothing suitable in the neighbourhood, she went, to my great satisfaction, to hunt in Suffolk, and here speedily found, and at once fixed, a little house with two acres of ground which she considered charming and exactly suitable. I have confirmed her judgment from the first. The whole place comes nearer to my ideal — a modest ideal, no doubt — than any place I have ever lived in. Apart from its special attributes Suffolk is more attractive and interesting to me than any other county in England, its climate seems to suit me better, and it was the home of most of my ancestors on both sides during at least several centuries. It is an additional pleasure that Françoise has come to love it almost as much as I do. I had never ventured to expect that I should spend my last declining days in Suffolk, and, as I lie in bed and gaze through the window at a prospect of which I never grow tired, I am well pleased to think it may be the last to greet my dying eyes. By a curious chance I happen here to be in the parish of Washbrook of which for a short time in the middle of the seventeenth century my ancestor George Peppen was the vicar, and the first time I was able to take a little walk I went to his charming old church and stood in his pulpit.

I no longer, it will be seen, enter into the details of my intimate life. It is still too near and too closely associated with those still living. It would be possible to tell of many beautiful experiences with various beloved friends of fine personality during these past twenty years, and if I do not write at length of the one who during that period has been nearest and dearest of all, that is not because I would fail to appreciate her wonderful and complex character, or even fail to observe her various points of resemblance to Edith, for whom she had genuine admiration, even physical points, and it was a school-fellow friend of Edith's who remarked that Françoise had the same hands. I have grown so close to her that the thought of possibly surviving her, since her health is not always strong, has become intolerable to me.

Nor will I enter into details of my external and literary life which during these years has pursued an easy and successful course, though with a more random freedom since the main tasks of life are over. It also proved — with no deliberate seeking on my part — much more financially profitable. At one time, through my American publishing friend, Mr. Doran, I was invited to write a short weekly article on almost (though not quite) any subject I pleased for the Hearst journals; the proposal hardly seemed sympathetic, and at first I refused. But eventually on reconsideration I agreed, and had no cause to regret doing so. One morning's work was frequently all required, and at one time, aided by a favourable exchange, it brought me in thirty pounds a week. Then, with but slight revision, I was able to make of the articles two widely appreciated volumes, *My Confessional* and *Questions of Today*.

Much more important was *The Dance of Life*, published in 1923. This book, planned a long time before actual publication, was mainly elaborated from essays written during the ten preceding years, and, without being deliberately so intended, I had in mind that, more nearly than any other book of mine, it would approach to being a statement of my philosophical outlook on life. It hardly seemed to me likely to find a large public. As regards England I was quite right, for here its sale has been quite small from the first, whatever the opinions held by good judges. But in America, to my surprise, the book met with a very different reception from readers of all classes. It became a recognised 'bestseller,' a unique experience for any book of mine. For one half-year the royalty that reached me amounted to one thousand pounds. The sale, moreover, was well sustained and continued even when the book was issued in cheap editions.

A much larger and more complex work, much more characteristic of the author, no doubt, in most eyes, appeared in 1927, a supplementary volume (that is to say Volume VII) of the *Sex Studies*. I regard it as scarcely, if at all, less important than most of the original volumes, though some of its contents were of much narrower scope, I could not have produced it earlier, since some of the subjects discussed I had only slowly learnt to grasp while others had only recently come to the front.

One book finally remains to mention: *From Rousseau to Proust.* Published in 1935, it will probably be my last book of any consequence. It brings together nearly everything of any interest which I have written on the literature of France, the literature to which, throughout life, I have given more attention than to any other. It is not, of course, intended to present any continuous development. Nor is the large space devoted to Rousseau meant to suggest any discipleship on my part. It simply means that during the past forty years I have come to regard Rousseau, not only as a most complex and interesting personality, but the most important and influential force to appear in our western world since Jesus.

I do not discuss in detail these latest twenty years of my life; they are not only too near, they are less closely related to the central facts of my life than the happenings of earlier years. But there is a reason why I may still, as I look back, finally say something about the deep and instructive lessons I learnt in that earlier life through my intimate association with Edith.

It has always been a pleasure to me to recall, as it was also to her, how, years after our marriage, when we were travelling down to Cornwall together, two strangers in the carriage, also going down to Saint Ives, inquired of friends, as we afterwards learnt, who we were. The Havelock Ellises, they were told. 'Oh, no!' was the rejoinder, 'they could not have been married, they were so interested in each other!' And the interest did not exclude, it was even bound up with, an acute interest on both sides in other people.

What from the eye of strangers, who saw only the surface, was 'interest,' was for me what I can describe as 'passion.' I have shown how the bond of sex in the narrow sense, which was never very strong on either side, passed out of our lives at an early stage, and therewith, according to accepted conventional notions, passion should have passed away. But it was not so, it was the contrary. During all the quarter of a century of our married life I constantly noticed, amid my various practical and emotional activities, how my love was ever growing deeper and more comprehensive, a spiritual love, if you will, yet also in the large sense a bodily love, for I cannot experience, or even conceive, any true love of the soul which is not also a love of the body. And that it was so also with her, even though it was her instinct, as it was also mine, to conceal the depths of feeling, I can have no doubt. It is not only my own assumed knowledge; it was the conviction, spontaneously given to me, of those who knew her. On her first voyage to America in 1914, she formed a friendship with a woman passenger who, as her swift instinct speedily divined, was secretly engaged to the captain and later married him. 'She always talked of you,' this friend wrote to me after her death, 'with such pride and such affection, as though the first freshness of married life had never become dulled. Perhaps you realise how much she idolised and idealised you, perhaps not.' And whether I fully realised I can never myself know. But I know something of all that was expressed in the cry from the hospital at Hayle: 'Havelock! Havelock!' of which after many years the echo still rings in my ears. 'There are no voices that are not soon mute; there is no name, with whatever emphasis of passionate love repeated, of which the echo is not faint at last.' I know it. The beautiful voice was soon to be mute. But the emphasis of passionate love in that name repeated in the distance still leaves an echo, only to die when I am dead. That constitutes the great discovery in love that I have made. Passion transcends sex. I shall never belittle the great roots of sex in life. I know I could not love any man as I have loved this woman. But I have discovered that the sexual impulse of physical attraction may pass away and give place to a passion that is stronger than it. That is a discovery with a significance for life and for the institution of marriage which has not yet been measured. And I smile when I see the ephemeral creatures of a day sneering at love. We who are not the creatures of a day, who live greatly, and do the work of the world, we are moved by love. So that rather than belittle love, we would even see a sense in the final extravagance of Dante, and end, as he ends, on the omnipotence of love, '*L'amor che move il sole e l'altre stelle.*'

I have always instinctively avoided superlatives in the language of love, for I know too well how common they are and how evanescent. I have never in my life, that I can recall, addressed anyone as 'Dearest,' however justifiably I might have done so; I have always felt we cannot rely on our feelings, and we cannot know whether what we feel today we shall always feel.

To an outsider who contemplates the life we led, it may seem at times an unnatural, uncomfortable, defective, and abnormal life compared to that of all the married couples who, to outward view, lead so placid an existence of smooth routine. Yet, when one is privileged to see beneath the surface of these lives, one realises that they are for a large part dead, with boredom gnawing at the core, unreal, paralysed, corrupt, selfish, fruitless. How few must the exceptions be! We at least were alive. It can rarely, indeed, have happened before that a person of the same vibratory emotional sensitiveness has been mated with a person of the same poignantly acute and manifoldly radiating energies. If we missed the placidity of inertia, we gained a greater measure than is given to most of that joy and pain which are the essence of life and we were spending our strength for what seemed to each of us the greatest causes in the world,

> 'to enrich
> The whole world with the sense of love and witch
> The heart out of things evil.'

Is it not enough?

Browning addressed the author of these words after her death as 'half angel and half bird.' Deeply as Edith in early life entered into the spirit of Elizabeth Browning, especially in *Aurora Leigh*, I would never so address her. I would sooner put it: 'O Lyric Love, half devil and half child.' For she was all love, generous and tender and passionate, and she was lyric aspiration, and she was half devil, mischievous, merry, sometimes instinctively cruel. 'Much of the angel and something of Billingsgate,' our friend Henry Bishop, the distinguished artist, once told her after an eloquent outburst. 'Devilkin' one of her friends affectionately nicknamed her, and she was more than half child, sensitive, proud, alive to the smallest joys and the smallest pains, poignant and pathetic.

To the pathos of her I am never quite reconciled. I am reconciled to her death, for I know that she herself was ready to welcome it. I am reconciled to live without her physical presence, for I could do that even while she was alive, and her spiritual presence is nearer than it ever was. But I am never reconciled to the pathos of this little woman with the temperament of genius, born before her time into a hostile world, an everlasting child, so eager and so sensitive and so trustful (for her acquired shrewdness and suspicion was but a reaction to her trust), wounded on every hand, tortured by the very make of her nature, and herself a torturer, yet to the end an absolute and adorable child — that I have never been reconciled to. I hold perpetual dialogue with myself. I repeat all the wise reasons why I should be at peace as she is at peace. Yet it never ceases to wring my heart.

It is in the inconsistencies of her temperament that I find the reason for the seeming inconsistence in my own feelings about her during the period immediately following her death. I tried to escape from the thoughts of her, often so sad, that streamed in on me from within and from without, and absorbed myself in work. Yet again and again it happened, after I had been in society and no thought of her had had room to intrude, that when I came away, at once, by no volition of my own or any suggestion from without, my scattered thoughts are gathered up together in a sweet nest of refuge with her. Nonetheless, with all the practical motives which I had to go to Carbis to occupy the cottage — which, moreover, she had often told me it would be to my interest to keep on in case of her death — or to dispose of the lease and furniture satisfactorily, the associations that clung round it were so poignant that I never even considered all the advantages of going, but felt as my grandfather Wheatley had felt when on his wife's death he had given away all that belonged to her.

For I can only repeat that she is still ever with me, and when, as at this moment, I recline on the lawn of my remote cottage garden, and the warm sunshine pours down on me, and I hear the birds and watch the apples swelling and bending from the laden branches, in this deep peace such as she loved, she lives in my spirit and by my side, she might be the butterfly that at this instant hovers close to my face. I am in eternity and can afford to smile at the simple souls who hope at some remote period after death to be able to recognise a sleek white-robed angel in heaven.

My love is a perpetual revelation to me, for it is so contrary to all I have heard of the transitory nature of love. My intellectual self looks on with an amused surprise while my real self throbs swiftly to any casual contact with the things she once touched, when I kiss her picture as I go to bed, when I cherish tenderly the things she herself had cherished. It is a perpetual revelation that, after I had lived with her tempestuously for a quarter of a century, in pain as well as in joy — that more than ten years after she is dead, love should retain its fresh original sensitiveness.

It may be true, as Bertrand Russell has said (in *A Free Man's Worship*), the past has a 'magical power,' but, as he adds, that power is not due to illusion: 'What was petty and transitory has faded away, the things that were beautiful and eternal shine out of it like stars in the night; its beauty, to a soul which has conquered Fate, is the key of religion.' If I now see less of what was 'petty and transitory,' I am the better able to see the rest, even though I never at any time failed to see it.

Intensely woman as she was in many ways, she had the loyalty, the sense of honour, the straightforwardness of a man, and indeed in a higher degree than all but the rarest men. Impulsive as she was, she had none of the incalculable abandonments, and shrewd as she could sometimes be, none of the incalculable reserves which may be observed in the women who are all woman, who may be adorable but scarcely such as one can ever lean on with all one's weight. Yet, while her deep instincts were so stable, on the surface she was restless, vivacious, fond of novelty, changeable, almost capricious, even in her affections, in a way that was not the fashion of my temperament, and, for her, mere habit was never, as for so many, itself a tremendous force. So that when I often look back now, I may sometimes feel like one who has been long tossed and buffeted amid the waves and at last thrown onto the shore, shipwrecked and naked, but able at length to rest on the firm ground,

> '*Liete, no, ma secura*
> *Dall antica dolor.*'

So at least I sometimes felt in the first year or two of my life alone, before the memory of old anxieties was swallowed up in a serene possession of its joy.

My life of a quarter of a century at Carbis is enshrined in memory as a dream of loveliness. I know that it was not so at any moment while I was living it. I know that the past tends to

> 'orb into the perfect star
> We saw not when we moved therein.'

I know that some of the most anguished moments of my life have been spent there, for these too come back to me vividly, so vividly that I have not even the strength to tell of them. But I know also that, of all the places I have ever lived in anywhere in the world, there is none that holds for me so many and so various and so magical visions of loveliness. I know also that nowhere have I carried out my own life-work so happily and so fruitfully, under the open-air conditions that suit me best, as in Carbis Bay. And in all the world there is no place so filled by manifold joyous activities of life, intimately mixed with the deepest experiences, of the woman who shared by my side the same glad receptivity to its loveliness and all whose pains and sorrows my heart partook of. It was her bright presence that first drew me to that spot and it was with her in my care that I left it forever a quarter of a century later. She is for me the living spirit that fills all Carbis Bay. I cannot imagine it without her; I could not revisit it, since she can never return.

I know well the defects of the woman I loved. I do not idealise her or experience any illusions. I remember nothing so poignantly as the sufferings I have endured, unless it is those I have, even innocently, inflicted. There can rarely have been anyone who has known much better or more variously than I have the beauty of the world, and absorbed it more eagerly, the beauty of Nature, of art, of human character and impulse. The memory of the torture remains. I could almost echo the words of Ninon de Lenclos: 'If I had known what my life was to be, I would have killed myself.' I see life whole, coldly, nakedly, all round, and though I am glad it is over, though I would not live it again, yet, now that I seem to view it whole, I view it with joy, even with ecstasy.

THE END

Index

Index